FIGHTING ALL THE WAY

BARBARA CASTLE

FIGHTING
ALL
THE WAY

M
MACMILLAN
LONDON

First published 1993 by Macmillan London

a division of Pan Macmillan Publishers Limited
Cavaye Place London SW10 9PG
and Basingstoke

Associated companies throughout the world

ISBN 0 333 59031 7

1 3 5 7 9 8 6 4 2

A CIP catalogue record for this book is available from
the British Library

Typeset by Cambridge Composing (UK) Limited, Cambridge
Printed by Mackays of Chatham PLC

TO MY FAMILY

CONTENTS

———— • ————

LIST OF ILLUSTRATIONS

———————— • ————————

BETWEEN PAGES 434–435

BETWEEN PAGES 562–563

PREFACE

————————— • —————————

I ALWAYS wanted to write this book. Having been born into a socialist family and taken part in the evolution of political ideas in this country for over half a century, I am often appalled by how little most people know about the development of left-wing ideas and the profound changes they made in society. I wanted to fill the gap from my own life. With my usual immodesty I also thought that people might be interested in what it is like for a woman to fight her way through the political jungle into the Cabinet. This belief is reinforced by the number of letters I receive from students, prominent academics and writers of political histories asking me what obstacles I met on my way to the top and what it was like to be there. In some ways therefore this book is an explanation of these political processes, but I hope it is much more than that. I believe that most politicians are formed, if not in the cradle, at any rate in the nursery. So I have tried to set out the influences which formed me into the politician which I became: my childhood environment, my school days, my time at university. Not least I have described the struggles I had to earn a living in the depression years of the 1930s and in the wartime years.

This record, therefore, goes far wider and deeper than my Cabinet diaries. When I entered the Cabinet I was excited and awed to be at the centre of power, and I decided I would keep a daily diary of what Cabinet government was like and what we actually said and did. My ability to do shorthand helped me here, much to the annoyance of some of my colleagues. But this was only part of the story. Politics is as much about character as it is about the blueprint of policies. It was important to set down the decisions we made and why we made them. It was equally important I believe to record what made us tick as people, and in my own case what made me a socialist.

So I have written a very personal record of the formative

influences of my life. In this I have been helped by the diaries I have kept on and off even outside Cabinet and the memorabilia I have collected for many years. I have also been helped by that remarkable body of people – the archivists. It was David James MA, District Archivist of West Yorkshire, who unearthed for me the accounts of the municipal battles in Bradford in the 1920s which I watched from the side-lines as a schoolgirl and who sent me an advance copy of his book *Bradford: A History* (published by Ryburn). It was P. Mudalier of the Inland Revenue who traced the record of my father's first job as an assistant surveyor of taxes in Sheffield in 1903 – at a salary incidentally of £130 a year. The Museum of Labour History in Manchester has been an invaluable source of reference to the old pamphlets and policy statements we poured out in my youth. I am indebted to the Bodleian Library in Oxford, which has provided me with essential research facilities, and to the research division of the House of Lords Library, which has fielded my queries with skill and patience. I am also grateful to the Joseph Rowntree Reform Trust for its financial support which enabled me to complete my research for the book.

My memory has also been recharged by a number of books, such as Ian Mikardo's *Backbencher* (published by Weidenfeld & Nicolson) in which the crusty old left-winger recorded biting accounts of the Bevanite years. Another such book has been Dr Elizabeth Bradburn's *Margaret McMillan: Portrait of a Pioneer* (published by Routledge). Margaret McMillan, the pioneer of nursery schools, was another of the influences on my early life. I must also register a debt to my mother, who died at the age of ninety-six. When I had the job of sorting out her possessions I found a large tin trunk packed to the top with letters her husband and children had sent her. I started to throw them all away until I realized that they were important records of pieces of British history. They included for instance a large number of letters I had written home during the war when I was confined to London as a local councillor in St Pancras, a member of the Air-Raid Precautions Committee and an air-raid warden in the Blitz.

I am also deeply indebted to my secretary, Joan Woodman, who skilfully fended off the people who were seeking to embroil me in speaking engagements while I was trying to finish this book. She stayed late many a night to help to get the typescript to my publishers. Another source of strength has been Jo Oxenbould, who worked for me for eighteen months helping me with my research. Her general political knowledge and flair for sussing out the sources of information I needed has been exceptional. There have been many others who helped me along the way. What has surprised me is how many people are eager to join in the chase. In writing this book I have been interested to discover how many want to know about their own roots and about the roots of the people who govern them. I hope this book will help to meet this need.

I also owe a very great deal to two outstanding editors – Richard Cohen and Roland Philipps – who guided my faltering footsteps through this literary enterprise with unerring judgement. Nor do I forget the skill with which Peter James weeded out any mistakes and inaccuracies that had slipped through the net. Authors are very dependent on people like these.

ONE

●

Early Influences

IN MY earliest memory I must have been about three years old. I was sitting on the back steps of a square little house, Beechhurst, in Love Lane, Pontefract. In front of me was a stretch of unkempt grass which we called a garden. It was divided from a cinder track by a high brick wall. Rediscovering Beechhurst several decades later I found it was a very modest house indeed, but to me it represented security and stability.

Across the cinder track was a row of houses occupied by miners from the pits of the surrounding area. My elder sister Marjorie, my brother Jimmie and I used to play with the miners' children and learned some colourful language from them. My mother used to recall how one day, after a rough and tumble on the cinder track with our boisterous friends, I pointed to my brother when we got home and lisped, 'Look at him. Isn't he a mucky little bugger?'

At this stage my mother was the dominant influence in my life. She was a William Morris socialist: ugliness must be turned to beauty, the spirit of pastoral England must never die. So every spring she created a maypole on our bit of grass and we children were taken into the dusty fields near by to pick milkmaids and anything else we could find to decorate the pole. My mother even looped it with ribbon, though where she got the money from I will never know, and we danced round it with the children across the track, who seemed unsure whether to giggle or gallop.

My father, Frank Betts, was a remote figure at the time. Tall, black-haired and big-boned, he was a forbidding presence

I

compared with my tiny, ash-blonde mother. He was a civil servant of unusual character, with a high-powered intellect which must have made him good at his job in the Inland Revenue because otherwise it is incomprehensible why the authorities should have tolerated his outrageously unconventional behaviour for so long. He was a one-man challenge to orthodoxy and I was brought up to believe that the duty of every free spirit was to challenge convention and question the smug assumptions of authority.

All my forebears were either Quakers or chapel-goers, including my father's father, who was a corn merchant in Coventry. Grandpa Betts ran a women's Bible class at Vine Street Chapel in Coventry for forty years – 'and never got one of them into trouble', my father remarked disparagingly at more ribald moments. Dad despised his father for what he considered his philistine narrowness. He never forgave him for having refused his son a classical education, sending him to some provincial 'college' (whose name I never learned) to study science. Dad used to tell us how he had ruined his chemistry experiments, teaching himself Greek instead of watching the Bunsen burners. He remained a passionate classicist all his life, striking up a friendship with Gilbert Murray, Regius Professor of Greek at Oxford, who encouraged this eccentric young intellect, winning my father's eternal gratitude by taking out for him a life subscription to the London Library, which Dad would never have been able to afford himself.

The relationship between my parents greatly influenced my life. The marriage was a stormy one, since my father, though intrinsically a kindly man, had a violent temper and a cutting tongue. Nonetheless, it was deeply enduring and this despite the fact that my father formed a close attachment outside marriage to a quiet, reflective and undemanding woman teacher called Nell, whom I never met. It was as though he needed a corrective to my mother's emotional intensity. To her we were all geniuses: above all, her Frank. The marriage held together for forty years because, backing her romantic view of us all, lay a tigerish determination to hang on to her mate and her young.

It was in Vine Street Chapel that my teenage father, dutifully attending as his father's son, first saw dainty little Annie Rebecca Ferrand, daughter of a rather incompetent, but highly esteemed, insurance agent in Bayley Lane, Coventry. Grandpa Ferrand had come down in the world. Descended from a prosperous Quaker bookseller, he was too kindly, unpushing and unbusinesslike to make a material success of life. It was my grandma, a tiny indomitable woman of strong if narrow views, who held the home together and brought up her daughter on twenty-five shillings a week. Grandma came from a working-class family and at the age of twelve had walked miles to work in a pen-filling factory. She had no use for fancy airs and 'all that book learning'. What mattered in life was to earn a living wage. Annie Rebecca was given no chance to acquire fancy airs. At the age of fourteen she was apprenticed to be a milliner. She had a gift for making picturesque clothes and trimming hats, and with her fragile prettiness was brought out from the workroom to model her creations for customers. Fortunately, she had her mother's spirit and on her way to work would slip into the outside lavatory in their backyard when her mother was not looking, take off her corsets and stuff them in her reticule, putting them back on again before she got home. She was already working out her own ideas about how to develop a healthy body for motherhood.

Although Gran was in some ways intimidating she was at heart a kindly woman, and we children enjoyed our visits to her cramped little home in Coventry. I was an imaginative child who firmly believed in fairies almost until my teens and I could find mystery and excitement in the most unusual places. I found it in the games we played in her tiny back room, playing a sort of dominoes with brightly coloured glass marbles which we moved around on a round wooden board or peering at faded photographs through a kind of bioscope which made the pictures appear three-dimensional. I even enjoyed running up and down the ginnel or narrow paved passage which separated her house from the next-door one, my footsteps echoing on its tiles.

I suppose I am indebted to Grandma Ferrand for a certain doggedness in my character. From my father I inherited a love of the romantic and of poetry. The young Frank would eye Annie

Rebecca hungrily across the Vine Street Chapel pews. His emotions poured out in verse. In 1900, when he was eighteen and she seventeen, he dedicated a poem to her which was the lodestar of her life. She could – and would on the slightest encouragement – recite it, word-perfectly, well into her nineties, thirty years after her husband's death:

To A.R.F.

To thee I bear the first fruits of my song
Not knowing whether in long years to come
It will be mine to thrill the hearts of men –
But these, my early blossoms hardly blown,
Lacking in glow and lustre, yet are yours,
Since they are all I have to give to you . . .

O song of mine! go not to her to plead –
Let her not think, that, vainly petulant,
I long to pluck my blossom in the bud
The fruit for my heart's hunger all unripe –
And striving, crush it. For this song is here
By right, an offering laid at her feet
Asking acceptance only, not return.

They were married in Vine Street Chapel in 1905. By then my father had become an assistant surveyor of taxes in Sheffield at a salary of £130 a year and my mother began the peripatetic life of a taxman's wife, moving from place to place, it being considered unwise by the Inland Revenue for a taxman to immerse himself too deeply in local life. The babies were not long in coming and with them the financial worries that always seemed to dominate our lives. First came Marjorie; then Jimmie. I myself was born in Chesterfield on 6 October 1910. Within a few months we were moved to Hull, then on to Pontefract, but I always retained a sneaking sense of identification with Chesterfield's crooked spire.

Even before their marriage my father had assumed his Svengali role of emancipating Annie Rebecca from her conventional

4

upbringing. His first step was to teach her to smoke, simply because it was considered unladylike. My mother responded enthusiastically to his tuition.

With Dad's sister Eleanor – the only auburn-haired member of the immediate family, from whom I probably inherited my red hair – she would cycle round Warwickshire in her bloomers and shock the respectable citizens of Stratford, a favourite haunt of theirs, by paddling in the Avon, showing her ankles. If there were any acts of defiance to be done, she and Eleanor were up to them.

Marriage gave my father the studious setting he required. His passion for reading dominated our whole lives. However cramped our home might be, Mother accepted that a room must be set aside to which he could retire with his pipe and a pint of his beloved bitter beer, leaving her to cope with us. His reading even invaded our mealtimes, for he would bring his books to the table, where we children were expected to sit mum so as not to distract his thoughts. 'Be quiet!' he would thunder at us from time to time as Mother vainly tried to suppress our giggles and childish whispering. Despite the inconvenience of his behaviour we never seriously questioned it. Respect for knowledge at whatever social cost was bred into us from our earliest days.

My father's literary appetite was voracious and catholic. He set himself the goal of reading every great piece of literature that had been written, wherever possible in the original, teaching himself a smattering of many languages. We children were brought up in an aura of Greek plays, Irish ballads, medieval romances and Icelandic sagas. They overflowed into his conversation and even into the names he gave us. Dad was reading *Tristram and Isolde* when my brother was born and the unhappy boy was christened Tristram to the jibes of his girlfriends, one of whom insisted on calling him Jimmie – and Jimmie he remained all his life. Marjorie was always known as Doddie or Dod because one day my father looking up from the book he was reading and, gazing down at his little daughter crawling around the floor, exclaimed, 'She's a Doddie Pole!' I have never been able to find anyone who could tell me who the creator of Doddie Pole may have been. I escaped relatively unscathed, having apparently been named after the redhaired St Barbara in an Italian triptych, a print of which was hanging on our walls.

Once Dad had made a new literary dicovery, he had to write about it, translate it or turn it into poetry. He used to bombard Gilbert Murray with his early efforts, and he even translated Greek plays with his help. Some of his writings were printed in modest little booklets, probably at his own expense, but there was great rejoicing when in 1911 Blackwell's of Oxford decided to publish a small volume of his verse, *The Iron Age*. In his preface to it Gilbert Murray wrote affectionately of Dad's bombardment of him with his latest literary offering: 'I never knew when next it might "blow in", or what new range or what new subject it would have swept into its range during the interval.' One thing was sure: 'it would be full of life and power and sympathy and curious erudition penetrated by imaginative brooding.'

We children were impervious to this great moment, but reading the book years later I discovered a poem which epitomized the socialism on which I had been brought up. It was based on an analogy with chess, of which he was a keen and skilful player, and was called 'The Pawns':

> Purple robed, with crowned hair,
> Caesar sits in a golden chair,
> And a proud, cold Queen beside him there.
> Knights in armour, many and tall,
> And the holy bishops throng the hall;
> Why trouble yourself with the pawns at all,
> Iscariot?
>
> Years agone, and a world away
> Lived One who did not praise the play,
> And he loved the pawns the best, men say,
> And he damned the pieces for their pride;
> So you sold him to be crucified,
> And bared unto the spear his side
> Iscariot

Knight nor bishop can resist
The pawns of this Antagonist
Whose countenance is dark wih mist.
The game goes on and will not wait,
Caesar is gripped in a deadly strait –
What if the pawns should give checkmate,
Iscariot?

My father's socialism was always imbued with respect for the ideals of Christianity, even when he was rejecting the detailed doctrines. When he snatched himself and my mother from their chapel background, he took them first into High Anglicanism. The colour and sensuality appealed to him, but he moved through this phase into rationalism and politics, leaving my mother behind in the Church. My parents struck a compact: we children should be free to choose whether we went to church with my mother or stayed at home with my father, immersed in his study of world philosophies. In our early years we stayed with my mother and the Church, where I and my sister at any rate were very devout. I was confirmed, went to confession, got up early for Holy Communion and fasted on Good Friday during the Stations of the Cross. I was always glad of the self-discipline my religious commitment taught me – particularly in Lent, when one voluntarily gave up the things one enjoyed most. I remember at a quite early age giving up raspberry buns for Lent. This was a real hardship because this substantial sugary concoction with a blob of jam in the middle used to sustain me on my long walk home from school. I can still feel the sinking sense of hunger as I pressed my nose against the cake-shop window, struggling wih my conscience and knowing that no one would know if I broke my vow.

Although my father left us free to make our religious choices we had some stern political moral values drummed into us. We were taught to despise the money-manipulators in the temple of life. The desire to make money was vulgar. Dad would not let us bring any literary 'trash' into the house such as comic cuts or pictorial Sunday newspapers, and if we did he would throw it on the fire. Above all, we were taught to align ourselves with the oppressed against the rich and powerful. We became increasingly aware of how many oppressed there were in the outside world.

I was four years old when the First World War broke out. This may be one of the reasons why we moved to Carlton Park Avenue, a leafy, undeveloped suburb on the outskirts of Pontefract. Everyone was nervously anticipating Zeppelin raids, and one Zeppelin did indeed penetrate as far as Pontefract. I can recall with photographic clarity being woken in the night by my anxious parents, of being wrapped in a blanket by the light of a candle hidden under the bed and carried out on to the allotment which abutted our house. There we flattened ourselves in the primitive air-raid shelter of the cabbage patch. The Zeppelin dropped a bomb harmlessly in Pontefract Park and the whole town trooped out the next day to gape at the bomb crater, of which we were rather proud.

My father was no pacifist. He had no doubt that the Kaiser was Attila the Hun and he rushed to join the forces. In another cameo of memory I can see him coming home to announce tragically that they would not take him because he was on important work and my mother clutching him as she exclaimed, 'Thank God!' Our life during the war then sank into a dull routine. My mother had increasing difficulty in feeding us. The concoction of hers we hated most was a maize pudding which was so distasteful that to get us to eat it she had to bribe us with a spoonful of our severely rationed jam.

The streets were full of men in khaki and my mother did her bit in providing comforts for them. One day she took me with her to the local barracks on some welfare errand and, young though I was, I was conscious of a sad and downbeat atmosphere. The jubilant jingoism of the early war days had gone. So had my father's enthusiasm for the war. He increasingly saw it as the product of competing imperialisms with nothing much to choose between them in their short-sighted folly. The attempt to cloak the horror and waste of war with bursts of 'Land of Hope and Glory', with its imperialist boastfulness, 'Wider still and wider may thy bounds be set: God who made thee mighty make thee mightier yet,' drove him to contempt. I dutifully shocked my friends by refusing to join them in singing it. Love of one's country, my father used to urge, should broaden one's vision, not narrow it. In one of his later articles in the *Bradford Pioneer* he mused upon this theme. 'The drums beat in our hearts (England, my England) and it is not easy to resist their call, but it is not right for grown men and women to sell the serious interests of humanity for an old song.'

The war had one great consolation for me: it stopped the development of Carlton Park Avenue. This suited my tomboy tendencies perfectly. The open spaces next to and opposite our house became a happy hunting ground for cowboys and Indians under the leadership of my adventurous brother, who alternately bullied and protected me. I followed him nervously as he shinned over the palings at the bottom of our garden into a private park, terrified at my own daring in trespassing. Gradually I learned to hold my own, carrying on a running war with a carrotty-haired boy who lived down the road. He would call after me, 'Ginger, you're barmy!', whereupon I would shout back, 'Cowardy custard, hair like mustard!', my first attempt at poetry.

As we children grew older my father sought more of our companionship, though on his own terms. Another of his passions was cricket and he would from time to time emerge from his study on to the piece of open ground to hurl hard cricket balls at us for us to catch. 'Cup your hands properly,' he would shout out to me when I muffed a catch and bruised my fingertips. We used to complain that we could never get into the one lavatory in our modest home because Dad would retire there with Wisden's Almanac and not emerge until he had learned a few more cricket scores by heart. In the end he could quote the scores of every notable Yorkshire cricketer back into the mists of time. Another bond between us was our devotion to dogs. Dad could even be prevailed on to take a few walks if there was a dog to exercise.

However, our most important contact with him was through the 'readings' which were a key feature of our upbringing. Every Sunday evening we would gather by the fire in his study to read the books he thought we should know about. I did not enjoy the

Iliad or the *Odyssey* – too many disembowellings. My turn came when we turned to William Morris' romantic novels. *The Waters of the Wondrous Isles* was pure magic. It had a witch who enthralled the beautiful Birdalone in the wood called Evilshaw, as well as a noble love story. My brother scoffed at this soppiness, but brightened up when he came to Morris' *The Roots of the Mountain* with the blood-curdling battlecry of its warriors: 'Death, death, death to the Duskymen!'

Our new home was a long walk from Love Lane Elementary School, to which my brother and sister went. My father had strong views about education, one of which was that every child in the land ought to be compelled by law to begin school life in a council school. Only in that way would everybody get an equal start in life and conditions in the school be improved. Conditions at Love Lane were pretty basic. We played on stretches of asphalt in front of the school and had to walk across the yard to the outside lavatories. The partitioned sections of their wooden seats were perched over a continuous channel which was flushed intermittently, and if one chose the wrong day to go to the lavatory the stench could be intolerable. 'If Nancy Astor had to send her children to Love Lane Elementary School,' said Father darkly, 'the lavatories would be flushed every day.'

Nonetheless it was a good school and one which had great attractions for me. The first day my sister and brother started to walk to school from Carlton Park Avenue I insisted on going with them, although I was only four and the normal starting age was five. The school obligingly found a corner for me in the infants' class where I sat modelling in plasticine, scribbling my alphabet and learning my sums. Another of my father's educational beliefs was that all children should be thoroughly grounded in the three Rs. It was cruel, he maintained, to send children out into the world without the basic tools to cope with it. He often praised Love Lane in that respect. The boys in the school were rough and I had to come to terms with them. We children got nits in our hair and my mother had to spend precious time in the evenings tooth-combing us. It was painful, but it did not detract from my devotion to the school.

When Marjorie was eleven and I nearly eight we were transferred to Pontefract and District Girls' High School. It had been
opened shortly after the war to provide secondary education for
girls, and at the laying of the foundation stone County Councillor
E. Talbot, chairman of the West Riding Higher Education Sub-
committee, pontificated on what this should involve. The aim of
girls' schools, he told an appreciative audience, should be 'the
production of womanliness'. The young woman of today was the
home-maker of tomorrow and he added that 'The sooner they got
away from the fact that only 2.5 per cent of the secondary-school
girls went to Girton or Newnham and remembered only the 97.5
per cent who required good, sound education necessary to make
them true womanly women the better.' The womanliness did not
extend to the school uniform, for which stern details were laid
down in the prospectus: tunic of brown serge with knickers to
match, a woollen blouse with high turn-down collar and sober
sleeves. No femininity anywhere. When my sister and I arrived at
the school the unlovely uniform was still *de rigueur* and the spirit
of County Councillor Talbot was not altogether dead.

The school was on a hill above the racecourse on which the
Pontefract races were held each year. This not only gave a touch
of excitement to our lives, but used to lead to blessed breaks in
school routine as we were hustled home early before the racegoers
below could conduct their nefarious practices. Some of them, we
were told in hushed tones, came from as far away as Leeds to
squander their money on gambling. The sinfulness must have
been catching for I was always in trouble – the ringleader in all
sorts of forbidden activities. On one occasion while returning
home from school I led my little band of followers on to the
sleepy suburban station at Tanshelf near the school. It had always
had an attraction for me and I found the freight wagon standing
in a siding irresistible, so we clambered on to it, to be discovered
by an irate stationmaster. I thought the whole episode was
innocent and natural, but the wigging I got from the headmistress
was intended to make me feel like a minor criminal.

Not surprisingly, the teaching we received was patchy and my
father, showing an intermittent interest in our education, would

from time to time conduct a campaign against the way we were being taught. The main object of his wrath was the elocution mistress. I was considered rather good at speaking verse and prose and was entered by the school in the inter-school competitions organized by the West Riding Educational Authority. One year I was almost torn apart by the battle between my teacher and my father as to how Walter de la Mare's poem 'Nod' should be declaimed. It began:

> Softly along the road of evening
> In a twilight dim with rose
> Wrinkled with age and drenched in dew
> Old Nod the shepherd goes.

My teacher belonged to that throb-with-emotion school of verse-speaking and I was made to declaim the verse like Donald Wolfit on an off day. Back home my father would have none of this hamming and made me recite the poem in a soft, lilting monotone which left the words to speak for themselves. Back at school duly de-elocutionized, I was severely rebuked by my teacher and made to put the throbs back in again. It is hardly surprising that my performance in the competition was a little confused and that I did not win the expected prize. My day was saved by the prose-reading, in which my teacher took no interest, so I was able to read as simply as I wanted to. I knew my father was right and have had a distaste for the unnatural arts of elocution ever since.

Despite the school's scholastic gaps I was deeply indebted to it for my grounding in two fields. The first was English grammar, in which I was drilled so thoroughly by a forbidding teacher of the old school that I retained a pedantic interest in it all my life. To this day I cringe at split infinitives and hanging participles, in which MPs seem to specialize at Question Time. I found that this pedantry stood me in good stead when I later studied German. The second was the drilling I got in French phonetics. Here again I was chosen to represent the school in inter-school French-speaking competitions. So I was put through my paces rigorously:

taught to roll my Rs, to make the correct ringing nasal sounds and to articulate my vowels distinctly, having been told that I would never speak French properly unless I was prepared to pull my mouth about. As a result my accent has always been the best part of my French. I am grateful to the two formidable ladies who sent me into the world so well equipped.

I was happy in Pontefract. Though in a mining area, it was a sleepy little market town whose place-names evoked its agricultural origins: names like Horsefair, Beastfair, Cornmarket, Sheep Street and Buttercross. To my delight it had a ruined castle in whose grim dungeon Richard II met his death. Not least it had Wilkinson's liquorice works, where I acquired a lifelong passion for the sweets. This was helped by the fact that there was a market garden in the middle of the town where Mother could buy liquorice roots at a penny a time for us to suck. When we were a bit more flush she would take us to the back entrance of Wilkinson's works, where those in the know could buy liquorice braid or telephone wires by the yard at wholesale prices. My current favourite is Pomfret cakes, which I dare not buy because if I once start on a packet I cannot stop eating until it is empty.

But I was drinking in politics all the time. I must have been receptive to it because I identified myself with all the political issues that were discussed in our home. For many years my father carried in his pocket-book a piece of paper torn from the back of an envelope on which I had scribbled my first election address – reputedly at the age of six. It ran: 'Dear citizuns! Vote for me and I will give you houses.' *Plus ça change* . . .

I was of course too young to be more than vaguely aware of the political and economic turmoil of the post-war years. The vindictive Treaty of Versailles meant nothing to me, except that I sensed something was wrong from my father's vitriolic attacks on the Allies' policy of squeezing the defeated Germans 'till the pips squeak'. Nor did I understand the significance of the Triple Alliance, in which miners, railwaymen and transport workers banded together to get their members some of the fruits of victory which had so far gone solely to the war profiteers. I only knew that Ernest Bevin and his dockers were our heroes for refusing to load the *Jolly George* with munitions designed for use against the struggling Bolshevik government, and that J. H. Thomas of the railwaymen was a villain for refusing to back the miners in resisting the coal owners' demands for a pitiless cut in wages. These hazy concepts suddenly came alive for me when in March 1921 the miners were locked out.

I had often travelled on top of the tram with miners returning home in their working clothes from the Castleford pits. There were no pithead baths in those days and to me these men with their coal-grimed faces were figures of mystery and power. The lock-out shook Pontefract, and the Labour Party rushed to their defence.

Practical as always, my mother set about ensuring that the miners were not forced back to work by their children's hunger. She organized a feeding centre in our kitchen and produced gallons of hot soup in the brick copper in which she did our weekly wash.

As a civil servant my father was forbidden to engage in politics publicly, but he adopted the device he was to deploy all his life of backing the causes in which he believed through his anonymous writings, through private political meetings in our home and through the production of challenging plays by local dramatic societies. His contribution was to take a performance of Galsworthy's *Strife* to the Miners' Hall in Featherstone to enliven the miners' black misery. It was here that I made my public debut, having been given the role of the maid who ushers the striking workers into the bosses' boardroom. I was supposed to fling open the door and announce, 'The men are here, sir,' but I was so nervous that I tripped over the sill and spoiled the whole effect. Nonetheless, as I looked down at the locked-out miners standing white-faced and sombre in the hall below, I lost my embarrassment in a burning sense of solidarity. When the men were forced back to work on lower wages at the end of June our whole family shared in the gloom of their defeat.

By this time my father had been promoted to inspector of taxes in the Bradford District and went house-hunting, returning home at weekends to the familiar domestic routine that meant so much to him. He wrote to my mother in one letter, 'Back Saturday late. Get me in four Tetley's Specials.' At last he found a house that suited us and I said goodbye to the leafy joys of Carlton Park Avenue.

TWO

———————— • ————————

Bradford

I WEPT the night before we left for Bradford. 'I will never become a town girl,' I told my mother passionately. She comforted me with her usual understanding gentleness. Nonetheless Bradford was an impressive city, even to my jaundiced eye. The contrast with Pontefract's sleepy little market town was stimulating and I soon responded to the grandeur of the stolid stone buildings in the city centre, dominated by the Town Hall. This imposing stone edifice had been erected in 1873 when Joseph Chamberlain was raising the banner of municipal enterprise in Birmingham. In those pre-Thatcherite days people of all parties in our big towns had a sense of civic pride and nowhere more than in Bradford, where the rough, blunt Yorkshire businessmen made it clear they were not going to be pushed about by Whitehall. There was no rate-capping then, so the issues of local spending became the stuff of raw class politics, which were to play a big part in my young life.

I even found the showers of soot romantic as they rained down on us from the surrounding woollen mills, blackening every building. I would watch fascinated as the particles of soot settled on my regulation white school blouse while I worked at my school desk. Industry to me was like a powerful giant who dominated millions of people's lives. I revelled in the thought of doing battle to extort a decent standard of living for those who worked under his thrall.

I also discovered the moors crowning the surrounding hills, up which Bradford's suburbs sprawled from the city centre in the valley below. As I grew older my great joy was to take a tram to the top of the hills and escape to the bracing air and lonely stretches of those windy heights. Later when I was at Oxford I wrote a nostalgic poem about my beloved moors:

Past stone and grass wind-chastened, I climb to the
    sky's clean edge
And the chained lamps of the town road sweep down from
    the tree-bare ledge.

Marjorie and I went to Bradford Girls' Grammar School (BGGS) and Jimmie to the boys' grammar school. My father was determined that all his children should have a grammar-school education, dismissing the secondary-modern school then available as a 'sausage machine'. Because of the great gaps in our education in Pontefract none of us qualified for a scholarship, so the cost of our education was to be a crippling burden on the family finances for many years. The main brunt fell on our mother, who had to do all the jobs we could not afford to employ other people to do for us, such as painting and decorating the house, washing and ironing for five people, cooking the meals and doing all the spring cleaning whenever my father would let her get at his precious books, mending our clothes or turning Marjorie's dresses into reach-me-downs for me, armed with nothing more sophisticated in the way of equipment than a dolly tub, a mangle, a Ewbank carpet-sweeper and an old-fashioned Singer sewing-machine. She was helped by a 'general' maid, a young girl who had to be supervised all the time. We had a succession of 'generals' while I was at home and it always seemed to me that Mother was helping them more than they helped her. More than once I found her hurriedly making a wedding dress for one of them who had got herself into the family way.

Of course, my father made sacrifices, too. He had to curb his passion for foreign trips and continental food and wine, though he usually managed a couple of weeks abroad (with Nell, as I discovered later). My mother was left to take us children to nearby seaside resorts like Whitby and Scarborough, where we stayed in cheap boarding houses and catered for ourselves. My great treat was when Mother bought salmon paste for us to take back for tea. She longed for my father to take her abroad with him and there were rows about this, as a result of which one year they went together to Paris. She talked about it all her life. One of my great satisfactions in later life was that when my father died in 1945 I was earning enough money as an MP to take her to Paris, where she nostalgically retraced her steps along the bookstalls of the Left Bank.

In my day BGGS was mainly peopled by wool merchants' daughters. Their families were Tory or Liberal, between which I could discern little difference. My Labour views stood out like a sore thumb. So did my passion for politics. 'Barbara and her politics' became a familiar jibe. I found an ally in Evelyn Carter, a scholarship girl from a poor home whom the other girls looked down upon. This was reason enough for teaming up with her, but Evelyn was a fellow spirit. Daughter of a blacksmith who had died prematurely, she was a keen Labour supporter. At election times we flaunted our red rosettes and walked round the school yard arm in arm as protection against the menaces of our schoolmates, who considered us little better than communists. Evelyn had a good brain and was obviously university material, but tragically she had to leave school at eighteen because her widowed mother could no longer struggle against poverty unaided. Evelyn became a typist in a firm of insurance brokers, which she hated. She married, but lost her husband through ill-health. I have kept in touch with her to the present day. She still lives in Bradford, where she is a leading spirit in a local history workshop in East Bowling producing booklets on a corner of Bradford's history.

Another consolation for leaving Pontefract was that my father's promotion meant we could afford to rent a larger house where my father could have his study or 'den' without cramping the rest of us. Our new home was a roomy doctor's house in the pleasant area of Toller Lane. We were intrigued to find it had a special side entrance with a waiting room which gave it an aura all of its own. It also had a garage which we used for storage, as we had no car. The extra space enabled my mother to fulfil her ambition to allocate each of us children a den of our own. My sister, being the eldest, was given a spacious attic. Jimmie was allocated a cellar which he got my mother to distemper red, adorned with the skull and crossbones in black. All that was left for me was the coalhouse in our backyard. My mother white-washed it and made it habitable with some bits of furniture, but as it had no window I and my school friends could use it without suffocating only if we kept the door open. This meant that our whispered secrets were always in danger of being overheard by the boy next door, crouching behind the dividing wall between our yards. One afternoon I persuaded my gang of friends to perform *Julius Caesar* in the yard. Just as I was declaiming 'Friends, Romans, countrymen' on our back steps, giggles behind the wall betrayed the fact that the wretched boy was listening in and, what was worse, laughing at us. I tossed my head and carried on.

At this time I took to scribbling. I gathered my good-natured band of followers in the coalhouse and told them we were going to start a newspaper. I was, of course, the editor and I gave each of them a bit of the newspaper to write. In the event few of them managed to produce anything and Evelyn and I ended by writing most of it ourselves. The enterprise did not last long. I also started writing novels. Like most writers I drew heavily on my personal experience, so the books were all dramas about school life with titles like 'The Madcaps of the Manor House'. My kindly mother listened patiently while I read out large chunks to her, assuring me that one day they would be published. They never got beyond the stage of being scribbled in pencil in exercise books.

In those days BGGS was housed in cramped quarters up a side street in the centre of town, but it made up in teaching what it lacked in facilities. I found that most of the girls in my class were far ahead of me in the syllabus, notably in maths, in which I had had only the flimsiest grounding in Pontefract. Anything more advanced than long addition was a closed book to me and I remember sitting miserably at the back of class trying to hide my ignorance from the bustling businesslike little body who taught us arithmetic. I succeeded so well that I never caught up with the other girls. I have always regretted this lacuna in my education as I believe that, properly taught at an earlier stage, I would have enjoyed maths instead of being afraid of it. Later, when I was preparing for school certificate, I decided to master geometry and algebra. Our teacher in those subjects was young and sympathetic and I wanted to shine for her, so I persuaded two or three classmates to stay behind with me after school to work on our theorems and draw the geometric diagrams on the board till we were at home with them. My ploy was so effective that to everyone's surprise I became quite adept in these subjects in class. Though no classicist I also enjoyed Latin because it gave me a key to my own language and even managed to get a credit in it in my school certificate as one of the six credits which enabled me to matriculate, the qualifying standard for entrance into university in those days. Brought up in a bookish atmosphere I found it easy to excel in English Literature and History. The moral of all this is that in education motivation is three-quarters of the battle.

But the biggest educative influence in my life was my home. My father was in his element in Bradford, both culturally and politically. Here at last was an informed and enthusiastic audience to share the erudition he had been bottling up. Our sitting room was soon devoted to 'readings' at which he and a circle of friends read Shaw's plays, Ernst Toller's *Masses and Man*, Chekhov and many more. As a shy schoolgirl I would only peep in at these readings, but though I was shy I liked to show off any new accomplishment. On one occasion, having learned to make puff pastry at school, I persuaded my mother to let me make a jam puff at home, where a reading was taking place. At the supper interval I marched triumphantly with it into the sitting room, only for our amused visitors to realize, as I had not, that it was barely big enough to give them all more than a few crumbs. I must have been a bit abashed by my reception, because the incident has stuck in my mind.

Bradford people had a strong civic sense. The stolidity of its no-nonsense businessmen, obsessed with making 'brass', had been leavened by an influx in the nineteenth century of German immigrants, mainly Jewish, who were attracted by the city's growth as a centre of the textile trade. They brought with them not only their mercantile skills but also their cultural tastes. Under their influence music and the arts flourished, so Bradford was notable for its subscription concerts, permanent symphony orchestra, two theatres, choral societies, amateur dramatics, arts club and a passable art gallery.

In one of his erratic bursts of interest in music my father would take us to Hallé Orchestra concerts in St George's Hall. His critical appreciation of music was pretty good. Before they were married, the eager young man wrote to his bride-to-be rhapsodizing about Bach's *Passion*, which he had just heard. The words tumble off the page. 'The beauty and the grandeur and nobility of the amazing tragedy comes out in Bach. The result is almost the greatest artwork I have ever encountered.' Mostly, however, he found music an interruption of the reading for which he never had enough time, and I have shared his priority, though I was deeply moved by Handel's *Messiah*, whose annual performance in St George's Hall was an event of considerable local importance to which we all went. My favourite part was the contralto rendering of 'He shall lead his flock like a shepherd'. Decades later when I was Sue Lawley's guest on *Desert Island Discs* I included it in my selection and found it as moving as ever. My father and I also responded to the robustness of Wagner's *The Ring*, though later in life I was to find most opera a bit tedious. Of course I make some exceptions, such as *Boris Godunov*, which I saw in Moscow, and the performance of *Parsifal* I heard years later at the Wagner festival in Bayreuth. Mostly I preferred to go to a play or a poetry recital rather than a concert or opera. Another of my *Desert Island* choices was Martin Luther King's speech – 'I have a dream' – delivered in 1963 to 200,000 civil rights marchers who crowded round him at the Lincoln Memorial in Washington. It stirs me as no music ever can.

One of the reasons for this bias in my taste was, I suppose, that I never heard music played at home, whereas I had access to a wealth of books on my father's shelves. I could raid them at will and developed catholic tastes. I adored Jane Austen and read every one of her books several times. Dickens, George Eliot and the Brontës were also favourites, stirring my imagination. I could never pass a rookery crowned by cawing rooks without thinking myself into Haworth Rectory's lonely environment, or see a garden with a high brick wall without expecting Estelle to arrive at the gate to summon a nervous Pip. Trollope never did this for me and I found Joseph Conrad cold, though I loved the exquisite writing of Joseph Hergesheimer's *Java Head*. I read my way excitedly through D. H. Lawrence and would even have read the banned *Lady Chatterley's Lover* if my father had been able to get a copy of it. I also devoured H. G. Wells.

I loved poetry too, much of which I learned by heart. Someone gave me an edition of *A Midsummer Night's Dream* illustrated by Arthur Rackham and I set out to memorize every line of it. I did not succeed, but I can still recite whole chunks of it if anyone will listen. I even dared to challenge my father's judgment from time to time, notably over Tennyson. Dad dismissed him as a pompous Victorian and would chant 'Come into the garden, Maud' derisively. However, having waded through *The Princess*, a lot of which was admittedly turgid, I came across lyrics which enchanted me:

> And come, for Love is of the valley, come,
> For Love is of the valley, come thou down
> And find him; by the happy threshold, he,
> Or hand in hand with Plenty in the maize,
> Or red with spirted purple of the vats,
> Or foxlike in the vine; nor cares to walk
> With Death and Morning on the silver horns.

Nor did I find the following particularly Victorian:

> Now folds the lily all her sweetness up,
> And slips into the bosom of the lake;
> So fold thyself, my dearest, thou, and slip
> Into my bosom and be lost in me.

Nonetheless Dad was a great help in developing my critical judgment. Already at the age of thirteen I was scribbling poems myself, though I tried to hide my efforts from my father. On one occasion he insisted on seeing a poem I had written about some foxgloves I had seen on a walk with Evelyn. It included the lame couplet:

> Deepest mauve against the green,
> What a lovely colour scheme.

'If it is,' said my father drily, 'you don't need to say so. It will be self-evident.' It was a piece of advice which made me blush at the time, but it improved my style.

As I grew older I explored foreign writers: Anatole France and American authors like Upton Sinclair and Sinclair Lewis. I sat up half the night squirming over the hypocrisy of Sinclair Lewis' evangelist, *Elmer Gantry*, as he seduced one trusting member of his flock after another. At school, with school certificate safely out of the way, I started to specialize in French, English and History for higher certificate and a bid for entrance to university. My tuition in French was excellent. One mistress drilled me in grammar, another taught me French speaking while a third, an attractive young woman called Miss Bradshaw, initiated me into the joys of French literature from Racine to the romantic poets. The latter intoxicated me as my father had been intoxicated by Swinburne in his youth, and I learned Lamartine's 'Le Lac' by heart. Though a romantic, however, I had a tough streak in me and one of my favourite poems was Alfred de Vigny's 'La mort du loup', which depicts a she-wolf, cornered in her lair with her cubs as her hunters close in on her, facing death with dignity. She admonishes the reader: struggle with life's problems with all your strength, then, as I do, suffer and die in silence. It was a philosophy I was often to recall in later life, not least when Hitler rounded up the Jews into the gas chambers.

But my dominant passion was politics, to which I believed literature should be the handmaiden. I could not have had a better place than Bradford in which to learn my left-wing socialism. It was there in 1893 that the Independent Labour Party (ILP) had been born, and we ILPers never allowed anyone to forget it. We had a proprietary interest in Keir Hardie, who had successfully challenged the established parties with his demand for a new party in which working men and women would represent themselves and no longer be dependent on the erratic goodwill of a few reformist Liberals to release them from the intolerable conditions in which they worked and lived. The courage and defiance of the man stirred my blood. I had seen how the wool merchants' daughters at school had looked down on Evelyn Carter, and I could imagine how Hardie felt as he entered the House of Commons in 1892 as the first independent working-class representative, braving the hostility of the top-hatted and frock-coated brigade in his tweed suit and cloth cap, declaring he would be his own man and sit on the Opposition benches whatever government, Liberal or Conservative, was in power. And his boldness had paid off. He had beavered away at detaching the old craft unions from their alliance with the Liberals and had been rewarded in 1906 when at last the unions joined with the socialist societies like the ILP and the Fabians to form the Labour Party.

In Bradford the ILP had kept up the momentum with its socialist Sunday schools, where the young were drilled in good socialist ethics, its Labour churches, which preached that socialism was merely Christianity in practice, its endless propaganda meetings and its local newspaper, the *Bradford Pioneer*.

In 1922, when we arrived, Bradford had become the political pace-setter of the Labour movement. It was the Bradford Trades Council which in 1916 had produced a programme of educational reform so powerful that it was adopted the following year by the Labour Party conference under the title 'The Bradford Charter'. There were plenty of Bradford bosses in those days who argued that workers did not need more than an elementary education to prepare them for a life of drudgery in the mill. The Trades Council would have none of it. It demanded the raising of the school-leaving age to sixteen, more government grants for education and the provision of free, compulsory education for all: no selection and no fees. Eminent propagandists like Philip Snowden considered it an honour to be invited to come and speak to us. As Colin Cross, Philip Snowden's biographer, put it, Bradford had become 'the veritable Rome of Socialism'.

Certainly the ILP was uncompromisingly socialist. Its object, declared at its founding meeting, was 'to secure the collective ownership of all means of production, distribution and exchange'. However, as my father's adherence to it showed, it was not a narrow or exclusive sect. Keir Hardie had mobilized a remarkable range of people for his pioneering cause: middle-class intellectuals as well as militant trade unionists, Fabians like George Bernard Shaw and Sidney Webb, brilliant orators like Annie Besant, heroine of the successful matchgirls' strike, woman-suffrage fighters like Emmeline and Richard Pankhurst. They were all united in their rejection of Victorian capitalism with its sweated labour, slum housing, unemployment, malnutrition and grinding poverty, of which I could see the evidence around me in Bradford. So I shared their desire to replace it with a new system in which the nation's resources should be used for the common good, instead of for private gain. They were not Marxists, nor was my father; I myself did not read *Das Kapital* till I got to university.

Interestingly, it was the Fabians, whom I later dismissed as dull pragmatists compared with the adventurous left, who provided the economic analysis to underpin Keir Hardie's socialist philosophy. Although they rejected Marx's labour theory of value and his revolutionary methods, they found an equal economic justification for socialism in the writings of the nineteenth-century economist Ricardo and his theory of rent. Ricardo argued that the accumulation of land and industrial capital in a few private hands had enabled the owners to monopolize in the form of rent the value which largely derived from the general progress of society and to exact a price for 'permission to use the earth' or 'leave to earn a living'. So the Fabians, too, called for the nationalization of the land and for the transfer to the community 'of such industrial capital as can be conveniently managed socially'.

It was Shaw among others who espoused their doctrine in Fabian tracts and it was Sidney Webb who in 1918 had helped Labour's general secretary, Arthur Henderson, to draw up the party's new and more unified constitution. Together they drafted the famous Clause IV which Hugh Gaitskell challenged in 1959 and about which there have been heated arguments in the party ever since. The clause defined the party's object as 'to secure for the producers by hand and by brain the full fruits of their industry and the most equitable distribution thereof that may be possible upon the basis of the common ownership of the means of production and the best obtainable system of popular administration and control of each industry and service'.

From my earliest days I accepted this as the guiding principle of socialism and, although circumstances have changed radically since the clause was drafted, I still believe it would be wrong for the party to drop it as though it were part of a disreputable past. It is in any case hedged around with Sidney Webb's practical qualifications – 'the most equitable distribution . . . that may be possible' and 'the best obtainable system of popular administration and control', yet it proclaims the principle that wealth is not created by individuals acting in isolation but is the product of the collective action of society. It is essential not to jettison that principle now at a time when private wealth is being promoted as never before at the expense of the collective needs of society. The Labour Party should emulate the Bishop of Durham, who continues to assert his Christian faith while shedding those doctrinal details which no longer seem appropriate.

Inevitably any challenge to the divine right of property was considered communist, particularly as the Bolshevik Revolution in Russia under Lenin was busy transferring land to the peasants and the control of industry to groups of workers employed in each factory, under the slogan 'All power to the soviets'. Though the ILP was far from being Marxist and indeed developed a bitter hatred of the communists in later years, many of us at the time, including my family, warmed to what Lenin was trying to do. I firmly believe that, if Lenin had not died in 1924, the Russian Revolution would have taken a different turn. Lenin deeply mistrusted Stalin and would have done his utmost to prevent him from inheriting power. Without Stalin the West would have been spared over forty years of cold war and the Soviet Union could have moved gradually through Lenin's New Economic Policy to a more relaxed and democratic form of socialism.

Nonetheless the anti-Bolshevik hysteria in Britain meant that we ILPers were dubbed communist. I learned to despise such political illiteracy and, as Lloyd George's post-war coalition government stumbled from one economic folly to another, the hysteria began to die down. As George Bernard Shaw pointed out in one of his Fabian tracts, the 1914–18 war had vindicated socialist precepts by 'compelling the government to supersede private commercial enterprise in several directions by direct state control'. Already by 1922 British socialism had lost some of its terrors and in the general election of that year the Labour Party won 142 seats and polled 4.25 million votes. In Bradford two prominent ILPers Fred Jowett and William Leach, were returned as our MPs.

To counter the rising Labour threat a number of reformist measures had been carried through, but most of them were merely permissive and the battle had moved to the municipalities. Here the ILP was in its element. 'Municipal socialism' became our battlecry and we campaigned so successfully that for many years we were the largest party on Bradford Council, with thirty-five seats out of eighty. Since, however, the Conservatives and Liberals ganged up in an Anti-Socialist Alliance to keep Labour out we found it almost impossible to gain control. Endless plotting took place in our sitting room.

It was there that I met some of Bradford's heroic municipal pioneers. One of the most venerable was Fred Jowett, a grey-haired but determined little man whose battles on Bradford City Council became legendary. Jowett had started his working life at eight years of age as a half-timer in a woollen mill. He had been brought up in one of Bradford's notorious back-to-backs with their communal outdoor privy middens serving a whole row of houses without benefit of water flushing and with the need to dig out the earth closets. By 1892 he had risen above his environment to become the first Labour man to win a contested seat on the local council. He used his office to campaign for the abolition of all privy middens and was so successful that his abashed fellow councillors made him chairman of the Health Committee. He also campaigned for free school meals for undernourished children. He was to become not only one of Bradford's Labour MPs in 1922 but a Cabinet minister when he entered Ramsay MacDonald's first government in 1924.

Another of my local heroines was Margaret McMillan, pioneer of the nursery school. She was before my time but the story of her struggle to transform the established views on education had a powerful influence on me. She came from a comfortably off family, but had leaped at the opportunity to come and work for the Bradford ILP for a pittance. In 1894 she was elected to the Bradford School Board, from which vantage point she joined Fred Jowett in campaigning for free school meals, managing to get them introduced into some Bradford schools before the 1906 Liberal government gave the local authorities the power to do so. She was equally successful with another of her pet campaigns: children, she argued, must not only be fed properly but be healthy if they were to benefit from their schooling. Board members thought she was obsessed with cleanliness, as she pounded away at them about the need for school medical inspections and school baths. Mercifully she was backed by Bradford's school medical officer, whom Jowett had managed to get appointed several years before it became compulsory. The medical inspections immediately proved her point. At one of them the officer found that, out of the 300 children examined, 100 had not had their clothes off for six months. As a result two school baths were opened, but the ILP pressed for more.

It also enthusiastically endorsed Margaret McMillan's new concept of education: it must encompass the whole child and the child's whole life. 'We must start with the babies,' she used to say. Nursery schools, therefore, were a vital link. Instead of confining small children in rigid rows of desks to learn by rote, we should set them free to learn through play and by doing things – preferably in the open air. Further, they must have a good meal inside them and their bodies must be clean. This was a revolutionary concept then and it took some fighting for. At last the 1918 Education Act enabled Bradford to open three nursery schools.

28

Margaret McMillan was vindicated when it was found at one of those schools that, of the initial intake of thirty-five children, only two were not suffering from lice.

My socialism, therefore, was built on simple precepts, as relevant today as they were then: you cannot educate children with empty bellies; equality of opportunity is meaningless without equal access to good health; your baby's chance of survival can depend on whether you live in a salubrious area or an unhealthy one (Bradford's infant-mortality figures bore this out); it is the wealthiest people who find the most plausible arguments for not spending money to put things right; if property feels itself threatened it will fight back ruthlessly and unscrupulously. All my experience has reinforced these views.

My father, enjoying himself hugely, soon took over the editorship of the *Bradford Pioneer*. He had to do so surreptitiously, but everyone knew who the 'F.B.' was who masterminded the paper and contributed weekly articles on everything from literature and art to cricket and chess. He had a gift for making his erudition readable and never wrote down to his readers. So the workers of Bradford were regaled with lively critiques of writers and artists most of them had never heard of, from the novelist Hergesheimer to the Japanese painter Hokusai. One of the most remarkable articles of his I read was on Jesus of Nazareth. Rationalist as he was, Dad was always deeply stirred by Jesus' personality and what he called the tragedy of his suffering. It was for others, Dad wrote in his article, to deal with Jesus the Christ. He wanted to write about Jesus the Man. And he did so with a sympathy and tenderness that was akin to reverence. My father never had any use for the purely carnal or materialistic. Life was a mystery and those who tried to fathom its spiritual side in whatever way should be treated with reverence.

Occasionally I rebelled against the endless talk of politics in our family, but these rebellions did not last long and politics always won. When I was thirteen I gave vent to my ambivalence in a jingle which my father, no indulgent critic, thought was lively enough to publish in the *Pioneer*. It ran:

The other day, I chanced to say,
In life there are to learn
So many things, and time has wings,
That one must need discern
Those that are best, and leave the rest,
The finer ones to fix.
'I'll not,' I said, 'bother my head
Concerning politics.'

My father said, from his wise head,
'What you have said is true,
Many would know, if time were slow,
Life's treasures through and through,
But time is short, and so we ought,
That with men we may mix,
To learn indeed the few we need,
And one is politics.

'All little deeds, and daily needs
Are ruled by politics.
Some new direction, at each election
You soon will help to fix.
Your daily life will teem with strife,
You'll get some nasty kicks,
You'll act the goat when you've a vote,
Devoid of – politics!'

I even took at an early age to lecturing my political elders. I was rising fourteen when in 1924 the first Labour government was formed. It was a minority government, Labour having won 191 seats, with the Liberals holding the balance of power. There had been a great deal of heart-searching in the party about whether Labour should take office in pawn to the Liberals, but eventually it was decided it could not shirk its first opportunity to govern. At a local party celebratory gathering I ran into William Leach, one of Bradford's three victorious Labour MPs, and with all the earnestness of youth urged upon him that the government should not compromise. It should try to implement the Labour programme in full and be prepared to be defeated if necessary. He dismissed my youthful advice with a metaphorical pat on the head, but, young as I was, I felt smug when eight months later the government fell – not in a bid to apply socialist policies, but as a result of its own confused blunderings. It had carried through a few good measures, notably the Wheatley Housing Act, which subsidized low-rent housing, but other social reforms were blocked by the Liberals. The immediate cause of its downfall was the Bolshevik bogey raised by the reactionary press when the government tried to negotiate a trade loan for the Soviet Union. 'No Money for Murderers,' screamed the *Daily Mail*. The damage was compounded by Ramsay MacDonald's inept handling of the Campbell case, in which an inexperienced Labour Attorney-General first brought a charge of incitement to mutiny against the communist journalist J. R. Campbell and then was forced to withdraw it.

Defeat in the election was ensured when the *Daily Mail* raised another red scare by publishing a letter alleged to have come from Grigoriy Zinoviev, president of the Communist Third International, to the British Communist Party, urging them to stir up disaffection in the armed forces. Once again Ramsay MacDonald vacillated and, though no one ever saw the original, the letter did the trick. The Tories romped home with a big majority, Labour lost forty seats and the Liberals were reduced to a pathetic rump. It was a bitter blow to my young dream. For the first time I began to wonder whether my hero, Ramsay MacDonald, might have feet of clay. I had worshipped him, as had the mass of Labour supporters. So great was my devotion that when he came to speak in Bradford and was mobbed by an enthusiastic crowd wanting to shake his hand I deliberately held back my own hand as he passed by me because I did not want to tire him. Now my hero had let me down. But my strongest reaction was the burning conviction that our opponents would always fight dirty and that politics would prove a rough business.

By this time I had grown from tomboyishness into puberty and was trying to come to terms with my own emerging sexuality. My parents were not much use to me, because they could not bring themselves to discuss sex with their children. My mother believed it should remain a sweet mystery. My father was a Rabelaisian puritan. His children were free to read any of his books they liked. He gloried in the prints of the naked Rubens women that adorned our walls, yet he was too deeply reticent to talk about the facts of life. I tried to find out about them in furtive discussions with my school friends, only to find that they were as much in the dark as I was. Yet my father was capable of great understanding. One day when I was in bed with a cold he came to see me and found me struggling to read Aldous Huxley's *Point Counter Point*. He could see that its cynicism about sex was distressing me and asked if I was enjoying it. 'No,' I replied miserably. 'Then don't read it,' he replied gently, taking it away. I was relieved he did not think I had let him down with my squeamishness.

But he had no understanding at all of my more frivolous teenage tastes. My attempts to keep in the fashionable swim, even if modestly, were frowned upon. When one day I came home with my hair waved by an older friend who was a hairdresser, my brother said I looked like a tart. I adored dancing and longed for some lessons to give me confidence, but Dad considered ballroom dancing 'common'. To console me Mother rustled up enough money to pay for some Greek dancing lessons, but these did not do my morale any good at all. The short Greek tunic did nothing for my teenage puppy fat and I suffered agonies of embarrassment in the changing room where I had to undress, because my shabby undies had to undergo the scrutiny of the other, smarter girls. I got my revenge at ILP dances, which were far more to my taste. One rapturous night, when the jazz music set my blood racing, I took the floor and found I could do the Charleston, untaught, with the best of them. I began to hope that I was not condemned to be one of life's wallflowers.

My hope was fortified when Mother produced the mystery play, *Everyman*, at St Mary's Church, to which we still went with her. I was the angel who comes to lead the dying Everyman to paradise. A young man with flaming red hair and flamboyant wings played St Michael. He seized his opportunity afterwards to kiss me behind the arras – a moment made all the more piquant because the vicar was talking to someone on the other side. The next day, plucking up my courage, I asked my parents whether I could bring the boy home to tea. Looking up from his books my father dismissed me witheringly with: 'Barbara and her boys!' This took me aback since I had no boyfriend. That had been my first kiss and was to be my last for some time to come.

Despite these discouragements Evelyn and I were not going to be outfaced and we pursued our little frivolities with zest, queuing for the sixpenny 'gods' at the Palace Theatre every Saturday afternoon. Any play would do as we sat entranced on our hard wooden benches in the balcony. But we did manage to see the Russian ballet and Shaw's *St Joan*. We were avid cinema-goers and haunted the Elite and the Coliseum in Toller Lane. I developed a teenage crush on Rudolf Valentino and followed his films around everywhere, never missing a showing of *The Sheikh* or *Monsieur Beaucaire*. When he died suddenly, I was inconsolable. I went to bed with his picture under my pillow and cried myself to sleep.

Our pursuit of beauty had to be conducted surreptitiously. With the aid of hints from any magazine I could lay my hands on we practised our beauty culture in the privacy of my bedroom, slapping oatmeal packs on our faces to clear the skin. Make-up was more difficult because we had to use makeshift materials. Evelyn has reminded me that we clubbed together to buy a sixpenny tube of Velouty de Dixor powder-cream, which we took it in turn to use. One day when it was Evelyn's turn it was raining hard and she arrived at school with white streaks running down her face amid the pink. I had to wash the whole thing off.

We also had fun of a more serious kind with the amateur dramatics in which my father became involved through the ILP Arts Guild. One of his productions was *The Insect Play* by the brothers Capek. Evelyn and I had walk-on parts. I was a moth, scorching my wings as I danced round the flame of life. She was a creepy-crawly of some kind. My father's productions always caused a stir, thanks in no small part to my mother's artistic skill as wardrobe mistress. Mother was not considered by the family to be an 'intellectual' but when the Guild produced a period play she was to be seen poring over vast tomes on costume and every garment she designed was historically correct down to the last paste buckle.

Despite his stern puritan values my father was not curmudgeonly towards the young. On the contrary, his great joy was to seek out talent among young people from restricted working-class backgrounds, and he would encourage them to express themselves in the columns of the *Pioneer*. He also invited a number of them to our house to discuss their hopes with him. Two of his protégés were Vic Feather and Mary Hepworth, whose potentialities excited him. Vic was a lively, good-looking lad a few years older than I was, and showed no interest in F.B.'s daughter, a freckled schoolgirl in school fustian. He was working as a counter-hand at the Co-op when my father discovered him. Mary was an attractive bosomy blonde with a flair for writing. She told me later that she and Vic, who were about the same age, at some time had had a 'thing' for each other but nothing came of it.

They both had familiar tales to tell. Vic was the son of a French polisher whose ILP loyalties and trade union activities had kept him more out of work than in. He was also a product of the socialist Sunday schools: a bright boy who had won a scholarship to Hanson Secondary School, where he had done well despite the fact that he had to eke out the family income as an errand boy while his mother sewed cheap shopping bags at the rate of one penny for four. His scholastic ability would have enabled him to fulfil his hopes of becoming a teacher if his father had not had a stroke. As it was he had had to leave school at fifteen and start weighing and filling sacks of flour in the Co-op. It would not have seemed conceivable at that time that he would one day become General Secretary of the TUC.

When I met him Vic was already showing unusual qualities. He was a cheeky lad who at the age of fourteen had hurled a brick through the windows of the Board of Guardians because his mother had complained of being insulted there when applying for relief. Rumour had it in Bradford that he once put sugar in the petrol tank of a Tory councillor's car, but I have not been able to substantiate the story. Certainly, years later he used to admit that as a penniless boy he had learned to 'ride the trams' and to judge when to jump on and off to avoid paying the fare. He had a great sense of humour, which showed itself in his cartoons and articles for the *Pioneer*. All his life he was to get out of corners with a suitable joke delivered in his plummy Yorkshire voice.

Forty years later, when he was General Secretary of the TUC and I was Secretary of State for Employment and Productivity, our paths were to cross officially. With sad shakings of the head but without malice, he led the trade union opposition to my *In Place of Strife*. One evening I lured him into a private dinner with me in a West End hotel to try to heal the breach between the government and the TUC. Typically, he evaded talking about my document, except to interject mournfully, 'Why did you do it, luv?' Instead he launched into reminiscences about my father. 'Your dad taught me a lot about art.' (Vic had by then become a modest but discriminating art collector.) 'He took me once to the Bradford Art Gallery and, pointing to a nude, said, "Look at that flesh. If you pinch her, she will bruise."' He also chuckled at the way my father taught him journalism, sending him out to dig up scandals about the Tory councillors. 'I owe your dad a lot.'

Mary Hepworth was another bright spirit whose potentialities had been blunted by poverty. She had won a scholarship to Salts Girls' High School, but was taken away at the age of fourteen to work in a baking-powder factory. By the time she came to our house with Vic she had found herself a job at the cash desk of the Co-op grocery – the Co-op being a haven of relatively good working conditions in those days. My father had been struck by the literary quality of a piece she had written for the *Pioneer* and urged her to try her hand at novel-writing, though without success. She married and had three children instead. Perhaps she was looking for the security which in fact she never found, as her husband died shortly after their third child was born. Dad continued to be her mentor for many years. She, like Vic, retained an abiding affection for F.B. 'Your father opened windows on the world for us,' she wrote to me a long time afterwards. 'He took us to art galleries, told us about Paris, talked books. It was like having your own private university tutor. Titian's *Bacchus and Ariadne* was the first picture I ever really looked at. F.B. was very keen on the French Impressionists, which Vic found a lot of airy-fairy nonsense, because he preferred strong drawing. He would have loved to have been a professional cartoonist.' She has remained a friend throughout my life.

At school an era of swotting had begun. By this time both my siblings were in university: Marjorie had gained a place at St Hugh's College, Oxford, and Jimmie one at Edinburgh to study forestry. My father was bitterly disappointed when his son eschewed classics and moved to the 'modern' side of the grammar school, but Jimmie was to make a name for himself in Africa, both as a forester and as an expert on rural development. Neither Jimmie nor Marjorie had won more than modest grants and the burden of supporting two children at university had stretched the family finances to breaking point. When I appeared on the scholastic scene my father said in desperation that I could not go to university unless I earned every penny of the cost, which I set out to do.

Financial constraints meant a change in our lifestyle. We moved from our comfortable home in Toller Lane to share a much smaller house with another couple. Family holidays became impossible until a friend helped us by offering to lend us her cottage on Blubberhouses Moor above Otley for a fortnight's holiday. We had, of course, to cater for ourselves in this remote moorland spot, so Mother and I were left to fill a large tin trunk with provisions. We lugged it by bus to Otley, at that time a quiet little market town, then humped it on foot up the steep hill to the moor and across tussocks of rough grass and little moorland streams. The enchanting cottage, with its living-room hearth open to the sky, stood in its own field and drew its water from a stone trough outside filled with icy cold water from a moorland spring. We would dash across the field in the chilly summer mornings to wash ourselves in the trough. That holiday was always associated for me with ice-cold water and the smell of Wright's coal-tar soap.

In my last year at school the new headmistress, Miss Hooke, astonished everyone by making me head girl. It must have been on the poacher-turned-gamekeeper principle. I was not particularly athletic, though I was quite good at netball and would have liked to have played tennis, but my family could never afford to buy me a tennis racket of my own. I also continued to shock everyone. When the sixth form wanted to make me a presentation and asked me what book I would like, I chose D. H. Lawrence's *Boy in the Bush*, one of the few books of his I had not read. I remember the strained look on the face of the form mistress as she said, 'But isn't it rather risqué, Barbara?' 'He is a great writer,' I replied loftily and got my book. Miss Hooke's daring gamble paid off when I won an exhibition in French to St Hugh's College, Oxford, and my name went up in gold letters on the roll of honour in our assembly hall.

To its credit, the school organized a weekly civics class for us sixth-formers. Compared with the discussions at home it all seemed very amateurish to me but it had its useful side when the form mistress tried to arrange debates. Getting girls to speak in public, even to their classmates, was an almost impossible task. I was practically the only one who would have a try, even though I did not do it very well. As a result when the boys' grammar school sixth challenged us to a debate with them I was called on to lead our tiny team. I was petrified, and with good cause. We faced a team of sophisticated and self-confident young men who were preparing themselves to become leaders rather than subordinates. The team leader delivered a witty, mocking speech which almost reduced me to silence as I mumbled my way through the few ponderous facts I had prepared.

Looking back I marvel at women's instinctive acceptance of men's belief in their own superiority. Mercifully this has begun to fade, but we have a long way to go. Some thirty years later when distributing the prizes at a girls' school I told the pupils that one of the most important skills they could acquire was self-confidence. They should not sit back and let the men monopolize the public argument. 'Shyness,' I told them, 'is a form of vanity. It means you are thinking more about yourself than about your subject and your audience. Put them first and your nerves will disappear.' It was a lesson it had taken me a long time to learn.

Denis Healey likes to recount that he was at the Bradford Boys' Grammar School when the famous debate took place, though he hastens to add that he is seven years younger than I am and so was not old enough to take part in it himself. If he had been I am sure he would have scored over me with great aplomb. Nonetheless, when we both became ministers in the 1960s I had no difficulty in holding my own with him, both in Cabinet and in public debate. I had found my nerve.

The climax to my school days came with the general election of 1929. The Bradford ILP fielded four Labour candidates: the veteran Fred Jowett, William Leach, William Hirst, a trade union official, and a newcomer, Norman Angell, who was chosen to fight the Tory stronghold of Bradford North. Norman Angell had won an international reputation as author of *The Great Illusion*, published in 1908, in which he had argued that war, far from benefiting the victors, damaged them economically. His analysis had been dramatically vindicated by the years following the 1914–18 war and the whole town was atwitter at having such a famous man in its midst seeking their votes. Even some of the mistresses at school wavered in their traditional allegiances. One of them said to me timidly, 'I know one should vote for the man and not the party, Barbara, but I am worried by some of your policies. Aren't you going to nationalize the Post Office?' She did not seem to realize that it was already a public monopoly.

I threw myself enthusiastically into Norman Angell's campaign, overcoming my shyness to go canvassing for him. On one such sortie I saw an elderly man digging in his front garden and approached him nervously. 'May I solicit your vote for Mr Norman Angell?' I asked. 'Well now,' he replied, leaning on his spade, 'is he an angel?' Swallowing hard, I recited a catalogue of his virtues as far as I could remember them. After a few minutes of this the man patted me on the shoulder. 'Run along. You've done well. I'm a founder member of the ILP.' I had joined the ILP Guild of Youth at the earliest qualifying age of sixteen, but I could not rival that.

The school decided to hold a mock election on the day before polling day. Of course, I had to be the Labour candidate since there were only a handful of Labour supporters in the whole school. As our small band pinned on our red rosettes, the atmosphere among our schoolmates became sulphuric and I wondered if it would come to blows. Our well-heeled opponents spattered the school walls with lavishly produced posters. We Labour supporters had no money and none of us could draw. Our posters were amateurish, to say the least, though I was proud of the slogan we thought up: 'Three Rs: Vote Tory for Reaction, Liberal for Rhetoric, Socialist for Results!' We also scored over them when I had the idea of asking all four Labour candidates in Bradford for a message of support. I knew we had hit the bull's-eye when I pinned the following message on the notice board: 'Because the Labour Party is the Party of Peace I trust that the Labour candidate will secure a huge victory.' It was signed 'Norman Angell'. In our election I polled seventeen votes out of a school of 600 girls. It was a record because Labour had never raised its head before.

I had my revenge the following day when Labour swept the board in Bradford, winning all four seats for the first time in its history. Nationally Labour had become the largest party in Parliament with 288 seats to the Conservatives' 261 and the Liberals' 57, and although it had still not won an overall majority it was about to form a government for the second time. I arrived at school bog-eyed having stayed up half the night listening to the results in Bradford's resplendent Victoria Hall and tried not to gloat over my schoolmates too obviously. I realized then that two days is a long time in politics.

THREE

•

Oxford

I WENT up to St Hugh's in October 1929 with a stack of new dresses Mother had lovingly made for me – unaccustomed sartorial wealth indeed! I arrived not knowing whether I would be home again within a few weeks. Our family finances had erupted into crisis when we discovered that my state, my city and my school scholarships were all valueless in money terms because under the prevailing means tests my father's income was considered too high for me to qualify for a cash payment. Only my Oxford exhibition provided any money, and that only £30 a year. With Marjorie now doing teacher training and Jimmie still at Edinburgh my father said desperately that he just had not the wherewithal to keep me at university. Mother, outraged at this threat to her youngest child, put on her tigress act. Armed with a sheaf of papers setting out our income and outgoings in meticulous detail she stormed in to see the director of education in Bradford Town Hall. Throwing the papers on his desk she declared: 'See for yourself! We haven't even a penny left to buy a newspaper.' As a result the Education Committee eventually decided to give me a scholarship of £50 for one year and to lend me another £50. There was great rejoicing when at last we learned that I could stay up – though, because I came down from Oxford in the depressed 1930s, that loan was to be a millstone round my neck for many years.

I had a love–hate relationship with Oxford. Like everyone else I fell in love with the dreaming spires, which seemed to me pure poetry in stone. In my first year I pursued all the normal fresher activities, cycling miles to explore the surrounding countryside, discovering the delights of the river and staying up half the night discussing life with my friends over cocoa in my room. I even got my half-captaincy in canoeing, a modest qualification which meant that I could manage a canoe alone. I used it to canoe myself down the river to Magdalen Bridge on a freezing May morning to hear the Magdalen choir sing madrigals from the college tower. I was no good at punting as I always managed to get a cascade of water into my armpits as I threw up the pole, so I developed the firm view that the only way to enjoy a punt was to lie back luxuriously while a competent man threw the pole in the air and slid it back effortlessly.

Despite these fresher enthusiasms I became increasingly restive in the cloistered and to me stifling atmosphere of a women's college. We had to sign out if we left the college in the evening and sign in again by 11 p.m. or be gated, losing the right to go out in the evenings for the rest of the term. The chaperone rules were positively Victorian. They reflected the days when women had to struggle to win the right to attend a university at all. When I arrived at St Hugh's our Principal was Miss Gwyer, a woman of formidable intellect who seemed to embody the belief that intellectual women should not be interested in sex. She laid down the law that her undergraduates should never be with a man alone. Whether on a walk, entertaining a man to tea or going on the river with him in a punt, she was always to be accompanied by a woman chaperone. When one of our braver spirits challenged the logic of this latter edict, pointing out that the river was a public highway, Miss Gwyer drew herself up and replied haughtily, 'There *are* creeks.'

The Principal was a tall gaunt woman with a beak-like nose which reminded me irresistibly of one of the gargoyles of Notre Dame, of which I had a set of replicas on the mantelshelf in my room. On one occasion, when one of my friends and I were discharging the obligation (which we had been told was customary) to entertain her to tea, I looked up at my mantelpiece and nearly burst out laughing at the likeness. It was not until much later that I realized Miss Gwyer had a keen wit hidden beneath that forbidding exterior. At one of the rare formal dinners the college organized for us in the dining room with the dons lined up *en masse* at high table, Miss Gwyer opened her after-dinner speech by remarking that she felt like Elizabeth in *Pride and Prejudice* with d'Arcy hanging over the piano while she played. I forgave her a lot for that.

Nonetheless St Hugh's seemed to me like a girls' boarding school and I had never wanted to go to one of those. In fact a number of the college students were the product of the most prestigious of those establishments: Roedean, Wycombe Abbey, Cheltenham Ladies' College. They were amicable enough, but they came from an alien world. My passion for politics was a joke to them and they enjoyed mimicking my northern accent. When I said, 'I am going to have a bath' (short Yorkshire vowel) they drawled back, 'Barbara is going to have a baath' (long-drawn-out southern A). My response was to broaden my accent still more. I was equally out of sympathy with the intense young women who had had a hard struggle to get to Oxford and whose one interest in life was to get a good degree as the passport to a good job. I had believed that university would be a place of stimulating conversation and the exploration of new ideas. I found neither in our Junior Common Room.

One of the intake from Roedean, a pretty, gentle girl called Audrey, had a room across the corridor from mine. She had been presented at Court and a photo of her in her regalia of long white gown, long white gloves and osprey feathers in the hair was prominent on her dressing table. Oxford certainly changed her, but not in the way her parents could have anticipated. She got God in the fundamentalist way which was invading Oxford at that time and developed the habit of bursting into my room in the middle of the night, kneeling beside my bed, clutching my hand and saying, 'Barbara, God is calling you. You have so much in you that is worth while. Come to him.' Restraining my irritation I would reply, 'Yes, Audrey. Thank you. Now go to bed and let me get some sleep.' She lost all interest in her looks and her parents must have despaired of her. I never knew what became of her but I doubt she made a society marriage. Missionary work in darkest Africa was more her line.

The cloistered life of a women's college was a by-product of the attitudes of the whole university. In those days Oxford was a closed and introvert community in which the lucky few expanded their egos as much as their minds and formed themselves into mutual-admiration societies. It seemed natural to them that it should spawn the nation's leaders and that those leaders should be predominantly male. For Oxford was openly sexist. Privilege, whether of sex or class, did not trouble it. Some dons made no secret of their resentment at the intrusion of women into their male preserve. One don, whose lectures I attended and whose name I mercifully forget, specialized in sardonic digs at his women listeners. On one occasion when he was dealing with the Directoire period of French history he raised a snigger among the young men in his audience by remarking, 'This name, I understand, has also been given to a certain type of women's knickers.' I was not amused.

I was indignant, too, when I found that women undergraduates were not allowed to be members of the Union Debating Society or to take part in its debates. We were expected to sit in the public gallery, cheering on the male gladiators doing battle below. I never went near the place while I was up and for a long time afterwards, when I had become an MP, I turned down invitations to speak in the debates as a privileged outsider. It was thirty years before I broke my rule when, incensed by the Union's overwhelming rejection of an attempt to remove the ban, I agreed to oppose a motion to the effect that women's emancipation had been a flop. The mover was Roger Fulford, author of *Votes for Women*, a history of the suffragettes, and I wiped the floor with him, as he admitted afterwards, sending me a copy of his book inscribed 'with respectful admiration'. I enjoyed myself hugely, taunting my male audience with their 'craven fear of being equal' and quoting Burke's dictum: 'An Englishman is the unfittest person on earth to argue an English woman into slavery.' The motion was defeated resoundingly but the ban was not lifted until 1963. Even by then Oxford was slow to move.

Sexual discrimination in my day even extended to the food. The men's colleges were well endowed, whereas the women's colleges were poor. The only time I had any good meals while I was in Oxford was when I was invited to private lunch parties in one of the men's colleges. The excellence of the meal was in startling contrast to the sparse fare we had at St Hugh's, which always left us so hungry that we used to supplement it with bread and cheese bought from the Buttery – a big drain on my meagre pocket money of two shillings and sixpence per term. I depended for any little luxuries on the food parcels Mother sent me from home.

More serious than these pinpricks was the effect on my studies of Oxford's failure to keep abreast with the outside world. On arriving at St Hugh's I had decided to switch from French to the new school of Politics, Philosophy and Economics (PPE) as more appropriate for the sort of life I planned for myself. I had been quite clear for some time that the only vocations I was interested in were politics and journalism. I certainly did not intend to become a teacher or a civil servant; least of all did I intend to become secretary to some great man. Unfortunately, when I arrived the new school was only five years old and was suffering from growing pains. Its introduction had been Oxford's stab at modernizing itself and frankly the university was not equipped for it. Life seemed to be a succession of disjointed lectures and tutorials, linked to an excessively long list of set books, with no one to give it a central theme. The only house tutor St Hugh's could find to allocate to me was a medieval historian, a plump, amiable little body who clearly had not a clue about the economic and political problems of the modern world.

Most of the lectures were deadly dull and the audiences soon melted away. The exceptions were the lectures by G. D. H. Cole, a university reader in economics, whom I had been brought up to revere as one of the outstanding socialist theorists of the time. His lectures were so lucid, elegantly delivered, well arranged and full of meat that they were a crammer's paradise and were always packed, but I never got to know Cole personally. I was invited occasionally to Gilbert Murray's house at Boar's Hill to admire the azaleas, but these were purely social occasions. He was charming about my father, but I was no classicist. I longed for an

44

adult with whom I could have the sophisticated political discussions I had had at home.

It was not until the middle of my final year that I was allocated the sort of tutor I had been looking for: Miss Headlam Morley. She had been a brilliant scholar at Somerville and had come to St Hugh's as an assistant tutor in politics, having already published a book on *The New Democratic Constitutions in Europe*. She was later to become the first woman to be elected to a chair in the university – Montague Burton Chair of International Relations – a tribute to her outward-looking mind. She came into my life like a breath of fresh air and stimulated me as she disciplined my looser lines of argument. Unfortunately she came too late to save my studies from the shambles into which they had sunk.

Of course Oxford life had its compensations. One of them was my discovery of two fellow spirits in St Hugh's with whom I formed a highly unconventional triumvirate. The first was Olive Shapley, who was to make a name for herself with innovative programmes and documentaries for the Northern Region radio of the BBC, though she herself had been reared in Dulwich and educated at the Mary Datchelor School in Camberwell. She was a tall gangling blonde with an infectious laugh, a lively mind and wide interests which embraced every creed and every race – one of nature's cosmopolitans. She attributed this to her Unitarian upbringing. She never knew who would be preaching at the Unitarian church she attended with her father. One Sunday it would be a rabbi, another a turbaned visitor. It was there that she first heard the Indian philosopher, Rabindranath Tagore, and when I met her she was deep into his teaching. I found it too mystical for my taste and not in keeping with the earthy doctrines of the ILP, but I warmed to her instinctive brand of socialism, with its total lack of racism or snobbery. It was this warm-hearted approach to life rather than any ideological devotion to communism which attracted her to the October Club which I eschewed. I sympathized with the Bolshevik Revolution as much as she did but always retained a cautious streak. It was typical of Olive's generous spirit that, when she had been widowed for the second time and her children had grown up, she opened up her large house in Manchester to Vietnamese boat people, giving shelter and support to twenty-five Vietnamese families who, thanks largely to her help, were eventually settled in worthwhile homes and jobs.

Olive and I laughed a lot and were natural rebels against the petty restrictions of college life. When the mood took us we broke the rules. One night, after we had been working till the early hours on our weekly essays for our tutors, we suddenly decided we must breathe the air of freedom. We had a sleeping partner in a St Hugh's colleague, Irene Yarwood, who had been educated at Dartington Hall and was as impatient of the rules as we were. As a third-year student Irene had been allocated a ground-floor room on the assumption that third-yearers would be 'responsible'. The sash window gave easy access to the garden and she would leave it open for us when she went to bed. That night we tiptoed down the garden to the Banbury Road gate – a hazardous enterprise since the gate was opposite one of the college hostels where a don had lodgings in order to keep a watchful eye on her charges. We shinned over the high wooden barrier, an exit made even more perilous because it was a brilliantly moonlit night. But our walk along the river bank that night was magical. The moonlight shimmered on the water and cows loomed up on us eerily out of the river mist.

Having found our escape route we used it several times. On one occasion we nearly met with catastrophe. We had decided to attend a dance in the town and had not asked for a late pass in case it was refused. Our long dresses made climbing the gate even more difficult. On our return at midnight we were trying to negotiate it when a policeman materialized out of the shadow. I was stranded halfway over the gate and could not escape. Our hearts sank. This was it! But all he said was 'Do you want a hand, miss?' and heaved me over the gate. We still bless his memory.

The third member of our triumvirate was Freda Houlston, a dark, strikingly attractive girl who came from a modest, middle-class family of whose conventional values Mrs Thatcher would have approved. She was not as light-hearted as Olive and I were, alternating between bursts of gaiety and moods of deep and almost sombre seriousness. She used to come with us occasionally to meetings of the Majlis, the mock parliament where Indian undergraduates threw themselves into rowdy and often disorderly debates. There she met a quiet and rather stolid Sikh with whom she felt an immediate spiritual affinity. They decided to write a book together, though I cannot remember what it was about, and most afternoons she went openly to his room in Hertford to work on it with him. An officious porter reported them. She had committed a heinous offence and was rusticated for the rest of the academic year as a punishment. But she was a girl of spirit and was not going to be brow-beaten. On her return she resumed her visits to Bedi, in the digs outside college to which he had moved, only this time she decided to give the disciplinarians their money's worth and started an affair with him.

Freda had a religious bent, however, and the clandestine relationship weighed on her. She fretted herself into a nervous breakdown, losing another term of academic work. When she eventually started on her final year I had finished mine and gone down, but Olive, who was still up, told me the rest of the story. Freda suddenly announced that she was going to marry Bedi and did so then and there. Olive was the only person from St Hugh's to attend the wedding, the authorities apparently not being certain whether to be thankful that she had been made respectable or shocked by her choice of spouse.

After their marriage Freda and Bedi spent a short time in Berlin and then went to India to live in the Punjab, where Freda helped Bedi to run a newspaper and bore him a daughter and two strapping sons. One of the sons, Kabir, became a film star of international repute. After starring in twenty-seven Indian films he was invited to Hollywood, where he appeared in *The Thief of Baghdad* and rose to the heights of a James Bond villain in *Octopussy*. Freda made a name for herself in India, where she embraced the Buddhist faith. She worked with Indira Gandhi, who as Prime Minister asked her to tour and report on conditions in the Tibetan refugee camps, where Freda lived for six months in a bamboo hut. Her work among the refugees won her the gratitude of the Dalai Lama, who became an admiring friend.

Freda also poured out articles and books and won a national prize for a children's book in Urdu. After Bedi's death she became a Buddhist nun. I lost touch with her but Olive, a great traveller, visited her in India several times.

My last memory of Freda before her death in 1977 was when she made a rare visit to London and I invited her to lunch with me at Westminster. She sailed into the House of Commons dining room in her flowing Buddhist robe, serenely indifferent to the covert stares at her shaven head. What her prim widowed mother made of all this I never knew.

Another consolation in my life was the Oxford Labour Club. We met in the backroom of premises on the High and it was always packed, as we were considered the most exciting club in the university. Even some young Tories, bored by the anodyne respectability of their own club, became members in order to hear the speakers we brought from Parliament and trade unions plus socialist philosophers analysing the stirring events of the post-war world. They were as fascinated by the Bolshevik Revolution as we were and when the club organized a showing of Sergei Eisenstein's film *The Battleship Potemkin*, his tribute to the naval mutineers of 1905, there were plenty of Tory bodies among those almost hanging from the walls. With the 1929 Labour government installed in power our club dominated the political life of the university. The only disappointing guest speaker we had was Vera Brittain, Shirley Williams' mother and author of *Testament of Youth*. We found her a bit limp.

The club was run by some lively spirits and I was elected one of its officers. We put on political skits at the end of term, in which I usually had a part. They were, of course, irreverent, even about our own leaders, and in one of them I was cast as Ramsay MacDonald's mistress and joined in the chorus in which we parodied a currently popular song with the words 'Life ain't half sweet on the government side of the street'. Lively as we were, only two of us, Tony Greenwood and myself, were to make our names in national politics. Tony had many advantages, being good-looking, attractive to women and a polished speaker. Not least he was the son of Arthur Greenwood, a much loved Labour

48

figure who was then Minister of Health in the Labour government, but Tony never stirred me. He was too smooth for me. I was more attracted to Owen Papineau, a swarthy, dynamic young man with whom I had a mild flirtation, though it did not last long.

I think what first attracted Olive and Freda to me when I arrived at St Hugh's was my campaign for sexual enlightenment. I was still pursuing my search for the facts of life and was indignant to find that my fellow members of the Junior Common Room seemed equally ignorant. Reading the *New Statesman* my eye was caught by an advertisement for a book on *Planned Parenthood* by Michael Fielding. I thereupon organized a whip-round in the JCR to raise the necessary six shillings and sent off for it. Explicit and illustrated with diagrams, it became one of the most thumbed books in the college, but the revelations did not immediately precipitate me into a life of sin. My knowledge of sex remained second-hand.

I was therefore as excited as anyone when the Labour Club invited Norman Haire to address one of our meetings on the subject in which he was an expert – sex. Everyone in Oxford seemed to be searching for sexual advice and his visit caused a tremendous stir. He was notorious for his frank books about sexual behaviour and the hall was packed – mainly with non-members jostling for a place. Haire spoke for an hour quietly, factually and unsalaciously. At the end he said that, if anyone had any problems, he would be glad to see them afterwards. The multi-political queue stretched almost into the High. We were delighted with the success of our meeting. But I did not realize what lay in store for me.

The next day Miss Gwyer summoned me. 'Betts,' she began (for some unknown reason we were always addressed by our surnames), 'I understand there was a meeting with Mr Haire at the Labour Club last night and that you are an officer of the club.' 'Yes, Miss Gwyer,' I replied, swallowing hard. 'Tell me what he said.' In an agony of embarrassment I went through the catalogue. 'He talked about love-making.' 'Yes and . . .' 'Contraception.' 'Yes, and . . .' 'Masturbation,' I blurted out, red in the face. The inquisition went on for a quarter of an hour. At last she released me from my misery. Leaning forward she patted my hand. 'Betts, you are pure, but there would have been people in that audience who are not pure. Now run along.' I escaped, furious.

The absurdity of those old attitudes is hard for anyone to appreciate today. In the 1960s, when I had become a Cabinet minister, St Hugh's made me an honorary fellow and I attended an honorary fellows' dinner as the guest of the new Principal, Rachel Trickett. She was no sex-kitten but she was of a totally different genre from the principals I had known, with a refreshing sense of humour, an approachable manner and a modern outlook on life. I took to her instinctively. On our way to dinner I asked if she was having any problems with student unrest. She replied that she was threatened with a 'sleep-in', because the undergraduates' boyfriends objected to being turned out of the college by midnight. She seemed unperturbed, even when we passed a couple locked in a passionate farewell embrace. The food at high table was excellent; so was the wine. I told Miss Trickett that one of the most encouraging manifestations of women's emancipation was that women's colleges now had their own well-stocked wine cellars and she agreed enthusiastically. I could not help thinking that there was no need for women's colleges to go co-educational when they could have such fun running their own show in the new liberated atmosphere. I believe that in Oxford they have lost something in doing so.

Later still I went back to St Hugh's to do a television programme for Mavis Nicholson. The idea was that I would sit in the garden with a second-year student comparing life in Oxford in her day and mine. The result was an eye-opener. The college was by then co-educational and the old restrictions on movement had gone. More revealing still was the cool way in which this pretty, self-possessed young woman told me of a booklet they all received on arriving at the university which contained among other things details of where to get advice on contraception. Miss Trickett greeted me like an old friend and invited me to lunch. Sipping sherry in her sitting room I mused on the contrast between the St Hugh's of my day and hers and told her how Freda, rusticated for an innocent relationship with Bedi, had come back determined to make it a full-blown one. 'Quite right,' said Miss Trickett approvingly.

In my second year my social life was dominated by my brother Jimmie, who had graduated in forestry at Edinburgh and had been sent to Oxford for a fourth year to polish him up for the Colonial Service. He did not have much time for Oxford, considering that its forestry department was not a patch on Edinburgh's. But his company was very welcome and he escorted me everywhere. On one occasion he took me to the theatre and was so attentive, finding me the best seat in the dress circle and plying me with chocolates, that one of my fellow undergraduates from St Hugh's would not accept that he was my brother and threatened to report me to the college for going out unchaperoned. Women's college life bred such pettiness.

It was thanks to Jimmie that I went to my one and only commemoration ball. These were the highlights of the university's social year at which undergraduates in white tie danced till dawn in flower-decked marquees with their glamorously gowned girl-friends. Jimmie had arranged a sixsome for the ball at Pembroke where his friend Ronald Harvey was resident. Jimmie escorted Olive, Ronald had his own girlfriend, while I was paired with Glyn Jones, another of Jimmie's friends, who was due to leave for the Colonial Service in Africa at any moment. Glyn was a gentle, sensitive, slightly built young man whom I rather liked, and the imminence of his departure lent a romantic poignancy to our short acquaintanceship. Later Glyn was to belie his modest manner by climbing the colonial ladder becoming, as Sir Glyn Jones, governor successively of Nyasaland, Malawi and Zimbabwe. Olive and I had not asked for permission to attend the ball because we knew it would almost certainly be refused, so we walked out of the college in the early evening without signing out and changed in Ronald's room. It was a tradition of the balls that, having drunk champagne all night, one drove out to John Fothergill's Spread Eagle Inn at Thame for breakfast. This we duly did, piling into Ronald's little four-seater car. The fresh morning air gave us an enormous appetite and – tradition again – the men had to push the ladies in their long ballgowns on the garden swings. We drove back to Oxford in broad daylight, Olive and I perched on the young men's knees and everyone all too obviously in evening dress. At Carfax Ronald had a noisy brush with a milk float, sending a few bottles crashing to the ground, and we were sure there must be a proctor lurking about who would discover us. To our relief Olive and I managed to creep back into St Hugh's undetected, to find that the 'please do not disturb' notices we had pinned on our room doors and the pillows we had tucked down our beds were undisturbed.

Such glamorous occasions were very rare. Oxford terms were short anyhow and the dreary expanse of the long vacations stretched in between. I spent the vacs at home because I could not afford foreign holidays. The family had moved to Hyde. As soon as his children's schooling was over, Dad had been transferred to the Stalybridge district, one of Lancashire's run-down textile areas. He regarded it as a punishment. Our new house was pleasant enough, having the advantage of being on Nottram Road, which leads to Glossop, a gateway to the Peak District, which consoled me for the loss of my Yorkshire moors. The empty days dragged on endlessly as I sat in my bedroom, looking out at a curious monument on a nearby hill called Werneth Lowe and trying to concentrate on my set books. I was amused one morning to receive a letter from an Indian prince, an Oxford undergraduate who had developed a crush on me. He wrote from Juan les Pins. 'Do join us here. The tennis is wonderful.' Impossible! I consoled myself with the thought that I was not much good at tennis anyway.

When the monotony became intolerable I would take the bus to Glossop, armed with a packet of sandwiches and accompanied by the dog, a shilling clutched in my hand. Sixpence of it went on the bus fare out. Usually, having walked miles to the Snake Inn on the pass between Manchester and Sheffield, a popular stopping point, I blew the other sixpence on a shandy, relying on being able to thumb a lift home. Whenever possible I had friends to stay with me. One year Olive came and, as she had a reputation for being a great outdoor girl, I took her on one of the thirty-mile walks with which I was familiar. To my surprise it knocked her out. Mary Clark was another visitor. One summer we decided to attend an ILP summer school in Derbyshire, cadging a lift there in a friend's car. When, as usual, our money ran out we had to walk home to Hyde, hoping to thumb a few lifts on the way. In any case it meant spending a night in the open air. The weather was wonderful and after a day's walking we wrapped ourselves in our coats and lay down optimistically under a sheltering tree. I had forgotten that English summer nights could be so cold and we rose at dawn, frozen. We searched around frantically for a farm cottage where we might get breakfast and eventually found one where the kindly occupants plied us with hot tea and food.

There was a welcome diversion in the summer of my second year when I was invited with another undergraduate to do a rural speaking tour on behalf of the League of Nations. We were supplied with a caravan in which we toured remote hamlets, pitching it on the village green for a night or two. From it we radiated out with our message, visiting the village notables such as the vicar and the squire to get their help in organizing a meeting at which we would enrol members. Even the vicar was not always friendly; the gentry were usually polite but cool. The locals, however, welcomed our stirring up things in their rustic fastnesses and, according to my letters home, most of our meetings 'went very well'. Even at Naseby, where we were expecting trouble, we scored a victory. 'We shall have a hard time with the Naseby vicar,' I wrote home; 'he's an Army man, damn him!!' In the event we won him round and he took the chair for us. We were particularly proud of the leaflet we distributed: 'UR invited to hear the ABC of the League of Nations. Don't be DEF to it. On THE GREEN, Naseby. If wet in the schools. Speakers the "CARAVAN GIRLS" (from Oxford).' No doubt we thought the 'Oxford' would help break down the resistance of the retired military men who seemed to abound in the countryside and who had no use for wishy-washy internationalism.

Despite the long empty days of the summer vac I was working only spasmodically. My first duty on going up to St Hugh's had been to sit a preliminary examination which one must pass in one's first two terms or be sent down. Since PPE was new, the only 'prelim' the university could find that was at all appropriate was Law and I had to sit down and master Roman law. In fact I rather enjoyed learning about *usufructus* and all the rest of it, and I passed the exam in my first term. Then something in me snapped. I had been swotting for exams since I was sixteen and I had had enough. I wanted time for the rest of me to catch up, and my finals were nearly three years away. My powers of concentration seemed to disintegrate. One afternoon in my second year when I was trying to work in St Hugh's library while the sunlit trees lured me outside my restlessness burst out in verse:

THE BOTTLED IMP

Crouching and impotent I dream, I dream!
Why all these books? I want to do and be.
My wandering mind throughout the world is free
But I am caught within the sluggish stream
Of study, a false shadow of a life
When there is waiting, calling for me
Strife worthy of my abundant energy.
Let me go out and fight: I will return
When wise Defeat has taught me how to learn.

It was in this desperate mood that I entered my final year. I seemed to be getting nowhere with my studies or my sexual development. With Olive moving serenely from one happy-go-lucky affair to another and Freda finding her soulmate, I was the odd one out. I decided the time had come for me to explore the mystery which seemed an open book to everyone else. I did it in the most reckless way possible, agreeing to spend the night with an undergraduate in his college room. He was a pleasant chap, though I was certainly not in love with him. I was not even particularly attracted to him, though he was to me, and I found his passionate pleading flattering. If we had been discovered I would undoubtedly have been sent down. I was saved by the student's scout, a naturally discreet man, who knew exactly what had been going on but turned a blind eye to the explorations of the young and kept mum. Nonetheless, it was a wretched experience which I was in no hurry to repeat.

The year was also darkened by the fall of the Labour government, on whose period of office we had pinned such hopes. The circumstances of its collapse hit us in the Labour Club like a body-blow. We knew it had taken power at a very dangerous time when economic crisis was sweeping the world, precipitated by the Wall Street crash of 1929, and we were prepared to make allowances, but what shattered us was that under Ramsay MacDonald's leadership the government had drifted helplessly with the tide and had made no attempt to apply its own alternative policies. I had to face the brutal fact that my former hero was not only weak, but vain, flattered by the attentions of duchesses and their social set. He had left Philip Snowden, his iron Chancellor of the Exchequer, to pursue policies of 'sound finance', by which Snowden meant defending the value of sterling as the overriding priority at the expense of everything else. There were plenty of voices to be heard urging that Britain should come off the gold standard, to which Churchill as Chancellor had shackled us in 1924, but Snowden would have none of it. He had the conviction of a fanatic and with his sea-green incorruptibility and powerful intellect he won respect even among the working people whom he represented as MP for Blackburn from 1906 to 1918. When I succeeded him there as MP twenty years later I found that the younger members of the party execrated him as a traitor while the older members mourned his loss. One old man told me he had always listened to his speeches spellbound because they were so 'intellectual'. He obviously thought I was not a patch on him.

So Snowden had no difficulty in getting his way with a bewildered Cabinet. He brushed aside those who argued that you cannot cure a depression by cutting demand still further. That seemed commonsense to rank-and-filers like myself, who instinctively believed that socialism meant using expenditure on public works to set unemployed men and women producing the goods and services people were crying out for. In 1936 Maynard

Keynes was to put these rather inchoate thoughts into the language of the professional economist in *The General Theory of Employment, Interest and Money* but to Philip Snowden any challenge to Treasury orthodoxy was anathema. When the young Oswald Mosley, then a socialist and Chancellor of the Duchy of Lancaster, advocated expansionist policies through public works, Snowden forced him out of the government, paving the way for the blackshirt movement which Mosley was later to organize. Snowden even ignored the advice of his own Economic Advisory Committee, on which Maynard Keynes and Ernest Bevin sat. Deflation was his only remedy and by December 1930 unemployment had risen to 2.5 million. Undeterred, he set up a committee under Sir Ernest May, chairman of the Prudential Assurance Company, to recommend further spending cuts to save the pound.

The May Committee report led to the most traumatic crisis in Labour's history. The Committee proposed savings amounting to £77 million, two-thirds of which were to come from cuts in unemployment benefit. Most members of the Cabinet, mesmerized by MacDonald's lectures about the need for 'sound finance', had already agreed to spending cuts of 10 per cent, but this was too much. With nearly 3 million unemployed already eking out a miserable existence on the dole, nine ministers refused to cut unemployment benefit. MacDonald's response, with the capitalist system crumbling before our eyes, was to defect to the enemy.

So 24 August 1931 was one of the blackest days in Labour's chronicles. MacDonald went to the Palace behind the Cabinet's back to tell the King, George V, that he was willing to help form a national government. Only three members of his Labour Cabinet went with him into the new government: Jimmie Thomas, who was already a villain in my family's political calendar, Lord Sankey, the Lord Chancellor, and Philip Snowden, whom many of us deeply distrusted. The rest of the Cabinet stood firm. A little belatedly, in our view, they had seen the light.

The response to MacDonald's defection was violent among the Labour rank and file, including the modest ranks of our Labour Club. As soon as Michaelmas term at the university started, we officers called an emergency meeting and to a packed

audience Tony Greenwood moved and I seconded that Mac-
Donald be deposed as our honorary president. Despite the influx
of a number of Tory undergraduates to defend the defector it was
carried overwhelmingly. We then organized a collection for the
coming election fight. As I took round my collecting box I came
to Sheila, MacDonald's daughter and a student at Somerville, who
was flattening herself white-faced against the wall. She turned her
head away and I left her to her misery.

Three weeks to the day from taking office, the national
government was to take Britain off the gold standard. This step
had none of the anticipated disastrous consequences. Prices did
not rise and unemployment began to fall. So Snowden's critics
had been right. Despite this endorsement of our left-wing views
the national government swept the polls. The Labour Club put its
pennyworth into the campaign, raising funds and organizing
open-air meetings in surrounding areas at which Tony Greenwood
and I spoke. Our efforts were in vain. Labour's ranks in Parliament
were decimated – 288 seats down to 52 – and of their leaders only
Clement Attlee, Sir Stafford Cripps and George Lansbury survived. The lesson I learned was that Labour governments cannot
win power or survive by adopting the economic policies of their
political enemies. I was to remember it all my life.

During all this excitement my academic studies had suffered
even more. As my finals drew near panic set in when I realized
how unprepared I was. I started a relationship with a young man
who was doing a course at Oxford, though he was not an
undergraduate, and who wanted to marry me. He was a nice
enough lad, but I certainly did not want to marry him and I am
not any good at casual affairs. I kept on this one mainly for
comfort, but it did not help. Emotionally and physically I was all
at sea. My written exam over, which proved less intimidating
than I had feared, I went away to a country retreat for two or
three weeks with my young man and some friends. The ostensible
purpose was to prepare for my viva: the face-to-face interview
with the panel of examiners which can make a good deal of
difference to one's degree. Like a relentless Greek tragedy everything went wrong. I did no preparing and we messed up the

journey back to Oxford so that I arrived for my viva tired and flustered, having driven through the night. I learned afterwards that I had been vivaed for a Second, but I was at my worst, answering the questions with truculent political generalizations instead of reasoned arguments. I knew I had thrown my opportunity away.

I was at home when the results came through. There it was in black and white: a Third. It was the final blow to my self-confidence. My father was desolated.

FOUR

—————— • ——————

The 1930s

I CAME back to Hyde in the summer of 1932 with my tail between my legs. I hated disappointing my parents after the sacrifices they had made, though my mother was as loyal and comforting as always. With the country in deep depression, unemployed graduates were ten a penny, so I lived at home with no prospect of a job. I did not want to be a teacher, even if there had been a chance. As always my sights were set on journalism and politics. Hyde had two local newspapers and I applied to both of them for a job. I got an interview at one of them. The editor seemed an impressionable man who was quite excited at the idea of having me on his staff and offered me a job at ten shillings a week. Naturally I jumped at it, but the paper folded before I could even start.

Hyde was a grim place in those depression years. All public development had come to a full stop so it was a town of drab streets in which the litter blew about in the northern wind. The only cultural life consisted of a run-down cinema. The most prestigious eating place was the UCP café – the initials stand for United Cow Products – that is, tripe. It was housed in spartan white-tiled premises with outlines of cows embedded in the tiles at intervals. Those who could afford it could get a cheap meal of tripe and onions. All I could afford to imbibe there occasionally was a cup of tea. The contrast with Bradford nearly broke my father's spirit.

As always I found my consolation in politics. My life centred round the Hyde Labour Club, which offered the camaraderie of billiards and cheap drinks. One of its offerings was Red Biddy, a potent drink of mysterious origin which at fourpence a glass could quickly catapult one into the stratosphere. I enjoyed the warm atmosphere, but I also took my politics very seriously. I started reading everything I could lay my hands on in the form of economic treatises, white papers and government blue books with an application I had never achieved at Oxford. The acquisition of knowledge had become relevant. The members of the Hyde Labour Party regarded me with a mixture of respect and suspicion. The women's section took me aback by asking me to talk about bimetallism, of all subjects, which was one of the panaceas being pedalled for our economic ills. The youth section asked me to give them a talk on economics. Following the collapse of the Labour government in 1931 some of the cruder versions of Marxism had become popular among the rank and file and my audience was shocked when I told them that one of the keys to our economic recovery was for Britain to invest more capital in her industries. Wasn't capital the engine of that hated capitalist system which had brought the country to its knees?, one truculent member demanded. Not necessarily, I replied. The accumulation of capital was essential to any economic system since it meant forgoing consumption today to invest in tomorrow's prosperity: what Aneurin Bevan was later to describe as not eating the seedcorn of tomorrow's harvest. Some of the more militant among them remained unconvinced, suspecting that Oxford had corrupted me. The encounter taught me that the party had to work out and proclaim far more clearly than it had done so far the alternative economic policies which we socialists were offering to the rigid communist philosophy and to the chaos of a capitalist free-for-all.

This fallow period in Hyde was productive in other ways. One of the jobs I took on for the local party was that of propaganda secretary. This meant humping our wooden speaking rostrum to Hyde market square every Saturday night to try to draw the attention of casual passers-by to our political message. It was my job, too, to induce already overworked local politicians and trade union officials to come and speak to us in these unpropitious circumstances. I remain eternally indebted to Ellis

Smith, a dogged little trade unionist from Eccles who helped me out time after time and never let anyone down. I was delighted when he was elected to Parliament for Stoke-on-Trent a few years later and still more so when he became Parliamentary Secretary to the Board of Trade after Labour swept back to power in 1945. He deserved both breaks, for he was one of the lesser-known stalwarts who built the party up again from the ashes.

The post of propaganda secretary also involved me personally in the most rigorous training in public speaking that any politician could hope for. Not only did I take the chair at these open-air meetings, but I became the speaker myself if those who had promised to come did not turn up. It was a fine cure for any speaking nerves. My wise old dad said to me, 'The only way to learn public speaking is to speak in public. You will make a fool of yourself at first, but you will suddenly realize you are a public speaker.'

As one of the few who were prepared to get on to their feet in public I was in great demand in the surrounding towns, particularly among the young socialists who were desperately trying to keep our propaganda going. On one memorable occasion I was inveigled into speaking in Ashton-under-Lyne marketplace. The young chairman leaped on to the back of the lorry which was our platform and introduced me with the words, 'Ladies and gentlemen, we now have a unique phenomenon: a woman wot speaks.' And speak I had to, trying to make myself heard above the passing trams.

All this initiation paid off when Susan Lawrence came to speak at an indoor public meeting in Hyde and I was asked to be one of the accompanying speakers. Susan Lawrence was one of Labour's middle-class intellectuals, an impressive figure who had won a national reputation as Parliamentary Secretary at the Ministry of Health in the 1929 government, and I was terrified. I worked on my speech for days, swotting up every statistic I could turn up in the blue books. It must have been one of the most encyclopaedic speeches the audience in the packed hall had ever heard. Susan Lawrence was late and I was in the middle of my flood of statistics when she arrived. I started to sit down but she waved me to continue. When I had finished she won my enduring gratitude by telling the audience, 'You have just listened to one of the future leaders of the Labour Party.' I made a vow then that if I ever became prominent I would go out of my way to give the same boost to the morale of the younger generation trying to follow me.

I had broken with my young man and my only companionship was with a member of the local party, a gentle meditative person with a philosophical bent. He was middle-aged and married and there was some raising of eyebrows among local members, but our friendship could not have been more platonic. Like me he was unemployed and desperately hard up. Our most sophisticated rendezvous was the UCP café, where we would discuss politics over a cup of tea. We both had a passion for dancing and once or twice he took me to Blackpool, the great windswept playground of the northern working class. We took shelter from wind and rain in the baroque edifice of the Winter Gardens, which incongruously organized tea dances in its vast ballroom. I shall never forget sweeping across the ballroom's nearly empty floor in his arms. He was an excellent dancer and I had to concentrate on following his steps. The song 'Tea for Two' has always brought nostalgic memories.

The continuing transformation of my life suddenly took an unexpected turn. I had filled some of my time on a secretarial course in Manchester. I never mastered touch-typing, though shorthand intrigued me and I acquired a reasonable smattering of it, which stood me in good stead in later years when I wanted to keep a verbatim record of conversations I had had – not least in Cabinet. My surreptitious shorthand scribbles were to provide the basis for my Cabinet diaries. I was still determined not to be trapped in a secretarial job, so I was delighted when one of our slight Labour acquaintances turned up at our house and said, 'If Barbara is not too proud, I can get her a job.' He was the north-western sales manager for Samuel Hanson and Sons of Eastcheap, prestigious wholesale importers of tea, coffee, tinned fruits and a range of confectionary from mint humbugs to crystallized fruits. Apparently the firm had acquired a new young director, a Mr

Dunning, who wanted to modernize its sales techniques by introducing a team to demonstrate its products in major shops and at trade exhibitions. He was looking for someone to launch a pilot scheme in Manchester. Was I interested?, asked our friend.

I jumped at it. Nervously I attended an interview with the directors, but as I left the room I heard laughter as Mr Dunning remarked, 'I would buy a whole load of mint humbugs from her.' So I got the job on the understanding that, if the pilot scheme worked, I would be brought to London to organize similar schemes across the country. I seemed on my way.

The reality turned out to be very different. I had to set up stall in Manchester's bigger shops, usually in a draughty doorway, where I was to accost customers coming in and out and try to persuade them to taste my wares. One of the firm's sidelines I had to demonstrate was crystallized fruits. The glossy boxes at two shillings and sixpence a time were not easy to sell in those depressed days and I would look out for any man with a fur collar to his coat and pounce on him, murmuring sweetly, 'Can I press you to a crystallized fruit?' Sometimes it worked, but more often it didn't and I got chilblains standing in the draught. One day our sales friend who had got me the job came to see how I was getting on and was horrified to find me blue with cold. He rushed out and bought me a woolly cardigan to put under my white sales-coat.

Occasionally the firm took a stand at one of the trade fairs in the area and I would make endless trial cups of tea for potential customers. On one occasion I spent a fortnight in the basement of Lewis' big store in Market Street, Manchester, selling Mr Pickwick's mint humbugs, one of the firm's sidelines. I had to dress up as Little Nell and was accompanied by a friendly older man parading as Mr Pickwick. It was warm enough in there, but by the end of an eight-hour day the airlessness and monotony had become almost unendurable. The stall next to ours was selling gramophone records and I must have heard the current hit 'Waggon Wheels', played several hundred times a day. Mr Pickwick and I alternated between bursts of sales enthusiasm and a sense of the utter pointlessness of the exercise, when we did not give a damn what sweets the great British public might decide to buy. I was outraged when the shop searched us each night as we left.

One point I noticed was that the more up-market the store the worse the working conditions were likely to be. Behind many a glossy shop-front there was a lamentable lack of staff facilities, and we assistants would have to eat our lunchtime sandwiches on upturned packing cases in unheated backrooms. Naturally, one of my first acts was to join the Manchester central branch of the Shop Assistants' Union, where I learned how difficult it was to organize the young women, particularly with unemployment hanging over them. I remember trying to sell my crystallized fruits in a small select flower shop in the heart of Manchester and one afternoon finding the young shop assistant in tears. It was her afternoon off and she had a date with her boyfriend, but the boss had come in at the last minute to say she must stay and deal with a sudden order which had come in for a wreath. Indignantly, I pointed out to her a statutory notice on the wall. 'Look, it makes clear that you are entitled by law to this afternoon as your regular half-day off. You should insist on it.' 'There are plenty more waiting to take this job if I don't do it' was all she would say through her tears. The thought of joining a union terrified her, as she knew it would mean she would lose her job.

I knew that she was right and that unemployment was the biggest enemy of the rights the trade unions had struggled to win for her. I suppose I also realized subconsciously that trade unions cannot defend working people single-handed. They need the support of a government whose aim is to bring unemployment down.

It was in Manchester that I met the man who was to give direction to my political life and meaning to my personal one for the next ten years. He was William Mellor, who had edited the Labour Party's paper, the *Daily Herald*, until it was taken over by Odhams Press in 1931, when he became part of Odhams' editorial management. I already knew of him as an influential figure of the left who had pioneered the concept of guild socialism with his close friend G. D. H. Cole. This movement reflected the disillusionment with parliamentary government among certain unions after the war – notably the miners and the railwaymen, who were determined to achieve the nationalization of their industries, by industrial action if necessary. Mellor himself advocated direct action by workers – not revolution in the streets but the use of organized industrial action to fight the capitalist forces which dominated Parliament. Guild socialism did not have much political impact, but the influence of its ideas lingered on in the form of Labour's belief in the right of workers to participate in the running of industry and the economy. It also helped strengthen the links between the party and the trade unions, which were never (as cynics still like to suggest) just a marriage of convenience, with the unions bringing the party a substantial dowry. Loyalty to the trade unions among the Labour rank and file was fierce and genuine, particularly as the politicians in Parliament had so signally failed to deal with the economic crisis of 1931.

The crisis deepened as the depression dragged on. Few people today can grasp the bitterness and frustration of that period. Unemployment hung like a black pall over the old industrial areas, destroying whole communities. Indignities were heaped on the poor through the household means test, which the national government had introduced as one of its answers to the slump. Under it any members of a family who were working were forced to contribute out of their wages to the pittance paid to those members who were unemployed. Aneurin Bevan, the fiery young MP for Ebbw Vale, told Parliament of cases in his own mining area where the household means test had broken up families. One young lad he knew of who had started work in the pit came home proudly one day to tell his family that he had increased his earnings by seven shillings a week only to have his rise deducted from his unemployed father's relief. Any luxury in the home, such as a piano, had to be sold before relief was given. Walter Greenwood caused a stir with his book *Love on the Dole*, which described similar schemes in neighbouring Salford. The play based on his book played to packed audiences in Manchester. Ellen Wilkinson, MP for Jarrow, whom we all knew as 'Red Ellen', herded her tattered, unemployed constituents on hunger marches, leading them all the way on foot from Jarrow to Westminster, describing Jarrow as 'the town that was murdered'. Dickens never described anything more brutalizing, but the government was not listening.

Worst of all was the growing threat to democracy. In 1933 Hitler was elected Chancellor of Germany. Mussolini's fascists were already installed in Italy. In Spain Franco was leading his army against the democratically elected Republican government. At home Oswald Mosley had formed the British Union of Fascists and was bringing his blackshirts on to the streets in provocative rallies. We on the left knew that the collapse of democracy could happen in Britain too, because there were many secret admirers of Hitler among the well-heeled ruling class and many would-be appeasers in the government.

I shared the growing anger at these developments. Following the débâcle of 1931 the Labour Party was in a ferment, with many of us seeking answers to the questions Why did it happen? How could we prevent a repetition in future? Could social democracy ever work in a capitalist economy? Some, like John Strachey, the upper-class socialist from a distinguished family, became converts to Marxism. By the time I came to hear of him John was a bogeyman of the right, having taken his restless brilliance into the service of the Communist Party, though he never became a member. He had startled the political world with the publication in 1930 of *The Coming Struggle for Power*, in which he argued that communism was the only alternative to barbarism. He was later to become a driving force behind the influential Left Book Club founded by Victor Gollancz, which was to make many people socialist in the 1930s. I became a member of the Club like thousands more.

The ILP moved in the opposite direction, to toy with Trotsky-ism. In 1931 its conference voted to disaffiliate from the Labour Party in disgust as its performance in government. The majority preferred to take their political purity unsullied into the wilder-ness. My family repudiated this move and was looking for a new left-wing non-communist grouping which would enable us to influence the Labour Party from inside.

Cole was one of the first to make a move. He set up the Society for Socialist Inquiry and Propaganda (SSIP), consisting of high-powered intellectuals, to act as a left-wing think-tank in the party. While I was still at university I attended one of its early meetings in Manchester. We met in the basement of a shop in Market Street and I remember how depressing I found not only the bleak meeting place, but the remoteness of the 'intellectuals'. They did not seem to be in touch with the real tough world I knew in places like Hyde. Cole obviously thought so too. He was always anxious to bring the trade unions and intellectuals together and had persuaded Ernest Bevin to become the chairman of SSIP. The split in the ILP gave him his chance to turn the think-tank into a wider pressure group. The minority in the ILP which opposed disaffiliation was led by Frank Wise, the party's leading economist, who now put himself at the head of the 'affiliationists'. Frank had not only a first-class brain which would have carried him far in the Labour movement if he had lived, but also an attractive personality. Having met him, I could understand why Jennie Lee, the glamorous young ILP MP for Lanark, had been in love with him for many years. I was no rival, as by then I was in love myself. Cole persuaded Frank to lead his affiliationists into a merger with the SSIP to form the Socialist League. To Bevin's chagrin Frank was elected chairman of the League, so Bevin walked out on it. I promptly joined the new body's Manchester branch. William Mellor had been a formative influence in setting up the League and became one of its leading propagandists. It was at a Saturday meeting in Hyde that I first encountered him.

I was impressed by him. Physically he was my kind of man: tall, black-haired, erect, with a commanding presence and strong, handsome features. It was clear from his dress that he had fastidious tastes and he stood on the platform in the dingy hall, groomed to his fingertips in his Savile Row suit, radiating authority. I could have dismissed all this, but what captivated me was his honesty: looking on the rows of rather shabby listeners, he boomed at them, 'I have just spent as much on my lunch as you earn in a week. How much longer are you going to put up with it?' It was not the sort of propaganda they had listened to before. My mother was in the audience with me and invited him home for tea. Our mutual attraction was immediate. He was soon back in Manchester inviting me to have a meal with him.

William proceeded to take me to a new world, one which included elegant little restaurants like Prince's off Albert Square, a favourite of Manchester connoisseurs in those days. He always chose a simple meal, and no spirits or cocktails, just half a bottle of fine wine. He introduced me to the glamour of late suppers in the Midland Hotel grill room, where I met theatre people who were trying out plays in Manchester before moving to London's West End. I also met theatre critics like the legendary Hannen Swaffer. Sometimes we would drive out to the country in a hired car. William did not have a car or drive himself – 'I belong to the car-hiring classes,' he used to say as he sat back in his seat with his immaculate white-gloved hands folded in his lap. When on one occasion we drove to Buxton's top hotel for afternoon tea he astonished me by complaining that the napkins were paper and not linen ones. 'What is this hotel coming to?'

All through this he was gradually restoring my self-confidence. It came to a climax over dinner one evening when at last I summoned up the courage to blurt out my terrible secret: 'I came down from Oxford with a Third.' He threw back his head and roared with laughter. 'I came down with a Fourth!' he said. Apparently as the son of a Unitarian minister he had been sent to Keble to read divinity with a view to entering the ministry, but he had hated it. I felt as if a millstone had fallen from my neck. If this brilliant man could get away with a Fourth why was I crucifying myself over my wretched Third?

I came increasingly to realize that William's fastidiousness extended through his whole personality. He rejected coarseness of any kind, not least in sex. He told me he was married with a young son, and this knowledge clearly held him back. As the electric currents flowed between us, he visibly controlled himself. Eventually it was I who led him to bed in our house in Hyde, where he was staying during a speaking tour. The next morning he went straight to my father and told him we were in love and that he was not free to marry me, though he hoped to be. My father said to me afterwards with a wry grin, 'I never expected a man to come to me and tell me that his intentions towards my daughter were strictly dishonourable.'

True to his word William went back to his wife to tell her what had happened and to move her gently towards the idea of divorce. Both he and I agreed that we did not want the rupture to be violent and were prepared to wait, but to all intents and purposes he became a member of my family. The more deeply he was in love the more anxious he was to help me to develop my whole potential. He became my intellectual mentor. One of his favourite precepts which he hammered into me was 'Think, think, think. It will hurt like hell at first, but you'll get used to it.' One day he brought me the selected works of William Morris, with the words, 'You could do a lot worse than to read that.' In it I found a poem, 'The Message of the March Wind', which was to run like a refrain through my whole life:

Now sweet, sweet it is through the land to be straying
'Mid the birds and the blossoms and the beasts of the field;
Love mingles with love and no evil is weighing
On thy heart or mine, where all sorrow is healed. . . .

Hark, the wind in the elm-boughs! from London it bloweth,
And telleth of gold, and of hope and unrest;
Of power that helps not; of wisdom that knoweth,
But teacheth not aught of the worst and the best.

Of the rich men it telleth, and strange is the story
How they have, and they hanker, and grip far and wide;
And they live and they die, and the earth and its glory
Has been but a burden they scarce might abide. . . .

Yet, love, as we wend, the wind bloweth behind us,
And beareth the last tale it telleth tonight,
How here in the spring-tide the message shall find us;
For the hope that none seeketh is coming to light. . . .

I also loved 'The March of the Workers'. As I grew more relaxed in my public speaking and learned to love my audience instead of being afraid of it, I would sometimes end my peroration with the last verse:

On we march then, we the workers, and the rumour that ye
    hear
Is the blended sound of battle and deliv'rance drawing near;
For the hope of every creature is the banner that we bear,
And the world is marching on.

It was not until much later that, having probed deeper into Morris and having read J. W. Mackail's biography of him, I discovered that he had been a member of Hyndman's Social Democratic Federation and a Marxist. True, Marx's labour theory of value gave him 'agonies of confusion of the brain', but he was an instinctive Marxist who knew from his own creative life that satisfaction in one's work is the key to happiness, which nine-teenth-century industrialization had destroyed for so many. 'If I were to work ten hours a day at work I despised and hated,' he declared, 'I should spend my leisure, I hope, in political agitation, but I fear in drinking.' Like John Ruskin, his mentor, he dismissed with scorn the 'great civilized invention' of the division of labour and often quoted Ruskin's words: 'It is not, truly speaking, the labour that is divided, but the men – divided into mere segments of men – broken into small fragments and crumbs of life.' Charlie Chaplin was to update this theme in *Modern Times*. Concern with the effect on human beings of the demands of the relentless conveyor belt was always part of my socialism and I believed we would never have a stable and happy society unless we found some way of relieving the monotony of workers' lives. So it has proved.

Being trapped myself in the monotony of a dull routine I rebelled. After eighteen months of peddling my wares round Manchester shops I wrote to Mr Dunning, the young director who had appointed me, reminding him that my job in Manchester was supposed to be only a pilot scheme and that I had been

promised that after an appropriate trial period I would be brought
to London. He replied immediately, 'Come and see me.' Within
hours I was on my way to London. From there I wrote home
ecstatically the next day, 'I've seen Dunning this morning and I
have been incredibly, deliriously promoted. I'm to be Sales
Supervisor, directly under Mr Maurice of the Publicity Department. I'm to be located in London permanently and I'm to get a
considerable rise in screw to be specified later.' (In the event it was
a rise from £4 per week to £5.) 'This is a job I can really make
something of,' I added, 'and it will be fascinating, too – involving
responsibility, initiative, organization and sales research.' Dunning
told me seriously at the end of my interview, 'You can make
yourself a big thing out of this.'

My euphoria was not to last long. Installed in my little office
in the firm's Eastcheap premises I found that Mr Dunning's writ
did not run as far as I had believed. The private-enterprise
bureaucracy moved in on me. I got on swimmingly with the sales
lads, who were eager for me to organize demonstrations in the
shops which they supplied, but they, just as I had, came up against
the brick wall of my immediate superior's scarcely veiled hostility
to the new ideas of salesmanship and to me as their instrument.
Within a few months I was writing to my mother, 'I am feeling
rather gloomy at the moment because I don't think this job is ever
going to get me anywhere. I am certain Maurice is trying to
sabotage it, even more so since I've read a letter I've just received
from one of the travellers whom I thought Maurice had told to fix
up demonstrations and who says Maurice has told him "not to fix
up anything definite".' In fact I had been allowed to arrange only
one demonstration in the whole of the winter of 1934 and had
been twiddling my thumbs. It was an absurd situation, but it
could not go on and I decided to have a last throw. With the help
of the travellers I drew up a memo setting out a detailed plan for a
nationwide network of sales activities. I sent it straight to the
directors, knowing that Mr Maurice would never forward it.
Retribution was swift: I had committed the unforgivable sin of
trying to beat the system. Mr Maurice had clearly put his foot
down and demanded that I be sacked. 'Either she goes or I do,' I

could imagine him saying. Anyway, sacked I was, having been given a useful insight into the hierarchical rigidities of private enterprise.

My vision of a brilliant business career had proved a mirage and I turned back to the consolations of politics, filling my days with work for the Socialist League, writing articles, organizing branch meetings and selling the League's paper, the *Socialist Leaguer*, late at night outside Russell Square Underground. Following Frank Wise's death, Stafford Cripps, the stern puritanical barrister, had become chairman of the Socialist League and moved into open confrontation with the Labour Party's National Executive Committee (NEC). The party leadership did not know what to make of him. Admired for his brilliance at the Bar, he had been brought in at the tail end of the 1929 government as Solicitor-General. The miners loved him for the masterly way he presented their case at the Gresford colliery disaster enquiry – free of charge. He was popular in the constituencies and could silence criticism by effective speeches in the House. His earnings at the Bar had made him a rich man and he was generous with his wealth, but he could show the high-handedness of the wealthy, as a number of us were to find. His integrity was not in doubt. He had a beautiful country home at Filkins in Gloucestershire, but he himself lived frugally in his small London flat in Whitehall Court. One evening when he invited me over to a discussion he offered to share with me his supper of sardines on toast. Nonetheless he irritated the leadership by his certainty that he was in the right. So they were torn: they realized the value of having such an outstanding advocate in the party's ranks, but changed their minds when he started advocating what seemed to them outrageous policies.

Nineteen-thirty-four was the first showdown year. In June the Socialist League produced its policy statement: *Forward to Socialism*. It bore all the hallmarks of William's conviction that there could be no common ground between workers who had nothing to live on but their labour and the property interests who dictated whether they should work at all. Private ownership of the means of production, it argued, was at the root of the economic crisis bedevilling the world. By definition it led to poverty and unemployment in an age of plenty because 'capitalism cannot distribute the goods it can produce'. The scramble for markets between competing private interests led of necessity to its final product: 'devastating war'. The emergence of fascism was a sign of 'capitalism grown desperate'. The answer was to replace private ownership of the land and the means of production by a new social order in which they would be owned by the community and run for production, not for profit. International co-operation between capitalist states rent by economic rivalries was a mirage. The only hope of peace, therefore, lay not in the League of Nations but in forging the unity of the working class throughout the world.

On this basis the League proceeded to table seventy-five amendments to the NEC's own document *For Socialism and Peace*, which was due to be debated at the Labour Party conference in October. Re-reading it I find the NEC document not too bad at all, though no doubt it had been pepped up to counter the pressures coming from the left. Its social policies, including the establishment of a state medical service, paved the way for the brilliant success of the 1945 Labour government in creating the welfare state. It also called for centralized economic planning and for the public ownership and control of the primary industries and services, notably the banking system, transport, coal and power, water supply, iron and steel and land. Much of this was achieved in 1945 but the National Executive's approach lacked the analysis of capitalism and the sense of urgency of the Socialist League's document, and the reforming drive of the Labour government petered out in 1950. Our amendments were designed to prevent any such retreat.

The task of moving the amendments fell on William, and I had never admired him more than when he went to the rostrum time and again to confront the open hostility of conference. The most controversial was on peace, collective security and the League of Nations. It declared that the League 'inevitably reflects the economic conflicts of the capitalist states . . . and cannot end war'. The only hope lay in co-operation between workers in every country to oppose the war plans of their own governments. The amendment concluded, 'The Labour Party . . . undertakes to

73

resist a war entered into by this government by every means in its power, including a general strike.' Since the NEC's document reiterated Labour's support for the League of Nations as the stepping stone to world government, the effect was electric. Arthur Henderson, who as Foreign Secretary in the 1929 government had been a keen advocate of collective security, was outraged. Confronting William in the corridor he said angrily, 'This reverses Labour's whole policy.' I was shaken by his fury, but William battled on unperturbed and won reluctant admiration for his courage and oratorical stamina. The votes in favour of our amendments were derisory.

A few months later our policy was severely tested when in September 1936 Mussolini invaded Abyssinia. The League of Nations, backed by the Labour Party, called for sanctions, but the Socialist League, true to its formula, opposed them. I began to have my doubts about our line when my brother, home on leave from his job as Assistant Conservator of Forests in Nigeria, berated me. Didn't we realize how bitter the colonial peoples were about this invasion and that they were demanding that sanctions be applied? I had no answer to that, but our argument that capitalist governments could not be relied on to make collective security work was soon vindicated by the British government itself, of which Baldwin had now become the head. Sanctions had been introduced with a flourish of trumpets, but the actual steps taken were pitiful. An oil embargo, for instance, would have stopped Mussolini's advance in its tracks, but it was deliberately excluded as too inconvenient for those applying it. 'The League of Nations', wrote Churchill in *The Gathering Storm*, the first volume of his history of the Second World War, 'proceeded to the rescue of Abyssinia on the basis that nothing must be done to hamper the invading Italian armies.' Mussolini's conquest went effectively unchecked.

Nor did Baldwin show any greater enthusiasm for stopping Hitler. In the general election campaign of October 1935, skilfully reading the national mood, which vacillated between the desire for action and dread of another war, he on the one hand talked about the need to build up our defences and on the other assured the Peace Society that 'there will be no great armaments'. His ambivalence was rewarded with a majority over all-comers of 249 seats. Labour gained 96 more seats, bringing its total to 154, but was still not much more than halfway back to its strength in 1929. The Liberals thought they had done well to get twenty-five seats.

On the personal side William's and my own prospects were darkening, too. After the Socialist League conference William had written to my parents to say that his wife was still refusing him a divorce, but that he would go on trying. Everything seemed to be conspiring against us. I was still out of a job and was earning a pittance from freelance journalism; and William's attempt just before the general election to get into Parliament in a by-election at Enfield had failed, though honourably. His defeat was followed by an immediate reckoning with Odhams. I reported it home in a letter to my mother. (All my letters were addressed to her with the footnote 'Please let Dad read this.') 'Yes, we *were* disappointed,' I wrote after the by-election,

> signs were so hopeful. But in Enfield on a 100 per cent left-wing programme, an increase of 5000 in the Labour vote is no disgrace. . . . But at the moment his and our future is badly in the melting pot. A definitive ultimatum has at last come that W. should go out of politics altogether or give up his job. . . . He had a long talk with Dunbar [managing director of Odhams Press] this afternoon and offered to resign from the Socialist League, but apparently that's not enough. . . . They want him to cease all writing, speaking or standing for Parliament. God he'll stifle if he has to do that! I say no. He says No. But it's the devil of a jam. He says he's been too long with Odhams to get a job elsewhere unless he sells out to Beaverbrook. If it were only a question of him and me, we wouldn't hesitate, but there's Edna [his wife]. I'm a bit low. . . . It's a ruthless world.

The answer to Dunbar was inevitably no and William's final dismissal came in January 1936.

The physical cost to William was enormous. I wrote home: 'Life is pretty grim at the moment. . . . It is hitting W. very hard

– having no place in the world and no money. Poor lad, my heart aches for him.' It was in this mood that he was persuaded by a Labour colleague on the London County Council called Wallis to put his redundancy money into launching a new local government paper. Labour was riding high in London. In 1934 Herbert Morrison had bucked the national trend by capturing a majority on the LCC and his successful administration had given a new fillip to local government. A new municipal journal was required to report the activities of local councils more vividly. So in July 1936 the *Town and County Councillor* was born, with me as secretary at £4 a week and William in general editorial control. There ensued three years of struggle to make it pay its way.

With the threat of war looming, it was certainly not launched at an auspicious time. In March 1936 Hitler had marched into the Rhineland. In July General Franco launched his revolt against Negri's Republican government. Alarm bells were ringing in Europe. At its Seventh Congress the Communist International called for a popular front to stop fascism. Popular-front governments had been established in France and Spain, and the formation of a united front against Hitler by all anti-fascist forces seemed a matter of common sense. The Socialist League, however, was not interested in joining forces with a handful of progressive Tories and middle-class Liberals. We believed that only a united front of working-class parties would stand firm against Hitler. The Socialist League therefore authorized Stafford Cripps and William to open talks with the communists and the ILP. Aneurin Bevan, who had never formally been a member of the League, agreed to join in. We knew the negotiations would be difficult, because the ILP was now openly hostile to the Communist Party, a hostility fed by the bitter relations between ILP fighters and the Marxist POUM in the Spanish Civil War.

William had been allocated the job of negotiating with the communists. I had by then, with William's help, moved from my lodgings in Taviston Street into a tiny service flat in Endsleigh Court near St Pancras. It was here that part of the unity talks took place when William brought Harry Pollitt, secretary of the British Communist Party, to have a meal with us. I found Pollitt an unexpectedly mild and pleasant man who did not fit the stereotype of a communist as portrayed in the Tory press. I was not only struck by his reasonableness, but charmed by the appreciative way he received my sausage and mash, the only meal I could manage in my pocket-handkerchief kitchenette. I warmed to him as a human being and was not surprised when his personal reaction to the non-aggression pact Stalin struck with Hitler a few days before Britain declared war was one of overt incredulity. He and his fellow communists had resisted fascism so bitterly that he was not prepared to switch overnight to denouncing Britain's attack on Hitler as an 'imperialist war'. For a time his position as general secretary of the British Communist Party was in the balance and he was not happy in the party again until Hitler invaded the Soviet Union in June 1941 and she was in the anti-fascist alliance again.

Eventually the three parties to the talks agreed a document which was accepted, reluctantly, by the Socialist League membership. In January 1937 the Unity Campaign was launched, along with a new left-wing weekly, *Tribune*, brainchild of Cripps, Bevan, George Strauss and others. Cripps became chairman of the editorial board and William was appointed editor. It was good to have him back in a mainstream journalist job again. He decided to keep on the *Town and County Councillor* in the hope of recouping some of the money he had invested in it, and I was put in charge of producing it. But his financial position was still precarious and marriage was as far away as ever.

During this fraught period one of my great comforts was the companionship of Michael Foot. He had come down from Oxford three years after I had and we met through the Socialist League. Though coming from a famous Liberal family – his father Isaac had been Liberal MP for Bodmin – Michael had become a dedicated socialist. I suspect he was the only member of his family genuinely to do so, though his brothers, Hugh (later Lord Caradon) and Dingle (a skilled barrister), were both later to accept posts in Harold Wilson's governments. I discovered that the best way to infuriate Michael was to remind him that at Oxford he had contributed a chapter to a symposium on 'Why I Am a Liberal'. It was as uncompromising left-wingers that we found ourselves in harmony. Michael himself, true to his rigid principles, refused office in Wilson's first government because he found it too right-wing and joined the Cabinet only in 1974 when the policies had changed.

When I first met him, shortly after I came to London, Michael was still at the chrysalis stage. Though taller than I was, he stooped slightly and his diffident air was heightened by his spectacles. He dressed casually, almost to the point of untidiness, but I took to him immediately. I liked the decisive cast of feature he shared with his brothers Hugh and Dingle, his acute mind, his bookishness and his enthusiasm for politics. I also liked the sardonic wit which was to make him such a good speaker and journalist, even though he occasionally used it at my expense. Michael knew of my relationship with William, whom he deeply respected, once describing him as 'the granite-like conscience of socialism', and, with William beset by work and financial anxieties – *Tribune*, like every other left-wing enterprise, lived on the edge of crisis – I was glad of this extra companionship, which made no sexual demands on me.

We were soon engaged in joint activities, both political and journalistic. We worked indefatigably for the Socialist League, learning our politics the hard way, speaking at sparsely attend-ed meetings on Hampstead Heath or at the windy corners of Mornington Crescent in St Pancras. Michael was a tub-thumping orator who had not yet acquired the finesse he was to achieve in later years. I struggled grimly against audience indifference. We wrote a joint column on trade union affairs for *Tribune* under the pen-name Judex. As Michael reminded me later, we wrote what William told us to. We were both hard up, as Michael was living on freelance journalism and I was having a struggle to pay my rent, so we found a cheap restaurant in Soho called Vincent's, where we could get a substantial dinner for two and sixpence a head, going Dutch.

I used to take Michael home from time to time for weekends with my parents or with my sister Marjorie, with whom I was very close. Marjorie was by then married, living in the midlands and starting a family. Michael had a second-hand run-down jalopy in which I persuaded him to teach me to drive. We used to circle round Regent's Park with me at the wheel until the custodians, attracted by my erratic driving, shooed us off. One Friday evening, as we set off for Leicester to spend the weekend with Marjorie, I insisted on taking the wheel and, brave man as he was, Michael sat beside me, trying not to put his head in his hands as I careered through quiet villages in torrential rain crying, 'What do I do now?' Some fairy spirit was protecting us and we arrived with me triumphant and still at the wheel. Later, when he moved up in the world, he got rid of his jalopy and there was no one else to give me driving lessons.

In January 1936 I moved from my service flat to a small top-floor flat in Coram Street, Bloomsbury, where the rent was extremely low. After the matchbox existence in Endsleigh Court it was paradise. Coram Street was a row of eighteenth-century houses of the type which give Bloomsbury its character. I loved the area with its little shops and quiet squares. My flat had no modern appurtenances, but the kitchen, despite its basic equipment, was big enough for me to cook something more adventurous than sausage and mash. The flat had no central heating and the floors were uneven, but it had a reasonable-sized sitting room, a little bedroom and an old-fashioned bathroom. To my delight it also had a stepladder leading from the tiny landing on to the roof, on to which Michael and I liked to climb on summer days to sunbathe precariously among the smoke-stained chimneypots.

William loved to come there whenever he could. So did Michael, who no doubt found it a pleasant escape from his lodgings. On winter evenings, when I had cooked us a meal, we would sit by the gas fire reading contentedly. On one occasion I found that Michael was deep in *Das Kapital* while I was immersed in *Martin Chuzzlewit*. When I revisited the area some years after the war I found to my distress that Coram Street had been pulled down to make room for a modern housing development. I could not really blame the St Pancras Borough Council, whose Labour majority was desperately trying to cope with an acute post-war housing shortage, because London University had committed equal vandalism on a beautiful row of eighteenth-century houses on the other side of Russell Square in order to extend its own buildings in Malet Street. But these depredations did grievous damage to a historic segment of London's life and should have been stopped.

Michael and I were both considered to be promising material by Stafford Cripps, so we became his protégés. Occasionally we were invited down to Filkins, but we shared a streak of irreverence, so we were not quite what Stafford hoped for. At Filkins we were expected to sit round with the family listening respectfully to the great man as his children seemed to do, but we were not very good at it. We were both fond of Isobel, Stafford's wife, a kindly, understanding woman, but she had had to learn domestic diplomacy, so we were the only people who ever challenged Stafford's arguments. Stafford was very fond of tennis and practised regularly on his own courts, so he had become rather good. During one of our visits he took Michael and me out to play against him and one of his sons. It was a daunting prospect but the devil got in us and by unspoken mutual agreement we set out to win. And win we did. It was a triumph of willpower over the objective facts because neither Michael nor I were much above the rabbit class. Stafford was none too pleased, for he liked to win.

Though I had a deep affection for Michael, as I believe he had for me, our relationship never developed into a romance. For one thing he was far too loyal to poach on William's territory. For another he was going through a difficult period, being plagued with acute asthma and its accompanying eczema, which must have inhibited him to some extent. As far as I knew he had no girlfriend, which explained why he could spend so much time with me. In the summer of 1938 we went on a holiday together in Brittany. Arriving at a small private hotel, we asked for two separate rooms. The *patronne* looked knowingly at us and said, 'I will give you these two: they have a connecting door,' which she promptly unlocked. We had a little giggle about this as we went our separate ways to bed. In the middle of the night I was awoken by the sound of Michael's desperate struggle for breath, and rushed into his room to find him in the middle of an asthma attack. Clutching his inhaler he waved me out of the room. The next day he was himself again and we did not refer to it. We arrived back in England at the very moment that Chamberlain returned from his Munich talks with Hitler, waving his bit of paper and saying, 'Peace in our time.'

Many years later, when we were political veterans, I had to sit next to Michael on Labour Party platforms and listen to him delight our audience with hints at a more salacious version of this holiday. It was, of course, a myth and I have never understood why Michael should have invented it. We were never lovers and I do not think either of us ever seriously thought of each other in that way. For one thing I was not beautiful enough to attract him sexually. Under that shy exterior there was a lover of beautiful women waiting to burst out.

As Michael himself admits, it was Nye Bevan, emerging as one of the leading firebrands of the left and one of the first to recognize Michael's potential, who turned the chrysalis into a butterfly. Michael had become closer to him than I ever did. Indeed, it was Nye who prescribed ultraviolet treatment for Michael's eczema and bought him the machine to apply it. It was Nye, too, who told Beaverbrook, the maverick proprietor of the *Daily Express*, of Michael's journalistic promise. Michael claims that Nye's prescription played a key role in curing his eczema. Be that as it may, the cure enabled him to enjoy the sophisticated new life to which Beaverbrook introduced him in 1938 when he offered him a job writing for the *Evening Standard*.

In his essay on Beaverbrook, which he published several years later in his *Debts of Honour*, Michael describes how he arrived at Cherkley, Beaverbrook's country home, to encounter a vision of an exquisitely beautiful woman floating by distractingly. He fell for her and, although she was the 'boss's girl', made a pass at her, though with what success he does not make clear. Michael was no longer the diffident, untidy figure I had known, but rapidly developing into a brilliant and self-confident journalist.

Nonetheless he still retained his integrity. Michael was one of those rare people who, like his hero Aneurin Bevan, could pass through the temptations of the fleshpots, enjoy them, learn from them and emerge unscathed. He stayed with Beaverbrook only as long as the views he was allowed to express in the *Standard* were compatible with his personal ones. Beaverbrook was a bitter opponent of Lord Halifax and the other appeasers and backed the brilliant attack on them by Michael and Frank Owen, then editor of the *Standard*, in their bestselling pamphlet *Guilty Men*. When Hitler invaded the Soviet Union, by which time Michael had himself become editor, Beaverbrook also backed his campaign for the opening of a second front. When later their policy paths began to diverge Michael left the Beaverbrook empire, more wordly-wise but still a dedicated socialist.

When Michael was swallowed up in Beaverbrook's embrace I inevitably saw much less of him. I was delighted by his success, but I missed his company and wondered if I would ever get anywhere myself. My own career was progressing modestly. With William tied up with *Tribune* and showing increasing signs of exhaustion, I was left in sole charge of *Town and County Councillor*. I enjoyed the experience, commissioning articles, editing them, drawing up the layout and planning new campaigns. The most exciting part was my monthly trip to the printers to put the magazine to bed. Printers are a friendly crowd and they helped this young novice in every way they could, showing me how to mark up copy and correct it on the stone. After that, producing an election address became child's play.

At this time I was elected to the National Council of the Socialist League, in which I was more active than ever, running the Unity Campaign from my flat, typing away at circular letters and arranging meetings. It was I who had to organize the protest when Mosley proposed to march his blackshirts through our area. All this activity got me well known locally and I was selected to fight a seat on St Pancras Borough Council; I was elected in 1937 as one of its youngest members. I immediately aligned myself with fellow spirits on the left and seven of us formed a ginger group to challenge the Labour Group's uninspired leadership. One of our number was Krishna Menon, who was later to become India's High Commissioner to London. Krishna was a gaunt, prickly man who had a chip on his shoulder because he was intellectually head and shoulders above the rest of us yet was barely tolerated by the majority of Labour Councillors. Our ginger group was devoted to him and, when the election for the leadership of the Labour Group came up, we proposed him as our candidate. He only got our votes, one of the stolider Labour councillors saying to me, 'Barbara, I know he is very clever, but what would the electors think of us if we could only find a black man to be our leader?' Krishna merely shrugged sourly and said, 'I told you so.'

Nonetheless when Krishna, who lived alone in circumstances of great austerity, scarcely bothering to eat, fell seriously ill, the motherly bodies of the local party bustled round at once to take care of him. They plied him with goodies, cajoling him to eat, and probably saved his life. They discovered that they were really quite fond of him. Their racial prejudice had been induced by the conventional attitudes of the time and did not run deep.

It was on the Council that I first received national publicity. I had been elected with two other young women and the elderly Tory councillors who ran the Council did not know how to handle this new phenomenon. They fell back on their instinctive mixture of chivalry and condescension, which I rapidly tired of. The Tory leader of the Council, Sir David Davies, was a kindly, fatherly figure, but when for the umpteenth time he replied to one of my attacking speeches with his usual ponderous compliment about 'the charming young lady' I saw red. Rising to a point of order I said, 'Mr Mayor, can questions of sex attraction or no sex attraction be left out of the considerations of this Council?' Sir David collapsed. I had used the forbidden word. I was surprised the next day to find myself on the front page of a number of national newspapers, complete with photograph. 'The Girl Who Bans Flattery' was the headline in the *Daily Mail*. 'Not Wanted – Sex Attraction in Borough Council Meetings' ran the *Mirror* story. Some time later when the dust had settled Sir David came shyly up to me after a Council meeting to say, 'I'm sorry if I upset you. I have been inundated with letters from Tory supporters asking me what is going on, but I did not mean any harm.' Then after hesitating for a moment he blurted out, 'I can't help it. You *are* charming.' William, puritanical as usual, said it was a pity my first incursion into the national news should be on such a theme. Personally I thought I had expressed an important point.

Like everyone else Stafford had become interested in what was happening in the Soviet Union and in the autumn of 1937 he put up the money to send me there to write a series of articles for *Tribune*. Re-reading them today I realize how much I had to learn journalistically. I faithfully reported what I was shown by my Intourist guide. Some of it was moving enough, as when I watched little children dancing in the former Imperial Palace, which had been turned into a kindergarten, but I did not write about my unofficial contacts, who were far more revealing than the official ones.

My first such contact was on the small tubby Soviet ship which took me from London to Leningrad. Stafford, no doubt fearing that he was subjecting me to physical hardship by sending me into the Soviet unknown, insisted on my travelling first class. It was a great mistake. I found myself isolated in the first-class saloon with a sporty Englishman who was going to the Soviet Union to buy racehorses, and even he disappeared when the choppy Baltic started to do its worst. I was not seasick, but I was bored, so I made my way down to the steerage quarters, where the rest of the tourists were housed. The steerage dining room was barely furnished, but it was clean and warm and alive with chatter. The ship's officers were eating there with their crew, sharing the same simple but ample food. After the meal we all, officers, ordinary seamen and visitors, gathered round the piano to sing international songs. This was the Soviet revolution in its early days, when the Bolsheviks set out to destroy class divisions and create an equal society. Sadly this period of classlessness did not last long.

My other insight came on my way home. I travelled back to London by train, passing through White Russia on my way to Poland and Germany, stopping overnight in Minsk. My hotel was a rustic timber structure whose dining room had an earthen floor. It was filled with large thickly clad peasants from the local collective farms enjoying an enormous meal. There was no other tourist but me as far as I could see and I was overwhelmed by the noise and physical exuberance. One of the diners came over to my table to ask my Intourist guide if he could take me to the cinema, and the guide was shocked when I refused. She therefore took me herself to see the film, *Peter the Great*, whose arrival had excited the town. The shabby cinema was packed by an equally shabby audience, which sat enraptured by the story of their country's imperial past. They shushed angrily when my guide insisted on whispering loudly into my ear an interpretation of what was happening on the screen. I got the strong feeling that the Russian people liked their rulers to be masterful.

On my night sleeper west I knew I had to pass through Nazi territory, but I had defiantly brought with me a copy of the Soviet constitution and a small bust of Lenin. On Edgar Allan Poe's principle that the best way to hide something is to put it in the most obvious place, I had packed these incriminating objects in my dispatch case and placed it prominently on the shelf beside my bed while heaving my trunk on to the rack above my head. At the German frontier I had my first contact with Nazi Germany. In the early hours of the morning there was thunderous knocking at my sleeper door and shouts of 'Offen!' 'Wait a minute,' I shouted back. 'I am not ready.' When I opened the door the Nazi frontier police poured in. 'Engländerin,' they commented as I cheeked back at them. 'Ja, Engländerin,' I retorted cockily. They told me to bring down my trunk and I told them to bring it down themselves. They rifled it in vain, exclaiming disgustedly, 'Alle Schuhe.' 'Ja,' I said, 'alle Schuhe,' and they stormed out muttering, with not even a glance at the dispatch case beside my bed.

I congratulated myself on my cunning but I knew that my bravado had been false courage, as I was in little danger. At Berlin station, where we changed trains, I came up against chill reality. I decided to have a look at Unter den Linden before my train went, but as I tried to leave the station I found the exit barred by a locked iron gate in front of which a crowd of passengers were waiting passively. I was trying to push my way through when I heard the sound of anti-aircraft guns and realized that a large-scale air-raid exercise was taking place. I had never seen any sign of air-raid drill in London and I knew then that Hitler meant war, that our turn would come soon and that we were not prepared.

At home the Socialist League plans for stopping Hitler were not going well. The NEC was dominated by the trade unions, which not only elected the trade union section of the NEC and effectively dictated the membership of the women's section by their votes, but had the right to vote for the constituency parties' nominees, thus ensuring that no one could get on to the NEC of whom they did not approve. They were for the most part cautious men deeply suspicious of left-wing ideas, and they proceeded to wheel out the party's disciplinary machinery against the Unity Campaign. In vain people like Harold Laski pleaded that the Labour Party should not rule out joint working-class action against Hitler before, as in Germany it was too late. Co-operation with the Communist Party was forbidden. Some members of the NEC, including Clement Attlee, argued for tolerance, but were overruled. The NEC declared that membership of the Socialist League was incompatible with membership of the Labour Party. We faced the classic dilemma: to go into the wilderness as the ILP had done or to stay in the mass movement on the NEC's terms. At a special conference in May 1937 the League faced up to this. Stafford wanted us to accept the inevitable. William wanted us to fight, but I made up my own mind. I gave a speech saying that we must disband the League but carry on the Unity Campaign as individuals. 'This is not a funeral,' I said, 'but a conscious political tactic.' It won the day. Stafford scribbled me a note congratulating me on my 'statesmanlike' speech. Naturally I was flattered, though I was not sure I liked the word.

I realized that Stafford was already changing tack in 1937. He had been impressed by the remarkable success of the Left Book Club, through which Gollancz had been urging the case for a popular front for some time. *Tribune*'s circulation had been disappointing and Stafford and George Strauss, its biggest benefactors, had had to pour a lot of money into it. They hoped that, by switching its support to the Popular Front, they might attract some of the Gollancz readers and enable it to pay its way. When

William stood firm against the change of policy he was forced to resign. Stafford's wealth had won again. With typical insensitivity he promptly offered the job to Michael Foot, then the assistant editor. Michael turned down the offer indignantly and at a meeting in my flat told William he was going to walk out of the paper altogether. Gently William persuaded him to stay at least until the paper had found another editor, which it did in H. J. Hartshorn.

Stafford's change of line did not do him much good. At the Bournemouth party conference that year the constituency parties won an encouraging victory when the trade unions were shamed into giving up their right to vote for the constituency nominees. The local parties promptly elected Cripps and left-winger D. H. Pritt to the NEC, but the trade unions were still in the majority. They feared the communists more than they did Hitler, and to them all 'fronts' were anathema. The Popular Front was blacklisted, as the Unity Campaign had been. Cripps pressed ahead regardless, launching a Peace Campaign and a Peace Petition with the help of his allies, Aneurin Bevan and George Strauss. Shortly before the war broke out and with Hitler at our door, they were expelled from the party on the insistence of the NEC, together with other Popular Front enthusiasts like George Trevelyan.

William and I were shocked by this short-sightedness, although we were never enthusiastic about the Popular Front, William sticking stubbornly to the view that the only enemies of fascism were the working class. In fact only one adventurous Liberal MP joined the Front. The Bournemouth conference had voted to support rearmament. William believed it was madness to give arms to a reactionary British government which might align itself with Hitler at any time. He was right in that, for Prime Minister Chamberlain and his Foreign Secretary Halifax continued to be appeasers to the very end. William also believed with many others that the Labour Party had sold the pass by its failure to resist the 'non-intervention' policy on Spain, which meant that Franco could call on all the arms he needed from his fascist allies, while the Republicans were denied arms from the Western democracies.

Later we learned that, while the NEC was denouncing all

'fronts', some of its members, notably Hugh Dalton and Herbert Morrison, were holding secret talks with a pro-Churchill group of Tory MPs which was anxious to stop Chamberlain. But nothing came of them. Thanks to political timidity by the official Labour Party and political treachery on the Tory right, Britain's resistance to Nazi Germany was touch-and-go.

In March 1938 Hitler invaded Austria. A month later Franco marched to victory in Spain. Britain drifted into war, because Chamberlain's 'peace in our time' agreement in Munich had only postponed the evil day. I started to write home for black-out material. We had not long to wait for the blow to fall. On 3 September 1939 Britain declared war. William and I clung to each other lovingly, but he was out of a job and deeply dispirited, so the last thing I wanted was for him to press for a divorce. We were immensely relieved that our timorous government had at last been forced to stand up to Hitler, and we prepared to play our part in the anti-fascist war. But I was under no illusions about what war would mean, and I dreaded it.

FIVE

•

War

THE WAR got off to an eerie start. Like most people in the country I believed that Hitler, having had his unchallenged way with the Rhineland, Austria, Czechoslovakia and now effectively Poland, would immediately turn his overpowering wrath on us. Frankly, I was terrified. I had read with horror of the massacre of civilians in Guernica, Barcelona and Madrid by Franco's bombers, aided by his fascist allies, Germany and Italy. I had said to myself, 'I would never be able to stand that.'

My anxieties were not made any lighter by my knowledge that Britain was entering this battle unprepared, politically and militarily. On civil defence, for example, the government's preparations were ludicrously inadequate. The first indications of this had been revealed during the Munich crisis when people were set frantically to work digging trenches in parks and stacking sandbags, in startling contrast to the efficient air-raid exercise I had witnessed in Berlin on my way back from the Soviet Union. This had all been part of the government's lingering hope that it might yet appease Hitler. When the Munich crisis had temporarily subsided, Labour had moved a vote of censure on the government in the Commons for what Herbert Morrison described as its 'tragic and wicked' lack of preparedness. Sir Samuel Hoare, Home Secretary in the still surviving Chamberlain government, was all complacency. He admitted that there had been 'deficiencies', but assured the House that all would be well now that Sir John Anderson had been appointed Minister of Civilian Defence. One million volunteers had already been recruited for civil defence, 30 million gas masks distributed, and Sir John was working out detailed evacuation plans. Typically, Hoare blamed the local authorities for the shortcomings, but I knew that on St Pancras Borough Council we were far more concerned about air-raid precautions than the government seemed to be. We lost no time in setting up air-raid warden training schemes, under which I qualified, and the ARP committee of which I was a member met frequently. After all, surrounded as we were by three main-line stations – Euston, St Pancras and King's Cross – we knew we were a major target for air attack.

What we also lacked was an adequate shelter policy, and I had been agitating together with our left-wing group on the Council for the deep shelters which Professor J. B. S. Haldane had been advocating. Haldane, a communist sympathizer and eminent scientist, had studied at first hand the effects of air raids on the civilian population during the Spanish Civil War and had reached conclusions on the best way to protect them, which he had embodied in a book *ARP* published in 1938. In it he argued that high explosive, not gas, would be the main threat. He pointed out that modern high explosives often had a delayed-action fuse and might penetrate several floors of a building before bursting and that therefore basements could be the worst place to shelter in. He stressed the deep psychological need of humans caught in bombardment to go underground and urged the building of a network of deep tunnels under London to meet this need and give real protection.

The government did not want to know. In 1939 Sir John Anderson, dismissing deep shelters as impractical, insisted that blast- and splinter-proof protection was all that was needed and promised a vast extension of the steel shelters which took his name. These consisted of enlarged holes in the ground covered by a vault of thin steel. They had, of course, no lighting, no heating and no lavatories. People had to survive a winter night's bombardment in them as best they could. In fact, when the Blitz came, the people of London created their own deep shelters: the London Underground. Night after night, just before the sirens sounded, thousands trooped down in orderly fashion into the nearest

Underground station, taking their bedding with them, flasks of hot tea, snacks, radios, packs of cards and magazines. People soon got their regular places and set up little troglodyte communities where they could relax. I joined them one night to see what it was like. It was not a way of life I wanted for myself but I could see what an important safety-valve it was. Without it, London life could not have carried on in the way it did.

On the first day of war it looked as if our fears of Hitler's intentions were to be justified when, within a few minutes of Chamberlain's broadcast announcing that we were at war, the sirens wailed. Even Winston Churchill, as he recounts in *The Gathering Storm*, feared the worst. Making his way with his wife to their allotted shelter, bottle of brandy in hand, he mentally congratulated the Germans on their promptitude and precision and was relieved to see that the government had made at least some elementary preparations as the barrage balloons climbed slowly into the sky. However, his shelter was merely an open basement, 'not even sand-bagged', he wrote, adding that as he stood at the door looking out on the empty street 'my imagination drew pictures of ruin and carnage and vast explosions shaking the ground. . . . For had we not all been taught how terrible air raids would be?' Silence in the sky and the all-clear soon showed that this time at any rate the warning had been a false alarm.

In my modest way I was going through the same trauma in my air-raid warden's post in Brunswick Square near my Coram Street flat. Since the end of August our post had been manned day and night and after four nights' consecutive duty with little sleep, and war ever more imminent, I temporarily lost my nerve. 'The war of nerves here is blistering,' I wrote home on 31 August, 'loudspeakers in the streets appealing for volunteers to fill sand-bags all night; Emergency Committee meetings (we had five hours of it last night); transport to office upset by evacuation.' In my letter I discussed how I could get home to Nottingham if war broke out. 'It would be hell here in war. I should have no money, no light, no cinemas and no boyfriends!' Two days later I am glad to say I had regained my equilibrium. On 2 September I wrote again: 'I shall *not* be returning just now – if at all. Now that we are working on full wartime rotas there is plenty to do and an obvious duty to perform. . . . I must be here to do my stuff.' The next day war came but not the expected hell. I was able to write home: 'Having prepared myself for four nights for sudden death I am beginning to relax and get a little rest. This is the oddest war – breaking all expectations.'

The oddity continued for several months. There were no air raids and little hardship. By the end of the year I was talking about coming home for Christmas, bringing valuable supplies of butter: 'there is no shortage of butter here'. It was not until January 1940 that food rationing was introduced and even then only for butter (4 ounces per head per week), sugar (12 ounces), uncooked bacon or ham (8 ounces), cooked bacon or ham (3.5 ounces). Margarine was not included and butcher's meat not rationed till March. It was all part of the government's attitude. Unemployment was still high and factories were far from operating at full blast. Yet the war news was grim. In April Hitler invaded Norway and Britain's attempts to come to the rescue ended disastrously. On 10 May Hitler swept through Holland, Belgium and Luxembourg and started bombing France. The House of Commons' patience with Chamberlain's dilatory war effort finally broke. His pathetic attempt to save himself by forming a national coalition government was foiled by Labour's refusal to serve under him. For a short dangerous spell it looked as if he might be succeeded by the Foreign Secretary, Lord Halifax, one of Michael Foot's 'guilty men', when Attlee and Dalton told Rab Butler that they would be willing to serve under Halifax.

But when Hitler attacked France they changed their minds: Winston Churchill must be in charge. It was fortunate that they did, for there would have been an outcry in Labour's ranks if they had taken office under the hated appeaser, Halifax. Instead there was relief when Attlee, Morrison, Bevin and Arthur Greenwood entered Churchill's War Cabinet.

The phoney war was at an end and the impact of the new government began to be felt immediately. An Emergency Powers (Defence) Act was rushed into law under which all citizens were required to place 'themselves, their services and their property' at the disposal of the government. Those not serving in the forces were mobilized in a nationwide Home Guard. Food rationing was tightened up. The butter ration was cut to 2 ounces, sugar to 8 ounces and uncooked bacon to 4 ounces. Margarine and other fats were included at last and – the cruellest blow of all – tea rationing was introduced at the devastating rate of 2 ounces per week. We were all exhorted to dig for victory. Exotic fruits like oranges, lemons and bananas almost disappeared from our diets.

But my main worry during the phoney war had been how to keep financially afloat. I had reduced my overheads by sharing my Coram Street flat with a friend from Hyde, Barbara Kenyon, but I lived from month to month uncertain whether I would have a job. By the end of 1939 the *Town and County Councillor* was lying punch-drunk against the ropes. The outbreak of war inevitably frightened advertisers off, just when the paper was beginning to pay its way. William had asked Stafford Cripps to take shares in the paper, which he had done, but showing his now familiar ruthlessness he had promptly removed William and his original co-director, Wallis, from the board in an attempt to get outside businessmen interested. In November my letters home were full of bitter references to the 'saintly knight's' manoeuvrings, which inevitably came to nothing. To keep his staff in a job William stepped in with an offer that he and Wallis would finance the paper for another three months and would settle all debts out of their own resources if in the end it had to be wound up. 'I revere William more and more as I see him face these difficulties,' I wrote home. 'The strain of the past fortnight was enough to make anyone crack up, but he has come through smiling, a little sourly, but still smiling.' I added, 'We are, in fact, staking our all on a short war.'

My long-suffering parents duly bailed me out, though they themselves had just taken on new financial burdens in the form of a succession of refugees: two Basque children, Aurelia and her younger brother Alfonso; a communist from Madrid called Manuel; and Elsa, a German refugee. When Aurelia and Alfonso left, my parents took in Aurelia's elder brother, Alberto. Years later Aurelia said to me, 'I don't know how your mother managed.

Your house was always full of refugees. You even brought home a bombed-out cat.'

Certainly my mother, tiny as she was, had enormous stamina. Aurelia herself cheerfully admitted that she had been a handful. She was fourteen when she came to us: dark, dynamic and determined to be a dancer. She had her wish at last with the help of a Spanish Relief Committee scholarship and was soon on her way to London to study ballet, taking Alfonso with her. Before long she was dancing in London shows. Two years later Alberto followed them to become a waiter. In the 1960s I was being entertained to lunch in the Connaught Hotel, one of London's most recherché eating places, when the manager came up to me. One of his waiters said he knew me. Would I mind having a word with him? 'Alberto!' I cried as he came shyly up to the table. We astonished the surrounding eaters by greeting each other as long-lost friends.

Manuel was a very different character. Communist he may have been, but I never met a gentler or more cultured man. Music was his passion and he had made a name for himself in Spain as a composer, becoming Under Secretary for Fine Arts in the Negrin Republican government. He had had a narrow escape as Franco's forces moved in on the capital and had to flee the country, eventually reaching England via France. He worked for a time with Basque children and Spanish refugees in London, until my parents were asked if they would give him a home. 'I can't wait to meet your new refugee,' I wrote home in January 1940 and when I did so I found him ensconced in the family as naturally as if he had known us all his life. To my father, with his love of all things Spanish, he had become like a second son.

Like the rest of the family I grew very fond of Manuel. His tastes were simple, contemplative and, I had to admit, male chauvinist. He would rise late and spend the morning sitting in his favourite armchair in his dressing gown holding court. By then my father had been retired from the civil service suffering from the early stages of Parkinson's disease, so Manuel's presence was a godsend to him. Together they translated Lorca's play *Marriage of Blood* (as Manuel named it) and supervised its production by the Nottingham Philodramatic Society, Aurelia playing the castanets offstage as part of the sound effects. The production shook the town with its vividness. While living with us Manuel fell deeply in love with the music tutor at Nottingham University, an English girl called Elizabeth Barnard, and I would come home to find him brooding over what he feared was unrequited love. In fact they were married in 1942. Years later I was intrigued to discover that their son Sebastian was as charming as his father, but not a bit political. He did not want to know about the civil war: that was the dead past.

Unmusical as I was I realized that Manuel was a composer of some significance. He was in demand from the Latin America services of the BBC and we were delighted when he was brought to London to do a regular job for them. I was prejudiced in his favour when I found he shared my reservations about opera, dismissing it as 'neither one thing nor the other: a bastard art'. When he died of a heart attack in 1954 I felt we had lost a member of the family.

In London I struggled to keep a roof over my head during the summer months of 1940, managing to place a few articles and complaining bitterly about the cavalier behaviour of *Picture Post*, which had a habit of commissioning articles and then not using them or paying for them. My most reliable source of income was trade papers like the *Tobacconist*, which did not pay well but were always glad to take what I sent them. I tried to become a political secretary and wrote to Labour members of the wartime government to offer my services, but to no avail. From time to time I was able to send a ten-shilling postal order home to discharge my debt.

Mercifully there were still no air raids and we were grateful for the peaceful nights, although we were all uneasily aware that it could not last. A quarter of a million members of the British Expeditionary Force had miraculously been brought back from Dunkirk and on 14 June German troops entered Paris. Mussolini had come off his fence a few days earlier and declared war on Britain. There were rumours of invasion in the air and the government issued leaflets warning us civilians to 'Stay Put'. On

18 June Churchill broadcast a stern warning to the nation: 'The Battle of Britain is about to begin.' The brunt of that battle in the first few months was borne by the incredible young men of RAF Fighter Command. We were aware of mighty air battles over southern England, but it was not until later that we realized what we owed to them. Göring had sent in the Messerschmitts of the Luftwaffe to smash Britain's air defences, as the first stage in the planned seaborne invasion of England. Despite more revelations of Britain's basic unpreparedness they failed, thanks to the unparalleled display of heroism by the RAF. Those of us waiting for the worst in the civilian frontline gratefully endorsed Churchill's immortal words: 'Never in the whole history of human conflict has so much been owed by so many to so few.'

Then our turn came. Forced to abandon his invasion plans Hitler turned his attention to civilians. On 7 September he unleashed his first attack on London with a daylight raid which I was relieved to find did not trouble me at all. The night was different. My personal Guernica had come.

For seven long hours 247 bombers dropped 352 tons of bombs on London, killing 448 civilians and seriously injuring 1600 more. I was not on the duty rota and had decided to get some sleep in the Anderson shelter which I shared with two neighbours. Instead I lay awake all night cursing the inadequacies of the government's shelter policy. I wrote home the next day: 'Last night was the nearest to hell I ever want to get. We slept in the Anderson shelter, open to the night sky, feeling there was nothing but a flimsy bit of steel between us and the horror of being able to feel every thud coming sickeningly nearer. . . . We thought the bomb which dropped near was our end. We heard it come with a rushing sound from a dreadful height.' In future I would sleep, if at all, in my own bed. 'No flimsy shelters that let you hear every sound. I don't want to hear my death coming all that way down to me through the night sky.' I added, 'I daresay we'll get used to it.'

I even added an anecdote. '"Aren't you frightened, Barbara?" Mrs Ashton almost sobbed at me in the middle of it last night. I'd been lying low, scared to open my mouth. (Fact is, I was biting a bit of blanket to keep my eardrums from being burst, like Manuel said.) Taking the blanket out of my mouth, I said in my best lecture-room voice: "I'm terrified out of my life, but I keep reminding myself of everything the articles say about air raids." And I gave her a nice little classroom talk on "Air raids sound worse than they are," which didn't convince me one bit. But I must say she took it very well.'

Mercifully my nerve steadied again after that first night. The following morning I emerged from the shelter expecting everything to be at a standstill, only to find life proceeding more or less normally. Night duty at the warden's post was a great comfort. Our head warden was a cheeky young Irishman who managed to laugh at everything and cheered us up. Every night when the sirens sounded I put on my tin helmet at a jaunty angle and carefully made up my face. I found that the great antidote to fear was to have something to do, even if only reporting an 'incident' in our area to HQ, trying to remember among the confusion the correct procedure for making a report. It did not make much difference because there were too many incidents for the services to cope with, as on the night when a shell burst a gas main just outside our post. The gas flared, a brilliant target, but no one came and we had to sit it out till dawn while the bombers circled overhead.

One night the all-clear came unusually early and, blessing the RAF, we decided to celebrate. The young Irishman led us to the back door of a public house. After knocking up the publican, he pleaded with him to sell us some beer. The publican did so and we had a riotous party in my flat. Two of the most effective members of our team were a couple of rather prim, mousey-looking women who shared a nearby flat. The Blitz transformed them. Whenever a bomb fell they were the first out of the post to report on it. On the night of the great fire raid on London on 8 December our area, too, was showered with incendiaries. Like a flash they had seized their buckets of sand and shovels and were out of the door, climbing on to roofs or any places where incendiaries had lodged. I followed, forgetting my fear in the satisfaction of dousing incipient fires. It was almost fun. One day the pair came into the post almost in tears. Their firm had decided to evacuate its staff into the countryside and they had to go. I envied them their escape to peace, but they were heartbroken. They had never had so much excitement and comradeship in their whole lives.

As the raids proceeded there was a new scare about gas attacks. Everybody had been issued with gas masks when war broke out, but now we wardens had been instructed to carry out exercises on getting in and out of full anti-gas protective clothing. We grouped into pairs for the purpose and one evening I found myself in the house of a gentle little woman in her sixties to whom I had been assigned. We spent two hours struggling in and out of the heavy gear and at the end I was exhausted. 'I'll make a cup of tea,' I said. 'No, my dear,' she replied firmly. 'I'll make it. You sit down. The old oak is tougher than the young sapling.' It was a phrase I never forgot, for I certainly found myself growing tougher and more resilient with the years.

For me the worst thing during this period was the loneliness and the lack of sleep. As the Blitz intensified, more and more firms evacuated their staff and more and more people, if they could do so, took themselves off to the countryside. My flatmate Barbara Kenyon was one of the first to disappear. So I was left living alone in my little eyrie at the top of 35 Coram Street with empty, echoing flats below me and in the surrounding houses. My only relief was my rare weekend breaks, either at home or with my great comforter Marjorie. She and her husband Alistair had moved to Wigan, where she had a job as personnel officer at Pilkington's glassworks, while Alistair was about to go into the army as a transport officer. It was a blessed solace to escape to Wigan and play with their three children, Sonya, Philippa and Hugh. Marjorie's warmth and her generosity to me created a relationship between us that few sisters have. It was a joy to stay with her, but the empty Coram Street flat seemed bleaker than ever when I got back. I saw little of William, who had now found a modest job on the *Daily Herald*. It was nothing wonderful, but at least it got him back into Fleet Street.

I thought of moving, particularly as I had no one to share the cost, but I had nowhere to go. Then came a respite. In November

I wrote home: 'I was just cleaning the flat out on Sunday morning and trying to maintain my morale, but feeling pretty lonely and blue, when William walked in! I was borne off to Hampstead for a hot meal and am sleeping there indefinitely with Thea, William's housekeeper (Edna and the young son having been evacuated) and her husband, despite the fact that William is on night shifts and except the nights I go on duty. I am confident that I shall be able to get a *lot* more work done in the atmosphere of a normal house, with normal facilities such as having a hot bath and hot food.' (Our gas had not been restored in Coram Street since the main was hit.) William thought it would be quieter in Hampstead, but the raids followed me there and we had some frightening nights in the shored-up living room in which we slept, but at last I was not alone. When my council and warden duties allowed I would go occasionally to Hampstead for company and a hot meal.

Gradually the pressure on London eased and the Luftwaffe turned its attention to the provinces. A succession of cities, including Liverpool, Plymouth, Bristol and Birmingham, had their baptism of fire, but none was as badly hit as Coventry. My heart ached as it became the victim of a reprisal raid for the RAF's attacks on Germany. Four hundred and forty aircraft flattened the centre of the pleasant, gentle city of Lady Godiva and Peeping Tom in which I had spent so many holidays as a child. St Mary's Church next to Bayley Lane, where my Grandpa Ferrand had had his modest, muddled office with its high desks at which the clerks used to sit on their stools, was burned out. The city centre has been rebuilt since then into a smart modern complex. The cathedral has been imaginatively recreated, combining modern themes with the incorporation of the burnt-out shell of the old building; Peeping Tom still spies on Lady Godiva from his corner window, but for me it can never be the same.

By January 1941 London's nights had become quieter, but the general misery of war went on. I was trying to write a book on the Blitz in which Gollancz had shown an interest, but in the clatter, uncertainty and discomfort I could not concentrate. On 26 January I wrote a letter home which epitomized the conditions under which so many Londoners were living after a raid: 'I got back to find the flat filthy and no Mrs Hide, though I had written to her. So I had to set to this morning and clean out the sitting room so that I could sit down somewhere without collecting bomb dust and soot. Then it was cold and the place looked so bleak and empty that I decided I must do something to make a home for myself. So I went out and bought a bag of coal and two bundles of firewood and made a good big fire and boiled a pan of water for a warm wash and even managed to make a rather smoky cup of tea. It was comforting, despite day-long alerts, with some local bangs and planes overhead.' My finances remained perilously uncertain. 'Everything is very expensive here, because I have to have so many meals out. This morning, for example I went to the ABC for hot breakfast which (though not too hot) cost me 1/7d.' Lunch was another one and sixpence; tea by the fire with bread and butter used up my last butter coupon. Together with midnight tea and sandwiches at the wardens' post (another ninepence) this brought my day's food bills to five shillings, with another one shilling and twopence for fuel on top. 'Luckily,' I wrote, 'I've been able to cash my cheque. As long as it lasts I can stay in London,' which I wanted to do because I had so many meetings. Occasional visits to Hampstead for free hot meals helped to keep me going.

Early in 1941 I got a break when Ritchie Calder asked me to help him with *Carry on London*, the book he was writing on the London Blitz. Ritchie was a brilliant journalist with a scientific bent, and a socialist. He was a fellow argumentative spirit and I got on well with him, with his delightful wife Mabel, who mothered me, and indeed with the whole family. I would go and stay with them at their home in Banstead, where Ritchie would keep me working so late that Mabel came in clucking anxiously, 'Ritchie, let the poor girl get to bed.' I did not mind, for that was the way I worked myself. I was supposed to be typing to Ritchie's dictation but he kept breaking off to ask me what I thought, and arguments began. When the book was published he sent me a copy inscribed: 'To Barbara Betts, without whose constant help and overcritical assistance this book would have been finished in half the time.' Well, it was his own fault.

I came back from Banstead to find the war entering a new phase. On 10 May Göring had his last fling at London with a massive night raid. German bombers made over 500 sorties over London, dropping nearly 800 tons of bombs. The chamber of the House of Commons was burned out by incendiaries and Westminster Abbey was damaged. I remember how terrible that was, but it was a last shot. After that the Blitz died away as Hitler turned his attention to starving Britain out in the U-boat war. Across Britain the Blitz had cost 60,585 civilian lives out of a total of nearly 147,000 casualties. Cities had been shattered and millions made homeless, but the industrial effort had hardly been checked. Ritchie came to see me again to say he had been invited to join the select band of professional communicators who were running the psychological war against the enemy. He would have to bury himself in a secret place in the countryside so hush-hush that even he did not know its whereabouts. He wanted to take me with him. 'Of course,' he said, 'I had to have you cleared with the security services. I am disappointed in you, Barbara: you've been passed.' I was tempted, but not enough to cut myself off from my political activities and Council work. As always, politics came first, so I said no.

I was just beginning to revel in the quieter nights when fate dealt me another blow. On 1 June clothes rationing broke on an unsuspecting population and I was aghast. My wardrobe was empty, my few items of clothing already shabby. For many penurious years my Christmas presents from the family, by request, had been essential articles like knickers, petticoats and office overalls to keep me in the minimal necessities. I remember how distraught I had been when in November 1940 my family had moved to another house in Nottingham lest a skirt I had left at home should be lost in the removal. I wrote to my mother desperately, 'If it gets lost the mainstay of my winter wardrobe will have gone.' I had been saving up the money I had earned from Ritchie to buy a couple of summer dresses and an autumn suit. Now I was presented with a book of sixty-six coupons to last me a year, and each pair of stockings would take two of them! A suit jacket, skirt and blouse would bankrupt me in the new coupon currency. How could I afford a warm winter vest? Salt was rubbed in my wounds when I went to stay with a well-to-do friend. She threw open her wardrobe, packed with expensive clothes, and remarked complacently, 'I can manage.' Manage! I did not see how I could clothe myself in the war years which lay ahead.

This personal calamity was soon dwarfed into insignificance when three weeks later Germany invaded the Soviet Union. To the commie-bashers it looked like nemesis. 'Serves the Russians right,' they said. Hadn't they given Hitler the all-clear with the Ribbentrop–Molotov Pact of August 1939? But some people's memories went back further than that. I myself had been shocked by the pact at the time, and it had split the British Communist Party. But later I had second thoughts and reported home, 'I learn that Aneurin Bevan thinks the pact was a brilliant move.' To most of the Labour leaders this was rank heresy, but later evidence was to prove that, not for the first or last time, Nye's grasp of events was more penetrating than other people's Pavlovian jerks. The first vindication came from Churchill himself a few years later in his book *The Gathering Storm*. In it he lays the responsibility for the pact fairly and squarely on Chamberlain, who, he complains, pussyfooted when, before the war broke out, Russia offered to form a Triple Alliance with Britain and France to stop Hitler's advance. Without such an alliance Britain could never have honoured her guarantee to Poland but Chamberlain seemed indifferent to the alliance's possibilities. One of the factors, Churchill believed, which persuaded the Soviet Union to sign the pact was that one of the principal sources of her munitions was the Skoda factory in Czechoslovakia, whom Hitler had overrun without the West lifting a finger in her defence. Ribbentrop, on the other hand, assured Molotov that the Soviets' supplies of munitions from Skoda would be safeguarded. The pact, therefore, became a simple question of self-preservation. 'There can . . . be no doubt', Churchill wrote, 'that Britain and France should have accepted the Russian offer. . . . The alliance of Britain, France, and Russia would have struck deep alarm into the heart of Germany in 1939 and no one can prove that war might not even then have been averted.'

Nearly twenty years later I was to hear the Soviet Union's version of these events from the mouth of Stalin's successor, Nikita Khrushchev. In April 1956 the Foreign Office, encouraged by signs of change in the Soviet attitude following Stalin's death, decided to invite Khrushchev and his colleague Marshal Bulganin to London to explore the possibilities of detente. As part of their programme Soviet leaders were invited to dine with the National Executive, of which I was by then a member, as was George Brown. It was soon clear that George had come spoiling for a fight. He pulled his chair along the top table till he was sitting directly opposite Khrushchev and sat muttering audibly all through his speech. The Soviet leader began moderately with a plea for 'confidence-building between us to safeguard peace'. But when he said, 'We should not waste time where questions of the peace of the world are concerned, and we are convinced that if the British and the French had understood us properly the last war might have been avoided,' George interjected at the top of his voice, 'May God forgive him!' And the balloon went up.

Khrushchev proceeded to harangue us for nearly an hour, letting out all the bitterness of history. 'Do you not know', he stormed at us, 'that when Hitler invaded Poland we made our troops ready to fight, but Poland would not let them through? We had an alliance with France which provided that, if Hitler attacked Czechoslovakia, we would fight. We took our troops to the frontier, but we would have had to fight alone. Britain and France sent a mission to us, but all they could do was drink tea. They were not prepared to come to terms with us. It is a fact that France and Britain at that time were trying to prod Hitler east. The alternative we faced was either to fight Hitler all alone or to find some other way.' Aneurin Bevan, who was sitting opposite me at a side table, said audibly, 'This is the best political speech I have heard for years,' but George Brown jeered and others looked unconvinced. Realizing that I was in at a big event I had been taking all this down in shorthand, scribbling on the backs of menus, on cigarette packs and anything else which came to hand. I stayed up most of the night typing it and took it into the *New Statesman* where John Freeman, then editor, wrote a strong leader on it, warning that Khrushchev's arguments should not be dismissed out of hand.

Now in June 1941, with Hitler's troops driving across the Russian frontier, there was an opportunity to learn from past mistakes. To his credit Churchill did not hesitate. Realizing that Hitler now faced the one thing he dreaded – war on two fronts – he unreservedly welcomed the Russians as allies in a stirring broadcast. He could not, however, change so quickly the ingrained prejudices of the British establishment. This was no time, he declared, to worry about Stalin's purges, disturbing news of which was coming through to us. With Stalin's help we could change the course of the whole war, and that must be the priority. His high-ups did not share his enthusiasm. Doubts were cast on the Soviet Union's battle-readiness, and Stafford Cripps, whom Churchill had sent to Moscow as ambassador in 1940, did not help dispel them. He did not get on well with the Russians. Those of us who knew him well could understand why. With his aristocratic high-handedness and administrative flair, he was irked by Bolshevik bureaucracy and secrecy, and we were not altogether surprised to hear that he was sending back reports which threw doubt on the Soviet Union's military reliability. This scepticism spread through the whole military command.

How far his initial coolness damaged the joint war effort it is hard for an outsider to judge, but on going through my papers to write this book I came across a revealing document which suggests it may well have held up effective co-operation for some time. It almost certainly helped to harden the British military command's resistance to the opening of the second front to relieve the pressure on the Soviet Union. It would certainly have fed Soviet suspicions of the West's motives in the war, which Khrushchev was still voicing nearly twenty years later. The document was a memo by A. D. Healy, foreign correspondent of the *Daily Herald*, about a private talk he had had in July 1941 with the First Secretary of the Soviet Embassy on the exchange of military missions between London and Moscow, and it was marked 'for the editor's information only'. Apparently the First Secretary had described, more in wry amusement than anger, the way the Soviet military mission had been treated when it arrived in London on 8 July. Its members had been met by officers of much lower rank than their own. They were not offered a meal on arrival and had to eat the food they had 'accidentally' brought with them. They were not provided with a car or a sleeping car, but had to travel to London in an ordinary compartment of an ordinary train. Two days later they had still not been supplied with food ration cards, for which they had applied well in advance, and had to share the Soviet Embassy's rations. Not wanting to sound too carping, the First Secretary added that the attitude of the public to the mission and comment generally on their visit had been 'very good', but he could not resist drawing the contrast with the treatment the British military mission had received when it went to Moscow. It had been housed in a former embassy as the guest of the Soviet government, provided with food, drink, special cars and even cigarettes.

Despite the petty response of British officialdom a Mutual Assistance Pact between the two countries was signed on 12 July. As the First Secretary had noted, the British people were in favour of it 100 per cent. They could sense that this might be a turning point in the war.

The gloomy doubts about Soviet battle-readiness were soon falsified. Whatever Stalin may have done to his people he had not broken their spirit and they resisted Hitler's onslaught even more stoically than the British had done and under worse conditions. In September the long agony of the siege of Leningrad began, as Hitler launched his surprise attack, encircling the unprepared and sparsely defended city, cutting its rail link with Moscow. When Finland seized her opportunity for revenge for the Soviet Union's earlier attack on her and declared war from the north, Leningrad's isolation was complete. With the Germans raining down bombs and shells and with the Russian winter approaching, no one believed that the city could survive. It did so for a miraculous 900 days and three winters of exceptional ferocity, a show of stoic heroism unparalled anywhere in the Soviet Union, even in Stalingrad, the story of whose resistance was to become legendary. A million men, women and children died in Leningrad, mainly from starvation and the bitter cold, but the people struggled on unaided, with Moscow unable to come to the rescue till the very end and the Allies preoccupied with their own concerns elsewhere.

Forty years later I visited Leningrad as a member of a delegation from the Socialist Group of the European Parliament. We were not surprised to find that the cemetery housing the million dead of the siege of Leningrad had become a sacred memorial. As we walked past the burial mounds, each containing a few thousand corpses, I was reminded of a visit I had paid to Buchenwald when it, too, had become a memorial. There, likewise, I had walked past huge burial mounds which bore inscriptions to the effect 'Here lie 10,000 Jews.' But the biggest impact on me came in the little museum at the Leningrad cemetery which contained photos of some of the victims of the siege and accounts of the conditions under which they had struggled to survive. A central exhibit was a pencilled diary kept by a little Russian girl, Tania, which recorded how her relatives died around her one by one until the last entry recorded, 'Now Tania is alone.' Just as the Soviet troops entered Leningrad her body gave up the struggle to subsist on starvation rations supplemented by the bark of trees, glue or anything else that would fill the aching hole, and she died. I was ashamed that I had ever bothered about such things as clothes rationing.

As news of these feats of endurance seeped through to Britain the suspicion began to grow that some people in the British establishment would not be too unhappy to see Russia expend herself unaided in tying Hitler down, and the clamour for the opening of a second front to relieve Russia's agony grew in intensity. Aneurin Bevan was its most vociferous advocate both in the columns of *Tribune* and in Parliament. He was rapidly emerging as the most challenging figure on the left of politics, a thorn in the flesh of the Labour leadership and the favourite bogeyman of the right-wing press. He was politically and physically the product of the South Wales mining community from which he sprang; of stocky build and defiant temperament he was blessed with the gift of Welsh oratory that could encapsulate the experience of less articulate people in a vivid phrase. He once summed up his socialism with the words, 'You can get coal without coal owners, but you cannot get coal without miners.' It was the sort of phrase to set alight the political imagination of the most moderate. He had climbed from the pits to Parliament by fighting the coal owners and it had left him with bitter memories of the struggles he and his fellow miners had had to wage.

This bitterness was to be the source of both his strength and his weaknesses. He came into Parliament with a heavy sense of responsibility to the people among whom he had grown up and to his own class, and it gave him an outsize courage which few other politicians possessed. I did not know him well personally at that time but I was stirred by the accounts of his one-man battles in the House with Churchill the Goliath. The audacity of it was breathtaking, for Churchill was our war leader at the peak of his authority and a hero to everyone else. In fact Nye had a good deal in common with Churchill. He had a fertile enquiring mind rather than an academic one. He had read voraciously in the Tredegar library while still in the pits, and he had Churchill's ability to tap the brains of people more expert than himself. He was not abashed by Churchill, whom he did not see as the military genius most other people did. There were plenty of military disasters in the Prime Minister's past to justify his doubts, from the Dardanelles débâcle in 1915 to the Norway fiasco of 1940. Now Nye was convinced that Churchill was throwing away the opportunity which Russia's entry into the war had brought. He welcomed the genial tone of Churchill's broadcast of 1941 but pointed out acidly that it offered Russia only 'any technical or economic assistance which is in our power'. Why not military assistance?, he demanded persistently.

Aneurin also deeply distrusted Churchill politically. He had warmly supported his replacement of Chamberlain, but was shocked when he proceeded to appease the appeasers by keeping so many of them in his War Cabinet. Even Chamberlain was retained as Lord President of the Council and Leader of the House, while the arch-Municheer, Lord Halifax, remained Foreign Secretary. Nor could Nye forgive Churchill's sudden assumption of the leadership of the Conservative Party in the middle of the war.

It was, he believed, an abuse of Churchill's position as head of a wartime coalition, particularly as the Tory Party had not put him where he was. His attacks on Churchill grew in intensity. In bitter debate after bitter debate he would stand in his place on the back benches, tossing back his lock of hair and stabbing an accusing forefinger at his victim, while gems of biting wit flowed out of him. 'In a democracy,' he wrote in *Tribune*, 'idolatry is the first sin,' and in the Commons he practised what he preached. When Churchill attacked him as 'a merchant of discourtesy', Bevan retorted, 'Better than being a wholesaler in disaster.'

Nor did he spare his own side. He attacked Labour's leaders for failing to get a clear declaration of war aims: it was not enough just to destroy Hitler. There must come into being the kind of post-war world which would prevent fascism's reappearance, and only an independent and vigorous Labour movement could create that world. The attempts of both Tory and Labour to muzzle the press infuriated him. 'You don't need to muzzle sheep,' he told the Minister of Information Duff Cooper when he threatened to introduce censorship in the early days of the Churchill government. So Nye was equally outraged when Herbert Morrison, who had become Home Secretary, threatened the *Daily Mirror* with suppression when it published a cartoon by the brilliant Philip Zec which showed a shipwrecked sailor clinging to an unexploded mine in mid-Atlantic, with the caption 'The price of oil'. The Cabinet found it offensive, though few other people did. In the furious Commons debate which followed, Bevan declared that Morrison was the wrong man to be Home Secretary. He had been for years the 'witch-finder of the Labour Party, the smeller-out of evil spirits'. It was not surprising that Nye was hated by many on his own side. He knew how to wound and he could use the power recklessly, even against colleagues. I believe that without this failing he might well have become leader of the Labour Party, as his growing influence showed when he matured in later life.

Nye was a highly cultured man who loved music, poetry, the arts generally, good food and wine. Above all he enjoyed good conversation and sparkling company. He found both in Beaverbrook's glittering gatherings at Cherkley, where writers like

Arnold Bennett and H. G. Wells rubbed shoulders with a catholic range of journalists and politicians from right to left. Legend has it that Brendan Bracken, Churchill's crony, once attacked him as a 'Bollinger Bolshevik, ritzy Robespierre, lounge-lizard Lenin'. Michael Foot dismisses this as invention, arising out of Nye's own jibe against Bracken's miserliness in the matter of wine. 'The best I ever had from you', he told him, 'I'd call bottom lower-class *Bolshevik* Bollinger.' Nonetheless Nye enjoyed the good life and was not ashamed of the fact. As his record showed, he sacrificed a good deal of it for his principles.

I never myself got into this social life. Although Nye and Jennie Lee, who had married a few years earlier, lived in Endsleigh Street close to my Coram Street flat, I saw little of them. This was partly because William and Nye never hit it off. Aneurin had been ambivalent in his attitude to the Socialist League and the Unity Campaign, and William suspected him of wanting to see how the cat jumped before committing himself. In any case I was not at ease in the sophisticated circle in which Nye and Jennie moved. Nye was fond of what he once called 'physical conversations', in which I gathered he frequently indulged. One morning I went round to their Endsleigh Street flat to talk over some political matter and found Nye sitting alone and listening enrapt to Beethoven's *Eroica*. As we talked he made an amorous pass at me from which I disentangled myself in some embarrassment and crept out, feeling like a small-town puritan. I was not, however, so puritanical as to allow Nye's difference in lifestyle to blind me to his political genius, and he was to be a guiding light for many years.

In the meantime my own finances had taken a modest turn for the better. In March 1941 Ernest Bevin as Minister of Labour started mobilizing women into essential work. I jumped at the opportunity to do something useful for which I would actually be paid and with 2 million other women I hurried to register. Offered the choice between the women's auxiliary services – ATS, WRNS and WAAF – and the civil service, I chose the latter: the idea of having to live in an all-female society reminded me too painfully of the boarding-school atmosphere of St Hugh's. I remarked to a friend, 'I don't mind sleeping with men, but I will not sleep with women.' In August, therefore, I found myself enrolled as an administrative officer in the Fish Division of the Ministry of Food.

We were housed in the *fin-de-siècle* splendour of the requisitioned Carlton Hotel in the West End – hardly an ideal working environment, since our offices were converted bedrooms which were interspersed at frequent intervals with enormous bathrooms. The only use we could make of these was for housing the fish which it was our responsibility to bring in from the four quarters of the globe. One bathroom was occupied by a bathful of snoek – an evil-looking fish from South Africa. We also had running battles with Iceland, from which we were trying to buy as much cod as possible. Iceland struck a hard bargain, demanding that we divert manpower and materials to producing the fish hooks she needed to catch the cod. We did not consider her as a particularly helpful friend. The head of the Fish Division was a Mr Adamson, a trim and affable little businessman who did not seem any more successful at these tricky negotiations than the rest of us.

What fascinated me was the continued fastidiousness of the British consumer even among all the stringencies of rationing. The Icelandic cod came to us in frozen packs of fluffed-up fish which looked – and tasted – like cotton wool, and the great British public would have none of it. I never discovered what happened to the evil-looking snoek and I do not remember tasting it myself. The Ministry's experimental kitchen worked overtime inventing ways of tarting up these unpalatable materials and doing it without benefit of normal embellishments like lemons or onions. One day when I called in at the kitchen the enthusiastic young women proudly displayed their latest invention – a parsnip cake. Parsnips, being sweet, could be used as a substitute for sugar. Unfortunately the cake made me sick.

The second impression was political. The Minister of Food at that time was Lord Woolton, former chairman or director of innumerable companies and banks, yet he knew as instinctively as any socialist that the only way to maintain morale in this civilians' war was by a rigorous policy of fair shares. Our remit in the Fish Division was: if anything edible moves, ration it. One of the more hopeful offers we got from Iceland was of herring and we knew that the prospect of an occasional kipper would enliven our meagre diets enormously. So we took what herring we could get and, since it arrived salted, distributed it to the kipperers, mainly in Scotland, with strict instructions to wash it thoroughly, then smoke it properly. I was given the job of working out a scheme for rationing these kippers, but after months of work I admitted defeat. We should have had to set up an elaborate machinery to share out four kippers per family per year. My regret at this discovery was tempered by the fact that most of the kipperers did not bother to wash or smoke the herring properly, so the final produce was not the delicacy we had hoped for.

My domestic arrangements at this time had also improved pleasantly. I had abandoned the attempt to hang on to Coram Street and moved into the top floor of a mezzanine flat at 44 Belsize Park Gardens. Two delightful people had come into my life: Donald Barber and his friend Jack, both from the world of retail distributors. They were tenants of the flat and, their wives having been evacuated, had enough room to let the top floor to me. They had been brought in by the Board of Trade to advise on clothes rationing and, being good Labour people, threw themselves into the exercise enthusiastically, staying up all hours to work out what should be the coupon value of the different articles of clothing. Being jolly people they got a lot of fun out of it. When I came in at night to find them hard at work, they would look up and chant in unison remarks like 'How many coupons for a long felt want?'

My finances were further eased when I found someone to share my attic. She was Stella Jackson, daughter of Tom Jackson, the redoubtable communist, but she herself did not seem to be particularly red. She was associated with all sorts of progressive causes, but never stridently. Her great value from my point of view was that she had a boyfriend who lived in the country and she used to come back from weekends with him laden with magnificent vegetables: beans, cabbages, great bulbs of fennel, even onions. And she was a natural cook who knew how to make the most of them. In our simple attic, the bath was in the kitchen, so I would often have the pleasure of soaking in the bath to the accompaniment of delicious smells from the vegetables she was cooking on the stove. On one occasion she came back with a load of tomatoes and we decided to throw a party at which we would serve the inestimable luxury of tomato soup. It was one of the most successful parties I can remember. Our friends squatted on the floor round our gas fire, drinking the cheap – and almost undrinkable – Algerian wine we had managed to obtain and were overwhelmed when we produced bowls of hot tomato soup. One of our guests, gulping down his portion, remarked in amazement, 'It is as good as Heinz.'

During this quiet period I was able to see a little more of William. One day he arrived to find that I had contracted mumps. My face was four-square. 'You have done it properly,' said the doctor admiringly. Every gland was inflamed full blast. William took me home to Nottingham, my head wrapped in a large scarf to avoid detection on the train. Mother sighed a little when she saw us because she was in the middle of her spring-cleaning, an awesome annual ritual, but of course she coped. I was in bed for four weeks, and had considerable pain in my womb for some weeks afterwards. Whatever the experts might say about mumps affecting only the reproductive mechanism of men, I am convinced that the king-sized attack I suffered was the reason why I never had any children, despite my efforts a few years later.

Then, in June 1942, William was taken ill with a duodenal ulcer. I had noticed for a long time how tired he looked. Now the years of strain had caught up with him. The specialist told him he must either take six months' complete rest or have an immediate operation. Worried lest he might lose his job, William chose the latter. When I visited him after the operation everything seemed to be going well and we rejoiced. Two days later I received a telephone call. He had collapsed and died. I was numb. My friends rallied round: Michael Foot and Ritchie Calder flanked me at the funeral like a protective bodyguard and Krishna Menon took me home afterwards. All I could do was to plod on with my work and politics. The mateyness of 44 Belsize Park Gardens helped ease the pain.

A new political interest now came into my life: the Beveridge Report. Sir William Beveridge had been appointed by Arthur Greenwood when he was Lord Privy Seal to survey and report on the existing national schemes of social insurance and allied services. I had done some work in this field with the Fabians under the guidance of William Robson and had contributed a chapter to the book he had compiled, but I felt I had got lost in a welter of technicalities. Then, on 2 December 1942, Sir William's report burst on the scene and by the clarity of its reasoning and the breadth of its vision transformed everything. It seemed at last as though we could bring some idealism into our war aims.

The Beveridge Report was to lay the foundations of social policy for the next forty years. Suddenly poverty was revealed as the avoidable scandal that it was. Before the war, said this pillar of the academic establishment, millions of people in our big cities had been living below subsistence level, mainly because of the interruption of their earnings through unemployment, sickness, disability or old age and in some cases due to the failure to link income to the size of the family. The reason for this lack of provision, he argued, was not lack of resources but the division of the responsibility for social security among a hotch-potch of schemes with limited coverage, different contribution conditions, different rates of benefit and a variety of means tests. Only comprehensive national provision, he argued, could tackle the five giants: Want, Disease, Ignorance, Squalor and Idleness. 'A revolutionary moment in the world's history', he wrote, 'is a time for revolutions, not patching.'

His detailed plan of action was based on such a compelling analysis that it was not to be seriously challenged for many a long year. It visualized a single compulsory insurance fund under a Ministry of Social Security to which all those working for a living, whether for an employer or on their own account, would have to contribute without upper income limit. All benefits would be flat rate and payable as of right at a level adequate to guarantee healthy subsistence. This was to be a 'national minimum' to which individuals should be encouraged to add by voluntary insurance and savings. Contributions were to be flat rate, too. The plan strongly endorsed the contributory principle because that 'is what the people of Britain desire'. Income was to adjusted to family needs through child allowances payable for all the children of those on benefit and for all children but the first for those at work. The latter would have to be included because otherwise the lower paid with large families would still be in want and would find that they were worse off when they were at work than when they were unemployed.

Sir William also firmly rejected means-tested benefits as a discouragement to saving, but recommended a state-financed system of national assistance for the few people in need who would fall through the insurance net. Special needs at birth, marriage or death would be met by maternity benefit and a death grant. A pension would be payable to women on retirement at sixty and to men at sixty-five, the pension to mature over twenty years. Postponement of retirement would lead to an increase in pension. The plan was based on two assumptions: first, that the state would take measures to reduce unemployment and so reduce the burden on the fund, and, second, that a national health service would be established by the government to provide comprehensive medical treatment for all citizens. Thus was born the concept for the provision of a safety net for all citizens 'from the cradle to the grave'.

The Beveridge Report sent a thrill through the Labour movement. Local parties, trade union branches and the Co-ops proceeded to organize discussion groups and weekend seminars on it in which I often took part. The message was carried to serving men and women through the Army Bureau of Current Affairs (ABCA), which was doing an excellent educational job in the forces with lectures on 'The British Way and Purpose'. Britain's fortunes had changed dramatically with the Japanese attack on Pearl Harbor at the end of 1941, which brought America into the war, and with Montgomery's victory over Rommel at El Alamein in October 1942. Suddenly it was possible to plan for a victorious peace. Talk of post-war 'reconstruction' was in the air and Labour's rank and file began to grow restive at the muzzling of political argument that was taking place.

Top: Frank Betts, Dad's father, loved cats. My father preferred dogs.

Bottom: My father on one of the rare occasions he was enticed into the countryside.

Gilbert Murray, Regius Professor of Greek at Oxford, who helped my
father translate Greek plays.

Top: I admire the daisy I have picked for our maypole in the fields around Pontefract.

Middle: At the age of about three I sit next to my brother on the front row. Marjorie is in the middle at the back.

A gathering of the generations: *left to right*, Jimmie, my mother, me and Marjorie. *At the front*, Grandpa and Grandma Farrand.

Top: Freda Houlston and I share a punt in Oxford, 1930.

Bottom: In my teens. I had at last persuaded my mother to let me 'bob' my hair.

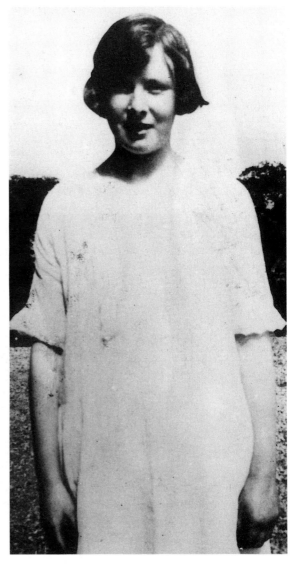

William Mellor, as I first knew him in 1934.

On the roof at Coram Street in 1934 where Michael Foot and I found
a suntrap among the tiles.

Ted and I gather for a wedding lunch with Nye Bevan, Jennie Lee
and two of Ted's *Mirror* colleagues.

Mum and Dad's golden wedding. Ted and I gather with other members of the family at
their cottage in the New Forest to celebrate.

CABINET

*Youngest of the four young women Socialist members of
St. Pancras Borough Council, Miss Barbara Betts, a fair-
haired B.A. in her early twenties, is the girl who refuses to be
flattered.*

*During a council meeting Sir David Davies referred to her
as " the charming young lady." Miss Betts objected.*

*" Leave the human interest stuff alone during administra-
tive hours," she commented yesterday.*

The problem was not only the electoral truce which prevented the contesting of seats in by-elections but the loyalty of the small group of Labour ministers to the coalition government whose decisions they were powerless to influence. When in the columns of *Tribune* Bevan warned that Churchill was seeking to embroil them in vague and non-committal versions of post-war reconstruction plans, they took it as a personal affront. Yet Bevan, with his usual prescience, could see that Churchill was hoping to persuade them to remain members of a post-war national government under his premiership. Under Bevan's leadership in February 1943, Labour backbenchers forced a debate on the government's attitude to the Beveridge Report and were outraged at the fence-sitting motion the government put down. The amendment they tabled calling for immediate legislation was denounced by the Labour ministers, but fifty-seven Labour MPs rebelled. The mood of defiance was carried further in the parliamentary report which Arthur Greenwood made to that year's party conference. Arthur had been reshuffled out of the government a year earlier but had been elected chairman of the parliamentary party by MPs who suspected he had been ditched because he was too left. He did not mince words in his report. 'The government's position did not convey any real enthusiasm,' it declared, adding, 'it was more unfortunate still that on the second day the Chancellor of the Exchequer laid stress on the necessity, when all the plans had been prepared and before any legislative action was taken, for the government to take stock of the financial position and the commitments that would arise'. This was the classic formula for delay, and the rank and file was now thoroughly alarmed.

The 1943 conference was to give me my great opportunity. For some years I had been nominated by my local party, South-East St Pancras, as their delegate, but each time our Labour candidate, Santo Jeger, had pleaded that he must be the delegate as otherwise he could not stand for the National Executive. The actual vote for the Executive that he received had always been derisory, so this year he stood down in my favour. I was a delegate at last.

No delegate has ever arrived at a Labour Party conference

more determined to get to the rostrum or more terrified at the thought of standing up before that large, stolid and critical audience. OK, I told myself, I could only make a fool of myself. I planned to charge down the gangway waving my order papers at every possible opportunity until I caught the chairman's eye. The chairman in question, A. J. Dobbs of the National Union of Boot and Shoe Operatives, was a kindly man, but born and bred to notice only men, so I went charging up and down in vain. Someone on the platform must have pointed my persistence out to him, for just as I was beginning to despair he called me to the rostrum.

My luck was in. The motion was on Beveridge and ranged round the rights and wrongs of the debate in the House. I began to enjoy myself. First, I turned sweetly to the chairman: 'Thank you, Mr Chairman, for calling me. I began to think there was no equality of opportunity for women in the Labour movement' – which ensured that he called me every time I stood up after that. Then I rounded on Arthur Deakin, formidable boss of the Transport and General Workers' Union, who with his fellow boss, Will Lawther of the Mineworkers, considered it his prerogative to bully conference. Arthur Deakin, I said, had attacked the rebels in the Parliamentary debate, but had not the trade unions rebelled against the government over the Trade Disputes Act? 'We of the rank and file of the constituency parties say to the trade union movement that the Beveridge issue is as axiomatic to us as the Trade Disputes Act is to them.' We were nauseated by the generalities about the brave new world. 'Jam yesterday and jam tomorrow, but never jam today.'

I had made such a stir that I had become a left-wing heroine and Nye began to take notice of me politically. He hurriedly organized a fringe meeting and I was invited to speak with the great man himself. This provided an interesting footnote to the conference. I had taken very seriously *Tribune*'s diatribes against the domination of party conference by the block vote of the trade unions and had been working for some time with William Warbey, an ally in many left-wing campaigns, on the details of a new party constitution designed, not to exclude the unions from a share in drawing up party policy, but to ensure that their views were expressed democratically. We therefore proposed that union votes in future should be cast through the local parties by individually affiliated trade unionists instead of through the block votes of nationally affiliated unions, though we later amended our proposals to allow half the union votes to be cast nationally in order to preserve each union's corporate political identity. In my innocence I believed that the fringe meeting would be the ideal place to launch our ideas, since I was sure Nye agreed with them. I was therefore surprised when he grew increasingly restive during my speech, refused questions and quickly closed the meeting down. I was even more surprised a few days later to read an article in *Tribune* by Nye himself advocating exactly the same line. I had a lot to learn about politics.

Undeterred, William Warbey and I continued our campaign, sending a copy of our memo to every member of the National Executive. Not one of them even bothered to acknowledge it. We were advocating 'one man one vote' fifty years ahead of its time. In those days it was considered one of the wilder mouthings of the left.

Nonetheless, my speech on Beveridge was to prove a milestone in my career. Garry Allighan, the *Daily Mirror*'s correspondent covering the conference, went back to the office and told the paper's night editor, a certain Ted Castle, 'There's a young woman, Barbara Betts, who's made a good speech. You ought to feature her.' So there I was the next day on the front page with a photograph of me speaking at the rostrum over the caption 'The Voice of Youth'. The picture showed me with a balloon coming out of my mouth containing the words: 'Jam yesterday, jam tomorrow, but never jam today.' This led to a comical interlude with my civil service boss, Mr Adamson. Sending for me after the conference he told me gravely, 'Miss Betts, I know that temporary civil servants have a good deal of political latitude, but you must not discuss commodity questions in public.' Suddenly it dawned on me that I had mentioned jam! I would not have believed that businessmen could be so politically illiterate.

That speech was also to change my personal life. Ted Castle, having put Barbara Betts on the front page of the *Mirror* at Garry Allighan's prompting, decided to come and have a look at her himself. I did not take much to him at first sight: tall, dapper, with a neat moustache, he looked a bit like David Niven, and I suspected him of being just a slick journalist. I gradually changed my mind. His marriage had broken up and he was waiting for his decree absolute, so he had a lot of time to spare for me. There then ensued one of the most unusual courtships in Cupid's history. He would meet me outside the Fish Division and listen with all the appearance of enthralled interest while I regaled him with stories about dehydrated mullet and fish hooks for Iceland, to say nothing of the mysteries of snoek. As a younger man (he was then in his early thirties), he had been very active in NUJ politics, organizing everything from press balls to strikes, and had been recognized as a bit of a lad, but I soon found that he was a serious socialist. The second great theme of our courtship was the Beveridge Report. We both of us signed up for local party and Co-op meetings to spread the word and would meet in the Great Northern Hotel afterwards to compare notes over a cup of tea. 'How many did you have there?' 'Ten.' 'Oh, I did better: I had twelve.'

I also found he was much braver than I was. On 15 June 1944 Hitler launched the first V-1 attack on London, and I found these pilotless bombs even more difficult to take than the Blitz bombs because they were so unpredictable and so impersonal. One could hear their engines clawing their way through the sky like rusty lawnmowers at any hour of the day or night. Suddenly the engine would cut, and one knew the bomb was about to drop. Ted took this all in his stride. One morning he told me he was walking along Aldwych to the *Mirror* office when a V-1 descended on the crowded bus in front of him. He picked his way through severed arms and legs, surprised at his own coolness and calm, but when he had tabled the story at the office he was violently sick. I was never cool and calm during these raids.

But what finally won me over to him was when I went to meet his parents in their modest country bungalow in a quiet beauty spot in the New Forest and fell in love with them. They were simple, gentle and devout people without a touch of worldliness and in Ted's dad I could see the man Ted would grow to be. In fact they were so alike physically, even to the bald patch on the crown of their heads, that it was almost comical. Dad was a professional gardener with miraculous green fingers, and gardening was to become one of Ted's enthusiasms in later life. Poor as he was, Dad always gave a tithe of his income to some good cause. What I liked about him and his wife was their lack of priggishness. Dad, indeed, was capable of a few innocent peccadillos. As a Baptist he was supposed not to swear, gamble or drink and the nearest he came to the former was to exclaim, 'Well, I'll be doiced!' However, we discovered that he engaged in a secret, weekly flutter on the pools, hoping that a win would enable him to buy a magnificent present for his adored Lottie. One year when we sent them away on a holiday, taking over the bungalow in their absence, Dad took Ted aside and whispered, 'If an envelope comes for me, Teddy, open it. I don't want your mother to know.' Unfortunately the Lord never rewarded him with a win. At Christmas we would slip him a glass of Cointreau, which he thoroughly enjoyed, pretending it was not alcohol.

These gentle people, I gathered, were a bit worried when their only son told them he was going to marry this Barbara Betts, who was already making a name for herself in politics. But after my first visit Dad said to Ted, 'Most women in public life are lambs in public, but lions in private. Barbara seems to be the exact opposite.' Mum, shy and more reserved than her husband, must have found it difficult to adjust to my fieriness but the only rebuke I ever had from her came when I was once fuming with impatience over something and she remarked gently, 'Barbara dear, it isn't intended.' It is a phrase I often repeat to myself and it helps. Ted and I both loved the countryside and the New Forest became one of our favourite stalking grounds.

We were married in the City of London registry office in London on 28 July 1944. With the V bombs falling we would not allow any member of the family to put themselves at risk, so it was arranged that Marjorie's husband Alistair, stationed just outside London, should give me away. On my wedding eve I met

Ted for a drink in a Fleet Street pub – he was never one for boozy stag parties. When he arrived he said to me, 'Do you mind marrying one of the great unemployed?' Apparently he had had a row with the *Mirror* over their decision to sack Garry Allighan, who had been running a column for the forces and who, they decided, had become rather careless about his facts. Garry was a friend and Ted was always loyal to his friends. So he had told the *Mirror* that, if Garry went, he would go too, and they had both been sacked. I smiled wryly to myself at the way I always seemed to team up with quixotic men, but I admired Ted's generosity of spirit, for I knew he was regarded highly at the *Mirror* and would have gone far. Fortunately Ted's nobility was rewarded the next day when Tom Hopkinson, editor of *Picture Post*, invited him to become his assistant editor, so I did not marry one of the great unemployed after all.

No one could have had a happier wedding day, even though Alistair did not turn up and we had to enlist the commissionaire at the door to be our witness. Later we discovered that we had chosen to get married just after Anglo-American forces had launched Operation Cobra to break out of the Normandy beachhead, and that all leave from the army had been cancelled without explanation. There was no wedding reception but Ted had arranged a small lunch party in the Savoy Hotel with Nye and Jennie, Garry Allighan and 'Bish' Bolam, another of Ted's *Mirror* friends. We even had a wedding photograph of our guests toasting us, but I have never had it framed – we were both simpering and looked our worst. The guests sent a telegram to Ted's parents: 'They've done it and they look very happy.' In the telegram to my parents Nye insisted on adding, 'God forgive them they know not what they do.' That day two flying bombs killed a total of ninety-six people; the first fell on a Lewisham shopping centre, the other on a Lyons Corner House tea shop on Earl's Court Road. The next day the private room we had used at the Savoy was gutted by a bomb, but Ted and I were on honeymoon in Buddock Vean, having travelled to Cornwall overnight by train from Paddington. The train was jam-packed with soldiers and passengers standing in the corridors and in the compartments without even enough space to sit down. In an inspired moment Ted had bribed the porter at the Great Western Hotel to find us seats. He did so and locked us into a compartment with eight other people who had had the same idea. Just before the train was due to leave a V-1 alert was sounded and we sat there, locked in, to await our fate. I decided it was not a bad way to end one's life, but the all-clear came without incident and the train left. I spent my wedding night with my head on Ted's shoulder, contentedly asleep.

By the beginning of 1944 local parties were starting to look round for the candidates for the election they felt could not be far off. I was delighted to find that in more and more constituencies the party's women's sections were insisting on having a woman on the selection list, though they came up against the customary resistance by the men. They gave the lie to the popular myth with which men like to protect themselves against equality. It was voiced to me that summer in the House by an elderly trade union MP with the words, 'I myself think you would make a good MP, Barbara, but unfortunately women won't vote for women.' Crewe Labour Party, for one, proved him wrong. Its women put forward my name and were so furious when the male-dominated selection committee refused to put me on the shortlist that they refused to work for the selected male candidate. The women of the Blackburn party were more successful. They threatened to go on strike, telling the men that they would no longer be the party's hewers of wood and makers of tea unless a woman was included in the final six. Appalled at the prospect, the men climbed down. In fact the women had no particular person in mind – they were merely acting on principle – so they turned to the party's regional women's organizer, Frances Kerby, asking her to give them the name of a 'good woman'. 'Try Barbara Betts,' she said. 'She made an impression at conference.' And so I was nominated. Unfortunately at this crucial moment the strains and stresses of war caught up with me and I succumbed to an agonizing attack of shingles, followed by acute appendicitis, which put me in hospital. I emerged a few days before the Blackburn selection conference. My doctor said I must not travel, but I insisted, and with the help of my solicitous husband I arrived.

And so in July 1944 I found myself in front of rows of men. I knew that Blackburn was a depressed area and that the local party was penniless. The other five people on the shortlist were sponsored male trade unionists who could bring a dowry with them from their unions. It seemed hopeless and it probably would have been if Blackburn at that time had not been a double-member constituency, which meant the selectors had two votes. As I stood, pale and shaky, before them I decided that cunning was my only hope. 'I want you to forget two things,' I began. 'The first is that I am just out of hospital. The second is that I am a woman. Just judge me as a socialist.' It did the trick, but only just. Inevitably they cast their first vote for a male trade unionist, John Edwards, the intelligent and articulate General Secretary of the Post Office Engineering Union, but they decided to use their second vote for the fiery young redhead whose fighting speech had attracted them. I had made it.

After the meeting the party agent, George Eddie, an upright Scot of great integrity, said to me sternly, 'In Blackburn we don't like career women who use their maiden names. When you go out of here you will be Mrs Barbara Castle.' And so I was from then on. My thirty-four-year association with Blackburn had begun.

SIX

•

Real Power at Last

ON 30 APRIL 1945 Hitler committed suicide in his Berlin bunker and a week later the German forces surrendered unconditionally. The British people erupted in a rapture of relief. The continuing war against Japan in the Far East seemed remote. All that mattered was that we in Europe had been liberated from attack, and the demand for a general election became irresistible.

As Nye had always predicted, Churchill wanted to form a national government under his premiership, but the Labour rank and file had the bit between their teeth and, whatever any Labour ministers might secretly have wanted, brushed the idea aside. Foiled in his attempt, Churchill changed his tune. Overnight, the 'national' leader turned into a vitriolic party politician and fought the election with a savagery which surprised even a seasoned complainer like me. If elected, he declared, Labour would set up a 'Geshtapo' as he used to pronounce it, always slurring his Ss. 'It is', he said in an election broadcast, 'inseparably interwoven with totalitarianism and the abject worship of the state.' In Blackburn, John Edwards and I hit back with relish, quoting speeches Churchill had made in the days when he was a Liberal and had described the Conservatives as 'the party of the rich against the poor . . . of the lucky, the wealthy, the happy and the strong against the left-out and the shut-out millions of the weak and poor.' We could not have put it better ourselves, we pointed out, yet this was the party Churchill now chose to lead.

Exhausted as I still was with the strains of war, the campaign recharged my batteries. The pace was hot: three or four factory-gate meetings by day, two or three schoolroom meetings every night, but we were buoyed up by the enthusiasm of our audiences. It was moving to see the shabby textile workers give up part of their precious lunch-break to come and listen to us outside the mill. The schoolroom meetings were always packed. There was never an election like it before or since. I had a pleasant moment of relief when Marjorie brought her daughter Sonya along for the declaration of the poll. Sonya was a pretty, blonde nine-year-old, proudly wearing a smart red coat. Ted, too, was blond and as Sonya walked between us a passer-by remarked admiringly, 'Doesn't she favour her daddy!', which made Ted smile. Some twenty-five years later, Sonya's son Mark was to attend another of his great-aunt's election campaigns. We have always been a loyal family.

The climax came with our eve-of-poll meeting when 3000 people crammed into Blackburn's largest public hall. We were very pleased when we were allocated Sir Hartley Shawcross as our main speaker, for he was a great draw. Shawcross was a tall, handsome, well-heeled and brilliant barrister who was to become Attorney-General in the ensuing Labour government and he exuded aristocratic self-confidence. We knew he was a right-winger and, some years later, he left the party when the going got rough, but he was the perfect antidote to Churchill's scaremongering. He had so many meetings to address that he arrived an hour late and the fort was held by the diminutive figure of George Tomlinson who, as MP for Franworth, had been Parliamentary Secretary under Ernest Bevin at the Ministry of Labour in the coalition government. The physical contrast between the two men made our socialist case for us, for George had the stunted growth of the weaver who had started his working life as a part-timer in a cotton mill at the age of twelve. He also had the indomitable sense of humour of the Lancashire working class. The audience loved his cheekiness. Teacher to her Bible class: 'Who put Joseph in the Pit?' Bright pupil: 'Please, miss, Ernie Bevin.' Or the story of the Lancashire lad who applied for a job in a butcher's shop and was sent away to get his character. Back he came and was asked if he had brought his character. 'No,' he replied, 'and I don't need it because I have got yours.'

A few years later, Attlee showed an imaginative insight few people thought he had when he made George Tomlinson Minister of Education in his government. Attlee believed, and rightly, that no one was more likely to fight for opportunity in education for everyone than the bright boy who had never been able to enjoy its benefits. I learned that George's civil servants not only had a great affection for him, but respected him as a minister. He had the satisfaction of presiding over the raising of the school-leaving age to fifteen, a step towards his goal of effective secondary education for all.

Despite the euphoria of the campaign, no one in the Labour Party, except Aneurin Bevan, believed that the party could snatch victory from the wartime Prime Minister. John and I were contending with Tory majorities of 3500 each and were not certain that we could win. Then on 26 July the news broke in an astonished press: Labour was in with an overall majority of 157 seats and nearly 3 million more votes than the Conservatives. John and I were both elected in Blackburn with majorities of over 8000 votes.

Perhaps now, I thought, selection conferences will realize that women candidates are not a liability. For the 1950 election the Blackburn constituency was divided into two separate seats – one, Blackburn East, being better for us, and the other, Blackburn West, less good. John was an excellent candidate and I got on well with him, but I could not help being pleased when Blackburn East chose me, perhaps because I had won a reputation as a fighter. I survived in 1950 and John lost.

Churchill never forgave the British people for what he considered their gross ingratitude. As leader of the Opposition, he concentrated his anger on the Labour government. For years to come the man who as wartime Prime Minister had declared that 'after the war this country will be bankrupt and the retiring soldier will have nothing to come back to' spent his time denouncing every piece of inevitable post-war austerity as due to the Labour government's mismanagement and every piece of our social legislation as 'socialist extravagance'. As I listened to him I became more and more in sympathy with Nye's attacks on Churchill, which had once seemed like treachery.

The Parliamentary Labour Party, which was summoned immediately to London to an excited meeting in the Beaver Hall, was unique in our history. The hall was spattered with young men in uniform, since sixty-eight Labour MPs, nearly a third of the new intake, had come straight from service in the forces, swamping the Tories' military claims. This, we pointed out, nailed Churchill's lie that Labour was less patriotic than the Conservatives. We got a thrill when the evening papers carried the headline 'Attlee for Potsdam', the meeting with Roosevelt and Stalin to continue the distribution of post-war spheres of influence between the victorious Allies, which Churchill had confidently believed he would be attending as Prime Minister. Attlee was elected leader by acclamation and we all crowded outside for the press photographs. As the youngest woman Member I was pushed to the front between Herbert Morrison and Aneurin Bevan, where I stood shyly, looking as overwhelmed as I felt.

There were twenty-three women MPs in the new Parliament: a record so far. We were proud of the fact that all but two of them were Labour. There was one Tory woman – Lady Davidson – and one Liberal – Megan Lloyd George, who was to become one of my favourites. Megan was petite, dark-haired and bright-eyed, with a great sense of fun. We could neither of us stand pomposity and on one occasion startled the staider occupants of the Lady Members' Room by dancing a can-can on top of two of the writing desks. She also had left-wing instincts reminiscent of the heyday of her father, whose memory she worshipped. When I remarked that she always wore blue, she replied that her father liked her in blue and had told her she should always wear it, which she did, faithfully from then on. She was also fiercely loyal to her mother and did not hide from me how much she loathed her father's mistress and second wife Frances Stevenson. Megan had a few affairs herself, notably with the Labour side. Her long association with Philip Noel-Baker was common knowledge, but

I also remember how devoted Dingle Foot was to her. He used to talk to me about her with great affection and it was these associations which eventually overrode her father's memory and brought her into the Labour Party in 1955. Dingle was desolated when she died of cancer in 1966.

With the Beaver Hall meeting over, I made my first contact with the Commons under Michael Foot's wing. Since Michael's father had been an MP many years earlier, Michael was less awed by the sacred precincts than I was and showed me round as though he had been an MP all his life. As he was proceeding to take me along the Members Only corridor we were stopped by a policeman who said to him, 'I am sorry, Mr Foot, you cannot take visitors there.' Michael replied haughtily, 'This isn't a visitor. She is Mrs Barbara Castle, MP.' The arrival of a record number of women MPs had obviously barely touched the consciousness of the guardians of this masculine institution.

I soon realized that this was not the only way in which the House of Commons was out of date. It was a relic of the days when government was run by wealthy amateurs. I had no desk, let alone an office, and had to stuff my working papers into one of the narrow lockers which lined the corridors and prepare my speeches in a corner of the overcrowded library. At £600 a year, the MP's salary was derisory. It was enough for me because I had a husband with whom to pool my finances, but it was penury for the married MPs from the provinces who had two abodes to keep – one in London and the other in the constituency – and had to cover their working expenses. One of the bravest things the new Labour government did was to increase the MP's salary immediately to £1000 a year, a modest enough sum in any case. Inevitably, this brought a torrent of abuse in the anti-Labour press which proclaimed, 'The first thing they did was to increase their own salaries.' I got the backlash of this from Tory hecklers in the constituency, to whom I used to retort, 'So you want to be ruled only by rich men with private incomes.' The smear was to pursue us for many years. Yet there was no secretarial allowance in those days and no free postage.

Nonetheless, our spirits were high as we trooped into the

chamber to hear the first majority Labour government's first King's Speech. We had fought the election on our policy statement, *Let Us Face the Future*, and had warned that the future would be very difficult. 'The nation', we wrote, 'wants food, work and homes,' but to produce them in the shattered post-war world would require 'the spirit of Dunkirk and of the Blitz sustained over a period of years'. We had to avoid the mistakes of 1918, we argued, when the introduction of a free-for-all by the Lloyd George coalition government had produced first a boom and then a slump, in which the returning soldiers were selling matches in the streets. So controls had to be continued for as long as necessary while the post-war reconstruction was carried through. Industry and finance had to serve the national interest; the Bank of England had to be taken into public ownership; efficient industries had to be helped to modernize; and essential industries like fuel, transport, iron and steel had to be taken into public ownership. Our first King's Speech went in at the deep end. The Bank of England was to be nationalized, the Beveridge Report implemented, a national health service set up, a housing drive launched and the hated Trade Disputes Act repealed. When two months later our booming new Chancellor of the Exchequer, Hugh Dalton, introduced the Bank of England Bill, he flourished *Let Us Face the Future* in the faces of the sullen Tories opposite and when we voted the strains of the Red Flag floated into the chamber from the government lobby. We were jubilant.

The prim Major Attlee was proving an unexpectedly courageous Prime Minister. He had begun by forming an adventurous Cabinet in which, while including a mix of the party's different political temperaments, he tilted the balance far less in favour of the right than Harold Wilson was to do in 1964. Attlee himself took charge of Defence, which none of us objected to. The most worrying appointment from the left's point of view was that of Ernest Bevin as Foreign Secretary. We knew him to be a cold warrior and I was afraid that he would make our relations with the Soviet Union even worse, as indeed he did. To make Hugh Dalton Chancellor, however, was a brave move, as he was known to harbour unorthodox financial views. The firebrand Emanuel

('Mannie') Shinwell was put in charge of Fuel and Power with responsibility for nationalizing the coal, gas and electricity industries. Another firebrand, Ellen Wilkinson, was given Education, where on her death in 1947 she was succeeded by George Tomlinson. Those two delinquents, Stafford Cripps and Nye Bevan, who had both been briefly expelled from the party for their Popular Front activities just before the war, were given key posts. Cripps became President of the Board of Trade with the job of rebuilding our export trade, an excellent choice because it was a post which called for all his intellectual grasp, administrative flair and ruthless drive. We were particularly delighted when Nye was made Minister of Health, responsible for two central planks of our policy: setting up a national health service and coping with the country's aching need for houses, of which nearly half a million had been destroyed or made uninhabitable by the war. Another popular appointment was that of the kindly, elderly ex-miner, Jim Griffiths, to become Minister of National Insurance, charged with implementing the Beveridge Report.

Coming up on the outside was a dark horse, Hugh Gaitskell. Though he had had administrative experience during the war and was then in his late thirties, he was not at first given a post in the government. He was known to be able, but had not made any great political impact. However, he was Hugh Dalton's protégé, his right-wing friends were pushing him and he was soon on the ladder to high office. Temperamentally, he could not have been more different from Nye and was to become one of his bitterest enemies, but in the early years of the government all was harmony.

Clement Attlee, in fact, was foxing everyone. He came from a conventional background and was deeply conventional himself. Rumour had it that his wife Violet was a Conservative. His socialism was certainly more Toynbee Hall than Marx. Yet he presided over what it is now agreed was the most revolutionary of all Labour's governments and he did it without benefit of the usual tricks of the political trade. He had no charisma, and Churchill, driven frantic by what the Attlee government was achieving, dismissed him contemptuously as 'a grub fed on royal jelly' – the royal jelly being office, which I have always argued can transform the most insignificant. Attlee, moreover, did not know how to communicate with his backbenchers. His clipped laconic sentences could dry up conversation within minutes. The key to the enigma of his personality lies, I believe, in the fact that he was a decent man who wanted to build a decent society. He took over the leadership of a party which had spelt out certain lines of policy and he was happy to follow them as long as the route was clearly defined. When, however, the tram lines led to the depot, as he believed they had in 1950, he had no revolutionary initiative of his own to carry the tram still further. So this successful Prime Minister led Labour into an unnecessary and tragic defeat a year later.

Ironically, I was one of the few backbenchers who was at ease with him. As an unreconstructed left-winger, I had no prospect of office and this did not worry me. So if I ran into him in the division lobby I could talk to him freely and naturally while other colleagues shuffling by could only manage a self-conscious 'Yes, Prime Minister' or two. Most of them avoided being trapped into conversation with him and, when he occasionally came into the dining room wondering whose table he should join, they looked the other way. One day when I saw him hovering by the door, I pulled a chair out for him next to me and was rewarded with the only blue story he was ever heard to tell. As we chatted he asked me if I had heard the one about the colony of female cats who got very excited when a male cat appeared upon the scene and invited one of them for a walk on the roof with him. When the chosen one came down, the rest crowded round to find out what had happened. 'Very boring,' was the reply. 'All he could do was talk about his operation.' I thought it was funny and I laughed with him.

On the Labour backbenches, we newcomers went into the fray with the dedication of King Arthur's knights. We were going to be above reproach. Michael Foot, who enjoyed a whisky as much as anyone, announced that he was not going to drink in the Commons, a spartan code he was later to modify when he discovered the delights of the Members' Smoking Room as the centre of political intrigue. In that famous room different political coteries marked out their regular territorial areas, left-wingers monopolizing a large round table in the corner by the window, over which Nye Bevan presided when he could escape from his ministerial duties. I was the first woman who dared to invade this traditional male preserve. I, too, enjoyed the political gossip and argument and was prepared to stand my round, but I did not go very often because I found the cost of assuaging the thirst of an ever-enlarging circle (the barman automatically served doubles) a bit prohibitive.

This was our only relaxation in an austere life. It was Labour MPs who initiated a new code: the weekly surgery in our constituencies to which local people could come with their worries and complaints, and no MP of any party has dared to ignore it since. It proved one of democracy's greatest safety valves.

At my first surgery I found the waiting room crowded with people anxious to avail themselves of this remarkable new opportunity. Demobilization, housing, pensions, poverty: the problems came pouring out and I went away awed by the size of the miracles the government was supposed to work overnight.

Blackburn itself, shabby and down at heel after over fifteen years of depression and war, was a symbol of the task which lay ahead, with its cobbled streets, dim street lighting, dilapidated schools and rows of terraced working-class houses in dingy backstreets. I almost despaired. When I first went there I could not find anywhere to eat unless a comrade gave me hospitality out of the family's rations, which made me feel guilty. The only hotel was bleak and uninviting with its cold bedrooms and linoleum-covered floors, but the people themselves exuded open-hearted friendliness. On one occasion when I tried to get a meal at the only café I could find and ordered the most promising item on the limited menu, the waitress leaned over and said confidentially, 'I wouldn't have that, luv, if I were you.'

Transport was particularly difficult. Petrol was rationed and few Labour people had cars anyway. So I had to travel everywhere by train, and the services were still erratic and far between. After meetings on Sunday evenings I would go to the station for the last connection to Manchester for the night train back. One night when I stood on the cold platform waiting for the delayed train from Hellifield to Bolton, where I would change for Manchester, the station master came up to me. Learning what I was waiting for he exclaimed, 'I wouldn't put a dog on t'Ellifield to Bolton!' I cannot remember how I eventually got to Manchester. A sleeping berth to London was almost unobtainable. Those of us in the know used to crowd at the far end of the London-train platform, hoping for the best. On one occasion George Tomlinson joined us. A Lancashire Tory MP remarked, 'I suppose you have a berth.' When George indicated that he had, the Tory sneered, 'Privilege!' 'Aye,' replied George cheerily and unabashed. 'Privilege. I've been waiting for it for a long time, and it's very sweet now it's cum.'

Hugh Dalton produced his first interim Budget with great panache. It was robustly socialist, raising income tax allowances, taking 2 million people completely out of tax and pledging the continuation of subsidies on essentials like food and clothing to keep the cost of living down. He also cut the standard rate of income tax by one shilling, a huge chunk in those days, and ensured that the wealthier would not benefit too much from that cut by raising surtax, making it more steeply progressive than before. We cheered rapturously, particularly when he said that wartime Budgets had been marked by a notable advance towards economic and social equality. 'If it was right for wartime, it is not wrong for peace. We must not give ground now, just when the men who won the war are coming home.' In his next Budget six months later he carried the war still more vigorously into the enemy camp with his declared intention to switch as much land as possible from private into public ownership by activating the provision in Lloyd George's 1910 Budget which enabled land to be transferred to the Treasury as payment for death duties, a provision which had barely been used. Dalton announced with a flourish that he would find £50 million to set up a national land fund, which could acquire such transferred land and pass it to non-profit-making bodies like the National Trust and the Youth Hostels' Association while compensating the Treasury for the death duties it had lost. Later, said Dalton, he hoped the Fund could be used to help create national parks. In an emotional peroration he described it as a 'thank-offering for victory', through which some of the loveliest parts of our land would become a war memorial. 'Let this land of ours be dedicated to the memory of our dead, and to the use and enjoyment of the living forever.' It was all music to our ears.

Like the rest of the 1945 intake I was anxious to make my maiden speech as soon as possible and I put my name down for the Debate on the Address in our first few days. In the event, I had to withdraw because my father, who had been in a coma for several months following a fall, was dying. It was sad that he never knew of my electoral victory and that I was never to see his saturnine face, fringed with shaggy hair, leaning over the public gallery. One of my last memories of him was his teeth. He had had a fine set of his own, which he had neglected, and eventually he had to have them out. He refused to wear his false ones because they irritated him, so his formidable dentures used to sit grinning at us on the mantelpiece.

When I could turn my mind again to making my maiden speech, I decided to slip it in unobtrusively at the quietest moment of the parliamentary week: the 4 p.m. Adjournment Debate on a Friday afternoon. I had balloted for this opportunity because I had had a lot of letters about the delay in demobilizing essential workers under Class B of the scheme which gave them priority. As I had anticipated, there were only two other MPs in the House, plus the amiable Minister of Labour, George Isaacs, who had decided to reply himself. The press gallery was apparently empty, so I let fly, quoting from a letter I had received from a constituent who complained that as a skilled bricklayer he would be better employed building houses at home than 'acting as a grease-monkey to worn-out Army lorries for a few hours each week'. The next morning I learned my first lessons in the art of parliamentary politics: never be deceived by an empty press gallery, and remember that a vivid phrase will get you anywhere. The word 'grease-monkey' had obviously caught the news editors' eyes and I was prominently reported in almost every newspaper.

The incident gave me an undeserved reputation as a calculating self–publicist. I had a flair for the vivid phrase, but it usually came spontaneously. It also gave me a name for rebelliousness, which I *did* deserve. Already within a few weeks of taking my seat I had voted against the government with a number of others in protest at its failure to introduce an immediate pensions uprating. The government argued that we must wait for the new National Insurance Bill, but we urged that the pensioners should not spend another winter in penury. Could there not at least be a special winter payment? Under this pressure, the government decided to bring in the Bill as its first measure of the New Year. Our protest had worked, but I was a marked woman from then on. John Edwards was soon given a junior ministerial job, but I was reconciled to being a rebel out in the cold.

The National Insurance Bill faithfully embodied the bulk of the Beveridge proposals. It transformed our social insurance system and of course we welcomed it, but some of us were perfectionists. I sat down with Sidney Silverman, the left-wing MP for Nelson and Colne, a neighbouring constituency, and together we drew up sixty-seven amendments for the committee stage in the Standing Committee, of which we managed to become members. Then Sidney went off to India on a parliamentary delegation, leaving me to move 90 per cent of them. I could not have had a better training in Standing Committee work, pitting my wits hour after hour against the Minister. One of the campaigns I supported was the Spinsters Pension Movement, which was particularly active in the north under the dogged leadership of Miss Florence White. Its aim was to get a retirement pension for spinsters at fifty-five on the ground that they were the women who had been deprived of the chance of marriage by the slaughter of the First World War and who had had to fend for themselves ever since. Having seen for myself the harsh conditions under which northern women had lived and worked between the wars, I had genuine sympathy for their case. I pressed it hard in Committee, but Jim Griffiths was adamant. Getting carried away one day I told him passionately, 'The Minister really will have to take the spinsters' bull by the horns,' which not unnaturally caused some hilarity – and got some publicity. I had not planned it – it was just that phrases like that flashed into my mind as I was on my feet.

Other of my amendments to the Bill were less spectacular. The one of which I am most proud, looking back, sought to make it compulsory for married women at work to join the insurance scheme instead of relying on their husbands' insurance to earn them a pension at a reduced rate, payable only when the husbands retired. In those unenlightened days it was assumed that most married women were dependent on their husbands' earnings, and even William Beveridge had caught the bug. He therefore proposed, as did the Bill, that married women should be permitted to contract out of the compulsory scheme, thus forfeiting their title to a pension in their own right. Freedom to opt out, it was assumed, was what most women wanted. They had to wait for their husbands to retire before getting a pension, even though they had probably retired earlier than the men. Worse still, they paid for the freedom to opt out by getting a smaller pension than the husbands if they did opt in and paid the full contribution all their working lives. From my contacts with married women workers in Lancashire I knew that the concept of 'dependency' was out of date. The textile industry could not have survived without married women's work and they were an independent lot, preferring to stand on their own feet. Besides, I instinctively rejected the whole concept of dependency, which visualized most women as satellites of men. I could not make any impression on Jim Griffiths, to whom, as an ex-miner, it was natural for the wife to stay at home, ready to feed her husband and scrub his back when he came in from the pit. I had to wait thirty years before, as Secretary of State for Social Services, I could abolish the married women's option.

On my arrival at the Commons, I had been pleased and surprised when Cripps invited me to become one of his Parliamentary Private Secretaries (PPS), the non-ministerial dogsbody who keeps the Minister in touch with backbenchers and the rank and file. Stafford had invited John Edwards to be his second PPS, not realizing we came from the same constituency. Typically, Stafford had decided he needed a man for the heavy administrative side and a woman to advise him on the complaints that were rolling in from women about clothes rationing and other problems caused by the shortage of raw materials. Nonetheless, I appreciated Stafford's invitation and soon found that 'women's questions' raised exactly the same administrative problems as men's questions did.

I learned a lot from Stafford about the art of government. As head of one of the largest and most complex departments, he was ruthless about saving time. When I started with him he called me into his office and said, 'I am always glad to hear what you have to say, but preferably do it verbally. If you must put it down on paper you must do it on half a sheet.' Though far from strong, having suffered for years from the intestinal trouble he incurred while working in a chemicals factory in the First World War, he drove himself and others remorselessly.

As part of his export drive he decided to do a tour of Lancashire, taking me along. It was a punishing routine. I remember emerging bog-eyed from our night train to find Stafford as perky as ever and apparently inexhaustible. 'I've had five hours' sleep,' he told me triumphantly on one of these occasions, as though it were a record. The textile industry had been one of four major sources of exports before the war – and before we had had to switch the textile workers to making munitions. Now we had to switch them back again. Someone in the Department had thought up the slogan 'Britain's bread hangs on Lancashire's thread', and this was the message Stafford carried to them, urging them to accept a return to double shifts. As I looked at those rows of shabby women workers in his audience who were weary from war work and longing for an easier life, my heart ached for them, but they took Stafford's exhortations stoically.

Stafford had no use for red tape and cut through civil service rigidities to get his way. When the inadequacy of women's corsets became a burning political issue it seemed to him natural to ask me to draw up a report for him. The protest campaign was headed by two formidable Labour women MPs, Bessie Braddock and Leah Manning, affectionately known as the United Dairies because their bosoms were on the ample side. Their complaint was that they had enough coupons for only one pair of corsets a year and that within a couple of months the corsets were out of shape. It did not take me long to get to the heart of the problem. Owing to the scarcity of rubber, manufacturers had been told they must make do with the synthetic variety. It was no use, I reported to Stafford, increasing the clothing coupons. Women did not want more corsets so much as corsets which did their job. It would be far better, I urged, to allocate some real rubber, however small the quantity, to the corset manufacturers than to waste other scarce raw materials, like cotton textiles, on corsets which the women only threw away. Stafford liked my report, but I never knew what happened to it.

I suspect the civil servants kiboshed it, just as Mr Maurice of Samuel Hanson and Sons had kiboshed my report on how to increase the company's sales. They were furious that this upstart backbencher should have been allowed to intrude on what they considered their exclusive area. Their grumbles must have gone all the way up the civil service hierarchy to the Cabinet Office, for Attlee intervened, circulating a memo sternly rebuking any attempt to give PPSs a role in drawing up policy. The experience made me a convert to the need for ministers to have a political *cabinet* on the French model. Ministers, I believed, should be entitled to draw on political advisers as well as civil service ones, and the political advisers should have the same status and authority. It was a theme I was to press even more urgently when I myself became a minister, together with my ally Tony Benn. We won some victories, but they were limited. Too many Labour ministers, I discovered, were in awe of the mandarins.

On 14 August 1945, the Japanese forces surrendered, but our rejoicings were muted by the horrors of Hiroshima and Nagasaki. The discovery that Attlee had approved the production and use of the atom bomb was to influence the party's split on defence in later years. The immediate crisis, however, was an economic one. The latent suspicion of American policy on the left was fired when exactly seven days later President Truman cancelled at a stroke the Lend–Lease arrangements with America which had provided us with the materials to keep fighting when we stood alone in 1941 and enabled us to become a key arsenal of the Allies when America joined the war. Not only were outstanding contracts cancelled but supplies of raw materials and food on their way to us on the high seas became immediately payable, either by cash or by credits to be negotiated.

As Attlee reported the news to a stunned House on 29 August, the bitterness of this mild-mannered man came bursting through. Under Lend–Lease, he pointed out, we had been encouraged to spend money abroad on the joint war effort without bothering about exports, since our imports of food and raw materials would be provided under Lend–Lease, with the repayment terms to be settled after the war. 'If the role assigned to us', he added bitingly, 'had been to expand our exports – we should, of course, be in an immeasurably stronger position than we are today.' No one was more stunned by the news than Churchill. 'I cannot believe', he told the House heavily, 'that it is the last word of the United States: I cannot believe that so great a nation, whose Lend–Lease policy was characterized by me as "the most unsordid act in the history of the world", would proceed in a rough and harsh manner to hamper a faithful Ally . . . who held the fort while their own American armaments were preparing.' Attlee assured him he was sending a team of Foreign Office experts and economists headed by Maynard Keynes, who had been made a peer in 1942, to Washington without delay to try to sort things out.

The Labour government now faced disaster. Immediately on taking office in July Dalton had warned the Cabinet that our balance-of-payments position was desperate. Even with the help of Lend–Lease and Mutual Aid from Canada, we had got through the war only by running down our gold and dollar reserves, selling overseas assets and accumulating debts with the sterling area countries which now hung over us in the form of sterling balances. We needed a minimum of $5 billion (£1250 million) to see us through until we could build up our export trade again. Keynes was optimistic as he set off for Washington, but it was soon clear that the talks were going to be tough, the American negotiators warning us that, the war being over, Congress was in no mood for philanthropy. We asked for a grant and that was refused. Nor could any loan be interest free. The $5 billion was whittled down to $3.75 billion, bearing 2 per cent interest, repayments starting in December 1951.

This was bad enough, but there was worse to come. None of the money was to be used to pay off sterling debts. Sterling balances were to be written off by voluntary agreement. (In the event only Australia and New Zealand were willing to help us, wiping off £20 million and £10 million respectively, a shining example of Commonwealth solidarity for which we rewarded them in 1972 by joining the EEC on terms which have done serious damage to their economies.) Another condition was that we had to sign the Bretton Woods Agreement designed to move to fixed exchange rates within five years and, worst of all, to make sterling convertible within a year. Only the most intense pressure persuaded the Americans to extend the period to fifteen months.

So we were faced with yet another attempt to cripple economic recovery by forcing us into a financial straitjacket in obedience to an orthodox doctrine which I knew had destroyed the 1929 Labour government. I have always been amazed by the power of this doctrine to blind people to the lessons of history. Every time it has been adopted it has caused economic suffering to millions and then has been abandoned without even an apology. I believe the explanation of this phenomenon is political. Growth brings hope to ordinary people, who begin to assert themselves. Deflation is a Tory weapon to bring them to heel. They are cowed into submission by lectures on the need for 'sound finance', as Snowden cowed the Labour Cabinet in 1931.

When the details were explained to the Parliamentary Labour Party meeting I was appalled. I could see the dangers standing out a mile. War-wounded sterling was to be forced into convertibility with the powerful dollar, which had emerged strengthened from the war, and this convertibility was to be achieved within fifteen months. I knew it could not be done and that our attempt to do it would cripple our recovery. Other colleagues on the left shared my anxieties and Dalton was sent round to do some heavy brainwashing, warning us of the horrendous austerity that would be necessary if we did not get the loan. I was not convinced.

I managed to get ten minutes with Stafford Cripps in the

tearoom. 'I am sorry, Stafford,' I told him hesitantly, 'but I cannot vote for the American loan – my conscience won't let me.' 'Then your conscience is wrong,' said Stafford briskly and spent the rest of the conversation swamping me with intellectual brilliance. I had no chance to answer before he hurried away, but I answered him in my own mind. I nursed a stubborn belief that in certain situations the weak have a power that they can exploit if they have the nerve. It could hardly be in America's interest to force Britain into a siege economy. How would she sell her goods to us if we could not afford to buy? I wanted us to call her bluff.

The two-day debate on the American loan was the most dramatic in the history of that Parliament. Hugh Dalton made as much of his case as he could, but I did not feel he was totally convinced by his own argument. The most powerful speech was made by Bob Boothby, later Sir Robert and then Lord Boothby, the maverick but charismatic Tory MP for East Aberdeen. 'Comparable terms', he stormed, 'have never hitherto been imposed on a nation that has not been defeated in war. . . . We shall have to increase our exports by 75 per cent over pre-war. If there ever was a chance of our achieving this aim, it has been removed by the conditions attached to the loan.' To anchor ourselves to an exchange rate of 4.03 dollars to the pound was 'an act of absolute insanity'. He was furious about America's insistence that we give up Imperial Preference. We were handing world economic power 'finally and decisively over to the United States'. It would have been better to go for a purely commercial loan at a higher rate of interest but without strings.

I listened enthralled. Though no great imperialist I had great faith in our expanding multiracial Commonwealth (early independence for India was on our programme) and I did not believe any other country would so lightly have weakened her links with her former territories. Moving to freer world trade was one thing. Robbing the weaker economies of the protection essential to their recovery was another. Socialism, I believed, had to find a way between the two.

When the vote came I was torn. I did not enjoy voting against my own government on a major matter of this kind. I hesitated, lurking behind the Speaker's chair while I made up my mind. Ted, sitting spellbound in the gallery, told me that they could see a drama being enacted below, as at last I moved across the floor of the chamber to the No lobby, only to be accosted by our venerable Chief Whip, William Whitely, who clutched my arm: 'Not *you*, Barbara!' 'I'm sorry,' I said and walked ahead. I found about twenty Labour MPs in the No lobby, most of them left-wingers like Michael Foot and Jennie Lee, whose presence was a clear indication of how Nye had voted in Cabinet. Churchill had decided that discretion was the better part of valour and called on his troops to abstain, but sixty of his MPs defied him and voted with the Noes. Nonetheless the government motion was carried by 345 votes to 98. As a final humiliation Congress took its time before agreeing to ratify the loan, making us wait seven anxious months. As some of us had predicted, convertibility proved a mirage and had to be abandoned two years later. Once again the folly of monetarists had been exposed.

In the bitter winter weather of January 1946 I made my first incursion into the outside post-war world. I had been chosen to go on an all-party delegation of six MPs to visit our troops in the British Army of the Rhine. Just before we were due to leave we received an urgent plea from the Foreign Office. Would we extend our journey to cover the Soviet zone of Germany? It was a startling idea since we would be the first foreigners – including journalists – to be allowed into the Soviet zone, but the Foreign Office was anxious to know what was happening there. Of course, we agreed and, bribed by extra clothing coupons to enable us to buy warm long-johns and other shields against the freezing cold, we set off.

It was eerie to be handed over to the Soviet authorities in the murkiness of battered Berlin. We were accompanied only by a young major of the British army. His presence was comforting, though what he could have done if things had gone wrong was far from clear. The head of the Soviet team was a large burly Russian whom we instantly nicknamed 'Colonel Black Death' because of his menacing air, which made him look like the caricaturist's version of the Russian bear. In fact he tried to be genial but we soon found that he was a seasoned drinker and his idea of hospitality was to get everybody drunk except himself.

Our first test came on the road to Leipzig, when we stopped for lunch. We ate in a cosy countrified guest house which was what I imagined a Russian dacha would be like. A motherly body waited on us. The food was plentiful and the vodka flowed. Most of us could cope, but not my Labour colleague Charlie Royle, the diminutive MP for Salford, where he had a butcher's shop. Charlie, a delightful chap, was once described by Herbert Morrison as the 'innocent butcher' because of the guilelessness of his left-wing views. He had never drunk anything stronger than orange juice and was not wise to the ways of the wicked world so, as Colonel Black Death kept filling his glass with vodka assuring him it was water, the result was predictable. Having grown more and more loquacious during the meal Charlie suddenly sprang on to the table and tried to do a Russian dance. Then, with a final 'Whoopee!' he disappeared, only his feet visible over the table edge. He had to be carried out and was extremely ill. The meal ended with someone putting on a record. The Colonel, gallantly pressing a bunch of artificial flowers into my hand, swept me into his arms for a dance on the carpet. As we both wore boots our feet caught in the heavy pile and I ended by almost riding on his feet.

I was sharing a car with a lively young Independent MP, William Kendall of Grantham. He was very quiet as we continued our journey. I snuggled down under the rug in the car. Later I learned he had been plotting revenge with two Tory members of our party, a brigadier and a young Tory peer. When we arrived in Leipzig I went thankfully to bed. Unfortunately my bedroom adjoined the dining room and I could hear a noisy gladiatorial contest going on into the early hours. The aim, I gathered, was for the three of them to drink Colonel Black Death under the table while not becoming incapable themselves. The next morning they told me proudly that they had succeeded. Breeding, they suggested, tells. Honour was satisfied.

Our next port of call, Dresden, was the biggest eye-opener. A few months earlier the beautiful and historic city had been the target of Bomber Harris' most savage saturation raid, one of the most inexcusable attacks on civilians by the Allies in which thousands of civilians had died and thousands more been seriously injured with little military effect, though the British people did not learn the details till much later. We were housed in a Soviet guest house on the top of a hill just outside the town, so we could only guess at the ravages below. I got some idea of them from my German chambermaid, one of the few survivors of the horror of that night. She did not talk much as she seemed cowed by fear, hunger and her memories. When I gave her a bar of chocolate I had with me she knelt down with profuse thanks and kissed my hand. Sitting in our guest house the adventurous young William Kendall and I grew impatient as we waited for the dilatory Russians to organize our day's sightseeing and decided to do a bit of exploring on our own. We slipped out unnoticed and caught a tram down the hill to the centre of the town. The other passengers eyed us curiously but their curiosity turned to alarm when a car full of furious Russians stopped the tram halfway down the hill and hauled us out. They were quite sure we were going to a concentration camp. The British major was very angry with us when we got back, saying that we had offended our hosts and made relations much more difficult.

Despite the brutishness of our 'arrest' on the tram, which had so frightened the German passengers, I had been struck by the Russians' obvious respect for their defeated foe. We had arrived at the city later the previous evening after a long cold drive and all I had wanted was a light meal and bed. Instead our hosts told us sternly that a performance of Wagner had been laid on at the Opera House in our honour and that we must go. The theatre was packed and we found to our horror that the audience had been kept waiting for our arrival for about three hours. This, however, did not dampen their enthusiasm as they listened enraptured to the performers standing in a row on the bare stage clad in rusty evening dress, singing their hearts out.

It was as though they were rediscovering their national identity, a mood with which the Russians clearly sympathized. They

143

had enjoyed the performance as much as anyone. This was their kind of music. It was my Russian escort who, when we returned to our seats after the interval, told me to put out my lighted cigarette, an instruction which the German at the door was clearly afraid to give. The next day I was to see great posters in the town: 'German people rebuild your fatherland.' I sensed an affinity of national temperament between the two nations which had been so bitterly at war.

Whatever else was happening I always kept in close touch with my constituents. Shortly after becoming an MP I decided I must learn more about the textile industry, in which so many of my constituents worked. I therefore spent a fortnight of my first summer recess trying to master the industry's problems and processes. The Manchester College of Technology's response to my appeal for help was magnificent. For my first week it laid on a team of instructors to give me an intensive induction course into what happens to cotton from cleaning and carding to finishing. It was personal tuition which I greatly appreciated. No one can get away in my presence with saying that teachers are a lazy lot. These people had given up part of their vacation to help me.

For my second week I wanted to work in a cotton mill and stay with a cotton worker's family. I approached Horrockses of Preston – 'the greatest name in cotton' in those days – whose gigantic mill dominated the centre of the town. Horrockses' sheets were to be found on the majority of the nation's beds, for the name was a hallmark of quality. It is an interesting commentary on the industrial transformation that has taken place since then that today most people look blank when I refer to Horrockses. The firm readily agreed to let me spend a week in the mill. I would report my impressions to them afterwards. Preston Labour Party then found me a cotton weaver with whom to stay. She was Anne Robinson, a pleasant, slight young woman who at first was a bit nervous about having an MP in her home, but soon got used to me. Her husband was a grocery hand, but she worked as a winder in one of the small local mills and could give me an insight into her lifestyle.

Thus accommodated I started one of the dampest weeks I have ever experienced. The Robinsons lived in a row of terraced houses and every morning at 6 a.m. an elderly knocker-up came down the street, tapping at bedroom windows with a long pole to wake us up, a service for which he got sixpence a week from every family. The house had only one living-cum-eating room, heated by a small coal fire, when it was lit. There was no bathroom, so we had to wash in cold water at the kitchen sink. Breakfast was a pot of tea, cereal and occasionally a small piece of bacon. On my first morning Mrs Robinson asked me if I would like to take a 'screw' of tea to work. When I looked blank she explained that at her mill there were no canteen facilities of any kind so the workers used to brew up their own tea at a hot tap specially provided for the purpose. 'I shan't need that,' I replied loftily. 'At Horrockses the firm provide us with tea.' Then out we went into the rain to queue for the bus. It rained every day that I was there.

Arriving at Horrockses I found I had to hang up my wet coat in a bare unheated room, so it was still damp when I put it on again at the end of the day. There was not even a mirror on the wall, an omission which angered me as much as anything. It seemed to downgrade the women, treating them not as human beings with pride in their own femininity, but as annexes to their machines. I then started my rounds. Management had arranged for me to 'work' beside a different girl at a different process every half-day. Of course I merely watched while they did the work, but all the time I was drinking in the character of mill life. At first some of the women were a bit suspicious of me as a possible management spy, but they were reassured when I slipped into the lavatory with them for an illicit smoke. One girl said to me, 'I'm surprised they put you next to me. I'm a trouble-maker.' I never heard her say anything particularly rebellious. Indeed, I was surprised by the general cheerfulness as the women chatted to each other above the clatter of their machines by lipreading. It was a way of life in which they had been brought up. Indeed, there was something exhilarating about the clatter of the machines, and I wrote a poem about it:

IN THE WEAVING SHED

Oh, the lashing of the picket
And the darting of the shuttle,
Oh, the trotting of the jacks
Astride the dobbie's head!
Watch the solid cloth grow
On the loom so featly
Maybe you'll earn some
Butter for your bread.

Thrump! go the big belts
Whirling from the ceiling
Dancing are the shafts
Above the lacy threads
Slap! goes the picker strap.
Bang! goes the sley home.
Maybe you'll earn some
Sheeting for your beds.

Grey cloth, bright cloths
Rolling off the loom beam.
Striped warp banded
To make a saucy skirt.
Gradely we're weaving
All the long day through.
Lancashire will see that
Britain isn't hurt.

When the time came for brewing up, the workers realized I was a genuine innocent. While the others lined up at the hot tap I waited patiently for the promised tea trolley. When at last it came and I hopefully held out my mug I found that the tea was cold and stewed, having done the rounds of several floors. One man remarked audibly, 'If she'll drink that, she'll drink owt.' He was right and after that I always took my screw of tea.

The day over, I put on my damp coat and went out into the rain to queue for my bus home, where Mrs Robinson had lit the fire and laid out our tea of tomatoes and potted meat. Afterwards I helped her with the domestic chores. I realized what drab lives these workers led: pathetically inadequate amenities both at work and in their homes. At the end of my week I enjoyed telling the directors of Horrockses what I thought of their primitive facilities. They seemed surprised, but they promised, 'We'll look into it.'

One evening Mrs Robinson and I braved the rain and went to the cinema. As we got wet again I was reminded of the Lancashire comedian's story of a cotton worker's day. In the morning he went to the mill ('It were rainin''), and came back home ('It were rainin'') to find a clothes-horse full of wet clothes round the feeble fire. Bolting his tea he went out to the nearby music hall ('It were rainin''), sat back in his seat, folded his arms and said to the entertainer, 'Now, you bugger, make me laugh.'

Certainly life for most working people was drab and hard in those early post-war years as the government wrestled with the shortages of everything from raw materials to foreign currency. I could sympathize with their impatience. Had we not won the war? Yes, but at enormous economic cost, which the countries that had most benefited from our heroism were not keen to share. America was busy building up Germany as a bulwark against communism and had not a great deal of time to spend on us. True, she redeemed Truman's outrageous behaviour over Lend–Lease by introducing the Marshall Plan in 1948, but the political damage to the Labour government had already been done.

The Opposition, of course, blamed the Labour government for the hardship and shortages. Various bodies were formed to plague us, of which the most vociferous was the Housewives' League, a collection of viragos who followed us everywhere, disrupting our meetings. Repeating to myself my favourite slogan, 'Always march towards the sound of gunfire,' I took the battle into the backstreets of my constituency, spending the parliamentary recesses organizing a series of street-corner meetings in working-class areas. My ever loyal Ted gave me what time he could, going ahead like John the Baptist with a loudspeaker to get me an audience. When I arrived I would find men in their shirtsleeves and women in their headscarves waiting at their doorsteps to listen to me. Standing on a borrowed chair, loud-speaker in hand, I said to them, 'You sent me to Westminster on your behalf. Now I have come to report back to you.' Sometimes the questions were startlingly well informed, as when one man in his shirtsleeves called out to me, 'What about Formosa?' I would never have believed that any working man in a Blackburn backstreet would be interested in America's installation of Chiang Kai-shek in one of China's offshore islands to conduct a running campaign of harassment against the new communist government. After that I learned never to underestimate the electorate.

Certainly the problems crowded in thick and fast. It was a shock when in 1946 John Strachey, transmogrified from a com-munist sympathizer into Labour Minister of Food, introduced bread rationing. It was a step we had not had to take even during the war but we weathered it when we found the reasons were honourable. There was a worldwide shortage of wheat in Europe and other areas. Agriculture had been devastated by war. The four great exporting countries – the United States, Canada, Argentina and Australia – had nowhere near a big enough exportable surplus to meet all needs. Hence the squeeze on us. We also had a duty to divert supplies to countries which were much nearer starvation than we were: India, Italy, Poland, Greece and Yugoslavia. We also had our obligation to the 20 million of our ex-enemies in the British zone of Germany. They were existing on a diet of 1000 calories a day and were showing signs of famine oedema. Any further cut for them could bring catastrophe. We backbenchers cheered this acceptance of human responsibility, which was in such marked contrast with the 1918 policy of 'squeeze Germany till the pips squeak'. We knew where that had led.

We were less proud of the fuel crisis which struck us in February 1947. True, the winter had been one of the coldest in living memory, with snow, fog and ice disrupting production and transport, but it was clear that Mannie Shinwell had failed to build up the pre-winter stock. The result was power cuts for all consumers for five hours a day for three weeks. I remember trying to powder my nose by candlelight in the ladies' room of a

restaurant to which Ted had taken me for a treat. Far worse was
the effect on industry and jobs. Unemployment rose temporarily
from 300,000 to over 2 million. The crisis left an impression of
imcompetence it was hard for us to live down.

Despite these setbacks the fighting spirit of the party was
strong and morale was high. Undeterred by economic handicaps,
the government continued doggedly with its programme. Electricity was nationalized, bringing power generation under one
single central body, the British Electricity Authority, and ending
the chaos on the distribution side which ever since 1919 had defied
reform by voluntary means. Fourteen area boards replaced nearly
600 companies, some private and some municipal, each with its
own tariffs, voltages and arrangements for the hire of apparatus
and each competing jealously with the other for the most lucrative
areas of supply and neglecting the unlucrative rural areas. The area
boards were charged with the responsibility of rationalizing the
muddle and bringing electric power to all who wanted it. Ted's
mum and dad were among the first to benefit. When I first visited
their little bungalow in the New Forest at Godshil our only
lighting was by oil lamps and Mum Castle had to struggle to cook
our meals in a shaky little oven fired by paraffin. After nationalization it was not long before we were revelling in the blessings of
electricity.

Then again Tom Williams' Agriculture Act had brought new
security to the farming industry. His Act turned its back on the
pre-war free-for-all which had brought many farmers to the brink
of bankruptcy. His system of deficiency payments gave the farmer
guaranteed prices while enabling the consumer to benefit from
lower market prices, the difference being met by the taxpayer.
The system was so popular that it endured through all governments until Ted Heath gave it up in 1972 in preparation for
Britain's entry into the European Economic Community. Instead
consumers were forced to support the farmers through shop prices
kept artificially high by taxes on imported food, the disastrous
formula of the Common Agricultural Policy. Consumers were
grateful to Tom Williams for keeping prices down, but the
farming community, instead of being grateful for its new security,

remained stubbornly Conservative. A popular music-hall joke of the time was of the man who, having farmed for thirty years, went to join his local Conservative Association. The secretary looked puzzled. 'May I ask why you have not joined us before?' 'I couldn't afford it under the Conservatives' was the reply. One of the government's great achievements was to keep food prices low. Essentials were rationed, but they were subsidized. British restaurants served low-priced, well-balanced meals, if a trifle dull. Despite the lack of variety most people enjoyed a healthier diet than before the war. Babies and children had priority. Free cod-liver oil, orange juice and school milk ensured that we were rearing a healthier generation than the country had yet known. 'If you want to see the success of this government,' Nye Bevan used to boast, 'look in the perambulators.'

Most heartening of all for many of us was Nye Bevan's success in bringing the National Health Service not only into being but into people's hearts. In doing so he showed uncharacteristic patience and consummate skill. The medical profession resisted the whole idea stubbornly. Tory MPs trooped into the division lobby to vote against it. There had been talk during the wartime coalition of setting up a health service of some sort, but Nye's comprehensive, centrally co-ordinated service, financed out of taxation and free at the point of use, was more than the Tories had bargained for. They openly yearned for a return to flag days and a mishmash of voluntary and municipal hospitals. To the very end GPs declared that they would not join the new service. The difficulties seemed insurmountable.

Nye eventually won through by the familiar device of divide and rule. He had an ally in Lord Moran, President of the Royal College of Physicians, who advised him among other things to win over the consultants by promising that they would be able to continue private practice while working for the NHS. Nye thought it was a price worth paying. The Labour movement never liked the compromise, and many years later when I was in charge of the Health Service as minister I was given the job of phasing pay beds out of the NHS. At the time, however, Nye was proved right. The consultants calmed down. The GPs continued to threaten to boycott the service but when Nye went boldly ahead and announced the appointed day they flocked to join.

The creation of the Health Service swept through the country like a liberating force. The sniping, of course, continued, but ordinary men and women stood ready to defend the miracle which had come into their lives. Elderly pensioners who had had to rely on sixpenny pairs of spectacles from Woolworths lined up for the first eye-test of their lives. The Opposition claimed that a lot of people were acquiring spectacles who did not need them but this was promptly dismissed by the opticians as nonsense. Prominent Tory propagandists like Isobel Barnett, later Lady Barnett, lost no opportunity to spread scare stories. One evening when I went to visit some friends I found them poring over their new toy – one of the first television sets – and heard Isobel Barnett asserting that people were going to their doctors for free cottonwool to stuff their cushions with. In fact most people treated their new rights with a respect that was almost awe.

Hugh Dalton continued to perform brilliantly at the Treasury, bringing great socialist gusto to everything, taking on the City and the Stock Exchange with his financial policy. Dalton was a big man in every sense of the word. Tall, with a powerful frame and booming voice, he dominated any company physically, but he was big, too, in his enthusiasms and prejudices and intellectual inventiveness. Strangely it was his elevated social background which helped to make him one of the most effective socialists in the government. As the son of a Canon of St George's, Windsor, who was tutor to the young princes in Queen Victoria's day, young Hugh spent his childhood in Windsor Castle and went to Eton and Cambridge, where he joined the Fabians. He thus came into politics equipped with the social self-confidence and intellectual credentials to challenge the orthodoxies of the establishment, a role which suited his robust temperament.

The most dramatic form of this challenge was his cheap-money policy, on which he was strongly supported by Keynes. He was not prepared, he boomed, to allow the rentiers to milk the post-war economy. So, backed by Keynes, he forced down interest rates, and got away with it. He halved the floating debt and substituted new long-term bonds at much lower rates of interest which reduced the cost of financing nationalization by government stocks. The *Economist* noted that his policy, aided by technical devices made possible only by the government's control machinery, had had a powerful influence on the financial structure. So Labour's controls had saved the taxpayer a great deal of money.

In his Budget of April 1947 Dalton was able to announce that the deficit, which had stood at £2200 million a year after the war ended, had been turned into a surplus of nearly £300 million, despite his cuts in income tax in his two previous Budgets and despite increased expenditure on education, housing subsidies, pensions, health and other social services. To us on the back benches it seemed like a miracle, and his stock was high. One of the key factors was a cut in defence expenditure, on which he fought a bitter battle in Cabinet. 'We cannot afford either the money or the men for which the Minister of Defence asks,' he told his colleagues, but according to his diary he found 'easy-going, muddle-headed irresponsibility' among most of them. Eventually he was given his cut, but only half of what he asked. It is interesting, in view of Dalton's later hostility to the Bevanites, how often he found himself on Aneurin's side in Cabinet. At one point he wrote, 'Bevan and I are on very good terms just now. I find him much brighter than most of them.'

Though I admired Dalton's courage and shared many of his enthusiasms, such as the national parks, for some reason I could not explain I was never quite at ease with him. Perhaps it was his staring eyes and overpowering personality. More likely it was the fact that all his protégés, notably Evan Durbin and Hugh Gaitskell, were unimaginatively right-wing. He liked to surround himself with young men whose interests he was generous in helping to promote, but judging by his occasional overtures to me his heterosexual instincts seemed normal enough though I was never one of his close circle. I suspect he was divided in his mind about me, since I had always belonged to a rebel group of which he thoroughly disapproved, and was to become an active Bevanite. No doubt he was a political mixture like many people.

Then in November 1947 disaster struck. Dalton became the

victim of his own temperamental exuberance. Walking into the Commons chamber to introduce his fourth Budget he was approached by one of the lobby correspondents, with whom he had a friendly and relaxed relationship. Asked 'What have you got for us, Mr Dalton?' he tossed the questioner a few crumbs, never suspecting that they could reach the journalist's newspaper before he was on his feet in the House. But technology defeated him and the paper appeared with details before Dalton had reached this part of his Budget speech. Quite correctly the Opposition seized on this and – equally correctly – Dalton accepted full responsibility. No one suggested that anyone had benefited financially by this slightly premature leak, but nonetheless Dalton resigned. In those days both government and Opposition followed strict standards of accountability which were to disappear in the Thatcher years when 'economy with the truth' in pursuit of political or commercial self-preservation were considered legitimate.

Dalton's resignation marked a turning point in the life of the government. He was succeeded as Chancellor by Stafford Cripps, flanked by Hugh Gaitskell as his Minister of State, an appointment which was to have far-reaching significance when Cripps resigned three years later on grounds of ill-health. Dalton's audaciousness gave way to Cripps' stern austerity. The cheap-money policy, bolstered by elaborate controls, was gradually whittled away. I have often wondered whether, if Dalton had not been forced out of the Treasury, the history of the next few years might have been very different. Not only might the disastrous rivalry between Bevan and Gaitskell have been avoided, but Labour's financial policy been more radical. For all his faults Dalton had the intellectual strength to stand up to the orthodoxies of the Treasury. Adventurousness went out with him.

SEVEN

•

Stirrings of Revolt

WITH THE Labour government achieving so much of its programme and with so many of the left's mentors – notably Bevan,
Cripps and Strachey – holding key posts in it, we on the left had
remained reasonably quiescent. There had been rebellions on
individual issues, in a number of which I had taken part, but no
organized challenge to the government's policy. Ernest Bevin's
pro-American line in foreign affairs and the government's meek
acceptance of the terms of the American loan precipitated a change
and brought the left together again in a coherent group.

One of our major worries was Bevin's pathological hatred of
communism. McCarthyite witch-hunts were sweeping America
and, by his attitude to the Soviet Union, Bevin was doing nothing
to mitigate them. It was hard at that time to stand out against the
near-hysteria evoked by the cold war, and those of us who did so
were liable to be dubbed Stalinists, though we were as critical of
Stalin's brutalities as anyone. The priority for us, however, was
to avoid the growing hostility between the superpowers from
developing into a hot war, particularly as both America and the
Soviet Union had developed the atom bomb.

Justification of our approach was to come from an unexpected
quarter, though we had to wait many years for it. Denis Healey
was at that time secretary of the Labour Party's International
Department and in that capacity he worked closely with Ernest
Bevin, who was one of his political heroes. In his autobiography
The Time of My Life Healey still rates Bevin as one of Britain's
greatest Foreign Secretaries, but he accompanies this with the

confession that they were both wrong in pandering to the American State Department's paranoia about the Soviet Union. He admits that under Bevin's influence he was a cold warrior. 'Like most Western observers at this time,' he writes, 'I believed that Stalin's behaviour showed he was bent on the military conquest of Western Europe. I now think we were all mistaken. We took too seriously some of the Leninist rhetoric pouring out from Moscow, as the Russians took too seriously some of the anti-Communist rhetoric favoured by American politicians.' Confession is good for the soul, but his cold-warriorship at the time helped to destroy party unity.

I always had a sneaking affection for Denis Healey, even at his most outrageous. I liked his rumbustiousness, a quality which adds richness to politics provided it is combined with intellectual insight and personal incorruptibility, as it was in Denis's case. He is an instinctive bully, but bullies always bring out the best in me and I enjoyed our clashes in Cabinet. His autobiography is a masterly piece of work and, as I read it, I chuckled over the cunning way he skates over his confessions of past mistakes, leaving the impression that they did not adversely affect events, though of course they did.

In 1945, another strong personality arrived on the political scene when Dick Crossman, the brilliant Oxford don, won East Coventry. He had never crossed my path before but we were to become close allies for thirty years. Dick had all the strengths and weaknesses of the don who decides to come into public life. Academic habits die hard and every political discussion tends to become a tutorial. He was often impatient of other people's judgments, including mine, but then I was often impatient of his. It was a stormy partnership but was, I believe, based on mutual respect. Certainly I loved him for the way he would use his first-class brain and intellectual clarity to scythe through political evasions, muddle-headedness and hypocrisy. Like Denis he was a bully, but I learned to stand up to him.

It was Dick who launched the first concerted attack on the government from the left. He was a Zionist and was appalled by Bevin's Palestine policy, but he was also bitterly opposed to his

155

part in promoting the cold war. In November 1947, Dick tabled an amendment to the King's Speech which fifty-seven of us signed. The amendment was a sweeping call to the government to 'review and recast its conduct of international affairs so as to afford the utmost encouragement to collaboration with all Nations and Groups striving to provide a democratic and constructive alternative to an otherwise inevitable conflict between American capitalism and Soviet Communism'. In his speech moving it he pointed to the 'remarkable contrast' between the government's domestic and foreign policies. At home it was vigorously pursuing its manifesto commitments. In foreign affairs it had given up the struggle to prevent the world being divided into two hostile blocs and was drifting into the American camp. No attempt was being made to break down the suspicions between the superpowers. Even when the Soviets were our allies during the war, we had kept them at arm's length. He had no time for the communist ideology because it destroyed democracy, but he had no time either for the Red-baiter.

Dick ended with a theme which Nye Bevan was to echo many times in the coming years. The only alternative to these two unacceptable ideologies was our socialist middle way. Bevin should offer the world 'that astonishing, constructive experiment we are carrying out at home'.

The debate was argumentative rather than polemical. There was no rancour: no personal attack. Attlee, replying in Bevin's absence in America, defended the government's record vigor-ously, but temperately. When the division was called we signa-tories followed the strategy we had planned in advance. We were not going to vote against our own government on this key issue. So we put in no tellers for the amendment and sat in our seats while Labour conformists and a large number of Conservatives streamed into the lobby against us. The result was nil votes for the amendment and 353 against.

Despite the care we had taken to keep down the political temperature, the press the next day gave us a foretaste of what in future we came to expect. My own local paper, the *Northern Daily Telegraph*, by no means the most vitriolic of our press critics, headlined its front-page story with the words 'Mrs Castle Joins the Rebels, Revolt Still Spreading'. And it adopted the tactic which was to become familiar of inventing a story in order to deny it, while leaving the impression desired. 'No Mass Expulsions Likely', it added. In fact no expulsions had been proposed. I was not even asked to resign as PPS, though when I went to see Stafford about my latest kicking over the traces, he said a little ruefully, 'Don't make a habit of it.'

There were two consequences of this 'rebellion'. The first was that it drew an excited response from the rank and file in the party, many of whom wrote in supporting us. The second was the hardening of Attlee's right-wing enemies against him, particularly among the trade unions. He had already incurred their disfavour by the emollient role he had played in the 1930s during the rows between Cripps and Bevan and the National Executive. Now, with Attlee failing to slap down the 'rebels' on foreign policy, the Big Three of the trade union movement, Arthur Deakin, Bevin's successor as boss of the Transport and General Workers, Will Lawther of the Mineworkers and Tom Williamson, the compliant head of the General and Municipal Workers, decided he must be replaced by someone who would be tougher with the left, though they had to bide their time.

Dick's amendment was to launch the first left-wing group of the post-war period, Keep Left, the precursor of many more. For some time Dick Crossman and a few left-wing cronies like Michael Foot and Ian Mikardo, MP for Reading, had been holding private discussions on Labour policy, aided by experts like Thomas Balogh and David Worswick. Ian Mikardo, a management consultant by profession and a born organizer, had been itching to turn these dilettante discussions into something more structured, but at first the others were unresponsive. It was the success of Dick's stand on foreign policy which made them change their minds. The first step was to put their ideas into print. At Easter 1947 they met in Dick and Zita Crossman's cottage in the Chilterns over the weekend and hacked out a forty-seven-page pamphlet covering the whole field of Labour policy. And so *Keep Left* was born. Published immediately by the *New Statesman* and endorsed by twelve other Labour MPs, it set the party activists alight. It is ironic now to note that one of the signatories was Woodrow Wyatt who, thirty-odd years later, was to become an ardent Thatcherite, writer of a scathingly anti-socialist column in the *News of the World* and one of Mrs Thatcher's promotions to the House of Lords.

The keynote of the pamphlet was its sense of urgency. The American loan was running out. There should be no more loans with political strings. Crisis faced us. The personality of the three men could be traced in the parts they wrote. Michael had clearly contributed the detailed indictment of the Tories for their pre-war neglect of Britain's manufacturing base: *Guilty Men* brought up to date. Mikardo's managerial bent can be traced in the draconian solutions the pamphlet urged: more cuts in luxury imports; ruthless diversion of raw materials and labour to essential industries; tax incentives to firms to modernize; speedier demobilization to release skilled men; the creation of a Minister of Planning with power to override other government departments. Any essential industry not operating efficiently should be taken into public ownership.

In retrospect the most interesting section is the international one. Having once again dilated on the dangers of a world divided into two power blocs, it reached the startling conclusion, almost certainly the product of Dick Crossman's fertile and roving mind: 'We are European now.' European unity must be the goal: only in this way could the European nations challenge the hegemony of the dollar and provide a counterbalance to the two ideological blocs. This was the only way, too, in which the problem of Germany could be solved. 'The greatest obstacle to European unity', runs the pamphlet, 'is, of course, the German problem.' Russia and America both feared a united Germany attached to the opposing bloc. France feared a strong Germany. Britain had to take the initiative in breaking the deadlock. 'History has shown that Europe can either be united under German domination, or else Germany must be reconstructed in the service of Europe.' The answer lay in an Anglo-French alliance to give the lead in constructing a European federation in which safeguards against

German domination could be secured and a counterbalance to the two superpowers built.

Thus it was from the British left, which was later vigorously to oppose entry into the EEC, that the first clearly articulated demand for European unity came. But it was a version of unity very different from that which eventually emerged in the European Community. The left wanted a federation binding the peoples of East and West Europe together in a European third force, independent of either bloc and building its own defence through a European security pact. We wanted the federation to pioneer a middle way between American capitalism and Soviet communism by planning its economy on socialist lines. By the time the Treaty of Rome was signed Europe had been frozen into rigid divisions by the cold war and any hope of renegotiating Potsdam had been abandoned. Germany had been split between the two blocs and the aim of the left had become to resist any attempts to reunify Germany by war, of which too many on the right still dreamed.

The publication of *Keep Left* brought a number of new Labour MPs into the little circle's activities, people like Richard Adland and Tom Williams. I began attending its discussions regularly. We did not attempt to organize a political cabal, but saw ourselves as a think-tank, though we hoped our various publications, whether in individual pamphlets or articles in *Tribune*, would influence local and annual conference. Sometimes we would meet in the House, sometimes in Dick Crossman's London home, sometimes in a modest Soho restaurant. Occasionally we would organize a weekend retreat to discuss in depth papers provided by our expert advisers, Tommy Balogh being the most prolific of them, plying us with erudite analyses of economic, industrial and international policy. These meetings were serviced mainly by Jo Richardson, Ian Mikardo's secretary, a beautiful young woman who set the MPs' hearts aflutter. Jo, after years of slogging as a backroom girl, started to assert herself and was elected to Parliament for Barking in 1974. She continued her advance, being elected first to the NEC, then to the Shadow Cabinet, becoming our Shadow Minister of Women's Affairs under Neil Kinnock in 1990, a post she would undoubtedly have occupied in his government if he had won the election in 1992.

Another young woman who helped us occasionally with the secretarial work, Betty Boothroyd, was to have an even more meteoric career. Betty was a jolly, plumpish Yorkshire lass who, in her early days, had had a brief spell as a Tiller Girl – an episode she was never allowed to forget. She also worked for me as constituency secretary for a few years until in 1974 she won a spectacular by-election in West Bromwich helped by my Ted. By 1979 she had become Deputy Speaker to the House of Commons and in 1992 was elected as the first woman Speaker in our parliamentary history. She presides over the proceedings with the briskness of a Yorkshire headmistress who intimidates her rebellious pupils and beats them into line.

Moral of these two careers: you never know what people are capable of until you give them the opportunity to show it.

The announcement of the proposed Marshall Plan in June 1947 relieved some of the Götterdämmerung atmosphere in which *Keep Left* had been produced, but there were still plenty of developments to cause us anxiety. There were ominous signs that Stafford Cripps was moving to a deflationary policy, backed by wage restraint. In February 1948, he produced a White Paper, *National Incomes, Costs and Prices*, in which he said there was no room for any increase in incomes at all and warned that 'if there were any increases they would not be allowed for in fixing controlled prices or subsidies'. There were also signs that the government was dragging its feet on some key issues, notably the nationalization of iron and steel. As we suspected, the Cabinet was deeply divided on this and Dalton gave the details later in his diaries: Morrison overtly opposed, Attlee unenthusiastic and even the Minister in charge of the Bill – George Strauss, Aneurin's former ally – halfhearted. Only Dalton himself, Cripps, Bevin and Bevan passionately believed that this cartelized and inefficient industry had to be brought into public ownership. The result was a succession of compromises and delays which were ruthlessly exploited by the steelmasters, aided by the House of Lords. The enfeebled measure which eventually reached the statute book with a vesting date late in 1950 was to succumb to the Tories' axe when they were returned to power. We became increasingly uneasy.

Nonetheless, though we in the Keep Left Group were a serious lot, we were far from being sombre. My most enduring memory of these left-wing years from Keep Left onwards was of camaraderie and a sense of fun. We seized every opportunity for comradely conviviality, though Dick Crossman was not as good at it as the rest of us. There were some lively spirits among us, such as Leslie Hale, who was one of the wittiest speakers – and certainly the fastest – in the House. There was Harold Davies, the cheeky MP for Leek, who could captivate the audience at any public meeting with his flow of psychedelic Welsh eloquence. There was Ian Mikardo, considered by the right wing of the party as the most sinister figure of us all. With his capacity for savage irony he excelled at making enemies, while the fact that his professional job involved advising firms how to trade with Eastern Europe inspired allegations that he was in pawn to the communists. Dr Edith Summerskill, one of our bitterest critics on the National Executive, used to refer to him disparagingly as 'the man in the brown suit', an epithet whose political significance we never understood, but those of us who worked with him knew he had all the warmheartedness of a Jewish poppa and a disarming ability to joke about his own race.

One of the highlights of the political year was the Christmas party which Ted and I gave in our Highgate Village flat. We loved entertaining and Ted with his extrovert exuberance was the perfect host. The entertainment on these occasions was a mixture of Mike Yarwood and *That Was the Week That Was*. Mikardo's Jewish stories set the tone of political irreverence. Harold Davies' star turn was a dramatic rendering of the Green-eyed Goddess of Katmandu. Philip Zec, still producing cartoons for the *Mirror*, was my special favourite as he parodied the Spanish song, 'Fiesta', in lugubrious tones, strumming on his guitar. Mike Foot was courting the beauteous Jill Craigie, a producer of documentary films, who used to corner Harold Wilson at our parties when he became President of the Board of Trade, and attack him for not doing enough for the British film industry. Michael used to be as brutal with her as he often was with me: 'Don't do that. No. Come off it.' The climax of the evening would be a competition between Geoffrey de Freitas and Jim Callaghan, our two guests with the longest legs. Lubricated by Algerian wine they vied with each other as to who could high-kick most of the little lampshades off our modest chandelier. Our political relationships at that time were still very catholic.

In the meantime I had changed ministerial masters. When Stafford was moved to the Treasury after Dalton's resignation Harold Wilson was appointed to fill his place at the Board of Trade. Stafford said to me that he was sure I would not be interested in going to the Treasury and that in any case Harold would take me on as PPS. I retorted proudly that I did not wish to be inherited with the office furniture, but in the event Harold was friendliness itself, saying that he hoped I would stay. Our paths had not crossed before. While I had been politically active during the war he had been acquiring a reputation as a brilliant young backroom boy in the job of Director of Economic Statistics in the Ministry of Fuel and Power. In 1945, having won the Ormskirk seat, he had been made Parliamentary Secretary at the Ministry of Works. By the time he was thirty-three he was in the Cabinet and a political phenomenon. Harold was a cherubic little man, inclined to be chubby, and his cheery approachability and Poirot-style moustache made it difficult to take him seriously. Nonetheless, we were all aware that he had a formidable mastery of statistics, a grasp of detail and an unrivalled memory for figures and dates. He was immensely proud of these abilities and in later years when he became Prime Minister for the second time lost no opportunity of reminding us that he had been President of the Royal Statistical Society from 1970 to 1973. When in those years he used to rattle off statistics at me I retorted by quoting reams of poetry at him. That silenced him, because he was numerate rather than literary.

We quickly built up an affectionate relationship, which was to endure for forty years. It was strengthened by the fact that we were both reared in Yorkshire, where they cannot tolerate side. We were both the products of grammar schools and modest-income families and had no time for the products of softly cushioned privilege. I was also attracted by the cheeky-chappie streak in him, since for a long time I have considered pomposity the cardinal political sin. I never found him conceited, as he was described by his enemies. On the contrary I sensed all the time that he was a mixture of dogged ambition and lack of self confidence. It was this, I realized later, which led him to prefer devious methods of getting his way rather than frontal attack.

In many ways Harold reminded me of my own Ted. He enjoyed – and sought out – the company of women, but he was no philanderer. The press never tired of hinting at a secret sexual life in the rumours in which Marcia Williams, his personal secretary, figured prominently. It was certainly an intriguing relationship which lasted through Harold's four stints as Prime Minister until he gave up politics. His left-wing friends in Cabinet including me used to muse over the power she had over him as she would storm into our occasional private talks with him, bullying and lecturing him. But I never had any reason to believe she was his mistress. He was too open about the relationship for that. On the day he took her on in 1956 he boasted to me that he had stolen her from Morgan Philipps, the Labour Party's general secretary, for whom she worked as a typist. It was a political conquest rather than a sexual one. He chortled that she was fed up with the right-wing stodginess of Labour's HQ at Transport House and was flattered by her desire to work for him. Later he told me she was going through a difficult patch in her marriage, was 'a bit neurotic' and needed his support. The support was mutual as he became increasingly dependent on her political loyalty. I liked her personally and thought she was good for him, stiffening his nerve against the political enemies with whose intrigues he was obsessed. If Mary Wilson resented Marcia's role she never showed it. More than once when I accompanied Harold as Prime Minister on a speaking engagement I would find Mary and Marcia chatting companionably in the bedroom of Harold's suite while the rest of us got on with our political scheming.

Certainly Harold never tried to seduce me. In the nearly forty years I worked with him all I can remember is one rather fumbling kiss. He liked a little flirtation, but it was verbal rather than physical. The only time I saw him get really flirtatious was when, as President of the Board of Trade, he became involved with the British film industry which he was trying to promote. He was like a schoolboy, dazzled by the glamorous film stars he met. In March 1950, the *Evening Standard* carried a picture of him at a dinner at Ciro's to celebrate a gala performance at the opera. He was resplendent in white tie and tails and obviously revelling in the company of the film star, Edana Romney, who sat beside him smiling seductively. Later, the diarist tells us, he danced with her, a pursuit in which he did not normally indulge. But there was a kind of innocence about it all. Shortly afterwards I was doing my duty on the second bench in the Commons during a debate about the film industry when he turned to me and said excitedly: 'She's in the gallery.' Here again he was so open about it that I did not believe he was having a secret affair. I never heard any more about Edana Romney after that. One of Harold's endearing traits was his desire to bring women to the fore. He was an instinctive feminist: the first Prime Minister to have two women in his Cabinet. Like Ted he never regarded women as rivals, but rejoiced in their success and was always trying to promote them to new opportunities. Such men are rare.

But I soon realized that under that easy-going exterior lay a shrewd political strategist. When he first got on to the front bench he was one of the dullest speakers in the House. From the bench behind him I watched him deliberately turn himself into a witty debater whom the Opposition feared. In due course his command of the House became masterly. I decided that he knew exactly where he wanted to go and had set his sights on the very top.

Life on the second bench was pretty tedious as I sat there night after night listening to technical debates. Harold never needed me to act as runner to consult the officials in their box since he always had the facts at his fingertips, but I had to stay late in case I was wanted. I was not too pleased, therefore, to discover that Harold's second PPS, Tom Cook, was accompanying him on his trips abroad to promote our export trade. Tom was a pleasant young lad who never seemed to be available to share the late-night chores, pleading that he had to get back to his Scottish constituency, though he always had time for these prestigious overseas trips to places like India. I decided that the time had come to go on strike and told Harold I must accompany him on his next trip or I would relinquish the delights of being his PPS.

As was his wont Harold capitulated to female pressure. I should go with him to Canada. I was delighted because promoting our textile exports would be high on the agenda and that would do me good in my constituency. Harold's Principal Private Secretary, Max Brown, later Sir Max, was not so pleased. Max was the model Private Secretary, gentle, considerate and firmly conscientious. He warned me that Canada was a pioneering country with a sexist attitude to women of which I would not approve. They simply would not know what to make of a woman PPS. Harold had better take me somewhere else. I brushed all this aside and we set out. But Max was right.

I did not mind it so much when, on our arrival in Toronto, Harold sent me round the shops to study how many British goods they sold and why they did not stock more, while he sat in a smoke-filled room talking the details of trade agreements. It was not that I was not interested in such negotiations – later as Minister of Overseas Development I was to engage in detailed negotiations over aid agreements with a wide range of countries and rather fancied my skill at it – but if I was not to be the top negotiator, I was happy to be a researcher. So round the big stores I went.

My researches revealed such elementary gaps in our marketing that British management sank still lower in my esteem. In one big store, which had laid on a 'Buy British' week in honour of our visit, I found one small stall draped with some undistinguished-looking towelling. The head of the store told me, 'Canadian housewives like their bathrooms to be colourful, with matching curtains, towels, bathmats and shower curtains. Only five per cent of the towels we sell are white, yet they form ninety per cent of your exports to us.' At another I was told that the colours of our dress materials were all wrong. Canadian women liked strong colours: not our muted beiges and washed-out mauves. The manager of another store complained that our delivery dates were often out of phase. His customers were very keen on our woollen goods, but the Scotch tweeds and other heavyweights had been arriving in the summer, while in the spring there was a shortage of Viyella and other lightweight goods which were in demand.

On my return to England I renewed my efforts to get our home textile industry to brighten up its ideas. I had always lectured the Calico Printers' Association in Manchester about the lack of good designs, particularly in the cheaper ranges. Now I carried my message to the firms in my own constituency. On one such visit I had begun to despair as I was shown length upon length of insipid materials: when I came across some cloths in strong colours and bold design my spirits rose. 'I like these,' I said. 'Oh these are for the West African trade,' I was told. 'They would not sell here.' Attitudes have changed since then, but it took decades to work the miracle.

Apart from my research the visit turned out to be disappointingly tedious. I was soon wishing I had listened to Max Brown: the Canadians did not know what to do with me. Our routine every day was the same, as we travelled from coast to coast across the provinces: a Rotary lunch to which I was invited and at which Harold made his set speech about strengthening trade links. An uninspiring meal and an uninspiring speech. 'I have listened to the same speech thirty-seven times,' I told Harold, 'and if I have to eat any more hunks of cold meat washed down with tepid coffee, I shall be sick.' In the afternoon there were trade talks from which I was excluded and in the evening Harold was swept off to an excellent ministerial dinner to which I was not allowed to go. I protested to the unhappy Max in vain. 'I am afraid these are always stag parties,' he replied. 'Wives are never invited.' 'I am not Harold's wife,' I retorted hotly. 'I am not even his mistress. I am his PPS.' 'They don't understand' was all he could say.

The further west we travelled, the deeper became the male chauvinism. As we approached Saskatchewan my hopes rose. The Co-operative Commonwealth Federation (CCF), the nearest thing to a Labour Party in Canada, was in power there and I was to meet my old friend George Cadbury, scion of the chocolate family, who had been active in Labour politics in London before he had come to Canada as political adviser to the CCF government. Surely the CCF's attitude to women in public life would be different? But it was not. George's wife Barbara had given up a promising career in Labour Party politics to come out with him. She was another Shirley Williams: intelligent, attractive, politically skilled and a fluent public speaker, but George told me she had not been allowed to hold any office in the CCF or become a candidate. She had not even been allowed to make any public speeches on its behalf: merely to train the men privately. Inspired by my outrage at all this George pulled strings behind the scenes and I was informed that I would be allowed to attend the ministerial dinner and that Barbara Cadbury was coming too – presumably to act as chaperone. We were placed side by side at the bottom of the table and spent our time shaking our heads over the men's obvious sense of vulnerability.

After a brief visit to Victoria, where I fell in love with the beauties of Howe Sound, we turned eastwards to Quebec. We flew in a small private plane which had been placed at our disposal by the Canadian government and was piloted by the Canadian RAF. As we flew over the Rocky Mountains, with their mile upon mile of snow-capped peaks, one of our RAF escorts sitting behind me leaned over and remarked, 'When we lose a plane on them thar mountains, we almost never find it.' 'Then next time I shall wear a scarlet petticoat,' I replied. 'That should be visible from the air.' We reached Quebec without incident, but there was a storm waiting there. The climax of our tour was to be a magnificent dinner at the prestigious Château Frontenac, where part of the Quebec Conference between Churchill, Roosevelt and Canada's Mackenzie King had taken place at a crucial point of the war in 1943. Harold had promised me that this time he would insist that I should be there. As I settled into my room in the hotel and sorted out my evening gowns, Max Brown came in looking wretched. I was not to go. It was to be another stag party, but a separate and equally good dinner had been laid on for me and the ministers' wives in an adjoining room. I exploded and threatened to return home by the next plane. 'You can't let the President down,' said Max miserably. I knew I couldn't and dressed sullenly.

The meal laid on for us 'wives' was superb, but as I gulped down the food I harangued the wives: 'Why do you put up with this purdah?' They responded eagerly: 'We don't like this treatment any more than you do, but what can we do?' 'You have your weapons,' I replied darkly. 'Have you never heard of Lysistrata?' From time to time one of the men, feeling guilty, put his head round the door to see how we were getting on. 'The food and wine are excellent,' was my reply, 'but that is not the point.' And I added, 'Je fomente la révolution,' to the women's cheers. I have never been back to Canada to see whether the stand I took had any effect.

As Hugh Dalton had already shown in his first Budgets, one of the devices on Labour's banner was national parks. It was a cause close to my heart. Ted and I were keen walkers and were rustic souls who had a natural affinity with the countryside. It was one of the things which brought us together. We developed the tradition of walking holidays. Ted was a Thomas Hardy fan and every Easter, after a weekend with Ted's parents, we would set off for Hardy country, rucksack on back. We would be furious when we found our way across some of the most peaceful stretches of Dorset barred by large army notices saying 'No entry – firing range'. We also had an affinity with the yearning of people who worked in the smoky industrial towns to escape into the open air. It had found expression before the war in such bodies as the Clarion Cycling Club, the Youth Hostels' Association and other manifestations of working-class demands for the right to explore the open spaces they believed should belong to everyone.

So Ted and I fell an easy prey to Tom Stephenson, the wiry, indomitable secretary of the Ramblers' Association, when in 1948 he invited us to join a Whitsun walk he was organizing among a group of Labour MPs to claim this right. Tom was deceptively gentle and slight in appearance, but he had a tough physique and a will of iron and was a perfect example of the little people who in those days battled against great odds to achieve big things. He had already enlisted the support of Hugh Dalton, who as an open-air fanatic had been elected the new president of the Ramblers' Association following his resignation from the Treasury – he was enjoying the comparative leisure of being Chancellor of the Duchy of Lancaster. He also had a constituency interest because the start of our walk had just been brought by redistribution into his Bishop Auckland seat and he was eager to arouse his new electors with his favourite access-to-mountains battlecry: 'We must not allow a few rich men to bar the way.'

The timing was apposite. The government was about to fulfil its election commitment to create a number of national parks. Lewis Silkin, Minister of Town and Country Planning, was drawing up his National Parks and Access to the Countryside Bill. Lewis was an improbable symbol of the hiker's friend. Portly, expensively suited and rather prim, he looked and was the successful City solicitor, but he had not forgotten the rambling days of his youth and the Bill delighted us with its comprehensiveness. It was something of a miracle to have any Bill at all in view of the many problems besetting the government, but here it all was: the creation of a number of national parks and areas of outstanding natural beauty, guaranteed access to the countryside, the safeguarding of footpaths and the designation of some long-distance walking routes. We wanted to be sure that the Bill did not get hijacked on its way to Parliament and was not watered down in any way.

There was also a more specific purpose in our walk. Tom had long cherished the ambition to forge the Pennine Way – a 250-mile continuous footpath stretching along the backbone of England from the Peaks to the Cheviots. We were to walk part of it, defying grouse-shooting landowners along the way.

The walk aroused considerable press interest. There were six of us MPs in addition to Hugh Dalton, and of course Ted came along. One of our number was Geoffrey de Freitas, then Under Secretary of State for Air, and we hoped he had come to spy out training grounds for possible release, but he told us he was there as president of the Nottinghamshire Ramblers' Association, so far-flung was the interest in the walk. The pressmen at first were sceptical. 'Are you really going to walk this route for three days?' one of them asked me and, when they found we were, a number of them trailed along with us. One newspaperman walked for two and a half days in a lounge suit, town mac and lightweight shoes and emerged from it looking as trim as when he began. We particularly admired the stamina of the photographers, who would dash ahead of us with their cameras and then spring out from behind rocks to catch the plodding cavalcade unawares. This was very hard on me as Ted and I had decided to pool our things into one big rucksack and take it in turns to carry it. I dared not risk being snapped without it and had to carry it all the way.

Hugh Dalton was another victim of the photographers' enterprise. When we came to a rushing mountain stream he turned to give me a helping hand over the man-sized stepping stones and was rewarded by a picture of it in one newspaper the next day over the caption 'Mr Dalton in difficulties'.

One of our aims was to get the right kind of national park. I for one believed that the loneliness and wildness of the mountains and uplands meets a deep spiritual need as well as providing the kind of physical challenge which can test character. We agreed with John Dower, one of the pioneers of the campaign for national parks, who produced a report on them in the last months of the wartime coalition government in which he urged that we must safeguard the 'beautiful and relatively wild' areas of our shrinking countryside. I knew I would grow old one day and not be able to walk those heights but I would prefer to keep my memories of the peace of those remote areas rather than invade them in a charabanc.

There was certainly plenty of physical challenge in our Pennine Walk. I captured the feel of it in an article I wrote for the *Spectator*:

> Forty-five miles in three days may seem poor going to the stay-at-homes [I wrote with the inspiration of that three-day walk still upon me], but, as one stalwart put it, 'vertical miles are not horizontal ones'. If you want to see the majesty of the Pennines, you have to scramble and strain for it, and risk the serious stumble and brave the snow-line, even in May. But grandeur is the reward, like the grandeur of High Force where the Tees hurtles over basalt bastions for nearly a hundred feet. There is even greater grandeur at Cauldron Snout looking, as well as

sounding, unparliamentary, for there is enough force to drive a dynamo where the long cascade thunders over the whinstone edge. And grandest of all is High Cup Nick, repaying the tugging scramble from Birdale with the sight of a dread, rock-walled gorge like a sword-cleft to the heart of the valley below, revealing the very roots of the mountains.

I also described the climb to Cross Fell:

The road from Dufton to Cross Fell forces the climber on and up over the slippery sides of Green Castle, across bog and high stone walls, past lesser ranges that seem formidable from below but are soon dwarfed as the road scales Dun Fell, under the slopes of Cross Fell itself. Here the snow clings to the rough grass and the wind bites. It is too cold to sit and eat, too cold to do anything but press on and upwards, keeping a watch for marshy patches and hidden holes that could snap an ankle. Is it worth it all? Why does one do this sort of thing? Here at last is the cairn and the answer – the cairn crowning the summit of 2,900 feet (the photographers dropped away a thousand feet ago), and the answer in the encircling view: the silver ribbon of the Solway, the Lakeland landmarks, Ullswater, Helvellyn and Langdale Pikes, the line of foothills passed on the way up two hours ago, and to the North, the Cheviot itself. Who would not walk with death and morning on the silver horns?

These walks were repeated for the next four years, covering the Lake District, Northumberland up to Hadrian's Wall, the Pembrokeshire coast, Brecon Beacons and the Peak District. On our second walk we even persuaded Lewis Silkin, who had been addressing a meeting on his Bill in the village hall, to walk a few yards with us for the benefit of photographers, which he did in smart town suit and polished shoes. We were fond of him and believed he had good radical instincts. He had already produced two major reforms in the New Towns Act and the Town and Country Planning Act of 1947. We knew his heart was in his latest measure, which he described as 'a people's charter for the open air', making the countryside 'theirs to preserve, to cherish, to enjoy and to make their own'. It was a good philosophy.

Despite this we were worried by what was happening to his Bill. Arthur Hobhouse, who produced a seminal report for the government in 1947, had urged that national parks should be truly national and that meant that they should come under a national parks commission which would appoint the majority of members of the local parks committees, leaving local authority members in the minority. At first Silkin was inclined to accept this view, but he came up against the resistance of his civil servants, who could see the role of their own Department being undermined. The Treasury too was hostile, fearing that a powerful national parks commission would want to spend too much. So Silkin was persuaded – or perhaps forced – to give the county councils the dominant role on the local park committees, only a quarter of whose members were to be appointed by the Commission which became purely advisory. In the Commons debate I pleaded with the Minister to give the National Parks Commission a more powerful role, but in vain, Silkin arguing that the Minister had power to intervene if the local parks committees did not do their job properly.

This unsatisfactory arrangement has had its inevitable result. The development of the national parks has been uneven, according to the strength of local interests. In some of them rights of access are still being resisted by local landowners. In others tourism is being promoted by local revenue-hungry councillors at the expense of John Dower's vision of 'beautiful and relatively wild' areas. The Minister's reserve powers atrophied in the Thatcher decade, when the rights of wealth, private property and profit-making were enthroned again. The Council for National Parks has been growing increasingly perturbed. So has the Countryside Commission, which has succeeded the National Parks Commission as the controlling authority. In 1989 it set up a panel under Professor Edwards to conduct a 'thorough review' into what was happening to national parks. To my delight, the report reinforced the concept of national parks as centres of 'physical challenge and spiritual refreshment' and called for the park committees to be reconstituted as independent national park authorities. The government promised that it would accept this change. At the time of writing, nothing has yet been done.

One outcome of our walks gave us complete satisfaction. Tom Stephenson achieved his ambition and three years after we walked it the Pennine Way became the first long-distance route to be designated. It was opened with a flourish by Hugh Dalton in the last days of the 1950–1 Labour government.

In 1948 I paid my first visit to America when the government sent me to the United Nations General Assembly as an alternate delegate. The journey over on the *Queen Mary* was heaven after British rationing and austerity, but my enthusiasm was dampened when I discovered I had been allocated to the Social Committee of the Assembly and that our main business there was to be a resolution outlawing prostitution. What on earth, I asked myself, had that to do with the growing threat to world peace? I was confident that I could deal with the problems of higher diplomacy at least as competently as Hector McNeil, who led the delegation under the towering shadow of Ernest Bevin. Hector was an affable young Scot who was very agreeable to everyone, but he seemed to have other preoccupations and the rest of the delegation did not see much of him.

We saw even less of Ernest Bevin, who was by then a very sick man. He was held in high regard by the Americans, but more for his past achievements than for his present ones. He would descend on the plenary sessions of the Assembly from time to time. Presumably he made at least one speech but it cannot have been a memorable one since I cannot recall a word of it. What I do remember is the awful moment when, sitting prominently in the front row of our delegation, he fell asleep during Dean Acheson's *tour d'horizon*. Press photographers hovered everywhere and one of them must have snapped him because the next day the *New York Times* featured a picture of the British Foreign Secretary sound asleep during a major speech by America's Secretary of State.

New York was an exciting shock. It left me half exhilarated and half appalled. I was intoxicated by the skyscrapers and by the magic view I got of Manhattan as I sailed round it in a boat. I also loved the atmosphere of 'get up and go', even though it produced so many pale faces, like those I saw in the drugstores we frequented for cheap meals. Drugstores, I decided, were one of America's great institutions, where the barmen served up expertly cooked fried eggs on rye bread in a flash. Since the British delegation was kept very short of dollars we always breakfasted in a drugstore on our way out to Lake Success, where the UN was then housed.

Our delegation was accommodated in the moderately priced Essex Hotel, whose name in large neon-lit letters was visible across Central Park. I noted with amusement that even in efficient America the lights of the two first letters had failed and remained invisible during our three weeks' stay. We were therefore mercilessly teased for living in the Sex Hotel.

I loved Central Park and liked to walk in it. This propensity of mine brought me up against the menacing aspects of New York life, whose atmosphere of fear I was later to encounter in Johannesburg. Americans warned me that I must never walk in Central Park alone, even in broad daylight. Druggies were everywhere and would stop at nothing, so I must hurry past anyone who tried to stop me on the street. One American woman pleaded with me to be very careful when I used a public lavatory, even in a reputable hotel. I must on no account put my handbag on the floor for a hand might appear under the partition which separated me from the next-door lavatory and snatch it away. It was many decades before this menacing atmosphere reached Britain in Margaret Thatcher's days.

My work in the Social Committee proved less dull than I had feared. We quickly dispatched the resolution which sought to make prostitution illegal. I noted cynically that the most ardent advocates were the Turks and the Arab delegates who, I thought to myself, were hardly known for sexual chastity. With the help of an excellent Home Office brief I argued that we ought to be pursuing not the prostitutes but the pimps and procurers. To my satisfaction this view eventually prevailed. I then got my first personal experience of the cold war. In a discussion on human rights the Soviet delegation and its satellites had tabled a resolution denouncing 'the discrimination practised by certain states against immigrant labour and in particular against labour recruited from the ranks of refugees'. It was not clear what the resolution was driving at until the Soviet delegate, Panyushkin, launched a vitriolic attack on Britain for 'forcibly' recruiting displaced persons in camps in West Germany and keeping them in conditions of Hitler-type slavery. Over 500,000 Soviet citizens, he alleged, were being prevented by force from returning to the Soviet Union. I saw red and started to draw on the Foreign Office brief I had intended to ignore. 'Why is the Soviet Union so interested in immigration?' I asked sarcastically. 'There are no applicants for the honour of entering the Soviet Union. What is more nobody can get out.' I reminded Panyushkin that, when the Soviet Union had invaded Poland in 1940, she forcibly transferred millions of Poles to labour camps in Siberia. The Ukrainian delegate sitting opposite me nearly spat in my face. I was still firmly opposed to a shooting war, but did not intend to let the Soviet Union win the verbal one.

I was particularly proud of what happened when the issue went to the Assembly's plenary session, at which I was determined to have the last word. A cat-and-mouse game then ensued between the Soviet delegate and me as we manoeuvred for the last place on the speaking list. I won, just as I won the argument. I left the debating chamber feeling elated, only to be brought down to earth when two American women came gushing up to me. 'We were listening in the gallery. You were marvellous!' they exclaimed, only to add, 'Whose side were you on?'

The most interesting contact I made during this visit and during another the following year when the government sent me out again was Eleanor Roosevelt, widow of the legendary President. She was a tall, almost ugly woman renowned for her good works and I went along to see her in critical mood because I had not much use for *grandes dames* and their do-goodery. Instead I found a shy serious woman with nothing of the *grande dame* about her at all. I also found that the causes she espoused went to the very heart of liberal policies. She was, for example, chairman of the United Nations Commission on Human Rights, which had just adopted a far-reaching international Declaration of Human Rights. I learned to respect her as a political force in her own right.

Back home Ted told me he had been sitting in the flat one night listening to the radio when my voice came booming over from Lake Success. 'If I had not known you,' he said, 'I would have thought you were a big woman.' All my life people who had heard me on television or radio have said on meeting me for the first time, 'You are smaller than we thought.' All that open-air speaking had apparently given me a more powerful voice than my size warranted.

Returning to British politics I found everyone preoccupied with the coming general election, since we had to go to the country by July 1950. Stafford Cripps was continuing his campaign on the need for austerity, but, with the dollar drain continuing and our reserves falling, he was forced to devalue in September 1949, the pound dropping from $4.03 to $2.80. It was obvious that it had been absurd to try to maintain such a high parity, but Cripps was shattered, accepting it as the failure of his own management. Thereafter devaluation was to become a badge of shame in Labour mythology, a view which was to lead Harold Wilson and Jim Callaghan into their disastrous decision not to devalue in 1964. For some mysterious reason Labour leaders had saddled themselves with an instinctive belief that they were less skilled than the Tories in economic management, even though the objective facts had proved – and continued to prove – the exact opposite.

The trouble was that the Cabinet ministers were tired men. The post-war economic struggle following the strains of a long war had worn them down. Bevin was a sick man, Morrison had been ill, Attlee was far from well, while Cripps was struggling with the intestine disorder, which was steadily worsening. He was to resign in October 1950 and died in 1952. The younger people, who had been kept out of Parliament in the war by the electoral truce, were not yet ready to replace them, and the ranks of young hopefuls with enough experience were thin. Defeatism was in the air.

Yet our achievements had been outstanding. In addition to the great stream of reformist legislation, no one in Britain had gone short of necessities. Unemployment had been kept down to just over 300,000 compared with nearly 1.5 million in 1939, when rearmament was already having an effect. Rents had been controlled. Our food prices were the lowest in the Western world. The cost of living had gone up by 75 per cent but average weekly earnings had doubled and benefits had been substantially increased. Our situation compared favourably with relatively prosperous countries like Belgium, where the cost of living had doubled. (In Italy it had increased fifty times.) Housing remained a problem, largely owing to the shortage of raw materials, but despite Cripps' cutbacks in his 1948 Budget we were still building 200,000 houses compared with an average of 361,000 between 1934 and 1938. Not least we had launched the free Health Service. But people were tired of food and clothes rationing, the drabness and lack of variety. In an attempt to cheer things up the government organized the Festival of Britain in Battersea Park, an imaginative effort, but no substitute for a bit of colour in their everyday life for which people longed.

In fact our standing in the country was still remarkably high and we had not lost a single by-election. Inevitably, however, the Opposition exploited every grievance ruthlessly and our own propaganda lacked bite. Our election address was a tepid document which revealed that our reforming drive had petered out. It continued to pay lipservice to the need to extend public ownership but without enthusiasm, and the list of proposed takeovers – chiefly sugar, cement and 'mutualization of industrial assurance' – appeared to have been picked out of a hat. The case for them was never made, so they seemed doctrinaire and irrelevant. It was hard for party workers to get excited about our programme.

In February 1950 Attlee decided to make a dash for it before the Budget because he did not think we could afford any sweeteners. Once again we were being purist to a fault, a mistake the Tories never made. The result was that Labour's seats fell to 315 against the Conservatives' 298, the Liberals' 9, and 2 for the Irish Nationalists. Leaving out the latter, who were inclined to switch their allegiance from side to side, our majority was down to 8. We had expected to lose some seats, but this was a blow we did not deserve.

EIGHT

•

The Drift to Defeat

THE EXASPERATING aspect of the 1950 election was that, though we had lost a large number of seats, we had polled nearly 1 million more votes than the Conservatives. So the majority of the electors had not rejected our policies, but we were up against the fact that our supporters were unevenly distributed throughout the country. It was to become a familiar problem; the extra votes we won went to swell already big majorities in the traditionally Labour areas, while the Tories made inroads in the more marginal ones. Yet the democratic arithmetic remained the same. Overall we had more support than they had.

The election result was not helped by the fact that in Chuter Ede the Labour government had had one of the most quixotic ministers in political history. Chuter Ede was a sternly upright man who as Home Secretary had proceeded to set up a boundary commission to redraw the boundaries of constituencies so as to bring them more into line with the size of their electorate. It was a perfectly correct democratic exercise but to proceed with it at the height of unprecedented post-war economic difficulties looked like a penchant for political suicide. As he did so, Churchill chuckled that the changes would cost Labour thirty-five seats in the 1950 election. Other commentators estimated the loss at eighty seats. No Conservative government would have followed such a purist line. They would have postponed the evil day till a more propitious moment, arguing with justification – as we should have done – that the population in those post-war years was in a state of flux due to demobilization and other changes and that we should wait until these movements of people had settled down.

There were other factors which influenced the result. They were expressed in the various inquests which were taking place. One of the most interesting appeared in the *Birmingham Gazette*, which commissioned Michael Foot and Woodrow Wyatt to discuss why Labour had lost and what should be done now. In the light of subsequent events it is intriguing to discover how closely they tallied in their analysis. Michael, of course, argued that 'Labour must now seek to portray much more clearly the vision of the new society which Socialism seeks to build.' Woodrow was more emphatic and more precise. The party's policy, he wrote, had been 'too negative', particularly over nationalization. 'It is largely nationalization', he declared, 'which has been responsible for fair shares.' And he added, 'It is Socialist planning that is necessary to maintain full employment.' He has eaten these words since then, but he struck an echo among many Labour people when he called for conviction politics.

The left, of course, conducted its own inquest. Just before the election the Keep Left Group had produced another document, *Keeping Left*, of which I was co-author with Dick Crossman, Michael Foot and others. Once again it was more philosophical than polemical. Michael's hand could be seen in the document's quotations from Colonel Thomas Rainsborough of Cromwell's Parliamentary Army and Gerald Winstanley of the Diggers. As Isaac Foot's son, Michael was a Cromwell fan and he had the same emotional devotion to the Levellers as I had to William Morris. They both gave us an almost religious view of the socialist cause, so we quoted Colonel Rainsborough in 1647: 'Really I think that the poorest he that is in England hath a life to live as the greatest he.' (Out of deference to Mike I ignored the 'he'.) From General Winstanley we took the words he used in 1649: 'I affirm (and challenge you to disprove) that the earth was made to be a common treasury of livelihood for all, without respect of persons.'

These were stirring words, which appealed to the idealism of Labour's activists and epitomized the most important dividing line between right and left. Man cannot live by statistics alone and the rank and file were hungry for a lead which made them feel that, despite the difficulties, the party and its government were carrying the country towards a new set of values and of human relationships. They had had that feeling in 1945 but it was threatened now by the pragmatists, who had no feel for political poetry.

Yet we in Keep Left had no use for the communists, whose initial idealism had been destroyed under Stalin. We were a highly individualistic bunch to whom freedom of expression and democratic institutions were the breath of life. Among our mentors was Professor Tawney, whose *Affluent Society* became one of the bibles of the left. Like Nye Bevan, Tawney believed that democracy had to be more than casting a vote every five years or so. We quoted from him in our pamphlet: 'Democracy is unstable as a political system as long as it remains a political system and nothing more, instead of being, as it should be, not only a form of government, but a type of society.' This would involve 'the conversion of economic power, now often an irresponsible tyrant, into a servant of society, working within clearly defined limits, and accountable to a public authority.'

So we called for a mixed economy in which power would be shared between the democratic representatives in Parliament and on local authorities, 'enlightened management' and the workers themselves. This, we warned, would call for a change of attitude across the board. 'Not only management, but the Labour movement itself, must be transformed to fulfil their new roles.'

One of the major issues then – as now – was the question of controls on which Churchill had fought the election and which was to become a familiar Tory theme. Labour's restrictions, Churchill had argued, were responsible for the shortages and the Tories would sweep away as many of them as possible. They would abolish rationing of food and even petrol, stop nationalization in its tracks and repeal the Iron and Steel Act before it could come into force, build more houses, start cutting taxes and bring the cost of living down. Since another general election could not be far away, it was clear that they would redouble their attack.

I was not surprised at the public's restiveness. Five years after the war had ended the meat ration was still only eightpence per head per week and with the cheese ration only 3 ounces per head it was hard to supplement the meagre meat meals. Rationing was part of the government's policy of keeping food prices down by subsidies.

Subsidies could not be open-ended but had to be limited to specific amounts. Cheap food was the holy grail of our economic and social policy and one could always get a cheer at meetings of Labour women by warning that food prices would sky-rocket if the Tories were returned to power and abolished subsidies. 'Do you want rationing by the purse?' I used to ask my audiences, who replied with a resounding 'No!' After one such meeting, however, I got a different view. A woman from my audience came up to me shyly and said, 'I did not want to ask a question, but I would like you to end food rationing because at the moment I am having to spend a lot of money on convenience foods. If we could have more of the basic ingredients, I could make more of these dishes myself. So even if their prices went up I should save money overall.' It made me think. Looking back I believe the Labour movement got itself locked into too many high-minded rigidities and was slow to realize where greater flexibility could be introduced without damaging our key priorities.

Nonetheless, I remain convinced that most of those post-war controls were essential if we were to balance our payments, build up our export trade and meet the community's essential needs.

As Harold's PPS I sat in on the President's discussions with his officials, and they were an eye-opener. For instance, I got a revealing insight into the hosiery industry. One of the big grievances among women at the time was the unflattering quality of the stockings they had to wear. Why could they not have more fully fashioned ones, of which they had 'consumed' 9 million pairs before the war? The answer, said officials, was that we had imported half of them and if we did so again the cost in foreign exchange would be prohibitive, particularly since the industry estimated that demand in a free-for-all would expand by at least another 3 million pairs.

The argument went round and round. Could we not, I asked,

expand output at home? Yes, said the Hosiery Working Party Cripps had set up, provided the government would fund the hard currency for the modern machinery needed to re-equip the industry, which would have to come from America and Switzerland. The truth, we discovered, was that the pre-war free-market economy had left the industry in parlous state. Two-thirds of its machinery was obsolete or obsolescent and half the remainder was on the way to becoming so. Harold agreed to go ahead with re-equipment in the hope that we could recoup some of the cost with increased exports of fully fashioned hosiery. But, he pointed out, this would mean directing some of the new production to exports, which would therefore not necessarily be available for home demand.

Another headache was pottery. Since the war the British housewife had had to put up with plain white crockery, since the sale of decorated pottery on the home market had been prohibited so as to make room for sales abroad. Naturally they complained, as did Dr Barnett Stross, Labour MP for Hanley, who pressed Harold to relax the ban. He may have thought that he was fighting the battles of the Potteries, but in fact the British Pottery Manufacturers' Federation advised us that any relaxation of the ban would mean a diversion of sales from exports to the home market. The ban stayed.

Faced with these grumbles, I decided to produce a pamphlet on *Are Controls Necessary?* As I dug up the facts I decided that they were. We could not, for instance, have built as many houses as we did or have given other essential buildings priority, if we had not licensed all building to ensure that the scarce raw materials went first into factories and low-cost houses to rent.

As the attacks on us grew wilder and more lurid I made it my business to help shoot them down. Sometimes I had the satisfaction of exposing the crasser inaccuracies, as when one of our most persistent persecutors, Major Turton, MP for Thirsk, declared in a debate that our imposition of purchase tax on children's clothes had helped to push up the cost of living. I was able to inform him that there was no purchase tax on children's clothing. 'Some Facts for Major from Barbara', the *Daily Herald* reported gleefully.

None of us on the government side wanted to keep on controls for controlling's sake. Chuter Ede as Home Secretary had swept away 227 Defence Regulations within his first two months of office. Harold had no hesitation about his own approach. At the beginning of 1949 he abolished clothes rationing and followed it with his famous declaration that he wanted a 'bonfire of controls'. This alarmed us in Keep Left as playing into the hands of the Tories. I, in particular, was worried that he had not made his announcement in the context of the role which our controls had played in building up Britain's economy and might still have to play in certain forms. I was perturbed, for example, by his apparent enthusiasm for returning the purchase of essential raw materials to private hands. He managed to suggest that private purchasing must always be superior, yet bulk-buying by the government and long-term contracts with Commonwealth governments had been a central part of our policy for keeping prices down. The UN's Economic Commission for Europe in its survey of Britain's trade position in 1949 had paid tribute to 'the influence of its bulk purchase agreements in restraining price increases'. Psychologically Harold had paved the way for abandoning this feeling.

We discussed all these matters in the Keep Left Group, helped by erudite documents from Tommy Balogh. Tommy, a Hungarian left-winger, had all the uncompromising intellectual logic of the continental socialist. 'Controls', he told us in one of his papers, 'retain their permanent importance (even if they can be handled more generously in the meantime) as the sole selective means of influencing exports and imports, i.e. maintaining balance of payments stability without general deflation (or inflation) in face of international fluctuations.' Those of us who had to live by the political realities always took Tommy's stern admonitions with a pinch of salt. Nonetheless, he had the capacity for putting his finger on some inescapable economic truths. If we managed to achieve full employment, he pointed out, inflation could be curbed only if wage demands were kept within the bounds of increased productivity. Yet decontrol, by stimulating the production of luxury goods at the expense of essentials, caused social inequality and undermined wage stability. Deflation and unemployment were then the only alternatives. It was a theme to which he was to return many times during the years I knew him.

I was to have an enduring affection for Tommy, who died in 1985. Infuriating as he could be, he kept forcing us back to a problem which has plagued successive governments. How does one expand the economy without running into inflation? Must deflation and unemployment always be the cure for runaway demands by all sections of the community? Labour governments were to have a more successful stab at it than others.

But it was international policy which was to cause the fateful rift which split the party in 1951. Once again, the argument was about the government's subservience to American policy. In March 1950 communist troops equipped with Russian tanks crossed the 38th parallel which divided North from South Korea, and America's reaction was instantaneous. At first her response did not seem like another manifestation of the cold war. North Korea was in clear breach of international law and the Security Council responded immediately to the South's appeal for assist-ance and called for the withdrawal of North Korean troops. When, therefore, America sent in forces to drive back the invader and Attlee announced Britain's support for the war, there was no murmuring in the party – or in the Cabinet. I for one saw no alternative. But when General MacArthur swept north of the 38th parallel far in excess of his United Nations remit and provoked a reluctant China into entering the war, the mood changed and the rumblings of a rift began.

Looking back it is tragic to see how easily the party split could have been avoided. Bevin himself could see the dangers of America's anti-communist phobia. He realized, for instance, that the communist revolution in China was a portentous event with which we must come to terms, and he had recognized the new government, rejecting the idea that the tough and confident men and women who had conquered this vast country would be willing to become mere stooges of the Soviet Union. So he opposed America's attempt to brand China as an aggressor in

Korea. Attlee, too, showed some independence of spirit and was cheered to the echo by our backbenchers when he announced he was flying to Washington to check up on the rumour that America was about to use the atom bomb against North Korea. Even the hostile press applauded what it called Attlee's attempt to 'stop a third world war'.

The West's relations with China, however, were severely damaged when America aligned herself with the regime's defeated enemy, Chiang Kai-shek, enabling him to dig in on the island of Formosa (known as Taiwan to the communist government) just off China's mainland, where he represented a permanent threat to the revolution.

Under the influence of McCarthyism, America's relations with the Soviet Union deteriorated to the point of hysteria. Yet, as long as our government continued to exercise a restraining influence, we on the left held our peace. We were well aware that the Soviet leaders were showing no desire to co-operate with the West. They had refused to take part in the Marshall Plan, and they had blockaded Berlin in 1948 in order to prevent the British, American and French from discharging their responsibilities in their own zones, so that the beleaguered Berliners had had to be saved by an Allied airlift. It was a dangerous period.

It was this awareness which held the party together. Even the government's decision to rearm did not at first break it. We Keep Lefters were certainly not pacifists and were resigned to the fact that the Korean war and Russian intransigence would inevitably lead to increased arms expenditure. The first increase of £100 million in March 1950 caused barely a stir, but as the arms budget shot up under American pressure it became clear that Britain was being entangled in a political assessment we could not accept. Bevin had begun to change his line, endorsing the growing assumption that the Korean war was merely part of Stalin's plan for military conquest of the West. Mannie Shinwell, as Minister of Defence, reinforced it with a lurid picture of 175 Russian divisions poised ready to strike. Churchill, of course, joined in enthusiastically. By September 1950, Britain's arms spending was inflated to £3600 million spread over three years and, in response to further American appeals, was pushed up yet again to £4700 million in February 1951.

Even then Nye did not kick over the traces. He had by now been moved to the Ministry of Labour and in that capacity had to make the winding-up speech in the key debate and justify the government's decision to extend National Service to two years. He did it in his inimitable way, warning that, if general direction of labour became necessary, it could apply to employers as well as workers 'and we shall deal equitably with both'.

Nonetheless he did not oppose the new rearmament figure – an act of loyalty which was to be quoted against him many times. One of his reasons was his anger at the Soviet Union's menacing attitude to Yugoslavia, a country which was practising a benign form of socialism of which he approved. 'Any threat to Yugoslavia,' he declared, 'which played an heroic role in resistance to Hitler aggression, is naturally a concern to His Majesty's government.' In fact, Nye's speech was full of indications of the train of thought that was to lead to his breaking with the government. He attacked Churchill for being as old-fashioned as the communists. Neither he nor they were facing the technical realities. The Soviets should have realized they could not sell their communist ideas in the industrialized West and Churchill should have realized Russia was in no position to wage war. Nye plugged what was to become his favourite theme. Steel was the key. 'I do not believe that a nation, however large its manpower, coldly contemplates launching 25 million tons of steel per annum [his estimate of Russia's production] against the combination of 100 million tons per annum' which the Allies could produce. Neither Churchill nor the party leaders, however, were listening.

Another divisive issue now raised its head. Should the West rearm Germany as an ally against the Soviet East? Churchill, carried away by his own propaganda about the Soviet threat, first launched the idea in Strasbourg in 1949 at a meeting of the Consultative Assembly of the new Council of Europe which he had attended as a delegate. Not surprisingly, his proposal terrified the French. They countered it with their own proposal for a

European Defence Community in which a West German component might play a part. Churchill, who had made great speeches
during the war about the need to build a United States of Europe,
backtracked when he realized he would have to put British forces
under the EDC. Even the French Assembly turned down the idea.
So we were left with the naked proposal to rearm the West's
section of Germany. Churchill challenged Attlee in the House,
'Does he still think the only Germans to be armed are the
communist Germans whom the Soviets have formed into a
powerful army in the Russian zone?' Bevin, who had originally
dismissed the idea of German rearmament as 'unthinkable', now
toed the line. So did Attlee, though more diffidently. The issue
was to become a *cause célèbre* in Labour politics. Differences of
opinion cut across the usual dividing lines. Hugh Dalton was
passionately opposed to rearming Germany; Denis Healey, a
devoted disciple of Ernest Bevin, accepted it. The left was to
oppose it tooth and nail.

These developments were anxiously discussed in the Keep Left
Group, where Dick Crossman told us that the issue of German
rearmament was far more serious than any of us realized. It would
stoke up German nationalism, which was already being fed by
America's treatment of West Germany as a favoured son in the
battle against communism. We could only guess at what was
happening in Cabinet, helped by *Tribune* editorials. Since both
Michael Foot and Jennie Lee were on the editorial board, it became
our political barometer as to what Nye thought.

Nonetheless, Bevan's resignation from the government in
April 1951 came as a shock to most of us. It had, we gathered
later, been precipitated by an explosive mixture of the political
and the personal. After five years' success in building up the
National Health Service, Nye believed with some justification that
he deserved to move higher up the government hierarchy. So,
when Cripps resigned on health grounds in October 1950, he
expected promotion and was outraged when Hugh Gaitskell was
moved almost automatically into the succession as Chancellor.
Another affront came in March 1951 when Bevin was forced by
Attlee to give up the foreign secretaryship, a post in which he had

hoped to die – he in fact died one month later. Nye was an internationalist by instinct and by personal contacts, and could legitimately have expected to be offered the job. Instead Attlee appointed Herbert Morrison, the Tammany Hall boss of London, in his place, an appointment which by common consent was disastrous.

Dalton, who was Morrison's second in command in the Labour delegation to Strasbourg for the Assembly meetings of the Council of Europe, was full of contempt for his uncouthness and insularity. It was Morrison who, without consulting his colleagues, committed the government to supporting the EDC on a visit to Washington in September 1951.

So the appointment rankled. Nye was not a calculatingly ambitious man: if he had been, Dalton believed, he could have become leader of the party. But he had proper confidence in his own abilities and the cavalier brushing aside of his value to the government must have reinforced his mistrust of its policies, notably its supine surrender to American pressure on the arms programme.

Later his critics claimed that he had imported the rearmament issue into the argument only at the last moment, which he denied. Proof of his assertions has recently come to light with the release of the Cabinet documents of that period. They show that he opposed the increased programme from the start, arguing that it could not be fulfilled. He accepted defeat at that stage, but salt was to be rubbed into his wounds when Gaitskell told Cabinet he was going to include charges on teeth and spectacles in his Budget to help pay for it.

It was too much. The principle of a free health service was at stake. The Cabinet records show that from the moment Gaitskell put his proposal to Cabinet Nye protested, manoeuvred and cajoled in an attempt to get his colleagues to reject it. In this he was supported consistently by Harold Wilson and fitfully by Jim Griffiths and George Tomlinson. Others tried to find a way out. Could not the decision be postponed till it could be seen whether the vast new sums earmarked for the arms programme could actually be spent? Gaitskell was adamant. When Nye threatened to resign if charges were imposed, Gaitskell retorted that he would resign if they were not, telling Dalton that Nye's influence was 'much exaggerated'. Nye was not the only one who warned that the earmarked money could not be spent and that the attempt to do so would do grave damage to our economy. Gaitskell himself had told Cabinet in January that the consequences of the new arms target would be severe: a desperate shortage of raw materials; disruption of exports and investment in key industries like engineering; a reduction in consumer living standards; the possible direction of labour. But all this was offset in his view by the political need not to offend the Americans.

Budget day, 21 April, found Gaitskell still unmoved. In the event his speech was a *tour de force*. Churchill congratulated him on a 'remarkable parliamentary performance . . . an honest attempt to solve the problems which lie before him'. Even our most critical backbenchers were impressed by the skill with which he balanced burdens and reliefs: sixpence on income tax offset by increased child and married person's allowances; the doubling of purchase tax on less essential goods like cars softened by its abolition on essentials like kitchen utensils; no increase in food subsidies to offset the rise in prices, but no cut either. He gave pensioners £39 million more and even found another £15 million for colonial welfare and development. Yet the very care with which he balanced the conflicting claims showed to us on the left that he could have avoided demanding £13 million from the NHS, which meant introducing charges for the first time.

Most provocative of all was his insistence that the increased expenditure of £690 million on rearmament in the current year was sacrosanct. 'The whole of this amount must be excluded from the economy field,' he declared. Later events were to make a fool of him and prove Bevan right when both the British and the Americans were forced to admit that their arms targets could not be reached. Still Nye hesitated to take the fateful plunge. A number of people – notably Hugh Dalton, John Freeman and Dick Crossman – urged him not to resign. But his closest associates – the little group which ran *Tribune* – were counselling him the other way, warning that he had already given way on so many things – housing cuts, the principle of prescription charges, rearmament itself – that if he vacillated now, he could find himself fatally compromised. Attlee, in hospital with a duodenal ulcer, made no serious effort to mediate. On Sunday, 22 April Aneurin Bevan, Harold Wilson and John Freeman resigned from the government.

Though I believed that Nye's intellectual argument was unanswerable, I felt uneasy about his mood. My uneasiness turned to alarm when, in accordance with tradition, Nye made a personal statement to the House the next day. He began well enough with a reiteration of his case against the new arms programme. The House stirred nervously as he said, 'It has for some time been obvious that raw materials, machine tools and components are not forthcoming in sufficient quantity even for the earlier programme.' But he lost his audience when, once again, his emotions ran away with him and he lapsed into attacks on Gaitskell which sounded embarrassingly like personal pique. The Chancellor, he claimed, knew perfectly well that the figures in his Budget were 'unrealizable'. The dental and spectacle charges were merely the little stone which could start an avalanche of attack on the social services: 'Where do you stop?' He capped it all with the assertion that there were too many economists in the Treasury 'and now we have the added misfortune of having an economist in the Chancellor of the Exchequer himself'. So bitter was the speech that it provoked interruptions from some backbenchers, unprecedented on these occasions. I sat appalled. I realized then that we backroom boys and girls of the Keep Left Group had acquired a leader who would put us on the political map, but at a heavy price.

The price continued to be paid the following day at a special meeting of Labour MPs in the Grand Committee Room, the gloomiest room in the neo-Gothic pile of Westminster. Sparks flew as one middle-of-the-roader after another rounded on Nye, accusing him of disloyalty and vanity. He reacted like a cornered animal, snarling back. He knew that once again he had allowed his emotions to carry him away to his own detriment. His bitterness was increased when Harold Wilson's personal statement in the House proved to be a model of diplomacy. Harold faithfully echoed Nye's reasons for their joint resignation, but he did it in such emollient style that he did not raise a murmur of dissent from the Tory benches opposite, even remembering, as Nye had failed to do, to express his 'deep sense of privilege' at having been able to play a part in 'the concrete achievements of the government'. As I listened to him I realized once again that this backroom boy had developed into a skilled strategist. This man, I told myself, is hell-bent on the leadership. I was also fascinated to note that, although MPs, a conventional lot, were pleased by Harold's conventional courtesies, his calculated moderation commanded less respect than Nye's blunderbuss sincerity. For his part Nye never trusted Harold again.

The biggest enigma in this resignation trio was John Freeman. John was a charismatic figure who from his first arrival in the Commons in 1945 had seemed to have a dazzling political career ahead of him. He was chosen to second the Loyal Address for the first King's Speech – the Commons' thanks to the sovereign for his speech. As he stood there in his major's uniform, erect, composed and competent, everyone felt his star quality. He was quickly appointed a junior minister, first at the War Office and then at the Ministry of Supply; much greater opportunities lay ahead of him. Now he had resigned and we all waited expectantly for him to carry the debate on to the high intellectual level of which we knew he was capable. Instead he made no personal statement at all, either in the House or in the press. In one stormy party meeting after another he stood against the wall, almost hiding himself behind the window curtains, but did not speak.

His later career threw some light on the mystery. He seemed to dislike exposure and was happier in expressing himself in writing, contributing articles to *Tribune* and, more congenially, the *New Statesman*, of which he became assistant editor in 1951 and later editor. He retired voluntarily from Parliament in 1955 – I felt thankfully. When later he entered the world of television he had a great success with his series of *Face to Face* interviews in which he excelled at drawing out his interviewees while obliterating himself. All one ever saw of him was his back. After years of studying his complex personality I decided he was afraid of giving himself too fully to anything or anyone. I once told him his motto ought to be 'Je me sauve'.

It was soon clear that Gaitskell had seriously misjudged the anxious mood of the rank and file. To his annoyance Nye became the hero and Gaitskell the *bête noire*. Of course he had his bands of devotees scattered throughout the party, but he never succeeded in getting elected to the constituency parties' section of the NEC, while Nye regularly topped the poll. Gaitskell's power base was the right-wing MPs, who were in a majority in the parliamentary party, and the Big Three of the trade unions, who loathed the left, despised Attlee and saw in Gaitskell the sort of leader who would hound the left as the NEC had hounded Cripps, Bevan, Strauss and others before the war. Since most of the rank and file were left, a bitter clash became inevitable.

I disliked Gaitskell intensely myself. The prim set of his mouth seemed to symbolize the primness of his political views – no adventurousness, no poetry. Nye's dismissal of him as a 'desiccated calculating machine' found an echo in our hearts. As Gaitskell's personality unfolded in later years I discovered sides of him I was not aware of in 1951. I found, for instance, that he was an emotional man capable of great political passion and I have always admired passion in politics, even when I did not approve of the ends to which it was being directed. I also found he could be a jolly man in private life. I came across this facet of him by accident when I was invited by one of Hugh's coterie to a social evening in his house. I went out of curiosity and found Hugh holding court with relaxed boyishness among his friends, perched on the edge of the kitchen table, cracking jokes. I also discovered that he was an enthusiastic ballroom dancer. One of the highlights of party conferences in those days was a grand ball given by the Mayor which everyone attended. Press photographers wove their way among the dancers, looking for a newsworthy picture, and found it on one of these occasions when Hugh invited me to dance. I whirled round with him in my ballgown, admiring the deftness of his feet, though I told Ted afterwards, that his style had been a bit too Palais de Dance for me.

Nonetheless I could never forgive him for precipitating a damaging split in the party which need never have taken place if he had been willing to show the slightest flexibility. The more that is uncovered about the events leading up to Nye's resignation the clearer it becomes that Gaitskell considered Nye to be not only expendable but a positive liability, despite his brilliant success in creating the NHS and the loyalty he had shown as Minister of Labour. The recently published Cabinet records of the period, for instance, reveal the unyielding hostility he showed to anyone who disagreed with him. Gaitskell had a streak of Crippsian rectitude, which one could respect, but it was combined with an intolerance of dissent which Cripps, himself so often a rebel, never felt. Gaitskell was to mellow later, but for many years his mixture of pedantry and prejudice led him to errors of political judgment which kept the party at war with itself.

Nye's resignation turned the Keep Left into the Bevanites. It led to a great upsurge of political activity in local parties, grouped around *Tribune*, which became our voice. The Bevanites were never an organized conspiracy. We had no formal membership. Nobody paid any subscription to any central body: instead they bought *Tribune* and raised funds for it. It was the medium through which we advised local parties what resolutions to table for party conference and how to vote on party policy. One of our most effective means of propaganda was the *Tribune* 'brains trust' modelled on the BBC's new programme of that name. We offered a panel of speakers to any constituency party willing to provide a hall and an audience, and local parties queued up for the privilege, providing us with enthusiastic questioners. I was often a member of the panel and found the experience exhilarating, not least when we skated on thin political ice on such issues as land nationalization or a socialist's attitude to the monarchy. The party leadership, dedicated under Morrison's influence to a cautious policy of 'consolidation', found our activities dangerous. We stubbornly believed that the only course for a reforming party was to live dangerously.

Another of our weapons was the *Tribune* pamphlet, of which we produced a spate over the coming months. The first, and perhaps the most successful, was *One Way Only*, which had a preface by Nye, Harold Wilson and John Freeman endorsing it, but of which Ian Mikardo claimed the authorship. Its purpose was to justify the resignations and it sold 100,000 copies. Subsequent pamphlets covered an amazing range of subjects. I wrote one on the textile industry called *Back to the Dole*. Geoffrey Bing, the brilliant KC and Labour MP, published an attack on the monopoly powers of the brewers in *Set the Pubs Free*. Harold Wilson wrote an economic treatise on *In Place of Dollars*. Roy Jenkins contributed a pamphlet in our early days. It was a bold statement of the case for a capital levy under the title *Fair Shares for the Rich*. To the leadership's annoyance it was clear that *Tribune* and the Bevanites had captured the ideological initiative.

During all this my own political fortunes had taken a dramatic turn. I had gradually been making a national name for myself by my speeches in the country and my activities in the House, but I was still considered a junior member of our left-wing team by people like Dick Crossman, who tended to patronize me. Nor was I ever one of Nye's intimates. But I soldiered on. As an MP I was entitled to attend party conference as an *ex officio* delegate and at the Blackpool conference in 1949 I managed to get to the rostrum during the debate on the party's policy document for the imminent general election, *Labour Believes in Britain*. In my speech I drew on the experience of controls I had gained at the Board of Trade. I warned conference that it was comparatively easy to share shortages fairly, but much more difficult to share abundance, for people became more selfish as production rose and goods came flooding back. That was the moment when we most needed the right controls. My speech went down well and Sam Watson, leader of the Durham Miners, congratulated me on it afterwards, hinting that if I ran for the women's section of the NEC I would have his support. Sam was one of the moderates of the trade union movement. Though no leftie he had no use for the loud-mouthed vulgarities of Will Lawther, his national boss. Nye Bevan used to consider him one of the trade union leaders with whom he could talk. Swallowing my principles, because I was against the women's section being in the pocket of the trade unions, I put up my name for it and, true to his word, Sam mobilized trade union votes in my support.

So at the Margate party conference in 1950 I found myself elected to the NEC along with Ian Mikardo, who had taken Michael Foot's place among the seven members of the constituency parties' section, Michael having decided that, as editor of *Tribune*, he ought to be free of the collective responsibilities of the NEC.

At my first meeting of the Executive Hugh Dalton waved to me to come and sit next to him. I did so reluctantly, as I would have preferred to sit with my left-wing friends. At every vote Dalton boomed instructions to me, which I ignored. Hugh said to me some time afterwards, 'Sam told me that it was my job to keep you in order, but I have failed.' It was soon clear that I had lost the trade union vote. I resigned myself to defeat at the next conference, but decided to go down fighting. As a gesture of defiance, I got myself nominated for the constituencies' section, to which no woman had so far been elected. I did not expect to win since most local parties argued, not unreasonably, that women were catered for by their special representation on the Executive anyway.

The result, however, was spectacular. When it was announced I found I had shot up to second place after Nye, who was top of the poll again. Ian was re-elected, pushing out Mannie Shinwell, who stalked out of conference in a fury and caught the next train home. So was Tom Driberg, who had managed to win constituency votes for a number of years – a surprising choice because he was the least populist of men, an aesthete with exacting tastes in food and style, who refused to make any concessions to anyone on either count and whose gay activities kept us in constant fear lest he should be found out. His success was due to the enlightened 'William Hickey' column he wrote in the *Express* and his reputation as a champion of all civil liberty causes, of which the abolition of the then highly restrictive laws on homosexuality was naturally one. Only three of the old guard – Morrison, Dalton, Jim Griffiths – were left in this section. The press headlined the 'Bevan Group Sensation' and Nye had to be dragooned somewhat reluctantly into posing for endless photographs shaking hands with me, his new lieutenant. No doubt the press thought that Nye had manoeuvred my election, which was far from the truth. No one was more surprised than my left-wing colleagues, who had not expected me to survive, particularly as Harold Wilson had failed in his election bid. I suspect my meteoric rise was due to the local parties' instinctive support of a David of the back benches who had defied the Goliath of the trade unions.

The press confidently predicted that the conference would be a bitter one and that the party would go into the election disunited. Instead Nye was at his most endearing, rousing conference to enthusiasm in a speech in which he praised Attlee and attacked Churchill as a threat to peace. 'I do not think Winston Churchill wants war,' he mocked. 'The trouble with him is that he does not know how to avoid it.' And he delighted his hearers with his emphatic restatement of his deeply held belief: 'We must avoid at all costs a repetition of what has happened to continental socialist movements. We must never carry doctrinaire differences to the point of schism.' In a belated stroke of sanity by the Executive (for which Dalton was later to claim most of the credit) he was put on a small sub-committee with Dalton and Sam Watson to rewrite the draft manifesto which Morgan Phillips as secretary of the party had prepared. The result was a document which all sections of the party could support. Even the hurdle of rearmament was safely negotiated with the words, 'The Labour Government decided without hesitation that Britain must play her full part in the strengthening of collective defence. Britain must be strong: so must the Commonwealth. But peace cannot be preserved by arms alone.' Once again Nye had shown that an integral part of his temperament was an instinctive working-class belief in the need for unity against the enemy. He was always ready to compromise if handled properly.

As Nye had hoped, his resignation revitalized the party. With the election approaching there was a resurgence of activity among the rank and file. Ted and I lived in Hornsey and our local party there buzzed with political activity. Hornsey was a Conservative stronghold, its MP, Captain Gammans, as true blue as you could find, but undaunted the Labour minority on the Council conducted a non-stop attack, exuding political irreverence and self-confidence. Its debates, in which Ted as an alderman played an outstanding part, regularly hit the headlines in the local press. Meetings over, the Labour team and its supporters would gather on the Town Hall steps to sing the Red Flag before adjourning to the local pub for camaraderie and conspiracy. I joined in whenever I could. These challenging tactics did not lose us votes. On the contrary we gained Council seats.

At this stage Ted and I decided it was time for us to start a family. When nothing happened we took medical advice. Physical examinations and studies of our family histories revealed no reason why we should not have a child. After some months a friend advised us to go to a German doctor she knew who specialized in the problems of infertility. It was a bad mistake. The doctor treated us with Teutonic solemnity. Ted was subjected to more tests and I was put on a course of injections with an extract from pregnant mares. When still nothing happened, the doctor turned himself into a psychologist, taking us aside in turn to probe our minds. When our marital relationship began to get rather strained we discovered that he had been telling Ted that I suffered from masculine protest; and telling me on the other hand that Ted suffered from a feminine one. We had had enough and we rebelled. Ted flatly refused to make love to any more jam-jars, while I declared that my buttocks could not endure any more injections from pregnant mares. We decided to let life take its course. I remained personally convinced that the trouble was due to my wartime attack of mumps.

Our lives were so full we had no time to mope over our childlessness. I used to say, 'I have 60,000 children in my constituency' – the electors I mothered and whose problems I tried to solve. We also acquired a proxy family when Marjorie and Alistair moved to London with their three young children – Sonya, Philippa and Hugh. There then began a long tradition of family Christmases. On Christmas Eve I would prepare a sumptuous children's tea in our Highgate Village flat. At a given signal ('Adeste, Fideles') Ted, surreptitiously clothed by me in red dressing gown and white beard of cottonwool, emerged shivering from our balcony, complete with well-filled sack. It took some years for the little ones to rumble that it was only Great-Uncle Ted. On Christmas Day Marjorie, an excellent cook, served a delicious dinner in their Putney flat. On Boxing Day it was our turn again and Ted took us all to a West End pantomime, reserving a box in which the children sat starry-eyed. The format of family Christmases has changed since then, as the children have grown up, but the tradition has never died.

In September 1951 Attlee decided to call the election before the rearmament programme could have its full effect. It was not an inspiring electoral campaign. Morrison's consolidation theme seemed drab when set against the Tories' promised cornucopia of blessings if only they were allowed to set the people free. The Conservatives won an overall majority of seventeen seats, but we were not disgraced. In fact we obtained nearly 49 per cent of the poll, a higher percentage than in 1945 – and gained 700,000 more votes than we had had in 1950. So more people had voted Labour than ever before – and we still polled 176,000 more votes than the Conservatives. One of our troubles was that the Liberals were squeezed out, being reduced to six seats; and, in straight fights between Tory and Labour, Liberal supporters clearly voted Conservative. In Blackburn, for instance, where I had a straight fight with the Conservative, Ralph Assheton, my own majority was almost halved. My deep-seated belief in the unreliability of Liberals as political allies against Conservatism was reaffirmed.

NINE

•

The Bevanite Battle

IT OFTEN happens in politics that defeat comes almost as a relief to the beleaguered supporters of the defeated government. A mood of exasperation takes over: 'Let the other lot have a try then.' That was very much the mood among Labour MPs in October 1951. For six years our government had struggled with intractable post-war problems, we felt on the whole very successfully, but it had had to endure the sniping of an Opposition which distorted every problem, belittled every achievement and blamed every difficulty on our incompetence. I for one was looking forward to hearing them eat their words.

We had not long to wait. One of the issues in the election campaign had been the meagreness of the meat ration. Within days Gwilym Lloyd George, the National Liberal who had been made Minister of Food, was cutting it still further, admitting that the Argentinians, on whom we relied for a substantial amount of our beef imports, were being very difficult. Butter and sugar rations were also cut. In the same debate Rab Butler, who had taken over Hugh Gaitskell's job as Chancellor of the Exchequer, echoed his predecessor's refrain: Britain faced a severe economic crisis which made austerity inevitable. In an Economic Statement in November he announced import restrictions, cuts in public expenditure and a rise in bank rate and hinted at worse to come.

Naturally we Bevanites were quick to point out the reasons for this change of tune. Butler's warnings about our economic situation exactly paralleled those which Gaitskell had given when advocating the enlarged rearmament programme. In other words, we could afford it only if deep cuts were made in other fields. Everyone in the House of Commons realized that if Labour had won the election and Gaitskell were at the Treasury he would have been making broadly the same speech as Butler. From this sprang the jibe in the press about 'Butskellism', which, by pointing out that the policies of the two men were practically indistinguishable, did not do the Labour Party any good. Butler, one of the shrewdest Tory political operators, who was all the more effective because he managed to appear as the statesman who was above party, rubbed in this point by acknowledging that in his Mansion House speech just before the election Gaitskell had warned that the economic situation was worsening. 'Those who listened to him', said Butler, 'could not have doubted that whatever government were returned to power an ugly situation would be bequeathed to them.'

All this was painful to Bevanite ears. We had no pleasure in saying 'We told you so.' True, we got a certain sour satisfaction from the admissions which now poured out of the government that the proposed increases in the rearmament programme not only could not be achieved, but had made our economic situation much worse. 'The main impact of the defence programme', Butler told the House, 'is on those industries from which any really substantial increases in exports must come.' He might have been making Nye's resignation speech for him.

But it was Churchill, the master mischief-maker, who most skilfully stirred the pot. Back in power again, he had taken on a new lease of life and there were no signs yet of the senility which followed his stroke two years later and led to his resignation in 1955. He knew that Bevan had been right in his calculations about the inability of British industry to meet the demands that the expanded rearmament programme would make on it and he enjoyed himself embarrassing Labour's front bench by admitting it. He echoed Nye's arguments almost word for word when he told the House that the country could not manage to spend the extra sums devoted to the arms programme on which Gaitskell had insisted. He even added saucily, 'This point was, I believe, made by the Rt Hon. Gentleman, the Member for Ebbw Vale

(Mr Bevan) after his resignation.' When Nye challenged him to spell out exactly what he meant, Churchill replied blandly that he did not want a debate. He was merely giving Nye an 'honourable mention in dispatches' for having 'it appears by accident perhaps not from the best of motives' been right.

Even more mischievous was Churchill's play over the atom bomb, which he knew was another divisive issue for us. Having attacked Attlee before the election for doing nothing to promote the production of a British bomb, he now heaped him with compliments and apologies. 'When we came to office we found a great deal of work had been done.' He even praised Attlee for agreeing to the establishment of 'the great and ever growing American air base in East Anglia for using the atomic weapon against Soviet Russia should the Soviets ever become aggressors', adding provocatively, 'We must realize that the step then taken by the Hon. Gentleman . . . places us in the front line should there be a third world war.' This provoked Attlee to protest, 'It was never put forward specifically as a base for using the atomic bomb against Russia,' but Churchill waved him aside. He had successfully inflamed two issues which were to tear the Labour Party apart – the bases and the bomb.

Furious as I was at Churchill's trickery, I had to admire his Puckish humour. Every backbencher trying to make their mark, as I was, always tries to score off the Prime Minister. In one debate on the Korean war I attacked him for not protesting to America about General MacArthur's bombing of North Korea. 'We used to think of the Rt Hon. Gentleman as a bulldog sitting on the Union Jack,' I declared. 'Now he has become a spaniel sitting on the Stars and Stripes of America.' Tory MP Ian Harvey snapped back, 'We know upon what flag the Hon. Lady is sitting and she is no dog.' But this was not Churchill's style. Running into me afterwards at the back of the Speaker's chair he bowed courteously and said, 'Your faithful spaniel salutes you.' He could always disarm his critics by laying on the charm.

Nye, too, laid on the charm. In fact, in many ways, he and Churchill were similar, which is why they knew how to score against each other so effectively. They both knew the technique of when and how to adopt an air of modesty. I learned this technique at first hand one year when Nye was due to address the annual conference of the Young Socialists. His train was late and I sat anxiously in the audience while a young socialist struggled to hold the fort. He was understandably nervous but was almost reduced to tears as the amplifying equipment kept failing in the middle of his sentences. When Nye got up to speak at last he said, almost tenderly, 'I would say to my young friend, do not worry that the loudspeaker failed. If it had only failed more often when I was speaking, I would not be in the difficulties I am in now.' I warmed to him, as did his audience.

Yet throughout this post-resignation period, Nye Bevan's mood remained curiously ambivalent. On the one hand the stored-up bitterness over his treatment at Gaitskell's hand was liable to break out at any time in some outrageous remark or rash unpre-meditated action, which drove his friends to despair. On the other, he remained as determined as ever not to organize a conspiracy, as though he was always looking for a way back to the party's centre of power. It seemed to us, who were his most faithful adherents, that he wanted Bevanism without the Bevan-ites. He hated teamwork and would sit brooding in his Cliveden Place flat with a few close allies from *Tribune*, notably his wife Jennie and Michael Foot. *Tribune* was the great outlet for his frustrations, in which he could express his political judgments and political philosophy. He was less interested in it as an instrument of political intrigue. It was left to people like Ian Mikardo, the Bevanites' most accomplished conspirator, to use the paper to give guidance to local parties on what resolutions they should table for party conference and how they should vote.

Nye's detached attitude irked Dick Crossman, who liked to be at the centre of things and in control. He countered the exclusivity of Cliveden Place by setting up his own political salon at his roomy, pleasant house in Vincent Square, conveniently close to Westminster.

The Bevanite 'conspiracy', therefore, such as it was, centred around the weekly lunches Dick organized at Vincent Square. It was open to any Bevanite MP to attend, and there were usually

about a dozen of us there, Nye himself attending only occasionally. Ian Mikardo and I were the most assiduous participants.
Some years later Ian wrote in his book *Backbencher*, 'I found these
little gatherings addictive. . . . The level and sophistication of
discussion, of political analysis and synthesis, tempered with wit
and enriched by relaxed good fellowship, were much above
anything experienced before or since.' I too enjoyed the stimulus
and comradeship and would slip into my favourite seat in the low
chair by the fire in Dick's homely but comfortable sitting room.
Zita rustled up sandwiches, Dick provided wine, and we all shared
the cost. Zita was a great favourite – a gentle person whose
accommodating manner hid a strong private personality. Dick
admitted cheerfully that only a saint could manage to live with
him.

It was through these lunches that Harold Wilson and Dick
formed an alliance against Nye's vagaries. Nye never really trusted
Dick, whom he considered too clever by half. He also suspected
that Harold was pursuing his own long-term interests. So planning the group's tactics for meetings of the parliamentary party
and the NEC could become difficult. Never was political plotting less organized. In November 1953, for instance, I wrote in
my diary, 'A strange NEC meeting in which Bevanites have cancelled each other out more than once: to the delight of the right.
This will strengthen their belief that there is some truth in the
rumour . . . that Nye has been trying to shed his Bevanite
associations.' This, however, did not alter their view of Bevan as
a deliberately disruptive element.

In fact, I noted that in our lunchtime discussions it was Nye
who more than once urged a cautious line. We did not deliberately
plan revolt but the NEC's view of us tended to become a self-
fulfilling prophecy. This is what happened in the famous 'revolt'
of fifty-seven Labour MPs against Churchill's Defence Estimates
of March 1952. In his Defence White Paper, Churchill had
admitted that the £4700 million arms programme he had inherited
could not be spent in three years as Gaitskell had planned and
would have to be spread over four years instead. Never missing
an opportunity of inflaming the Labour Party split, he added that

the delay would not reduce the overall arms expenditure. In the party meeting Dick pleaded that the total arms programme should be scaled down in view of the evidence which had come to light about its disastrous effects on the economy, but our motion to that effect was defeated heavily. Instead, the Shadow Cabinet, on which there were no Bevanites, decided that the party should abstain on the White Paper's arms programme but add a rider declaring that the House had no confidence in the ability of Her Majesty's government to carry it out. Nothing could have been more provocative. In effect it was saying, 'Any rearmament you can do, we can do better.' An appeal by some of us to Attlee to mediate and find a compromise met no response. At an emergency meeting we Bevanites discussed anxiously what we should do. Dick was all for our tabling our own compromise amendment on the lines we had suggested to Attlee and vote for it. Nye opposed this as an open defiance of the party line. Instead, he argued that we should claim our constitutional right under the party's rules to vote against the government motion and abstain on the party's on conscientious grounds. Dick complained that this was so moderate the press would not be interested, but the majority of us supported Nye. So fifty-seven Labour MPs marched into the lobby against the government and sat in their seats as the Opposition amendment was called.

The effect was more electric than any of us had anticipated. The press trumpeted this as a major Bevanite revolt and a bid by Bevan for the leadership. Attlee was furious and for a time expulsions were in the air. An irate party meeting wanted to throw us out but we were saved by middle-of-the-roaders, of whom John Strachey was now one, who deflected the fire from us by proposing that the PLP should consider reimposing Standing Orders to enforce stricter discipline. So we lived to fight another day.

The relations within the parliamentary party and on the NEC now degenerated into a bitterness the party had never known before. Arguments were no longer listened to on their merits, but were accepted or dismissed according to the source from which they came. Looking back, I now accept that the Bevanite row helped to keep the party out of office for thirteen years. Voters only see the conflict and cannot be expected to follow the niceties of the internal arguments. I came to realize that the whole art of the left-winger in politics lies in identifying with the bread-and-butter issues in which the man and woman in the street are interested and persuading them that only radical solutions will meet their needs, as William Beveridge did in his seminal report. Nye Bevan, despite his temperamental eruptions, realized this far more than the Gaitskellites with their moderate policies ever did – policies which did not enthuse anyone at the bottom of the pile.

The bitterness came to a head at the 1952 annual conference at Morecambe. Gaitskellite MPs and the Big Three of the unions were out for our blood and the litmus test of our support was the vote for the constituency party section of the NEC. A roar went up when the result was announced: Herbert Morrison and Hugh Dalton out, Harold Wilson and Dick Crossman in, giving us six seats out of the seven. Only the kindly Jim Griffiths remained of the old guard.

What the result showed most of all was Hugh Gaitskell's unacceptability to the rank and file. As third runner-up after Morrison and Dalton he polled 330,000 votes to Nye's 985,000 and my 868,000. Even his detested enemy Mikardo got twice as many votes. The result highlighted a serious constitutional issue. Attlee's retirement could not be long away. The parliamentary party, which at that time selected the leader, would undoubtedly plump for Gaitskell as his successor, as would the big battalions of the trade unions, but how could the party be led by a man who could not win the support of the people in the constituencies who did the work?

The trade unions' response at Morecambe was to redouble their ferocity against the Bevanites. Two of the Big Three lost no time in voicing their menaces. The message of Arthur Deakin of the Transport Workers was that the unions paid the piper and would call the tune. He retorted to a heckler, 'You know you would listen if you wanted to get money from the trade unions.' Sir William Lawther of the Mineworkers rubbed it in. 'You can have the happy assurance', he told delegates, 'that the block vote and the money that is provided will be used in the direction that we think is in the best interests of our membership.' When heckled mildly from the floor he yelled back, 'Shut your gob!' Later when bringing fraternal greetings from the TUC he dismissed the Bevanites' objections to rearmament as spurious. 'What most people are thinking is that there is a great struggle for leadership going on,' he declared. 'Organization has been set up – well, organization *will* be set up to counteract that.' What interested me was how calmly the press took this naked display of trade union power. All that mattered was that the big battalions were using their muscle behind what the Tory press considered the right policies. It was not until the big unions swung left, with Frank Cousins becoming General Secretary of the Transport and General Workers' Union in 1956 and Hugh Scanlon elected President of the Amalgamated Engineering Union in 1967 that the newspapers began writing angry editorials about the iniquity of the block vote.

Nye's main interest during this stormy period had been a contemplative one. He was one of those politicians who are never satisfied with scoring debating points, however good they may be at it. They draw their strength from their power of analysis of the political forces at work in society and the purposes for which they are in politics. Following his resignation Nye had been struggling to put his analysis and purposes into a book, which was published in 1952 under the title *In Place of Fear*. To the fury of the left I adapted this title for my White Paper on industrial relations, *In Place of Strife*, which I produced as Secretary of State for Employment some sixteen years later. They were outraged that I should call Bevan in aid of my proposed reforms but, having read *In Place of Fear*, I was convinced that I understood what Bevan was about better than they did.

The most striking thing about the book is Nye's passionate allegiance to parliamentary democracy. Direct action as the road to power was a mirage. He had devoured Marx and other left-wing writers in the Tredegar Working Men's library which the miners had financed, but he had swallowed nothing whole. Marx, he wrote, had been right about some things, but not about

Parliament. This made Nye all the more impatient of the archaic proceedings and rigid conventions of the House of Commons. With its busts of former statesmen around the walls, its vaulted roofs, stained-glass windows and time-honoured ritual it was designed, he believed, to cow the board schoolboy newly arrived as an MP and make him feel he was in church. He is expected, Nye argued, to worship in that most conservative of all religions – ancestor worship. And he admonishes the newcomer from the working class: 'The first thing he should bear in mind is that these were not his ancestors. His forebears had no part in the past.' His job was to use Parliament to build a different present.

Some of the book's reviewers complained that Nye had not spelt out the administrative detail of how he would build the New Jerusalem. That did not worry me. Far more important was his ability to illuminate the principles which have inspired reform in every age. Democracy, he believed, was in danger as long as the main centres of economic power remained in private hands. This meant Parliament had the responsibility and private property the power, so Parliament became 'the public mourner for private economic crimes'. Its authority was undermined, for 'people have no use for a freedom which cheats them of redress'.

Nye's analysis made a permanent impact on my political thinking. As the Labour Party struggled with the problems of office and the frustrations of opposition I found his principles increasingly relevant. I was struck, for example, by his rejection of doctrinaire rigidity. Democratic Socialism, he argued, is based on the conviction that 'free men can use free institutions to solve the social and economic problems of the day, if they are given the chance to do so'. But the methods used must be flexible. The student of politics must not claim universality or immortality for his ideas or for the institutions through which to express them. 'His Holy Grail', wrote Nye, 'is the living truth, knowing that the truth being alive must change.' It was this principle which inspired my proposals in *In Place of Strife*. The trade unions, being an expression of the living truth, must learn to change their role. It also put me at odds with the intolerant doctrines of the hard left, which played such a distinctive role in the 1970s and 1980s. It alienated me from Tony Benn, who, though an out-and-out individualist himself, lent the aura of his approval to a wide range of hard groups from Stalinists to Militant, ignoring Nye's warning that politicians must not become the prisoners of rigid dogmas and old words, 'for if they are out of touch with reality, the masses are not'. I believe that, if Nye had not died in 1960, the left would have spoken with a very different voice.

In the 1980s I also found Nye's aphorisms a powerful antidote to the Thatcherite philosophy that gripped the public mind. I believe that if only our political leaders at that time had had Nye's capacity to spell out a socialist analysis of a changing world Margaret Thatcher would never have been allowed to capture the moral initiative. His view of the importance of the individual, for example, put hers to shame. He quoted Dylan Thomas: 'after the first death there is no other'. He elaborated this in terms which summed up a political truth: 'If our imaginations could not enter into the depths of each personal tragedy we would build up a society indifferent to global tragedy.' This was a definition of the caring society which Margaret Thatcher never understood. To her the individual was a digit in the market economy. It was in keeping with her philosophy when she declared she would be prepared to use the H-bomb first.

Nye was one of the few people who grasped the size of the problem which faced a Labour government trying to create a more equal society. Our first problem lay in the adaptability of our political enemies. 'The principal study of the more politically conscious Conservatives', he wrote, was to find an answer to the question: 'How can wealth persuade poverty to use its political freedom to keep wealth in power?' And he added, 'Here lies the whole art of Conservative politics in the twentieth century.' That is why he pleaded with the party's leaders not to become 'symbol worshippers', but to develop a political art to counter this.

Nye was also one of the few to grasp that collective action was at the mercy of economic theories which were systematically destroying it. 'The chief characteristic of the modern Competitive Society', Nye wrote in 1952, 'is the feverish accumulation of property in private hands.' He realized, as few political pundits did, what effect this had on the ability of Labour governments to finance their reforms. Since the state had given up any wealth-creating initiatives, all wealth had first to flow through private hands and the public Exchequer had nothing in it that was not wrung from the reluctant taxpayer. All public expenditure therefore was seen not only as an interference with the rights of the individual, but as 'the enemy of the process of capital accumulation'. In the battle between communal need and private greed, Nye argued that the balance of power lay with the taxpayer, because he controlled the votes which elected the government. Nye sometimes discussed with me his anxiety about the growing resistance to taxation as epitomized by the Poujadist movement in France. He would say to me that if Labour governments were ever to acquire the funds they needed for the communal services and the redistribution of income we should have to find ways of raising money at source before it was distributed into private hands. I used to brood about this problem, but we never solved it. We did not even succeed in hammering home our central thesis that wealth is never created by individuals single-handedly and that part of that wealth should belong automatically to the community which provided the infrastructure which made its creation possible. Our failure to do so left the door open for the triumph of the Thatcherite philosophy that private wealth-creation must be paramount and that all government spending is robbery. To my alarm the party's reaction to it in recent years has been to join the chorus of demand for saving 'taxpayers' money'. We have barely challenged the new doctrine of setting the people free from their responsibility to the community to whose services they owe so much of their own opportunity.

Despite the setbacks and difficulties Nye remained robustly confident about the rightness of his socialist analysis. 'The influence of ideas on social events is profound,' he wrote, 'and is not less so because things turn out differently from what we expect.' He had no use for the faint-hearted or cynical. His words should be emblazoned on every Labour banner nationally and locally. 'Disillusionment is a bitter fruit reaped only by the intellectually arrogant.'

A considerable part of the book was written in Yugoslavia, to which Nye and Jennie paid a visit as President Tito's guests in the summer of 1950. In his search for an alternative to the cold war Nye had lines out to all the leading non-aligned statesmen of the world, Pandit Nehru and Tito becoming close personal friends. Tito was a man after Nye's own heart – a brave and brilliant soldier who had led his partisans in heroic resistance to Hitler and who was now equally robustly refusing to be swallowed up in Stalin's empire. In his book Nye described the arm's-length relationship which Tito had developed with Stalin as 'one of the most valuable political mutations in all history'. Yugoslavia was the first communist country to reject the Soviet Union's claim to be the 'leading nation' of the revolution with the right to impose her ideas on everyone else, a dogma which conflicted with Nye's belief in the sacred virtue of flexibility.

Largely thanks to Nye's lead Yugoslavia had become a symbol of hope to 'soft left' socialists. Enthusiasm for Tito's regime grew when in 1950 he opened her frontiers to foreign visitors. Dick and I decided we had to seize this opportunity to study the regime at first hand. So in the summer of 1951 Dick and Zita, Ted and I became part of the first batch of tourists to brave the physical hazards of post-war Yugoslavia. As the first influx of tourists was small we travelled, explored and ate with the local people and shared the shortages and hardships of their lives. We also shared their sense of exuberance.

Hardship number one was transport. We sailed down the Dalmatian coast in one of the battered boats which had just been dredged up out of the waters into which it had been sunk by war. There were few amenities and we camped on the deck with a crowd of young Yugoslavs on a trade-union-financed holiday. We also shared with them the most nauseating lavatory it has ever been my lot to use. This put me off more than it did Dick, who joined lustily in the singing, led by a young lad who sat perched on the railing strumming an instrument.

Roads in the rural areas were few, winding and narrow with crumbling surfaces. The alternative of flying – where flights were available – was even more challenging. Dubrovnik airport had a kind of crazy charm. The airfield was a stretch of rough grass on which a peasant woman grazed her sheep, shooing them out of the way just in time as a plane came in to land. The field was ringed with mountains, so take-off was even more hazardous. I held my breath as with a great heave the plane just cleared the mountain tops.

Dick, bursting with energy and enthusiasm, took charge of our itinerary. The compliant Zita, Ted and I tagged submissively along. It was Dick who insisted on touring Diocletian's palace at Split in the broiling midday sun. It was he who found a delightful little seaside resort where the only other visitors seemed to be Yugoslavs on their free holidays. Our small hotel was primitive but clean. The water ran dry and the electricity failed from time to time, but our bedrooms looked down on a tree-shrouded courtyard where we ate at trestle tables with the rest. When the evening meal was over the tables were cleared away, a two-piece orchestra appeared and the young people danced and sang till the early hours. Here again it was Dick who discovered the Island of Love – a tiny, rocky islet not far from the shore to which we were ferried by fishing boat. We had the island to ourselves, so Dick, Ted and I swam naked in the pellucid sea. Dick insisted on being photographed standing stark naked on the top of a rock, while Zita, to whom the lack of shade was troublesome, sat beside him swathed from head to foot in a white muslin shawl as a shield against the scorching sun.

We had, of course, asked to see Tito and were just giving up hope when at almost the last minute the message came: he would see us in his villa in Zagreb the following day. Panic ensued. Zagreb was several hundred miles away. How to get there? No plane was available. The journey by train on the single-track line would take a couple of days. There was nothing for it but to hire a car. Our ferocious-looking driver took his remit to get us to the President on time very seriously, driving his rather ramshackle car at top speed along the winding coast road with nothing in the way of barriers between us and the steep cliffs plunging far down to the sea below. At every hairpin bend we prayed to St Christopher. Mercifully he heard our prayers.

The most striking thing about our visit to Tito was its informality. The President's unpretentious villa seemed to be guarded by only a single sentry at the garden gate. If any other guards were lurking in the bushes we did not see them. In his pleasant sitting room Tito was protected only by an interpreter and his alsatian dog. A rather short, stocky figure in a holiday sweater, the first impression he gave was of boyishness. He greeted us with great friendliness and answered our questions freely and off the cuff: there had been no demand that they should be submitted in advance so that he could be briefed for the awkward ones. Tito's answers were as impromptu as everything else in Yugoslavia, one of the main ingredients of his great charm.

He was only too happy to spell out his disagreements with the Soviet Union. Communist bureaucracy, he told us, was 'the worst bureaucracy in the world'. He would have none of it. Special shops for the privileged communists were being abolished, the free market was creeping in here and there. His victory had been won by an alliance of peasants and partisans and he meant to keep it that way. Collectivization of the peasant? 'It is far better to entice him into the co-operative farms voluntarily.' Less than a quarter of the peasants were yet in co-operatives, but he believed they would increasingly see the advantages. Smallholdings here and there would remain in private hands. Nationalization? 'In the beginning we went too far and tried to take over everything. The state could not run some of these small businesses and our people did not like it when they found they could not get a drink in a café or buy a packet of needles in a shop.' He was going to do more to encourage the individual specialist. I told him how delightful it had been to find bright little shops inside Dubrovnik's old walled town and yet the beauty of this remarkable piece of Venetian architecture had been preserved intact. Yes, he said, those shops were privately run, but he would never allow commercialization to ruin the environment. No bill hoardings; no ugly shop fronts or garish advertisements. Could it be, I wondered, that Yugoslavia was on her way to finding the magic mix between freedom of enterprise and state intervention to prevent its abuse?

One of Tito's obsessions was the possibility of conflict

between the country's diverse ethnic groups. He had been able to keep them together in resistance to a common enemy. Now, he told us, he wanted to find a way of welding them into a nation without over-centralizing everything. Two of Tito's closest colleagues – Milovan Djilas and Vladimir Dedejer – were to complain a few years later that he had betrayed his own ideas and allowed the country to get into the hands of a rigid communist bureaucracy which Djilas was to denounce in his book *The New Class*, only to be imprisoned for his pains. I have never been able to satisfy myself how far Djilas's accusations were justified or how far the centralism was essential in keeping together the country's traditionally warring elements. The horrors of ethnic strife which followed Tito's death in 1980 proved that while he was alive he had succeeded in one of his aims at any rate.

At home the Tory government was still struggling with post-war austerity. Its stock had fallen when Butler had introduced his second bout of austerity in his Budget of 1952, raising bank rate to 4 per cent, tightening controls on imports of consumer goods, increasing petrol tax and entertainment tax, slashing food subsidies and cutting the currency allowance for foreign travel to one of the lowest levels since the war. But this was no pre-war troglodyte-type of Tory government. Every member of it, including Churchill, was anxious to dispel the image the Conservatives had acquired of being a party of warmongers opposed to the welfare state. Ministers were aware that Labour's post-war reforms had bitten deep into the national consciousness and they were out to modify Labour's politics gradually rather than attack them frontally.

The most significant expression of this school of thought was the production of a new One Nation doctrine by a group of Tory MPs who had just come into Parliament. They included Iain Macleod, Angus Maude, Robert Carr, Enoch Powell and Edward Heath. They had a social conscience, admitting that the state had a responsibility for ensuring a minimum standard of living for everyone as a safety net. Economically, they wanted more freedom of action and less state control. Butler himself wrote an approving foreword to the pamphlet which they produced and proceeded to soften the austerity of his 1952 Budget by increasing family allowance, raising war pensions, introducing an excess profit levy and taking 2 million people out of tax through higher tax allowances. It was as a result of the One Nation influences that in their 1951 election manifesto the Tories had pledged themselves to build 300,000 houses a year, thus stealing one of the key items of Labour policy. It was notable too, that the victorious Tories had made no move towards mass privatization. Steel and road haulage were denationalized, but Labour had been ambivalent about them anyway. The rest of the public sector Labour had created was left untouched.

In this atmosphere it was difficult for the Opposition to strike sparks. Even Butler's earlier announcement that charges in the NHS were to be made permanent and new ones introduced did not give the Opposition much purchase since its own hands were not entirely clean. Nye, of course, attacked the announcement savagely, though he did so diplomatically, so as not to reopen old wounds in the party, arguing that what the Labour government had done reluctantly the Tories had done with relish because they hated the NHS. Iain Macleod, waiting his chance on the back benches, seized the opportunity to leap to stardom with the most violent attack on Nye any of us had ever heard, lambasting him for a 'vulgar, crude and intemperate speech' and taunting him with the fact that the charges were being levied under the Labour government's own legislation. Unfair as it was it was a parliamentary masterpiece from a man who had hitherto been noted only for his brilliance at bridge. A delighted Churchill made him Minister of Health shortly afterwards. Listening to Macleod I commented that this was the Tory whom, with his subtle and cultivated mind, Labour should fear most. I believe that, if he had not died prematurely in 1970, he would have gone to the very top.

But by 1953 none of this cleverness might have availed the government if the world economic situation had not changed. The world was emerging from the post-war doldrums. Following currency reform the German economy was going from strength to strength and Japan was beginning to emerge as a major economic power. World trade was reviving and with that revival the terms of trade swung in our favour. It was their adverse nature which had helped precipitate the economic crises of 1947 to 1952. Now, as the *Economist* pointed out in its review of 1953, import prices had fallen by 14 per cent and export prices by only 4 per cent, giving the 'fortunate' Mr Butler an increase in real income of between £200 million and £300 million to play with. The improving trend enabled him to reflate and industrial production had surged upwards by 5 per cent, bringing the total increase in national wealth to over £600 million. Consumers got their share of this and spent it happily, enjoying, said the *Economist* 'a greater increase in real incomes than in any other year since the war'. This cloaked the effect of the rise in food prices which had gone up every time the rations were increased without benefit of food subsidy. But there was more to eat and people had the money to pay for it.

The result was a marked change in the national mood. I found this when I went to the Durham Miners' Gala in July – the most prestigious event in the trade union calendar. To my astonishment I had come second after Clem Attlee in the miners' ballot for speakers at the gala – another upward step in my career. 'Scared stiff,' I wrote in my diary, 'as everyone tells me how important this occasion is.' As I watched the swirling mass of miners and their wives singing and dancing behind their lodge banners down the narrow Durham streets, I determined to make a fighting speech though 'I'm so tense I'm afraid I will fail.' In the event I made a speech that, though not my best, was sufficiently passionate to hold the crowd, which began to drift away when Herbert Morrison followed me. 'He's contradicting everything Barbara said,' a miner's agent remarked to Hugh Dalton sitting next to him on the platform. Dalton recounted the story to me afterwards with some amusement, but I could not help noting that what I had said – including a passage about the need for more public ownership – was official party policy. The crowd seemed to enjoy my speech, even if some on the platform did not. Will Lawther, who was disgruntled at not having been elected a speaker that year, informed me gleefully that he had stolen a march on all of us by making a speech that morning at some lodge ceremony in which he had dismissed us left-wingers as 'smart alecs' who talked 'poppycock'.

Nonetheless, back at the charming County Hotel I met nothing but friendliness. Indeed the alcoholic amorousness of some of the miners' delegates became embarrassing. Even Will Lawther was civil, if cynical. 'I have been saying', he told me, 'that we ought to have you plead our wages claim: you really believe the cost of living has gone up.' I retorted that the figures proved it had. 'Ah no,' he replied. 'The answer to us is in the shopping basket. I know it from Lottie [his wife].' I travelled back to Darlington station by car with Mannie Shinwell and Arthur Horner, General Secretary of the Mineworkers, who conducted a conversation across my silent form. My diary reads: 'Mannie on me: "She's too charming. That is why I dislike her. I always dislike good-looking women because they take it out on us men." Arthur: "Do you think Bevan is the alternative to Attlee?" Mannie: "No. I think Morrison is, I don't say he ought to be, but that's the way our Movement is."' I had had enough cynicism for one day.

In more ways than one, 1953 was a turning point in Britain's post-war recovery. A succession of events boosted the national morale. George VI had died the previous year and the country was captivated by the dewy-eyed, dedicated young girl who succeeded him to the throne. The Coronation ceremony was a great romantic jamboree, with the Church revelling in its position at the heart of it. The occasion caused some problems for the Bevanites, for we were either republicans or muted monarchists, who feared the resurgence of 'ancestor worship' which Bevan had denounced. Our attitude to the monarchy became a stock question at *Tribune* brains trusts. I noted in my diary, 'I am in trouble for a reply at last weekend's brains trust at Lowestoft to the question: "What should be a socialist's attitude to the coronation?" JF [John Freeman] led off with a flat: "We should deplore it." I said, "I hoped this would be the last coronation of its kind, so unrepresentative of the Britain of ordinary people." The audience applauded, but I had no doubt I was in the minority, and I had to admit: "Today's show was certainly magnificent pageantry." '

The romantic aura continued throughout the year. Edmund Hillary and Sherpa Tensing made the first ascent of Everest. Gordon Richards won the Derby. Stanley Matthews inspired Blackpool to win the FA Cup. The Ashes were wrested back from the Aussies for the first time for twenty years under Len Hutton's captaincy – a professional, not an amateur, we Bevanites noted approvingly. Hillary, Richards, Hutton were all knighted as they came like latterday Walter Raleighs to lay their conquests at the feet of their sovereign. Was this, people asked, the dawn of a new Elizabethan age?

The national intoxication was supplemented by a relaxation of austerity in our personal lives. Rab Butler had increased the travel allowance to £40 per adult per year, which made it possible to consider foreign trips again, provided one travelled frugally. Ted and I therefore planned a modest gastronomic tour of France with two long-standing friends, Kenneth Robinson, Labour MP for St Pancras North, and his wife Helen. They were delightful company, lovers of books, of good conversation and of good food and wine. Kenneth was to become Minister of Health in Harold Wilson's 1964 government and later Chairman of the Arts Council, but he always remained a relaxed human being with wide cultural interests.

We started our search for good food at the Île d'Oleron, where we had a superb cheap meal of seafood at a fishermen's simple restaurant. Then on to the Dordogne, where we splashed out on a couple of days at Père Bonnet's hotel, whose prestigious restaurant looked out over the valley from its high vantage point. There we were joined by two other fellow spirits, the Labour MP for Deptford, Dick (Sir Leslie) Plummer, and his wife Beattie, who were old friends of both families. Dick was still bruised by the failure of the scheme for growing groundnuts in East Africa on a commercial scale, of which he had been put in charge by Creech Jones, Labour's Colonial Secretary, when it was launched with such high hopes in 1946. The Tories chortled and jeered when it foundered under climatic and other difficulties, but we refused to apologize for it. It was one of the first attempts to bring economic development and self-reliance to this part of Africa. It had undoubtedly been launched on too ambitious a scale, but we had gained invaluable experience and the area had gained a port, a network of roads and railways and the clearance of a vast expanse of bush. The groundnut scheme laid the foundations for commercially successful enterprises which were to follow it.

Dick's disappointment had not dulled the ebullience of his spirit nor his skill as a raconteur. He kept us hilariously entertained with a succession of funny stories and his accounts of life on the *New Statesman*, whose board he had joined. Things there, he told us, were chaotic, because Kingsley Martin, still editor, was 'going mad'. The company was losing a lot of money on Ganymede Press, Kingsley's pet.

I was doing quite a bit of writing for the *New Statesman* at that time and attended its Monday editorial meetings, so I could understand what was happening to Kingsley. He was a brilliant editor who gave the paper a distinctive character it never achieved under any other predecessor or successor, including Dick Crossman and John Freeman, both of whom lusted after the editorship. Kingsley made the *New Statesman* the most successful left-wing magazine in the market but was tortured by a mixture of self-doubt and vanity. He was particularly proud of the Diary he wrote for the paper every week. On one occasion, when he had cast around for ideas for material, I gave him a story which pleased him so much he asked me to write it up. It was a good Diary note and he was glad to publish it, but at the same time he resented the fact that he had not written it himself. He went to considerable lengths to prevent me from getting any acknowledgment.

On one of our explorations of the beautiful Dordogne valley we came across Josephine Baker's château, in whose grounds she had created a leisure park of distressing ugliness. 'When the French go vulgar,' I noted in my diary, 'they go with unrivalled thoroughness.' To take the taste out of our mouths we visited the caves of Lascaux, famous for their superb prehistoric wall paintings. They were so beautiful and well preserved that Kenneth decided they were a fake. Since the caves had been discovered only in 1940 he asserted that Picasso must have spent the war down there painting them.

To recoup some of the extravagance in which we had indulged at Père Bonnet we decided to motor across country looking for one of the lorry drivers' places of call, for which France was famous. We found an excellent one at Quatre Routes, some fifty miles beyond Beynac and delightfully untouristic. Here we were housed simply but comfortably: pension 900 francs (about 12s 6d) per head per day with superb food and good red wine *compris*. The only drawback was that our rooms overlooked the farmyard and at night our ceilings were thick with large, manure-gorged flies. Fortunately, the ever resourceful Beattie had brought some fly-spray with her and sprayed our rooms for us before we went to bed. Kenneth introduced me to the powerful writing of Henri Montherlant by lending me *Les Jeunes Filles* and I became an addict from then on. It was good to indulge one's palate and expand one's spirits in such excellent company.

Back home I found Nye worrying lest the Tories should spring an election while the economic situation was reasonably good. He was therefore conducting himself with care. He had decided he should run for the Parliamentary Committee and just scraped on to it in 1952, though at the bottom of the poll. At the 1953 party conference his role had been scrupulously conciliatory. Once again the Bevanites dominated the elections to the constituency-party section of the NEC. Nye and I came top with over 1 million votes, Harold climbing to third place and Dick rising to sixth place above Mikardo. 'Dick immensely relieved,' I wrote in my diary. 'Said so unashamedly.' Despite these victories by the left, I noted that the atmosphere at conference was unexpectedly harmonious except for Hugh Gaitskell, who was bitterly disappointed by his failure to get elected by some 100,000 votes. 'He has reacted most sourly,' I wrote. At the Parliamentary Committee elections for the 1953–4 session Nye moved up to ninth place and it looked as though the old wounds had been healed. It was not to last. A few months later Nye shattered the new peace by one of his acts of passionate impulsiveness. I was not there when it happened as I was spending an extended and much needed Easter holiday with Dick and Naomi Mitchison in their rustic Scottish retreat in Carradale. I returned to find the Bevanites in miserable disarray. Once again, Nye had been right in substance and wrong in tactics and had managed to split the Bevanites as well.

The occasion, I gathered, was a statement by Eden in the House to the effect that Britain was being pressed by the Americans to enter a united front against communism in the Far East. The US Secretary of State Foster Dulles, alarmed by the success of Chinese-backed communist insurgents in French Indo-China, was coming to London to press for the setting up of a South-East Asia NATO to contain China. Attlee's response to the statement had been non-committal and the House was astonished when Nye had suddenly sprung to his feet, fought his way along the front bench to the dispatch box and declared that the statement would be 'deeply resented' by the majority of the British people and amounted to an attempt to impose European colonial rule 'upon certain people in that area'. The snub to Attlee was obvious. There had been uproar in the party and Nye had resigned from the Parliamentary Committee. To the Bevanite Group's amazement Harold Wilson, the runner-up, had moved into Nye's place, apparently on Dick's advice and against the advice of most of the Bevanites.

In the House I ran into Dick, who clutched at me like a drowning man, obviously feeling guilty about his own part in the affair. 'If you'd been here,' he assured me, 'you would have been terrified about the mood into which Nye was drifting: a position which was leading him logically out of the party.' Would I go and talk to him? Nye greeted me cordially and was glad to pour it all out. He insisted that, when he intervened on the front bench, it had never occurred to him that it was a snub to Attlee. His resignation was forced on him. At the Parliamentary Committee, after the incident, Attlee had announced his conditional acceptance of SEATO; Nye had strongly opposed this, so he had walked out. 'I believe the Indo-Chinese situation is very dangerous and I had to regain my freedom to deal with it.' He was furious with Harold and Dick. 'Never once did Harold come and see me: he was too busy conspiring with D.C.' As for Dick, you could not trust him. He would never lunch in his house again. John Freeman came in at this point and together we gradually brought Nye into a better mood, persuading him to attend the lunch the following day. He did so, to Dick's relief. Gradually the storm blew over, but the rift between Harold and Nye was never really healed.

One of the issues which bound us together again was German rearmament. In April the Americans had exploded the H-bomb in the Pacific and it was clear to everyone that a dangerous new factor had entered into the world situation which made it imperative to heal the breach between East and West. Undismayed Foster Dulles seemed determined to widen it. He chose this moment to insist on a German military contribution to Western defence and sent an ultimatum to his European allies threatening an 'agonizing reappraisal' of American policy unless they stopped dithering about the setting up of the European Defence Community with a European army in which German divisions would play a part. The Labour Party was deeply divided on the issue. Many non-Bevanites were unhappy about the American line, notably Hugh Dalton, though his xenophobic slogan 'No Guns for the Huns' was not to anyone else's taste. Attlee had become a reluctant convert to the idea on certain rather general conditions on which he did not insist too forcefully. Gaitskell and Morrison were passionate advocates, Gaitskell because of his ingrained devotion to the Americans, Morrison because he argued that we could not deny Germany the full panoply of national sovereignty, including arms. Yet it was the growing nationalistic fervour in the Federal Republic under Chancellor Adenauer's leadership which alarmed most of us.

The Bevanites led the campaign on the issue in preparation for the coming party conference at Scarborough. Some of us, led by Nye, published a Tribune pamphlet, *It Need Not Happen Again: The Alternative to German Rearmament*, which had a big influence in the constituencies. It certainly was not an anti-German document. We recognized Germany's right to be reunited, provided it could be achieved peacefully, but that meant winning Russian assent, which would certainly be unobtainable if a united Germany were then to join the Western alliance against her. Russia, we argued, had a right to security as much as anyone else. It would certainly not help to break down Soviet suspicions if we were to rearm the Western half of a divided Germany, which might then be tempted to try to reunite by war. The German problem, therefore, could be solved only in an atmosphere of detente, and this should be the West's overriding aim. No more American holy crusades against communism. Instead, we needed a peace strategy aimed at moving steadily towards global and not just German disarmament.

When the French Assembly voted to postpone discussion of EDC indefinitely it was obvious to any objective observer that the scheme was dead. Ironically it was Pierre Mendès-France, the most progressive Prime Minister France had had since the Popular Front, who gave it the *coup de grâce*. He was a forceful personality – author of the famous phrase 'To govern is to choose.' Brought into office when France was reeling from the fall of her garrison at Dien Bien Phu in Vietnam, he tried to railroad a number of difficult issues through the Assembly, and on EDC his masterfulness boomeranged. It was about this time that Henri Hauck, Labour attaché at the French Embassy, a delightful man and a good friend, telephoned me to plead that the British left should drop its opposition to EDC in order to help Mendès-France. Mendès, he urged, though no socialist, was the only independent-minded Prime Minister France could hope to have. If he fell, the alternative would be a government in America's pocket and there would be nothing to stop Foster Dulles rearming Germany behind everybody's back. I had to point out to him that Mendès' policy was to integrate Germany into the Western alliance, and that was something we could not support. Henri had more success with Denis Healey, still in his cold-warrior mood and a keen supporter of German rearmament. I noted in my diary that he made the best speech for the platform's case at conference, his main point being the need to save Mendès-France's government. 'He is clever,' I wrote, and I did not mean it entirely as a compliment. We had never expected to win against the massed battalions, but the result was much closer than we had dared to hope. The platform's resolution was only carried by 250,000 votes out of 6.25 million and the Bevanite resolution was lost by not much more. We could clearly claim a moral victory.

Unfortunately, much of the effect was thrown away when Nye embarked on another piece of political private enterprise. Arthur Greenwood, the party's treasurer, had died and Hugh Gaitskell saw this as a way to get on the National Executive with the help of trade union votes. In the Bevanite group we accepted this situation philosophically, until Nye suddenly told us he intended to run for treasurer. In vain we pleaded with him that he had no chance and that, by giving up his seat in the constituency section, he was effectively throwing away his seat on the NEC. Nye was adamant and even started counting the votes he believed he would get from the trade unions as a trade unionist. We could none of us understand the source of these illusions, for after the row over SEATO the result was predictable. Gaitskell romped home with a majority of over 2 million votes. Even Nye's own union, the Mineworkers, did not vote for him. Nor did the Transport Workers or the Engineers.

Equally galling was the fact that Harold Wilson slipped effortlessly into Nye's old position at the top of the constituency poll. I retained my second place and Tony Greenwood filled the vacancy Nye had left, coming third. I was furious with Nye for manoeuvring himself into the wilderness: no seat on the Shadow Cabinet and now no seat on the NEC. Dick Crossman, with his usual brutality, declared that this was a piece of self-destruct. But my heart ached for Nye as he faced the 2000-strong Tribune rally the following night. I noted in my diary that his speech showed 'obvious strain'. Half of it bewildered his audience as much as it did me. He seemed to be arguing that he had run for the treasurership in order to lose because 'power at the moment is outside the NEC'. This naturally infuriated Dick: if that was so, had those of us who had struggled to get on to the NEC with Bevanite votes been wasting our time? A meeting of a few of us was hurriedly called in Dick's room in the hotel after the rally. There Dick challenged Nye angrily. Once again it was Harold Wilson who soothed things over, suggesting a 'division of labour' was involved, a formula at which Nye clutched thankfully.

Bewildering as his speech was, it ended with one of those flashes of sanity which illuminated the political landscape for me. 'All I am pleading for in foreign affairs is time,' he told the audience. 'Every year gained is a year further from catastrophe. We should take no step that is irrevocable.' It was wisdom like this from this brilliant but baffling man which made me forgive all his human weaknesses. He had his full quota of them, as I observed sitting next to him on the conference platform during his last day as a member of the NEC. I could see what he did with the letters which were passed up to him, tearing up the attacks, as every sensible politician does, and pocketing the compliments. 'I have made a discovery about him,' I wrote in my diary. 'His favourite doodle is writing his own name.' There are few top politicians who are not egoists.

Despite these setbacks the Bevanites had scored one important political victory. For some time we had been inspiring and organizing a flow of resolutions from the constituency parties to the NEC denouncing America's threats to the Chinese government and calling for China's admission to the UN. Our campaign, helped by the death of Stalin at the beginning of the year, was so successful that a resolution had been passed at the Margate conference of 1953 urging the party to send a goodwill mission to China and the Soviet Union. The right-wingers on the NEC were in a trap. They could not prevent Morgan Phillips, secretary of the party, from carrying out his remit by writing to the People's Republic of China suggesting the visit. Even so they fought a rearguard action to reduce the visit's significance as much as possible. When the Chinese invitation came, Sam Watson wanted us to turn it down on the ground that the Chinese were only 'playing politics'. Their next move was to send a delegation of only eight, instead of the thirty which the Chinese had proposed. (One trade unionist wanted to send only four.) Finally an attempt was made to send the delegation via Hong Kong instead of Moscow, a suggestion which was rejected merely on the grounds of cost. In May 1954 the delegation, led by Attlee, set off for Moscow, with Nye himself as the only Bevanite. The NEC knew there would be trouble with the local parties if they left him off.

The visit was violently attacked in the ranks of Tory MPs and in the Tory press but in the event it went without untoward incident. Even the two days in Moscow produced useful results in the form of an acceptance by the Soviet hosts of an invitation to dine with the delegation at the British Embassy, the first time our Ambassador, Sir William Hayter, had managed to induce them to come to the Embassy. Another useful discovery was that the Soviets' anxiety about the visit to China was almost as great as that of the Tory press, since they feared any attempt to drive a wedge between the two regimes. The delegation's report on the China visit was cautiously statistical rather than analytical, which was safe politically. It did however record that all the members had been impressed by China's drive for industrial development, which led them to the sensible conclusion that it would be a mistake to assume that communism could be contained militarily. That at least was progress.

The visit had other encouraging effects. A few months later the Chinese government was lifting the Bamboo Curtain still further by organizing a second delegation, this time a mixture of Labour MPs, trade unionists, artists, doctors and scientists. I jumped at the opportunity it offered and in October 1954 found myself *en route* for Peking via Moscow among some very congenial company. The journey to Moscow by plane took the entire day. Every time we touched down for refuelling we were ushered into a VIP lounge where a motherly body in full skirts and white cap was waiting to pour us libations of vodka accompanied by mountains of caviare. It was all very exciting at the first go, but by the end of the day I did not want to see another granule of caviare. What struck me was how Victorian it all was – red chenille curtains draping the doorways to the airport lounge, red chenille tablecloths sweeping down to the carpet. At one stop I noticed that even the wireless set was draped in red chenille. It was the same on the aeroplane, where the seats were draped with covers down to the floor, as if to hide their legs as the Victorians did. I assumed that revolutions must breed a hankering for tradition as an antidote to the new uncertainty.

At Prague, where the plane touched down, we ran into two

bold American Congressmen who were braving the disapproval of the current American political ethos by coming to find out the realities of the Soviet system for themselves. Apparently they had simply applied to the Soviet Embassy in Washington for visas and had got them without difficulty. This was all the more surprising since, although one of them, Congressman Fisher of Texas, seemed innocent enough, the other was Congressman Battle of Alabama, who confessed to me shyly that he was the author of the notorious Battle Act. That Act, which banned the grant of American aid to any country shipping strategic materials to the Soviet bloc, epitomized America's determination to prosecute the old war by every means. Representative Battle (a Democrat) was a charming, good-looking American in his late thirties who argued with us pleasantly in the plane all the way to Minsk. We all gathered round him in friendly dispute while stern officials checked our passports and cross-examined the Americans suspiciously. I was called in to act as interpreter between the stewardess, who spoke French, and the officials, who spoke nothing but Russian and who wanted to know who had invited the Americans. I said nobody had. The authorities had just given them visas because Russia was an open society. There was nothing the officials could do in the face of that, and the Americans were very grateful that I had got them through. We parted having cemented Anglo-American relations, and I hope Soviet–American relations as well, though of that I felt less sure.

In Moscow we were to find the same lack of revolutionary artistic creativity. 'Soviet realism' vied with the traditional drapes. The accoutrements at the enormous new Moscow University made the watercolour painter in our party, Denis Matthews, almost physically ill. 'These are the worst paintings I have ever seen,' he whispered to me, and he upset our guides by shaking his head sorrowfully over the vast ungainly murals of Soviet youth. They assured us that Soviet people liked this sort of thing. It was a relief that evening to attend a performance of Prokofiev's *Romeo and Juliet* at the Bolshoi. I noted in my diary that the performance was 'overwhelmingly beautiful', with Ulanova an enchanting Juliet. The Soviet authorities were immensely proud of these showpieces.

Sir William Hayter and his team confirmed my impression that there was no shortage of food and that the supplies of other necessities were not too bad. The butcher's counter at the Gastronome, Moscow's biggest food store, was full of meat. The Moscow Underground and other public buildings were spotlessly clean. There was nothing like the deterioration I was to see thirty years later when the crumbling of the Soviet economy brought Gorbachev to power. Sir William also had good news politically. The atmosphere, he told me, had already started to improve when he arrived a year ago. He was convinced that the Soviet authorities wanted a rapprochement with the United States, with whom they felt they had much in common: size and a crude love of power.

It was the size of the country which struck us as we resumed our journey to Peking. Flying east across the Russian Republic, the Tartar Republic and Siberia, we could see how mad Hitler had been ever to imagine he could conquer this vast territory. All the Soviet government had had to do was to move its industry into the enormous hinterland – to Kazan, Sverdlovsk, Krasnojansk, Irkutsk, Omsk, Novosibirsk. Here were the hidden reserves of Soviet strength, a huge sphere of influence. Even when we arrived at Ulan Bator, capital of Outer Mongolia, we found that the airport and other signs were written in Cyrillic script.

The flight to Peking took us over snow-covered mountains, brown valleys and bare hills, until suddenly there it was: the Great Wall of China magically stretching for 3000 miles along the razor edge of the bare hills. 'No better than Hadrian's wall,' I remarked loyally. Impression number one on arriving in Peking was of the functional effectiveness of the new hotel in which we stayed: simple and almost spartan but meeting all our basic needs. Impression number two was of the sexlessness of our women guides. The uniform of all the officials who looked after us – a blue dungaree boiler-suit – was unisex. Some of our party who tried to make typical Western overtures to our women guides were sternly rebuffed. 'No sex, please, we're communists.' They seemed severe. Yet the children we saw during our trip were some of the happiest I have ever met, extrovert, laughing and emotionally at ease. When we arrived at the Pei Hai nursery in

Peking, formerly the Winter Palace, the stolid males of our party were taken aback when we were engulfed by a bevy of small children who ran towards us with open arms, their pigtails bobbing, climbed up to our shoulders and threw their arms round our necks, shrieking with delight. I saw one stout trade unionist hurtling down a slide with some of the eager children in tow, while other children entertained us with a little dance in which I joined. One of the teachers explained the phenomenon to me. Chinese babies, she told us, are carried everywhere slung against their mother's back and so are in close contact with her body all the time during babyhood. She believed this gave them a sense of security which bred affection, happiness and trust.

We encountered tradition again on a visit to the Peking Opera. With its stylized mimicry, elaborate ritual and flat intoning of the words it is not to everybody's taste, but I loved it and, more importantly, so did the Chinese audience. The gallery was packed with workers in their blue boiler-suits who revelled in the formal costumes and traditional routine, cheering the familiar episodes of comic relief. Like me they loved the acrobatic mime of a twelfth-century battle between lavishly dressed peasants and imperial troops, as well as a long operatic piece called *The Black Whirlwind*, which depicted a revolt by heroic nobles against the Sung dynasty. It was like a showing of *Peter the Great* in Minsk all over again. Not for the first time I realized that the leaders of revolutionary upheavals fall back heavily on tradition to allay their followers' anxieties. Even in social democratic Britain most Labour Party supporters find the existence of the monarchy makes them – or used to do – feel more secure.

Most of our delegation found the Peking Opera tedious. I was therefore glad to find that I had an ally in the artist Stanley Spencer, who sat behind me chortling so audibly that it could be heard throughout the little theatre. After the show I had a long conversation with Stanley in our hotel. He was a robust, untidy man, bursting with enthusiasm, and I warmed to him. He was in the middle of painting *Christ Preaching at Cookham Regatta: Listening from Punts*. He told me he was obsessed with a consciousness of Christ: 'I *feel* him. I know him personally. In the painting I want to show him moving among ordinary people, the life and soul of the party, out-regatting the regatta.' The methods and mechanics of art did not interest him: 'If my soul feels it, the painting is all right.' He had fallen in love with China, painting Ming tombs and sketching Chinese faces. But he was nobody's stooge. He told me with a chuckle that he had been asked by our hosts to give a lecture at the Peking Arts School. As good communists they no doubt expected him to give a child's guide to methodology. Instead he refused to discuss art methods and just talked about himself. I tremble to think what they made of him.

Another insight into the nature of the Chinese revolution came the following day. Mr Chang of the Ministry of Foreign Trade had told us that the Americans' embargo on the export of 'strategic materials' to China whether by America or by her allies was being made to cover everything which might help to build up the Chinese economy. Yet British firms like Austins were only too anxious to expand trade and had signed a contract with the Chinese government to supply large quantities of trucks. The deal had fallen through because the British government would not give them the necessary export licences. We would have dismissed this as propaganda if we had not visited the huge dam and reservoir being built ninety-two miles north of Peking, which would supply the city with water and electricity. There we found that every item of building equipment was listed as a 'strategic material'.

After a night journey by train I woke to see what looked like a procession of blue-coated ants hurrying to work along a tall embankment against the rising sun. As we emerged into the huge excavation of the reservoir hundreds of the blue ants were scurrying about, digging up earth with shovels and carrying it away in panniers slung on long poles across their shoulders. It was like a scene from the Capek brothers' *Insect Play*. There was not a piece of earth-moving equipment to be seen, no heavy drilling or firing machines, no bulldozers, no excavators – no trucks even, only donkeys laden with brushwood, presumably to mop up the mud. The only encouragement to both humans and donkeys was from the music-while-you-work programme, on the loudspeakers, which regaled the toilers with moralistic themes. Typical was the lament by a peasant girl who had been cruelly treated by a landlord. Another lament was from a man who expressed his passionate desire to go and fight in Korea. 'This song is very popular,' our guide assured us solemnly. But what overwhelmed us all the time was the massive human effort that was being made. At the side of the dam a hydroelectric plant was rising of which the Chinese were very proud. It was their first big water-conservation scheme. The trade union members of our delegation, such as Arnold Hardy of the Foundryworkers and George Doughty of the Draughtsmen and Allied Technicians, were appalled by the prospect of all this having to be done by hand. 'Every piece of equipment these people need comes under the American embargo,' one of them remarked sourly. We found the same picture in the factories we visited, which the Chinese government was struggling to modernize, though the Russians had done their best to help.

When we arrived in China the Formosa crisis was at its peak. The language of Peking had become more belligerent. We began to understand why as we flew south-west along the line of the Yangtze river to Chungking, 1000 miles away. This, we were informed, was where Chiang Kai-shek had made his last stand before being overwhelmed. The reconstruction of houses and factories was going on feverishly, notably in the steelworks, where Chiang's retreating forces had destroyed the blast furnace, power plant and open hearth in pursuit of a scorched-earth policy. Before air links were opened in 1946 the only contact the 50 million people in this remote area had had with the rest of China was by the Yangtze river itself, all passengers and freight being carried in sailing boats. Even the rolling stock for the new railway had to be brought that way. Many of the homes were mere hovels of bamboo and mud or just plaited straw, a legacy of the old regime. It was not surprising that Peking writhed at the thought of its old enemy sitting on an island only 400 miles from the Chinese coast, protected by the American Seventh Fleet, supplied and trained by the Americans. From this vantage point and other little offshore islands the Nationalist forces harassed shipping along the coast and, according to foreign journalists we talked to in Shanghai, showered leaflets on the mainland to incite revolt. How long could this situation last?

We put this question to Chou En-lai, the Prime Minister, who gave us two hours of his time before we left Peking. The impression he left with us was one of shrewdness, resilience and informality. He was the most Westernized of the Chinese leadership, having spent his youth as a student in Paris in the 1920s. I sensed that little escaped his subtle mind. Though he spoke English he insisted on talking to us through an interpreter, but corrected his interpretation from time to time. Chou En-lai assured us he wanted to open doors to the West. China would soon be sending a chargé d'affaires to London. Student exchanges and other contacts should be organized on a growing scale. On Formosa his attitude was one of lighthearted mockery of the United States, which was, he declared, 'morally isolated'. There was no barrier to peace in the Far East except the belligerence of the United States. We left, encouraged in the belief that the Bamboo Curtain was being rolled back, hopefully for ever. But it was not to be. In December America concluded a mutual defence treaty with Chiang Kai-shek. She marshalled countries like India, Ceylon, Burma and Indonesia into a treaty they did not want, to protect Asia against communism. China's overtures to the West died away. Ten years later the cultural revolution sent the Bamboo Curtain crashing down again.

At Shanghai our delegation split, the majority going north to Manchuria, while three of us – a Dr James, Charlie Royle and I – went south to Canton and Hong Kong to take the quicker route home. So we found ourselves for two days and a night on the Shanghai–Canton Express, a little Western enclave in a Chinese community. On this train we learned far more about China's 'new democracy' than from all the statistics that we had been given about the new constitution, the People's Congress and People's Courts. We did not belittle the changes in political rights that had been made. We knew it was a fact, for instance, that the status of women had been transformed overnight. From being the slaves of their husbands they had become people with property rights and the vote at eighteen. And we had proof that it was not all theory when we met the Vice-President of the All-China Textile Union and found she was a woman. As Charlie Royle and I remarked, the Weavers' Association at home had not managed to put a single woman on its Executive. I had also noted that there were far more women members in the People's Congress than in the British Parliament.

Nonetheless we were under no illusion that this was Western-style parliamentary democracy. How could it be when 80 per cent of China's population, after years of Nationalist rule, was still illiterate? But on the Shanghai–Canton Express we were intro-duced to the regime's grass-roots democracy. The first guiding principle was the passion for cleanliness. Hygiene was king. Our 'soft class' bunks may have been made of wooden slats with horsehair mattresses, but the coach conductor was down our corridor with his broom and flyswats at regular intervals. The second guiding principle was physical fitness. In the morning I awoke to the sight of passengers doing their bending and stretch-ing exercises on the platform. The third guiding principle was the Suggestions Book, which we discovered by accident. We were assured that the chief conductor and his staff, which consisted of two nurses, the coach conductor and the restaurant personnel, were not allowed to go off duty at the end of the journey before they had considered the suggestions and produced their reply to them. One entry moved us particularly. It ran:

> The conductor in our coach is enthusiastic and has a sense of responsibility. He has been very helpful. Four of us make this comment. But one official in Souchow station had a bad attitude towards an old woman who was a soldier's mother. She bought a ticket for the slow train, but in fact boarded the express and the official wanted her to pay excess fare. The passengers criticized his attitude and, under pressure from the masses, the official agreed to solve this problem by consulting a higher official.

The upshot was that the old woman was allowed to stay on the express without paying the extra fare. The chief conductor's entry concluded: 'The matter will be reported to Souchow station and I hope passengers will continue to criticize and uncover abuses.'

Another entry, much to our relief, called for the loudspeaker to be turned off at night. Comment: 'The suggestion is accepted and will be carried out. In future the conductor will wake passengers individually on request during the night.' We were able to check at first hand that the system worked, and by the time the spotless train steamed into Canton station one minute ahead of time we were thinking how much pleasanter travelling by British Rail would be if only they had a Suggestions Book.

Heading for home, we saw little of Hong Kong before we ran into a typhoon, which kept us immured in our hotel bedrooms playing cards. We stopped off in Burma on the way back, and this gave me the chance to cross-examine Burmese ministers about their attitude to communist China. It was, they said, one of 'suspicious friendliness', but they saw no hope of peace in American policy, which was 'all suspicion and no friendliness'.

We returned to find the prospect of a general election looming near, despite the fact that the government still had eighteen months to go. Rationing had been finally abolished in 1954 and Harold Macmillan as Minister of Housing had triumphantly announced that he had achieved his target of 300,000 houses. But derationing had pushed up prices, and after an improvement in 1953 the balance of payments was moving into the red again. It was obviously in the government's interest to make a dash for it.

This was all the more apposite since the Labour Party had plunged into one of its major rows. Once again I was on Nye's side on the substance of the argument while almost despairing of his ability to handle the dispute tactically. Once again, too, the row was over defence policy, only this time the whole dimension of defence policy had changed following America's explosion of an H-bomb in the Pacific in March 1954.

Nye, as usual, put his finger on the key issue by pointing out that Churchill's Defence White Paper in 1955 visualized the H-bomb being used as a response to the threat of any military attack including a conventional one. That, Nye pointed out, would mean the destruction of the globe. He stressed this in a passionate speech in the defence debate. 'We have either to agree with our enemy', he said, 'or commit suicide.' So why not negotiate with them

233

before the nuclear-arms race went any further? So far so good, but Nye then went on to attack the amendment tabled by Labour's front bench, which accepted the development of thermonuclear weapons as a deterrent without stating specifically whether a Labour government was prepared to use H-bombs first. It was this issue which was to bedevil the discussions about the H-bomb for years to come and lead to the creation of the Campaign for Nuclear Disarmament. CND argued that the adoption of a first-strike policy was an integral part of the concept of the H-bomb as a deterrent, since in nuclear warfare the chance of a retaliatory strike was small. He who does not strike first may not live to strike at all.

Nye's mistake was that his attacks on the Opposition's amendment were almost as savage as his attacks on Churchill's motion. What, he asked, was the difference? The amendment accepted that thermonuclear weapons must be part of a deterrent policy, but did not say whether a Labour government would use them in a first strike. He challenged Attlee on this point and, when Attlee failed to reply, sat in his seat with a considerable number of Bevanites when the amendment was called. Party loyalists took this as a personal attack, and right-wingers launched a campaign to get Nye expelled from the party. Gaitskell joined in this campaign enthusiastically.

Actually the Bevanites were divided on Nye's tactics, and a number of them, including Harold Wilson, Dick Crossman and John Freeman, voted for the party's amendment. Whatever my doubts about Nye's behaviour, I knew I must abstain because his policy approach was right. The battle went all the way up to the National Executive Committee, where we on the left found an unexpected ally in Clem Attlee, who, in his quiet way, dug in his heels against Gaitskell's determination to get Nye expelled. We carried by one vote Attlee's motion to refer the issue to a committee of eight. I was the only Bevanite member on it and I admired his persistent stand on behalf of sanity. Together he and I drafted a motion rejecting expulsion but calling on Nye to give certain assurances about his future behaviour. The full NEC dared not turn this down. So Nye was saved by Attlee's distaste for Hugh Gaitskell's bigoted destructiveness.

In his Budget of April 1955 Butler paved the way for the election with 6d off the standard rate of income tax, 3d off the lower rate and increased tax allowances. In the following month the government went to the country, claiming that industrial production and investment were rising and that 'Tory Freedom Works'. Labour responded with a moderate manifesto, whose main emphasis was on a Policy for Peace (including, I was glad to note, the evacuation of China's offshore islands by Chiang Kai-shek and the admission of communist China to the UN). The only proposals on nationalization were to renationalize steel and road haulage and to bring 'certain sections' of the chemicals and machine-tools industries into public ownership. It skated over the defence issue, supporting past actions but undertaking to 'submit all problems of defence to a searching enquiry'. The only concrete commitments on the social side were to abolish all charges in the NHS (another recognition of Nye's influence) and to institute an annual review of pensions.

Our moderation did not save the day. Labour lost 1.5 million votes to the Tory's half a million. What worried me was that the poll dropped from 82.5 per cent in 1951 to just under 77 per cent: always a bad sign in a democracy. As I wrote in an article for the *Star* newspaper, 'The most significant thing about the general election was the lowness of the poll. What happened was that there was no swing either way, just a general sag.'

But the sag comprised some individual tragedies, the worst from my point of view being Michael Foot's defeat at Devonport. I myself narrowly escaped tragedy. When Ted and I arrived at the count confidently expecting victory, we were met by George Eddie, my agent, with a distraught face and the words 'Ted, she's out.' It is always a traumatic moment for an MP but I braced myself to face it philosophically, my main reaction being that I would now have to second the vote of thanks to the Returning Officer instead of moving it – an ignominious role. Ted told me afterwards that his first thought had been: 'What shall I do with her when I have her at home all the time?' As these thoughts went through our minds George came back, mightily relieved. There had been a recount and I was in by 500 votes. It was the lowest majority I was to experience.

Later I discovered what had gone wrong. I had 10,000 Catholic voters in my constituency, and Cardinal Hume, the great Catholic prelate from Liverpool, had issued an edict from the pulpit denouncing all Bevanites as communists. In obedience to this the local priests had been on the doorsteps telling the faithful that, as good Catholics, they could not vote for me. 'Right,' I said to myself, 'I too can get on the doorstep and I will fight back.' I had to tread warily, winning back Catholic approval by supporting government help for Catholic schools. It worked like magic but I knew I had sacrificed one of my principles since I did not approve of denominational schools. But I doggedly refused to join the Catholic campaign against abortion. Later I voted for David Steel's enlightened 1967 Abortion Act and resisted intense pressure to change my mind. It was a rough ride but I survived.

TEN

•

Not in Arthur's Day

THE ELECTION result left the Bevanites unhappy and confused. I, for one, was prepared to admit that splits had damaged the party electorally. Dick, the supreme pragmatist, had lost patience with Nye's temperamental vagaries and had drawn closer to Gaitskell, so relationships within the group had become strained. Harold Wilson, I noted, was cannily keeping an eye on his own opportunities. Nye himself was divided between his innate desire for unity and his refusal to give up his principles. The outlook was not promising.

Yet the next few years were to see changes which gradually put the party on the road to power again. Nineteen-fifty-five started badly for Nye, as he once again left himself open to humiliation by running for treasurer at the party conference. He was resoundingly beaten by Gaitskell. Despite this, I noted that he was obviously restraining himself at conference, taking no part in the public debates and being goaded into an explosion only in the private session, when an inquest was held on the reasons for our defeat. Only a saint could have failed to react to the trade union bosses, led by Bill Webber of the General Council of the TUC, who declared that our defeat was due to the 'antics of the left'. Nye was no saint and he sprang to the rostrum to declare that our defeat was due to the party's witch-hunters. Had they not tried to expel him from the party just before the British people went to the polls? 'What a prelude to a general election!' he stormed. 'I was deeply humiliated.' There was pandemonium as the constituency delegates rose to their feet to cheer him. It was not Nye's fault that the 'private' session was not private at all and that the row captured the newspaper headlines the following day.

The ostensible purpose of the private session had been to discuss the report which Harold Wilson had been deputed to produce on the party's organization. It was a brave report, which denounced the party's amateurish organization as a 'penny-farthing machine'. The trade unions mistrusted it as another piece of machination by the left, though the constituency parties welcomed it as expressing many of their demands, for example on the need to build up the agency service. In the end, conference merely referred back the report for further discussion by the NEC. Harold, a wise man, was undismayed. He had already built his power base by becoming chairman of the Organization Sub-committee of the NEC, which he knew would enable him to pursue his reforms. He was prepared to bide his time.

Gaitskell skilfully exploited the row the following day with the most emotional speech conference had ever heard him make. He defended nationalization and spelt out his socialist faith with unaccustomed passion, as though deliberately setting out to refute Nye's description of him as a 'desiccated calculating machine'. He, too, got an ovation. At the Tribune rally that night a hall packed with Nye's devotees waited for a pyrotechnic display of sarcasm from their hero. None came. Instead there was some gentle raillery. So we were now all agreed that the Labour Party's aim was socialism, he mocked. 'We have had it asserted in unmistakable terms, by every element, that our objective is the establishment of a socialist society.' Excellent. We had even had recognition of the achievements of the nationalized industries. 'We are a bit late in praising them, but at least we have come round.' But the mockery was very low key and some of the audience went back to their hotels disappointed. Personally I noted with satisfaction that Nye had decided to come in out of the cold and stay out of it. There might be some lapses of temperament, but he was tired of martyrdom.

Amid all the press excitement about the clashes between Nye and Hugh Gaitskell, my own personal triumph at the eve-of-conference rally went unnoticed, except by David Low in the

Guardian. Low's cartoon depicted me as Joan of Arc throwing her shield before a reluctant Dauphin of France in the guise of Attlee, head down and doodling away – which was the position Attlee had maintained throughout my speech, I was afterwards told.

My inspiration came from the increasingly insolent alliance between right-wingers of our party and the Tory press to oust Attlee as leader and put Gaitskell in his place. It was a mixed inspiration of fury and of fear and I am always at my best when my emotions are so strong that I lose self-consciousness. I knew that if there were an immediate leadership election, nothing could stop Gaitskell triumphing again and I wanted to give Nye time to play himself in again in his new conciliatory mood. I had been to see Attlee just before conference to plead with him to resist the pressures and hang on for another year. I knew that Gaitskell was not Attlee's favourite and that in his unassertive way he had a soft spot for Nye, as he had for me. Attlee listened to me in his non-committal way and I knew that if someone else did not fight his battles for him, he would not fight them for himself.

My speech, therefore, was a ringing challenge to the plotters, though I did not name names. We must not, I told the audience, allow the Tory press to become the party's king-makers. We must choose our own leaders and it was for Attlee himself to decide 'when we should thank him for his great services and say goodbye'. I ended by quoting Morris' 'The Message of the March Wind', which I knew by heart, and a couplet from his 'March of the Workers', my favourite:

> For the hope of every creature is the banner that we bear
> And the world is marching on.

The audience knew exactly what I was driving at and I was mobbed. To be the subject of one of Low's brilliant cartoons was immensely gratifying, though I was mildly disappointed when the press and my Executive colleagues did not bother to attend. I knew I had made one of the speeches of my life, and so did the audience. *Tribune* accompanied its report of the rally with a picture of Ted smiling broadly as I received my ovation, over the caption 'That's my gal!'

The only press coverage I got, apart from *Tribune*, was by Beverly Baxter, Tory MP for Southgate, who was doing conference sketches for the *Evening Standard*. He wrote that my speech was the star turn of the rally and that I had 'set out to play La Vengeance in a smart Bond Street frock'. The headline the paper put on his piece was 'How They Love Barbara: She HATES So Well', which I thought was a bit of a libel on my gentle William Morris.

My hopes that Attlee could be inveigled into carrying on for another year were dashed when he resigned in December 1955. In announcing his decision to the parliamentary party meeting he made it clear that he had effectively been forced out. I knew it was his own fault for having failed, not for the first time, to fight vigorously enough against the manoeuvres of which he disapproved. His resignation made my heart sink in my boots since it was clear that Gaitskell would romp home in the ballot for the succession. In those days the party's leader was still chosen exclusively by the Labour MPs, the majority of whom – though they often made Bevanite noises in their constituencies – were Gaitskell fans. Gaitskell had also skilfully won over some of the doubters by his speech at the party conference. Opposed by only Nye Bevan and Herbert Morrison it seemed inevitable that he would win. My only consolation was that he would be better than Morrison, who still nurtured the belief that he was entitled to the leadership. I liked Morrison personally more than I did Gaitskell, but his Tammany Hall qualities, which had worked so successfully on the LCC, would be disastrously narrow in the national field.

Our only hope, it seemed to me, was to get as big a vote for Nye as possible and live to fight another day. I was therefore appalled to learn on my return from a visit to Kenya on the eve of the election that Nye was part of a conspiracy under which he would stand down in Morrison's favour if everyone else (meaning Gaitskell) would do the same. Nye's motives were obvious – Herbert was the older man and could prove a useful temporary stop to the Gaitskell bandwagon. Nonetheless I was shocked. This was Nye being that which he had once accused Dick Crossman of being – too clever by half – and it boomeranged. Gaitskell cantered in on the first ballot with 157 votes to Nye's 70, while a shattered Morrison limped home in third place with 40 votes. Under our rules it was enough to have a simple majority, a system which would have kept Margaret Thatcher in power if it had obtained in the Conservative leadership election in November 1990. Nye's vote was far from derisory and in my view would have been higher if he had not muddied the waters with his intrigues over Morrison. I do not believe that cynicism pays in politics.

The leadership contest left no bruises. Nye had always known in his heart of hearts that Gaitskell must win and that he had thrown away some of his own opportunities. He was now out to mend his fences and the process was made easier by two developments in British politics. The first was the revelation that the economic euphoria on which the Tories had won the election was phoney. We did not have long to wait before Butler's extravagance in his pre-election Budget came back to haunt him. A run on sterling in the summer forced him to slap on hire-purchase controls and in October he was driven to introduce a supplementary Budget which took back all the extra purchasing power his pre-election Budget had given the voters. Butler's aura as an economic magician vanished, and it was evident that he could not cope. In December 1955 he was replaced by Harold Macmillan. The Tories hoped a new magician had arrived upon the scene. Macmillan had an attractive air of aristocratic insouciance, combined with a reputation as a moderate reformer as a result of his book *The Middle Way*. There was no doubt that he had been profoundly influenced by his experiences as MP for Stockton-on-Tees in the 1930s and that he was determined to prevent mass unemployment if at all possible. Yet as Chancellor in the economic situation he inherited in 1955 he had no choice but to continue Butler's deflationary policy, cutting public investment, suspending investment allowances for private industry, raising bank rate, restricting purchase credit. We could not help saying, 'We told you so.'

By this time Churchill had at last been persuaded to resign. We had all watched with sadness as he had become increasingly doddery. He was another example of a top political leader who could not face reality and relinquish power. In April 1955, he had been succeeded as Prime Minister by Anthony Eden, the spruce, charismatic Foreign Secretary. Eden had won an exaggerated reputation for courage and integrity by his opposition to Chamberlain's appeasement policy and his resignation as Foreign Secretary in 1938. I had never been impressed by his matinée-idol type of charm, suspecting that it hid an intrinsic weakness, and so it proved. He was to do more than anyone else to bind the Labour Party together by his disastrous conduct of foreign policy.

Eden's greatest blunders related to the Middle East. The whole area was like a powder keg, with two lighted brands waiting to be thrown into it. The first was the Arab states' hatred of Israel and the second was the rising tide of nationalism in the Arab world, which threatened the survival of the authoritarian ruling class. Eden did not know how to deal with either of them. His major concern was to safeguard Britain's supplies of oil, and his way of doing it was to support the old discredited regimes, a policy which was to inflict almost fatal damage on Britain's influence in the Middle East and on the security of Israel.

Though I was no Zionist, I always had an instinctive alignment with Israel. I was haunted by the horrors of the holocaust and could identify with the Jews' hunger for status and security. At the same time, I had sympathy with the Palestinians who had been turned off their land and out of their homes so that the new state could be formed. It was one of those problems which, like Northern Ireland, seemed almost insoluble. The only hope lay in the gradual building of mutual understanding between the two sides.

When Ted and I visited Israel about this time, we were struck by the country's idealistic motivation. The most prominent expression of this were the kibbutzim, community settlements where the members voluntarily joined together to live for each other and not themselves.

The kibbutzim varied in size and organization. In some of

them communal living was carried almost to religious lengths, with the members pooling their resources and drawing out of the pool what the other members thought they were worth. In others the standards were less austere. But all of them reflected the belief that individuals fulfilled themselves better in a collective society than in a competitive one. One young couple we met in a small kibbutz told us that under its rules they put their children in the collective nursery from their earliest months while they went to work on the farm or engaged in other kibbutz activities. I was rather shocked by this, but they assured me it worked very well. Their children learned to grow up in a community, but spent all their evenings and spare time with their parents, who were free to devote their whole time and attention to them, helped by the fact that they could eat communally. Everyone certainly seemed to be very relaxed. We were also enchanted by the political philosophy of the Ben Gurion government, which was expounded to us by MPs and leaders of the Israeli Labour Party, Mapai. They saw Israel as a 'centre of excellence' in the Middle East from which it would spread its know-how throughout the Arab world, helping the Arab peoples out of their poverty and backwardness. I knew from my African contacts that Israel at that time was considered one of the most selfless and dedicated contributors to the progress of the developing countries, particularly in Africa. I could understand the pride of socialist Jews like Ian and Mary Mikardo in the new homeland. Mik and Mary were delighted when their daughter Ruth and her husband, both of whom had been brought up in England, launched their married life in a kibbutz.

But there were also worrying aspects. Beneath the pastoral peace the atmosphere was always tense as waves of hatred washed in from the surrounding Arab states. On a return visit a few years later I stayed at the kibbutz of Na'am with a Mapai MP who had at one time been Ben Gurion's deputy. As he showed me round the farm I noted he carried a gun. Na'am, he told me, was only six minutes from the Jordan border, so one had to be prepared. Even more worrying was the common determination to throw the new homeland open to any Jew in any part of the diaspora. Such a commitment, I realized, confirmed the Arabs' belief that the State of Israel must, by definition, be expansionist. How else would she find room for another 3 million Jews? Our Israeli friends assured us that their country's technological skills would enable even a small area to accommodate all of them. Certainly, the pace of development was staggering, as Ted and I found when we went to see the vast new town of Beersheba, which was rising dramatically in the undeveloped expanse of the Negev. This was the conquest of the desert in its most impressive form, achieved by a willingness to endure hardship and overcome obstacles. We were not likely to forget our visit: after a day revelling in the hot sun, we were plunged into the freezing cold of the desert night. Our hotel, though modern and comfortable, had no central heating. We ate our evening meal in the dining room in our overcoats, our teeth chattering, and at night piled every garment we possessed on top of our bedclothes and clung to each other in a desperate attempt to get warm enough to sleep.

One evening after our meal we were invited to attend a youth rally in the huge new meeting hall. This, too, was unheated and the cold was so intense we could not manage to sit there for more than a quarter of an hour. The enthusiasm of the audience must have kept the listeners warm for they seemed ready to stay there half the night. These young people were not going to submit to the Arab threats to drive them into the sea.

But, though Ted and I admired the pioneering spirit we met throughout Israel, we believed it would be unwise of the West to ignore the Arabs' problems, anxieties and growing determination to assert themselves.

I was therefore glad of the opportunity offered me in January 1953 to tour the key centres of the Arab world as part of Émile Bustani's cavalcade. Bustani was a large, genial and wealthy Lebanese businessman and Progressive MP in the Lebanese Parliament who combined a shrewd assessment of his own business interests with a genuine desire to promote greater under-standing between the Arab world and the West. He was an Anglophile and for the preceding three years had taken two or three British MPs on an intensive tour of the Middle East at his own expense. This, of course, enhanced the standing of his

Construction and Trading Company in the eyes of the sheiks and the officials of the British oil companies who were out in force wherever we went, but which also gave the selected MPs a unique insight into the influences at work in the area. The tour in which I participated was his most ambitious yet. There were six of us: John Freeman and I formed the Labour contingent, together with Jimmie Johnson, the stocky MP for Rugby who looked like a scrum-half. The Tory Members consisted of Burney Drayton of Skipton, a trade consultant, and Stephen McAdden of Southend, who was in leather goods. They were rounded off by the big and burly Brigadier Terry Clarke. A less military brigadier I have yet to meet.

As we set out I thought we were rather a motley crew but in the event we fused into a harmonious and pretty effective team. Each of us found his or her own niche. Brigadier Clarke proved invaluable in inspecting the guard of honour which awaited us at every port of call. I for one would not have known what to do. By common consent, we gave John Freeman the job of conducting our press conferences, which he did with consummate skill, keeping the nervy Arab journalists happy while not giving anything away.

My main role seemed to be to chat up our sheik hosts, on whose right hand I was always placed at our ceremonial meals. I was always struck by the courtesy and respect with which they treated me while keeping their own women out of sight. I was always the only woman present. I soon learned the correct drill: how to sit cross-legged on the floor with reasonable elegance, how to tear pieces of meat from the whole roasted sheep that was put in front of us and scoop up handfuls of aromatic rice – always using my left hand and never my right, as custom demanded. I even managed to avoid eating the proffered delicacy of the sheep's eye without offending our hosts.

One of my privileges was an invitation from our hosts to penetrate the purdah in which they kept their women. There used to be murmurs of envy from the men in our party as I disappeared behind the curtain into the women's quarters. They obviously thought I was being introduced to some glamorous harem. The reality was very different, as I told them later. On one occasion I found the Sheik's new child-bride, a timid slip of a girl of about fourteen, confined in a rather depressing room at the back, furnished, as all these sheik palaces seemed to be, with luxurious carpeting and rows of rather ugly Western-style armchairs lined up against the walls. Keeping a watchful eye on the child-bride was her stern-looking mother-in-law, making sure that the only life the girl had was in her husband's bed.

Stephen McAdden, with whom I shared a car in our cavalcade, allocated to himself the responsibility of looking after me, which he did with such sensitivity that I realized he was much nicer than the brash Tory I had always found him in the House. His solicitousness for my wellbeing even extended to jumping out of the car when we arrived at a new desert outpost to take aside some Arab official shrouded in his burnous to ask delicately what ablution facilities there were for the lady member of the party. His chivalry saved me a good deal of discomfort and embarrassment. As a Lebanese picture magazine put it, I was 'toasted and deferred to'; it added that I displayed 'as much charming aplomb as is generally attributed to her Queen'. This addendum caused some amusement among our group, but the first statement was certainly true.

We arrived at Lebanon in a Comet, on which we discovered Attlee, on his way to a socialist conference in Rangoon. We were met by an enthusiastic Émile Bustani, who swept us off to Beirut for a few luxurious days in the most prosperous and modern city in the Middle East, whose way of life seemed immutable. The contrast between Lebanon then and now still haunts my memory. Some years later Émile himself was to die in a mysterious accident when his plane crashed into the sea. Many who knew him believed he had become a victim of Arab politics.

We soon understood, however, that this was to be no tourist trip. We were switched to Bustani's de Havilland Rapide for an intensive tour of Jordan, Syria and Iraq, including a quick descent on the Trucial States of the Persian Gulf. Émile wanted his money's worth and at the end of each exacting day would say to us, 'We leave in the morning at first light.' This meant that somehow, after a short night's sleep, we had to be crossing the tarmac to our plane promptly at 5.00 a.m.

It was easy for Westerners to fall under the romantic spell of the desert, particularly on a guided tour like this when the substructure of poverty, disease and backwardness was kept out of sight. It was intoxicating to visit the archaeological treasures of the area: Balbek, Petra and ancient mosques. It was romantic for me to be carried across the eternal fires at the Kirkuk oilfield, where the flickering flames from the oil-soaked ground never die out. Above all, it was exciting to achieve my ambition and mount a camel, on which I managed to travel, somewhat uncomfortably, for a few hundred yards, ignoring the warnings of my male colleagues that it was probably covered with fleas. Remembering my teenage infatuation with Rudolph Valentino, I could happily have ridden off into the undulating, mysterious sandy wastes. I was not surprised to learn that the Foreign Office was full of Arabists.

One of the most enjoyable parts of the trip was our visit to Qatar. It was not only that we flew down the Persian Gulf over the clearest deep-blue water I had ever seen, but that awaiting us was a delightful and untypical Foreign Office character in the form of Christopher Ewart-Biggs, the Political Representative for Qatar and Bahrain. Tall, lanky, with a drawl and a monocle disguising a high intelligence, Ewart-Biggs epitomized Lord Peter Wimsey, one of my favourite fictional characters. His presence in this tiny sheikdom of 16,000 inhabitants, whose capital, Dohar, looked like a midwest shanty town, indicated its importance to Britain, producing as it did the finest-quality oil in the Gulf and lying across strategically important routes. In his drawling voice Ewart-Biggs recounted to us his long battle to civilize the local sheik. When he first started making his official calls the sheik had a habit of regularly spitting on the carpet at his feet. After some energetic play with his monocle Ewart-Biggs managed to convey to the sheik that that was not a practice of which he approved. Thenceforth the sheik would lift the edge of the carpet and spit under it.

When we paid our official call the sheik's behaviour was impeccable, and he did not spit at all. I could only assume that the monocle had been working overtime.

I was next to hear of Ewart-Biggs some twenty years later when, as Ambassador to Dublin, he was assassinated by the IRA. I felt I had lost someone I knew and liked personally.

But everywhere we went we felt the stirrings of trouble beneath the romantic surfaces. The Arab leaders we met made no attempt to hide their hatred of Israel, repeating the refrain 'Give us arms.' They blamed Britain for Israel's existence. 'Israel would never have happened if we had had arms.' The oil companies we talked to expressed anxiety. In Lebanon two managers of the Iraq Petroleum Company (IPC), Mr Ryland and Mr Dickson, told us they were trying to negotiate a new agreement with the government and were angry with Bustani because his Progressive Party was demanding better terms than President Chamoun was ready to accept. The situation, they said, was explosive. In Damascus the British Ambassador told us that the IPC was having the same trouble with the Syrians, who were demanding a fifty–fifty agreement, which the IPC thought too generous.

Most worrying of all from my point of view was Eden's failure to appreciate the growing revolt against the old regimes. Émile was generous in allowing us time to meet some of the dissidents. In Baghdad we had a long talk with the opposition leaders, who complained bitterly about Britain's support for the repressive regime of Nuri Said, who, they claimed, was practically living at the British Embassy. Britain, they told us, was opposed to any moves towards the liberalization of the regime for fear of endangering her oil supplies, but it was a short-sighted policy.

It was not long before they were proved right. One of our official visits in Iraq was to the young King Faisal, which did not produce anything very enlightening. This time I was lucky to pay a courtesy call on the King's aunt, who was, of course, in purdah. The Princess was a beautiful woman elegantly dressed in Western clothes and very articulate. When I said politely that I found Baghdad very interesting she retorted, 'I hate Baghdad.' Apparently, she lived for her annual visit to Paris, where she could study the latest fashions, wear Western clothes and move openly in society. I found her excellent company, frank, poised and amusing in her faultless French. Two years later I was shocked to learn that she was among those members of the King's household assassinated with him and the Crown Prince in a military coup launched by Brigadier Abdul Karim Kassem. I was also intrigued to learn that Nuri Said had been assassinated along with them. So much for the alleged subtleties of British diplomacy.

I returned home conscious of the need to accept far-reaching changes in the Middle East. I found that Eden was more deeply embedded than ever in the old attitudes. He was now busy taking on Gamal Abdul Nasser, who had seized power in Egypt in 1954. The Foreign Office had been horrified, for Nasser represented the mood of rebelliousness they dreaded. They had felt they could handle his predecessor, Colonel Neguib, even though he had dethroned King Farouk, but Nasser was a new type of Arab: defiant and self-confident. He was not the favourite son of everyone in the Arab world, but all Arabs had a sneaking admiration for his assertion of Arab rights and his call for Arab unity. They also admired his determination to fight the poverty of his people by modernizing the backward Egyptian economy. Central to his development plan was the building of a High Dam at Aswan which would irrigate the banks of the Nile and provide electricity for Cairo. But he could do it only with outside financial help.

Significantly he turned first to the West for assistance, thus belying the instinctive suspicion in the Foreign Office that he must be a communist. Typically Britain and the United States did not seize their opportunity to increase their influence in this vital area. Having toyed for some time with the idea of offering loans, they got cold feet and withdrew the offer in July 1956. Nasser's response was spirited. He promptly nationalized the Suez canal, arguing that its revenues were the only alternative source of money available to him to build the dam. I visited Aswan a few years later, when it was under construction, and the only equipment I saw on the building site was Russian.

The reaction in Britain was hysterical. The canal was one of

Britain's vital trade arteries and here was this dangerous man with his foot on our jugular. At first there was all-party unity in the House of Commons to condemn his action. Gaitskell aligned himself with the government in denouncing this new Hitler, and even Nye joined in the condemnation of Nasser's action, explaining later in *Tribune* that he believed that Nasser had the right to nationalize the canal but that all strategic waterways should be internationalized. Gaitskell and Nye united in demanding a negotiated settlement and when the suspicion grew that Eden was planning the use of force against Nasser in collusion with France and Israel, they broke the united front with the government and moved into the attack. By the time the party conference met in October 1956 they were working together to promote the same policy.

This was one of the factors which was to make the conference a turning point in Bevan's career. Some of us were worried when he decided once again to stand for the treasurership. We knew that some of the union old guard were muttering that this time they would destroy Bevan once and for all. Nye also faced a formidable opponent in George Brown, who at his own request had been nominated by his union, the T & G. George Brown was a more than usually complex character, truculent, loud-mouthed, with a tiresome chip on his shoulder because he had had to leave school at fifteen to become an odd-job boy. This fed his venom against the Bevanites, whom he contemptuously dismissed as 'a bunch of intellectuals'. Nonetheless he was an exceptionally able man and a good parliamentary performer who had made a name for himself shadowing defence. Nye's great consolation was that, thanks to Sam Watson, the miners had nominated him this time, and Sam was mustering what support he could among the other unions. But it was obviously going to be a close thing.

The development which probably did most to change the situation was the election of Frank Cousins as General Secretary of the Transport and General Workers' Union. Yet, like so many things in politics, his election was a piece of luck. When Arthur Deakin had died the previous year he had been succeeded by Arthur Tiffin, and Frank had become Assistant General Secretary.

Even that appointment was a surprise to many, for Frank was an outsider. Apparently he had won over the Executive by a remarkable speech setting out his ideas for revitalizing the union. A few months later Arthur Tiffin died suddenly and Frank swept into the job with the biggest majority ever registered in such an election in the union. Members seemed to have got the message that the union had to accept fundamental change.

Conference soon got the same message. Looking back over Frank Cousins' long career, with which I was associated most of the time, I have no doubt that the greatest contribution he made to the Labour movement was to start the break-up of the monolithic power of the big union bosses. Frank was a democrat, which was why he was such an enthusiastic trade unionist, and he was going to be governed by the majority decisions of his members and their delegates. Not for him Arthur Deakin's bludgeoning of his delegation, or the trading of block votes among a few top men in smoke-filled rooms. I often found Frank excitable and difficult to work with, and I had many bitter clashes with him when I became a minister, but through it all I retained an affection and respect for him which I hope he returned.

The new atmosphere Frank created obviously helped Nye. It was not that Frank was going to switch his union's vote to Nye, even though – being a left-winger himself – he wanted to do so. Solidarity demanded that the vote should go to the union's own member who had asked it to nominate him. Nor did Frank do any arm-twisting. The smaller unions realized that they were free to follow their own preference, without being steamrollered by the old guard. One of the most revealing examples came when the Distributive Workers voted for Nye against the T & G's nominee. Far from being punished, their President, Walter Padley, was elected handsomely to the trade union section of the National Executive. As one delegate remarked to me, 'It could not have happened in Arthur's day.'

This, in fact, became the theme song of the conference, repeated again over the issue of German rearmament. Two years earlier Gaitskell had attempted to expel Nye from the party on the ground that he had refused to accept a 'majority' vote of conference on this issue, yet we all knew that this narrow 'majority' had been secured by Arthur Deakin's pressure on the Woodworkers, who had wanted to vote the other way. This year we had the remarkable spectacle of the platform climbing down on a motion from the same Woodworkers. This called for an agreement with the Soviet Union on the reunification of Germany through democratic elections, accompanied by the withdrawal of forces by East and West. The platform knew it could no longer rely on the block vote of the big unions to push it through. I wrote in the *New Statesman* at the time, 'The rigid alignments of the past few years have been broken down and their going has liberated suppressed ideas and new comradeships – as well as a new will to power.' Frank also pioneered acceptance by the unions of the importance and rights of the constituencies. It was a symbolic moment when he went to the rostrum and announced himself: 'Cousins, Sutton and Cheam Labour Party and Transport and General Workers' Union.' That, too, could not have happened in Arthur's day.

The highlight of the conference came on the Tuesday morning with the result of the election for treasurer. It was announced that Nye had won with the respectable margin of nearly three-quarters of a million votes. The hall went mad. Delegates scrambled over chairs to get at him, sitting modestly in the body of the hall. He was hugged, kissed, thumped on the back. This was no ordinary demonstration of affection. It was the product of a surge of relief that at last the party could be united as it had not been for four years. At that moment even the surliest of the old guard recognized that Nye Bevan was indispensable.

The elections contained an added bonus for me when I topped the poll in the constituency party section for the first time. I could only assume that it was due to the success of my speech at the conference rally the previous year. I was interested to note that Tony Greenwood came second, pushing Harold into third place. I could see Harold was annoyed and I could not blame him. I considered Tony Greenwood a lightweight with more charm than principle.

'Bevan – Labour's Second Most Powerful Man', ran the *News*

Chronicle headline after the result. Nye's long sojourn in the political wilderness was at an end. He was not to be opposed as treasurer again. In the elections for the Shadow Cabinet he climbed from seventh place to third, showing that he had broken the ice barrier between him and the majority of Labour MPs. He was now in a position to claim the post he had wanted as Shadow Foreign Secretary, and this time Gaitskell recognized his right. It was the beginning of a remarkable partnership.

On 29 October the simmering Suez crisis came to a head in one of the most insane ventures a British government has ever entered into. Israeli forces attacked Egyptian positions in Sinai while British and French forces launched air attacks and paratroop landings on Egypt herself. It was clearly a prearranged plan, though Eden continued to deny collusion to the very end. Labour MPs erupted in a fury I had not seen since the war. It was not only that the Prime Minister was lying to the House. They were astonished at the folly of it all. Here was the British government aligning itself with the hated Israelis in an act of aggression against an Arab nationalist who had shown no signs of wanting to block the West's free passage through the canal and every sign of wanting to increase the canal's shipping revenues. There could not have been a better recipe for inflaming passions in the Middle East.

Labour's was a brave stand, but a risky one. As soon as British troops became involved, the party protested against this breach of the UN Charter, only for its protests to be drowned in a wave of public jingoism. Nonetheless, the party battled on under Gaitskell's and Nye's dual leadership. Nye addressed a huge rally in Trafalgar Square on the theme 'Law Not War'. In an uncompromising broadcast, Gaitskell demanded Eden's resignation as the only way to 'save the honour and reputation of our country'. In the Commons there were such stormy scenes when Labour moved a vote of censure on the government that the Speaker was forced to suspend the sitting for the first time in twenty years. I was proud of the party's determination to stand by its principles regardless of the electoral consequences.

We were saved when the ridiculous enterprise collapsed

ignominiously thanks to the open hostility to it shown by the United States. America's attitude led to a run on sterling, with which Britain could not cope. A few days after Gaitskell's broadcast, Eden announced a ceasefire. The humiliation shattered him physically and a few months later he retired on health grounds, making way for Harold Macmillan.

There were two lessons I believed we had to draw. The first was that Britain would never again be able to launch a military enterprise without being assured beforehand of the backing of the United Nations in general and the United States in particular. The European alternative, in the shape of France's collaboration in the Suez crisis, had proved a broken reed. Even today, when European federalists are trying to build up the European Community as a powerful third force, there are no signs, as the Gulf war showed, that Europe could act independently.

The second lesson was that courage is the most important ingredient in politics. Any government or politician unable to ride a burst of short-term unpopularity will not survive for very long.

In the parliamentary inquest on the Suez affair, I was able to produce evidence that Eden's aim from the outset had been to destroy Nasser, using the alleged threat to the canal as an excuse. On 19 October, the British government had requisitioned a commercial broadcasting station in Cyprus, Sharq al Adna, for use as a propaganda instrument in a war which did not start until 30 October. What alarmed me was the government's use of the station to promote a policy of which it had kept Parliament in ignorance. The Arabic service of the BBC, which the Arabs trusted for its impartiality, was squeezed into a corner and the air saturated with hate propaganda against Nasser and with attempts to rouse the Arab world against him. The result was, of course, counter-productive. The station lost its Arab staff and most of its listeners, while the British government lost its credibility.

I had employed my usual device of demanding that transcripts of Sharq al Adna's broadcasts be placed in the Commons library. From these I found to my astonishment that the attacks on Nasser continued even after the ceasefire. When Tony Benn, who was also researching this subject, and I made this known the supply of transcripts suddenly dried up, allegedly because of 'technical difficulties'. I wrote up the shameful story for the *New Statesman*, pointing out that the government had deliberately tried to corrupt the independence of the BBC and that its first attempt would not be its last. Mrs Thatcher later proved me right on the first point if not the second. Her methods of attack were more subtle and oblique, but the independence of the BBC is still not safe.

The Labour Party's new unity over foreign affairs did not extend to defence policy. America's explosion of the H-bomb in the Pacific in 1952 had, in Churchill's words, changed 'the whole character of war'. As other countries hurried to catch up, it also led to a reckless pollution of the atmosphere. For a time the party remained united in demanding an end to testing by both sides in the cold war, but when Britain exploded her own bomb on Christmas Island in April 1957, the party split. Should we keep the bomb as a card to play in disarmament negotiations or abandon it unilaterally?

The issue dominated the Brighton conference. The 127 resolutions had been merged into three, of which the Norwood resolution became the flagship of the unilateralists. It demanded that the next Labour government should refuse to test, manufacture or use nuclear weapons. This was more than the trade unions could stomach, and the resolution was defeated by nearly 6 million votes to three-quarters of a million.

Frank Cousins, himself a unilateralist, had to bide his time, dutifully accepting that he was bound by the decisions of his union's last biennial conference. But the drama of the occasion lay not in the size of the vote against, but in Nye Bevan's role in answering on behalf of the National Executive.

For some time, Nye's attitude to the bomb had been ambivalent. Shortly before conference he had returned from a talk with Malenkov's successor, Khrushchev, in the Crimea, telling us he had been assured that a Labour Party decision to stop the testing – and by inference the manufacture – of the British bomb would evoke a helpful response from the Soviet Union. By the eve-of-conference meeting of the NEC he had changed his mind. When Ian Mikardo and I moved that we accept the Norwood resolution he suddenly declared that repudiation of nuclear weapons could affect Labour's relations with every other country in the world and that we should reject Norwood out of hand. I was shocked, but still believed he would modify this line when he came to speak to conference.

Instead, he intensified it. It was one of the most fumbling speeches I had heard him make as he groped his way through the moral dilemma which faces every politician who has to deal with the H-bomb. What was the best way to lift its shadow from the world? His followers were shattered when he almost shouted that a Labour Foreign Secretary could not be sent 'naked into the conference chamber'. We should not abandon it, but negotiate it away.

His misery was painful to watch, and delegates sat silent as his agonized cry went out: 'I knew this morning that I was going to make a speech that would offend and even hurt many of my friends. Of course. But do you think I am afraid?' He lost their sympathy again as he got carried away, as he often was when on his feet, by his own oratory, dismissing the desire to ditch the British bomb as an 'emotional spasm' which would lead to a 'dangerous negative polarization' of the world. The uproar was renewed and Ian Mikardo and I were not the only ones to attack him afterwards. He strode through the attacks with defiantly jutting chin.

Nye's dramatic *volte face* did him no harm politically. In the next election for the Shadow Cabinet he topped the poll, and even his friends forgave him in time, admiring his courage in saying what he believed. His speech inspired the launch of the powerful Campaign for Nuclear Disarmament, which was born a few months later in the home of Canon Collins of St Paul's Cathedral. Its hallmark became the annual march to London from the nuclear research station at Aldermaston, to which hundreds of anxious people flocked from all over the country, mothers pushing babies in prams and elderly citizens struggling along on sticks. Heading the marches was always Michael Foot, accompanied by his shaggy white bitch Vanessa, of doubtful lineage but delightful temperament. I once told Michael I was reporting him to the RSPCA for making the dog walk eleven miles each day on hard tarmac, but he pooh-poohed the idea as he would pooh-pooh anything with which he disagreed, asserting that the dog revelled in every mile.

I joined the CND because I believed it was an expensive and dangerous folly for Britain to produce her own bomb. The idea that we could ever have a bomb which was independent of America was ludicrous. We were dependent on her for the know-how and technological development, and to use the bomb independently of her would be an act of suicide. To argue that without the bomb we would go 'naked into the conference chamber' was to encourage the proliferation of its manufacture by every country which could manage it. But I was never very active in CND, nor did I join in the marches, except for one year when Ted and I decided we must walk a few miles from Aldermaston to Reading to show solidarity. My reservations were due to my distrust of single-issue campaigns, which seemed to me to oversimplify complex situations. I agreed with Nye on this, that our efforts should be concentrated on strengthening the Labour movement as the forum in which the interrelationship between defence and foreign policy could best be argued and the militarists prevented from dominating our lives.

But a flame had been lit which would not be put out and was to sear the party for many years to come.

ELEVEN

—————— • ——————

Death Throes of Empire

ONE OF the consuming interests of the Labour left in the 1950s was colonial freedom. The tide of anti-imperialism and self-determination was flowing strongly in some unexpected quarters of the world. I was drawn to it naturally by my upbringing and by the influence of my brother Jimmie. He was an extrovert who could make friends with a cosmopolitan range of people and who despised racism. During the time he was at Edinburgh University we never knew whom he would bring home next. Once or twice it was a friendly little African called Tungi. My mother affectionately named her coal-black miniature poodle after him. Fortunately Tungi the student took this as a compliment. Another frequent visitor was a large beaming Turk called Sidki. Sidki had a motorbike on which he once took me a hair-raising ride to the seaside. I remember clinging to him desperately as he raced at full throttle all the way to the sea.

When Jimmie went to Nigeria for his first job as a forester he became absorbed in the problems of Africa, which, I slowly began to realize, were not only economic but political. I found it hard to grasp at first that the African natives with whom he went into the bush to preserve and plant trees had minds and traditions of their own and were getting restive under white rule, which was at worst brutal and at best patronizing. It was through Jimmie, too, that I became aware of the new currents of thought on colonial development which were swirling around, particularly in the Fabian Society, and of the number of outstanding people who were challenging the old paternalist approach: Dudley Seers, senior economics lecturer at Oxford and economic adviser at the UN; the *Observer* journalist Colin Legum and his wife Margery; Basil Davidson, author of *The Awakening of Africa*; and Norman Leys, who as far back as 1931 had written *The Last Chance in Kenya*. I had, of course, worked with Tommy Balogh in the old Keep Left days, and he was now pioneering ideas on rural development and delivering great iconoclastic swipes at the establishment and its paternalistic approach to colonial affairs. Tommy was to become one of my invaluable mentors when I got into government.

But a key influence in getting me involved in the fight for colonial freedom on the floor of the House was Fenner Brockway, Member for Eton and Slough. To begin with I had been prejudiced against him by my father. In the 1930s Fenner had been one of the dedicated purists labouring as a speaker on the ILP circuit and had stayed at our house. His saintly air and slight touch of self-righteousness irritated my father, and after one of Fenner's visits he snapped at me, 'That man thinks he is Jesus Christ.' Later I discovered that that was unfair and that Fenner could enjoy modest indulgences in wine and women as much as anyone. True, he firmly believed that he was right, but this had the advantage of immunizing him against the fury of Kenya's white settlers which he had managed to arouse. He was also totally devoid of racial prejudice and this gave him a unique ability to get on close personal terms with the considerable number of Africans who had found their way to Britain as students or to find jobs: men like Jomo Kenyatta, author of a scholarly study of the Kikuyu tribe called *Facing Mount Kenya*, and Tom Mboyas, head of the Kenya Federation of Labour, who was doing a course of study at Ruskin. They included a few hand-picked promising Africans whose university courses were being paid for by their colonial governments. This was not always as liberal a policy as it sounded since they were not allowed to get ideas above their station. A typical example was Herbert Chitepo, an African from Southern Rhodesia who was sent to university in England on the strict understanding that he did not study the one subject he wanted to: law. Once there he kicked over the traces, switched courses and, with the help of left-wing lawyers like Dingle Foot and D. N. Pritt, he qualified for the Bar.

My last doubts about Fenner disappeared when in 1950 he went on a remarkable visit to Kenya, accompanied by Jomo Kenyatta. At that time racial prejudice was strong in most of Africa and certainly in Kenya, yet here was a white British MP not only travelling with a suspect troublemaker but actually refusing to stay in the regulation white hotel in Nairobi. Instead he accepted an invitation from ex-Chief Koinange to stay at his bungalow in an African reserve. Kenya's white settlers were outraged. They had been shocked enough when Kenyatta had married an Englishwoman during his long stay in London, but this was too much. A white journalist from Nairobi descended on Fenner in the bungalow and asked him if he realized how shocked the white settlers were that he should have stayed with a native instead of the Governor: the first British MP to do so. In fact, as Fenner told us later, the bungalow was very comfortable and his only moment of embarrassment had come when Koinange, having presented him to the tribe as a blood brother, indicated to him that this meant he was entitled to share the chieftain's five wives.

What impressed me was that, amid all this camaraderie, Fenner had the courage to challenge one of the Kikuyu's worst practices, their treatment of women. One day as he walked with Kenyatta to the Chief's bungalow he pointed out that the women were walking behind carrying his luggage and other heavy burdens on their heads. He also pointed out, gently no doubt, how barbaric was the practice of female circumcision, which was designed to make sexual intercourse unattractive to the women of the tribe so as to keep them chaste. That took moral courage.

So did Fenner's return to Kenya two years later when the horrors of the Mau Mau uprising had broken out. Jomo Kenyatta was arrested, as was ex-Chief Koinange. Thousands of Africans, high and low, were rounded up into detention camps. Kenyatta had been warning for some time that the Africans' land hunger, due to the appropriation of their best land to form the White Highlands while they themselves were herded into overcrowded reserves, was leading to unrest that was becoming uncontrollable. Nonetheless the atavistic forms the uprising took, with a hundred European farmers being hacked to death, and women and even babies mutilated, blotted out all political arguments. The security forces were swollen with an influx of temporary officers whose remit was to root out Mau Mau suspects, force them to confess and if necessary detain them indefinitely. Yet Fenner went back after the declaration of the emergency. He did not believe that either Kenyatta or Koinange was the sort of man to support Mau Mau and showed his solidarity with them by spending his first night at the ex-Chief's bungalow to reassure his anxious wives. For the rest he argued with anyone who would listen that the only real solution to this horrific throwback was to meet the legitimate grievances of the Africans.

This was the kind of courage I liked and I became a ready recruit when Fenner set up the Movement for Colonial Freedom in 1952, drawing together a number of other bodies he had helped to launch, such as the Congress of People Against Imperialism. Most of the left became sponsors, including Harold Wilson, Tony Wedgwood Benn (as he was then known) and Tony Greenwood. Never before had colonial issues been raised so persistently and so knowledgeably in the Commons. Of course, there were some reactionary backsliders in the party, notably Patrick Gordon Walker, who had been Commonwealth Secretary in the 1950 Labour government and as such had a pretty dismal record. It was he who had exiled Seretse Khama from Bechuanaland for marrying a white woman, Ruth Williams, on the ground that it would disrupt the life of the tribe of which he was chief. I found his whole approach to colonial issues disastrously obtuse, stuffy and insensitive. I was not surprised when he fell an easy prey to the pressures of the Commonwealth Office establishment, which had convinced itself that the best way to solve the post-imperial problems of central Africa was to lump together three highly divergent African communities – Southern Rhodesia, Northern Rhodesia and Nyasaland – in a Central African Federation which would inevitably be dominated by Southern Rhodesia. To anyone who knew anything about central Africa it was a recipe for catastrophe, because Southern Rhodesia was the citadel of racially prejudiced white settlers, whereas Northern Rhodesia's white population consisted mainly of workers who had come to make a good living from the copperbelt and might be returning home. As for Nyasaland, one of the poorest countries in Africa, it had no tradition of white domination, no pass laws, no racial discrimination. It had been included by the architects of the Federation simply as a way of getting a poor country off their hands. The Labour Party wobbled for a time, but eventually came out against Patrick's prescription and when in 1953 the Conservative government decided to impose the Federation on Africans, most of whom did not want it, we moved into the attack. One of the main purposes of the Movement for Colonial Freedom was to oppose the Federation tooth and nail.

By 1954, therefore, colonialism was fighting its last battle over large tracts of Africa. In East Africa Kenya was rent apart by Mau Mau. In central Africa Southern Rhodesia's obvious determination to run the Federation for her own ends had inflamed African opinion in Northern Rhodesia and above all in Nyasaland. The reaction of Conservative ministers to these situations was as obtuse, arrogant and dishonest as Eden's had been to Suez. The principal culprit was the Colonial Secretary, Alan Lennox Boyd. He was a Guardsman type of a man – physically imposing and imbued with the conviction that the British ruling class, both at home and overseas, could do no wrong. He was to become my main target of attack for five years and I was rather proud of what I had achieved by the end of it.

I was brought into personal conflict with him by a series of accidents. Evidence was seeping back into Britain from Kenya that things were going badly wrong with the security forces' handling of the Mau Mau emergency. Anxiety was brought to a head by the resignation in December 1954 of Colonel Young, Commissioner of the City of London Police, who had been seconded to advise the Kenya government on the running of the Kenya police. I had not previously heard of Colonel Young, but he proved to be one of the most remarkable men I have ever met: a policeman of high rank who saw his job as a sacred trust to enforce the rule of law with total impartiality. His resignation from his Kenyan post sparked off a dramatic debate in the House of Lords in which legal luminaries like Lord Jowett, who had been Solicitor-General and then Attorney-General in the post-war Labour government, teamed up with the Church in the form of the Archbishop of Canterbury to reveal the horrendous abuses of the rule of law which had been going on. The security forces, we were told, had been swollen by an influx of temporary district officers with the powers of magistrates. Worse still the Kenya government had authorized the establishment of a Home Guard manned by 'loyalist' Africans with extensive police and judicial powers. Some judges in Kenya were beginning to protest, and Lord Jowett read out in the Lords the words of acting Judge Oram in the Kenya High Court about the treatment of an African detainee in Ruthagathi detention camp:

> It appears that there exists a system of guard posts manned by the headsmen and chiefs, and that these are interrogation centres and prisons to which the Queen's subjects, whether innocent or guilty, are led by armed men without warrant and detained and, as it seems, tortured until they confess to alleged crimes, and then are led forth to trial on the sole evidence of these confessions.

It was a situation which illuminated Colonel Young's complaint. Though Lennox Boyd had refused to publish his full report, Young managed to get enough into their agreed statement to indicate that what he was after was a police force in Kenya totally independent of the government, acting as 'impartial custodians of the law' – with the bobby, as in Britain, answerable to no one but the common law. It was because his whole concept was alien to that of the Kenya government that he resigned. Judge Oram had revealed some of the consequences of the Kenya system, but Alan Lennox Boyd remained unmoved. When some of us, including me, followed up the Lords debate with questions in the Commons, he brushed us aside. There had been some abuses, he admitted, but the Governor of Kenya was correcting them. We must not forget the horrors of Mau Mau and so on. There was no need for him to publish Colonel Young's report.

By the time the House rose for the summer recess, we had not managed to shake his imperturbability one jot. It was then that I came across a story tucked away in the corners of the British press to the effect that a Kikuyu, Kamau Kichina, had been flogged to death while in police custody. I managed to ferret out more details with the help of the invaluable House of Commons library. The legal records revealed a picture of behaviour so horrifying that one could not imagine it happening in a British colony. Kichina had been employed at a police station manned by two European police officers, Fuller and Waters. When some money disappeared he and a fellow African were accused of taking it to pass to the Mau Mau, which they denied. After successive beatings and threats, Kichina's fellow accused 'confessed' and allegedly led the police to a small cache of money. At the end of five days Kichina died still protesting his innocence.

At the preliminary hearing the Resident Magistrate, Mr Harrison, delivered the following diatribe against the two police officers:

> Throughout Kamau's captivity no effort was spared to force him to admit his guilt. He was flogged, kicked, handcuffed with his arms between his legs and fastened behind his neck, made to eat earth, pushed into a river, denied food for a period and left out for at least two nights, tied to a pole in a shed not surrounded by walls with only a roof overhead and wearing merely a blanket to keep out the cold.
>
> For a day or two at least before his death it appears that the deceased's condition had deteriorated to such an extent that he could no longer stand or walk properly. He used to collapse on the ground and had to be assisted out of vehicles.

He concluded:

> He was never brought before a magistrate in the proper manner and he received no trial whatever, the right of all British subjects.

Thus he must be deemed legally innocent of the offence. Such conduct from police officers who should respect the law and set an example to others and protect the public is intolerable.

I was not surprised, therefore, to read that at the inquest the police officers had been charged with murder. It was a shock, however, to discover that by the time of the preliminary hearing the charge had been mysteriously reduced to causing grievous bodily harm. Mr Harrison did not seem too upset by this, merely telling the men that they were 'fortunate'. He proceeded to impose sentences – eighteen months' imprisonment – so derisory that the Supreme Court felt obliged to intervene to increase them. Even so my legal friends in the Commons told me that the new sentences of three and a half years' imprisonment for causing grievous bodily harm were outrageously lenient.

Two other Europeans who had been privy to what was going on, Chief Inspector Coppen and District Officer Bosch, whom Mr Harrison had proposed to fine £25 and £10 respectively, also had their sentences reviewed, Bosch being committed to six months' imprisonment. But by this time Inspector Coppen had slipped out of the colony unscathed.

I was convinced that a massive cover-up was going on. My first step was to raise the case at the September meeting of the National Executive, which passed my resolution demanding an enquiry. I followed it with a seething article in *Tribune*: 'Labour to Fight Kenya Thugs'. By the time Parliament reassembled in October Lennox Boyd was furious. He admitted the facts in a statement for which I asked, but he insisted that the case, though deplorable, was an 'isolated' one. The Governor of Kenya was taking steps to ensure that it did not occur again. I was wrong in suggesting that Colonel Young's resignation had anything to do with cases like this and, no, he could not publish his resignation report. The charges against Fuller and Waters had been reduced 'in consequence of the medical evidence', but he would not put that evidence in the library.

This was totally unsatisfactory. There were some questions that were crying out to be answered. What had happened between the inquest and the preliminary hearing which had led to the charge of murder being dropped? Why was the man who had overall responsibility for the treatment of Kamau Kichina while in custody – Mr Richmond, a regular, fully trained member of the Colonial Service – not being punished at all? It was not that he had not known what was going on. He had been to the police station a couple of times during the five-day torture of the man. He must have seen that he could barely stand. Lennox Boyd had told me that the Governor was considering whether any disciplinary action was necessary, but this was not good enough. How could the Colonial Secretary assure us that cases like this would not recur when those who were responsible were not being brought to account impartially?

One of my characteristics, which some consider a fault, is that I do not let go. In his autobiography, Roy Jenkins dismisses it rather disparagingly as my 'obsessiveness'. But I have always known the dangers of sensational campaigns. One must be sure of one's facts. Was I exaggerating this time? I asked myself. Was this really an 'isolated' case? I decided there was only one man who could tell me this: Colonel Young. I did not know him and he did not know me. On an impulse I rang him up at his headquarters. To my surprise he came to the telephone immediately. To my greater surprise he agreed readily to lunch with me and did not even flinch when I suggested we might meet at St Stephen's Tavern, the favourite haunt of busy MPs and parliamentary journalists because it is just across the road from the House of Commons. He was just as I had visualized: big, imposing, authoritative, fearless and frank. He answered all my questions in a clear voice, indifferent to the fact that MPs and journalists at nearby tables could overhear. He had, he told me, resigned because he had not been allowed to introduce proper policing methods in Kenya. Abuses were rampant and would continue as long as the Kenya police controlled part of the administration instead of enjoying the same independence as the British bobby under common law. This is what he had introduced in Malaya when Attlee's Colonial Secretary Arthur Creech Jones had sent him to deal with the same problem there, and it had worked, but the Kenya government would have none of it. The Kamau Kichina case had not surprised him at all. He was delighted when I said I was trying to get to Kenya to carry out some enquiries of my own and said he would give me an introduction to Duncan Macpherson, who had been his Assistant Commissioner in Kenya and was still serving there.

On 1 November I was on my way to Kenya, having persuaded Hugh Cudlipp of the *Mirror* to send me to follow Colonel Young's trail. Hugh had one of the liveliest minds in Fleet Street, with a flair for investigative journalism. The *Mirror* was at its prime in those days and enjoyed nothing so much as taking a subject off the beaten populist track and making it interesting to its mass readership. He got quite excited when I told him of my conversation with Young and I felt a heavy responsibility to unearth the truth about what was going on. I also had to make it interesting.

I decided to proceed circumspectly, seeing all the right people first. So the Nairobi *Sunday Post* was able to report that within an hour of my arrival I was talking to Kenya's Finance Minister, Mr Vasey. High on my list was a visit to Sir Evelyn Baring, the Governor, whom I found very courteous and charming, but as ineffectual as I had feared. Next I spent four hours with Kenya's Attorney-General discussing the implications of the Kamau Kichina case. He was frank with me and I was impressed by him. But I had pledged as a condition of the interview that I would not repeat any of it, so I was unable to defend myself properly when on my return Lennox Boyd attacked me in the House. By the end of my first week the *Sunday Post* reporter wrote approvingly that I was 'charming, essentially good-humoured, and much better informed on Kenya than many left-wing visitors we have had.' He added, 'It is difficult to imagine her a rampant, raging Bevanite and her disarming manner is an invaluable asset to her. But I think this is not a little deceptive.' Not for the first time I realized that there are advantages in being a woman in politics. Most men are vulnerable to a little femininity, and many are unsure how to cope with it particularly when it is combined with what is considered a masculine strength of will.

The white settlers, however, proved a tougher nut to crack.

The *Sunday Post* reported that I wanted to meet them, but they did not want to take me on. To my disappointment, they refused to come out of their laagers. At my first official engagement, a summer party, the reporter wrote, 'only one European turned up, apart from the press'. Actually I counted five, but his perception was broadly true.

I had not, of course, neglected what the whites in Kenya liked to describe as 'non-Europeans', the African and Asian communities. I had made early contact with Gaya, who was deputizing for Tom Mboya at the African Federation of Labour while Tom was in London. Gaya was a spirited young African who was bursting with African grievances. Through him I met Gem Argwings-Kodhek, the first African lawyer to qualify in Kenya. He specialized in criminal law and devoted himself to taking up cases of suspect Mau Mau detainees. I also made a point of seeking out Mr Mangat QC of the East African Indian National Congress. He was touchingly grateful for my visit because the Asians, he told me, felt caught between the Africans, whose cause they supported, and the whites, who were prepared to give them preferential treatment which they refused the Africans. I realized one night how right he was to be worried about the Africans' hostility when Gaya and some of his friends took me on a mad ride through Nairobi in their battered jeep. Gaya spent all his time complaining of the government's preferential treatment. 'Look,' he declaimed to me excitedly in one African location, 'not a single African shop in this area, only Asian ones.' And he chanted almost monotonously, 'Oh, how I hate the Asians.'

This did not prevent me from moving after a couple of days from the New Stanley Hotel to the home of a Mr Desai in a pleasant suburb of Nairobi where Fenner had stayed during most of his second visit to Kenya. Mr Desai was a friendly if frightened little Asian businessman, who had thrown his roomy house open to any Asian, African or European who cared to come. It was there that I held open court as a succession of complainants against the white regime came streaming through. Mrs Desai, a gentle woman, was the perfect hostess, unruffled by the influx and taking care of my every need. Everyone seemed to have some story about the brutality of the police. Only a few yards away from the house, I was told, an African boy who had climbed a tree to escape a security-forces raid had been shot at to bring him down. Mrs Desai assured me it was true.

The highlight of my visit, however, was my meeting with Duncan Macpherson. True to his promise Young had written to him and he was as ready to talk to me as his former boss had been. Our meeting had all the appurtenances of a James Bond film. The only place for us to talk, he told me, was Kenya's National Park, safe from prying eyes and ears among the wild animals. And so I found myself in his jeep, watching the animals prowl at a safe distance while we talked. Macpherson was another prototype of the British policeman at his best – a sturdy Scot, frank, open and direct. He was fuming against the political interference he encountered every day. Young had put him in charge of a new Criminal Investigation Department (CID) to follow up any abuses which came to light. He was still doing the same job, but he came up against frustration at every turn. Yes, there had been a cover-up over the Kamau Kichina case, as in many others. That sort of thing was still going on. More power to my elbow in exposing it.

After that all that remained to me was to try to unearth the evidence. A friendly Nairobi journalist advised me that I could find the records I needed in the library of the Supreme Court. As I had expected, the inquest proceedings gave the game away. The murder charge depended on the evidence of Dr Brown, to whom as medical officer at the Tumu Tumu mission hospital Kichina's body had been brought. Fuller and Waters had tried to mislead him from the start, telling him that Kichina had died by poisoning. Later that day Richmond called to assure Dr Brown that Kichina had been 'perfectly well' when he had seen him just before his death. As a result Dr Brown did not carry out the post-mortem until the following day when he found the body carried the marks of extensive injuries: multiple weals, swollen limbs, a knife wound and areas where the skin had been removed. He sent the organs to the government analyst, who reported that he could find no signs of poisoning or disease. Dr Brown therefore told the inquest, 'In view of the negative findings of the government pathologist I am of the opinion that the injuries must have caused death. . . . There was no evidence of death from any other cause.'

It was on this testimony that the murder charge was based. At the preliminary hearing it was clear that he had been leaned upon. Did not the delay in conducting the post-mortem mean that he might have missed something? He began to hedge. 'It is imposs- ible to be explicit about the exact cause of death.' He did not oppose the reduction of the charge, but still added doggedly, 'On the other hand I did not find any other cause of death.' The legal records also revealed that Mr Richmond, as I suspected, had been implicated up to the hilt. He had not carried out the actual flogging, as Fuller and Waters had done, but he had in effect incited it, calling on *barazas*, meetings of village elders, to tell them that he knew Kichina had taken the money and that unless he was made to confess and the money was found the whole village would be punished. He had even impounded 100 cattle and seventy-two goats from the village to show that he was serious. At one of the *barazas* Kichina had stood only a few yards from him, and he had barely glanced at him, though witnesses testified that Kichina was already so weak that he could barely stand. It was impossible to believe he did not know how his orders were being carried out. A 'loyalist' African corporal who witnessed one of Waters' severe floggings of the two accused said to him, 'Both these prisoners are going to die.' Waters replied, 'That is nothing.' Yet no charges, not even as yet a disciplinary one, had been brought against the man with overall responsibility.

I still had to prove that this was not an 'isolated' case. Gem Argwings-Kodhek assured me that beatings and other breaches of the law were still going on and that innocent people were being rounded up. I decided I must visit a detention camp and talk to the detainees. The Governor raised no objection but, when I arrived at the camp he had suggested for me, a high-handed district officer was waiting to take charge of me. On my saying that I wanted to talk to some of the detainees alone he replied haughtily, 'I cannot allow that. These men are dangerous. A woman must not be with them alone.' I replied equally haughtily,

'I am not a woman. I am a Member of Parliament.' To that he retorted, 'Madam, I can only go by appearances.' I had to give him best and spent a futile morning trailing round the camp with him and feeling like minor royalty as I exchanged distant courtesies with the men crouching in their compounds. Some eight years later I was to meet a number of them again in the gardens of Government House, as we celebrated Kenya's Independence Day.

Then at last Gem brought me a case of ruthless brutality which would really lend itself to proof. The father of a young boy had been to see him saying two European police officers had descended on his home, picked up his son and driven off with him. They returned the next day with the boy's dead body, saying he had been shot while trying to escape. Gem had gone with the father to the inquest, where the police officers had admitted killing the boy and the court was told the CID would investigate. Before it could start its enquiries the father had been rounded up together with some friends who had been helping him and detained in Manyani camp. Would I go and visit them? I agreed readily and this time the commandant arranged for me to interview the men in his office, though with a district officer lounging in the doorway within earshot. There then ensued a pantomime which was the proof I needed that gross perversions of justice were still going on. The men denied that their detention had anything to do with the boy's death, though they also denied being Mau Mau. The father even denied that the boy had been killed by European police officers, though I had seen the inquest report in which they admitted it. Unfortunately I could only speak to them through the prison's official interpreter, so the men's replies may have been doctored, but in any case the CID's enquiries had been successfully aborted and I could understand Duncan Macpherson's professional fury at not being able to do his job.

I was still anxious to hear as much of the other side as possible and so was pleased when Michael Blundell, Minister of Agriculture and leader of the European elected members of the Legislative Council invited me to visit him in his White Highlands home. Michael was a curious side-shoot of colonial rule, intelligent enough to realize that white privilege could not continue indefinitely and progressive enough not to join forces with the bigoted white settlers in resisting it. But he was a bluff, blunt man on whose reactions one could not always rely. During Fenner's first visit to Kenya Blundell had denounced him in the Legislative Council as a 'communist'. During Fenner's second visit he was ready to co-operate with him in trying to create reconciliation between the races. Later he was to write disparagingly about me in his autobiography as someone who had come to Kenya with a closed mind, but in fact I rather took to him.

His home in the White Highlands made me understand what the white settlers were being expected to give up. It was a spacious, comfortable house built on the hillside with a stupendous view of the Rift Valley spreading out below. The air was fresh and so cool in the evening that log fires burned in the open hearth. I could see why Michael was sometimes tetchy, wondering whether he was going to lose all this and even more whether he ought to do so, but I preferred his bluff, blunt manner to the soapy smoothness of the Evelyn Barings. Later I learned he had formed the New Kenya Group, which argued that the new Kenya must be multiracial. After independence he gave up politics and went back to his farm: and there *was* a farm to go to, despite his earlier fears, because after independence there was no great appro-priation of white property. In fact, the progress towards land reform was painfully slow. I found in my political life that most revolutions peter out very quickly – a lot of sweeping demands before power is gained, and a strong dose of realism afterwards. That is why timidity is such a bad guide for those who are frightened of change.

The day before I was due to leave Kenya, Gem came to ask me to do another piece of detective work. So I found myself driving out of Nairobi with him to a remote rendezvous. As we arrived a group of men materialized nervously out of the under-growth. They were, they said, traders in a nearby village whose goods and equipment had been impounded by the tribal police for their Home Guard post. When they had been screened and cleared of association with Mau Mau they asked for their property back or for compensation. For their pains they had been taken to the

Home Guard post and beaten up. At my request they took off
their shirts and showed me the weals upon their backs. The best
description of the scene came in a letter from a colonial officer
which had been forwarded to Jimmie by a third party to whom it
was addressed. Jimmie in turn forwarded it to me. It ran:

Dear Hilda
. . .
Have you seen Barbara Castle since she got back?
Perfectly amazing was the scene on the last morning of her
stay in this country, when I ran into her by chance, examining
the naked backs of Africans by the side of the main road to
Nakuru, for Clement Argu [sic]. I was roped in to witness the
scars.
'For goodness sake, Clem,' I said 'if we are going to examine
naked Africans in broad daylight with a European woman in the
party, can't we go behind those bushes over there, or at least go
down some sort of side road? Anybody in the Colony may come
along here at any moment.'
'No,' said Clem, firmly. 'If we go behind those bushes we
shall all be shot.'
So the main road it had to be. God knows who saved us. I
took the precaution of going straight to the D.C. telling him
what had actually happened.
I believe anyhow that she had a jolly good run for the
money, all things considered: and she certainly saw as much of
what matters as can possibly be seen in Kenya in a fortnight.
Definitely, I call her 'tops'.
Love
John Miller

I found when I got back to London that Lennox Boyd did not
share these sentiments. The *Mirror* had done me proud and had
splashed my articles under headings such as 'What Price Justice:
Kenya Land of Fear', and he was awaiting his chance to get back
at me. 'Some of us do not have the advantage of writing articles
in the *Mirror*,' he snarled at me in his speech on our first encounter

in the Commons and launched into a personal attack on me for
what I was supposed to have said to the Attorney-General during
our private talk. It was a grave mistake. The House of Commons
does not like a minister who loses his temper and Labour
Members, who were in an uproar of solidarity, were able to seize
on a constitutional point: how could MPs ever go abroad and
do their investigative duty if uncorroborated accounts of what
they were supposed to have said in private talks with ministers
were to be quoted in the House? The Speaker stopped the row
by indicating that we could thrash it all out in an Adjournment
debate the following week. The parting shot came from Irene
Ward, formidable scourge of the left from Tyneside: 'Is my
Rt Hon. Friend aware with what contempt responsible public
opinion in Kenya will regard the conduct of Mrs Castle?' I was
sorry the Speaker's intervention prevented Lennox Boyd from
answering.

Some of his own people must have got at him because by the
time of our debate Lennox Boyd was as mild as milk, apologizing
for having quoted a private conversation: 'I made a mistake in
what I did.' He made other conciliatory moves. He would place
in the library the full medical records of the Kichina case. A
disciplinary enquiry was being held into Richmond's conduct and
he would let us know the result. But he gave no sign whatsoever
of a fundamental change of attitude. It was clear to me that the
old complacent cover-ups were still going on. I had, for instance,
told him that Gaya had been arrested as soon as I left Kenya. He
assured me that it had had nothing to do with my visit: it was a
theft-of-money charge again, all too painfully familiar. As for the
men I had seen in Manyani camp, the Attorney-General was
satisfied that 'there was no connection between the father's detention and the enquiries by the CID into his son's death'. When I
referred him to the inquest report on the boy's death, he was taken
aback. He had obviously never heard of it and promised he would
'look into it'.

I was even more suspicious about the saga of Richmond. I
knew that the establishment would find a way of looking after its
own. In February Lennox Boyd informed me that Richmond had

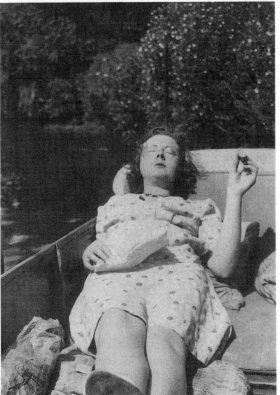

Above: Power at last. Harold Laske – Chairman of the Labour Party – addresses the newly victorious group of MPs.

Left: On a punt in Oxford, but with Ted on the pole this time, 1944.

The photograph Ted Castle put on the front page of the *Daily Mirror* during the Labour Party conference of 1944 which led to a marriage and a parliamentary seat.

My first general election in 1945 and the strain of the wartime years shows.

On one of my first journalistic efforts in 1945 when I was sent by *Picture Post* to interview the new Prime Minister, Clem Attlee.

Electioneering with John Edwards in 1945 with Ted at the wheel.

John Edwards and me with Sir Stafford Cripps and his wife Isabel when, as President of the Board of Trade, he made us his Parliamentary Private Secretaries.

On becoming a new MP in 1945 I break into TV with Michael Foot on *In The News*.

Always a keen walker, I hold my own with Hugh Dalton, Ted, Arthur Blenkinsop MP and Tom Stephenson, pioneer of the Pennine Way, in blazing the trail.

At the UN in 1949, I sit next to an American delegate.

One of the lighter moments on my tour of Canada with Harold Wilson in 1947, when we escaped from the boring routine of Rotary Club meals.

Nye Bevan congratulates me on my election to the constituency section of the NEC, 1951.

With Zita Crossman and Ted, Dick Crossman and I take advantage of the first interviews that Marshall Tito of Yugoslavia gave to foreigners in 1951.

I always enjoyed dancing at the party conferences, even with Gaitskell in the stormy fifties.

been dismissed the service, and I was sure he had taken his pension rights and other perks with him. But I had not expected rehabilitation to be so swift. Not long afterwards my contacts in Kenya informed me that Richmond had reappeared in a top job with the white-dominated Aberdare County Council as, of all things, African Affairs Officer. When I tackled Lennox Boyd about it in the House he was at his most truculent again. The appointment, he told me, was a matter for the Aberdare County Council and not for him, but he could not resist adding his own personal piece of Richmond whitewashing: 'In fairness to Mr Richmond it ought to be clear that his offence was limited to what was described as a misguided effort to avoid incriminating other officers. Personally speaking I am glad that he has been given another chance in life.' I knew then that nothing had changed in Kenya and that other Africans would be flogged to death.

My visit to Kenya had launched me journalistically. Up till then I had done a lot of work for the *New Statesman* under Kingsley Martin's editorship. Kingsley was a vain man and more than a touch neurotic, but none of us who worked with him had any doubt that he was a great editor with a unique flair for knowing the things that would interest his readers and for attracting interesting people to write about them. I had also written regularly for *Tribune* and occasionally for other journals like the *Spectator*, but this was the first time I had made a splash in the national press. Typically it was Dick Crossman who blazed the trail for my next journalist debut.

Having written regularly for the *New Statesman* for twenty years, during ten of which he had also written a weekly column for the *Sunday Pictorial*, Dick got the academic's urge to leave his ivory tower and go populist. He therefore severed his connection with the *Statesman* in order to concentrate on producing a major column for the *Daily Mirror* three times a week, for which he had negotiated a lucrative contract with Hugh Cudlipp. It was a dangerous thing for him to do politically, for Dick was as compulsively provocative in his journalism as he had been in his tutorials as an Oxford don, and this got him into trouble with the party. A classic example was a column he did for the *Pic* in which he implied that the trade union leaders were not up to their job: he was hurt and bewildered when they turned on him. He wrote mournfully in his diary a few days later, 'Quite suddenly my column in the *Sunday Pic* has become the special object of detestation in the Party.' It was one of Dick's many gaffes which he spent his political life trying to live down. How many would he produce writing for the *Mirror* three times a week? But his decision to do so meant a beneficent fall-out for me: shortly afterwards the *Pic* asked me to do the column in his place.

I was, of course, delighted, but also nervous. It was a great challenge to follow Dick who was a much more practised and confident journalist than I was. One prospect, however, encouraged me. I had noted that Dick had always been able to exact perks from his employers in the form of frequent visits abroad to cover any area or incident in which he was interested. Thus emboldened I suggested I might launch my column with a visit to the treason trial in South Africa, where 162 men and women, black, white and coloured, were on trial for their lives. Ever since Verwoerd's Nationalists had launched their apartheid regime in 1948 I had been increasingly worried about its cruelties. This was the first great showdown and we ought to cover it. I also suggested I should then go on to visit Southern Rhodesia and the other countries of the Central African Federation, where trouble was brewing up. The *Pic* agreed instantly.

I arrived in Johannesburg in January 1958 to be met by a young reporter from the *Sunday Post*. He carried with him a letter of welcome from his editor, Frank Collins, saying he hoped the room he had arranged for me at my hotel was OK. If not, would I let him know and he would pitch into the management. If there was anything else I needed I should let him know. Since the *Sunday Post* had no links with any British newspaper, this was impressive. It was my first introduction to the mad-hatter teaparty which was South Africa: friendliness in unexpected quarters and everything acted out against a backcloth of violence. I had an example of this as the young journalist drove me to my hotel. We passed the recumbent figure of a black African in the middle of the road, and I said instinctively, 'He's hurt and we must help

276

him.' 'He may be shamming and waiting to mug us as soon as we bend over him,' was the reply. 'It happens all the time.' I learned later that in Johannesburg no one went out alone after dark.

The next morning I presented myself promptly at the Drill Hall where the treason trial was being held, flourishing my press pass. Any fears that I might be refused entry were quickly dispelled. On the contrary, the police officer at the door waved me to the best seat at the press table with the greatest friendliness, merely saying mildly that I was not supposed to be carrying a camera, though he did not confiscate it. The Kafka-like confusion between nightmare and reality continued throughout the day. The Drill Hall was a ramshackle building with a corrugated-iron roof, an almost comically informal setting for an important trial, with the accused lined up in rows in front of the magistrate's chair, so near to the press table that I could almost touch them and could certainly chat with them. There was a supreme moment of irony when Lionel Forman, barrister and writer, passed to me from his seat among the accused a copy of a book he had written with Solly Sachs called *The South African Treason Trial*, which they had published in England and smuggled into South Africa. Not only was no attempt made to intercept the book on its way to me, but the clerk of the court obligingly acted as courier. I had to keep reminding myself that the men and women in the dock had been ruthlessly and arbitrarily rounded up. Dorothy Stanley, for instance, a nursery-school teacher, told me that she and her husband had been woken up and arrested at four in the morning, with no time to make arrangements for their three children aged three to eight. Later the charges against them had been withdrawn, with no reason given, but her husband had lost his job. Two lawyers, Duma Nokwe and Joe Slovo, who had been briefed for the defence, were themselves arrested before the trial began and were in the dock with the accused.

This was a preliminary hearing to see if the charge of treason, a capital offence, could be made to stick. The government was not playing about: it was deadly serious. Mr Maizels, who was leading for the defence and dominated the court both physically and intellectually, told me he thought the government would have to drop the treason charges, but would then proceed under other statutes, such as the Suppression of Communism Act, under which the accused could get ten years. The authorities had already released 61 of the original 162 and steadily continued to release others. 'It is always possible', Maizels said to me, 'they may narrow it down to about a dozen people who could not deny they were communists. Ruth First, for instance.' And the government could always bring in new laws to catch more people in its net. No one could feel safe.

In view of all this the accused were astonishingly relaxed – almost ebullient. They enjoyed cheeking the authorities, as when they all insisted on using the Non-Whites' entrance to the dock, rejecting the segregation laws the government was trying to enforce. At the beginning of the hearing, they told me, they had been herded into a cage at the back of the dock surrounded by sixteen armed guards, who had prevented the defence lawyers from entering it, insisting that they must talk to their clients through the wire mesh. One of the accused hung a notice outside the cage: 'Danger: Do Not Feed'. The authorities' discomfiture turned into defeat when every member of the Bar in court refused to proceed unless and until the cage was removed. Maizels told me that, despite the regime, the black man could get more justice in South Africa than in Southern Rhodesia because most magistrates were drawn from the Bar rather than from the administration, as they were in the colonies. 'As in Kenya,' I thought to myself.

I had a long talk with the young lawyer Nelson Mandela, not as well known in those days as Oliver Tambo, whose chambers he shared, but already making a big impression on the Court. He was a man of extraordinary dignity and lack of bitterness, in spite of which – or because of it – he was assuming a natural leadership among the accused. He knew what he wanted and was quietly determined to get it. He had been arrested for his part in the Defiance Campaign of the African National Congress (ANC) and had been campaigning against apartheid legislation like the Group Areas Act. He and Oliver had at first been given permission to have their chambers opposite the law courts, but then the net had tightened and they had been given peremptory notice to move out of the white area. Like Maizels he was convinced that somehow or other the government meant to get its way.

And so it proved. In March 1961 the three judges in the special criminal court which had been set up to try the remaining accused found them not guilty on the ground that the prosecution had not proved they were conspiring to overthrow the state by violent means. It was only a breathing space. Three years later Mandela and others were sentenced to life imprisonment under a new Act which the government had rushed through. This defined sabotage so widely and so loosely that no activist against the regime could escape. In 1964 Nelson Mandela disappeared from view to Robbin Island, though not from the thoughts of the people he had inspired.

It was true that many aspects of apartheid appeared comical, but I soon found that life was no laughing matter for any African. Peter was my guide, a gentle young African lorry driver who lived in the African location of Alexander Town and had volunteered to show me round the shops so that I could see how they treated their customers, even in establishments which catered mainly for Africans. We were soon laughing at the absurdities. At one big store, blacks and whites were going up the escalators together, but when we tried to enter the lift the black operator waved Peter out with the admonition that the African lift was round the back. We found it among the ashcans – a lift for goods and 'natives' all in one. As we rode in it together we discovered that its operator was white. This pantomime was repeated in store after store, and I became genuinely bewildered about what were the guiding principles behind apartheid. Was it that the races must be physically separated? If so, why a black boy operating a white man's lift? The rudeness of whites to blacks extended to me because when I was with an African at one counter the white assistant ignored the African women waiting ahead of me and asked me what I wanted. When I replied, 'These ladies are before me,' the assistant tossed her head and strode to the other end of the counter, where a white customer had just appeared. I felt a deep pity for the poor whites of South Africa, who had to bolster their self-esteem in this way.

But I felt an even deeper pity for Peter, who suddenly became nervous. 'It is getting late,' he said. 'I must get back.' He had not got his pass with him and he knew he could be picked up and whisked back to the reserves without his family even being informed. On my return to my hotel I received a telephone call from his frightened wife. 'Barbara, where is Peter? I am afraid they may have taken him.' Mercifully, that turned out not to be the case.

I found that even a religion could be a political crime in Nationalists' eyes. Within twenty-four hours of my arrival in Johannesburg (so I wrote in my diary), I had broken the law. 'My crime? I had gone to church. It was crowded with Africans.' The government had just promulgated a law prohibiting mixed church congregations. The Churches were immediately up in arms, the Archbishop of Cape Town, the Right Rev. Joost de Blank, declaring that he intended not only to ignore the law, but to admit non-Europeans to his church schools. Indignant white members of his Anglican congregation wrote to the *Sunday Times* that he had done 'irreparable harm' to race relations in South Africa. But I found the same mood of Church defiance everywhere. Trevor Huddleston, as priest in charge of the Anglican mission of Sophiatown and Orlando, had blazed a trail of multiracial worship from 1943 to 1955. It was in Orlando in the church still known as 'Trevor's church' that I committed my crime. There was a different officiant at the altar, but Trevor's spirit still lingered there. Everyone seemed to be enjoying themselves. 'An African choir sang its heart out behind me,' I wrote in my diary. 'African women in their best go-to-church hats knelt all around. Black toddlers craned their curly heads to stare at the altar.' When all this awe got too much for them they erupted into the aisle to do a jig, and nobody stopped them. I noted that a white man and his young son were there too, ready to resist Nationalist wrath.

I found the same eruption of happiness at the Community of the Resurrection's mission at Rosentenville, presided over by Father Jarrett Kerr, who was on the list of people and things I must see which Trevor had given me before I left London. When I arrived there I found a group of informal and not noticeably reverential men who plied me with tea and fruitcake and asked me if I had brought the latest issue of the *New Statesman*, which apparently they all read avidly. Martin Jarrett Kerr knew how to use his cloth to cheek the authorities. It was he who took me on a tour of the African locations, lifting his cassock high above the muddy ruts in the obviously 'unadopted roads' with which he was clearly familiar. It was he who introduced me to the Union of African Artists, which organized rock-and-roll groups in the townships. On one memorable night he took me to a Non-Europeans Only performance of an African ballet. ('We have signed you in as a committee member because of the law'), throwing his head back in sheer delight as the African penny-whistle band came on the stage – symbol, I wrote in the *New Statesman*, of 'light-hearted defiance of crippling poverty'.

Then there was Father Hooper, a lively, fearless young priest whose home was a sanctuary in the troubled area of Zeerust. Many of the African women bravely risking arrest and assault to resist the hated pass laws were his parishioners, and it seemed entirely natural that they should meet their legal advisers on his premises. His white parishioners thought otherwise, but, as he drove me into the reserves in his Land Rover (affectionately known to the Africans as 'God's Pick-Up'), I could see he did not care. He had been sent to convert the African to the Christian God, 'who was not to be mocked by apartheid'. A few weeks after I met him he was banned from the African reserves and could no longer carry on his missionary work or try to protect his parishioners. He was eventually forced to move to Tanzania. My visit to Zeerust was attacked in the House of Assembly, and the government rushed through a law making it illegal to enter a reserve without permission from the Native Commissioner. 'That means', Father Hooper wrote to me, 'nobody has access to observe what is going on behind our local iron curtain.' He was soon to be banned himself under the same law.

And yet, despite all these manifestations of ruthless, arbitrary power, it was with a sinking heart that I left South Africa for Southern Rhodesia. In a strange way there was something honest about South Africa: the Nationalists made no attempt to hide their aims or to disguise the policies needed to enforce them. The line was clearly drawn and everyone had to decide on which side of it they stood. The process involved risks so great it almost led to light-heartedness. One had made one's choice and there was nothing to do but joke about it. And in doing so one soon identified one's friends. I was surprised and heartened by the relative enlightenment of the English-language Sunday newspapers in Johannesburg and I was naturally delighted when Frank Collins wrote to my bosses on the *Sunday Pictorial* to say, 'she worked like a ruddy Zulu', adding, 'By all means send more reporters like Barbara. They write good copy, and by God, they make it, too!'

In fact there was an exuberance about South Africa, manifested even in her most tragic moments, which I had not met elsewhere. It was as though the overt oppression brought out the courage to resist it.

My last memory of Johannesburg was of visiting the offices of the sadly depleted Labour Party to meet its chairman, Jessie Macpherson. It was Saturday morning and the offices were almost empty. We heard a knock at the door and there stood three Africans. They had come, they said, with some money for the Treason Trial Fund. When Jessie told them the offices were closed, their faces fell. She asked if they could come back on the Monday. Impossible. Would they leave it with her? They hesitated, clearly weighed down with responsibility. Eventually they agreed on condition that they were given a signed and stamped receipt. How much was there? 'More than three pounds.' It had been collected by six women at a municipal women's hostel, and their part in the donation must be made clear on the receipt. At last all was ready and they counted out the money: £11 18s 2d, most of it in small change. It was a fortune! As I looked at their thin bodies under their cheap mackintoshes, at the earnest black faces under severe berets, I knew I could not be on anyone's side but theirs.

It was a shock, not a relief, to go to Salisbury. The atmosphere was so stiflingly smug. Not much Afrikaner stock here, but great dollops of Anglo-Saxon hypocrisy. The in-word, I found, was 'partnership' with the African. Any suggestion that the whites practised apartheid was pooh-poohed, yet I discovered that Salisbury had a Land Apportionment Act worthy of Johannesburg which prohibited any African from owning, leasing or occupying land outside the blacks' own areas. When Herbert Chitepo became the first Southern Rhodesian African to qualify at the English Bar, the Federation government had to amend the Act to enable him to open an office in Salisbury, and a special dispensation was rushed through to enable him to use the Whites Only lift in the Supreme Court. Chitepo was one of a number of outstanding young Africans who were coming to the fore through any loopholes they could find. The special Acts and dispensations which had been pushed through to make an exception in his case filled him with contempt. The only things the Europeans were interested in, he told me, were 'wealth, comfort and power'. They would not abdicate any power unless their wealth was threatened. And in the meantime there was much more separateness practised than 'partnership'.

White liberals I talked to in Salisbury told me that under the Natives (Urban Areas) Act they were not allowed to house an African servant under the same roof: the 'boy' had to live in a *kia* at the bottom of the garden and was allowed to have his wife with him only if his employer was willing to employ her too. If she should have a baby, they told me, they were obliged by law to send her back to the reserve. I found evidence of a colour bar every-where: Africans were forced to make their purchases outside a shop through a hatch in the wall; newly built Post Offices with separate entrances for blacks and whites; separate cinemas for whites and blacks. Nor was it only the 'natives' who were snubbed. I discovered that the Assistant High Commissioner for India was unable to get his hair cut in Salisbury. The whole unhappy atmosphere was highlighted for me by an incident I witnessed when shopping in Salisbury's main street. A white youth in a jeep came careering down the street and suddenly decided to make an illegal U-turn. This brought him face to face with an African out for a ride on his new bike. 'Get out of the way, you black bastard,' yelled the youth. The African did so – just in time.

I saw enough in those few days to realize that the attempt to impose a Federation on Northern Rhodesia and Nyasaland would end in disaster. A tour of the northern territories brought more evidence. How could the civil servants and politicians who had pressed this idea, I asked myself, not understand that the three

countries were as different as chalk from cheese? Southern Rhodesia was a colony which had been conquered for the benefit of
the white settlers. Northern Rhodesia and Nyasaland had never
been conquered. Their African populations, led by their chiefs,
had voluntarily put themselves, as protectorates, under the care of
the British; they had been promised that, when they were ready
to rule themselves, power would be handed back to them. Now
they felt betrayed. They knew they would be sucked into the orbit
of Southern Rhodesia, with the racial discrimination laws they did
not have and her links with South Africa. The pundits in Whitehall
and Westminster argued that most Africans did not know or care
about federation and that trouble was being stirred up by a few
agitators in the towns. I did not find this true even in Southern
Rhodesia, where the Africans had less to lose from federation and
more to gain. Local ANC officials told me there was a general
feeling of uneasiness. 'To the African the Federation is race
discrimination,' one of them said to me.

Once again I found that the missionaries were better guides
than the civil servants, particularly as to what was going on in the
villages where their parishioners lived and where they had
pioneered education for Africans through their mission schools.
To a man they were opposed to federation. Prominent among
them was the Rev. Andrew Doig, a Church of Scotland missionary of many years' standing. He was another upright, dedicated
Scot, of whom there seem to be many in Africa, who was never
going to compromise his principles. In every village, he told me,
there was someone with a relative who had worked in South
Africa and brought back stories of the pass laws. These things
counted more than any economic or constitutional arguments. He
was so obviously trusted by the Africans that he had been
appointed to represent African interests in the Federal Assembly.
Like many of his fellow missionaries he had been over to London
to lobby MPs against the Federation. Shortly after I left Nyasaland
I learned that he had resigned from the Federal Assembly in
protest against its disregard of African interests.

Another brave spirit was Dr Colin Morris, minister of the
Chingola Free Church in Northern Rhodesia. He was in London

when I arrived in his country, joining in the general anti-Federation lobbying, but I learned about the sermons he had preached to his mainly white congregation denouncing the federal idea, as a result of which he became known as the Fighting Parson. When I returned home I met him and took to him instantly. He was a lively and outspoken young man and, when I asked him if he would address a meeting in my constituency to try and bring home to the people of Blackburn the significance of these obscure events in a faraway country, he agreed immediately. As I remember we had a good attendance at the meeting we addressed together at the premises of the Methodist church in Blackburn. I treasure the letter he sent me on his return to Chingola. Apparently the Federal Minister of Law and Education, Mr Julian Greenfield, had been outraged by his statement that the partnership policy of the Federation was 'the biggest confidence trick in political history' and had denounced it as a 'wicked attack on Europeans in this country'. Colin's letter noted, 'I am still living down the Blackburn meeting. One can get away with sodomy, blasphemy and adultery, but to speak on the same platform as Barbara Castle puts one completely beyond the pale as far as the white Raj is concerned.' Later Colin Morris was to become director of religious broadcasting for the BBC and then regional controller of the BBC for Northern Ireland. When in 1991 he was retired from the latter at the age of sixty, I was glad to find him as lively as ever and to welcome a fellow spirit into British politics.

I returned from Northern Rhodesia well equipped to expose the speciousness of colonial constitution-making. I had found how easy it was to distract attention from reactionary principles by a welter of confusing detail, some of which sounded plausible. The amendment to the federal franchise was a case in point. Theoretically it opened the door to African advance, but in practice it pitched the property and educational qualifications for the vote so high that few Africans could meet them. Even the creation of seven reserved seats for Africans elected on a special roll was a fraud, partly because the qualifications, though lower, were still too high to enfranchise many Africans, and partly because European voters were entitled to vote for candidates on the special roll.

The amending Act was so blatantly discriminatory that Sir John Moffat, head of the African Affairs Board of the Federal Assembly, tried to get it ruled out as unconstitutional, claiming that 'the Europeans have it both ways: the African is having it neither way'. The Africans were not fools, and they realized that the chips were stacked against them. The rosy forecasts of the Federal authorities about a great advance towards African emancipation were exposed as the nonsense they were when it was found that only seven Africans had registered on the special roll in Nyasaland, fifty-three in Northern Rhodesia and 560 out of a total electorate of 62,000 in Southern Rhodesia, where – because most Africans were better off – more should have been able to qualify.

I learned then how essential it was to keep one's eye on the ball. If the Federal authorities had really wanted to promote a steady and systematic African advance they would have concentrated their priorities on expanding their educational opportunities. Yet the Director of Education in Nyasaland told me that places had been provided for only a quarter of the African children in government-assisted schools. The missionaries had provided as many school places as the government, but that still meant that only half the children got any schooling at all, some only to junior primary level, while the number passing to secondary schools was minute. A development plan to improve matters had been cut back savagely due to 'lack of finance'. On that basis it was clear that it would take generations for Africans to clear the educational hurdle of the Federal Franchise Act. Yet the hunger for education was acute, as I found when Grace Karumbe, an instructor at the Teacher Training College which the Church of Scotland had set up, took me into the bush to meet some women from the villages. They stood in a circle round me while I made a speech. Being at a bit of a loss what to say to them, I asked them what message they would like me to take back to England. To my surprise the answer was 'Give us education for our girls.' It was the emphasis on 'girls' which delighted me.

The Federal authorities claimed that, despite all this, progress was being made, and they cited the admission of a handful of Africans to Salisbury University as a 'great advance'. This, of course, raised the familiar problem of how to house these black students in a white area and involved more amendments to the law to enable them to have their own hostel in the university – segregated from the whites, of course. The white students were obviously not too keen to learn about the black ones. A minor crisis was caused when it was discovered that one of the African students was a girl. After protests from parents of the white women students, she was at first put in the African men's hostel, until it was realized that this was 'inappropriate'. So segregated arrangements were hurriedly made for her in the women's area. It was clear that the 'great advance' towards African emancipation was going to be very slow. In any case, as Herbert Chitepo put it to me sourly, there was nothing to stop the Federal government from moving the franchise goal posts if too many Africans started to qualify.

It was a lesson I was to remember when Harold Wilson, having taken office as Prime Minister shortly after the collapse of the Federation in 1963 and faced with a Unilateral Declaration of Independence by the now isolated Southern Rhodesia, started his long saga of constitution-mongering with Ian Smith in an abortive attempt to make the latter's UDI respectable. I was sure of one thing: we could not trust any white government in Southern Rhodesia.

Not for the first time in the course of my trips to Africa, I ended my visit with a public-relations exercise. The idea was Andrew Doig's. When he attended meetings of the Federal Assembly he told me he always stayed in Meikles Hotel, Salisbury's most prestigious whites-only establishment. Why should not he and I dine there, taking with us Wellington Chirwa, one of the specially elected Africans in the Federal Assembly representing Northern Rhodesia? I jumped at it. Chirwa was clearly nervous, but braced himself manfully for the humiliation he believed awaited him. I then encountered British colonialism at its most astute. The manager, seeing us cross his sacred portals, blanched, but did not throw us out. Would we wait in the lounge until a table was available? We sat there for over an hour, Chirwa cautiously drinking only orange juice. Eventually when the restaurant was almost empty we were shown to a table in a corner hidden by a large palm.

Despite the manager's discretion the news caused a furore. My friend Frank Collins of the *Sunday Post* did his stuff, splashing a story from his Salisbury correspondent to the effect that some diners had threatened to walk out when we appeared. One man, said the report, had phoned his local paper to complain in outraged tones, 'There's a munt in Meikles.' Another man told the reporter, 'It was the sight of a white woman which annoyed me. I don't think I should have minded so much if he had been with other natives or with a white man.' I left the country with demands ringing in my ears that next time I should be declared a prohibited immigrant.

In the meantime reports continued to trickle in from Kenya. My fears that more Africans would die in her detention camps were justified, but Lennox Boyd still brushed them aside as 'isolated incidents'. However in March 1959, news came through of one of the most blatant cover-ups of those 'incidents'. The press carried stories of the death of eleven African detainees in the Hola camp, the official explanation being that they had died 'after drinking water from a water cart'. I might have been forced to accept this innocent version like everyone else if I had not received a telephone call at the Commons from D. N. Pritt, the left-wing QC who was in Kenya representing the African detainees. 'It is a pack of lies,' he told me. 'These men were flogged to death by their wardens.' I hurried to the Commons library to sift through the court records for the evidence. Late one night I rose to my feet in an adjournment debate to report what I had found, trembling so much from anger I could barely get out my facts. I was followed by Enoch Powell who was equally outraged. His cold logic clinched our case and Lennox Boyd, pressurized by Labour's front bench, was forced to admit the truth. It was a classic case of misrule by a colonial government and the quality press seized on it. I was glad I had been to Kenya and opened my mind to what was happening. I felt proud when David Wood, the political correspondent of *The Times*, reported my speech with the words: 'She gives no quarter, nor does she ask any.' I would like this to be my epitaph.

TWELVE

•

Chairman-Designate Meets Makarios

IN OCTOBER 1957 I was elected vice-chairman of the party and chairman-designate. In the Labour Party the job of chairman is mainly a symbolic one. He or she is elected each year by the NEC on the principle of Buggins' turn. The next two people in line with the longest periods of unbroken service on the NEC are chosen as chairman and vice-chairman almost as of right. They serve for the following year, at the end of which the vice-chairman is usually confirmed in the chairmanship automatically.

The chairman's chief job is to preside over the party conference – no easy ride. But the job also brings a certain prominence which can be of importance during crucial periods such as a general-election year. So it has been known for the NEC to manipulate the Buggins'-turn principle from time to time to avoid embarrass-ment. In 1957, however, the principle seemed to play into the hands of the NEC, where the majority were anxious to keep two undesirables out of the limelight in the anticipated election year of 1959. The first was Tom Driberg, who had served for one year longer than I had. By choosing him in 1957 they ensured that his chairmanship was safely out of the way before the election year. The second was Ian Mikardo, who was pressing hard on my heels. By making me chairman-designate for 1958 he could be made to wait. Whatever my faults I was considered a safer electoral bet than either of them.

It was as chairman-designate that at the conference of 1957 I replied to a debate on the party's policy for smaller colonial territories. I was also chosen to reply because I was a member of the Colonial Sub-committee of the Executive, on which I had helped work out the Labour Party's line on the complex problems of these small communities. It was a combination of circumstances which was to plunge me into the bitterest controversy I had yet experienced.

The theme of the policy document was that all colonial territories large or small had the right to eventual self-determination. The smaller territory in which everyone was interested at that time was Cyprus, where the government's clumsy policy had set this once peaceable island aflame. The government seemed to have learned nothing from the Suez fiasco. All that concerned it was to find a substitute for the bases which its folly had forced it to surrender in the canal zone. Cyprus, the third largest of the Mediterranean islands, straddling the strategic routes from the West to the Middle East and beyond, seemed ideal. Britain had acquired Cyprus from Turkey as a result of the Conference of Berlin in 1878. The island became a Crown colony in 1925, shortly after Turkey had renounced all rights in it in the Treaty of Lausanne. Britain had established two sovereign base areas there. Now Harold Macmillan was set to compound Eden's mistakes over Suez by turning the whole island into a British base, regardless of the views of the inhabitants.

It was a policy which defied everything the Labour Party proposed for the smaller territories. Its implication was that self-determination was a luxury the Cypriots must forgo. In 1954 Henry Hopkinson, Lennox Boyd's deputy at the Colonial Office, had made this clear when he announced that the government intended to impose a constitution on the island which was such a pale imitation of self-government as to be laughable. Challenged by Jim Griffiths, from Labour's front bench, as to when Cyprus would be able to run her own affairs Hopkinson had replied firmly, 'There can be no question of any change of sovereignty in Cyprus,' adding, 'It has always been understood and agreed that there are certain territories in the Commonwealth, owing to their particular circumstances, which can never expect to be fully independent.' It was the word 'never' which had roused the island into armed rebellion as Colonel Grivas, a right-wing retired army officer with political ambitions, launched a bloody and effective guerilla war against the British government through his National Organization of Cypriot Fighters (EOKA). Before long, 35,000 British troops had to be imported into the island to deal with it.

Most of us in the party had an instinctive sympathy with the Greek Cypriots. The debate at conference demanding self-determination for Cyprus was led by Lena Jeger, MP for Holborn and St Pancras, who had many Greek Cypriot friends, both on the island and in her constituency. I had met some of these friends in her St Pancras flat, notably a watercolourist whose paintings of pastel-coloured houses in narrow streets against a blue Cyprus sky enchanted me (I bought two of them). I had never been to Cyprus myself, but I knew that 80 per cent of her population of half a million were Greek and only 17 per cent Turkish, so her culture was basically Hellenic and Christian. Turkey had annexed the island in 1571, but Cyprus' 300 years in the Ottoman Empire had made little impression on her way of life. The main language was still Greek and the religion Christian. Any future for it had to recognize the predominantly Greek character of the island, with due safeguards for the rights of minorities. In fact, I was assured, the communities had lived together peaceably for years.

Unfortunately Grivas had played into the hands of the British government by his demand for *enosis*, or union with Greece, which would mean the assimilation of Cyprus into Greece politically and economically. This enabled the Macmillan government to argue that, if Greece was to be brought into the picture, Turkey had a right to be brought in too. This had long been one of Macmillan's main aims. Though Greece and Turkey were both members of NATO, the NATO military strategists had always argued that Turkey was a more reliable ally against communism than Greece – another judgment that was to be belied in April 1967 when the fascist colonels took power in Greece. This belief in Turkey as a natural ally of the West, despite her consistently bad record on issues of human rights, was to persist for many years.

Another characteristic of British diplomacy was that it always looked for a scapegoat for the troubles it had created. In Suez the scapegoat had been Nasser, in Cyprus it was Archbishop Makarios, the Ethnark or national leader of the Greek Cypriots. Makarios was a formidable opponent. No one doubted his charisma or his abilities. Son of a Cypriot shepherd, he had started life as a shepherd boy himself, but it soon became clear that this was not his natural lot. At the age of thirteen he was a novice at the Kykko monastery, and he went on from there to climb the academic ladder, being awarded a scholarship by the World Council of Churches to study theology and sociology at Massachusetts University. He returned to Cyprus to assume a natural leadership of his people. His commanding physical presence in long flowing robes and flowing beard, combined with an air of religious authority, gave him an influence which became a threat to the British government.

The whole panoply of British diplomacy moved into action to discredit him, to break his spell not only over his own people, but over world statesmen who were watching the situation in Cyprus with some anxiety. The impression had to be spread that he was the evil force behind Grivas' murderous policies.

In pursuit of this the British government adopted one of its familiar devices for dealing with leaders of unrest. In 1956 it exiled Archbishop Makarios to the Seychelles, which was no great hardship to him because, as he told me when I met him afterwards, he fell in love with the island and bought a house there for his retirement. From the British government's point of view, however, it was a great mistake because it left Grivas free to follow his own methods without restraint. The result was an escalation of violence. One of the great question marks over the Cyprus situation was how far Makarios was involved in Grivas' activities. To incriminate him and justify his exile the British government published in 1956 what it claimed were Grivas' captured diaries, but the publication did not help them very much. The diaries were full of Grivas' complaints about Makarios dragging his feet. 'I began to believe,' Grivas wrote, 'that Makarios did not want to use force at all and that he had merely yielded to pressure in going that far.'

By the time I had to reply to the Cyprus debate at conference, the situation there had reached crisis point, with the publication by Macmillan in June of a new plan for Cyprus. It was grandiloquently called 'An Adventure in Partnership', but to the Greek Cypriots it was the first step towards partitioning the island between Greeks and Turks, a goal which they suspected the government had long had in mind as a means of entrenching Turkey in this vital base. Under the plan communal affairs would be dealt with by two separate Houses of Representatives, but responsibility for other internal matters would rest with the Governor's Council. This Council would include representatives of the Greek and Turkish governments, who would also advise the Governor on external affairs, defence and internal security. At the appropriate time, and subject to safeguards about the bases, Britain would be prepared to share the sovereignty of the island with her 'Greek and Turkish allies'.

It was a clever trap and not surprisingly the Greek Cypriots rejected it out of hand. Macmillan, however, had the bit between his teeth. He descended on the Greek and Turkish capitals like an avenging angel, telling the two governments that they had no choice but to accept the plan. Those of us in the party who were interested in colonial affairs had no doubt that the plan was the first step towards partitioning the island and that this would involve a carve-up as brutally clumsy as anything contemplated by Ankara. Turkish villages were scattered among Greek villages all over the island and they could not be separated geographically. Partition could be achieved only by chopping the island in two regardless of the rights of the Greek majority or of the damage it would do to the relationship between the two communities. We were therefore dismayed when the reaction of Labour's front bench was ambivalent.

Once again Nye Bevan was in the front line. He was far too intelligent not to realize the purpose and effects of Macmillan's policy, but the Shadow Cabinet's main preoccupation was to get this awkward problem solved before Labour came to power.

In the Commons debate Bevan trimmed, to my and others' dismay. Having so recently returned to the party's fold, he was anxious not to seem to rock the boat. So he urged the Cypriots not to reject the plan out of hand but to negotiate the changes. Macmillan, incidentally, showed no signs of being willing to contemplate any negotiations. Indeed he announced that the Turkish representatives would arrive in Cyprus on 1 October.

It was against this background that I made my fateful speech to party conference. The party's Commonwealth Officer, John Hatch, an uncompromising anti-colonialist, had been following the situation closely. In fact he had been out to Cyprus the previous year and had sounded out Makarios on the need for the Greek Cypriots to abandon Grivas' demand for *enosis* and go for the island's independence instead. In a report to the NEC he had implied that Makarios might be willing to consider various alternatives. John had produced the brief for my reply on behalf of the Executive, which contained the fateful words: 'We are not like the Tories talking about a vague and misty future when we talk about self-determination coming to Cyprus. We shall endeavour to complete this freedom operation for the people of Cyprus during the lifetime of the next Labour government.' This firm commitment did not go unnoticed among Greek Cypriots. Above all it attracted the attention of Makarios, who had become increasingly anxious about the trap into which he felt the British government was manoeuvring his people. This was a vital clue to what happened next.

I was at home with Ted at our country cottage in Buckinghamshire in the summer of 1958 when I got a phone call from Athens, where Makarios, though still in exile, had been transferred from the Seychelles. It was from Spyros Kyprianou, Makarios' right-hand man, who was to follow him as President of Cyprus when the Archbishop died in August 1977. I had never met either Kyprianou or Makarios and was rather taken aback when Kyprianou said Makarios wanted to see me urgently to discuss the situation in Cyprus. Could I come to Athens? I hesitated. I have never minded taking risks in a cause in which I believe, but I have a canny streak in me which always makes me suspicious of being used for someone else's propaganda purposes, whether by Eastern European governments or anyone else. John Hatch, however, thought I should accept Makarios' invitation. Ted added his wise counsel. I should go on two conditions. First, I should make it clear I would visit Turkey as well as Athens and Cyprus and see members of the Turkish Cypriot as well as Greek Cypriot communities. Secondly, I should pay my own fare. So I arrived in Athens on 14 September. I had taken the precaution of seeing both the Greek and Turkish ambassadors in London before leaving. I also had a briefing session with Foreign Office officials. Lennox Boyd himself clearly did not think my visit was of any significance.

Kyprianou met me at the airport. He was a dapper little man, polished and poised, but he greeted me with genuine warmth and whisked me off to see Makarios, who was waiting for me at the Ethnarchy. It was the first time I had met the 'wily prelate' whom everyone had warned me against. He sat there, a dignified figure, and I could already imagine the comments that would be waiting for me from hostile quarters when I got home. 'She fell for his enigmatic charm: being a woman, of course she would.' Our first meeting was very businesslike and guarded on both sides. 'We will not accept any intervention by a third party,' he told me firmly, 'whether Greece or Turkey.' I pointed out that it was he who had brought in the Greek government by endorsing *enosis*, so he could not be surprised that the Turkish government wished to be brought in too. He did not demur. I asked him if he was willing to accept John Hatch's plan for an independent Cyprus within the Commonwealth: no partition and no union with Greece. He said he was, on conditions, but he feared that the British government had made up its mind to go ahead with the Macmillan plan whatever compromises were offered it. We agreed that I should sound out the Greek, Turkish and British governments and that we should meet again as soon as possible.

Somehow I managed to keep a daily diary of the hectic events of the next few days. If I had not done so even I might have believed afterwards that I had dreamed it all. My first call was on Roger Allen, our Ambassador to Greece, whom I had met in the old days during my visit to the UN. He was obviously deeply impregnated with the government's pro-Turkish line and received with scepticism my account of what Makarios and I had agreed.

The idea had been mooted before, he told me, but Makarios had never been willing to commit himself openly. When I said that this time he was prepared to do so, he changed his ground. 'It was amusing,' I noted, 'to see how instinctively he thought in terms of what Turkey would say, never once what Greece might think.' We parted cordially, Allen assuring me that he would immediately cable Lennox Boyd on Makarios' statement. He added, 'If they don't do anything, don't blame me. It won't be because I have blackballed the idea.'

Even more illuminating was my talk with Mr Riddleberger, the American Ambassador. He was most interested in what I had to report but doubted whether the British government wanted a compromise. 'Can you tell me what is the hurry about 1 October?' he asked. 'I cannot for the life of me see why Macmillan is rushing things so. On his visit here, it was not negotiation, it was the slapping of papers down on the table. I have never seen anything like it in my whole diplomatic career.' But Macmillan had warned the Americans not to interfere.

Next I called on Constantine Karamanlis, Greece's National Radical Union Prime Minister, at his official headquarters. I wrote in my diary:

> I was saluted smartly all the way up the steps and along the corridor. Flunkeys rushed to clear my route, a TV camera whirred and altogether I felt like a Foreign Secretary-elect! My arrival was obviously an event. Karamanlis received me in a large room with his interpreter. Both were charming and handsome men, Karamanlis' smile being positively benign. We sat down on a large leather settee and he patted my hand every time he got excited.

When I unfolded my plan for independence for Cyprus instead of *enosis* he nearly jumped for joy. 'He caressed my hand fondly,' I wrote, 'and cried "We accept! We accept!"' The *enosis* claim, he assured me, had never come from Greece. They wanted no rights in Cyprus, but if their Greek brothers there said they wanted to unite with Greece he could not turn them away: 'I have told the

British time after time we do not want Cyprus.' But he had a domestic audience to think of and had to tread warily. When I told him of the statement Makarios was prepared to make, he kissed my hand with delight and almost kissed my cheek, begging me to keep him in touch with developments.

My next port of call was Ankara. The first thing which struck me about Turkey was her poverty. I flew in a dirty little local plane of the Turkish airline. 'It smelt,' I noted, 'because Turkey is obviously too poor to afford paper bags for people to be sick in and the person who had occupied my seat before me had had no choice but to be ill down the seat in front.' At the frontier a particularly brutal customs officer purloined most of my cigarettes, and an American who took the next seat as we continued in the plane was muttering in fury, 'This country could not last a minute without aid and look how they treat you. Just downright arrogance.'

In Ankara, things brightened up, although my hotel, the Ankara Palast, was shabby and none too clean. In the evening, I attended a fascinating dinner given by Patrick O'Reegan, Britain's Information Officer, at which I met Bülent Ecevit, opposition deputy for Ankara, and other Turkish opposition leaders. Though not unreasonable, the Turkish guests obviously did not believe that the Greek Cypriots would ever give up *enosis*. The next day I got the authentic Turkish view from Melih Esenbel, Permanent Secretary at the Foreign Office, who had a long talk with me in the absence abroad of the Prime Minister and the Foreign Secretary. He was a neat little man whose trim good manners hid an implacable will. Turkey, he assured me, had written guarantees from the British government that partition remained the government policy: Turkey had accepted the Macmillan plan only as a step towards it. Partition in any case was a British idea. To Turkey it was a poor second best. What did Turkey want then, I asked: the whole island? Apparently, the answer to that was yes. What about the Treaty of Lausanne? Turkey, he said smoothly, had signed that on the assumption that Britain would remain in Cyprus. If Britain left, Turkey would have to protect her own strategic interests.

I grew irritated as I began to realize the House of Commons was being misled. Macmillan had assured MPs that his plan was an alternative to partition. Now it was clear that the Turks had been promised that this was the road to it. Once again the government had deliberately lied to Parliament.

I flew on to Cyprus. There had been high hopes among the Greek Cypriots when Sir Hugh Foot had replaced Field Marshal Harding as Governor a few months earlier. Sir Hugh had a liberal reputation like the rest of his famous family, and I for one believed that his arrival meant that British policy would become more flexible. I was sure he would recognize the importance of Makarios' statement to me and try to build upon it. I was soon disabused.

Sir Hugh was a big, genial man with a warm, disarming smile. He had the Foot cast of strong features and the family streak of moral seriousness lightened by the sense of humour all the Foot brothers possessed. He greeted me affectionately, knowing of my close association with Michael and Dingle and of the political work we had done together. After a long career in the Colonial Service, he was more polished and formal than the rest of the clan.

I spent two hours with him, and of course he was charm itself. But any hopes I had that he was looking for a compromise were soon dashed. I was dismayed by the smooth way he deflected my attempts to get his response to Makarios' statement, outdoing Roger Allen in diplomatic evasiveness. I realized then how exposed my position was, so I set about covering my flanks, asking him who he thought I ought to see while in Cyprus. He gave me a list of both Turkish and Greek Cypriots, and at this point volunteered the information that I would receive a lot of complaints from Greek Cypriots about rough treatment by the troops after recent incidents. Some of these would be false, others exaggerated, but some would have substance. There had, for instance, he told me a little uneasily, been an example the previous Saturday, when Greek villages had been searched following the killing of a British soldier in an ambush. Some damage had been done to property and some injury to the villagers themselves, though not as much as the Greek Cypriots claimed. He then made this astonishing statement: 'I do not mind so much if the soldiers get a bit rough when they are engaged in hot pursuit. What would worry me is if they started to do it in cold blood.' I could not imagine any such statement coming from Colonel Young. To him the law was the law and discipline was discipline, whatever the provocation. I could sense a laxity of control which fell below the standards my model policeman had laid down.

But I had not come to Cyprus to talk about detainees. I was determined to concentrate on my prime objective: the destruction of the Macmillan plan. So I readily followed Sir Hugh's advice. Part of it was that I should make a point of visiting Greek and Turkish villages.

He did not suggest, nor did I, that I should spend any of my short stay in visiting the British troops. Instead I gladly visited as many villages as possible, both Greek and Turkish, being garlanded with flowers by the Greeks and handed perfumed bouquets of jasmine by the Turks. They seemed equally glad to see me and I could believe Makarios' claim that Greek and Turkish Cypriots, left alone, could live perfectly well together. But *enosis* had poisoned the atmosphere.

I came up against communal politics again when I dined with the leaders of the Turkish Cypriots: Dr Fazil Kutchuk, their leader, Osman Orek, a lawyer, Umit Suleiman and Consul-General Ishin. We spent a pleasant evening on the terrace of a Turkish restaurant and the conversation, though lively, was amicable, which it might not have been if Rauf Denktash, Kutchuk's deputy, had been there, as he was to prove the most intransigent of the Turkish Cypriot negotiators. But once again it emerged unequivocally that they had accepted the Macmillan plan only as a step towards, and not as an alternative to, partition. 'Whatever the British government says, we are determined to have partition,' they told me.

The rest of my short stay in Cyprus was spent meeting Greek Cypriots and listening to their woes. There was one idyllic interlude when I lunched with Charles Foley, editor of the *Times of Cyprus*, and his wife in the garden of an open-air restaurant under the lemon trees. Another guest was Peter Benenson, a London barrister and leading light in Justice, who was passing through. Charles Foley, who had been foreign editor of the *Daily Express* before coming to Cyprus in 1955 to found the newspaper, was a tall, elegant, witty man and an excellent host, always ready to entertain the succession of Labour and progressive notables who passed through the island in the search for a solution to the Cyprus problem. As I sat drinking the local wine in the dappled sunshine of the lemon trees, I thought what a tragedy it was that this predominantly Greek island with its little villages in the hills, where one ate black olives and drank the rather strong, resinous wine, had become the pawn of hard, militaristic, international politics.

It was not the purpose of my visit to enquire into the conduct of the security forces in this emergency. I was also aware that the Greek Cypriots were excitable and had brought a lot of their troubles on to their own heads. But I was conscious that at my instigation their Ethnarch was about to renounce their sacred goal of *enosis*, so I could not afford to appear indifferent. I sat in the Ledra Palace Hotel listening to a stream of complaints about the brutal handling of Greek Cypriots by the troops. I even persuaded a reluctant Hugh Foot to allow me to visit a detention camp and talk to detainees alone. I compiled a great dossier about what they told me and said I would present it to the Governor.

On my last morning I allowed myself the indulgence of a swim with Peter Benenson round the rocky Mediterranean shores of Kyrenia. I wrote later in my diary, 'As we milled about in the water and looked across its perfect blueness at the distant hills of Anatolia, we agreed what a tourist paradise and gold mine the island could be if only the emergency were removed.' Our swim was followed by a drink in the hot sun, lunch with Mrs Foley and a mad dash to the airport accompanied by Mossman of the *Daily Herald*, a sympathetic chap who was nonetheless after his journalistic pound of flesh. In the few minutes we had at the airport he wanted a quote about what view I had formed of the treatment of Greek Cypriots by the security forces. I thought I was playing safe when I repeated what Sir Hugh had said to me almost word for word. I believed, I said, 'that the troops were permitted and even encouraged to use unnecessarily rough measures after a shooting incident on the grounds that they were engaged in hot pursuit.' 'Encouraged?', queried Mossman. 'I withdraw that,' I said, though I privately believed that Sir Hugh's attitude did nothing to restrain it. Nonetheless, despite my withdrawal, the word 'encouraged' went down the line. I boarded my plane confident that I had successfully avoided the pitfalls in this tricky area.

At Athens airport, I was greeted not only by Kyprianou but by a young man from the Greek Foreign Office bringing a personal welcome from the Prime Minister and accompanied by clicking cameras. 'And then I knew the plan was really on,' I wrote in my diary that night, 'and that Makarios was going to do his stuff.' I had read in the Cyprus press that he had spent four hours with the Greek Cabinet that morning, and I could guess what had been discussed. Kyprianou told me my appointment with the Archbishop was within the hour. Mercifully, I had managed to change into something moderately respectable on the plane. But I had not had time to wash the salt off my face and had to content myself with putting another layer of powder on it instead.

Thus patched up I walked into Makarios' room at the Ethnarchy to find a battery of television cameras awaiting me. 'I sat there,' I noted, 'wishing the ends of my hair had not started curling all the wrong way after my swim.' But Makarios and I posed obediently, endlessly shaking hands and looking into each other's eyes. 'He is an expert in this kind of thing,' I wrote in my diary,

> managing to appear as though he is smiling straight at you while really curious shutters are going up and down over his eyes. Nonetheless I like him. His gentleness, coupled with a steeliness of purpose, was very impressive. I do not think 'wily' is the right word for him. He obviously cares deeply for his Greek Cypriots and is always thinking out his next moves on their behalf. His almost film-star poise (he arranges his robes and his hat with the elegant motions of a model) is misleading for it disguises what I think is a very real sincerity. And if he uses his

wits, who can blame him? It is the only weapon a small power has against a big.

With the cameras out of the way, Makarios opened his hands in a warm gesture of welcome and asked 'What is the report?' I replied, 'Bad.' The British government did not seem to want to know. His eyes narrowed when I told him of Esenbel's statement to me in Ankara that the Turkish government had written assurances from the British that the Macmillan plan meant partition. The only hope, I told him, was for him to make a clear renunciation of *enosis* through me. He agreed, but at first tried to suggest that the interview should be in the form of a question by me asking what his reaction would be if the Labour Party were to propose the abandonment of *enosis* in favour of independence for Cyprus within the Commonwealth. I turned this down firmly. It would look as if we were playing party politics. The only course was for him to volunteer a statement, which he eventually agreed.

I was sent away with Kyprianou to type out on my little portable, which I carried everywhere, the statement I believed he should make, which I was to bring to Makarios for approval the following morning. So I typed away until 11 p.m., tired, hungry and still caked with sea water. When I had finished, Kyprianou took me out for a much needed meal in an excellent open-air restaurant. He then took me on to a nightclub where I saw more revealing striptease than Paris could produce. Kyprianou sat there correct and unperturbed while a bath was brought into the middle of the floor in which a beautiful naked Greek girl bathed herself seductively. I decided that this was an important part of my education in the complications of international diplomacy.

The next day went like a fantasy. Makarios agreed my draft statement with slight amendments. I had, before coming, entered into a rough arrangement with the powerful American agency BUP, whose editors got very excited when I relayed Makarios' statement to them over the transatlantic line.

All that remained that day was to make my promised visit to Karamanlis. It was even more of a fairy tale. 'The whole Greek army', I wrote in my diary, 'was lined up to salute me and I was ushered deferentially along corridors amidst excited comment. I felt more like a diplomatic Mata Hari every minute. Once again Karamanlis almost embraced me as I entered his room.' When I told Karamanlis what Makarios had agreed he almost panicked for a moment. When I added that what Makarios had agreed was being issued the same day, he rallied to say 'I accept it too,' though he hoped the Labour Party would endorse the plan before he had to endorse it. I hoped so too and was reasonably confident that it would, because what I had achieved was in line with what John Hatch had been pressing on the National Executive for some time.

The next day, I flew home, quietly proud of the fact that I had helped to achieve a turning point in the history of the Cyprus tragedy. There it all was in the newspapers. The BUP had done its stuff and there were splash headlines about Makarios' change of line, accompanied by pictures of us looking into each other's eyes. I did not mind overmuch that the whole idea was put down to Makarios. This after all was the condition I had insisted on with him. But I was a bit peeved later when BUP declined to contribute a penny towards my expenses because I had refused to give them an exclusive, insisting that the story should get the widest possible coverage. But I was buoyed up by the knowledge that what I had achieved was completely in line with Labour's policy.

I had reckoned without the minefield of politics. The only press interest which awaited me on my arrival in London concerned not what I had said to Makarios but what I had said about the troops. I doubt if the press would have taken much notice of my carefully chosen words if one of my right-wing enemies on the National Executive, Jim Matthews, had not seized the opportunity to pose as a patriotic defender of the British troops by launching a personal attack on me. Matthews was the dour left-baiting national officer of the General and Municipal Workers' Union, whom I disliked intensely and who I am certain hated me. He actually volunteered a statement to the press to the effect that my remarks about the troops were 'deplorable' and a 'stab in the back' for our serving men. Naturally enough, the press made a meal of it. 'BABS' BOOB' screamed the *Daily Sketch* headline in its boldest-possible type. The *Daily Mail* had it that I had been denounced by a 'Party chief', the *Daily Telegraph* by a socialist, descriptions by which few of Jim Matthews' colleagues would have recognized him. The *Mail* was not the only paper to suggest that the row might cost me the party chairmanship.

It could be argued that if I had been a more seasoned politician I would have refused to take any interest in the Greek Cypriots' complaints and risked alienating them at a crucial stage in my talks with Makarios. Certainly if I could have foreseen what would happen I would have refused to make any comment at all, but this error of judgment, if it was one, can happen to the most cautious of politicians, and the only thing to do when it happens is to ride out the storm defiantly. To be attacked by a hostile press is not the greatest tragedy that can happen to a party which is challenging its way to power. On the contrary, it has the saving grace of drawing public attention to what one has to say and gives one the opportunity of turning the tables on one's critics, as I did later in press interviews and on television. The best defence is always to attack, as Mrs Thatcher was to teach us dramatically thirty years later. Caution does not always pay in politics.

No such fighting spirit was shown by Hugh Gaitskell when I went at my own request to report to him on my visit. He was backed by Nye, Jim Griffiths and Jim Callaghan and I did not get a word of sympathy or support from any of them, just a united front of cold disapproval. They refused to see Makarios' offer as a hopeful development: in fact they were clearly annoyed with me for fouling their line of support for the Macmillan plan. After grilling me for over an hour, Gaitskell emerged to tell the press that my visit to Greece, Turkey and Cyprus, and my statement to the press, had been made in my personal capacity and not as a party representative. The Labour Party, he declared, was horrified by the brutal murders perpetrated by the terrorists and appreciated that these soldiers were operating under great strain. As for the wider issues of policy, they would be considered by the National Executive.

The press had another bonanza the following day when I was variously described as having been 'rapped', 'carpeted', 'rebuked' and 'disowned'. The only person who leaped to my defence was Tom Driberg, who, in his role as chairman of the party, criticized Jim Matthews for making a personal attack when personal attacks were expressly prohibited by party rules.

It was not a pleasant experience but I was not too downcast. I knew that the deal I had done with Makarios would be warmly welcomed by conference and that few unions would relish Jim Matthews being cast as their mouthpiece. And so it proved. There was not a murmur of a suggestion on the Executive that I should not be confirmed as the next year's chairman and I was re-elected to the NEC with an increased vote, though in second place, Tony Greenwood having climbed to the top of the constituency section the previous year. Hurried moves were made by the party managers to restore the image of party harmony by setting up a photocall for me having an amicable cup of tea with Jim Matthews, smiling at each other as though we had been bosom friends for life.

True, I was not allowed to speak on Cyprus at conference. To most people it would have seemed natural that I should have been given a small slot to explain exactly what Makarios had said to me, but Gaitskell would have none of it. Instead, Nye dealt with the Cyprus issue in the debate on foreign affairs and made a belated recognition of the importance of the Makarios offer by saying it should be 'sincerely examined', although he carefully did not mention my part in it. I had my chance at a fringe meeting on Cyprus organized by the Movement for Colonial Freedom, at which I was received enthusiastically by a large audience. Unfortunately, my speech was drowned by a group of Empire Loyalists who heckled and shouted all the way through my speech and had to be bundled out. This gave the press the diversionary story they were looking for, and lurid copy was filed about how violently interrupters were dealt with at Labour meetings. So blinkered were the press that they missed the most human story of all: that some of the alleged violence came from my own Ted in one of his peppery-old-colonel moods. When one Empire Loyalist shouted 'Traitor!' at me several times, Ted leaped across rows of seats to

305

get at him, seized him by the collar and shouted, 'No one calls my wife a traitor!' He had to be pulled off by the stewards, who allowed the frightened heckler to escape.

My nastiest moment came when we conference delegates were returning home. As a crowd of us streamed off the conference train at Euston on the Friday night, floodlights were suddenly flashed into my face, microphones pushed under my nose and voices demanded behind whirring cameras, 'What do you say about the murder of Mrs Cutliffe, Mrs Castle?' It was the first time I had heard that a British sergeant's wife, mother of five children, had been shot in the back while shopping at Famagusta that morning and her woman companion seriously wounded. I was shattered. How could I explain in such circumstances that this was just what I had been working to avoid? All I could murmur was 'Tragic, terribly tragic,' but the incident was used to build up hatred against me once again. 'Well, Barbara, what do you say now?' was the front-page lead in the next day's *Sketch* over a photo of me with my mouth open, looking stupefied. What the British press did not report was that Mrs Cutliffe's murder released an orgy of retaliation by British troops, who went through Famagusta rounding up every Greek Cypriot male, dragging some of them out of their homes with uncontrolled brutality and smashing windows. Charles Foley was later to write in his book *Island in Revolt* about these reprisals that my comment 'on the licence allowed to troops in Paphos a month before had been proved justified by 250 new Cypriot casualties and four deaths' (one of them a British serviceman accidentally shot in the turmoil).

It would be foolish to pretend that this media pressure is not unnerving or that it does not have its immediate political effect. But in my political experience it is remarkable how short-lived these exaggerations of emotions are. If one can only keep one's nerve and plug away at a reasoned argument, the natural fairness and common sense of the British people rally to one's side. That is what I found. Two months later, I was astonished to receive a Christmas card from the Royal Argyll and Sutherland Highlanders serving in Cyprus. I examined it, front, back and sideways, convinced that I would find a snide satirical message tucked away somewhere, but there was none – merely the conventional printed message 'With every good wish for Christmas and the New Year' and handwritten below it 'President and Members, Sergeants' mess'. Who sent it and why I shall never know, but its message was confirmed during the general election campaign the following year, when my opponents were trying to exploit to the uttermost the attack I was supposed to have made on British troops. A young soldier who had been serving in Cyprus came to me and volunteered to speak on my platform in my defence. He told the audience in simple terms that most soldiers who had served there did not support the attacks that had been made on me. They did not feel I had done anything against the troops when I had been in Cyprus. Naturally I alerted the national newspapers to the fact that he was going to speak in my support, but none of them reported him. His speech did not fit into their election scenario.

On my return from Cyprus I had sent a message to Lennox Boyd to say I was ready to meet him at any time to report on my talk with Makarios. But he was in no hurry. Not until three weeks later did he agree to see me, by which time Macmillan had already rejected Makarios' offer and said he intended to press ahead with the imposition of the Macmillan plan. Hugh Foot had already shown which way the wind was blowing: twenty-four hours after my talk with Makarios he broadcast to the people of Cyprus, declaring, 'We must not be deflected by violence from the policy which we know is right.'

But outside Britain other world leaders were reacting differently. Paul Henri Spaak, Secretary-General of NATO, who had since August been pressing his own alternative plan to the Macmillan one, took Makarios' offer seriously. At the NATO General Council he proposed that the Macmillan plan should be put in cold storage and a conference of interested parties convened by NATO to consider alternatives. There then ensued convoluted manoeuvrings by the British government both in NATO and at the United Nations to stop its allies from accepting Spaak's initiatives. The dramatic climax came when the foreign ministers of Greece and Turkey, Evangelos Averoff and Fatin Zorlu, at a meeting in Zurich, decided to cut the corners and settle the messy affair themselves without the benefit of British face-saving. The result was an agreement that Cyprus should become an independent state with both *enosis* and partition excluded, an agreement which Macmillan was forced to accept. A conference was called in London to embody it.

At Lancaster House on 19 February 1959 Cyprus became an independent state, with a Greek Cypriot president and a Turkish Cypriot vice-president, her independence guaranteed by Britain, Greece and Turkey. Britain renounced her sovereignty over the island except for her two bases, and a Treaty of Alliance was signed between Greece, Turkey and Cyprus in which they undertook to defend Cyprus's territorial integrity. So those of us who had been insisting that a compromise was possible had been proved right.

Makarios kept his word to me but I learned at second hand that he was worried about a number of points in the new constitution, notably the blocking power over legislation given to the Turkish vice-president. He feared, with some justification, that this could keep communal hostility alive. Nonetheless, after a night of anxious cogitation, he signed the agreement and the following year became President of the new independent state, with Dr Sadil Kutchuk as Turkish vice-president. A miracle had been achieved.

For some time after the settlement there was peace in Cyprus and the tourist industry flourished, as Peter Benenson and I had hoped. A few years later Ted and I decided to taste its delights and spent and idyllic fortnight there, starting in a transformed Kyrenia. We swam in the blue sea from the rocks surrounding our hotel, fell in love with the picturesque little harbour and drove into the hills to drink resinous wine in the cafés of the peaceful Greek villages. I even learned to dance the Zorba with the help of the proprietor and his daughter in a simple little open-air, jasmine-scented nightclub, very different from the one to which Kyprianou had taken me in Athens. We did not like Famagusta as much. It had a superb sandy beach but this was flanked by a row of tall modern hotels which kept the sun off it in the afternoon. This was a tourist development of which we did not approve.

During our stay, I decided I would like to see Makarios, who, like most sensible Cypriots, spent the hot season in the Troodos Mountains. Our phone call to him brought a warm response: he would send his car for us. Our drive into the mountains was nerve-wracking, as the Archbishop's driver went at breakneck speed up the narrow roads. We were told by Greeks afterwards that Makarios was driven everywhere at 100 miles an hour as a precaution against the many assassination threats which he recieved. Makarios himself appeared to be unchanged – serene and as enigmatic as ever, with his film-star poise – but he treated us cordially. He admitted to us that he was worried about the way things on the island were developing. The relationship between the two communities was still too tense. He admitted, too, that the rush into tourism was inadequately controlled. When we complained about Famagusta he agreed that it was an example of the lack of planning laws. I had the feeling that in any normal situation he would have made an excellent prime minister, but the situation was not normal and I sensed he felt under constant threat.

When I next went to Cyprus, Makarios was dead, victim of a heart attack in 1977. His death must have been hastened by the attempted coup against him in 1974 by emissaries of the Greek colonels led by a right-wing Greek Cypriot, Nicos Sampson, who had never accepted the Lancaster House settlement. I was taken to the Presidential Palace in Nicosia to see the bullet marks on the walls inflicted when an attempt had been made to capture Makarios and murder him as a traitor to the Greek cause. Ironically, he was saved then by the British forces stationed in Britain's Akrotiri base, who gave him refuge and smuggled him out of the island. The Sampson coup failed, bringing the colonels' regime in Greece down with it, but it gave the Turkish government the excuse it had been looking for to move in its troops and partition the island, drawing arbitrary lines through Greek areas, forcing their inhabitants out of their homes and settling Turks from the mainland in their property. Kyrenia came under Turkish occupation. Famagusta, also annexed, became a ghost town. Nicosia, the capital, was split between the two communities by frontiers patrolled by armed guards. Cyprus became a military battleground instead of a tourist's paradise. If Macmillan had backed Makarios' change of line, built up his authority against the right-wing elements who were pressing for *enosis* and kept the Turks under control, the tragic partition of Cyprus need never have taken place.

The foreign ministers of the European Community have unanimously condemned Turkey's aggression, but nothing happens. Negotiations in the United Nations to find a settlement drag on futilely. Turkey digs in her heels, conscious that she is still the darling of the NATO strategists. Whatever the mistakes made by the Greek Cypriots, they are not a patch on the blunders of British diplomacy.

THIRTEEN

•

Defeat and Resurrection

UNPERTURBED BY the succession of colonial fiascos in Cyprus, Hola and Nyasaland, Macmillan sailed into the election campaign with great panache. He proceeded to demonstrate the manipulative skills which Harold Wilson always watched with envy. A heady mixture of principled statesman and political charlatan, he appreciated the importance of the feel-good factor at election time long before the phrase entered into the common language of party strategists. He knew that foreign-affairs issues did not win or lose votes. What mattered was what people felt in their stomachs, not their principles. He therefore set out to rig the economic scene regardless of the real state of the British economy.

I watched his performance in the House and on television with a growing sense of helplessness. He was a consummate performer in both media. With his aura of aristocratic unflappability, he managed to give the impression that all was well, when in fact Britain was still struggling with the aftermath of the Suez débâcle. The austerity measures which Macmillan himself had introduced as Chancellor of the Exchequer in 1955 had had to be extended for another year because of the continuing run on sterling, and for the first time in British history the government had had to seek a loan from the International Monetary Fund to replenish its reserves. It was hardly a picture of brilliant political management.

So precarious was Britain's situation that when Macmillan succeeded Eden as Prime Minister in January 1957, he allowed Peter Thorneycroft, his newly appointed Chancellor of the Exchequer, to continue a policy of such restraint that by 1958 Britain's annual rate of growth had sunk below 1 per cent. This was too much for Macmillan, the man who as early as 1938 had argued for expansionist policies in *The Middle Way*, and for the populist politician who could see electoral disaster looming. He decided that Peter Thorneycroft had to go. This abrupt change of line outraged the rest of the monetarists in the Treasury team, Enoch Powell and Nigel Birch, who resigned in protest, a development which Macmillan dismissed as a 'little local difficulty'.

The way was clear for some electoral scene-setting. In Derick Heathcoat Amory, Macmillan found a more pliant Chancellor, who put the austerity policy into reverse and, as a climax, produced the election Budget of April 1959. It was a cornucopia of goodies: cuts in income tax, cuts in purchase tax, the restoration of investment allowances and the lavish releasing of the post-war credits, the IOUs issued by the government to savers during the war which up to now had been honoured only gradually by successive administrations. The result was an inevitable consumer-spending spree as people rushed to buy the capital goods they had been denied for so long.

It was a tactic with which the Labour Party was becoming familiar, and once again it worked. Voters did not stop to ask where the money for all this had suddenly come from or how long it would last. Macmillan was in his element in the part of Santa Claus, expansively assuring the electorate that they had never had it so good. A Tory election broadcast showed a modest home inhabited by a family on a modest income who suddenly had a little car in the garage, a washing machine in the kitchen and a new television set in the sitting room. Nye remarked in the House, 'The Prime Minister has an absolute genius for putting flamboyant labels on empty luggage.' But the luggage was not empty: it was merely that its contents had been bought on the never-never and there was no assurance that they would not be taken back as they had been in 1955.

The Labour Party struggled against this irresistible tide by seeking to modernize the presentation of its policies. I was the first on the NEC to welcome its decision to call in our friend, Hugh Cudlipp of the *Mirror*, to advise us on how to communicate.

As a former employee of the paper I had long been distressed by the turgid verbosity of our party's policy documents. My Ted, a *Mirror* product too, had revolutionized the layout, not only of my election addresses, but of those of any Labour candidate who appealed to him for help. So I approved of the mock-up of the election manifesto that Cudlipp's team produced. It was in the form of a booklet with a glossy cover in green, white, red and black, its every brief section indexed with a little tab.

Then again we had spent a record sum, for us, on a poster campaign: no less than £20,000. It was about one-tenth of what our opponents spent, but it had at least enabled us to make a limited appearance on the hoardings. Again we had begun to cultivate the (for us) neglected art of the photo-call. As chairman of the party I was whisked around all over the place, and our most dramatic climax came when I went to the airport to welcome Hugh Gaitskell and Nye Bevan back from a Moscow trip which they had undertaken as part of our election campaign. We produced a dramatic photograph of me in the middle holding their hands triumphantly aloft which got a very good press coverage.

There were of course members of the hairshirt brigade in the party who disapproved of all this razzmatazz. I was never one of them. I had been irritated for years by the party's total indifference to appearances. I did not at all mind the rough and tumble of our party conference debates which, in my view, contrasted favourably with the smooth insincerity of the managed debates of the Tory conferences. I believed – and still do – that the democratic virility people saw on the screens during our conferences was a plus. But I also believed that people needed to see a bit of pageant, too. I was tired of struggling on to the platform with other members of the National Executive at the opening of the conference while an organ in the background droned out a far from rousing tune. I was sick of sitting at a trestle table on the platform which was thinly draped with red muslin and of snagging my stockings on its rough underside. I did not see why we could not combine political sincerity with a little presentational panache. I wanted a few frills, but fire in the belly too.

But none of these efforts saved us from defeat. We knew we

would have an uphill struggle against Macmillan's brilliant stage-management, but the size of the Tory majority was a shock. Although the swing to the Tories was surprisingly only 1 per cent it gave them a majority over Labour of 107 seats. The Liberals, though polling 1 million more votes than before, returned the same number of MPs. This was, of course, good ammunition for the electoral reformers, who were just beginning to raise their heads, but I remained stubbornly of the view that our first-past-the-post system reflected the national mood and certainly saved us from the political fragmentation of countries in Europe which subordinated great swings of political opinion to their search for arithmetical purity. I had no doubt that the majority of the British people wanted to gamble on Macmillan's miracle, that the Liberals bored most people to death and that the Labour Party deserved to lose. We had had no strategy to offset the arts of the supreme stage-manager. We had made no imaginative attempts to alert the men and women on the factory floor to the dangers of Britain's insidious industrial decline. We had not even mobilized the moral vote, which could have laid us up psychological treasure in our reformist heaven. Instead the motto was caution, caution, caution – as our leaders' reaction over Cyprus had shown.

The final recipe for electoral defeat was produced by Gaitskell, who, in a speech at Newcastle which he delivered without consulting the Campaign Committee, promised on the one hand that the next Labour government would increase old-age pensions (which had not been increased for years) and build new hospitals, while undertaking on the other hand that there would be no increase in income tax and that purchase tax on essential articles would be abolished. It was a recipe for winning the incredulity – even the contempt – of the electorate.

Ian Mikardo lost Reading, Lena Jeger lost St Pancras and Michael Foot was not returned to the House. I myself not only survived at Blackburn, but actually increased my majority from the alarming 500 in 1955 to 2500. This was interesting in view of the fact that the Tories thought they had got me on the run over what I had said about the troops in Cyprus. They devoted one of their election broadcasts to this, in the course of which Chris

Chataway claimed that I had accused the soldiers in Cyprus of the 'torture' of Greek Cypriots. I was so furious about this distortion that I slapped in a libel writ. I later realized that this was a mistake because it gave the press an excuse not to report anything on Cyprus which seemed to justify my line. I should have let it ride, because most of my voters did not believe it anyway.

Stafford Cripps had always argued that it was impossible for any socialist in Britain to win a political libel case. I felt that withdrawal would be taken by the press as a confession of guilt, so I went ahead when the election was over. Stafford, however, was right. The judge was Mr Justice Sachs, son-in-law of Lord Chief Justice Goddard who was noted for his right-wing views. Sachs' summing-up was hostile, but the jury clearly wanted to find for me. They kept coming back for definitions of 'torture', because they did not see how my words about the soldiers being permitted to use 'unnecessarily tough measures when engaged in hot pursuit' bore the remotest relationship to the Oxford Dictionary definition of torture as 'the infliction of severe bodily pain as punishment or method of persuasion' or alternatively as the infliction of 'severe or excruciating pain . . . anguish, agony or torment'. Sachs found a form of words in some obscure dictionary which might be held to cover my remarks and sternly sent them back again. After two or three hours they returned to report unhappily that they had found for Chataway. My solicitor, David Jacobs, was furious and told me, 'If you were a wealthier woman I would advise you to appeal.' But that I could not afford to do.

It was a blow, particularly as we faced legal costs of £8000, a fortune in those days. Yet we emerged to meet the press smiling as buoyantly as if we had won. 'Don't worry, love,' said my loyal Ted cheerfully. 'We'll sell the house.' We were saved by Morgan Phillips from his sickbed, where he was recovering from a stroke. I had often been a thorn in his side but he volunteered immediately to launch an appeal in the party to pay my costs. The response was generous, so we didn't lose the roof over our heads. It was an example of the party's comradeship in adversity which has always warmed my heart.

The party's third electoral defeat in a row inevitably had a shattering effect on our morale. What had gone wrong?, everyone began to ask. At a long meeting of the National Executive we all came in with our pet theories. No one this time could blame the Bevanites, because Nye had healed the split. So the right-wingers seized the opportunity to demand a further watering down of the party's already diluted policies. Nationalization, they argued, was the millstone around our necks. People would not have it and it had lost us votes. Nye listened for a long time and then came in quietly. What we had to realize, he told us, was that people always rationalize the reasons for voting as they do because they want to make their real reasons appear respectable. The reasons why we lost this time were obvious. Nationalization was irrelevant. Working men and women were enjoying a whole range of new satisfactions for the first time since the war, and the very fact that these satisfactions were financed on the never-never and were therefore precarious merely made them the enemy of change. This was the challenge the Labour movement had to face.

Turning to 'my trade union friends', he rebuked them gently for not spending as much time and energy on educating their members on these wider political realities as they did on pursuing short-term sectional interests. We had allowed our political opponents to set the worker as consumer against the worker as producer, whereas in a civilized society the two would be seen to be interdependent, because the worker–producer was a consumer, too. I never forgot his final warning: 'The trade unionist votes at the polls against the consequences of his own wild-cat strikes.' It was a theme I was to hammer home in my own document *In Place of Strife*.

The key inquest, of course, was held at the delayed party conference shortly afterwards. Our normal conference had had to be suspended because of the election, so I found myself presiding as chairman over a two-day rump conference at Blackpool at the end of November. It was one of the most harrowing and yet inspiring weekends I have ever spent. To begin with I had to write out my chairman's speech in time for it to be distributed to delegates as they assembled – something which was wholly contrary to my style. The occasion clearly warranted more than the routine platitudes and I stayed up half the night trying to write the speech, riddled with doubt about the validity of every word. I arrived on the platform the next morning convinced that it would be a flop. Instead, to my astonishment, it was one of the major successes of my political career.

Somehow my message got through as I analysed the superficiality of the capitalist boom we were going through and the failure of the government to build a strong and well-balanced society. 'You cannot', I argued, 'separate moral issues from economic ones. The morality of a society is not created in a vacuum: it springs from the way it organizes its economic life and distributes its rewards.' The Macmillan government had failed to do either properly. 'Today we are making more TV aerials than houses to put them on. Millions of pounds are spent encouraging our children to eat more sweets per head than any children in the world while the government starves the school dental service.' Macmillan would never have won the election if he had persisted with the policies he had pursued up to 1958. 'It must be unprecedented', I jibed, 'for a Prime Minister to seek a mandate to stop carrying out his own policies.' And I ended with a challenge to conference:

> Are we prepared to affirm that what Nye has called 'the commanding heights of the economy' must be publicly financed under public ownership? Of course this does not mean we want to nationalize everything from atomic energy to pin-table saloons. But it does mean that the community must control, inspire and finance new industrial developments.

What Nye called 'the commanding heights of the economy' had to be publicly financed and under public control.

Of all the compliments I received at the end of my speech the one which gave me most gratification was from the old sceptic Dick Crossman, my oft-time critic, who in one television interview awarded me the accolade of Woman of the Year, saying I had stolen the show from Bevan and Gaitskell 'by making what is usually a purely formal introduction the most powerful speech of the conference'. He noted with glee in his diary, 'What really did Hugh [Gaitskell] down was the contrast between Barbara's attack on the Tory economy and his own apparent complacent acceptance of it as satisfactory and stable.'

I was less successful, however, in my conduct of conference. The only hall available in Blackpool at that time was a cinema, which meant that, although the platform was flooded with television lights, the body of the hall was sunk in sepulchral gloom. A feature of our conferences, of which delegates are very jealous, is that, apart from the movers and seconders of resolutions and amendments, speakers are not selected beforehand and in theory everyone in the hall has an equal chance to speak. In practice, of course, the chairman knows that there are certain obvious people who must be called, such as a union boss in a debate closely affecting his union, but woe betide the chairman who does not strike a fair balance between union and constituency delegates, between the famous and the unknown.

My trouble was that in the gloom before me I could not see a thing. All I could do in selecting speakers was to point wildly into a corner of the darkness below me saying 'You' and hope that somebody appropriate would emerge. By the alchemy of politics the person who usually emerged was one of the high and mighty like Frank Cousins, because everyone sitting around him assumed I was playing favourites and must be indicating him. Sometimes when I located an area where constituency delegates were sitting, half a dozen delegates would spring up in answer to my 'You' and argue among themselves while I struggled to identify my choice more precisely through the gloom. The result was chaotic, and my chairmanship was badly panned in the press. The most hilarious comment appeared in the *Spectator*'s Notebook whose author wrote that my chairmanship 'was so fantastically bad that I was moved to inquire plaintively at one point whether the job could not be handed over to Sir Arthur Comyns Carr, whose memorable ineptitude in the chair at the Liberal Assembly at Torquay could be at any rate partially excused on the grounds that he is twenty-nine years older than she is and slightly hard of hearing'.

But all these stresses and strains were forgotten as Nye rose to wind up the great inquest. Hugh, Nye and I sat on the platform like a ruling triumvirate, Hugh on my right and Nye on my left. I had opened the debate with my chairman's speech, which had roused the delegates. Hugh had followed the next day with a speech obviously designed to tone down some of the enthusiasm for public ownership which I had inspired. He had begun with a long laundry list of economic facts which had bored the audience: not for the first time I wondered how a man so able could be so pedestrian. But the sting was in the tail. Nationalization, concluded Gaitskell, had been the major vote-loser and he served notice that he was out to rewrite the party's holiest text – Clause IV of the constitution – which Sidney Webb and Arthur Henderson had drafted forty years earlier. Its demand for 'the common ownership of the means of production, distribution and exchange' was out of date. As Nye had said, we needed to control 'the commanding heights of the economy', but how far we had to go at any one time was 'a matter for discussion'. Public ownership was not an end in itself, but the means to an end, and not the only means and perhaps not a means at all.

Delegates had been muttering angrily about his speech ever since and it looked as though this conference might provide the very split which the press had been predicting was bound to come.

So when Nye rose to wind up, both press and delegates craned forward expectantly. Was he going to stir the pot? Whose side was he on? They underestimated the Nye I knew so well – the man who could charm his way out of any difficulty if he had a mind to, and this time he was out to avoid the split the press was hoping for. So he teased us all. Even at his board school, he told us, he had been taught Euclid's proposition that if two things are equal to a third thing, then they are equal to each other. I had quoted Nye's 'commanding heights of the economy'; so had Gaitskell. So if Euclid's proposition were correct, Hugh and I were both equal to him and therefore to each other. 'So we have a kind of Trinity,' he said mischievously, adding in his seductive Welsh lilt, 'What does that make me: the Holy Ghost?' Conference collapsed in laughter. The crisis had passed, and delegates went home feeling that the forces of unity were stronger than those of disunity. I was not the only one who believed that it was not beyond the bounds of political possibility that Nye might after all become leader of the party.

Indeed Nye with his 'commanding heights of the economy' formula had done more to reinterpret Clause IV than Hugh Gaitskell could ever do. The formula was a sensitive response to the intellectual struggles going on among the left as we faced the growing complexities of the modern economy. Few of us had ever wanted to impose a centralized command economy on Soviet lines. It had produced some dramatic scientific and technological developments, such as the sputnik, the first-ever satellite to be launched and the pioneer of the space age, which was now circling the moon to the envy of the West, but it had failed to respond to consumers' desire for choice in a whole range of daily necessities. As production and people's expectations became more sophisticated I for one realized that central planning and control had to be limited to setting the broad economic parameters and that the satisfaction of consumers' more detailed needs was best left to the play of supply and demand in the market. In fact most of us had long accepted the need for a mixed economy, and the main argument with the right was about the size of the public sector and whether it should have any industrial role at all. There was already a move in certain sections of the party to embrace the whole Tory philosophy that the market was king and that market forces should decide the priorities in values of economic policy. Nye's formula was a safeguard against those who argued for the total abandonment of government powers and government responsibility in the industrial field.

Seven months later, Nye Bevan was dead. Without any of us realizing it, perhaps not even Nye himself, stomach cancer must already have started its inroads into his life. One of the last big speeches I heard him make in Parliament was in the Queen's

Speech debate in November when the triumphant new government met Parliament for the first time. To me it was the epitome of his political genius. He was relaxed and genial. Yes, the government had won a very big majority, but what were they going to do with it? He warned Tory MPs, who had come to taunt but had stayed to listen in silence, that the government was failing to solve 'the central problem falling upon representative government in the Western world': how to persuade the people to forgo immediate satisfactions in order to build up the capital equipment on which future economic strength depended. The Labour government had failed to solve this problem because, while devoting the resources necessary to long-term development, it had sacrificed its parliamentary majority. The government was failing the other way round – it had kept its parliamentary majority at the cost of the country's long-term needs. And he returned to his favourite theme, which I had heard him expound in so many speeches: we must educate the voters in a democracy not to eat the seedcorn of tomorrow's harvest, because otherwise democracy will fail. His taunt against the government was that it had not even tried.

Nye's death united the House of Commons. It is always claimed that the House is at its best on these occasions. Nye would have said it is at its most hypocritical, but there was a genuine emotion as the tributes were paid, as though even Nye's most bitter opponents realized that a dynamic democratic force had gone out of British politics. Macmillan's tribute was simple rather than sonorous: 'he was sometimes harsh, but never trite. . . . He expressed in himself, his career and his life some of the deepest feelings of humble people throughout the land.' Even Gaitskell was inspired to one of his rare bursts of eloquence:

His death is as if a fire had gone out, a fire which we sometimes found too hot, by which we were sometimes scorched, a fire which flamed and flickered unpredictably. But a fire which warmed us and cheered us and stimulated us. A fire which affected the atmosphere of our lives here and illuminated all our proceedings. Now that it has gone out, I think we are peculiarly conscious of the change, of a certain coldness and greyness that has come.

Churchill, who still occupied the special seat on the government front bench reserved for him, though he was no longer capable of taking part in debates, sat with bowed head. One copy-seeking journalist wrote that he wiped away a tear. That I do not believe, though I do believe he would have delivered the most moving tribute of them all if he had still had control of his faculties. I myself fought back my tears unsuccessfully.

Ironically, the death of Labour's most controversial figure did not lead to party peace. I had written in the *New Statesman*, 'Nye Bevan is dead and the emotions I feel are despair and love.' I felt despair because I feared a resurgence of the old bitterness that would split the party again. Gaitskell proved me right, and proceeded to give full rein to his two major flaws: stubborn dogmatism and a pedantic obsession with detail. The first bitter fruits were reaped in a battle over defence policy, which came to a head at the 1960 party conference. It was a battle which most of us thought need not have taken place.

The occasion was the tabling of a resolution on nuclear weapons by Frank Cousins' union, which he had won over to his unilateralist line. Frank was rapidly establishing himself as the leader of the trade union left, but the resolution was not a frontal attack on Labour's official policy. It did not call for our withdrawal from NATO or make any specific reference to the British bomb. It called for the cessation of nuclear tests, but so had Labour spokesmen. Its most controversial item was the demand for 'the complete rejection of any defence policy based on the threat of the use of nuclear weapons'. Even here there was room for argument as to what it meant. Clarity of phraseology was never Frank Cousins' strong point and some of us urged that 'no threat of the use' of nuclear weapons was entirely compatible with Labour's 'no first strike' policy. Nonetheless, Gaitskell immediately saw in it the sinister hand of CND and rushed into a public denunciation of the resolution and of Frank Cousins and all his works, thus engendering a personal enmity between the two men. It was as though Gaitskell had a psychological need for another political demon to take Nye's place.

George Brown was as taken aback as anyone by Gaitskell's stubbornness. As our defence spokesman he was aware that the whole of the government's nuclear strategy was in the melting pot following the cancellation that year of Blue Streak – the British missile which had been intended to put us in the independent nuclear deterrent league. In the House a few months earlier George had taunted the Minister of Defence, Harold Watkinson, and his colleagues for having spent three years and £65 million before discovering that Blue Streak's liquid fuel system was so slow in firing that it could be blown up by the enemy before even leaving the launching pad. He also added that this failure meant that Labour might have to reconsider its attitude to the British bomb. A review of our defence policy was thereupon conducted by a joint committee of the TUC and the NEC; Dick was a member, but I was not. It produced a statement which, compared with previous official policy, went a remarkably long way to meet Cousins' points. It called, for example, for a review of NATO's strategy to ensure that the West would never be the first to use the H-bomb nor base its strategy on threatening to do so. It demanded an end to British tests pending an international agreement to end all tests and opposed the establishment of Thor nuclear missile bases in Britain. Most remarkable of all was its statement that the 'Blue Streak fiasco has shown that Britain cannot maintain herself as an independent nuclear power. In future the provision of the thermonuclear deterrent must be left to the USA.' George Brown endorsed the statement enthusiastically.

If Nye Bevan had lived, I believe agreement could have been reached at conference on the basis of accepting both the Cousins resolution and the joint statement, which could be held to interpret it. That is what George Brown was pressing for. He wrote an article for the *New Statesman* denouncing those who wanted a showdown with the words: 'What damned nonsense is all this.' Dick Crossman circulated a memorandum to the Executive saying that the joint statement and the Cousins resolution were compatible and that we should accept both. Tony Benn engaged in one of his pieces of private enterprise with which I was to become familiar, emerging as a peacemaker at the eve-of-conference Executive meeting and urging that even at this late hour Gaitskell and Cousins should meet to settle their differences. When this was turned down he resigned from the Executive and told the press waiting outside the meeting room that he had done so as a protest against the fact that 'so many of the party's leaders can view the prospect of a split with apparent unconcern'. Naturally it hit the headlines and left his normal political allies, not for the last time, wondering if they had been politically remiss in not resigning too.

Despite these efforts the Executive proceeded to vote down the Cousins resolution by thirteen votes to seven. Because we knew this was going to happen four of us – Harry Nicholas, Tony Greenwood, Tom Driberg and I – voted against the joint statement, although we agreed with a great deal of it. It was carried by thirteen votes to four. Looking back with hindsight and the wisdom of later years I think we were wrong and should have voted for both of them. After all the joint statement met us on the major point: that it pledged a Labour government not to use the H-bomb first or to support a NATO strategy based on the threat to do so. This effectively weakened the deterrent principle, since in nuclear war the first strike could well be the decisive one. Yet few political leaders of any party were prepared to say openly that they were ready to start a nuclear war, with its disastrous consequences for everyone, before a nuclear attack had been made on this country. The exception in this as in so many other matters was Margaret Thatcher, who, when asked during her premiership if she would be ready to use the A-bomb first, replied with a decisive 'Yes.' My own view was that the threat of retaliation was one thing, but nothing could justify a British government being the first gratuitously to launch the nuclear holocaust on the world. To me this was a moral issue on which there could be no compromise.

Despite all this turmoil, the debate in conference was by common consent magnificent. Speakers on both sides faced up to the complexities of nuclear policy with an honesty no other party had shown. I wrote in the *New Statesman* afterwards, 'Nobody listening to the debate could fail to be proud of the Labour movement: this was democracy at its best.' And I asked those who wanted to stifle future debate, 'is it now suggested that after last week's stirring display of democratic discussion, the Party should suddenly start modelling itself on Tory Conferences?'

So reasoned were the arguments that Gaitskell might well have won the day. He even opened by listing all the points on which we were agreed, but the medieval-schoolman streak in him got the better of him and he launched into a remarkable attack on Cousins, accusing him of guilt by inference. Some people might say, he argued, that the meaning of his resolution was not clear, but it was clear to him. Whatever the words said, it was inspired by those who wanted to lead us into unilateralism and neutralism. To cap it all, Gaitskell threw down the gauntlet of defiance to conference, warning that Labour MPs would never accept the Cousins resolution whatever conference said. He ended with a dramatic peroration: 'There are some of us, Mr Chairman, who will fight and fight and fight again to save the party we love.' I have seldom heard a more effectively counter-productive speech. At one stroke Gaitskell had damaged two of the causes he held dear. In the first place, conference proceeded to adopt the Cousins resolution and reject the NEC statement, though by a narrow majority, and even narrowly carried the Amalgamated Engineering Union resolution, the only one to demand Britain's unilateral renunciation of nuclear weapons. In the second place, he widened the breach between conference and the parliamentary party and intensified the determination of the rank and file to break the MPs' monopoly of the election of the leadership.

Defence was not the only issue on which Gaitskell was determined to pursue his stubborn course. His attempt to reform Clause IV of the party constitution had ended ignominiously. No one on the National Executive wanted to know. Even his trade union friends could not understand why at that delicate time he should want to pick a quarrel over theology. They preferred their credo to be left intact and for it to be applied pragmatically. In July the NEC had decided not to proceed with any amendment to

Clause IV but to publish a 'Statement of Aims' in the annual report which included the declaration that the 'social and economic objectives [of the party] can be achieved only through an expansion of common ownership substantial enough to give the community power over the commanding heights of the economy'. Gaitskell had had to swallow this, and conference accepted it.

Altogether, therefore, I felt it had been a satisfactory conference, partly because I had been elected to the top of the constituency poll once again – no doubt the result of my previous year's chairman's speech.

By 1961, however, some of Gaitskell's trade union allies who had deserted him the year before began to think it was time he reasserted his authority. To snub the leader once when he was being unnecessarily obdurate was permissible. To continue to humiliate him was politically dangerous. In any case, Gaitskell's political allies had mobilized themselves more effectively against the left through the Campaign for Democratic Socialism, using the journal *Socialist Commentary* as their vehicle. At the 1961 conference, therefore, the tables were turned on the unilateralists. The Executive under George Brown's influence had produced a new statement of policy which called for 'multilateral and comprehensive disarmament' and declared categorically that the West could not renounce nuclear weapons as long as the communist bloc possessed them. In riposte, Frank Cousins tabled the same Transport Workers resolution as in 1960. The NEC statement was carried by nearly 3 million votes, while the Cousins resolution was lost by roughly the same amount. The only point to be salvaged out of this *volte face* was the continued demand that Britain cease the attempt to remain an independent nuclear power. But enduring damage had been done by the row. Policies on defence had been polarized, the party's own leader had cast doubt on the value of public ownership and the rift between left and right had deepened. The party had become almost unmanageable.

The Macmillan government in the meantime had run into its own problems. Once again, the economic engineering for electoral purposes had come unstuck. Even we on our benches had been mesmerized for a time by Macmillan's elegant air of certainty, but now the belief began to grow that Supermac might be an ordinary mortal after all. Heathcoat Amory's electioneering Budget of 1959, like Butler's pre-election Budget of 1955, had promised what the government could not deliver, and within a year, faced with another sterling crisis, he had had to rein in the credit boom. His replacement by Selwyn Lloyd, who was considered a lightweight and a bit of a joke by the House of Commons, did nothing to restore confidence. By 1962, unemployment had risen to the alarming figure for those days of 800,000 and the unions were aflame as a result of the Chancellor's clumsy attempts to manoeuvre them into pay restraint.

In this situation, Macmillan turned his eyes to Europe, where the European Economic Community of the Six had got off to a flying start. The larger market had stimulated their economic growth considerably in the first five years of the Community's existence. Britain had already helped to form the European Free Trade Association (EFTA) in 1959, together with Austria, Denmark, Norway, Portugal, Sweden and Switzerland, but some people had begun to wonder whether we were not missing out on what was already being called the 'economic miracle' of the EEC. There was also the temptation for beleaguered prime ministers like Macmillan – and later Harold Wilson – to believe that by joining a larger organization they could distract the voters from their failure to solve their own economic problems and palm off some of the responsibility. In August 1961, therefore, Macmillan announced that Britain had made a formal application to join the EEC.

The decision had not been an easy one to reach because, in the debates on whether Britain should apply which had been taking place during the previous twelve months, it had become clear that there were deep divisions in both parties on the issue. There was a powerful clique in the Labour Party, led by George Brown and Roy Jenkins, then merely a backbencher but already making a name for himself as an impressive parliamentary performer, who were passionately in favour of Britain's membership. On the other hand, the left wing of the party and most of the Shadow Cabinet were deeply concerned by the effect Britain's entry would have on the Commonwealth. Concern for its members was part of our anti-imperialist ethos. We were proud of the way former British colonies were progressively moving into a free association of independent states, a process we were actively encouraging. Having exploited these countries for years as colonies, were we now to turn our backs on their needs to save our own economic skin? On the government side some forty Tory MPs, led by Peter Walker and Derek Walker-Smith, were digging their heels in against entry, rushing to the defence of the Commonwealth, though their main concern was with its white members, the Anzacs who had fought beside us in two wars, ignoring the rights of the black and coloured soldiers who had done the same.

In such situations of indecision, fanatics seize the reins. This is what Heath did, when as Lord Privy Seal and with special responsibility for foreign affairs, he was put in charge of the negotiations in Brussels. Heath was in many ways like Gaitskell: able, insensitive, opinionated, his pedestrian plodding illuminated from time to time with flashes of genuine passion – passion which both he and Gaitskell were to show on the Common Market, though on different sides. Heath became obsessed with Europe. Not for him any nit-picking over details of the Treaty of Rome or any attempt to query its major policies. The Common Agriculture Policy did not worry him: nor did the fact that other members of the EEC raised most of their tax revenue through VAT, levying it on essentials like food. All he wanted was for us to join at any price. To him the ideal of a Europe united by an almost mystical bond became sacrosanct.

I had never had any doubts about where I stood on Britain's membership of the EEC. Immediately Macmillan made his application, I launched an Anti-Common Market Committee with my Labour MP colleagues Douglas Jay, Edwin Gooch, John Stonehouse and Bill Blyton, a stolid miners' MP. When the *Daily Herald* ran a two-day debate for and against our entry, I contributed the piece 'Why I say KEEP OUT!' My main argument was that the Common Market did not help world trade or the development of more backward economies. Its hallmark was the common external tariff, behind which a few rich countries were determined to protect their own interests at the expense of the rest of the world. We would have to put levies and tariffs on food and other imports from Commonwealth countries which had hitherto sent them to us duty free, while we let in all Community goods freely in their place. The offer of a few concessions did not alter the basic principle that there would have to be a fundamental shift in our loyalties.

My worst fears were confirmed by the progress of Heath's negotiations in Brussels, which I reported in the *New Statesman* from time to time. France was adamant. She wanted Britain in only as a market for her agricultural goods and insisted that her farmers needed the protection of a high-food-price policy, supported by levies on all imported food. There could be no concessions for the Commonwealth except in the form of a transitional period during which Britain could switch from the deficiency-payments system introduced by Tom Williams, coupled with its accompanying imports of cheap food, to Europe's high-food-price policy. Even here France was fighting for a shorter transitional period.

The National Executive was as divided over this issue as the Shadow Cabinet. The result was the tabling for the 1962 party conference of a non-committal statement setting out five conditions which must be met before we could accept entry. The only one of substance demanded 'strong and binding safeguards for the trade and other interests of our friends and partners in the Commonwealth'. Conference accepted the statement without a vote but not before Gaitskell had electrified his audience with another of his dramatic acts of defiance – this time against his own friends. Having dismissed the economic arguments as evenly balanced for and against, he denounced the whole concept of a federal Europe. 'It does mean', he declared, 'the end of Britain as an independent European state. . . . It means the end of a thousand years of history.' His pro-market friends were appalled, while I, for once on Gaitskell's side, cheered. The battle-lines had been drawn for fourteen years of argument in the party.

Three months later de Gaulle saved the day for both parties by vetoing Britain's application. He at any rate had grasped the enormity of the switch Britain was being asked to make: 'You who eat the cheap wheat of Canada, the lamb of New Zealand, the beef and potatoes of Ireland, the butter, fruit and vegetables of Australia, the sugar of Jamaica – would you consent to feed on continental, especially French, agricultural produce, which would inevitably cost more?' He knew that in our place the French would have refused. Heath's response was to declare that 'We in Britain are not going to turn our backs on the mainland of Europe or on the countries of Europe.' Britain's application was left on the table. The moment of decision had merely been postponed.

But there were some substantial satisfactions for me among these dramas. One of the achievements of which I was proudest at that time was the forcing of South Africa out of the Commonwealth. The massacre by the South African police of seventy peacefully demonstrating Africans in Sharpeville in March 1960 had sharply brought home to the man and woman in the street the horrors of apartheid, and some of us had been taking action. The Anti-Apartheid Movement, which had been set up in 1959, had some success in inspiring a boycott of South African goods and when in 1961 I was invited to become its president, its honorary secretary, Abdul Minty, and I hatched even more ambitious plans. Abdul was a delightful man – gentle, of slight build and high intelligence. His quiet manner hid a resolute dedication to fighting apartheid, and we entered into a partnership which developed into friendship and affection. Though our paths seldom crossed after I became a minister in 1964 and particularly after I went into the European Parliament, the sense of comradeship always rekindles instantly whenever we meet.

Anger against South Africa had also been mounting in the Commonwealth, so Abdul and I set our sights on the Commonwealth Conference due to take place in Lancaster House in March 1961. We knew that Macmillan, despite his stirring speech to the South African Parliament in 1960 warning them that 'the wind of change is blowing through the continent: whether we like it or not the growth of national consciousness is a political fact', was working inside Lancaster House to keep South Africa in the Commonwealth just as he had opposed the boycott of South

African goods. We could only assume that his heart was in the right place, but that his head was telling him he must not do anything to upset the British commercial and industrial interests which had invested in South Africa. Our only hope was to shame other Commonwealth prime ministers into branding South Africa as unfit to be a member of a multiracial body.

Demonstrations, we knew, were often counter-productive, not least because way-out groups have a habit of latching on to them. Our plan therefore was for a silent vigil outside Lancaster House lasting forty-eight hours, night and day, without a break, to coincide with the main part of the conference. For two or three weeks Abdul and I had sat in a little interview room in the basement in the House of Commons working out the details. It was essential that the protest should be newsworthy, so we approached bishops, actors and actresses, writers, journalists, scientists, professors, MPs, members of do-good organizations of various kinds: any public-spirited person we could think of, though we prayed for a few prominent ones. The rotas took some organizing. We divided the forty-eight hours into shifts of four people a time and asked our notables whether they would give us two hours and at what time of day. The response was heartening, though it soon became clear that Abdul and I might have to do most of the nightshifts ourselves. In the event stalwarts among Labour and Liberal MPs and among the do-gooders helped us out. As a reward for the night-vigilants a back-up group of helpers ran a little buffet round the corner where they could refresh them with hot drinks and sandwiches.

We impressed on everyone that they must stand in line in total silence. We even had stewards ready to march off any hooligans who might appear. To complete the effect we copied the South African black-sash movement and equipped everyone with a broad black sash on which appeared in large white letters the words 'Sharpeville' or 'Lange', another township where a bloody massacre had taken place. As the limousines rolled into Lancaster House for the conference on the first morning of our vigil, we could see the black or white faces staring out at us curiously through the car windows, because accounts of our vigil had already appeared in the press. A few days later, South Africa was out of the Common-wealth. We gathered that for two days a fierce debate had raged at the conference in which South Africa had come under heavy fire from all the other countries and in which the Canadian Prime Minister, John Diefenbaker, had proposed that a Bill of Rights should be adopted by all the members of the Commonwealth, which would obviously have ruled out South Africa. The follow-ing day, Dr Verwoerd announced his country's withdrawal. We were jubilant, convinced that our vigil had helped to raise the temperature and so make it impossible for South Africa to stay in.

One of the compensations for being in opposition is that one is less tied to the House by draconian Whips. I took advantage of this to go on some exploratory foreign trips which the *New Statesman* helped to finance. For instance, I spent some time in Paris studying French planning, which had been so successful after Jean Monnet had set up the Commissariat au Plan in 1945 that even Selwyn Lloyd was showing an interest in it. Its driving force had been France's belief that her industrial weakness before the war had contributed to her ignominious collapse in the face of Hitler's onslaught, and de Gaulle had kept up the momentum by responding eagerly to the planners' battlecry 'modernization or decadence'. In intensive talks with Massé, head of the Commissar-iat au Plan, with technocrats in the Ministry of Finance, with trade unions and with Mendès-France, I learned how France had laid the foundations of her post-war economic growth by a drive to revitalize her basic industries: coal, electricity, transport, steel, cement and agricultural machinery, the first three of which were nationalized. The right had been demoralized and discredited by its association with Vichy, and as a result it was possible to carry out strong interventionist policies. Renault's works, for instance, had been taken over without protest because its owner had been a collaborator.

When I talked to Mendès-France, however, he put in some caveats. Over a delicious lunch, he told me that he thought the limits of indicative planning had been reached. He was a high-powered, dynamic little man, who as chairman of the Commissar-iat des Comptes, which had helped to finance the Plan. 'Planning is a set of choices,' he told me, echoing one of his pet themes, but the choice must be backed by the power to enforce it. What interested me were the views I was given of the effect on French planning of EEC membership. The young technocrats of the Commissariat had already told me they were afraid that membership would limit their freedom to plan. One of them told me, 'We hope that French industry will continue to look to the French government as it has always traditionally done, but I admit that logically it will increasingly look elsewhere.' He added mournfully, 'I have never been *chaud* for the Common Market.' Mendès-France put it even more bluntly. He had opposed France's membership because the Common Market was based on orthodox liberal economic concepts of the kind which prevailed in Germany. He wanted a coherent collective European policy for investment and planning: 'If Great Britain would come in with this idea, it would transform the Common Market.' On my return I wrote an article for the *New Statesman*: 'Le Plan: Miracle or Myth'. Harold Wilson told me a couple of years later that he had been greatly impressed by it. It was one of the factors which had made him decide to include me in the Cabinet.

I was in Cairo in January 1963 when Hugh Gaitskell died. The *New Statesman* had agreed to send me to Egypt for a fortnight to study President Nasser's schemes for land reform. I had never shared Eden's categorization of him as a demon. He was to me a symbol of the 'wind of change' that was blowing through the Middle East and I wanted to find the truth about what was happening. As I sat in my hotel room waiting with what patience I could muster for the labyrinthine Egyptian civil service to produce my itinerary, the phone rang. It was the young woman who was in charge of me during my visit: 'Please accept my condolences for the death of your leader.' I was stunned, having been unaware of the mysterious illness which had struck Gaitskell down. Dazed, I wandered out into the sunlit streets and into the bazaars. In one souk an Arab sitting cross-legged behind his wares leaned forward and said to me in good English, 'Please accept my sincere sympathy for the loss of your great leader.' I thought to myself, how insular we British are! How absurd that we should be conditioned to look down on these dignified people as near-barbarians. I received the same condolences a few days later in a flower-decked tent at the Aswan dam, where an excited crowd of Arab workers awaited the arrival of their President. The dam had been completed mainly with Russian money, and now the Egyptians were ready to move on to the second stage, of which Nasser was to lay the foundation stone: the building of a power station which would double Cairo's electricity supply. Despite Britain's disgraceful record over Suez I was greeted by the crowd with great friendliness.

Back in Cairo, where I had a long talk with Nasser, I met the same courteous sympathy for Gaitskell's death. I had not realized he was so widely known and respected and thought once again what a pity it was that his obvious qualities had been marred by his streak of stubbornness. Nasser was tall, with a commanding presence, but without bombast: no military medals or uniform, a fatherly figure as his children came in to say good-night. As we sat in a modestly furnished room in his presidential palace, he spoke freely of his hopes and fears and described his almost insurmountable difficulties. Yes, he wanted all his peasants to have their plot of land, which he hoped the irrigation of the Nile would help him to achieve. Yes, he wanted to house the city workers properly. I wondered at the arrogance of the West that it should take upon itself to try to destroy this man.

I returned home to find electioneering for the succession to Gaitskell in full swing. There were three names in the ring – George Brown, Harold Wilson and Jim Callaghan – Tony Greenwood having been persuaded by the left not to run in order to avoid splitting the left-wing vote. It was an all-male cast again. In recent years, journalists have often asked me why I have never been leader of the Labour Party and if I would have liked to have been. Certainly, if I had nursed such an ambition, Gaitskell's death might seem to have offered as good an opportunity as any. I had a high and not unsuccessful political profile and was popular with the constituencies. Harold Wilson had not yet established himself in the party's affections and even some of his friends were uneasy at the skill with which he had navigated his way out of political controversy since his resignation from the government in 1951. So why did I not have a go? The truth is that the idea never occurred to me – or to anyone else. For one thing the Labour movement was still deeply imbued with the instinctive assumption that in the natural order of things you choose a man. More important was my own political attitudes. My trouble was not so much that I was a left-winger as that I had been brought up to despise time-serving and to be outspoken to the point of abrasiveness. I believed that a Labour government which wanted to turn society round would have to be ready to face unpopularity so one had better learn to face it now where principle demanded it. My uncompromising attitude went down well with the party workers in the country, but not with most Labour MPs, who needed far more delicate handling. I was not very good at this. I enjoyed a friendly cup of tea with colleagues in the tearoom but to spend hours there on small talk was tedious. I had too much to do.

Harold Wilson, on the other hand, had become a past master at this art and carried it to lengths which worried me. He once told me proudly that he had just returned from a trip abroad with a parliamentary delegation whose Labour members were mainly fierce anti-Bevanites and had ingratiated himself so successfully with them that they had elected him their leader. It struck me as a strange expenditure of nervous energy. No doubt, I told myself, such conciliatory tactics were essential to someone who was seeking votes, but what worried me was the question: if he started placating his enemies so lavishly at this stage, what would he do in government?

Nonetheless, Harold's technique paid off during a campaign in which the old Gaitskellites opposed him bitterly. Despite George Brown's noisy demands that, as deputy leader, he was automatically entitled to the succession, Harold polled 115 votes on the first ballot to Brown's 88, Callaghan being eliminated with 44 votes. Two days later the party meeting assembled with bated breath to hear the result of the second ballot. Where had Callaghan's votes gone? It was soon clear that 29 of them had gone to Harold, whose vote rose to 144, and only 15 to George. So most Callaghanites had decided that Harold was a safer bet. They must have thought their judgment was justified when a few moments later we watched an extraordinary scene. George Brown, making no attempt to disguise his fury and disgust, muttered that he would have to consider his position as deputy. Harold could easily have let him go and no one would have worried overmuch. Instead, he heaped coals of fire on George's head. Turning with every appearance of affection to George, he begged him to stay as deputy. This magnanimity obviously irritated George still more, and he disappeared. Personally, I thought Harold had over-egged the reconciliation pudding, but the meeting loved it. The collective sigh of relief was almost audible. It was clear that a new era in the party had begun. The dominant motif of Harold's leadership – his determination to keep the party together at all political costs – had been born. I could not help wondering where that would leave the left – or Harold's own freedom of action, come to that.

It was also the start of a new era in British politics. The Macmillan government ran into a series of difficulties which Harold Wilson proceeded to exploit brilliantly, showing a mastery of the House he had never shown before. In a panic response to the government's growing unpopularity, Macmillan had sacked a third of his Cabinet the previous year, including Selwyn Lloyd, in the Night of the Long Knives and had brought in Reginald Maudling as Chancellor. Maudling had a 'hail fellow well met' approach and a good brain which, with his reputation as a progressive, made him popular. But he was trained as a barrister and it was soon clear that his knowledge of economics did not run deep. His Budget of 1963 caused some concern in financial circles when he announced that he was going to cure the balance-of-payments deficit by expanding the economy without doing anything to make Britain more competitive. Harold, with his telling mixture of taunting debater and serious economist, was increasingly to have a field day at his expense.

In March 1963 another blow struck the government. For some time, the newspapers had been full of stories that a government minister was having an affair with a call-girl, Miss Christine Keeler, whom he shared with a Russian officer. Macmillan, revealing the serious flaw in his unflappability, pretended not to notice in the hope that the scandal would go away. We all knew that the Minister was Jack Profumo, Minister for War, and that the Russian was Captain Ivanov. I was furious. I was the last person to want to hound a politician for a sexual affair, as I knew that this could cover half the Cabinet of any government, but there seemed to me to be a genuine question here of national security. What would the press have done if a Labour Minister for War had shared a call-girl with a Russian officer? I believed it made Profumo the sort of security risk which would have brought immediate action by a Labour prime minister. Attlee would have sacked him immediately. At a private dinner which Ted and I gave in our Islington flat for Dick Crossman, Harold Wilson, George Wigg and a few others, I told them that I intended to raise the matter in the House. Dick and George, who had been hesitating, decided to come in too.

In the House, all three of us moved into the attack. Macmillan fended us off skilfully until I asked the direct question: 'Was it true that the Minister of War was involved?' Dick and George were not too pleased with me. Here they were trying to handle the matter with parliamentary delicacy and I came in being crude. But my question brought Profumo to the dispatch box the following day to declare that there had been 'no impropriety whatsoever' in his relationship with Miss Keeler. We all knew that to be a lie, but Macmillan sat on the front bench beside him, complacently accepting it.

It was the beginning of the end for both of them. Six months later, Profumo confessed that he had lied and resigned 'with deep remorse'. Harold Wilson moved in immediately to indict Macmillan for the laxness of his control over national security, with such telling effect that the old man was cowed. I never felt like gloating over Profumo's personal tragedy. If he had not lied to the House of Commons I believe the whole House would have forgiven him. His wife, the actress Valerie Hobson, stood by him loyally and Profumo submerged himself from public view in good works at Toynbee Hall. Some years later I ran into him at some reception, where he was standing in a corner unobtrusively. I went up to him and greeted him warmly. 'Why don't you come back into politics?' I asked him impulsively. 'Oh no,' he said, and ducked away.

But Harold's greatest moment of triumph was his speech to the party conference in 1963. We all sat spellbound as he painted a picture of the technological changes that were taking place, how the Tory Party was not even aware of them and how only socialism could harness 'the white heat of the technological revolution' to public ends. We were not training enough scientists but, worse still, we were not using those we had. In Tory Britain, 12 per cent of the new PhDs were going abroad for work each year. 'We are not even selling the seedcorn,' he said scornfully, 'we are giving it away.' The whole conference was inspired with a new hope and will to win. A few days later Harold Macmillan, who was in hospital recovering from a prostate operation, resigned. The Tory Party's 'customary processes of consultation' were then brought into play in order to choose his successor. Harold could not believe his luck when they chose the fourteenth Earl of Home from the grouse moors of Scotland, even though he would have to resign from the Lords and win a Commons seat before he could become prime minister. To some of us, it looked like political suicide. Harold Wilson had made the whole country aware that it needed more scientists or at least economists. Alec Douglas-Home, a kindly man, was clearly an aristocratic amateur. He confessed that he had had no training as an economist and at one stage even admitted that he did his sums with matchsticks. After that it was mayhem on the floor of the House of Commons as the bright grammar-school boy pitched into the effete country landowner. Slowly the country began to stir out of its innate conservatism. To make matters worse for the government it was clear by the summer that Maudling's dash for growth was in trouble, and Harold predicted a record balance-of-payments deficit of some £800 million.

In September 1964, Douglas-Home went to the country, Harold Wilson conducted the election campaign with tireless skill. On 16 October, Home conceded defeat. We had won, but only just. Labour had gained 317 seats to the Tories 304, but there were 9 Liberals, giving us an overall majority of only four. It was one of the closest results in modern British election history.

338

FOURTEEN

———————— • ————————

Revelations of Government

ON SATURDAY morning, 17 October, Harold Wilson summoned me to Number 10. I was in my dressing gown in our little cottage in Buckinghamshire and not really expecting a call. Most of the key appointments I knew would have been made on the Friday and I was never one to assume I would get a job. When the summons came there was a flurry to get dressed. My hair needed shampooing and I had no hat, so I used one of Marjorie's. Mercifully, Ted was at hand to drive me up to town.

My main feeling as I walked through that famous door at Number 10 was one of exhilaration. Harold was sitting at the long oval table in the Cabinet room hugely enjoying dispensing the fruits of office. 'Minister of Overseas Development,' he said and paused mischievously. 'In the Cabinet, of course.' I was overjoyed. For some months I had been shadowing overseas-development questions on the front bench at Harold's request and had worked out a detailed policy in this field with my colleagues in the Fabian Society. One of our main themes had been the need to set up this new co-ordinating Ministry and give it Cabinet status. Now here it was and I was in charge of it.

I freely admit that the whole paraphernalia of taking office was enormous fun. This is the most dangerous point for any minister. I do not think anyone who had laboured in the Lord's – or Labour's – vineyards for so long with only hard times as a reward could feel anything but a thrill of 'We've arrived' when the whole British establishment opened its welcoming doors. This is where one must decide resolutely not to inhale. Of course, I enjoyed the novelty of going to Buckingham Palace for the swearing in. Like the rest I had been through a rehearsal at the Privy Council office, instructed that I must never turn my back on the sovereign but advance to her from the stool allocated to me, on which I had to balance myself precariously on my right knee. On reaching the sovereign, I had to kneel again and kiss hands, then retreat backwards to my own place. Since the stools were arranged in strict order of seniority I was at the very back and my return journey was hazardous. My day was saved by three things: the first was the clumsiness of public schoolboy Crossman of Winchester, who almost fell off his stool. The second was the story told to me by one of the Palace organizers of the ceremony about an earlier Conservative initiate who had taken his instructions so seriously that he had crawled up to his sovereign all the way on his knees, almost making the Queen laugh outright. The third was the aplomb of the Queen herself who, I gathered, had many a private laugh at the antics of her subjects. After we had all weaved our way back through the minefield of footstools to our places, she remarked sweetly, 'Poor Mrs Castle, she had so far to go.' After that I saluted her as a natural human being whom fate had forced into a formal life.

One of the great ceremonial occasions into which we were initiated is the Guildhall Banquet, at which the Lord Mayor of the City of London welcomes the new Cabinet. It is a glittering spectacle – gold plate on the tables and tiaras on many a head. Cabinet ministers must wait in line to be announced and then advance through a double line of aldermen and their wives to the Lord Mayor, waiting to greet them on the dais. Ted and I were last, and as we came forward the official announcer, who had never seen any of us before, proclaimed in a stentorian voice to the expectant gathering, 'Her Majesty's Minister of Overseas Development and Mrs Castle.' When we reached the Lord Mayor, who was enjoying the joke as much as anyone else, Ted bowed and said, 'Call me madam.'

Looking back I can see that the dominant characteristic of this period was my innocence. I had not realized how completely the civil service was in control. It was not that I had led a sheltered political life. I had spent nearly twenty years at the heart of party infighting and been privy to all the intrigues of smoke-filled rooms, but nothing had prepared me for the interdepartmental intrigues which lay ahead or the civil servants' determination to keep control of them. So when I walked into Number 10 for my first Cabinet meeting I had in my innocence assumed it would be like a glorified meeting of the National Executive Committee, in which we, the elected, would thrash out the policy decisions and pass them to our staff to carry out. Instead I found that every policy decision which came to Cabinet had first of all been mulled over by a committee of officials from the departments involved who had struck bargains designed to reconcile their conflicting interests. They then agreed on how to brief their respective ministers, whom they brainwashed successfully into believing that their prime duty was to fight for what their civil servants told them was their 'departmental interest'.

I was to suffer from this time and again. I usually knew before I went into Cabinet how the chips were stacked and that no argument I might advance in the wider interest of the government as a whole could prevail against the departmental brainwashing that had taken place. The longer I stayed in government the more convinced I became that the system was upside down. Why, I used to ask myself, should not the Cabinet meet first, work out the collective interest and how our sectional interests fit into it, and then pass our decisions down the line for the civil servants to apply administratively? To have put the idea forward boldly in Cabinet would have been like blaspheming in church. Later, when we had all got more experience and wrung a bit more freedom of action from Harold, it was too late to break the mould.

One of our troubles was Harold Wilson's instinctively conventional approach. He had been a backroom boy himself during the war – and a good one – so he had a natural appreciation of the work that civil servants do. When he became Prime Minister, flanked by a charming and co-operative Cabinet Secretary in Sir Burke Trend, and backed by a Cabinet Office trained to service his every whim, his appreciation turned into something dangerously like an uncritical acceptance of the status quo. Any sympathy he may have had towards Nye's dictum that 'The first essential in the pioneers of a new social order is a big bump of irreverence' soon disappeared. Cheeky chappie he may have been, but he never seriously challenged the establishment.

Another problem, I soon realized, was the power of the Treasury. I have never been one of those who ignore the importance of budget-balancing. I know that the major responsibility of any government is to enable its country and its people to pay their way. But I also know that any minister, given his or her share of the overall budget, would mobilize specialist expertise to help them spend it wisely. That, after all, is what they are appointed for. What I objected to was that, in drawing up the national budget and distributing it, only one form of reckoning was used: that of the accountant with his short-term arithmetical calculations. Ministers found themselves arguing with a succession of chief secretaries and Treasury officials about the right way to spend what money was available, knowing that the Treasury's only bottom line was an accountant's one. The result was some short-sighted decisions on public expenditure which my own experts would have avoided if only we had been able to spend a little more money immediately in order to save a great deal more in the slightly longer term. In many of these agonizing public expenditure encounters, Harold did his best to help me and other ministers with whose policies he agreed, but I discovered that every Prime Minister in the end backs his Chancellor, whose word in Cabinet is law.

There were battles which some of us ministers conducted in our own departments. Roy Jenkins, when he became Home Secretary in December 1965, told me of the bitter struggle he had with his formidable Permanent Secretary, Sir Charles Cunningham, who insisted that any briefing of the Home Secretary by any responsible civil servant lower down the line must be vetted by him before it reached the Minister. My problem at the Ministry of Overseas Development (which became known as the ODM as the Ministry of Defence had collared the acronym MOD) was rather different. Since my Ministry was new, there was no incumbent Permanent Secretary for me to inherit, but I readily agreed to take on Sir Andrew Cohen, Director-General of the Department of Technical Co-operation, the nearest the Conservative government had got to giving overseas development a distinct identity. Sir Andrew was a great hulk of man and the shyest to hold office I had ever met. As Governor of Uganda from 1952 to 1957 he had made a name for himself as a liberal administrator, but had blotted his copybook in the eyes of progressives by conniving in the exile of the Kabaka of Buganda, Mutesa II for refusing to co-operate with the protectorate government over its federation policy. I therefore decided to keep a sharp eye on him.

On the weekend of my appointment Andrew came out to the cottage to pay me a courtesy call and was in such an agony of shyness that I could hardly get a word out of him. No doubt he was embarrassed at having to deal with a woman minister: his wife Helen, a delightful person, told me many months later that Andrew used to swear that he would never work for a woman. She was astonished at the change I had wrought in him. We developed such a good working relationship that we became affectionately known in the Department as the 'Elephant and Castle'. Nonetheless, we had many battles of will. Though a gentle and courteous man, he was capable of almost desperate doggedness in resisting any of my ideas that he considered too way out. I got used to his coming into my ministerial room almost literally wringing his hands over one of my latest choices of policy or people and saying wretchedly, 'I know the decision is yours, Minister, and that you must do what you think right, but I should be failing in my duty if I did not tell you how unhappy your decision makes me.' I would listen patiently and then send him away, still distressed.

I soon learned to resist what I came to call the civil service's 'companionable embrace'. On my first Monday morning, when I arrived at the Ministry – housed in a modern office block in Stag Place, Victoria – I found my top civil servants waiting at the door to welcome me. Upstairs in my pleasant ministerial room with its view over Buckingham Palace gardens, my in-tray was piled high with documents. I learned afterwards that civil servants spend an election-campaign period studying the manifestos of the contestants and preparing alternative briefs ready for whomever wins. I looked at that pile of paper and decided not to read a word of it. If I had done, I should never have had time to work out my own policies and put my own ideas across. Instead I told Andrew to study the Fabian pamphlet that I and others had produced. As a result the lone receptionist at the Fabian Society's modest rooms in Dartmouth Street was startled the same morning to see a government dispatch rider roaring up on his motorbike demanding to purchase six copies. These were then circulated through the Department like a newly discovered version of the divine writ.

I certainly intended to preach a new credo. Until then Britain's aid programme had been fragmented among a cluster of departments: the Colonial Office dealing with dependent territories; the Commonwealth Relations Office dealing with those which had become independent; the Department of Technical Co-operation, which dealt with the non-financial side of aid; the Foreign Office, which considered itself the arbiter of the political purposes of our aid; and the Board of Trade, which was interested only in promoting British exports. Over all brooded the Treasury, which had a finger in every pie.

The result was that the aid programme was unplanned and uncoordinated and was far more concerned with the interests of the donor than with those of the recipients. I was delighted to be in a position to end all this and establish a revolutionary new principle: that the purpose of aid was to promote the development of the backward countries of the world and that all other considerations must be subordinated to this test.

This inevitably brought me up against a whole phalanx of vested interests. Things were not made any easier by the fact that the Opposition had denounced the changes. Almost before I had drawn ministerial breath, I had to make my debut at the dispatch box to explain the role of the new Ministry, and I faced a front bench crowded with former holders of high office: Rab Butler, who had just ceased to be Foreign Secretary; Duncan Sandys, the recent Colonial Secretary; Robert Carr, ex-Minister in charge of the Department of Technical Co-operation – all waiting to pounce. Naturally I was a bit nervous, but I am always my best under attack and I enjoyed myself. My sweetest moment came when Butler rose to ask me magisterially who would take over the Foreign Office's aid responsibilities. I replied crisply that I would. He looked as though the heavens would fall, but I got some good press comment for my firm reply.

A few months later Iain Macleod returned to the attack, though more wittily and far less ponderously than Butler. Macleod was always one of my favourites on the Tory front bench. He never indulged in political buffoonery, and I knew him to be dangerous, wielding the rapier rather than the blunderbuss. I was introducing my first Bill to the House – a measure which among other things encouraged expatriate British officials to remain in the service of developing countries by underwriting and financing the standards of service which would encourage them to stay. I was wise enough to begin by paying tribute to the fact that Macleod himself had launched the Overseas Service Aid Scheme when he was Colonial Secretary in 1961, though I pointed out gently that my scheme went further than his. He reciprocated by saying that he welcomed my Bill and would support it, but then proceeded to tease me about the new Ministry. 'We have not so far', he told the House, 'been able to find a satisfactory answer to the question: "What exactly is she up to?"' Was this elaborate new Ministry going to do something new or was the Rt Hon. Lady merely a 'bird in a gilded cage?' I joined in the laughter when he added, 'I use these words in an ornithological and not a personal sense.' This was the kind of tourney I relished, in which the most skilful argument won the day. I was immensely saddened when Macleod died suddenly in 1970 at the age of fifty-six. He represented Toryism at its best, before the yuppie generation of young Tories came in with Margaret Thatcher and worshipped around her throne.

The *Daily Mail* enjoyed itself with Macleod's ornithological reference, publishing a cartoon of me with a birdlike neck squawking in my cage, but as its report of the debate also added that I had made a 'splendidly reasonable appeal on behalf of hungry countries', I felt that honours were even.

Setting up a new Ministry was an absorbing task. In taking over the aid responsibilities of so many different departments I inevitably took over numbers of their staff. Their sensitivities had to be dealt with gently and some new slots filled. Here I found the advice of Tommy Balogh invaluable. Harold had made him Economic Adviser to the Cabinet, so he was at the heart of events, where he loved to be. He was round to see me in a flash, full of dire warnings about the manoeuvres of the establishment. 'Barbie,' he would say – it was his pet name for me – 'you can't appoint so and so to such and such a post. He's a terrible reactionary' or 'he knows nothing about development'. It did not do to swallow Tommy's advice whole and none of us who worked with him ever did, but he had a brilliant way of illuminating dark corners and an unrivalled knowledge of the civil service, seeming to be acquainted with all the top men – and the top women – personally. Since I had no knowledge of the civil service personnel at all and had never worked with them, I found his insights a great help.

Tommy was also an expert on overseas development. It was to him that I owed the appointment of Dudley Seers as head of the Economic Planning Department which I set up. I was no great economist myself, but I had a profound belief that political decisions should be based on economic realities and that politicians should be aware of the economic cost of their policies. I was therefore one of the first ministers – perhaps the first minister in the new government – to recruit economists and other outside experts to my Ministry. The 'generalists' of the civil service reacted with traditional suspicion, even resentment at first, but they got used to it.

In the ODM, they even got used to Dudley Seers. Andrew, who had been hovering with a list of 'safe' names for the new post, was horrified when I told him whom I had in mind, obviously considering Dudley far too left-wing, despite the high reputation he had gained as economic adviser at the UN. I had to go through one of Andrew's hand-wringing sessions, but I stood firm. Dudley soon won him – and the Department – over by the excellence of his work. In appearance he had the look of a cuddly teddy bear, but this was deceptive. He knew exactly what he wanted to do and his hug could be lethal if anything got in his way. With my approval he recruited a remarkable group of experts who had devoted their lives to the problems of the developing countries, including Paul Streeten, Fellow of Balliol College, Oxford, and Associate of the Oxford University Institute of Economics and Statistics, who became Dudley's deputy. Paul was a gentle and diplomatic man who charmed everyone. Cambridge economist Robin Marris and Peter Ady, his senior assistant, were other members of the team. The quality of the documents they produced and the advice they gave raised the status and morale of the whole Ministry.

I was always lucky in the outside advisers brought in because they all had a flair for breaking down the resistance of the career civil servants, which could have been troublesome. Dudley, for instance, had the bright idea of organizing a weekend seminar at which the economists and the heads of departments would get to know each other and exchange ideas. The Labour peer, Gavin Faringdon, another gentle soul who was renowned for his generosity, lent us his beautiful eighteenth-century house at Buscot Park for the weekend. Gavin was an aesthete, who had furnished the house in keeping with the period, down to the last hand-basin. The house looked out on an extensive park complete with grazing deer, lake and romantic bridge. The administrators may have felt a little constrained at first among this socialist elegance: I do not know how they made out in Gavin's famous four-poster beds but as the weekend wore on everyone thawed gradually, and uninhibited discussions took place on the papers the economists had prepared. At the end everyone voted it a great success as old resentments melted away; one of my regular civil servants asked if the venture could be repeated in six months' time. I would have liked these seminars to take place on a regular basis, but it did not prove possible.

A major task of Dudley's team was to advise the countries to whom we gave aid on how to make the best use of the aid available. Dudley, or one of his aides, therefore always accompanied me on my foreign trips. While I conducted formal talks on aid strategy with the ministers concerned he would be chatting up the ministers' backroom boys, advising them on how to draw up a development plan suitable for their country's needs. Some of the discoveries we made were hair-raising. In some countries the alleged 'plans' were merely a list of wildly optimistic projects; in others there was no development plan at all. Money was just spent *ad hoc* as it came to hand. I thought to myself that we British were in no position to criticize. For years we had been dispensing aid *ad hoc* without any co-ordination between the aid-giving Minister and agencies and without helping the recipients to plan their development properly. Yet Rab Butler and Iain Macleod had presumed to query the need for the new Ministry!

For my first few months I was so absorbed with departmental work that I only superficially followed what was happening in Cabinet. Other ministers experienced the same phenomenon. In fact Dick Crossman, busy with his housing programme as Minister of Housing and Local Government, admitted to me that it was nearly a year before he began to function as a member of Cabinet, comparing himself unfavourably with me as I had become concerned much earlier than he had about the major developments that were going on in government policy. Nonetheless I was always uneasily aware how many major policy proposals by other ministers I had to take on trust because I had not read the detailed documents. Excessive workload is an abiding problem of Cabinet ministers, who struggle to be full members of Cabinet as well as conscientious departmental ministers. The answer, I argued, was for each minister to be allowed to appoint a political *cabinet* on the French model – a small group of people outside the civil service on whose political judgment he or she could rely. They could read all the Cabinet papers – not just the departmental ones – and brief the Minister on anything controversial that was coming up.

At first, therefore, the economic crises through which the government was going flowed over my head. I was aware that when, as Harold put it, we had 'opened the books' we had found that Harold's warning during the election had been right and that Britain was facing a record balance-of-payments deficit of over £800 million. As a result of Maudling's 'dash for growth' sterling was under threat. I had been vaguely disturbed to learn that during the first weekend after the election, Harold as Prime Minister, Jim Callaghan as Chancellor of the Exchequer and George Brown as head of a new Department of Economic Affairs (DEA), set up ostensibly to balance the power of the Treasury, had met at Number 10 to decide the economic strategy which was to dominate the life of this government. Sterling, they decided, must be defended at all costs. Labour must not be associated with devaluation once again. That decision having been made without consulting the rest of us, a tough deflationary policy was the only choice we faced.

I had also been disturbed by Jim Callaghan's speech introducing his first Budget in November 1964. There was nothing wrong with the Budget's contents. We had kept our promise to the pensioners, giving them a big increase, the first they had had for many years, and we had announced that prescription charges would be abolished; so two of the party's sacred cows had been safeguarded. Knowing the economic mess we had inherited, I had no objection to Jim's austerity measures to pay for them: 6d on the standard rate of income tax and an immediate increase of 6d per gallon on petrol tax. But what alarmed me was the wider tenor of his speech. Our Queen's Speech had contained the ominous phrase: 'At home my Government's first concern will be to maintain the strength of sterling.' Now Jim was embroidering it in Powellite language of financial orthodoxy. We must restore Victorian values and pay our way. No more borrowing. Sterling must be supported at all costs. He sounded like a stern uncle lecturing a bunch of profligates.

As I listened I asked myself if we had learned nothing from the 1930s, when Philip Snowden had wrecked the Labour government by clinging to the gold standard. Had we totally ditched the expansionist policy for which we had always called? Maudling's mistake, it seemed to me, was not that he went for growth but that he failed to accompany it with the measures either of taxation or of government intervention that would make it work. Everyone knew, for instance, that our currency was overvalued and that direct government measures were needed to strengthen our industrial base. I believed that October 1964 was the ideal moment for the government to devalue, when it had the balance-of-payments crisis to justify it. I became increasingly convinced that the rigid alternative being forced on us would not work – and so it proved.

I was therefore unhappy about the economic and political context in which we started our period of government. We had in effect handed control of our policy over to the City, and Lord Cromer, Governor of the Bank of England, was quick to take advantage of that. He did nothing to staunch the run on sterling which followed Jim's Budget. No one could say the Budget was inflationary because increased taxes had balanced increased spending. Our crime was not that we were squandering money, but that we were redistributing it. The Governor was interested not in a balanced budget but in a conservative one. He weakened sterling by publicly demanding savage cuts in public expenditure, particularly in the social services, and accused the government of being 'profligate'. Harold muttered that he would never accept that a democratically elected Labour government could not be allowed to carry out Labour policies, but he was trapped. Most of the Cabinet were not privy to the secret discussions that were taking place. I for one was unaware that meetings of the inner cabal of ministers were held at Chequers during the weekend of 21–22 November, at which it was decided to raise the bank rate by 2 per cent as part of an exercise to persuade the reluctant Governor to raise a loan from the central banks. That bought us time.

Most of the Cabinet – particularly us spending ministers – were on the fringe of these events. From my lowly position at the far end of the Cabinet table, I struggled to follow what was going on, hampered by the fact that the intimate discussion between the inner four at the middle of the table – Prime Minister, Chancellor, Minister for Economic Affairs and Foreign Secretary – was almost inaudible to those of us sitting below the salt. My consolation was that my neighbour was Ted Short, who had been made Chief Whip. Ted was a kindly, honest man with a sense of humour and we would exchange ribald whispers and irreverent little notes. Ted was particularly interested in the rambling old cottage – Hell

Corner Farm – in the Chiltern hills which my Ted and I had just acquired. I tried to draw him pictures of it with its irregular contours and tiled roofs sweeping almost to the ground. We were due to move in during the summer recess and I would distract myself during the duller moments of Cabinet by making lists of the equipment we had to get. On one such occasion, Harold turned to my end of the table and said sharply, 'No note-taking in Cabinet.' On my way out at the end of the meeting, I stopped by Harold's chair and mischievously showed him what I had been writing. It ran: 'Decide colour of lavatory seat.' After that, I was able to get away with a good deal of note-taking in Cabinet.

By January 1965 developments in the Labour government had become so traumatic that I decided I would keep a regular Cabinet diary. The shorthand I had acquired during my years of unemployment in the 1930s, though far from perfect, proved invaluable. It meant that I could scribble outlines nonchalantly on bits of paper during Cabinet discussions and type them out afterwards. In this way I was able to capture some of the lighter sides of Cabinet as well as pinning down what my colleagues had said and how they had voted, which some of them were anxious to forget afterwards.

I did not spend all my Cabinet time in frivolities. As the months went by I became increasingly convinced that my analysis was right and Harold's wrong. I could not for the life of me understand why the government did not immediately produce a strategic five-year plan telling the country what our political and economic objectives were and how we hoped to advance towards them year by year. This would have enabled us to hold out the vision of the sort of society we wanted to create while rubbing in the message that each social advance had to depend on the economic progress we had made. Instead we seemed to approach our difficulties piecemeal.

There were many excellent things in the Queen's Speech in addition to the promise of the long-term review of pensions and the abolition of prescription charges. These included the establishment of Regional Economic Planning Councils, the creation of a Land Commission to acquire land more cheaply for public purposes, the nationalization of steel, the repeal of the Tory Rent Act of 1957 which had decontrolled private rents (and incidentally forced Ted and me out of our Highgate flat as its rent sky-rocketed), leasehold enfranchisement, law reform and the setting up of an ombudsman. Not least it provided for a state-run redundancy-payments scheme which compelled employers to contribute to a central fund and pay agreed levels of redundancy compensation, thus extending to all workers the cushion against adversity which under the existing voluntary schemes had been the privilege of the few. We had fought the election on the need to come to terms with the 'white heat of the technological revolution', which we knew would entail a lot of restructuring and upheaval as we modernized industry. The move to give all workers the statutory right to a sum of money – sometimes quite a large sum – to cushion them against the first impact of unemployment was one of the most enlightened social reforms of the century, one which the Tories dare not reverse, not even Mrs Thatcher. Indeed, it is unlikely that she would have got away with the massacre of jobs during her monetarist period without violent riots had it not been for our scheme.

But, excellent as all these measures were individually, we did not manage to present them as part of a cohesive plan or a coherent philosophy. True, Harold had sketched out the image of a modernizing government by creating three new ministries – DEA, the Ministry of Technology and ODM – but we were all prisoners of the government's commitment to maintain the value of sterling at all costs, which made it impossible to challenge the Treasury veto on our policies. George Brown at DEA made a good start with the setting up of his Regional Economic Planning Councils, but his National Economic Plan was a flop. Dudley Seers dismissed it to me as perfunctory, a mere catalogue of optimistic predictions instead of a plan of action. In any case its target of 25 per cent growth over the next five years was clearly in conflict with the priority it continued to give to eliminating the balance-of-payments deficit, and the plan itself admitted as much. Ironically, George's greatest success was in persuading the employers and trade unions to join with the government in a Joint Statement of Intent in which they all agreed that the machinery should be created to keep the movement of prices and of 'money incomes of all kinds' under review.

This was followed a few months later by the setting up of the Prices and Incomes Board (PIB) under Aubrey Jones, who had been Minister of Supply in the Macmillan government. Aubrey was a sensibly moderate Tory, who in Thatcherite terms would be called a 'wet', but his appointment caused considerable unease among the trade unions. The unions were still anxious to co-operate with the Labour government but were becoming increasingly uneasy about the orthodox path it was following. Jack Jones, the rising star of the Transport Workers and their representative on the NEC, pointed out to me sourly that the PIB had been set up before the National Plan had been produced. He suspected – rightly as it turned out – that the government was on the slippery slope to a statutory prices and incomes policy as the central feature of its economic strategy. Later George Brown was to become a bitter opponent of the deflationary policies which he himself had helped to launch during that fateful weekend of October 1964 – but for which he conveniently blamed Harold Wilson.

One of Harold's most imaginative appointments was to make Frank Cousins Minister of Technology. Frank himself told me he was reluctant to take the job, but he had campaigned for Harold's succession to the leadership and did not want to let him down. Personally, I thought it was an excellent idea. If the Labour government was to create a new, more egalitarian, down-to-earth society it needed to bring in people with an inside knowledge of industry from the shop floor and reflecting the views of the rank-and-file trade unionists. Frank, however, was never happy in his strange new environment. I gathered from Tommy Balogh and others that Frank's civil servants respected him as a competent minister, but he hated his appearances at the dispatch box and found the Union Debating Society atmosphere of the Commons totally alien. During the whole of 1965 I had to nurse him through his growing discontent, and when, in July, Jim Callaghan introduced a whole new package of deflationary measures, including a cut in our housing programme, hire-purchase restrictions and limits on private investment, I had to restrain him from resigning on the spot. I myself was battling for more money for overseas aid in the most hostile atmosphere anyone could face. I managed to get a modest increase, but Jim threatened that it might have to be recouped by reductions in future years.

The whole agonizing process was made bearable only by the fact that Cabinet unitedly agreed that we should cut the bloated defence programme we had inherited from the Tories. Since Harold was not prepared even to discuss the shedding of some of our worldwide commitments, we concentrated on economies in weaponry. Denis Healey, however, as Defence Secretary, was not going to be a party to any serious cuts in equipment. He was a brilliant and ruthless operator on his own behalf and not too scrupulous about drowning opposition with a flood of expertise, whose validity we might suspect but were not equipped to refute. Cabinet eventually agreed to cancel the British strike reconnaissance plane, the TSR2, though we left open the question whether we should buy the American swing aircraft, the F111, in its place – which Denis was clearly determined we should do. I voted for the cancellation, though my heart sank. The TSR2 was made in Preston and a number of my Blackburn voters travelled there to work on it. There would inevitably be an outcry, which I was prepared to face, but I was not prepared to have the savings on the TSR2 squandered on the F111. That battle lay ahead.

Nonetheless, I was hugely enjoying my work at the Ministry. The tighter money became, the more important became our work to spend it wisely. I found a vivid example of this when I visited Pakistan and India in January 1965. One of the costliest items in my aid budget was the huge steelworks at Durgapur in India. Steelworks, I discovered, were a virility symbol to emerging countries. They all, large and small, wanted one of their own, regardless of whether their economy could support it. In India's case the situation had been saved by a remarkable Scottish engineer, Douglas Bell, who had been put in to run the works. I took to him immediately. He was obviously one of those rare management geniuses who can combine a compulsive efficiency with a human rapport with his workers. He had got the plant working to a high level of output, despite the snags with which he had to deal. One of these, he told me, was the lack of back-up factories to supply small parts and do repairs. I realized how absurd it was to spend millions on the main plant before these essential ancillaries were in place.

I took Paul Streeten with me on the trip and together we discussed India's fourth five-year plan with the Planning Commission. India was a relatively advanced country and the members of the Commission knew their job, but unfortunately most of the aid I could give them had been swallowed up by Durgapur. In any case they, too, had some grandiose ideas, and the main thing in which they were interested was the extension of Durgapur. In my talk with the Indian Prime Minister, Lal Bahadur Shastri, in which I was accompanied by Sir Paul Gore-Booth, our High Commissioner, I had to explain to him that our balance-of-payments difficulties at home made a big increase in the aid programme impossible. I left Durgapur on a note of sadness. Douglas Bell told me he was being replaced shortly by an Indian manager (he was knighted the following year). He was not bitter about it and perfectly understood that no country with any national pride could tolerate indefinitely the running of its major prestige project by a foreigner. The move towards Indianization was perfectly legitimate. But both he and I knew that there was no Indian sufficiently well trained and experienced to do what Douglas Bell had done. I came back conscious once again of how uncoordinated our aid programme had been, with one department deciding to finance Durgapur and another being responsible for the essential technical assistance and training. My predecessors had just put in Douglas Bell and hoped for the best.

Checking up on the latest state of play in Durgapur I find that it remains the main plant of the Steel Authority of India, but it is operating below its rated capacity and is still struggling with persistent management problems, which prevent its steel from being internationally competitive. Tragically my Economic Planning Division broke up when I was moved to another Ministry.

One of my moments of real joy came when in June 1965 I announced to the House of Commons that in future our loans to the poorest developing countries would be interest-free. It had taken a bit of a battle to persuade the short-sighted pundits at the Treasury that they would lose nothing since it was clearly impossible to expect countries with an abysmally low income per head to pay interest on their debts even on favourable terms. I am glad to say that Jack Diamond, as Chief Secretary to the Treasury, brushed aside the obscurantism of his own officials and supported me. The excellent people in the American aid agency, AID, with whom I had worked closely in international conferences, were delighted, telling me that they had been fighting the same battle with their own government, so far unsuccessfully, and that my victory would give a great fillip to their campaign. Unfortunately, all these years later we have still not learned the lesson that it is folly to lend money for development which is then swallowed up in paying interest on previous loans. The failure of rich nations to wipe out the debt burdens of the poorer nations is one of the scandals of the modern world.

One of my problems in trying to promote public interest in overseas development was Britain's underlying racial prejudice. This was far more widespread than politicians would admit. It was epitomized in the cartoons by Cummings in the *Daily Express*, who lost no opportunity in depicting me as a 'nigger lover' who was squandering British taxpayers' hard-earned money on feckless blacks. The paper had a field day when Dr Hastings Banda came to visit me at ODM shortly after I became Minister. It was part of my job to receive visits from Ministers of newly independent governments to discuss their development programmes and what we could do to help. Normally it was a pleasure. I was particularly delighted to receive, for instance, the delegation from Kenya, which comprised a number of my old African friends among the detainees as well as Bruce Mackenzie, Minister for Settlements, the only white man prepared to take a job in the new government. I was all the more delighted because they had come for help with their land-reform scheme, which involved the purchase of white Kenyan farms for distribution to Africans.

The arrival of Dr Hastings Banda, now Prime Minister of an independent Malawi (formerly Nyasaland), was a different matter altogether. I had, of course, campaigned with him for his country's independence, but he had long ceased to figure on the freedom fighters' calendar of saints. He had not only set up a ruthless personal dictatorship in Malawi, but had also made ingratiating overtures to South Africa. I would have loved to keep him at arm's length, yet I could not refuse to see a Prime Minister from a Commonwealth country. As usual the cameras were there in force as I greeted him, and to my disgust he seized his opportunity to hit the headlines by turning my handshake into an embrace, putting his arm around me and cuddling his face up against mine. It would have been an impertinence from any official visitor, but from him it was intolerable. I tried to pull away and laugh it off but the *Express* had got the moment it was waiting for. It blew up the picture of the embrace to fill half a page. Cummings produced another of his cartoons. This showed Banda flying across the room to embrace me at my desk, while Harold Wilson (standing in the doorway) says to Patrick Gordon Walker, his Foreign Secretary, 'Babs seems such a hit with the Africans, it's a pity we didn't drop her on the Congo to pacify the rebels.'

The result of this publicity was a shoal of the filthiest letters I have ever received. One of my correspondents scrawled across the enlarged photograph 'Disgusting. Sooner these people are out of office the better for all decent white people. It makes you ashamed of been British.' Another scrawl ran, 'Gosh you do love nigger boys. Hope this fellow had a bath recently.' Another writer excelled himself: 'If a dirty animal is allowed to do this sort of thing in full public what goes on in private? It's cheap cows like you that let the nation down.' The incident was hardly conducive to persuading the nation to spend more on aid.

But I was able to draw consolation even a short while afterwards. I had taken the precaution of recruiting a practising journalist from Fleet Street to strengthen my information team, whose members, being career civil servants, had more conventional attitudes to publicity. Once again I consulted Ted, who suggested Chris Hall, a lively young spark from the *Sun*, formerly the *Daily Herald*; a very different paper from the *Sun* we know today, it was sympathetic to Labour's cause. Chris proved a godsend. He was an abrasive young man and has always had views of his own, which he is not prepared to compromise. But he believed strongly in what I was doing and kept an eye open for news angles which would help. He found an ideal one in Tanzania, which I visited in April. As part of my tour I went to see the model village of Upper Kitete, in which British aid had helped to finance the settlement of 100 African families. While I talked to villagers, Chris dived into one of the huts and emerged with an African baby, whom I took in my arms. It was a gift for the photographers and the result was a picture of me smiling broadly as I held the little black baby close to me. Even the *Express* could not resist using it, giving it prominence with the caption 'A cuddle in the sun'. The accompanying text described me as a 'mother figure', which made a pleasant change.

Later Chris's quick-wittedness saved me from a rather less welcome experience. From Dar-es-Salaam I went over to the island of Zanzibar, which had merged with Tanganyika to form Tanzania. My visit was a political act in itself since Zanzibar's First Vice-President Karume and his Revolutionary Council were Marxists and, as such, highly suspect in the British Foreign and Colonial Offices. So was Julius Nyerere, President of Tanzania, because he had promoted the union. One of the causes of suspicion was that Julius always wore a simple Chinese-type shift and trousers, even on state occasions; another was that he was prepared to accept help from the Chinese, who were insinuating themselves throughout Africa into the vacuum left by the inadequacies of Western aid. Personally I could not blame him. I was certainly not in a position to give him much aid, and in his shoes I would have looked for help anywhere I could get it. One of the purposes of my visit, therefore, was to end the coolness which had grown up between Tanzania and the British government. I did it by telling a press conference that my government welcomed the union and that I had come to discuss the use of the outstanding £150,000 of aid due to Zanzibar, which had been frozen by my predecessors.

Zanzibar is an attractive island. Karume, dressed in a smart Western-style suit, greeted me cordially. We climbed up a path fringed by flowering bushes to a vantage point above the sea and held our meeting in a hall open to the refreshing sea breezes. While I talked to Karume, Dudley Seers sought out the Chinese who were supposed to be drawing up the island's development plan. He found one Chinese official sitting in a small office who seemed to have no very clear idea of what the plan should be about. Karume and I were getting on famously when I was startled to receive urgent signals from Chris Hall. He had noted that the chandelier under which I was sitting housed a large bird's nest from which I was likely to receive droppings at any time. Many years later he told me that he had for long been dining out on his story of how the expression on my face changed when his message at last got through and how I edged myself diplomatically out of the firing line. The visit ended amicably with an agreement to spend the £150,000 development grant on a secondary school and an automatic telephone exchange for the island.

The highlight of the visit was the evening I spent with Julius Nyerere. He had given a reception for us at Government House, and when the other guests had left we drifted into the garden, where we were joined by Trevor Huddleston, who, after being forced by his Church to leave South Africa, had come to Tanzania as Bishop of Masasi. Years afterwards Trevor and I agreed it was one of the most memorable evenings we had ever spent. We sat chatting in the balmy evening air, and the friendship of the old Movement for Colonial Freedom days gradually reasserted itself as we listened to the bitterness which poured out of Julius. He accused the Labour government of failing to confront the growing arrogance and racialism of South Africa and Southern Rhodesia. I hope I calmed him down. I certainly felt a great deal of sympathy with what he said.

These two issues were coming to dominate our Cabinet discussions and I was increasingly unhappy about my colleagues' attitude to both of them. Economic pressures had made cowards of us all – or most of us. I had reluctantly agreed that we should fulfil the contracts which our predecessors had entered into with the South African government to supply sixteen Buccaneer aircraft, plus the spare parts, but I did so on condition that we could reject the order for another sixteen which they wished to place with us. I had, however, been outraged to learn that Lord Caradon, formerly Hugh Foot and now our representative at the United Nations, was under instructions to veto an Afro-Asian resolution in the Security Council calling for mandatory economic sanctions against South Africa. Eventually I won on that, but only to the extent of persuading our government to abstain. We were still in the clear on South Africa, but only just.

Now Southern Rhodesia was emerging as another threat to black rights in Africa. The break-up of the Central African Federation in 1963 had brought independence to Nyasaland and Northern Rhodesia. Southern Rhodesia, however, had reverted to colonial status – a situation which clearly could not last. The problem was how to agree the terms on which she, too, could be given her independence while guaranteeing the democratic rights of her African majority. When Labour was in opposition we had had no doubts about that at all. We had bitterly opposed the constitution which the white-dominated government had introduced and had declared that independence should only be granted to a colonial country on the basis of majority rule. 'No independence before majority rule', known as NIBMAR, became our battlecry. At first the Conservative government had been ambivalent, but when the right-wing Rhodesian Front swept to power in the election of 1963 and Ian Smith replaced Winston Field as its leader in April 1964, even they began to be alarmed, and just before the general election Sir Alec Douglas-Home endorsed our line.

In our first months of office Ian Smith's threats of a Unilateral Declaration of Independence (UDI) hung over us and the way seemed clear for Harold to rally a united House of Commons against Smith. Instead, to my dismay, Harold was engaged in an extraordinary show of vacillation, one moment declaring that he would ensure that UDI brought severe economic retribution on Rhodesia's head, the next sending his emissaries scurrying around to try to persuade Smith to change his mind and accept a compromise. It was soon clear to everyone but Harold that this was a hopeless exercise. Though persistently snubbed by Smith,

Harold pressed on with his overtures undeterred. Apparently he could not see that every rebuff weakened his own authority and strengthened Smith's. So when in November 1965 a cocksure Smith announced UDI at last, Harold had no effective weapons left with which to counter him.

Faced with Julius Nyerere's diatribes, I had defended the government as stoutly as I could, but as we talked I had become vividly aware of the threat an independent racialist Southern Rhodesia would present to the northern states. Southern Rhodesia would be progressively integrated with South Africa and together the two countries would exercise a stranglehold on black governments. This view was urged on me also by Kenneth Kaunda, an old friend, whom I went on to visit in Zambia. This gentle Christian did not seem tough enough to be President of such a turbulent country, but he was buoyed up by a strong belief in moral rectitude. I described him in my notes as 'informal, but with great natural dignity'. It was thanks to him that I was in Tanzania at all, because he had sent Harold Wilson a message urging him to do everything possible to support Julius Nyerere. He greeted me by saying how much he had appreciated Harold's quick response in sending me.

Kenneth was obsessed with anxiety about the grip Southern Rhodesia would have on the lifelines of the front-line states if UDI took place. We were joined for a time by Seretse Khama, who in 1956 was allowed to return to Bechuanaland (later known as Botswana), where he became leader of its independent government. He was anxious to develop his country's cattle industry and expand trade, particularly with Zambia, but the cattle had to be driven across a corner of Southern Rhodesia, which could be blocked at any time. He desperately wanted the Bechuanaland road to be extended to the Zambian border and the pontoon over the Kafue river replaced by a proper bridge. Kenneth's plea was that we should support the building of the Tanzam railway, the project for a 1320-mile railway from the Copperbelt to Tanzania which he and Julius were promoting as an essential escape route from the clutches of Southern Rhodesia. He was unhappy about Julius's contacts with Peking and the suggestion that the Chinese should build the railway. He would far rather, he told me, that it was financed by us. Harold, with the typical warmth which endeared him to me, had responded eagerly to Kaunda's overtures and wanted us to help. I told him that my experts had already looked at the railway scheme and did not believe it could be made economically viable. 'The need is political as much as economic,' Harold replied sadly and asked me to look at it again. He was right, of course, but I knew we could not accommodate a project of this size within the aid money I had available. It was no use our wishing the ends unless we also wished the means. (Later the Chinese were to build the railway.)

I returned to London anxious to help these beleaguered countries as much as possible and determined that we must not sell out to Southern Rhodesia.

The tragedy to me was that Harold, who was so instinctively in tune with progressive causes, should have got himself into a situation in which he seemed to be dragging his feet on all the issues about which his allies on the left cared most. Outstanding among these, of course, was Vietnam. It was to cause more anger among his normal supporters than any other issue, including economic policy. For some reason which was hard to fathom at the time, Harold became emotionally embroiled with America. He came back from an early visit to Washington full of the friendliness he had been shown by Lyndon Johnson (LBJ), who had become President on the assassination of John F. Kennedy. He had the sense, however, to resist LBJ's plea for Britain to send in troops – a course which would certainly have been rejected by Cabinet.

Harold lent him moral support to the furthest extent he could. It was clear to most Labour Party workers – and to many Americans as well – that this was not only an immoral war, but one that America could not win, however many Vietnamese peasants she napalmed or however many of their growing grounds she defoliated. Despite mounting protests from Labour MPs, which some of us – notably Tony Greenwood, Frank Cousins and myself – voiced in Cabinet, we could not get Harold to dissociate himself and the government from America's actions in Vietnam. I began to suspect that under Harold's cheeky-chappie exterior and acute statistical brain there lay a deep sense of insecurity.

Another manifestation of this lack of self-confidence lay in his treatment of his political enemies. We on the left had noted wryly how he had distributed power in his government. Of course he had included a number of his left-wing friends – Dick Crossman, Frank Cousins, Tony Greenwood, Gerald Gardiner, Fred Lee and myself – but we were mainly in peripheral posts, while he had reserved the central positions of power for the right-wingers who had done their best to keep him out of power. The supreme example of this generosity was George Brown, who was to be the sharpest thorn in Harold's flesh.

George had one of the best brains in the Cabinet, but he was tragically unstable, emotionally, physically and politically. He was a maverick who believed he was a law unto himself and who had no sense of personal loyalty. It was George who was to plunge us into another bruising showdown with our backbench MPs and further dent Harold's authority.

The issue was steel, which in the Queen's Speech we had said we would take into public ownership, a nettle we had been failing to grasp ever since 1945. In Cabinet George had protested that he was in favour of 100 per cent public ownership, even though two of our Labour MPs, Woodrow Wyatt and Desmond Donnelly, were demanding that we should merely go for a 51 per cent state holding in the existing private companies. (Both MPs were to defect from the party later.) Since our majority in the Commons was only four, these two votes were crucial in the coming debate on the Steel Bill, but George gave every appearance of being determined to stand firm. Our Whips started marshalling the sick and wounded for the vital vote. I myself was in University College Hospital recovering from a sinus operation and the press had a field day, photographing me emerging to vote with tubes up my nose. At least the sick were spared the ordeal of going through the division lobbies. We sat in our cars in Speaker's Court while the Opposition Whips came and checked on us, enabling our own Whips to 'nod' us through. I sat waiting anxiously for the result of the division, until the electrifying news came through that the rebels had voted with us and we had won by four votes! We were all jubilant until we learned the reason. George had made a secret deal with Wyatt and Donnelly off his own bat and without consulting anyone. He consummated the deal in a winding-up speech in the debate with the assurance that he was prepared to 'listen' to alternative proposals for giving the government control of the industry. The rebels knew he was ready to climb down.

It was a direct attack on Cabinet decisions and on Harold's authority. And it was unnecessary too, for, even if the rebels had voted against us – which was far from certain when the chips were down – we should still have won with the Speaker's casting vote, which by convention always goes to the government. Labour backbenchers were totally demoralized. Dick and I were furious and tried to get a vote of censure on George passed in Cabinet, but Harold wriggled away from it. He told us privately that George was a cross he would have to bear in the interests of party unity until George destroyed himself, which he eventually did. But Dick and I were drawn closer together by our alarm at the damage which Harold's obsession with the need to keep the party together at all costs was doing to him and the government. We respected him for it, but we believed he was going about it the wrong way.

The attempt to deal with Ian Smith's UDI in November 1965 was to dominate discussions in Cabinet, but a few weeks later I was distracted by a dramatic change in my own status in Cabinet. On Tuesday, 21 December Harold sent for me. He was, he told me, very concerned by the fact that the government had not got an effective transport policy. Tom Fraser, the Minister, was a fine chap, but transport was not his field. 'I need a tiger in my tank,' said Harold darkly. 'I want you to take the job.' I was appalled. I loved ODM and the people I worked with there and believed I was making an impact on international aid policy. As I moaned Marcia, whom he always consulted, put her head round the door and said with an air of authority: 'You've got to do it, Barbara.' 'May I talk it over with Ted?' I asked desperately. 'Of course,' said Harold. 'Come and see me first thing in the morning saying yes.' Ted was sympathetic, but firm: 'It is a challenge you can't refuse and you can't let Harold down.' In bed I was cheered up by an idea that occurred to me. Harold did not know that I could not drive. (I had not followed up those driving lessons Michael Foot had given me thirty years before.) In fact I had underestimated Harold. When I walked cheerily into his study the next morning with the words, 'Prime Minister, of course I want to help you, but you don't realize—' he interrupted me. 'I know,' he said. 'You don't drive,' adding with a twinkle, 'I think that is a good thing. We cannot have Ministers of Transport knocking down people on pedestrian crossings.' And so I said my tearful farewells at ODM and took on the job I did not want and which, in the event, I enjoyed more than any of my ministerial posts.

FIFTEEN

•

Full Steam Ahead

To walk into the Ministry of Transport was like entering another world. To begin with the Ministry was sited in St Christopher House, an ugly flat-fronted building overlooking Southwark Street, along which the roar of traffic was a constant reminder to me of the problem I was supposed to solve. If the environment was macho outside, so it was inside the Ministry. When I walked into my office the first morning the atmosphere was almost glacial. In the first place I found that my Private Office was manned exclusively by Scots, resentful of this Sassenach woman who had ousted their beloved Scottish Minister, Tom Fraser. In the second place the Permanent Secretary, Sir Thomas Padmore, had gained a reputation for indifference to his job and knew that one of the conditions I had laid down to Harold Wilson in accepting my new post was that he should be replaced. Thirdly, I found that the Ministry was dominated by highway engineers. They were competent and courteous, but their lives were centred round the expansion of the roads programme and they suspected that I had other loyalties, like the development of public transport and the salvaging of the railways – so I was not 'sound on roads'.

My first few weeks were dominated by various embarrassments. I asked Harold if the Ministry could be moved nearer to the House, but he did not hold out much hope. My Private Secretary, Bill Scott, who had been devoted to Tom Fraser, barely troubled to hide his hostility to me, even taking it upon himself to decide which of my instructions to my officials he should pass on. Although by convention a minister is allowed to choose his or her

Principal Private Secretary, Bill Scott proved as difficult to move as Sir Thomas, and it was several months before I was able to exercise my choice. A rather comical embarrassment was that they could not find a ladies' lavatory near to my ministerial room: women clearly had had no important role on the ministerial floor. They solved the problem by requisitioning a nearby gentlemen's lavatory for my use, so I would wash my hands in a large space lined with men's stand-up facilities, wondering where the civil servants I had displaced had had to go. (When some months later my new Private Secretary, Richard Bird, a more congenial spirit, insisted that a properly equipped washroom should be provided for me where I could wash and change in comfort, some of the press carried snide stories to the effect that the first thing this woman Minister had done was to have a lavish boudoir built for her own use.)

But my major embarrassment was Sir Thomas Padmore. He would confront me at every opportunity about my declared intention to have him moved, saying he would fight me all the way. Tom Fraser's shortcomings, he declared, were not his fault. 'I am not prepared to be the sacrificial goat for a weak minister.' I made innumerable appeals to Harold to keep his promise and have Sir Tom moved elsewhere, but by now Harold, having lured me into his transport net, had other preoccupations and referred me to Sir Laurence Helsby, head of the home civil service. It soon became clear that Sir Laurence was no friend of mine, telling me smoothly that Sir Thomas was too senior a civil servant just to be pushed out. An alternative post of equivalent status had to be found for him. No such post was found while I was Minister of Transport.

The moral of this situation seemed to me to be that ministers are expected to go to the dispatch box at the House of Commons to take personal responsibility for every detail of the work of their departments without having any power of hire and fire of the people who are carrying out their policies. Another moral I drew from this whole business was that Harold Wilson was not very good at standing up to his own top civil servants, whose skills and protestations of loyalty seemed to dazzle him. He should, in my view, have instructed Sir Laurence to find another post for Sir Tom – and quick. To do him justice Sir Thomas struggled within the limits of his comprehension to support my changes in ministerial policy, but I longed for a permanent secretary who would guide my new initiatives because he believed in them, instead of just accepting them.

The task I faced was gargantuan. In pleading with me to accept the post Harold had said to me, 'Your job is to produce the integrated transport policy we promised in our manifesto,' adding characteristically, 'I could work something out myself, given half an hour.' This was an over-simplification de luxe. Integrating transport sounded easy, but I soon found I had walked into a minefield of confusion and conflicting interests. To begin with, my Department had no tradition of, or instinct for, planning transport as a whole. Its work, I discovered, was compartmentalized under three deputy secretaries dealing respectively with highways, urban policy and a miscellany in which railways were lumped in with ports, shipping and nationalized road transport. It seemed a chaotic system to me and when I asked Sir Thomas who co-ordinated the three sections and whether there were policy meetings under the Minister, he replied, 'Your predecessor did not have that way of working. Any co-ordination took place round my table.' I registered that in future they should take place round mine.

I also discovered that the idea of having economic advice built into the policy-making machinery at every stage was strange and new. They employed, Sir Thomas admitted, half an economist in Michael Beesley, who worked half-time for us. When I asked when and how they consulted him my top officials replied sheepishly that they would stop him in the corridor and ask his views. Michael Beesley, I decided when I met him, was a competent chap who was only to anxious to be used, but was not given an opportunity. This became apparent when I asked my highway engineers what criteria they followed in drawing up the roads programme. They replied that there were always more projects in the pipeline than there was money to do them, so every project was a priority. Later I found that my highway engineers had a test for selecting the next stretch of major road to be built. It was called TAL (Traffic and Accident Loss): an assessment of the economic cost of working time lost, periods in hospital and so on caused by congestion or accidents on one road compared with another. This seemed to me to freeze the existing pattern of road development, which was broadly north to south, radiating out from London. No one had done a cost–benefit analysis of this pattern of road building, while environmental assessments had barely been heard of at that time. I had to pit myself against the pressures of the 'roads first and foremost' lobby and the daunting expertise of my highway engineers.

But I also had to pit myself against some of the over-simplifications of my own party members and the vested interests of rival unions. The Labour Party had always believed that the only way to keep traffic moving in this small island with its congested cities was to plan transport as a whole. Only by integrating all traffic movements under a central plan and common ownership could we avoid waste and overlapping, make the best use of our resources and protect the environment. In the heady days of the post-war Labour government the job of carrying out this policy had been given to the MP from the Co-operative movement, Alf Barnes. He was a quiet, efficient man and he proceeded to embody it in his 1947 Transport Act, which, by the time I took over, had become the ark of Labour's transport covenant.

His method was to set up an umbrella organization, the British Transport Commission, with five divisions responsible respectively for road transport, railways, inland waterways and docks, London transport and hotels. All existing public undertakings were vested in it and it was given powers to acquire all road haulage concerns except owner–operators. The nationalization of the railways presented no difficulties. It had long been clear to most transport experts that Britain needed a national rail network, so there was no great outcry when the various regional companies were absorbed in the British Railways Board. Road haulage presented much greater difficulties. Freight was being carried on British roads by a large number of lorry operators with small and often inefficient fleets. Many of the lorries were not even road-worthy and the conditions under which the lorry drivers worked were a hazard to their own and other people's safety on the roads. Alf Barnes set out manfully to bring them together in a publicly owned subsidiary of the Commission, British Road Services. It proved an expensive job. The Labour government, always conscientious, and harried by the Tory benches, agreed that the owners should be properly compensated. The result was that the Commission acquired a number of vehicles which ought never to have been on the roads anyway. Many years later, I talked to the owner of a medium-sized firm in my Euro-constituency, who told me that the foundation of his modest industrial fortunes had been laid when his small fleet of rather dubious lorries had been bought out under the 1947 Act. The Tory MPs, who were demanding even more lavish compensation, knew how to look after their own.

When the Labour government fell in 1951, its transport policy was put into reverse. The cry then was that integration should come to an end and competition be restored between road and rail. What interested me was how gingerly our successors approached this task. In the first place, they made no attempt to denationalize the railways since the establishment of a national network had proved popular. They did not even manage to privatize road haulage since, here again, the creation of a national network of services on long-distance routes had proved popular with industry. Industry, being pragmatic, realized that it was more economical to have a central organization planning to ensure that lorries going with one load could pick up another load for the return journey, instead of coming back empty as most of the smaller fleets run by private operators did. At first, the British Transport Commission was instructed to sell all its road haulage assets, but by 1956 it had managed to dispose of only 528 vehicles out of a total of 6111 in the long-distance services. The government therefore bowed to the inevitable and when it wound up the Commission in 1962 it transferred the assets of British Road Services, including some road passenger services, shipping assets and travel agencies, to a new body, the Transport Holding

370

Company, still publicly owned but legally obliged to operate on commercial lines. The company had flourished under the dynamism of its cocky little managing director, later chairman, Sir Reginald Wilson, of whom my officials spoke with awe. When I made an early point of meeting him I found him bouncing with self-confidence. I respected him for that but realized I should have to handle him carefully.

My trouble was that the party wanted me to restore the 1947 Act in its entirety, including the renationalization of all road haulage, yet I knew this attitude was out of date. To begin with there had been a dramatic switch of traffic from rail to road. The number of private cars had leaped from 2 million in 1947 to 8 million, and my experts were forecasting an increase to 18 million by 1975. The number of lorries on our roads had risen from 1.5 million to 4.5 million, and I had no intention of trying to buy them up. Nor did I intend to recreate the British Transport Commission with its five separate Executives. I had a hunch that this structure gave the appearance rather than the reality of integration, and this suspicion was confirmed some time later when I got around to meeting Lord Hurcomb, the original chairman of the Commission. He was by now eighty years old, but I noted in my diary that he was 'remarkably fluent and clear-headed'. He confirmed that although the Commission had published a comprehensive report on the finances of its Executives, it had left them to go their own sweet way.

What worried me more was the effect of the road-transport explosion on British Railways. My predecessor at Transport, Ernest Marples, had not dared to try to sell them off. Instead he airily instructed them to pay their way, regardless of the fact that there was no level playing field between road and rail and that the motor car did far more damage to the environment. If the railways wanted to compete with the road, he told them, they would have to cut their costs, and he appointed Dr Richard Beeching, formerly chairman of ICI, whom he had made chairman of British Railways, to show them how. Beeching's report was awaiting me on my arrival at the Ministry. In it he argued that one-third of the total route mileage would have to be cut out, involving the closure of 2000 stations and 3000 miles of track. Closures had already begun and there was uproar among Labour's rank and file, which has always been pro-rail. Inevitably, the rail unions were up in arms and resolutions opposing any further closures were passed by conference. Even the transport workers supported them out of solidarity, but only halfheartedly since their own interests lay in road transport and they secretly thought the railways were out of date. In a private moment, Frank Cousins once said to me scathingly, 'If I had my way I'd close the whole lot down and put everything on road.' It was a sentiment he would never have dared express publicly, but it did not make my job any easier.

I had to walk through these pitfalls warily, however. It was obvious to me that there would have to be some trimming of routes that were built before the age of the private car, but I was equally determined not to allow market forces to destroy a railway system on which so many people were dependent, to say nothing of the effect on the environment of turning the traffic carried by the railways on to our already overcrowded roads. When I met Dr Beeching shortly afterwards I found I was up against another formidable personality. He was a quiet man without bombast, but he exuded a cold logic against which emotional protests would have little effect. I was in a man's world all right, and I had to impose my will on it.

It was against this background that I started to work out the party's new transport policy. As at ODM my first step was to set up an Economic Planning Unit. At Tommy Balogh's suggestion I interviewed Christopher Foster, Fellow of Jesus College, Oxford, who had specialized in transport, and offered him the job of heading it. He was young and a bit brash but full of ideas and enthusiastic about my approach. I suspected he had plenty of personal ambition, but he was not in my view necessarily the worse for that. Sir Thomas, anxious to prove he was not rocking the boat, concurred in his appointment eagerly.

But before I was more than three weeks into my planning process the National Union of Railwaymen (NUR) jumped the gun, threatening a national railways strike. They had rejected the Railway Board's offer of a 3.5 per cent pay increase, which had been endorsed by the Prices and Incomes Board, and discontent was being fomented by a couple of communists on the union Executive. There then ensued one of those 'beer and sandwiches at Number 10' negotiations for which Harold was so much derided in the press. In fact he was rather good at them as he enjoyed meeting the rank and file on informal terms, and it often worked. The only trouble in this case was that, as the discussion with the NUR Executive dragged on into the night, we discovered there were no sandwiches. Harold was furious, having two days earlier ordered food to be provided in case the persuasive efforts of George Brown, Ray Gunter as Minister of Labour and myself failed to get a quick result. Marcia Williams was sent scurrying round to Number 11 to borrow bread from the Chancellor. She returned armed with sausages and pies and more beer from the local pub and the atmosphere grew more relaxed.

Harold seized the opportunity to call on me to explain what I was doing in my new Ministry. The day was saved when I was able to assure the worried delegates that I was drawing up a new transport policy and that the hated 1962 Act the Tories had passed would go. Sid Greene, the NUR General Secretary who was patently anxious to get a settlement and not harm the government, welcomed what I had said and made the most of it. The communists were isolated and we had won.

All my ministerial life I remained a devotee of the 'beer and sandwiches' technique – though preferably not at Number 10. We gradually persuaded Harold that the Prime Minister ought not to become involved in these tortuous arguments, though there is no doubt that his cheeky-chappie accessibility kept him personally popular with our working-class voters and the unions, even when they were irritated by the policies of his government. Labour, I believed, had one of two choices: we could either treat the unions as our partners in a pluralist democracy, listening to them even when they seemed most unreasonable and spending endless time trying to win them round, or we could repress them saying, 'We are the boss.' Edward Heath was the first to try this second method of running the country, and he failed disastrously.

I also had to deal with an urgent issue on the road-safety side.

One of the most exciting parts of my job was the chance it gave me to reduce road deaths and injuries, which were rising alarmingly. Prominent among the causes of this increase was drinking and driving, and the Department under Tom Fraser had prepared a Bill introducing the breathalyser. It was my duty to approve its contents and pilot it through the House. In doing so I made two main changes in Tom Fraser's Bill. The first was to abandon his proposal for random tests. Some commentators suggested that I had been forced to yield to pressure on this in Cabinet, but in fact the change was my own choice. I knew that the breathalyser would arouse great antagonism among motorists. The individual-liberty brigade outside the House was already denouncing this invasion of personal freedom, and I believed the case for random testing had to be watertight. My road-safety experts persuaded me that it was not. If police were thin on the ground and if they scattered their testing too widely they would be likely to get less results than if they concentrated on situations in which there was *prima facie* evidence that the driver had been drinking. Secondly, the police themselves were worried about the effect that arbitrary testing might have on their relations with the public. Most important of all from my point of view was what I called 'the lone woman driver in a lonely lane' syndrome. Mugging and rape had not then reached the dreadful heights they have now, but nonetheless there were plenty of women who would be nervous about being stopped, either by day or at night, by a man or men purporting to be police officers doing a bit of breath-testing, when they might not be what they seemed.

I therefore decided that the police should be entitled to breathalyse only where the driver had committed what in the Ministry's jargon was called 'a moving traffic offence' – for example, if he or she had shot the lights – or where the police officer, having stopped a driver for any reason, detected signs of alcohol on their breath, or there were other indications that alcohol had been consumed. I remain convinced that this was right at the time, though later, when the novelty of the new law had worn off and drivers were increasingly defying it, I voted as a backbencher in the House for random testing. And, if I were Minister of

Transport today, I would certainly introduce it – with appropriate safeguards against arbitrary behaviour by the police. I would not, for instance, give them 'total discretion' about when to test, but would lay down guidelines including provisions which would prevent individual police officers exercising this new authority.

The most important change I made in Tom Fraser's Bill was over the penalty. A tough deterrent was essential and I knew that fining was not enough. I therefore introduced automatic disqualification from driving for twelve months for any driver caught with more than 80 milligrams of alcohol per 100 millilitres of blood. This brought a ton of bricks upon my head. Mark Carlisle, one of my Tory shadows on transport, moved an amendment to give the court discretion to reduce the disqualification period in the case of a first offender where there were 'mitigating circumstances'. Another amendment would reduce the period to six months where the driver depended on the car for his or her livelihood. I stubbornly refused to make the penalty discretionary, on the ground that I was not going to let anyone have a first go at taking the risk of killing someone. Magistrates, I reminded the House, were notoriously lenient towards driving offences on the principle of 'There but for the grace of God go I.' I even had some opposition from my own side, but I won. Some twenty-five years later I was on a Sky television discussion programme with Norman Tebbit, the dangerously abrasive Thatcherite MP, and Austin Mitchell, the witty Labour MP for Grimsby. The producers warned me beforehand, 'Norman always goes for the jugular,' but to my surprise he suddenly launched into a public tribute to me over the breathalyser: 'I opposed you at the time, but you were right and I was wrong. It was the most important thing you did.'

As I had anticipated, the breathalyser, when it was finally launched in 1967, caused a stir throughout the land. My postbag was full of abusive letters, usually anonymous. One of them, scribbled on a torn bit of paper, ran: 'You've ballsed our darts matches up, so get out you wicked old B.' It was signed '3 Regulars'. Another grubby epistle showed a dagger dripping with blood over the words: 'We'll get you yet, you old cow.' One

Christmas card wished me an 'evil Christmas and a whole year of unhappy days', adding, 'These are the views of the public, you bitchy old cow.' Other letters were more conciliatory. One of them gave me an interesting insight into the mentality of the British male. It was from a woman who wrote, 'Thank you for giving my husband back to me. He used to leave me at home when he went to the pub, now he takes me with him to drive him home.' Another from a 'lifelong Conservative' in Norfolk congratulated me on what I had done and told an amusing story about his young son at school. The class had been asked who was the patron saint of travellers and one boy wrote, 'Barbara Castle.' It was the only time in my political life I had been canonized.

In fact the breathalyser brought me a number of comical experiences. I became the *bête noire* of publicans, some of whom were heard by friends of mine declaring that they would not allow 'that woman' to set foot in their establishment. I overheard one of these publicans myself when one weekend Ted and I were walking on the Berkshire Downs with a couple of friends. We dropped into a little village pub in the Vale of the White Horse, one of our favourite walking areas. I sat in a corner while Ted and the rest went to the bar to order shandy. The publican said to them grandiloquently, 'I had Barbara Castle in here the other day. I refused to serve her.' We suppressed our smiles and did not disabuse him, but when we arrived at the Bell Inn in Faringdon for the night we told the story with some relish to the genial host, an old friend of ours. We learned later that the story spread through the Vale like wildfire, heaping the unhappy publican at Woolmer with embarrassment. Ten years or so later when Ted and I did the same walk and slipped into the garden of the same pub at Woolmer for a midday snack, thinking that the whole thing would have blown over long ago, the publican heard I was there and came out into the garden to apologize. He was, in fact, a decent chap who had been caught in the wave of prejudice which followed the introduction of the breathalyser.

Ted behaved magnificently through all this. A convivial man, he enjoyed a drink in good company but he imposed a self-denying ordinance on himself, drinking only tonic water, which he did not like, at parties and in pubs to which we had to drive. While appreciating his loyalty I could not help noting to myself with a smile that he was paying the price of having discouraged me from learning to drive. We were a one-car family and he did not want me borrowing the car. In fairness to Ted, I must admit I never clamoured to learn to drive. I was a born drivee, which was just as well since all my life the car was to me a place where I could relax, enjoying the view, having a snooze, reading my newspaper or writing my next speech. In any case, Ted was always ready to drive me anywhere. His circumspection over drink-driving was invaluable, because the press tracked us everywhere. They would turn up at our local pub in the country, camera in pocket, disguised as innocent drinkers at the bar, but hoping to catch Ted driving me home after a couple of pints. They went away frustrated because we usually walked back anyway.

Ted's and my reward came when we got the first year's figures for road accidents since the breathalyser had been introduced. My Department had estimated that the breathalyser would save 200 lives in its first year. In fact we found that road deaths were down by 1200. Some of them were due to the fact that the 'moving traffic offence' provision in the Bill had made the mass of motorists drive more carefully to avoid being breathalysed. But the effect of the drinking restriction was proved to me when an electrician came to our cottage to do some work for us. He brought with him his dad, who, he said, wanted to tell me of his own experience. The father was an ambulance driver in London and he told me that before the breathalyser their night's work had a regular pattern. As soon as the pubs closed the accident figures shot up and they were operating at full stretch. Now, he said, they spent the night playing cards. This first dramatic impact of the new legislation obviously did not last, which was why I later believed we should tighten up the law, but it sent my personal popularity zooming up the political scales.

One memory stays with me. Shortly after the new law came into operation I was making one of my regular journeys from High Wycombe to Marylebone when a large West Indian ticket collector at Marylebone seized me by the lapels. 'Do you know what you did to me?' he said with a synthetic air of menace. 'I was the very first person to be caught by your breathalyser.' 'Then I saved your life,' I replied sweetly. We have been good friends ever since.

Another road safety measure on which I had set my sights was the wearing of seat belts. Experience in other countries had shown that this reduced the seriousness of accidents and could save lives. Few cars already on the road at that time were fitted with them and I had to start inserting them into as many of the older cars as possible. I also had to persuade those passengers who had them in their cars to use them. It was not as lurid a battle as over the breathalyser, but there was a good deal of resistance all the same. Some of it came from the government drivers themselves. My own protested vigorously that the belts impeded their driving or hurt their bosoms. Nor did I get much support from my Cabinet colleagues for my campaign. They obviously thought it was another piece of Barbara's dictatorial attitude. One of my most contemptuous critics was Harold Lever who objected to such nannying. I felt I had turned the corner when one day after an editorial meeting at the *New Statesman* he took me back to the House in his opulent car. 'Barbara,' he said, 'you have a convert. The other day the son of a friend of mine was catapulted through the windscreen when a car rammed him from behind. Now he will be handicapped for life.' The seat belts having been fitted it was left to subsequent governments to make the wearing of them compulsory, a measure for which I always voted in the House. Today even the former critics belt up automatically.

I had not been in my new job for three months when Harold decided to go to the country. We had all been aware that we could not carry on for long with a majority of only four but there was no certainty that we could improve on it when the general election was called in March 1966. Sterling was still under pressure and the Governor of the Bank of England had been pressing us to raise the bank rate another 1 per cent to 7 per cent. Fortunately, we had not listened to him, having learned to treat the Bank's advice with scepticism. Labour MPs, however, were still restive about Jim

Callaghan's deflationary measures of the previous July. Austerity was still the rule. Nonetheless we sailed home in the election, increasing our overall majority to ninety-seven. Our share of the vote rose from 44.2 per cent in 1964 to nearly 48 per cent and all our ministers were returned. By contrast Ted Heath, who had supplanted Alec Douglas-Home in the Tory leadership a year earlier, had his majority in his constituency nearly halved, and the Conservatives lost four former ministers, including Peter Thorneycroft and Christopher Soames, Churchill's son-in-law. The Liberals' share of the vote fell from 11.1 per cent to 8.5 per cent. History shows that the Liberal vote usually falls when Labour is polling strongly, which explains why in an election campaign the Liberals, despite their alleged radical views, concentrate more of their vitriol on Labour than on the Conservatives. This also explains, in my view, why the Liberals will never progress from being a temporary protest vote against all governments to being a serious and consistent national force. This is true of all breakaway movements from Labour, as David Owen was to discover some twenty or so years later.

Two things about the election result worried me. The first was that the poll was relatively low. The second was our growing obsession with the balance of payments as the most important economic indicator. Good trade figures in February had enabled us to claim that we had 'halved the deficit', but what mattered with the public was that we had kept unemployment down to 241,000 – as near to full employment as one can get in a modern economy. I feared that the elimination of the deficit by deflation would force unemployment up and that we could not survive as a Labour government by ignoring the other economic indicators of employment and growth. I was determined to continue the fight on which some of us were engaged to persuade Harold and his co-conspirators to abandon their attempt to maintain the value of sterling at all costs. Some of us also noticed that one factor in our victory had been Harold's genial and unassuming personality. The country seemed to like its new type of Prime Minister: the bright boy from the lower-middle class who had made his way by virtue of his own abilities.

The Tories had been looking for the same type of appeal when they elected Ted Heath as successor to the upper-crust Alec Douglas-Home. They were to repeat it later when they opted for Margaret Thatcher to follow Heath, and for John Major to follow her. The claim had become 'We are all classless now.' Harold had set a new trend.

Though we now had a more comfortable majority, life in government was not much more comfortable. The pressure on sterling remained merciless, even though our economic perform-ance had been far more impressive than our predecessors'. There was clearly an intrinsic political bias against a Labour government in financial circles and among financial commentators. We used to have discussions in Cabinet about the mysterious nature of 'confi-dence' in sterling. In July 1966, for instance, when we had just settled a damaging seven-week seamen's strike, the pressure on sterling was so great that we had to rush through another series of crisis measures, including raising bank rate to 7 per cent, a wages and prices freeze and further cutbacks in spending programmes. 'Confidence is a curious business,' Harold mused in Cabinet. 'One can never be sure what effect one's actions may have.' Take the seamen's strike, he went on. One would have thought the government's determination to stand out against excessive pay increases would have strengthened confidence. Instead, all that sterling-holders had noticed was that the trade figures had suf-fered. Short-termism had damaged us again.

The menacing shadow of PESC (Public Expenditure Survey Committee) dominated our lives. An intimidating body of civil servants had been set up by Selwyn Lloyd as Tory Chancellor in 1961 to co-ordinate the spending plans of the different departments into a realistic whole in the light of prospective growth, and thus arm the Chancellor against the pleas of departmental ministers. The Labour government added a refinement to this torture by setting up a new committee of non-departmental ministers under the Chancellor to arbitrate between the competing claims. The committee, ironically known as the Five Wise Men, consisted at the outset of George Brown, Frank Cousins, Ray Gunter, Douglas Houghton, Chancellor of the Duchy of Lancaster, and Jack

Diamond, Chief Secretary to the Treasury. Our problem was that the economy could not afford public spending plans greater than those the Tory government had postulated for the next few years. They had inflated these figures just before the general election, as they always did. This meant that if we wanted to make room for our own new policies we either had to change the Tory priorities, thus infuriating the Minister whose Department had been promised certain increases, or push the spending figure up. As a result our spending programmes grew by nearly 5 per cent in our first year, and even after Jim's cutbacks in 1965 the increase was still running at 4.4 per cent. As Jim warned us a year later, the demands we had all put in would have led to a jump in spending in 1967–8 of nearly 10 per cent, which our growth rate could obviously not sustain. In such a situation every minister fights his or her corner stubbornly. Failure to do so is considered weak and tougher ministers jump in eagerly to take advantage of it. This time we were able to coalesce against a common enemy. As the pressures mounted we all turned our attention to defence. Here again Denis Healey, a likeable man but totally unscrupulous in battle, managed to give the impression that he had cut more deeply than he had actually done, though later we were to call him to sterner account.

Harold Wilson and his inner circle had a problem. In the interests of backing up sterling they had to give the impression that public expenditure was being tightly controlled, but the more they succeeded in giving that impression the more they demoralized their own backbenchers and party rank and file, who wanted to know why the City should dictate our policy.

What was in the end to cause us the greatest anger was not public expenditure cuts, but prices and incomes policy. Since George Brown had persuaded employers and unions at the very outset of our government to sign a Statement of Intent – that they would keep price and wage increases under voluntary control – he had been taking the government down the slippery slope to a statutory prices and incomes policy. The six-month wages and prices freeze which was included in Jim's deflationary package of July 1966 had in fact conceded the principle, since the Act which was introduced to embody it contained in its notorious Part IV the provisions to enforce it, if necessary by fines. It was the publication of the Bill which had finally led Frank Cousins to resign, insisting that this was entirely the wrong way of going about things and threatening to lead a campaign against us.

Looking back at the heated discussions over the Bill in Cabinet, it is fascinating to see the sides we all took then. Dick Crossman argued powerfully that the Bill's inquitous Part IV would mean that if a trade unionist struck in favour of a pay increase which the employer was not allowed by law to concede, he could be fined, and would go to prison if he refused to pay the fine. I backed him, urging that the best way to put a curb on wage increases was to freeze prices, because then the employer would be unable to find the pay increases. George Brown, however, was adamant that the new powers were essential to enforce the standstill and that the TUC wanted the statutory backstop behind them to ensure that everybody played the game. The Bill went through the House to a chorus of protests from a number of our backbenchers, led by Frank Cousins. As the prices and incomes policy developed, the chorus was to grow.

With the pressures on the economic side so intense it seemed to me a tragedy that Harold expended so much of his political credit on his unpopular policies on Rhodesia and Vietnam. It might be essential to force our rank and file to accept economic realism, but, I asked myself, could we not give them a little idealism in other fields to keep up their morale? Yet the party waited in vain for any condemnation of American policy on Vietnam. Instead when in February 1966 President Johnson announced that he was resuming the bombing of North Vietnam, which had so outraged our people, they had to suffer the indignity of hearing their own Foreign Secretary, Michael Stewart, say that 'Her Majesty's Government understand and support' his action.

I believed Michael Stewart was sadly miscast as Foreign Secretary. He was a decent, honourable man who had good radical views on a number of social service issues, notably education, but in foreign affairs all his radicalism disappeared. He not only sympathized with America's policy in Vietnam, but fell prey to his Department's phobia about communism. I had had a long battle with him when I was at Overseas Development about the Russians' alleged manipulation of UNESCO (the UN's Educational Scientific and Cultural Organization) for political purposes. His officials were obsessed with this idea. My officials, who had worked with UNESCO, could find no evidence of it. Michael's reiteration of this theme helped to feed America's prejudice against UNESCO, which was already running strong.

Michael's statement led to an explosion of anger among our backbenchers, and 100 Labour MPs cabled Senator Fulbright, Chair of the Senate Foreign Relations Committee, protesting against America's action. The anger was echoed in Cabinet, where on 4 February 1966 I noted that we had 'the most spirited wrangle yet on Vietnam'. The violence of the reaction shook Harold and induced him some months later to make a statement in the House dissociating himself from the American bombing of oil installations near Hanoi.

Unfortunately this show of independence did not last long: Harold was too deeply committed to LBJ. This was partly due to the way the Americans had flattered him during his visits to Washington. LBJ's friendliness had boosted his morale – and all politicians need a bit of that. He also pressed some familiar arguments: America had been very helpful in supporting sterling, LBJ could not understand why Britain did not send in troops, and so on. The arguments convinced neither me nor large numbers of our people in the House.

Harold's answer to our restlessness was to launch a succession of abortive 'peace initiatives' in Moscow, Hanoi, the Commonwealth and anywhere else where they might seem plausible. These initiatives always foundered on America's intransigence, which prevented us from testing whether any negotiation with Hanoi would have been possible. Typical of these efforts was Harold's decision to send his Parliamentary Private Secretary, Harold Davies, on a secret mission to Hanoi in July 1965. It was characteristic of Harold Wilson that he should choose one of his old Tribune friends as his PPS. These were the people with whom he felt most at home as his praetorian guard against the right.

Harold Davies had been a frequent visitor to Hanoi and knew Ho Chi-minh well. What Wilson hoped to achieve by this visit was never clear to me, since it was obvious that Hanoi's price would be an end to the American intervention in Vietnam, which Harold would not accept. In the event we never knew what might have happened because the 'secret' trip was leaked by someone unspecified and Harold Davies's interviews were called off by Hanoi. According to my diary Harold Wilson was not too disappointed at the failure of the mission because he was satisfied with the 'gesture' he had made. I began to realize that he felt himself a prisoner, not only of the Americans, but of the right-wing majority in his Cabinet and was sending out signals to his friends of the sort of policies he would like to pursue if he were free.

The trouble as I saw it was that Harold had made himself his own prisoner. During all the time I served in his governments I believed his political instincts were the same as mine, which is why I remained loyal to him. But he drove his friends like Dick Crossman and me almost to despair by his failure to capitalize on his support in the party and by his propensity to put himself in the power of his political enemies. His motive was honourable enough – his determination to avoid the searing splits which had kept the party out of office for thirteen years – but he carried the process too far, demoralizing the party workers and damaging himself.

Our only hope of surviving as a government, I believed, lay in taking a strong moral line over issues of principle, and that meant opposing this barbarous war, which was increasingly shocking world opinion, including growing numbers of Americans. Standing up to LBJ would have won us more friends in America, not fewer.

But the issue on which I came nearest to resigning from the government was Rhodesia. The issue brought out all the contradictions in Harold's character. He was certainly no colonialist and his support for the African cause was genuine, but he ran in fear of the racialist prejudices in Britain, which could flare up at any time. Many white Rhodesians had relatives or friends in Britain; they certainly had a powerful voice in Parliament, where the Rhodesia lobby of right-wing MPs jumped to their defence at every opportunity. Were not these whites our 'kith and kin', as those scruffy Africans were not? Harold knew his opponents and believed that this was a bandwagon on to which the Tory front bench would climb if the going got tough.

From the very start, therefore, Harold sold the pass by making it clear he would not use force to bring the illegal regime to heel. All Ian Smith had to do was to sweat it out. When I raised this point in Cabinet, asking why we did not send in the troops to suppress this colonial rebellion as we had done so often elsewhere, Harold referred me to Denis Healey as Minister of Defence. Denis treated me to one of his brilliant logistical arguments: our nearest troops were in Aden, too far away to intervene quickly, so Ian Smith would be able to annex the Kariba dam before they could arrive, depriving the neighbouring African states of vital water supplies. I was in no position to query his military assessment, but I knew that Harold (and probably Denis) would never have been a party to using military force anyway.

What angered me was that Harold never seriously tried the alternative. Yet, as Trevor Huddleston pointed out to me from Tanzania, there were some he was sure would do more to stop Smith. We should, for example, initiate UN action to protect the Kariba dam and spell out our intentions more definitely to the Rhodesians. '1) Majority rule in 5 years; 2) All Europeans who wish to leave will be financially assisted in the UK if they are genuinely of UK origin (not SA!); 3) Civil servant to lose all rights if they continue to serve Smith; 4) Massive educational pro-gramme, etc.' I thought this made sense. Harold, however, thought he could trump the 'kith and kin' ace by persuading the Governor of Rhodesia and his civil servants to refuse to co-operate with this 'rebellion against the Crown'. They were certainly unhappy, but they were not going to risk their professional lives when Ian Smith was clearly getting away with UDI. Harold did not offer them the inducements I urged him to do in Cabinet. Even the sanctions we imposed were halfhearted, being limited at first to sugar and tobacco, Harold resisting pressure from our own side for oil sanctions to be added to the list. He also opposed the imposition of mandatory sanctions by the UN. It was not until

Smith executed three African resistance leaders in March 1968 that international anger forced Harold to back mandatory sanctions, and he was not too concerned when they proved not to be enforced effectively. His earlier claim that economic sanctions would topple Smith in 'weeks not months' vanished in thin air.

Harold, therefore, spent his time trying to persuade Smith to amend the racialist 1961 constitution, which the Labour Party had vociferously opposed when the Rhodesian leader had brought it in. Harold enjoyed constitution-making and considered himself rather good at it, so he scribbled out endless complicated provisions which he said would safeguard African advance and democratic rights. He sent endless envoys to Smith armed with these documents, finally entering the fray himself in direct negotiations with Smith which took place on our warships *Tiger* and *Fearless*, which he persuaded himself did not constitute a breach of his own pledge not to negotiate with an illegal regime. These warship negotiations inspired a number of witticisms in the press. A couple of years later when I was myself engaged in protracted negotiations with the TUC over my industrial relations document *In Place of Strife* Franklin produced in the *Mirror* a cartoon of me marooned in mid-Thames under London Bridge with George Woodcock, General Secretary of the TUC. We were sitting on a coal barge and the caption ran: 'They'd run out of warships.'

Smith enjoyed himself playing cat and mouse with the British Prime Minister, one moment hinting at concessions and the next withdrawing them. I spent agonized hours following these negotiations in Cabinet. After one report back I passed a note to Ted Short: 'If we sold out on this I should resign.' He scribbled back, 'You would not be the only one.' But in fact I was often isolated in Cabinet. The majority was anxious for a settlement at almost any price in our own economic interests. Ian Smith was certainly not going to accept the principle on which the Labour Party used to base its policy and which was insisted on by the Commonwealth prime ministers. When I used to remind Cabinet of the party's commitment to NIBMAR (no independence before majority rule) the reaction was not unlike a Bateman cartoon. Most of my colleagues lost patience with what they saw as my endless nitpicking, and my doggedness irritated them. Dick complained that my speeches in Cabinet were too long, and he may have been right because when I get on one of my conscience's hobby-horses I do not get off easily. On one occasion I seized the opportunity of a talk with Harold in his study in Number 10 to say to him quietly, 'You do realize, Harold, that if the Rhodesian negotiations go the wrong way I shall have to resign?' He replied with typical indiarubber cheerfulness, 'I would resign myself.' In the event we were both saved by Smith's intransigence. After the abortive *Fearless* talks, even Harold accepted that he should make no more overtures to Smith.

My great consolation through all these anxieties lay in working out my transport plan. Never have I had a more stimulating assignment. I was determined to face the facts, but not the facts tinctured by the prejudices of my officials or of my political opponents. My Tory predecessor, Ernest Marples, was a director of the road construction company, Marples Ridgeway, both prior to and after his stint at Transport, so it was not surprising that he had imprinted on the Department a belief in the superiority of road over rail. Even the Railways Division of the Ministry was temperamentally inclined to accept the Beeching cuts. What I had to do was to convince them that road and rail must be complementary. It was not a question of being anti-motor car. Since I now spent my weekends and holidays in a remote country area I was the first to realize the social value of the mobility which the car brought into so many people's lives. I was not, however, prepared to allow the motor car to destroy the railway system and other forms of public transport on which people without a car depended for their mobility. The roads lobby's only answer to congestion was 'build more roads'. To me that was not the whole answer, only part of it. I loved the countryside and wanted to find a way of protecting it and our environment generally to the greatest extent possible.

It was not an easy remit. But I was also only too aware of the constraints on public expenditure, which grew steadily worse during my time at the Ministry. The railway deficit was running at £159 million and it was hard to resist my officials' pressure to close uneconomic lines which were barely used. After one long discussion round my ministerial table about the proposed closure of a particular line which was being fiercely contested by the local people, an official from the Railways Division said to me, 'It really would be cheaper, Minister, to give all the passengers £2000 towards buying their own car.' (That £2000 is equivalent to around £16,000 today.) I was also aware that some of those people who protested most loudly were increasingly using their own cars anyway. At a conference of railwaymen, who were opposing any more closures, I challenged my audience: 'Hands up those of you who came here by car.' Sheepishly about two-thirds of them put up their hands. Another amusing encounter was with John Betjeman, who wrote to me with a poetic plea to save a certain rural line. I was, he suggested, forcing people to sit in 'diesel-scented traffic jams' in country lanes. At 2 a.m. one morning I was going through my Cabinet box and found the reply the Department had produced for me to sign. It was so stilted and pedantic that I tore it up and, tired as I was, scribbled down my alternative. It contained the words: 'Unfortunately people *like* sitting in diesel-scented traffic jams. What am I supposed to do: force them on to the train at the point of a gun?' He wrote back at once: 'What a jolly good letter!' After that I felt he was my friend.

Gradually my ideas began to crystallize. In this I was helped enormously by two outstanding parliamentary secretaries, Stephen Swingler and John Morris, whom I eventually persuaded Harold to promote to ministers of state. Stephen Swingler, MP for Newcastle-under-Lyme and a left-winger of my own ilk, had already made a name for himself in the Department under Tom Fraser, discharging a parliamentary secretary's late-night chores at the dispatch box with great skill. I chose John Morris, then at Power, when Harold said I could have another junior minister to ease my load. He was a Welshman and a lawyer, with shrewd judgment and a good mind, and though naturally equable he adapted himself to my more fiery temperament with great good humour. On one occasion, when I had routed a sneering journalist from the *Railway Review*, John said to me, 'Let me say this. I wouldn't be married to you for any money, but you will be Prime Minister one day if your health holds out.' I had a warm affection for both my ministers and we made a harmonious and effective team.

The most urgent job facing us was to decide what size railway network we wanted to preserve, to what extent it should be subsidized and how to transfer more traffic from road to rail. The existing situation gave us the worse of all worlds. The size of the railway deficit demoralized the staff and, since some of it was due to British Rail being forced to keep open uneconomic lines on social grounds, it was hard to say how much of it was due to operational inefficiency. Stanley Raymond, chairman of BRB, was a touchy man and I had to handle him carefully. At my request he gave us a demonstration at the Ministry of the sort of network he would like to see. Seventeen thousand miles of track, he told us, had already been reduced to 15,000 and was due to go down to 8000 if the rest of the Beeching cuts went through. He wanted a network of 11,000 miles, the minimum needed to maintain important feeder routes. He made an impressive case and I accepted it. In return, I persuaded him to accept, though clearly reluctantly, my decision to set up a Joint Steering Group of experts from the Department and from his own Railways Board under the chairmanship of John Morris to enquire into the finances of the railways. Its main task would be to identify and cost the 'socially necessary' lines: those which should be retained for social reasons and which would have to be subsidized. Once the subsidy had been fixed and paid, British Railways would be expected to conform to strict financial targets set by the government. Raymond knew perfectly well that another point of the exercise was to put the spotlight on the management of British Railways, which, my officials kept hinting to me, was in a mess.

Our next step was to win over the railway unions, who were also bristling with suspicion. Here again Raymond was masterly. He invited us over to his head office, where he had prepared a big map showing the network as it would have been under Beeching and what it would be under the new policy. The unions were clearly impressed, even though they faced the loss of another 3000 passenger miles of rail. I intervened to say passionately that I wanted them to hold their heads high and not be dragged down by a deficit, some part of which at any rate was not their fault. After a silence Sid Greene, emollient as ever, said in his slow drawl, 'I am very pleased with what I have heard. Clearly there is going to be a very good future for the men who are left in the system. Our trouble is, as I expect you know, the men who will not have a place in it.' He was particularly pleased that we had explained it all to them, 'not like when the Beeching Report came out and the first we heard of it was when a copy was put into our hands two hours before publication'. Other union leaders echoed him, the man from the Associated Society of Locomotive Engineers and Firemen (ASLEF) saying almost pathetically, 'You must help us with our members.' We knew that we had won and that all our effort and expenditure of time had been worth while. I was confirmed in my belief that the country's industrial relations troubles were primarily due to the high-handedness of management, which seeped so easily over from the private sector into the public one.

John Morris did an excellent job chairing the Joint Steering Group on railway finance. The innovation on which I had insisted of including a working railwayman on the team despite my Department's doubts proved a success. The concept of 'socially necessary' lines which had to be subsidized was to endure through subsequent Tory governments. So was the detailed scheme for applying it which the Steering Group worked out.

Road transport was a more difficult one to solve. Having decided that I was not going to renationalize road haulage firms I had to find other ways of controlling the industry and dealing with the cowboys who filled our roads with ramshackle vehicles whose exhaust fumes polluted the atmosphere. My first device was what we called 'quality licensing', under which licences could be refused to firms whose vehicles did not meet our tough new standards of roadworthiness. I also got my Department working on all the possible ways in which we could switch freight from road to rail. One way was by encouraging private firms to acquire private sidings from which they could ship their goods directly on to rail, and I suggested that in future planning authorities should refuse to sanction industrial estates on greenfield sites unless they were positioned next to the railway line wherever possible.

I also wanted to encourage the use of freightliner terminals. The freightliner concept had been one of Beeching's most brilliant ideas, highlighting the fact that the movement of small consignments of goods by rail could never be economical unless they were first collected together in containers at assembly points which could put them on high-speed trains. I endorsed this idea enthusiastically and could see that in order to get as much freight on rail as possible the terminals would have to be open to all-comers, private or public. In order to integrate the movement of freight by road and rail still further I finally decided to set up a National Freight Corporation to take over responsibility for all the publicly owned freight operators, including the freightliners. My idea was bitterly opposed by most of my Department as well as British Railways, but it seems to have worked.

My greatest obstacle was the rail unions, who were jealous of the rights of their nationalized industry and did not see why private road hauliers should exploit this exciting innovation the railways had produced. I reasoned with them in vain, even breaking with the civil service convention that the mountain always comes to Mohammed by going to a meeting with the NUR Executive at the union's headquarters in Marylebone Road, the first Minister of Transport, I gathered, ever to do so. But thanks to the influence of the communists on the NUR Executive, the terminals remained closed to private hauliers and the press had a field day chanting, 'Open the terminals!' Harold was plagued with questions in the House.

By March 1967 I decided I had had enough. Raymond suggested he should just open the terminals and risk a strike, but I said we must make one more effort to win by argument. Strikes do not come cheap. The crunch came at a marathon meeting in my ministerial room at which Raymond, John Morris and I wrestled with the NUR Executive for some ten hours. Their stumbling block was the Tartan Arrow road haulage company, a private company which was planning to develop its own private sidings for putting its goods on rail. This to railwaymen was the final insult, threatening as it did to put some of them out of work. One of the NUR representatives argued that railwaymen had accepted redundancy after redundancy; now they were fed up. 'When the railways get a new development at last, it is handed over to other people.' The fact that Reginald Wilson's publicly owned Transport Holding Company had just acquired a 100 per cent holding in Tartan Arrow did not make any difference. This was a development which would help other transport workers, not railwaymen, the NUR complained, and strike they would.

John Morris then had a bright idea. Why, he said, should not British Railways acquire Tartan Arrow and so keep it in the railway field? I thought this was going too far, but that a 50 per cent acquisition might be possible, if Reginald Wilson agreed. Reginald was on holiday in Switzerland and there ensued frantic efforts by my Private Office to track him down. When I got him on the phone he agreed immediately. 'I am quite happy to do anything you think is right,' he said obligingly. He was as anxious as anyone to get the open terminal issue settled amicably. The solution pleased me as a step towards the integration of road and rail. It also did the trick with the unions, and by 10 p.m. we had achieved our agreement to open the terminals. I could not believe we had at last removed this obstacle. Sid Greene was patently delighted and even the communists looked relieved. I called them all into my room and we celebrated over a drink.

A relieved Harold was on the phone immediately to congratulate my team. He repeated his congratulations fulsomely in Cabinet the following day. He always liked to give me a boost there when he could. I suspect he thought he had found a trouble-shooter and was already planning to move me on to another trouble spot as soon as he could.

There was an amusing sequel. That evening I was supposed to have been accompanying the Queen at a concert in the Queen Elizabeth Hall on the South Bank. Tied up as I was, I had asked Ted if he would deputize for me and convey my apologies to the Queen. As soon as the agreement was reached, I raced into my 'boudoir' to change into a long evening dress in five minutes flat, hoping I would arrive in time to give my apologies personally. I swept up the circular wrought-iron staircase at the Hall to where the Queen was taking some light refreshment and I was puzzled by the gawping which accompanied my ascent. Ted soon enlightened me, whispering, 'Do you realize that your zip is not done up?' Since the zip went all the way down from my neck to the bottom of my back, I must have been revealing all my underwear! The Queen with her usual tact had pretended not to notice.

That summer Ted persuaded me to take our holiday in Ireland. He was one-quarter Irish himself and had always wanted to take me there. I had resisted, saying that I represented a wet Lancashire constituency and wanted to go somewhere where I could dry out. I did not, however, regret our decision. It rained most of the time, of course, but the air was so relaxing and the people so friendly I did not care. We stayed in Ernie Evans' little hotel in Glenbeigh near the Kerry coast where that remarkable restaurateur produced some of the best meals I have ever eaten. After dinner we would gather round the piano in the bar hung with photographs of the famous and with oil paintings while a local lass, Mary, strummed away at revolutionary songs. Daring as ever Ted asked her to play 'The Sash my Father Wore', which she did without batting an eyelid, wittily parodying the words with her own anti-Orange ones. I began to understand why people went to Ireland for a holiday.

While we were there I received a telephone call from Marjorie Proops, formidable agony aunt of the *Daily Mirror*. She told me that in a public opinion poll I had come out top of the ministerial rating and she wanted to write a Top of the Pops piece about me. Could they send out a photographer? When he arrived Ted and I were just setting out for a bit of pony trekking in the hills. I had not been on horseback for twenty years, and then only precariously, but I was sure those gentle animals would be kind to me. The photographer followed us and the result was a picture of me in the *Mirror* merrily waving the reins about with my bottom sticking out. I could imagine the comments back home: 'That woman cannot ride a pony, let alone drive a car.'

Emboldened by my success over open terminals I decided to

take further steps to switch freight from road to rail. I therefore introduced the concept of 'quantity licensing' under which all vehicles of over sixteen tons gross weight would have to obtain a licence for journeys over 100 miles. The licence would not be granted where it could be shown that the freight involved could be carried just as economically by rail. This proposal was too much for my officials, who opposed it bitterly, but Stephen Swingler and Chris Foster backed me manfully. When a few months later Harold moved me to another job, my successor, Richard Marsh, dropped this provision from my Transport Bill. This was not unexpected, as I regarded him as a languid cynic who was certainly not my favourite man. I was not surprised when he defected from the Labour Party some years later.

My White Papers on policy rolled out in an endless stream and I spent many long nights putting them into simple language. My aim was to strengthen the role of public transport by making it as convenient and comfortable for passengers as possible. To this end I set up Passenger Transport Authorities in the conurbations responsible to the local authorities and charged with the job of integrating the local road and rail services and supplementing them with any other forms of public transport services they thought fit. As MP for Blackburn I had had many unhappy experiences of arriving at Manchester Piccadilly station on a dark wet night and having to wait in the rain for an infrequent bus to Manchester Victoria to catch a connection there. How on earth, I used to ask myself, can we get people to use public transport more if we subject them to such miseries? Why cannot I take a lift at Piccadilly station down to an underground railway that will take me in speed and comfort to Victoria? I wanted the new bodies to build attractive modern interchanges and other links between road and rail. The conurbations were enthusiastic about the idea and many went ahead, showing great enterprise and initiative. Years later some of them told me how saddened they had been when my Tory successors watered the concept down in their 1985 Transport Act.

Money, of course, was always a problem. To help the new

bodies I gave them powers to engage in all kinds of money-making activities in their interchanges, from bookstalls to coffee stalls. I did not see why public authorities should be expected to provide the expensive infrastructure and not be allowed to make money to help pay for it. This provision riled Peter Walker, my Transport shadow, as much as anything in my proposals and, as soon as I was moved on, it was dropped from the Bill.

One of my jobs as Minister of Transport was to approve the line of route for extensions to motorways. I always found this a very difficult task because I hated any disturbance of the country-side. Matters were made worse by the fact that the line of motorways was decided section by section as money became available. The result was that the next instalment was dictated by what had gone before, without a proper assessment of its environmental effects. This meant that engineers were able to dominate the argument.

I met this problem particularly over the proposed extension of the M40 down Aston hill on the edge of the Area of Outstanding Natural Beauty in which I lived. The suggested route lay through a nature reserve and carved a yawning gap through a hillside I had walked and loved. I was appalled, but my highway engineers insisted that this line was preferable to one slightly to the north, and they told me that the Landscape Advisory Committee supported them. As I lived in the area I did not feel I could press my objections, and I reluctantly acquiesced. When Peter Walker succeeded me as Minister of Transport after we lost the election in 1970, I wrote to ask him to have another look at the proposed route because he was freer to do so than I had been. In his autobiography some years later, Walker made a snide reference to my letter, suggesting that I had been pressing a personal interest without disclosing it. Taken aback, I invited him to tea in the House of Lords, to which I had by then transferred my political activities, explaining that I could not understand what had provoked his attack. He responded with great friendliness and said he would look the letter up. When he had done so, he wrote apologizing for having been unfair. So I was cleared, but I remain concerned that the wider effects on the environment are not being taken adequately into account as we drive more and more roads through our shrinking countryside.

A more certain source of satisfaction was what I was able to do for the canals. I had always been fascinated by inland waterways. I had been on a couple of canal holidays with Jimmie and had been struck by how quickly one could escape from drab industrial surroundings as one slipped between the hedges lining the towpath in a flat-bottomed boat. I believed that messing about in boats was a leisure activity which should be increasingly available to everyone. I was therefore horrified to discover that one of the Treasury's money-saving exercises in 1967 involved closing down miles of inland waterways which were no longer commercially viable. I was alerted to the danger by a vocal band of canal enthusiasts led by a certain Mr Monk, whose main political weapon was verbal vitriol to be thrown in the faces of all politicians. I did not need any kind of threat to launch me into the attack because my heart was in their cause. Getting money out of the Treasury at that moment of economic crisis was like the proverbial getting of blood out of a stone, but when I moved in on Jack Diamond, who as the Chief Secretary to the Treasury was responsible for cutting public expenditure, I found he was human after all, or as human as his job allowed. I got him to agree to give me enough subsidy to keep open 1400 miles of non-commercially viable canals for pleasure cruising; we called them 'leisureways'. Jack stipulated, quite rightly, that the job of opening up and maintaining further stretches of disused canal would have to fall on the voluntary bodies. In fact the voluntary canal societies have responded magnificently, as I found when as Euro-MP for one of the Manchester area constituencies I was made president of the Huddersfield Canal Society and attended their annual canal festival. I was saddened when some years later Jack Diamond followed David Owen's misguided lodestar out of the Labour Party, because I believe that at heart he was one of us.

When my White Paper on inland waterways was published I enjoyed one of the few rewarding moments in a minister's battle-scarred life. I walked into my ministerial room to find my civil servants staring at a large bunch of red roses from the vitriolic Mr Monk, who had been a thorn in all our sides.

Gradually my comprehensive Transport Bill came into shape. I was told it was the longest Bill to date in parliamentary history. Stephen, John and I entered into our parliamentary battle with zest, ready to work all hours. But my life at Transport was nearing its end. I was in the middle of guiding my Bill through Parliament when I was caught by another economic crisis facing the government. On 16 November 1967 we ministers were called to a sombre Cabinet in which Harold announced that he and the Chancellor had decided that sterling could no longer be defended at its present parity and would have to be devalued by 14.3 per cent. The forbidden word had surfaced at last! Of course, those of us who had been pressing for devaluation for the previous three years were relieved, but it was not unalloyed joy. I for one thought we were merely putting ourselves into a different strait-jacket. I had always wanted us to float the pound. But devaluation carried one bonus. A few muddled days later Jim Callaghan decided that he should resign as Chancellor. In the ensuing Cabinet reshuffle, Harold decided to appoint Roy Jenkins in his place, probably reluctantly because he always believed Roy was conspiring against him. I thought this was a misguided view: if anyone was conspiring against him it was Jim.

In some ways, Roy was to prove as orthodox a Chancellor as Jim. Devaluation, he was soon telling us, made deflation more, not less, necessary. It was the familiar Treasury refrain. Whatever the economic situation, argued the mandarins, the only course of action was to deflate. I got so irritated by this that I adapted the saying of Dorothy Parker, the American wit: to the Treasury everything worth having in life was illegal, immoral or inflationary. That was all I heard from them while I was in government. Roy had some saving graces. He did not flap about in panic, as Jim had tended to do. Moreover he was tougher in distributing the sacrifices than Jim had been. When within a couple of months he told Cabinet that we had to reduce demand by £1000 million, he sweetened the blow by asserting that civil and defence cuts must be on a parity. The battles in Cabinet were long and bloody, and our morale was low. The loss of three by-elections on 28 March, with a big swing to the Tories, was a body-blow. Dick and I had been pressing Harold for a long time to set up an inner Cabinet, and now the crunch had come. There must, we agreed, be a fundamental reconstruction of the Cabinet.

When we challenged Harold we discovered that he had come to the same conclusion, but I was dismayed when I learned the part he wanted me to play in it. His first plan was that I should become Lord President of the Council and Leader of the House, concentrating on the collective strategy of Cabinet, and a member of the inner Cabinet he would now set up. I was not impressed by this idea since I knew that the government's strategy was dictated by the Treasury. 'Why not put me at DEA?' I asked. There I would be level-pegging with the Treasury in working out and presenting policy to Cabinet. 'Roy Jenkins won't hear of it,' he replied. Shortly after, Roy had a personal talk with me in which he admitted frankly that this was so. He described his refusal as a compliment. This split in responsibility did not work, he told me. It had been bad enough with George Brown, but it would be impossible with a 'strong minister' like me. His reaction proved that I had been right to turn down the post of Lord President.

Harold's next idea was that I should become Minister of Labour in Ray Gunter's place because I was, he said, 'good at getting on with the trade unions'. I recoiled in horror, telling him fiercely, 'I am not prepared to become Margaret Bondfield Mark II.' Margaret Bondfield, the first ever woman in the Cabinet, had been Minister of Labour in Ramsay MacDonald's government in the 1930s, and as such had always been an ogre of the left. 'I will change the name of the Ministry,' Harold assured me desperately. I left him conspiring with Dick Crossman, who, very content with his own new job at Social Security, was anxious for me to agree.

Ted and I were at Windsor Castle for the weekend, having been invited by the Queen to dine there with a number of other guests from the political and diplomatic worlds and stay the night. We were just admiring the view of Windsor Park from the windows of our suite when Dick Crossman telephoned. He had arranged with Harold that if I took on the job of Minister of Labour I should become First Secretary as well – a post Harold had offered to Dick. I was taken aback at Dick's generosity. The First Secretary had no special duties: it was simply a question of rank. It meant I should be moved up to become one of the inner top four of the government. I decided that the new status would make all the difference and that I could not refuse. But, I insisted, the name must be changed from the class name of Minister of Labour to one which would reflect my intention to switch the whole emphasis of prices and incomes policy from negative wage restraint. It must be seen as the way to a higher standard of living by making it possible to expand the economy without inflation and by encouraging productivity. Above all it must apply to everyone. Harold agreed.

And so on 4 April 1968 I became First Secretary of State and Secretary of State for Employment and Productivity, the new name I had chosen for the sort of positive job I wanted to do.

I wrote in my diary, 'I am under no illusion that I may be committing political suicide. I have at last moved from the periphery of the whirlwind into its very heart. And yet I knew I couldn't do anything else. If I go down in disaster, as well I may, at least I shall have been an adult before I die.'

SIXTEEN

•

In Place of Popularity

THE FIRST evidence of my change of status came when I entered the Cabinet room and found I had been moved to the inner circle with a seat next to Denis Healey, opposite the Prime Minister and Roy Jenkins as the new Chancellor. At least this meant I did not have to strain to hear what they said, but I missed the camaraderie and conspiratorial interchanges with my colleagues lower down the table.

Harold had said to me when persuading me to take the post, 'You will have two of the best men in Whitehall: Denis Barnes and Alex Jarratt.' As Permanent Secretary, Denis Barnes was certainly a welcome relief from Sir Thomas, being a matey and informal man who was soon calling me Barbara. He radiated relaxed common sense towards industrial relations, and Harold, for one, believed he was 'one of us'. Alex Jarratt was composed of tougher intellectual material. He had made a reputation for himself as Secretary to the Prices and Incomes Board since 1965. Aubrey Jones thought highly of him and was not too pleased when he was seconded to my new Department as Deputy Secretary with particular responsibility for the prices side of prices and incomes policy. I worked happily enough with both men.

I was also lucky in my Private Secretary, Douglas Smith, and my Chief Information Officer, Charles Birdsall. Douglas was a tall, quiet, authoritative man with a sense of humour whom I took to immediately. He was slightly older than most of the young high-fliers who pass through Private Offices and had a long experience in the Department. A product of Leeds University, he

had the northerner's nous. I found comfort in his shrewd judgments and his obvious understanding of the crown of thorns I had
taken on. I pleaded with Denis Barnes to leave him with me as
long as possible. When at last in Douglas' own interests I had to
agree to let him be promoted into another job, I felt I had lost my
right arm. He ended up, very appropriately, as chairman of
ACAS, the Advisory, Conciliation and Arbitration Service which
the Labour government set up in 1974.

Charles Birdsall was charming and, I was told, the most
competent Chief Information Officer in Whitehall. He was an
eager, rather cherubic little man who exuded enthusiasm for his
job. He mothered me, fighting my corner against the press, and
was tireless in his duties during the long hours we often had to
spend during weekends at the Ministry dealing with the threats of
major strikes. I remember one weekend when we were incarcerated in our building in St James's Square without food. He came
bustling into my room to suggest he should go to Wheeler's
restaurant, not far away, and bring us all their best provender and
a bottle of wine. 'Charles,' I rebuked him, 'you cannot go out to
Wheeler's, through the press who are besieging us, and come back
with oysters and wine.' Unabashed he went off and brought us
back some smoked salmon sandwiches instead. I was particularly
glad of his unflinching support because Chris Hall had refused to
come to Employment with me, saying it was not his line of
country. He stayed at Transport, where I prayed he might have
some influence on saving my policy, but he left the Department a
few months later with a considerable loss of salary to become
secretary of the Ramblers' Association, where his heart really lay.

Charles was hovering around me protectively at my first press
conference, but it went quite well. There was an amusing moment
when one of the journalists said to me, 'Ray Gunter described his
job as a bed of nails. How would you describe yours?' After a
moment's frantic thought, I replied instinctively, 'A springboard.'
'To the premiership?' chipped in Peter Patterson of the *Sunday
Telegraph* naughtily. 'Oh God,' I replied, 'don't saddle me with
that!' and we all laughed.

But pleasant and helpful as all these people were, I soon

grasped that they could not save me from the trap into which I had allowed myself to be caught. I was the victim again of my impulsive streak: I wanted to help Harold and the Labour government, though it was vanity to imagine that I could single-handedly turn a negative economic policy into a positive one. My trouble was that I was constitutionally incapable of turning down a challenge, however risky, and once I was embroiled in anything I wanted to make it work. On one occasion when I was in the middle of my troubles I was taken out to lunch by Alan Watkins, the newspaper columnist who had been making a series of attacks on me in the *New Statesman*. I had never warmed to him, because I thought he had a good opinion of himself. He certainly did not have one of me. 'You are a dangerous woman,' he said to me. 'You are a button-pusher like Kennedy, and I don't like button-pushers.' Presumably he meant that I liked to get things done, and I replied that one could push good buttons as well as bad. 'Doesn't matter,' he replied, 'I am just against activists.' Here I now was, pushing buttons once again and finding the challenge riskier than I had visualized.

Before I could turn round in my new job, let alone work out new aspects of policy, I was on my feet at the dispatch box moving the Second Reading of the Prices and Incomes Bill 1968, the next instalment in the government's statutory prices and incomes policy. It formed part of Roy Jenkins' post-devaluation strategy, which was based on the argument that wage restraint was more important than ever if we were to achieve export-led growth and not just a short-lived consumer boom. I had had no part in drafting the Bill, which I had inherited from Peter Shore, formerly responsible for prices and incomes policy at DEA. I liked Peter enormously. He was a gentle, courteous man of high intelligence whose wife Elizabeth was a doctor in the Department of Health and Social Security. They were both natural political allies in our left-wing group. But Peter had not been a success at DEA. Harold did not think he was tough enough, which was why I had been brought in to carry his Bill through Parliament against the growing opposition of Labour backbenchers and trade unions.

So there I was at the dispatch box, urging support for a measure of whose importance I was far from convinced. The new Bill not only renewed for another eighteen months the powers of the original 1966 Prices and Incomes Act, which our people had been promised would be temporary, but strengthened them. The government's existing power to demand the advance notification of proposed pay and price increases and to refer them to the Prices and Incomes Board for a report on their acceptability remained, but the power to delay the increases for seven months was extended to twelve months – a hefty period. For the first time, too, the legislation fixed a ceiling of 3.5 per cent for pay and price increases. I had insisted in Cabinet that there would have to be an exception from the ceiling for productivity deals which the Board accepted as genuinely increasing productivity. We also included a power to cut existing prices where the Board recommended that this should be done. The Bill also prevented 'excessive' increases in rents and dividends.

I made the best case I could for this in my new role. The renewal of these powers, I argued, was taking place in a different context. We were no longer urging wage restraint as part of a deflationary policy to underpin the artificially high value of the pound, but to make the alternative to deflation – devaluation – work. My shadow at Employment, Robert Carr, had some fun at my expense. 'So the Labour government had actually *wanted* devaluation?' he mocked. Nor did I convince our MPs on the left, who refused to accept that wage increases were the cause of inflation and had tabled an amendment to that effect which the Speaker, in the event, did not call.

This approach to incomes policy was endorsed and encouraged by the trade unions. When I went to Employment, the major unions had come under aggressive and highly effective left-wing leadership. Frank Cousins, already a rebel against the government, had a militant lieutenant in Jack Jones, who was in charge of the dockers. Son of a Liverpool docker himself, Jack was a man of iron integrity who had dedicated his life to the cause of trade unionism, which he believed was best promoted by industrial militancy. Some of the people in my Department believed he was a communist, but I did not, and his co-operation with Labour's 1974 government proved me right. So did his dedicated work, on retirement, for the pensioners. Nor was there any sign of it in his autobiography *Union Man*, published in 1986, where he would have surely boasted of it if it had been true. A month before I took over my new job, Hugh Scanlon, the other 'terrible twin', was elected President of the Amalgamated Engineering Union (AEU). His election undoubtedly owed something to the backing of the communists in his union, but here again I believed it was an over-simplification to brand him as a member of the party, as our Security Service liked to do.

Indeed, I had nothing but contempt for the Security Service, whose reports landed on my desk from time to time. Harold Wilson became convinced that sections of the Service were plot-ting against the Labour government in general and him in particu-lar, shadowing the private lives of his aides and even rifling their offices and flats. I had no direct experience of this myself, but the publication of *Spycatcher* by Peter Wright in 1987 showed that Harold's allegations were not just the inventions of a neurotically suspicious man. What struck me about the Security Service from the reports I received was its amateurishness. The facts its officers gave were thin and obvious. One report, for instance, on a dispute we had in the motor-car industry, solemnly informed me that Hugh Scanlon had been anxious for a settlement! The judgment of anyone who could submit this as a serious piece of 'intelligence' could not be trusted on anything. In fact my conciliation officers, led by Conrad Heron, knew far more about the influence of the Communist Party in industrial affairs than the Security men marooned in their foetid atmosphere of conspiracy.

Conrad Heron, the Deputy Secretary in charge of industrial relations, was one of the most remarkable civil servants I was to meet. He was kindly, shrewd and above all knowledgeable, since he knew exactly which trade union officers, local and national, were under communist influence and how to outmanoeuvre them. He was backed up by an equally shrewd team, including Andy Kerr, the Chief Conciliation Officer. I learned to rely on their judgment in all the disputes with which I had to deal because, like me, they had no Pavlovian reaction to the word 'communist', realizing that many local communist officials were doing a dedicated job in the factories, even if a misguided one. Equally, like me, they were determined not to allow the communist policy to disrupt the economic struggles of the Labour governments. What always struck me about my new Department was how strong was the tradition of conciliation and how unhappy most of my officials from Denis Barnes downwards were about the rigidities of the prices and incomes policy.

The unions were not prepared, therefore, to help me get the new Bill through Parliament. My problem was intensified when the Chief Whip, John Silkin, told me he had put on to the Standing Committee through which the Bill had to pass two of my out-and-out Labour opponents on the policy, Ian Mikardo and Ted Fletcher. John Silkin was another of my agreeable left-wing friends. He was married to Rosamund John, the beautiful star of those early English post-war films, who was as enchanting in private life as she was on the screen – and she was as left-wing as he was. John argued that the left had to feel that it had had its say. I was not too pleased with his relaxed and tolerant attitude: he did not have to stay up night after night dealing with their practised delaying tactics, as I had to do. Nonetheless, we eventually won through and to the government's intense relief got the Third Reading of the Bill by a majority of forty-four – far more than we had dared to hope for.

Much of this success was due to my Joint Parliamentary Secretaries, Roy Hattersley, who had been Parliamentary Secretary to Ray Gunter, and Harold Walker, a stocky little man from Doncaster who had come into Parliament from the shop floor. He looked like a boxer and behaved like one at the dispatch box, delivering some telling blows. Later he was to become an untraditional Deputy Speaker in the Commons, but a very effective one.

Roy Hattersley was more of an enigma. When I agreed to go to DEP, Harold said I could have a different Parliamentary Secretary. I said that I wanted to keep Hattersley; Harold frowned. 'You know he is a Jenkins man,' he said. 'Everything you say will go straight to the Chancellor.' I replied that I would judge as I found. I wanted a competent team and everyone told me Hattersley was competent. And so he proved. He always loyally carried out my policy, even when he disagreed with it. I never found any evidence of his conspiring with Roy Jenkins. Indeed, Roy Hattersley was a dove on prices and incomes policy, which hardly made him a Jenkins sycophant. To this day I believe Roy Hattersley is his own man, though what that 'man' involves I have never been quite sure. He has radical instincts on issues like freedom of the individual, but I am far from clear about where this puts him in the spectrum of those who want a fundamental change in the distribution of economic power. He is no leftie, but then he is no conformist either. I was sorry that our election defeats robbed him of the chance to reveal his true character.

The Bill out of the way, I was determined to exploit to the full the power it gave me to tackle excessive price increases, encourage productivity deals and help the low paid. In this I found a convinced partner in Aubrey Jones of the PIB. Aubrey was another enigma. Though a former Conservative minister, even of the moderate years of Conservatism, he was almost austerely dedicated to the success of the prices and incomes policy. He also appreciated that the policy could not work unless I managed to persuade my fellow departmental ministers to make a regular flow of price references to the Board. But on the whole other departments found reasons why the price increases proposed by their own industries should not be referred. Aubrey was always suggesting new types of reference, such as distributors' margins on the goods they handled. He argued, with perfect logic, that if prices went up as a result of devaluation, it should not automatically follow that distributors' margins should go up too. His report on this was radical, but it came up against Treasury resistance to anything which did not reduce demand by cutting purchasing power.

On one occasion when I protested to Harold about the failure of my colleagues to back my drive for price references, he said to me rather sheepishly, 'Some economists argue that the best way to control inflation is to let prices rise.' Right, I thought, then why have I been given this assignment to sell a prices and incomes policy? If the aim is only to reduce demand, the best way would be to do it openly and frankly through the Budget, instead of getting people like me to spend hours splitting hairs over who has or who has not exceeded the norm or produced some real increase in productivity. The ham-handed policy I was asked to operate alienated our people more than a budgetary policy which distributed the sacrifices fairly would have done.

But I soldiered on doggedly. For one thing, I believed in the principle of a genuine prices and incomes policy. I could not see how it was possible to plan the economy without controlling demand, of which wage demands form a part. Every government has an incomes policy of some kind.

When a few months later, Vic Feather, the pawky young Yorkshire lad of my youth, succeeded George Woodcock as General Secretary of the TUC, he said to me in one of our private arguments about prices and incomes policy, 'Give it up, luv, and let the Chancellor do his worst.' Ten years later, Margaret Thatcher was to show what that worst could be: the ruthless application of monetary policy which pushed unemployment up to the highest levels since the 1930s and almost destroyed the trade unions. It was that which I wanted to avoid.

I therefore set out with renewed determination to highlight the positive side of the policy. In particular I wanted to help workers to make the fullest use of the productivity deals which could provide them with a loophole from the 'norm' of 3.5 per cent. I had therefore set up a Manpower and Productivity Service to advise on how this could be done and was delighted when George Cattell of Rootes agreed to become its head. George was a great asset and pleasant to work with, a liberal in industrial relations, with an inside knowledge of industry, having held high managerial posts in Rootes. He made a big impression on the Industrials, as we called the industrial correspondents, a cynical breed of men, when I introduced him to them at a press conference. The result was some very favourable press comment, for a change.

In fact I had scored my second bull's-eye in two days, having shaken everyone by my appointment of Jim Mortimer to the PIB two days earlier. The Industrials knew what a coup this was in silencing my Labour critics, since Jim was a full-time official of the Draughtsmen and Allied Technicians' Association (DATA), which was later to merge with the AEU, and to which a number of our left-wing rebels like Stan Orme then belonged. Jim's left-wing credentials were never in doubt, nor were those of his union, which had been one of the small minority to vote against George Brown's Statement of Intent at a TUC special conference three years earlier. When I told George Woodcock of my intention to appoint Jim, his bushy eyebrows shot up. 'Well, I am in favour of experiments – very interesting. Of course, he is a communist.' When I shook my head, he added, 'Well, he certainly was and I think still is. But I don't say he is any the worse for that.' In the event, Aubrey had nothing but praise for his work on the PIB.

Later, Jim was to head ACAS, and he won widespread respect for the impartial and constructive work he did there, thus providing another example of how right Nye Bevan was in denouncing the 'demonology' of politics which puts labels on people which owe more to prejudice than to fact.

The restraints of the prices and incomes policy involved me in endless industrial disputes as the unions struggled to demonstrate that the settlements they had reached were within the criteria. Sometimes it nearly broke my heart to have to turn down increases won by workers who were certainly not lavishly paid. One almost comical example was the building workers, who had persuaded their employers to pay them an interim increase of one penny an hour, which I feared would take them over the ceiling. So it proved, and I had to freeze it. The 'builders' penny' became a by-word at my expense. On one occasion when we had all been incarcerated in the Ministry for another long weekend and were congratulating ourselves on having avoided another national strike, Douglas Smith said to me with his usual dry humour, 'Secretary of State, we ought to strike ourselves a campaign medal with bars to commemorate each success.' In some of these disputes we managed to lift the argument above the mundane details of who got this or that to a higher level of social policy. In fact, it was two such disputes which fired my determination to force the macho male chauvinists in the Treasury to accept the principle of equal pay.

The first was the strike of women sewing-machinists at Ford's factory at Dagenham. These were the women who had to do a heavy job machining the upholstery of the car interiors. They went on strike complaining that they had been cheated under the firm's job-evaluation scheme, which in their view had not properly assessed the value of their work in relation to that of the men. The strike threatened the firm's production of cars and Ford appealed to us to settle it.

My usual role when a major strike was threatened was to sit back and let my conciliation officers deal with it, but there is nothing more interventionist than a prices and incomes policy, so there would be moments in a complicated dispute when my officials would call me in or I would insist on going in.

We set up a committee of enquiry under Jack Stamp, our favourite trouble-shooter, but he made the mistake of announcing that it would be in private, so the women refused to co-operate. As we were getting nowhere, I asked for a report. Our problem, I discovered, was that no less than five unions were involved through the National Joint Council (NJC) at the factory, so the situation was snarled up by inter-union rivalries. The NJC had approved the job-evaluation scheme, so most of the unions were only too anxious to co-operate with us, because the last thing they wanted was for the whole evaluation process to be reopened. But Reg Birch, a communist organizer of the Amalgamated Union of Engineering and Foundry Workers (AEF), saw the chance to make trouble and declared that his union could never oppose the principle of equal pay – an issue which no one, not even the women, had raised before. It was stalemate. 'Right,' I said, 'I'll see the women myself.' Douglas Smith, good civil servant that he was, looked nervous, but he complied. He managed to track down the unions involved and it was arranged.

I proceeded to set the scene as informally as possible, saying to Douglas Smith that these women were decent working people with a grievance and not the enemies of society. Douglas entered into the spirit of the whole enterprise, pushing back my ministerial table and arranging a circle of chairs. When the women arrived they were taken aback as I sat down among them and offered them a cup of tea. They had arrived full of suspicion, fired by their formidable ring-leader, Rosie, who was not going to have them done out of their rights. Nor was I prepared to surrender the criteria of the prices and incomes policy.

As we talked I found what the trouble was all about. They believed – encouraged by their communist shop steward, a Mr Friedman – that there had been a second job-evaluation report more favourable to them which the firm had suppressed. I called in Mr Blakenham, the factory's personnel officer, a reasonable but worried man. He managed to convince them that this was not so. Clearly impressed, the women were uncertain what to do. Rosie said defiantly that they could not go back empty-handed or else they would not get their fellow workers to call off the strike. At this point Mr Blakenham took me aside to say that the firm had been worried for some time about the large differential between men's and women's pay at Dagenham: nothing to do with the job-evaluation scheme. At Dagenham women automatically got 85 per cent of the men's rate, whereas they got 92 per cent at other Ford factories. The firm would be only too willing to close the gap. I consulted Conrad Heron, who told me we could justify this under prices and incomes policy as the firm had reassessed the economic value of the women's work. A quick call to Number 10 for approval and it was agreed. The women were delighted and the unions relieved that the job-evaluation scheme was intact. We parted the best of friends.

Blakenham had thanked me profusely on behalf of the firm, but I was savaged by the Tory press the following day for having undermined the Chancellor's brave austerity. I knew – because people in the know told me – that the Treasury was gunning for me as too soft on prices and incomes policy. But I did not care. The dispute confirmed me in my beliefs: first, that in a free society the best way to deal with communists is not to suppress but to outmanoeuvre them; second, that industrial disputes are about human beings and that governments should not try to keep out of them; third, that many strikes are about genuine grievances and are often workers' only way of drawing attention to them; finally, that equal pay was an issue that the Labour government could not ignore much longer.

The Ford women's dispute entered into trade union hagiology. Over twenty years later Ron Todd, then General Secretary of the Transport Workers, commissioned a commemorative plate. He invited me to attend a ceremony at Transport House to receive my plate. Most of those Ford women were there, including Rosie, and we embraced affectionately. Their pride was great to see and I did not mind that my own name had been tucked away at the back of the plate. This had been their hour.

It was the pay dispute in the engineering industry which clinched my belief that the Labour government had to act on equal pay, prices and incomes policy or not. Hughie Scanlon, newly elected President of the Engineering Union, was out to win his spurs and had put in a substantial pay demand. As usual I left it to Conrad Heron and his team to keep an eye on the negotiations, and as usual it ended up in my ministerial room.

Jim Fielding, leader of the Engineering Employers' team, thought he had brought peace when he put all the money he had available into an offer of £19 for the skilled men, the group in which, he rightly assessed, Hugh Scanlon was really interested. But this left only £13 for the women, who were at the bottom of the pile. For years the union had tolerated a pay-structure hierarchy which descended in the following order: skilled workers, semi-skilled, labourers and women. The employers' offer made the discrepancy even more glaring and Marion Veitch of the Transport Workers, the only woman in the union negotiating team, rebelled and said she would denounce the agreement to the press unless the women got a better deal. Scanlon, a cunning negotiator whom the employers feared more than the communist Reg Birch, promptly discovered the importance of equal pay and demanded a move towards it, on top of his pay demand.

I was in a trap. Nothing would please Hughie more than to break on the issue. Equally the employers insisted that they had already put on the table all the money they could afford. I called in Jim Fielding and lectured him. He must now tell Scanlon that he was prepared to renegotiate the deal within the same sum to give the women more. Fielding looked terrified at the very idea, but I persisted and he gave in. It worked. Hughie was outraged and stumped off, threatening a strike. After a few anxious days of waiting the message came: the union would accept the employers' original offer. There would be nothing more for the women and no strike. I knew then that left to themselves the unions would never do anything serious about equal pay and that the government had to legislate.

These subtle issues were not appreciated by the party conference. By October 1968 hostility against the prices and incomes policy exploded in a spectacular defeat for the National Executive when Frank Cousins' resolution demanding the total abandonment of the policy was carried by some 5 million votes to just over 1 million. I had the wretched task of opposing it on behalf of the National Executive, knowing that the Executive itself had only just missed supporting it, the government's face being saved by the casting vote of Jennie Lee as chairman. I made a poor speech. The floor was not listening. Even my announcement that I was setting up a working party on the future of the policy was brushed aside as irrelevant. I sensed that even my Cabinet colleagues were backing down, and I wrote in my diary, 'This leaves me carrying an immense can. I have got to go on justifying a policy which three-quarters of the Cabinet no longer believe in.' I knew, for instance, that even Roy Jenkins was ready to ride roughshod over the policy in order to avoid a damaging strike, as he had shown over the 15 per cent claim by the ships' tally clerks a few months earlier.

I was therefore astonished when, despite my association with the hated policy, I was voted to the top of the constituency section of the National Executive again, climbing up from third place. I was to stay at the top the following year as well. Harold Wilson got a standing ovation for a fighting speech which showed him at his best. So conference was telling us it was against the policy, but not against the government. I also felt most delegates were divided in their minds over economic policy. Few of them could swallow

412

Hugh Scanlon's sweeping assertion that no wage claim could ever be inflationary. They disliked wage restraint, but could not think of an alternative.

It was in this atmosphere that I had to deal with the Donovan Report. We were plagued by a rash of unofficial strikes which were turning public opinion against the trade unions, while Ted Heath was having a field day directing that public irritation against the government. The Tories had long been clamouring for curbs on the unions, and a group of Conservative lawyers had drawn up a complicated legal framework for controlling them which had been published under the title *Fair Deal at Work*. Two years earlier, Harold had sought to fend off these attacks by setting up a Royal Commission under Lord Justice Donovan, to enquire into 'relations between managements and employees, the role of trade unions and employers' associations . . . with particular reference to the Law'. To cover his flank with the unions, Harold made George Woodcock a member of it. Other members were Sir George Pollock, an industrialist, Alf (Lord) Robens, chairman of the National Coal Board, independent specialists like Hugh Clegg, a former member of the PIB but at the time Professor of Industrial Relations at Warwick, Eric Wigham, industrial correspondent of *The Times*, and Andrew Shonfield, Director of Studies at the Royal Institute of International Affairs. Their report was awaiting me when I took over my new job.

The report was surprisingly relaxed and had George Woodcock's fingerprints all over it. It started from the premise that the right way to avoid strikes was to improve the machinery of collective bargaining and ensure that there were effective conciliation procedures in every plant. Reform must be voluntary. An Industrial Relations Commission (CIR) should be set up representing both sides of industry to advise how it could be achieved. Legal restraints did not work. The report therefore rejected the proposals in *Fair Deal at Work*, in particular the suggestion that collective agreements should be made legally enforceable, arguing sensibly that, if they were, the unions would never enter into them and anarchy would result.

Behind this approach lay the assumption that workers should

have the right to organize in voluntary associations like anybody else and to fix their own rules as long as they were in accordance with natural justice. Industrial relations should be treated pragmatically. The report even justified the closed shop on the ground that it helped the employers to know with whom they were to negotiate. The major dissident note was struck by Andrew Shonfield in a minority report in which he wanted the proposed Industrial Relations Commission to have powers to enforce its findings on such issues as inter-union disputes. The majority, however, insisted that it should be purely advisory.

I approached the report with an open mind. I was glad it had rejected the Tories' legalistic approach, though I could not see it doing much to help with the problem of wild-cat strikes in the short term. My first step was to consult the TUC, the CBI and the PLP. There was little help from any of them. At my meeting with the TUC, George Woodcock sat on his hands, drawling that they had not come to make any proposals, merely to find out what I intended to do. The CBI, led by John Davies, denounced the proposals as totally inadequate. My consultation with the PLP was sparsely attended and I remarked cynically that MPs were interested in meetings only where they could attack the government's decisions. To ask them to make decisions themselves was a bit below the belt.

My mood of exasperation was heightened by two disputes which I found impossible to justify. The first occurred at the Girling Brakes factory, where twenty-two machine-setters downed tools without warning because they refused to accept instructions from a chargehand of another union. As they were key men producing a key component for the motor industry, their action led to 5000 workers being laid off, some of whom protested publicly at the behaviour of the machine-setters. As usual we set up a court of enquiry, but the strikers refused to give evidence. I inspired one of our Labour MPs to put down a Private Notice Question to me in the hope that the adverse publicity would force Hugh Scanlon to act. It worked and eventually Scanlon persuaded his four shop stewards to get the strikers back to work. Ted Heath made great political capital out of all this and I began to feel that I would have to strengthen the Donovan Report.

The second dispute threatened the launching of the newly nationalized steel industry as a result of rivalry between two unions over the question who should organize the clerical workers in the industry. On the one hand stood the powerful steel union under Dai Davies, who had the ear of the TUC; on the other there were two clerical workers' unions who did not see why Big Brother should be allowed to take their natural membership away from them. Both contestants had the power to disrupt the industry and threatened to go on strike if they did not get their way. Lord Melchett, chairman of the British Steel Corporation, and Ron Smith, his director of personnel, came to see me pleading that they did not care which unions they recognized so long as they could get on with their job. The dispute dragged on miserably for months before it was resolved.

My final consultation took place at the government's austere residential establishment at Sunningdale. I was put in a spartan room and had to take my morning bath in a cold tiled bathroom across the corridor, from which I emerged shivering. On one occasion when I stayed there I asked timidly whether I could have an early-morning cup of tea in my room. This was clearly against the rules, but the management stretched a point for the Secretary of State. After waiting in vain for my cup of tea to arrive, I found it congealing outside my door when I emerged for my bath. Someone had dumped it there silently.

Nonetheless on this occasion it was a stimulating weekend, to which I had invited people who could speak both for the employers and for the unions, as well as for the government. It was Peter Shore who suggested that the answer to our problems might lie in taking power to impose a conciliation pause during which the two sides to a dispute could be brought together to talk over their differences and at least try to avoid a strike. It seemed common sense to me and I jumped at it.

Back in the Department I could see my ideas taking shape. I firmly believed in the Donovan concept of the workers' right to organize themselves in trade unions and in the Donovan argument that we ought to strengthen unions not weaken them. So I wanted to raise the status and rights of trade unions, but I also believed I had the right in return to ask them to accept greater responsibilities in preventing the needless disruption of the country's economic life.

And so *In Place of Strife* was born. I worked out the framework with the Department and then took the draft home to our Islington flat to work on while Ted went to bed. I wanted to find the right language to express my philosophy. There were, I wrote, inevitably conflicts of interest in industry: we must try to ensure that they did not develop into damaging strikes. There was nothing wrong with strikes in principle. 'The right of a worker to withdraw his labour is one of the essential freedoms in a democracy' and 'the existence of this right has undoubtedly contributed to industrial progress and to the development of a more just society'. But the strike weapon was so important it should not be abused. About three-quarters of the days lost through strikes were lost through unofficial ones, which formed 95 per cent of all industrial disputes. They were often more disruptive than major official ones because of their unpredictability. They could have a disproportionate effect on modern industry. We needed to improve conciliatory machinery. In the majority of firms consultation procedures were defective or did not exist at all. But conciliation was a two-way process. To correct this, we needed to improve the status and organization of the trade unions, encouraging mergers into fewer and larger unions so as to minimize inter-union disputes, giving them funds for the training of their shop stewards and strengthening the role of the TUC. Only in this way could we eliminate industrial anarchy.

To the Tories this doctrine was heresy. They were outraged when I proposed to give workers the statutory right to belong to a trade union for the first time in their history and to encourage employers to institute the check-off, whereby workers agreed to have their trade union dues deducted from their pay packet. They scoffed at my idea of a Trade Union Development Fund to help finance the merger of smaller unions and the training of their staff.

My left-wing friends, on the other hand, were appalled when I demanded a *quid pro quo* from the trade unions. It was in fact a modest one, as all I asked was that the unions should co-operate in avoiding unnecessary strikes. The whole purpose of my proposals was to remove the causes of many strikes by providing an alternative. In the case of unofficial strikes, for instance, where workers had downed tools without any conciliation procedure having been used, workers would be called on to suspend their action for twenty-eight days to enable conciliation to be tried. The first obligation would be on the employer to reverse any arbitrary action such as a sudden dismissal which might have caused a strike. That done, however, it would fall on the workers to agree to a 'conciliation pause'. Enforcement in both these cases would be by fines. If that failed the strike could be resumed.

Secondly, I wanted the power to demand that a secret ballot be held before an official strike was declared. Thirdly, I wanted the power to enforce the findings of the Industrial Relations Commission in disputes about union recognition. Normally this would cause no problem with the unions since they were only too glad to have an anti-union employer forced to recognize a union. However, where two or three unions were disputing which of them should be recognized the situation became more complicated. They did not want to have imposed on them a CIR ruling as to which of them should be recognized, because they preferred to fight it out. I wanted to avoid the disruption this caused and proposed that either employer or union could be fined for ignoring the findings of the CIR.

In all this I rejected the idea of bringing in the courts. These modest powers would only be activated at the discretion of the Secretary of State, who was answerable to Parliament.

As I finished redrafting my White Paper in the early hours, a sleepy Ted came out to make me a cup of tea. I told him I was stumped for a title which would reflect the philosophy I was trying to set out. 'Why not "In Place of Strife"?' said Ted, and I hugged him. It was a brilliant adaptation of Nye Bevan's *In Place of Fear* and was totally justified. Had not Nye himself warned of the limitations of industrial action, particularly in a situation of economic crisis? 'To render industry idle as a means of achieving political victory was hardly an effective weapon in such circumstances,' he wrote. My left-wing friends who considered themselves Bevanites and who were getting ready to smite me hip and thigh were furious. They considered my title a piece of *lèse-majesté*. In fact I was convinced that Nye would have been on my side.

Harold was delighted with my ideas. He was shrewd enough to realize I had drawn the poison out of Heath's attacks without surrendering the rights of trade unionism. 'You haven't so much out-Heathed Heath as outflanked him,' he chuckled. He started planning how he could get my draft quickly through Cabinet and decided to set up a small *ad hoc* ministerial committee to deal with it. He was already showing signs of being far more hawkish than I was. Strikes were an issue on which he felt vulnerable to Ted Heath's barbs.

I decided that my first step must be to take George Woodcock into my confidence. Labour MPs and the trade unions had been immensely relieved at the mildness of the Donovan Report and they knew that they owed that to George Woodcock's influence in drawing it up. 'Just stand by Donovan' became a favourite battlecry of the anti-reformers. I knew that if George Woodcock damned my proposals I would have to give them up.

Instead I was taken aback by the warmth of his response. There was nothing in my proposals, he told me, which need alarm the trade union movement. Indeed he hinted then and later that I had closed some loopholes in the Donovan Report. Yes, he would try to convince the TUC of this but he exacted a price. I should, he urged, take the Finance and General Purposes Committee of the TUC equally fully into my confidence before I went to Cabinet. Only in that way, he believed, could I persuade the unions I was not conspiring behind their backs. He assured me I could talk to the Committee in complete confidence.

I decided to take his advice – wrongly as it turned out. The union leaders listened to me in sullen silence, held back only by George Woodcock's restraining presence. As soon as the meeting was over Frank Cousins rushed out to give a damning indictment of my proposals to the waiting press, though he had silently acquiesced when I insisted before the meeting that I was talking to them all in confidence.

Another failure of judgment? Perhaps it was, though in fact the unions' behaviour merely endorsed the validity of my criticisms of their high-handed attitude. Nor do I believe that if I had played my hand more discreetly it would have made any difference to the outcome.

Cabinet had to make up its mind on what it would do about the Donovan Report and about the unofficial strikes, which were worrying all of us. It was the last thing most ministers wanted to do and they wriggled and writhed as my proposals were discussed. Dick Crossman, furious at having been left off the *ad hoc* committee on my White Paper (by accident, as it turned out), led the attack with a venom which surprised my officials. Jim Callaghan joined forces with him enthusiastically, saying that penal powers would never work and asking why I did not stick to Donovan. I pointed out that the report recommended that all unions should be obliged to enter themselves on the new register it proposed and the majority of the Commission wanted the protection of the 1906 Trade Disputes Act – the historic foundation of trade union rights – withdrawn from those which did not register, a far more draconian penalty than anything I had proposed. Jim did not want to know and he had a small covey of backers, including Dick Marsh and Ray Gunter, the last of whom had never forgiven me for replacing him at the Ministry of Labour. But I, too, had my allies, notably Roy Jenkins, whose only proviso was that my legislation should be rushed through immediately as he did not want the consultations dragging on. I resisted this strongly as out of keeping with my approach, and I won. I had welcome support from Tony Benn, who had been brought into the Cabinet as Minister of Technology in 1966 and who knew what havoc even a small strike could cause in the complex network of modern industry. On 14 January 1969, my White Paper was approved by Cabinet.

But still the argument dragged on. The trade unions mobilized support in the National Executive and the parliamentary party, and many Labour MPs, who had not been particularly upset by my proposals when I first explained them to them, joined in what had now become a holy crusade against Barbara. *Tribune* joined in the fray and Michael wrote a piece in the paper headed 'The Maddest Scene in Modern History'. In it, he declared that historians would look back with amazement on Harold Wilson's and my 'declaration of war on the trade unions'.

Jim continued his rearguard action to undermine the decision of Cabinet, even defying the principle of collective responsibility to the extent of voting for a trade union resolution in the National Executive opposing my proposals outright. George Brown was outraged by Jim's disloyalty and told him so. When he heard of it, Harold threatened dire sanctions against Jim, but they did not materialize.

Faced with such open war, Harold and I were now deep in a conspiracy. Whatever others did we were not prepared to budge and, if Cabinet backtracked on its decision, we would resign. It was no empty gesture. I, for one, knew I was too deeply implicated to be able to accept a defeat now. Harold could easily have extricated himself but he had entered into the spirit of the battle enthusiastically. I got the impression that the idea of resigning over an issue like this positively appealed to him. We both sensed that the feeling of the rank and file was far more ambivalent than the thunderings of the trade unions and their sponsored MPs would suggest. I addressed a number of party meetings on the issue, speaking as well as I had ever done, and I could see I had made a mark. After one such meeting Peggy Herbison, the beloved and respected former Minister of Social Security, came up to me and said, 'You're right, Barbara. Stick to your guns.' I could not help wishing she had said that openly. I also kept getting encouraging messages from George Woodcock, who told Denis Barnes that my White Paper was 'excellent'. He also told me privately that I had let the unions off lightly. Here again, I wished he was saying this kind of thing publicly.

So Harold and I decided to dig in our heels. We believed this was a crucial moment in the party's relations with the trade unions. If we were to allow them to refuse to change any of their procedures in the national interest, the government was effectively their prisoner. Harold proceeded to hammer home this point in the endless consultations he conducted with them. We had made it clear that the powers of enforcement we wanted to give the Secretary of State were reserve powers, only to be used if the TUC had not been able to achieve the conciliation we were looking for. It was to be given the first chance to settle a dispute. This provision annoyed some of the more anarchical unions as much as anything I proposed. We knew in my Department that some unions positively welcomed unofficial strikes because they often won concessions without the unions having to find strike pay. Other unions resented TUC interference in their affairs as much as interference by the Secretary of State. Freebooting was their way of life.

Harold loved talk and he enjoyed nothing more than the intimate discussions he held with Vic Feather in his study at Number 10. Harold and I, who had developed a contempt for our vacillating colleagues, used to toss each other notes across the table during Cabinet meetings. One of his notes read, 'What are you doing tonight, baby?' Me: '1. Meeting of IR Committee immediately after Cabinet; 2. Meeting with my officials to start drafting my speech, Daddy!!' Harold: 'Don't be a spoilsport. I was wondering whether you'd like to come and see my etchings – with Vic Feather!' In fact, I spent a number of evenings in Harold's study with Vic Feather as they talked round and round the issues, trying to find the basis of an agreement, sipping brandy and puffing companionably at cigars. Vic was obviously trying desperately to find a way out. Indeed the most remarkable thing about the whole *IPOS* episode was the anxiety of the unions lest Harold should indeed resign. I used to excuse myself from these late-night sessions, and go to bed.

My main contribution to our joint campaign was to carry the argument out into trade union conferences, where, to my surprise, I was usually greeted as a friend and not an enemy. Typical was the conference of the Metalworkers' Union. They gave me a standing ovation after my uncompromising speech, but when I had a drink with some of their Executive members afterwards, one of them said to me, 'You were magnificent, but you know we are all mandated to vote against you, so it won't make any difference.'

Another dramatic moment came when I addressed the annual conference of the Scottish TUC – a tough body of industrial militants. As I boarded the ferry to Rothesay, my civil servants warned that there was going to be a walk-out against me on the boat. On the contrary, I was fêted with the greatest friendliness. At the conference itself, I knew I would be up against a hostile atmosphere and I was nervous. But as I stood up on the platform in a new scarlet dress, I said to them, 'I am in my true colours here today,' which raised a sympathetic laugh. The audience of toughies sat on their hands during my speech, but the industrial correspondents reported that I had survived.

One of the most moving moments in my campaign came when I was flown from Rothesay by helicopter to visit the Rootes factory at Linwood. Management was waiting to greet me and sweep me along a red carpet to their office in the factory. At this point, I saw a crowd of Linwood workers leaning over a wire fence some distance away from the helicopter pad. 'Come in at the workers' entrance, Barbara,' one of them shouted and, wheeling off the red carpet, I replied, 'Of course.' As I went along the wire fence, shaking hands, one lusty young lad called out 'Gi'e us a kiss, Barbara!' and, to the delight of the crowd, I obediently lifted up my face. The next day I was horrified to see from the press photographs that I had been showing my petticoat.

So successful were our joint efforts that the TUC began to move. In June 1969 it called a special congress at Croydon to consider a document called 'Programme for Action' to deal with both inter-union disputes and unconstitutional strikes.

It was a document unprecedented in trade union history, proposing tough action by the TUC to deal with inter-union disputes and declaring for the first time that 'workpeople are constitutionally in the wrong if they strike before the procedure is exhausted'. The document was carried with a majority of 7 million votes, and the press went out of its way to praise the great steps forward the TUC had taken.

Again, this would have been a let-out for Harold if he was

looking for one, but again he was enjoying being tough. I also suspect he was enjoying tormenting what he considered the weaklings of Cabinet, among whom Roy Jenkins was now prominent, having lost his nerve. I was out of the country in Italy, enjoying a holiday with Ted and the Crossman family, which Harold had urged me to take, promising to call me back if there were any interesting developments in our discussions with the unions. Instead, I discovered to my horror on my return that in my absence he had issued a press statement *over my name* rejecting the Croydon overtures as totally inadequate. I would certainly have advised him against this if I had been at home. As it was, I had to ride it out with him as he declared that nothing less than a change in the TUC's rules to embody these Croydon commitments would do.

The discussions with the TUC reached their climax in a protracted meeting at Number 10. In fact, having taken this tough stance, Harold conducted the negotiations with considerable skill. It was a contest of giants, with the trade unions clearly anxious lest Harold should resign, yet doggedly convinced that they could not accept rule changes. They were afraid of creating a precedent, and said, 'We would not like to discuss a rule change with any other government.' Jack Jones pointed out that it was possible to get binding commitments without a rule change on the lines of the Bridlington Regulations of 1939, with which the TUC successfully stopped poaching by one union upon another.

It was Hughie Scanlon, however, who clinched the argument. He had had a long struggle, he told us, to get his National Committee to accept the concessions he had already made. If he went back to them for a rule change he might lose everything. If we were to accept a binding commitment by the TUC on the lines of the Bridlington agreement, he would not have to consult his National Committee again. I rushed back to my waiting officials, and Conrad Heron was impressed. The Bridlington agreement, he assured me, was not just a form of words. There had never been a case in which unions accused of poaching had not obeyed the TUC's ruling. Faced with that we knew we had to accept. And so it was agreed, the long hours ending with a

Solemn and Binding Undertaking by the TUC in the actual words of the rule change we had proposed.

Harold and I returned to the Cabinet which we despised. Its relief at the agreement was patent, as was its shamefacedness, Roy Jenkins admitting later that he had not played a particularly noble role. The press, of course, derided an agreement which they dubbed 'Solomon Binding'. I crept back to the Department feeling deflated. In the car, I said to Douglas Smith, 'Do you understand why I wish I was going back as the Minister who had resigned?' With his usual sensitivity, he said he did. The trade union movement's hostility now turned on me. Harold was forgiven, as though he had played no part in it, while Jack Jones denounced me as 'totally politically discredited'. Certainly, my popularity among Labour MPs had taken a nosedive, but I did not complain. I had known at the outset what I was letting myself in for and did not regret what I had done. The TUC carthorse had stirred indeed and I was prepared to pay the price for that.

I got consolation from a surprising quarter when shortly afterwards at a dinner party of the Socialist International at Eastbourne, George Brown moved the toast to the retiring General Secretary and suddenly reached out to me across the crowded room. He started his speech, 'I wanted to begin by saying a few words to Barbara. I know that the last few weeks must have been a misery. But you have achieved a marvellous result. Barbara, you have been magnificent.' I was overwhelmed.

Business in the Department felt flat after the drama we had been going through. The trade unions demanded a short Industrial Relations Bill which included a few of my goodies, such as the right of appeal against unfair dismissal, and nothing else. They would not even consider including the Donovan proposals that members of a union should have the right of appeal to an independent review body if they felt they had been unfairly treated by their own union. Nonetheless, Vic Feather scrupulously kept the TUC's part of the bargain, intervening as an intrepid fire-fighter in unconstitutional disputes, and he undoubtedly helped us to avoid several strikes. But I felt the trade union movement had done itself great harm by its 'hands off us' attitude and would pay the price under a Tory government. I also knew I had wrecked any chances I might have had of getting to the top.

Just before the election was announced, Peter Patterson had written an article in the *Spectator* under the heading 'Whatever happened to Barbara?' I was, he claimed, 'the most successful woman politician in British political history' and in television interviews not very long before had been 'only slightly coy' at the suggestion that I was ambitious to become Labour's first woman Prime Minister. Since then, he wrote, my eclipse had been 'rapid and complete'. He had no doubt about the reason. 'Trade union memories', he asserted, 'are a great deal longer than anyone else's in politics, and it is unlikely that Mrs Castle will ever be forgiven for her assault on their privileges and prerogatives in her ill-fated White Paper "In Place of Strife".' He also noted that my political colleagues seemed only too glad to abandon me to my fate.

Undeterred, I tried to salvage something from the wreck. I had been giving serious thought to how we could encourage voluntary wage restraint as the only alternative to the Tory policy of keeping wages down by pushing unemployment up. I had recruited as my economic adviser Derek Robinson, senior research officer of the Oxford University Institute of Economics and Statistics, who became the economic adviser to the Research and Planning Division which I set up. He was on my political wavelength and had had some practical experience of our problems at the Prices and Incomes Board. It was Derek who at one of my Sunningdale Conferences on the future of prices and incomes policy had pointed out that workers could not be expected to forgo wage increases which helped push up the value of a company's capital assets unless they shared in that increase which their restraint had helped to produce. His argument seemed to me to be unanswerable and I asked him to give me a report setting out the details of his plan. This he was only too keen to do but he kept complaining to me that he was getting no backing from the Department in working out a detailed policy, though convinced that a feasible plan could be produced. It was May 1970 before he was able to put before me a rough outline of his proposals to present to the Inner Cabinet. Once again I got permission to pursue the idea but once again it was too late.

By the spring of 1970, election fever was in the air. The balance of payments had moved into surplus and so had our national accounts. We did better than expected in the municipal elections and we had an average lead over the Tories of 3 per cent in five consecutive polls. In March the independent National Institute of Economic and Social Research called on the Chancellor to reflate the economy by £650 million in his Budget. Dick Crossman and I, advised by Tommy Balogh, pressed for the more modest figure of £400 million, but even that was too much for Roy Jenkins' financial rectitude. 'I had sweated much too hard to turn the balance of payments', he wrote later in his autobiography, 'to put it all at risk by a give-away Budget, which in any event I regarded as a vulgar piece of economic management below the level of political sophistication of the British electorate.' In fact, our supporters in the country would have been glad of a bit more populist vulgarity. So would some of us in Cabinet but all he was prepared to concede was a minuscule reflation of £150 million, a poor reward after the 'two years' hard slog' he had been calling for. Tories are not so purist.

Roy had developed a technique for deflecting criticism. He would take one or two of his intimates like me aside before the Budget to give us an advance outline of his proposals under the strictest pledge of secrecy. It was an effective way of silencing us. How could I, for one, deliver a penetrating economic analysis, unarmed by expert advice and faced with Roy at his most courteous over a private drink? I made a few critical noises in Cabinet about the stinginess of the Chancellor's attitude but I was no match for him, and Roy had no difficulty in getting his proposals through.

Despite the discouragement of the Budget, the momentum towards a June election grew. I preferred October, but realized that press speculation about an early election was becoming a self-fulfilling prophecy. Harold went into the campaign exuding relaxed self-confidence. Ted Heath, stiff and uncharismatic, was getting a bad press and the polls continued in our favour. But as I toured the country I was made increasingly uneasy by the atmosphere I found. Quite early in the campaign I wrote in my diary: 'I don't believe these poll figures. . . . I have a feeling there is a silent majority sitting behind its lace curtains, waiting to come out and vote Tory.' My hunch proved correct. Ted Heath snatched victory from the teeth of the polls with 330 seats to Labour's 287. The Liberals lost seven of their thirteen seats. Our most notable casualty was George Brown at Belper, but for many of us the saddest result was the defeat at Cannock of Jennie Lee, who had been a first-class Minister for the Arts.

I had one consolation. Just before the general election I had managed to get an Equal Pay Bill through Parliament. Once again it was the women who made the running. It was only made possible when Labour women MPs, led by Lena Jeger, tabled an amendment to the government's latest stab at a Prices and Incomes Bill to demand that the pay norm should not apply where a pay settlement included a move towards equal pay. I was sitting miserably on the front bench trying to pilot through a measure with which I was far from happy when Roy Jenkins came and sat next to me. 'We are going to be defeated on this amendment,' I told him trying to suppress my glee, 'unless you allow me to announce that I am drawing up proposals to phase in equal pay over the next five years.'

No doubt suspecting he would not be Chancellor during this period, he agreed. And so the Equal Pay Act 1970 was born. It was far from perfect but it established the principle on which later refinements could be built. I knew that if we lost the election our Tory successors would be forced to proceed with it.

The 1970 election was lost by Labour apathy, our vote falling by 5 per cent to a slightly lower level even than in 1959 and nearly 1 million less than we had polled in 1966. I remain convinced that Roy Jenkins' Budget was the primary cause. This view was endorsed by Peter Jenkins, one of Roy's fans, in a commentary on the election headed 'How Roy Muffed It' in which he argued that he could have safely relaxed his austerity a bit more. Harold's conduct of the campaign was a major contributory cause. There was no barnstorming as in 1964, no vision, no political analysis, no prospectus of future policy, only Harold dispensing presidential bonhomie.

What annoyed me most was our failure to proclaim our achievements, which were substantial despite the economic difficulties – the Equal Pay Act, the Open University, the legal aid scheme, and many more. We had turned an inherited deficit of £372 million into a surplus of nearly £500 million by the end of 1969. Despite restrictive policies, we had averaged an annual growth rate of just over 3 per cent. Unemployment had risen, but was still only 600,000. Inflation, which had been running at 4.8 per cent at the end of the Maudling era, was 4.7 per cent at the end of 1969. It was a mixed bag of achievements – and Treasury restrictions had had a palpable effect on the levels of growth – but it was better than our predecessors had achieved, and was to make the achievements of our Tory successors, Ted Heath, Margaret Thatcher and John Major, pale into insignificance. Yet they manage to cling on to power. Their secret weapon is their instinctive belief in their right to rule, so they describe their disasters as economic miracles, while Labour becomes apologetic if it fails to produce the millennium in one month. It is a lesson which Labour governments must learn if they are to survive.

SEVENTEEN

—————— • ——————

Fighting Back

THE ELECTION over it did not take me long to clear my office at
DEP. The consolation on these occasions is the kind letters one
receives. One of the most generous I received was from Conrad
Heron; the most surprising was from Martin Jukes, the President
of the Engineering Employers, which expressed gratitude for 'the
friendly and co-operative way in which you have listened to us on
matters affecting the industry'. It added poignantly, 'None of us
will forget that you were a tower of strength to us in the difficult
negotiations in 1968 over our long-term agreement.' I could
imagine what Hughie Scanlon would have said if he could have
seen that!

But the most remarkable letter – viewed from the perspective
of later developments – was from Bernard Ingham. When on my
move from Transport I lost Chris Hall and was looking for his
successor, it was suggested to me that Bernard had been a very
effective Information Officer at the PIB. Aubrey did not want to
lose him but could be persuaded to let him go. It was also hinted
with departmental discretion that he was a Labour man. I found
him a rather cuddly, but stolid Yorkshireman. I did not find his
draft speeches exciting, except for a memorable one he drafted for
me to deliver at the Institute of Directors' annual jamboree in the
Albert Hall at which the captains of industry sit *en masse* with
expensive lunchboxes on their knees. It was this stolid Yorkshireman who produced the phrase which was to shake this comfortable assembly: 'Power has passed to the shopfloor,' adding that
management had better come to terms with it. My officials were

not too happy about this, but I used it in my speech with dramatic effect. I decided this man had smouldering fires beneath his Yorkshire exterior.

His letter to me was unexpectedly warm, stressing how much he valued the two years' work he had done for me. 'I doubt if it is possible', he wrote,

> for me to work harder over a period of two years, to learn more, and ultimately to derive so much enjoyment and satisfaction out of it. . . . These two years will, I am sure, go down in the history of Government and the Department as a traumatic but richly rewarding experience for all involved because you made the Department think as it had never thought for a long time; made it question its whole purpose; introduced a new constructive concept of conciliation; and brought together in one cohesive whole all those manpower services like employment, training and SHW [Safety, Health and Welfare] which formed the heart of the old Ministry of Labour.

I never discovered what precipitated his transfer of political loyalties when ten years later he became Margaret Thatcher's devoted mouthpiece. Perhaps he is one of those men who enjoys working for a woman provided she will stand up to him.

I was personally relieved to have a breathing space. The pace of work for a minister is so intense that the little satisfactions of life, like dawdling through St James's Park when the crocuses are out, have to be sacrificed to the imperatives of Cabinet and departmental timetables. Of course I had enjoyed the perks of office, such as a government car standing ready to rush me anywhere I wanted to go. More valuable still were the government drivers. I always asked for a woman if possible, because she could act as a kind of wife, able to cope with any crisis such as the laddering of the ministerial tights or the loss of the ministerial lipstick, slipping out and buying the necessary replacements. I had a number of delightful women drivers, full of character and initiative. It was they who begged me to give them my weekly shopping list so that they had some activity to fill the long waiting hours in Private Office while their Minister was tied up in meetings. Thanks to their ministrations I learned what it must be like to be a man in public life with a wife to relieve him of the little daily chores.

I also missed the back-up I got from the civil service. In those days backbench MPs were not provided with personal research facilities and it was bliss as a minister to be able to call for expert briefing on any point I wanted to pursue. My Private Office kept me cocooned from the outside world, sifting out unwelcome visitors and planning every detail of my day. On official visits I travelled like the Queen, not needing to carry any money since one's Private Secretary would buy the tickets, pay the hotel bills, tip the hotel staff and even settle small personal accounts for drinks, presenting one with the account discreetly afterwards. Travel has never been so carefree since.

Nonetheless my freedom came like a breath of bracing air. The first time I travelled on a bus after the election I felt a curious sense of liberation, much as William Kendall and I had felt when we escaped from the Russians on to that Dresden tram. I also knew how dangerous the civil servant's control of a minister's life could be, cutting one off from contact with the outside world. Departments felt that they owned their ministers and that any outside interests must take second place. I even had a struggle to get time to see my constituency secretary or to visit my constituents. On one occasion I exploded to my Private Office, 'These people put me here and you did not.'

After I left the Ministry, I was invited to address a seminar for senior civil servants at Sunningdale on the relationship between ministers and civil servants and I had let fly on my favourite theme. The trouble with the civil service, I told them, lay in its excellence, which gave it the feeling that it had the right to swallow up the Minister in what I called its 'companionable embrace', running and organizing every moment of the Minister's day. The power of the civil service, I argued, lay in its continuity, its knowledge that the Minister might be here today but would be gone tomorrow, leaving the civil servants still in charge. Reforming ministers, therefore, struggled against the 'loneliness of the short-distance runner' and the balance must be redressed by injecting political advisers into their entourage. Apparently my contribution was tape-recorded and Harold Evans, the brilliant reforming editor of the *Sunday Times* until Rupert Murdoch took over, splashed it across two pages under the title 'Mandarin Power'. When some four years later I was back in office at Health and Social Security one of my officials said to me shyly, 'I was at Sunningdale. I got the message.' So did Harold Wilson, who at last allowed us to appoint the political advisers some of us had been pressing for ever since we got into office. I was amused to note that those in my audience who were most supercilious about what I said were the Foreign Office mandarins.

Loss of office also enabled me to enjoy to the full the delights of our rural retreat in the Chilterns, mysteriously called Hell Corner Farm. The farm's name was on the Ordinance Survey map and we never found out its origin. There were stories of witches associated with the neighbourhood, but ours were always friendly, if a bit mischievous. My mother, whom we housed there for some ten years, used to sit by her open doorway looking at a picturesque dead tree among the encircling foliage and remark, 'My witch is smiling at me.'

We had acquired the cottage when Marjorie died at the tragically early age of fifty-four. As the family sat in a mourning circle after her death her younger daughter, Philippa, turned to me and said, 'You must be our proxy mum.' Ted thereupon looked around for a family gathering ground. The old cottage had no damp course and the large garden area was full of nettles, but taming it was Ted's great hobby, as he increasingly inherited his father's love of gardening. The rising young generation of the family fell in love with it, particularly at Christmas time when we decorated the beams with ivy, holly and old man's beard and Great-Uncle Ted presided over the dinner table with avuncular geniality. The possession of a country home enabled us to indulge our passion for dogs. A succession of cocker spaniels, golden, black and white and blue roan (Ted would have preferred bull terriers) led wonderful lives, going long walks with us and chasing rabbits and deer – mercifully always ineffectually – through the surrounding woods.

In July 1969 Ted and I celebrated our silver wedding at Hell Corner Farm. It was an idyllically hot summer's day and our guests, drawn from our wide range of political, journalistic and local friends, sprawled on the grass while Ted and I struggled to keep the wine from boiling point. Typically, Harold found time from his prime-ministerial duties to bring Mary Wilson along, and Marjorie's elder daughter Sonya was furious when she discovered a *Daily Express* photographer trying to snatch a candid-camera snap over our garden hedge. She went out and berated him so fiercely that he disappeared, which was just as well because shortly afterwards the deck chair in which we had installed Harold collapsed under him and he sat engulfed. I could imagine what the cartoonists would have made of that.

Although saddened by our electoral defeat we waited with interest to see how Ted Heath would cope with the problems with which we had been struggling. At first it looked as though we were going to suffer a complete reversal of Labour's policies. Just before the election the Tory Shadow Cabinet had met in secret conclave at Selsdon Park to work out its strategy. From its deliberations emerged the picture of the new 'Selsdon man' – precursor of the Basildon man of the later Thatcher years. He was the flag-bearer of the 'incentive society' in which tax cuts were to be financed by cuts in public expenditure, industry made to stand on its own feet, government intervention dramatically reduced, prices and incomes policy abandoned and the 'monopoly power' of the trade unions smashed. Indeed, when Heath won the election his Chancellor, Anthony Barber, lost no time in putting this blueprint into effect.

The policy comprised not only a catalogue of measures, but a new philosophy. The aim, Barber told the Commons in introducing his first Budget, was to secure 'fundamental reform of the role of government and the public authorities'. The changes were sweeping and followed a pattern which was to become familiar. Barber cut income tax by 6d (two and a half new pence) and then got some of the money back by increasing charges on a wide range of public services: prescriptions, school meals, rents, even museum charges. Subsidies of every kind were cut. Investment grants to industry gave way to depreciation allowances, which provided most help to successful firms, and the capital programmes of the nationalized industries were reduced. Quangos like the Consumer Council were abolished and all Harold Wilson's modest interventionist measures to help the modernization of industry, such as the Industrial Reconstruction Corporation, bit the dust.

Every one of Labour's social policies was reversed. Universal benefits were to give way to means-tested ones. Instead of the increase in family allowances which Heath had promised during the election, Barber introduced a means-tested family income supplement to help low wage-earners with children. Grants to public transport were cut back. Even the subsidy for cheap welfare milk was abolished.

We sat appalled on the Labour benches, believing that the counter-revolution had begun. But we had reckoned without the complex character of Edward Heath, which was to dominate the politics of the next four years. Heath was a middle-of-the-road Tory who wanted to goad his party into more modern attitudes and stir up sluggish management to become more competitive. It was typical of him that as Secretary of State for Trade and Industry just before the 1964 election, despite fierce opposition from his own side, he had abolished retail-price maintenance, a restrictive practice dear to shopkeepers. But he was no monetarist and did not believe in using unemployment as an instrument of policy. Some years later Peter Walker, who had been at Selsdon Park and became Secretary of State for the Environment in Heath's government, told me that it had been an accident that Heath had become identified with Selsdon man, because he had not been a prime mover in drawing up the policy. Others were far more anti-interventionist. Iain Macleod, for instance, had already indicated to the Commons that a Conservative government would pay for income tax cuts by cutting investment grants for industry. The

Women MPs of all parties campaign for equal pay, 1954.

Dick Crossman, Tom Driberg and I follow Attlee into the National Executive meeting to save Bevan from expulsion, 1955.

Top left: Mobbed by an enthusiastic audience at the Labour Party conference of 1955 after a speech I made in Attlee's defence.

Top right: Fateful Athens meeting with Makarios in 1958 when I persuaded him to give up Enosis.

Bottom right: I return from Cyprus in 1958, a 'Red'.

Top: I unite the old enemies, Hugh Gaitskell and Aneurin Bevan, as we launch the general election campaign of 1959.

Bottom: Delivering the chairman's speech at the 1959 Labour Party conference. Nye Bevan listens attentively.

Top: Fenner Brockway and I give a warm send-off to Joshua Nkomo and his friends as they return to the battle in Central Africa, 1960.

Bottom: Revisiting my first school – Love Lane Elementary School, Pontefract – in 1962, I find little has changed.

Above: I try to laugh off
Dr Hastings Banda's exuberant
embrace in 1965.

Left: As Minister of Overseas
Development I cuddle a baby in
an African village during a visit
to Tanzania.

I launch the breathalyser in 1967.

Two Ministers of Transport together. Monsieur Pisani of France and I discuss
the Channel Tunnel in 1966.

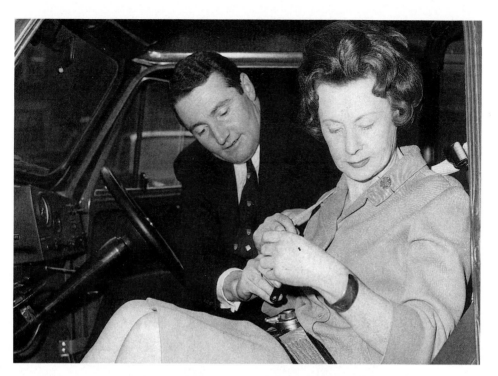

Launching the seatbelt campaign, 1967.

The *Daily Mirror* catches the Minister of Transport pony-trekking in Ireland in 1967.

I find solace in walking with Ted on the Scarborough sands at a stormy
Party Conference in 1967.

only overtly monetarist speeches were coming from Sir Keith Joseph, whose star as a right-wing guru was beginning to rise. Heath was inveigled into issuing a statement on Selsdon's decisions which others had effectively drawn up.

Heath's trouble was his inability to enter into human relationships. He was a reserved and probably deeply shy man, a bachelor who lived alone, consoling himself with the music which he loved. Peter Walker, who admired him, told me that Heath could be rude and dismissive even to his friends. I encountered this side of him more than once. When Selwyn Lloyd, the new Speaker, gave a reception at which I ran into the Tory leader I noted in my diary that he 'looked through me as though I did not exist'. Even at a lunchtime reception which he himself gave at Number 10 he was incapable of behaving like a normal host. Trying to make polite conversation I said to him sympathetically, 'And you are top for Questions today, Prime Minister.' Once again he looked through me and turned away without a word, leaving me wondering whether he had even been listening. His friends said to me in justification, 'The explanation for Ted Heath is that when he went home there was nobody waiting for him' – of either sex.

Heath was a man clearly divided against himself. It was not surprising, therefore, that he plunged into a number of U-turns of policy which were to cost him not only the premiership but the Tory leadership. The first came when Barber's Budget failed to produce the stimulus which the government had hoped for. Growth remained flat. Industry was worried by the deflationary policies and failed to invest. Workers were surly as they found the Barber package had left them worse off. Heath had fought the election on the pledge to bring down prices, yet his own policies had deliberately pushed them up. One of the key factors had been his decision as a keen European to adopt the Common Agricultural Policy of the EEC even before we joined. He abandoned Labour's deficiency-payments scheme for farmers in favour of taxes on imported food, which sent food prices escalating. He also introduced the European system of VAT in place of our own more selective purchase tax. When as a result of all these developments

435

unemployment rose to nearly 1 million Heath decided the time had come to reverse some elements at least of this economic strategy.

Expansion now became the order of the day. Heath cut taxes, lifted hire-purchase restrictions and reflated generally. When this brought a record balance-of-payments deficit and a sterling crisis, he floated the pound, something which I for one had tried to persuade the Labour government to do, in vain. Most astonishing of all was his change of attitude towards industry. When the prestigious Rolls-Royce company ran into difficulties and faced collapse, Heath stepped in to nationalize it by the unprecedented device of a one-clause Bill. I particularly relished the moment when my old sparring partner of the CBI, John Davies, who had been transmuted into the Minister for Industry, introduced an Industry Bill giving the government wide powers to bale out the 'lame ducks' of industry and to acquire shares in those companies in return for financial help.

It was a policy which could work only with the co-operation of the trade unions, whom Heath now set out to conciliate. But it was too late. In another of his curious inconsistencies he had given the Conservative lawyers their head in drawing up a mammoth Industrial Relations Bill designed to tie the unions hand and foot in a complex legal straitjacket. It was the most savage piece of anti-union legislation the country had known since the beginning of the century. Labour MPs waded through its complicated formulae with a sense of disbelief that a sane government could attempt to impose such a policy. The first provision gave workers the statutory right *not* to belong to a trade union, thus enabling the 'free rider' in a factory to benefit from the terms and conditions the union had won, without having to accept any of the obligations of solidarity. The closed shop was out, even where employers were willing to concede it. The Bill compelled unions to register under strict rules drawn up by a new registrar. Failure to register meant the loss of all traditional trade union rights. Collective agreements became legally binding. Any employer or union member with a grievance against a union could take the union to a new Industrial Relations Court set up by the Bill under a High Court judge. This court had the power to mulct trade union funds for a long list of unfair industrial practices. The Bill even reintroduced the doctrine of 'agency', under which a union could be held responsible for the action of any of its members – a doctrine which the House of Commons had rejected some sixty-five years earlier as a threat to the very existence of trade unions. The government was not 'curbing the power of the unions', but castrating them.

The whole Labour movement and the unions were outraged by this Bill, which was as destructive of workers' rights to organize in self-defence as could be found in any totalitarian state. It was in direct conflict with all that Donovan had argued, and with all that I had proposed in *In Place of Strife*. Inevitably the Tories tried to claim that they were merely following the path which I had pioneered.

The question then arose as to who should lead our opposition to the Bill from our front bench. Everyone, particularly my left-wing critics, assumed it could not be me, though I had been elected to the Shadow Cabinet in 1970 without their help. Had I not given Heath his alibi with my own proposals, and so rendered my attack vulnerable? The Bill's whole approach was repugnant to me. I could not bear the thought of our spokesmen going on the defensive over *In Place of Strife*. Harold was dubious when I told him that I must lead, but he had the courage of his loyalty. In the tormented aftermath of our agreement with the TUC, he had said to me, 'You and I must keep together. I am the only friend you have and you are the only friend I have. I'm like the elephant: I may appear to forget but I never do.' And so he reluctantly agreed that I should lead the battle.

It was an exhilarating, but intimidating experience. Perhaps I was too sensitive but I was conscious of a latent hostility among my Labour colleagues and the experts we brought in to advise us. Nonetheless I pressed ahead, collecting a good front-bench team to help me, which included Eric Heffer, the left-wing Liverpudlian who had been among the most vocal in condemning *In Place of Strife*. He was only too willing to serve when he found that our policy was to oppose the Tory Bill root and branch. I faced the toughest test of my parliamentary life as I prepared my Second Reading speech on the Tory Bill. I wrote in my diary: 'A cold terror has seized me.' I was tense with anxiety and so was Ted, leaning over the gallery.

It was not my greatest oratorical performance, but I knew my stuff and spoke with conviction. I sat down to a great cheer. Eric Heffer said to me, 'Magnificent! Quite first class!' My Ted was radiant with relief. Ted Leadbitter, Labour MP for Hartlepool, came up to me to say, 'All the doubts about your leading have now disappeared.'

But this was an exaggeration. The mutterings against me continued. On one occasion, after talking to the trade union group, I commented in my diary on the 'bitterness and almost savage hostility' that was shown to me. Vic Feather did not attempt to hide his feelings, telling Harold, in front of me, that on industrial relations matters I was 'a liability'. I wrote of all this, 'It is probably the price I shall pay for honesty all my political life.' And so it proved.

In 1970 I scraped on to the Shadow Cabinet, though at the bottom of the poll, which Jim Callaghan topped easily. In 1971 I dropped to joint runner-up with Eric Heffer, getting back when Roy resigned from the Shadow Cabinet, leaving a vacancy. By 1972, with all my hard work on the Industrial Relations Bill behind me, I felt more secure, particularly because I had given up shadowing Employment when the Bill got through and moved to social services. In the event, I was knocked off again, this time more catastrophically, dropping to third place among the runners-up. Ironically, Reg Prentice and Shirley Williams topped the poll, both of whom were to leave the party a few years later, Reg Prentice to emerge as a Conservative MP and Minister for Social Security in Mrs Thatcher's government and Shirley to become a founder member of the Social Democratic Party.

I had never seen Harold so angry and so moved as he was by my 1972 defeat. When the result was declared, he swept me off to his room for a drink, raging against the 'rats' who had humiliated me like this. He was at his most endearing, talking to me as an old friend for whom he had always had a great affection. He said impishly that if our friendship had always been merely platonic, that was not his fault. Ian Aitken of the *Guardian*, always a fellow spirit, wrote to me indignantly, 'I don't know why I should pay my subs to a party which puts you off and makes Reg Prentice top. Perhaps I should join the Young Liberals at the age of forty-six!'

One of my consolations was to enjoy the mess into which Ted Heath's Act had got him. Heath had appointed Sir John Donaldson President of the new Industrial Court, and Sir John proceeded to apply the provisions of the Act with legalistic rigidity, defending the sanctity of the powers of his court as though they were written on tablets of stone. The result was a succession of pantomimes which revealed better than we had been able to do that industrial relations in a democracy are relations between free human beings and not an appropriate matter for the courts. Ted Heath had been reluctant to face the fact that, if he wished to break the spirit of the trade unions, he would first have to smash them economically through the unemployment which Margaret Thatcher was later to use.

So the unions, united as never before, set out to wreck the hated legislation and succeeded brilliantly. Major unions like the Transport Workers and the Engineers refused to register, even though it meant that they lost their legal rights. Weaker unions, like the Seamen, who dared not risk losing their rights, were expelled from the TUC. The unions withdrew from all concili-atory agencies like the CIR, and the TUC called on them not to recognize the court.

Within months the Act was in tatters. When Hughie Scanlon refused to call off a strike for union recognition at Con Mech (Engineering) Ltd and the court sequestered £100,000 of the union's funds, public opinion was shaken, but Hughie unrepent-ant. The government itself provided a touch of farce. Faced with a threatened rail strike over pay, it applied to the court for a compulsory secret ballot, believing that the majority of railway-men were against a strike. Instead they voted six to one for a national strike and the government was forced to climb down, agreeing to give them another £32 million. But the classic case which discredited the Act was that of dockers up and down the country 'blacking' lorries which carried goods to container depots outside the ports, because they could see their own jobs disappearing. It was the sort of situation in which I and my conciliation officers would have moved in immediately, trying to find a solution which recognized the rights of all involved. But Sir John's remit was to apply the letter of the law, which he did enthusiastically, fining the union for contempt when the blacking did not stop.

The union took the case to the Court of Appeal, where Lord Denning ruled that the dockers were not acting as agents of the union and revoked the fine. Undeterred, Sir John, to the consternation of the government, then proceeded against individual dockers and arrested three of their shop stewards. Disaster – and a nationwide dock strike – were averted only by the wheeling out of a mysterious figure, the Official Solicitor, of whom none of us had heard before. As a result of his intervention, the Court of Appeal hurriedly set the arrests aside. But the legal juggernaut rolled on. As the picketing continued, Sir John committed five London dockers to Pentonville, which brought 85,000 workers out on strike. There was uproar in Parliament, and the House of Lords hurriedly reversed the Court's findings, making the union, not the individual dockers, once again liable and cancelling the arrests. The Official Solicitor was wheeled out once again to convey this to Sir John, and the unrepentant dockers, released from prison, were carried shoulder high by an enthusiastic crowd outside Pentonville.

Judges like Lord Devlin became restive, complaining that the courts were being used to make judgments on matters which were really political. 'The prestige of the judiciary', said Lord Devlin, 'is not at the disposal of any government.' Even Sir John himself admitted that parts of the Act had been 'thoroughly misconceived'. The Act was consigned to the dustbin of history and no Tory government was to try to revive it.

Heath was in a corner of his own making. He had to do something about inflation, which was soaring, fuelled by his own policies. In desperation he made another U-turn. He had fought the election on a scornful rejection of Labour's prices and incomes policy, declaring, 'We utterly reject the philosophy of compulsory wage control.' But it was not long before he was eating his words. I watched fascinated as he was driven along the road he had condemned us for following, starting with a wages and prices freeze and moving relentlessly to a full statutory prices and incomes policy, fixing 'norms' and setting up a Prices Commission and Pay Board to enforce the rules. His transformation was complete. Gone was the talk of the 'incentive society' for the rich. In its place he urged the need for the fairer society. In his incomes policy he went to far greater lengths than we had done to help the low-paid, proposing a 'norm' for pay increases which combined a flat rate with a percentage element. On prices he accepted the TUC's suggestion for 'threshold agreements', under which every 1 per cent increase in prices above 6 per cent would lead automatically to an increase in wages. When the TUC raised the question of pensions, he offered a Christmas bonus for pensioners. But his earlier Selsdon Park policies had created the wrong scenario and the unions were not listening. A series of major strikes shook the economy, and the government – except in the case of the postal workers – came out worse. More working days were lost through strikes than at any time since the general strike of 1926. In February 1972, after a seven-week strike which had forced Heath into declaring a state of emergency, the miners won a spectacular wage increase of 25 per cent.

Ted Heath had succeeded magnificently in healing the breach between the Labour Party and the unions. Shortly after the election we set up a Liaison Committee consisting of representatives from the TUC, the NEC and the parliamentary party to sort out our disagreements privately and, we hoped, harmoniously. As a regular attender I watched the politicians and the trade unionists skate round the problems which caused us so much difficulty. Industrial relations was the least of them. We agreed unanimously that the next Labour government would repeal Heath's Industrial Relations Act outright. Inflation was a bigger headache. Here again we all agreed that a Labour government would never again introduce a statutory prices and incomes policy. No one concurred more thankfully than I did, because I had been through the agony of trying to enforce one. But we politicians knew that, if we expanded the economy without any agreement over wage restraint, inflation could get out of hand. Would not the unions at least help us to secure voluntary restraint? At first they bridled at the very idea but gradually an uneasy agreement emerged in a document entitled 'Economic Policy and the Cost of Living', which indicated that the unions would 'respond', by inference hopefully, to a tough government action to control price increases. The concept of the 'social contract' had been born, under which the unions accepted for the first time a share of responsibility for making economic policy work in return for being given a share in drawing up that policy. I began to feel a new sense of hope.

Heath could not match these developments. When he added refinement after refinement to his prices and incomes policy, the unions responded by demanding a complete reversal of the Selsdon strategy. When they called for a lower rate of VAT, the abolition of automatic rent increases and of levies on imported food, higher pensions and family allowances and above all the repeal of the Industrial Relations Act, Heath rebelled, insisting that these were matters for government. The unions were, in fact, demanding partnership in government, a demand which was to draw the battle line between the parties for the next twenty years.

Faced with Heath's flounderings, the monetarists in the Tory ranks were coming to the fore. They had found a protégé in the attractive young MP for Finchley, Margaret Thatcher, who sat at Keith Joseph's feet. I had been impressed by some of the speeches she had made in the House. Ted Heath had put her into his Cabinet as Minister of Education, and the general opinion got around that she was a rising star. Many MPs, particularly on the Labour side, were put off by her conventional social graces, which never seemed quite genuine. I noted of her mannerisms in my diary, 'I am interested in Margaret's technique. She enters the room radiating charm and embraces everyone in a cocoon of courtesy. But she gives nothing away.' I experienced this technique at first hand when I went to see her in her Department about a constituency case. To my surprise she was waiting outside the lift to receive me, for all the world like Penelope Keith in *To the Manor Born*. She ushered me on to her sofa and poured me out a cup of tea. I was reminded of the way I myself had received the Ford women machinists. The main difference was that I did not send them away empty-handed as she did me. That encounter with her made me realize there was a core of hardness under the social charm.

What worried me during this period was Harold's mood. Following his election defeat he seemed deflated and detached. The only thing that seemed to keep him going was the brandy and water he sipped incessantly, even presiding over the Shadow Cabinet with glass in hand. Dick and I were appalled at his casual attitude to the role of leader of the Opposition. At one point Dick complained to me that Harold was not doing his homework as leader because 'All he is interested in is his memoirs.' Harold was, it appeared, contracted to write a book, with which he had become obsessed. I myself had begun negotiations with Harold Evans for the serialization in the *Sunday Times* of extracts from my Cabinet diaries when they eventually appeared. I had come to the decision to publish them because Dick had made it clear that he was going to publish his own Cabinet diaries as soon as possible and I was not prepared to leave the field clear for the Crossman version of history. But I was shocked by Dick's decision to publish while crucial political battles were going on in which his colleagues were engaged. I intended to remain on the battlefield, unlike Dick, who had accepted the editorship of the *New Statesman* and talked about going into the House of Lords. I did not want to harm Labour's fight. As a result, the *Sunday Times* had to wait through two general elections encompassing another period of Labour government and ending with our return to Opposition again before I would authorize publication in 1980. In the meantime, I had to admit that the publication of Dick's diaries had done no harm to Cabinet government and a great deal of good in letting the voters know what was going on at the heart of power.

It was the issue of the Common Market, as we called it in those days, which stirred Harold into a show of life again, though in his own devious and convoluted form. Heath had lost no time in making an application for Britain's membership. He was already halfway there through changes in British domestic policy, such as adopting import levies on food and introducing VAT. He was soon announcing triumphantly that he had negotiated satisfactory terms and was going to press ahead with the necessary legislation. Harold was in a trap. Those of us who had served in Cabinet knew that, led by George Brown, he had been trying to negotiate his way into the EEC as Prime Minister, as shown by his appointment of George Thomson, a fanatical pro-European, as Minister for Europe. He had been thwarted – as Harold Macmillan had been before him – by the veto of President de Gaulle, who had argued with some prescience that our economy was not strong enough for the strains membership would put on us. Britain relied on large imports of cheap food, a lot of which came from the Commonwealth. Membership would mean we would have to switch to dearer food from the EEC, hopefully most of it from France. I admired de Gaulle's logic and accepted his conclusion that association with the Six would be a better bet for Britain than full membership. Now Heath had negotiated a long transitional period to soften the impact of the blow.

Harold knew he would have accepted the terms if they had been offered him, even though they did not include any of the fundamental changes, such as amendments to the CAP, which the Labour Party conference had been demanding. I commented to Dick Crossman that successive British prime ministers of both parties seemed to have given up hope altogether of solving their own economic problems and were anxious to shift the responsibility to someone else. The economic expansion which followed the creation of the Common Market of the Six in 1957 seemed to indicate that the solution lay in a bigger market, even though the initial economic spurt had petered out. The advocates of Britain's entry were not bothered about the small print. Heath, for example, assured doubters that British sovereignty was not in jeopardy since Britain would be able to veto any developments she considered contrary to her national interests. This was being economical with the truth, to say the least of it, since the European federalists, of whom Heath was one, had no intention of tolerating the national veto for long. Britain was being edged into member-ship by a series of similar dishonesties.

Harold, however, was well aware that a majority of Labour MPs and almost certainly the Shadow Cabinet were opposed to membership. So was a majority of the unions, led by the giants like Frank Cousins' Transport Workers. Feeling against entry was running high among the rank and file, and Heath's terms would clearly have been rejected by conference. I myself had been against the idea of Britain's membership for some time. I welcomed the Franco-German reconciliation as much as anyone and approved the creation of the Community of the Six, but I did not believe the formulae of the Treaty of Rome would suit Britain economi-cally or us as socialists. Economically, we would lose our biggest competitive advantage of cheap food while exposing ourselves to unfettered competition in manufactured goods from more indus-trially efficient countries like Germany. As a socialist, I feared that the Treaty's free-market philosophy would undermine a Labour government's power to plan our economy and help our own industries.

I also resented the pro-marketeers' sanctimonious attempt to label us 'antis' as Little Englanders. 'You are little Europeans,' I used to retort. What was internationalist about a group of rich nations insulating themselves against the needs of the rest of the world behind a common external tariff wall? To me the CAP was the supreme symbol of the rich countries' selfishness. First they pushed up the price of food by keeping out imports from countries which could produce it more economically, then when food became too dear for many of our own people to buy they dumped the resulting surpluses on the world market with the help of export subsidies. They were totally indifferent to the effect this had on the economies of developing countries, which depended on their food exports to keep them afloat. Harold always grew uneasy when confronted with arguments like these.

Harold also faced a new and highly effective opponent in Tony Benn, whose political star was rising as mine was on the wane. By 1971 he had climbed to second place in the poll for the constituency section of the NEC, pushing me down to third place.

For some time my attitude to Tony Benn had been confused. I was one of the few people who applauded his fight to change the law to enable him to renounce the peerage he had inherited from his father, Lord Stansgate. It was an epic battle which I enthusiastically backed at a time when a lot of other people were sneering at what they considered a piece of eccentricity. I was also dazzled by his brilliance in analysing what was wrong with our society and his skill in promoting his ideas, but I had an uneasy feeling from time to time that something was not quite in focus. Ted, carried away by one of Tony's speeches, said he believed that Benn would become leader of the party one day, but I had begun to have my doubts.

Now my doubts came back again as he started to change his line on a number of policies. At one stage he had supported Britain's entry into the EEC, talking rather vaguely about the need to create a 'technological Europe'. Now he had become one of the most vocal of the anti-marketeers. His opposition became almost mystical. After one of his Common Market speeches in the Commons, I wrote in my diary that he had risen to 'stratospheric, philosophical heights. . . . I still mistrust his judgment but I admire his courage.' After another of these speeches I became more critical. He had, I noted, 'made an astonishing speech which leaves the House bewildered though impressed by his virtuosity. . . . Once again, one feels uneasily that he is a bit mad.'

I preferred Michael Foot's style. Following Bevan's death, Michael had returned to the House as Member for Ebbw Vale and was clearly determined to be a worthy successor to his hero. He had always been a competent speaker in the House: now he set out to become a great debater. I watched his technique with admiration tinged with envy. He would walk into the chamber whenever he had time to spare, picking up on his way in a copy of the document that was being debated. He would read it quickly as he sat on the bench, listen to a few speeches, and then join in with some penetrating analytical point. The technique worked. 'Nye's mantle has fallen on him,' I noted after a masterly contribution Michael made to one of our debates.

Tony Benn also revoked his support for *In Place of Strife*, though, to do him justice, he never taunted me with it as others did. He put himself at the head of the movement to give more power in the party to the rank and file. He had just scraped on to the Shadow Cabinet by a whisker but despite this, and despite Michael Foot's success in rising to fourth place, it was clear that the parliamentary party was moving to the right. Following the general election, Roy Jenkins had triumphed in the election for deputy leader and his supporters were gathering strength. The Tribune Group became alarmed. It produced a pamphlet, *Labour – Party or Puppet?* in which it challenged the right of MPs to be a law unto themselves, ignoring the views of the local party which put them there and claiming the exclusive right to elect the party leader. This, it argued, should be the prerogative of the party conference. These views were to be institutionalized in the Campaign for Labour Party Democracy. Tony had not signed the pamphlet but he was to annex the cause, as he often did.

One of the signatories was the new young MP for Bedwellty, Neil Kinnock, who had come into the House in 1970 and promptly joined the Tribune Group. He was staunchly left-wing but without rancour, and I warmed to his light-hearted boyishness. He voted faithfully with his Tribune friends but I never heard him make a personal attack. His jocularity – pointed up by Welsh wit – was a pleasant change from the customary vitriol.

The pro-marketeers in our party, though in a minority, were a formidable force. They had the strength of single-mindedness, being ready to sacrifice all British political issues to their European ideal. They could also see the issue as a weapon against Harold, whom they had never forgiven for snatching the leadership when their beloved Gaitskell died. They were also the custodians of orthodox financial policies, which they wanted to see reinforced on a European scale. Their attack on Harold was persistent and merciless, egged on by an enthusiastic press. They sensed that Harold was going to come out against Ted Heath's terms and in a famous speech in Birmingham Roy Jenkins delivered a scarcely veiled attack calling for 'honesty and consistency' in European policy, to press applause. George Thomson, with all the authority Harold had given him as Minister for Europe, declared publicly that Heath's terms were exactly what Harold would have negotiated. Two years later he was to give up British politics to become a European Commissioner on a large salary.

I watched Harold's agony with a mixture of exasperation and sympathy. I could not understand why he refused to fight. At party meeting after party meeting the pro-marketeers stole the show, mobilizing their forces in surprise attacks while anti-marketeers, out of loyalty to Harold, tried to keep the whole debate low key. At a special conference of the party on Europe called by the National Executive in July 1971, Harold made a speech which I described in my diary as 'a rambling, undignified affair which I found embarrassing'. John Macintosh, an ardent pro-marketeer, made a passionate and effective one. Nonetheless, the reference at the back of the Executive's motion that we should oppose Heath's terms was lost. The party split had deepened without Harold having given any leadership either way.

In despair, I went to see him to beg him to come out fighting. I got my first insight into the streak of obstinacy in his character. He agreed that it was war and that his enemies were plotting against him, but he was not going to change his tactics. 'I know perfectly well what I am doing,' he told me, 'and I wish some of you would stop worrying. My one job is to keep the party united. All along I have believed my duty was to be the custodian of party unity.' He was determined to avoid a return to the splits of 1959. On the Common Market, he continued, 'I know I have to come out against, but in my own time and my own way. I am about to go through the worst three months of my life. The press will crucify me.' It was almost a noble decision to adopt an ignoble role.

He then let slip the first indication of the resolve he had clearly made to resign as leader at the first appropriate opportunity. He assured me he would bring the party out of this crisis united, 'and then I am seriously considering giving up the leadership. Why should I go on? It has been hell!' I realized that, whatever else Harold could be accused of, it was not of hanging on to power for its own sake.

His predictions about the press were fulfilled. *The Times* carried a leading article declaring that he must never again become Prime Minister, and even his ally, the *Mirror*, which was pro-Market, complained that he was allowing himself to become a 'tethered sacrificial goat' to party unity. But Harold stumbled on in his own way, leading the party in the House against Heath's terms when a few months later the Tory leader tabled a motion approving them. No less than sixty-nine Labour MPs, headed by Roy Jenkins, defied the Labour whip and voted for the government motion, giving Heath a majority of 112. This treachery caused immense bitterness. The rift in the party was now so deep it was hard to see how it could ever heal.

The pro-marketeers fired another warning shot by getting Roy Jenkins re-elected deputy leader later in the year, though Michael Foot ran him close. The situation was saved by Roy Jenkins himself. In 1972, he resigned the deputy leadership, leaving his supporters dismayed. His public reason was that Harold had accepted Tony Benn's idea that Labour should pledge itself to hold a referendum on Heath's terms if it were returned to power. Roy denounced this as a constitutional monstrosity, but I believed the real reason for his resignation lay in his political daintiness. I wrote at the time, 'I have an instinctive feeling that, although Roy would like to be leader, he is both too intelligent and too refined either to intrigue seriously or to go in for the kill.' He just wanted to leave the battlefield.

My ejection from the Shadow Cabinet had left me out on a political limb. Some people on the National Executive made friendly overtures. Frank Allaun, always a gentle Tribunite, said to me, 'Barbara, I wish you had never gone to DEP. More than one trade unionist used to say to me that you ought to be leader of the party. Of course your Bill altered all that.' In a charming letter Harold urged me to stay in his front-bench team, but I declined, explaining that I wanted to be free to make more speeches in the country. I had had enough humiliations to last me quite a while.

Thinking over my defeat I had to admit I had not been performing particularly well in the House for some time. One of the reasons was my anxiety about Ted's health. He had always had a dicky heart since he had had streptococcal rheumatism as a young man. Now he had developed breathlessness and was in and out of hospital. I would slip away from the front bench to go and see him in the Royal Northern Hospital at any hours I could manage during the day or later at night, often having to excuse myself for my absences. Robert Carr, reading in the press that Ted was in hospital, sent me a sympathetic note. In these human situations the House of Commons always closes ranks. I knew my work suffered but I wrote in my diary, 'Politicians become barren creatures unless they can have their human priorities.'

The tests on Ted ended in open-heart surgery in the National Heart Hospital. It was a perfect demonstration of what the NHS was all about. One day when I visited Ted in the public ward he said to me, 'One of your constituents is over there,' and I found a man who had been sent from Blackburn for the same heart surgery. We had a matey chat. On another day I arrived to find they had taken out all Ted's teeth, which had become focal points for infection. He was sitting in bed irritable with hunger because all they had given him to eat was a salad, which he could not chew. After that I ferried him in crème caramel and other edibles.

But I did not care. The operation, performed by Donald Ross, one of the most eminent heart specialists in the country, was a success and saved Ted's life. What was the lack of a few amenities compared with that? When I ran into Donald Ross after Ted was safely in intensive care, I could have kissed his hand. He said to me proudly, 'This operation would have cost you £8000 in the United States' – and that was in the 1970s. How much more today?

In the meantime, Heath was struggling with his economic difficulties. There was a touch of irony in the event which clinched his downfall. In September 1973 the miners, who had come out against his pay policy at their annual conference, decided they must recoup the pay they had lost since their last settlement in 1972, and started an overtime ban. They knew they were in a powerful position because the crisis in the Middle East had forced up the price of oil to heights we had none of us known before.

Heath declared a state of emergency – his third. Arguing that coal supplies were low and must be preserved, he restricted the use of electricity so that we were all shopping by candlelight, and he put industry on a three-day working week. Undeterred the miners' union balloted its members on a national strike: on a high poll 81 per cent voted for a strike. Heath, believing he had the country with him on the issue of 'Who governs Britain?', called a general election for February 1974.

Unfortunately for Heath his desperate throw was defeated by one of his own creations: the Pay Board. In the middle of the election campaign it produced the 'relativities' report for which he had asked, designed to show how miners' pay stood in relation to that of other workers. It revealed that the miners had indeed fallen behind in their wage increases as they had claimed. I also had a field day in Blackburn with the press when I discovered – as other Labour MPs did in their own areas – that the local power stations had such large reserves of coal that the introduction of a three-day working week had been unnecessary. The fire went out of Heath's campaign. Disaster was heaped on disaster. The CBI called for the repeal of the Industrial Relations Act because it was 'surrounded by hatred'. Enoch Powell shook the country by declaring that he had used his postal vote for Labour because it was the only party offering the people the chance to vote in a referendum on the Common Market. The *coup de grâce* came three days before the poll with the publication of trade figures showing a deficit of £383 million, which *The Times* described as 'the largest monthly deficit the country has known'.

So Heath's lead in the opinion polls, which continued right up to polling day, melted away. His gamble had failed. The question 'Who governs Britain?' had brought the answer: 'You've made a mess of it anyway!'

EIGHTEEN

•

The Baptism of the Social Contract

NO GOVERNMENT can ever have taken office in more difficult circumstances than we did in 1974. Harold Wilson had justified his unheroic stance on the Common Market by holding the party together and leading Labour to victory for the third time. But though we were in office, we were not in power. Labour had won only 301 seats to Heath's 297, but were 34 seats short of an overall majority. We were dependent on the goodwill of fourteen Liberals, cock-a-hoop at their increased number of seats, seven Scottish Nationalists, two Plaid Cymru and twelve Ulster Unionists. Heath at first refused to relinquish power, trying to lure the Liberals into a coalition with a seat in the Cabinet, but it was in vain. The Queen, therefore, sent for Harold, with whom she had always had a relaxed and friendly relationship.

The economic situation could not have been more discouraging, with inflation rising and industry still on a three-day working week. Not only had the balance-of-payments deficit risen to the astronomical monthly figure of £243 million, the largest ever recorded, but the explosion of oil prices, which had darkened Ted Heath's final days, broke against us with full force, adding nearly £2500 million to our oil-import bill in our first year. As Nicky Kaldor, back as one of Harold's economic advisers, pointed out to me, the oil-price increase hit not only our balance of payments but those of other countries as well, syphoning off an extra $60 billion into the pockets of the oil-producing countries, whose economies were too backward to absorb it. Unless therefore this surplus was pumped back into the world economy through loans and other means, it was bound to contract international trade and drive the world into recession. Unfortunately, few statesmen were prepared to hammer this lesson home, preferring to fall back on their traditional competitive deflation.

Despite the precariousness of our situation there was a buoyant atmosphere as we met for our first Cabinet. Harold set the tone by his obvious determination not to repeat old errors but to adopt a less conspiratorial style of government. Cabinets, we were told, were to be more informal: ministers were to be referred to by their Christian names instead of as the Minister for This or That. I thought this was important because it would encourage us to work together collectively as comrades instead of confronting each other with our departmental interests. I was also delighted when Harold told us we could appoint political advisers, for which a number of us had been pressing for so long. The walls of Jericho had fallen without our having to give another peep.

Most remarkable of all was Harold's success in getting Michael Foot into his Cabinet and as Secretary of State for Employment too. This man, who had attacked me so fiercely when I was in the job, was now in charge of industrial disputes and trying to get the unions to accept wage restraint. I never found what made him change his mind – it was a point on which he was bound to be sensitive. I suspect that like many of us he had been doing a lot of thinking in the previous four years and had realized that mistakes had been made on both sides – by backbenchers and trade unions as well as by the Labour government, and that we had to learn to work together more closely if we were to be returned to power. Hence Michael's acceptance of a share in ministerial responsibility, which he discharged with an almost passionate loyalty. I was amused as he became as ferocious a guardian of incomes policy as ever I had been. His left-wing credentials, coupled with his steadfastness, were a great asset to the government.

The composition of the rest of the Cabinet seemed reasonable. I believed that Denis would prove a more flexible Chancellor than Roy Jenkins had been and that Roy would be a very liberal Home Secretary. So he proved to be, though it was not the post he had wanted. He had set his heart on being Foreign Secretary, a job

which Harold had given to Jim Callaghan. I was always fascinated
to observe which people Harold would stand up to and those to
whom he would capitulate. He had capitulated to Roy Jenkins
when he opposed my going to DEA because he feared him then
as a rival who had to be kept sweet. Now he was standing up to
him because he considered him discredited. I believed that Jim
would be slightly more liberal than Michael Stewart as Foreign
Secretary, though it was a job I would have liked myself. I
flattered myself that, despite my directness, I had been rather good
at negotiating with foreign governments as Minister of Overseas
Development and with both sides of industry when at Employment because I knew when to be tough and when to turn on the
charm. But the idea of appointing a woman as Foreign Secretary
was too much even for Harold's feminism. Failing that, I was
quite happy with my new job of Secretary of State for the Social
Services.

For me there was one great gap in the Cabinet. Dick Crossman
had died shortly after the election. I had watched sadly over the
previous months as he struggled with stomach cancer. Our last
meal together in the House had been very poignant as he barely
touched his food and had only a couple of sips of the wine I
bought him. On his death I wrote in my diary, 'A great abrasive,
tonic force has gone out of my political life. We had often
quarrelled, but there was a mutual appreciation between us which
made an enduring bond.'

Harold had recovered his fighting spirit, declaring that we
would press ahead with our full programme and daring the
Liberals to do their worst. Our first Queen's Speech, therefore,
was uncompromising. We had fought the election on our Social
Contract with the unions as the best hope of winning their co-
operation in restraining excessive wage demands, and in the
Speech we set out to fulfil our side of the bargain. The hated
Housing Finance Act, with its compulsory rent increases, was to
be repealed and, in the meantime, the rent increases the Act had
imposed for 1974 were frozen. In obedience to union pressure we
declared that we would repeal the Industrial Relations Act in its
entirety, increase pensions and other benefits, keep the price of

key foods down by subsidies, legislate on equal status for women, press ahead with comprehensive secondary education and abolish the despised museum charges. The speech also outlined our long-term policies such as bringing development land into public ownership, new measures to regenerate industry and devolution of more power to Scotland and Wales. Even the enemy *Daily Mail* ran the headline: 'Labour's new package leaves few loopholes for the Opposition.'

Denis Healey entered into the new mood with his usual exuberance, throwing himself behind the Social Contract and refusing to allow our minority position to cramp his style, but he was too canny to allow his enthusiasm to run away with him. He was a shrewd operator and I had always admired his combination of intellectual grasp and political verve. Nonetheless he was no sentimentalist and was unscrupulous in getting his own way. It was difficult to place him ideologically. He was more of a pragmatist than a philosopher. If he was now embracing the Social Contract as a political necessity I felt he could switch direction any time it suited his economic strategy and thought he could get away with it. I decided that he must be watched carefully.

In his first Budget in March, he walked a tightrope between discretion and egalitarianism, cheerfully providing for a record increase in pensions and other benefits, earmarking £500 million for food subsidies and raising the tax threshold for the lower paid by increasing personal and child allowances. But he warned Parliament that this was no time to expand the money supply, which he proudly claimed he had brought under tighter control than for many years. Government borrowing under Heath, he warned, had risen to over £4000 million and had to be cut back. So he increased corporation tax, brought more people into the higher rates of tax and increased the highest rate of all from 75 per cent to 83 per cent. For the first time, he introduced a ceiling for mortgage tax relief, cutting it off on properties worth over £25,000. But he also put 3p on the standard rate of income tax, bringing it to 33 per cent, and put VAT on petrol, sweets and ice-cream. The effect of his Budget, he told the Commons, would be to reduce demand by the modest sum of £200 million; any more savage deflation than that would only damage the economy. He therefore announced that he had negotiated a ten-year loan from the foreign banks of $2.5 billion, telling the House that 'borrowing is more sensible in economic terms than trying to cut imports by massive deflation', though he added, 'but it is not a soft option'.

In the event he turned out to have been too deflationary. Firms began to complain that their cash flow was drying up, and unemployment was running at 575,000, a figure which shocked us in those days. Commentators like Peter Jay, economics editor of *The Times*, complained that the Bank of England was superimposing a financial crisis on an economic one by contracting the money supply too drastically. It was a familiar story and Denis responded to it by means of an interim statement in July the following year in which he set out to stimulate growth and encourage industry by relaxing dividend control and doubling the Regional Employment Premium, which was designed to stimulate investment in the development areas. The great worry was inflation. On the whole the unions had played fair with their wage demands, even though the oil-price explosion had pushed up import prices. Ironically the most inflationary element on the wages side was the 'threshold agreements' which Ted Heath had introduced in an attempt to win over the unions. Under these, every 6 per cent rise in prices automatically triggered off a 1 per cent increase in wages. With world prices soaring up they added internal inflationary pressure to the external one. His first priority, therefore, was to do everything possible to keep prices down. He cut VAT from 10 per cent to 8 per cent, where the standard rate stayed until Margaret Thatcher nearly doubled it in 1979 in order to make room for her income tax reductions (later John Major raised it again to 17.5 per cent to pay for the concessions he had been forced to make on the poll tax). Healey also found another £500 million for subsidies to bring down the retail price of food and £150 million for domestic rate relief.

It was a package designed to narrow the gap between rich and poor, and neither Tories nor Liberals dared attack it frontally. We knew we could not struggle on for long as a minority government and decided to go to the country in October. Both opposition parties played it cautiously in the election. This time Heath promised to amend the Industrial Relations Act 'substantially' and called for national unity, an appeal echoed by the Liberals. But with the economic situation so menacing, it was no walk-over for us. Though we gained 19 seats, bringing our total to 319, with the Tory seats dropping to 277, the 39 seats won by the 'other parties' left us with an overall majority of only three.

Particularly worrying for us was the growing strength of the Scottish Nationalists, who threatened us in our political heart-lands. When I visited Scotland, for example and I went to Cumbernauld, I found our local Labour people perplexed and anxious about the inroads the Nationalists were making and I was not surprised when they gained four seats in the election, bringing their total to eleven. The Nationalists were less rampant in Wales but they gained one seat, bringing their total to three. The awkward squad from Northern Ireland was still twelve strong, giving them a grip on events which was to cause us some uncomfortable moments. There were two consolations for me in the result. Our vote had risen to 39.2 per cent while the Tories had dropped to 35.8 per cent, their lowest in recorded electoral history. In Blackburn my majority rose to over 7000, my highest yet.

But the man who was really worried was Ted Heath. In October *The Times* had declared, 'It is not possible for Mr Heath to remain as Leader of the Conservative Party,' and he had been living on borrowed time. When the Tories lost the October election, their third defeat under him, Tory backbenchers moved in on him. The 1922 Committee, which was their voice, had already prepared for a leadership contest by drawing up a new procedure. This provided that unless a candidate obtained the votes of at least half the Conservative MPs on the first ballot, a second ballot would be necessary in which newcomers could join.

There then ensued something very near to farce. Heath was outraged that he should be challenged and his anger cowed his obvious rivals – William Whitelaw, Jim Prior and Geoffrey Howe – into standing back. But the monetarists had got a stronger grip on Tory MPs than any of us realized. Most Labour people were surprised when they put up Margaret Thatcher as their candidate. We were even more surprised when she defeated Heath on the first ballot by 130 votes to 119. 'I felt a sneaking feminine pleasure,' I wrote in my diary. 'Damn it, that lass deserves to win.' She had dared to put her head above the parapet, risking annihilation, while the gentlemen of the party lay low. Their decision to emerge and fight in the second round now that she had paved the way merely swung more Tory doubtfuls to her side. On 11 February 1975 she skated home on the second ballot with a majority of seventy votes over William Whitelaw, her nearest rival, who would probably have won the contest if he had dared to put his hat in the ring earlier.

I realized then that we had in our hands a powerful political personality in Margaret Thatcher. 'I can't help feeling a thrill,' I wrote in my diary, 'she is so clearly the best man among them. I have been saying for some time that this country is ready and more than ready for a woman Prime Minister.' She had that combination men fear most: a brain as good as most of theirs plus a mastery of the arts of femininity. On her victory she appeared dewy-eyed before the cameras. 'She lends herself with grace and charm to every piece of photographer's gimmickry,' I wrote. I had no doubt that there was a rough politician beneath that demure exterior. I had no doubt either that the men would not be quite sure how to deal with her.

I watched with fascination how Harold in his first parliamentary encounters with the new Tory leader adapted his style into an unaccustomed gallantry. So did her backbenchers, whom I described as behaving like 'knights jousting at a tourney for a lady's favours . . . making an unholy row at every opportunity'. But what I noticed too was how unsure she was in her new job. Like many a leader of the Opposition, challenging a government which seemed confident in power, she was tense and uncertain of how to handle it. On one occasion when the Tories were after the government's blood, I noted, 'She sat with bowed head and detached primness while the row went on: hair immaculately groomed, smart dress crowned by a string of pearls. At last she rose to enormous cheers from her own side to deliver an adequate but hardly memorable intervention with studied charm.' Roy Jenkins, sitting next to me, groaned and I said, 'She's not quite real, is she?'

No one seeing her then would have foreseen the mastery she developed over the House as Prime Minister. She was not very effective in opposition, treating Harold Wilson gingerly. But all the time she was proving what I have always believed to be true – that performance in opposition is no clear indicator of what a leader is capable of achieving when given responsibility. Office maketh the man – or woman – and many politicians have gone underrated because they were never given the opportunity of power.

Our hold on power was still precarious. Despite this we entered two years of the most important social reforms since the Beveridge Report. I was lucky because so many of them lay in my field of the National Health Service and the social services. As one of the main custodians of the government's side of the Social Contract I was able to get a great deal of my own way in Cabinet. I was helped by two excellent ministers of state. Brian O'Malley, whom I put in charge of the social services, became a close personal friend. He had come into the House via the Musicians' Union and ran his own dance band for several years. This gave him a sense of humour which made him good company and we shared many a bottle of wine together over a conspiratorial meal. As often seems to happen with musical people he had an actuarial mind, which proved invaluable when I set him to work on the state earnings related pension scheme the government was pledged to introduce.

David Owen, whom I entrusted with the health side, was a different character. Reserved and sometimes arrogant, he could switch from the genial to the morose at lightning speed. He was handsome and knew it, and I would catch him glancing at his reflection in my windows as he walked up and down my room. Nonetheless he could be pleasant company when he was in a sunny mood. He was a keen European and a Jenkinsite, but that did not worry me as long as he worked as a loyal member of my team. This he mainly did, particularly when we were dealing with the medical technicalities of the Health Service, on which he was an expert, having served as a hospital doctor in St Thomas' Hospital and as a research fellow in its medical unit. I had less confidence in his political judgment and I often had to pull him back into line on such issues as the role of private medicine in the NHS. On the whole, however, it was remarkable how well we got on together considering that he belonged to the tightly knit political clique of pro-marketeers while I was an active anti-marketeer.

When Harold told us we could appoint a political adviser I was at a loss. The permission had come so suddenly that I had no one in particular in mind. Ted, who was then an alderman on Islington Council, strongly recommended young Jack Straw, who had made a name for himself as a lively President of the National Union of Students, had qualified at the Bar and was then proving a very effective Islington councillor. When I met him I found him boyish and unstuffy, a left-winger with his feet on the ground, and I took to him.

Jack did more than any other political adviser to get the civil service to come to terms with this new type of animal. The idea of bringing party activists into the inner citadel of ministerial power was totally alien. Civil servants are trained to distance themselves from the party political side of a minister's life. Apart from the Prime Minister, Foreign Secretary and Home Secretary, ministers are left to fend for themselves when they go to their constituencies or on any visit which is not an official one. On one trip to Blackburn I ran into a visiting American who was astounded to find a Cabinet minister wandering around alone and unguarded. It could not happen in the States, he told me. Sometimes the civil servants' circumspection led to comical situations, as when I attended the annual dinner of the Bradford City Labour Party, together with Vic Feather, another Bradfordian. I was then Employment Secretary at the height of my dispute with the TUC over *In Place of Strife*, so the situation had some piquancy. My Private Secretary conducted me to the door of our eating place and then melted away. An hour or so later he was back, hovering in the doorway and sending me frantic messages.

Apparently Yorkshire Television had learned of the historic moment following the dinner when Vic and I were photographed circling the dance floor in each other's arms. They wanted an interview with us both. When we agreed my Private Secretary moved in again. This had become an official occasion relevant to government policy, so all the arrangements fell to him. The interview over, he disappeared again. Civil servants get used to behaving like the Cheshire cat.

My departmental officials, therefore, viewed Jack's arrival with deep suspicion. Thanks to his tact and the co-operation of my understanding Principal Private Secretary, Norman Warner, the suspicion was gradually whittled down. Civil servants got used to the fact that Jack, having signed the Official Secrets Act, was entitled to see all the documents which came to me and to give me a political, as against a civil service, briefing on them. They had already become used to ministers bringing in their own chosen experts from outside as I had done in all my previous ministries. In my new field I had a remarkable range of specialists to draw upon. The most outstanding was Brian Abel-Smith, Professor of Social Administration at the London School of Economics. He had worked with Dick Crossman when Dick was put in charge of Social Services in 1968.

When I phoned him and asked, 'Will you come and work for me?' he replied simply, 'Of course.' Brian was a gentle person, though with firm ideas on the sort of society he wanted a Labour government to build, and he had an unparalleled mastery of the details of social policy. He brought with him Tony Lynes, who had been Secretary of the Child Poverty Action Group and had close connections with other radical spirits in this field, such as David Pichaud and Peter Townsend. They acted as my conscience, often giving uncomfortably critical assessments of government policy. No one could have described them as party hacks, for they lived in the academic's perfectionist world, while I had to struggle for my share of the money available with colleagues who were struggling with equal determination for their own priorities. Sometimes I had to bring my experts down to earth, while equally they kept reminding me of Labour's first principles.

One of my main jobs in my new Ministry was to bring our concept of social security up to date. Society had changed fundamentally since Beveridge's day. Inflation had made his flat-rate contributory pension inadequate for providing enough to live on in old age and various forms of supplementing their income had been introduced on the basis of a means test. Family allowances had been inadequate to keep out of poverty the large numbers of wage-earners with children. The one-parent family, barely heard of when Beveridge was drawing up his report, had become commonplace. Most of the disabled were being denied the chance of leading a full life. Far too many groups were still living in poverty. How could we restore dignity and security to their lives, given – as I knew only too well – that resources were limited?

Our whole team rejected means testing as the solution. The Tory argument that this was the best way of targeting help at those who needed it most was, we knew, a fallacy. Even the poor have their pride and many would not ask for what they considered to be charity. Others were inept at playing the system and getting what they were entitled to, so the welfare state had become more of an asset to the middle classes than to the poor. The failure of Tory targeting had been demonstrated by Ted Heath himself when, instead of increasing family allowances as he had promised, he introduced a means-tested family income supplement (FIS). Nearly everyone was only too glad to draw family allowance whereas the take-up of FIS was only 50 per cent and stayed around that figure for many years.

The answer, we believed, lay in universal benefits as a right, of which the NHS was a brilliantly successful example. So we worked out a scheme for what we called 'functional means testing', whereby people paid for their benefits through taxation or contributions when they were fit and at work and drew them as a right when they became old, ill or unemployed. The test of their need would be, not income, but the situation in which they found themselves.

We started with the pensioners and widows. With almost 2 million of them on supplementary benefit, they formed the largest area of poverty. Cabinet had no hesitation in keeping our election promise to lift the single pension from £7.75 to £10 and the married couple's pension from £13.50 to £16, a 25 per cent increase, the largest they had had since national insurance was introduced. Officers of the National Federation of Old Age Pensions Associations, which had its headquarters in my constituency, were startled. They were notoriously 'true blue' and could not believe Labour would carry out its promises. One of them said to me, rather grudgingly, 'We never thought you'd do it.' I suspect most of them continued to vote Conservative.

But we went further. In the past, pensions and benefits had been increased only spasmodically. Now I proudly piloted through the House a Bill tying the government's hands by binding it to uprate pensions and benefits every year in line not only with the rise in prices but with the increase in average national earnings, whichever was more favourable to the pensioner. It was right, I told the House, that these groups should share in rising national prosperity. If wage-earners got more, they should too. The value of this earnings link was demonstrated when Margaret Thatcher abolished it in 1980. Eleven years later we calculated that if she had not done so a single pensioner would have been £14.55 a week better off and a married couple £23 a week, enough to make many of them independent of means testing.

But we wanted more than a patchwork solution. One of the biggest divisions in our society was in the pensions field, where an increasing number of white-collar workers in the professions and in the more progressive private firms were able to earn super-annuation payments which enabled them to retire in comfort, while most manual workers were left to rely on the basic pension. I was outraged when I learned that some railway workers, under the British Railways Board's occupational pensions scheme, had been taking home, after forty years' service, the magnificent additional sum of 2s 6d a week. Dick Crossman, when in charge of the social services, had beavered away at this anomaly. In a masterly speech to the 1967 Labour Party conference, he had urged that we had to get rid of 'apartheid in old age' and worked out a national superannuation scheme to cover everyone. But his plan was too complicated and had stirred up resistance among some of the unions as well as in the pensions industry. Yet the party remained committed to the general principles he had laid down. It was my job to pick up where Dick had left off and produce a scheme which was acceptable and workable.

I could not have done it without Brian O'Malley. We had no hesitation in rejecting the pathetic reserve pension scheme which my predecessor, Sir Keith Joseph, had put on the statute book just before the election. His scheme not only provided an inadequate pension, but failed to protect it against inflation. Worse still, it gave women lower earnings-related pensions than men for the same contributions, on the grounds that they retired earlier and lived longer. I had great fun on the Standing Committee dealing with his Bill, taunting him for his actuarial aridity. Women, I told him, lived longer than men because they lived more frugal and hardworking lives and should not be penalized for that. If men lived more virtuously they might live longer too. But, despite my teasing, he would not give way.

Together Brian and I set out to produce a new scheme to cover the 12 million workers who had no occupational pension. The aim was to give every worker inside and outside the state scheme a guaranteed minimum pension on retirement up to a ceiling equivalent to half the average national earnings. This meant that no worker, manual or white collar, need be dependent in old age on means testing, while anyone who wanted to provide additional security on top was free to do so. Any contributor was free to contract out of the state scheme into a private one, but on condition that the private scheme provided an equivalent guaranteed minimum pension and on the same conditions which we laid down for the state scheme.

The key condition was that every year the pension must be increased in line with the rise in the cost of living, something few private schemes guaranteed and which we proposed the Treasury should help them achieve through a Treasury supplement. But we worked out other refinements too, and my usually staid officials got excited as we worked on them. An important provision was that, although people would be expected to contribute throughout their working lives, their occupational pension would mature in twenty years, and each year of contribution would be reflected in the value of the pensions, so those who retired before they had completed twenty years would still get some benefit.

Brian grappled with the details while decisions of principle kept coming back to me. I told him sternly, because he was a bit of a male chauvinist, that women had to have a fair deal at last. We had to get rid of Beveridge's concept of women's dependency, the idea that women only went to work for pin money and that the husband was the main breadwinner. Coming from Lancashire, where married women dominated the textile industry, I knew how untrue that was. We had to help them to stand on their own feet and ensure that they got equal treatment when they did so. The married women's option had to go, because under it married women who went out to work could decide not to contribute for their own pension but rely on their husband's contributions to provide them with a reduced pension when he retired. In future, all women who went to work would pay the same *pro rata* contributions as their husband and would receive equal benefits in return, even though they were entitled to retire five years earlier. I knew that this was discrimination in their favour, but I argued that men had been discriminating against women for centuries and it would not do them any harm to wait until we could afford to bring down the retirement age to sixty for them as well, which we certainly could not afford to do then. No private pension scheme, I ruled, would be approved as an alternative to the state scheme which did not give its women employees exactly the same right to join as men or which did not provide equality of treatment in every respect, including perks.

Research had shown that one of the largest groups living in poverty were widows, for whom adequate provision had not been made in Keith Joseph's scheme. The provision we made for them in ours was the most generous yet known. Not only did they inherit 100 per cent of their husbands' pension entitlement, but they were able to add to it the value of any contributions they had made themselves when at work – up to the ceiling. We even included a modest step towards a pension for widowers, a cause dear to my heart since I had studied the new pension scheme which was being introduced for MPs. Under it I found that although I had drawn the same salary as my male colleagues and paid the same contributions, their widows would automatically receive a pension as of right when their husbands died, whereas my husband would receive nothing, unless he was 'incapable by reason of age or bodily or mental infirmity of earning his own living and was wholly or mainly dependent' on me. This was grossly unfair to Ted, who had stoically put up with my inability, as MP and Minister, to pursue my normal domestic activities, and I told the Commons so in vigorous terms. MPs sheepishly admitted that my case was unanswerable and I won some minor concessions, but no government then was prepared to accept my logic because of its implications for civil service pensions.

My officials shared our excitement as our scheme took shape. It was Tony Crocker, one of my more elderly under secretaries, who gave the Bill its final touch. In most private schemes the pension was based on a final salary, because most white-collar staff reached the peak of their earnings in their final years. For manual workers the opposite was often true. Miners, for instance, often reached their working peak at the coalface in their middle years and ended their working days as surface workers, earning less. The final-salary formula was no use to them, and we worried about how to deal with this. Almost stuttering at his own daring, the shy Mr Crocker said to us, 'Why not base the pension on the twenty best earning years?' Brian and I jumped at it: another good piece of egalitarianism.

All this, of course, had to be paid for by higher contributions. There were mutterings from the Opposition that people would not be prepared to accept this increase, but we believed that they were wrong as most people would be prepared to pay more for greater security in old age, and we were proved right. The Tories were nonplussed about how to deal with our mammoth Bill, because they knew it was popular. They fell back on the argument that the scheme was so ambitious that it would run out of funds, but this was scotched when the Government Actuary's report showed that the scheme would be viable at manageable cost. Our crowning moment came when Frank Byers, Liberal Leader in the

House of Lords and chairman of the Company Pensions Information Centre, publicly congratulated us on the scheme and threw a party in our honour to celebrate the passing of the Bill. We knew we had produced a model example of how state and private interests could co-operate for the general good.

There was rejoicing in the Department too, when the Bill became law. Our staff, at all levels, had thrown themselves into it. Brian and I thereupon decided to give two 'pensions parties' which would enable all those involved in the production of the scheme to celebrate. We gathered that it was unprecedented for ministers to entertain their civil servants high and low – not forgetting the drivers – when they got an important piece of legislation through Parliament, but we did not care. At the party at Hell Corner Farm, Brian stood tirelessly in my kitchen carving ham, tongue, chicken and other delicacies, while our civil servants strolled round the garden in the sunshine, food and drink in hand. It was Brian's and my idea of a civilized society.

Brian and I were uneasily aware that our scheme did not help those who would have retired before it could come into effect in 1978. We were discussing the possibility of crediting them into the scheme so that they would receive some at any rate of its benefits, when disaster struck. I was sitting on the front bench at Question Time flanked by my two lieutenants, Brian and David, when Brian suddenly said to me thickly 'Take the next Question,' which he was due to answer, and disappeared. It was so unlike him that I could not grasp what was happening and sat stunned. I was grateful to David Owen, who said to me, 'I'll take Brian's Questions.' He did so with cool competence while I tried to collect my wits. Question Time over, I rushed out to discover Brian being hurried in a wheelchair to St Thomas' Hospital across the road. His last words to me were 'Don't tell my wife,' which was of course absurd. Kate doted on him and was at his bedside within hours. Apparently, he had had a subarachnoid haemorrhage, which can happen even to a young man, as he was, of forty-four. For three days, he was in a coma, watched over by Kate and their delightful young daughter Elizabeth, but he never came out of it. Everyone in the Commons was shocked by his sudden death, and tributes to him poured in. But none could adequately express my deep sense of personal loss.

As we struggled on without Brian, the next group to which we turned our attention was the disabled. With his usual political flair, Harold had appointed Alf Morris, MP for Wythenshawe, as Minister for the Disabled. Alf had put the disabled on the map as never before in his promotion as a backbencher in 1970 of the Chronically Sick and Disabled Persons Act which, for the first time, forced politicians to take note of the right of disabled people to lead as normal a life as possible. It drew attention to the importance of such simple things as providing ramps instead of steps outside public buildings to allow access by people in wheel-chairs. I thought I had got the message when I organized a meeting of the disabled in Blackburn to discuss the Act. I soon realized that I needed educating as much as anyone else, for I discovered to my horror that we had booked a hall for the meeting which had no ramp, so the disabled would not have been able to get into it. We hurriedly changed the venue, though it was difficult to find a suitable building with a ramp. My next shock came with the first question at the meeting: 'This is supposed to be a meeting for the disabled, but you have made no provision for the deaf.' Frankly, I had not even thought of them.

Alf Morris was a mild but dogged man, who gave me hell as he fought for a new charter for the disabled. I got irritated with him sometimes as he demanded the impossible and kept us in ministerial meetings for hours, demanding that every disabled person should be presented with a free car, in place of the invalid tricycle provided for those who could drive. Eventually, after a long wrangle, we struck a compromise by giving all disabled people a reasonably generous mobility allowance to spend on any form of transport they desired. We also introduced a non-contributory invalidity pension and an invalid care allowance for those who had to stay at home to look after a sick, elderly or disabled relative. It was far less than either Alf Morris or I wanted, but I was heartened when the Disablement Income Group gave us a sherry party at which Mary Greaves, a former president, congratulated me on what we had achieved for the disabled: 'Such a breakthrough.'

With my Blackburn *faux pas* still in mind, I turned my attention to the deaf and, to the Department's surprise, invited Jack Ashley, MP for Stoke-on-Trent South, to become my Parliamentary Private Secretary. At the height of a promising career as MP and television producer, he had been suddenly struck by a mysterious virus which left him stone deaf almost overnight. Jack fought back with great courage, announcing that he had no intention of resigning as an MP. Instead he insisted that Parliament provide him with the mechanistic aids he needed to do his job. He was delighted by my invitation, and so was Harold. This was the kind of humanistic socialism in which Harold believed. Thanks to Jack's pressure, I persuaded the Treasury to give me enough funds to set up the Institute of Hearing Research, upon which he had set his heart, to conduct and co-ordinate multi-disciplinary research into hearing problems. It became part of our co-ordinated plan for helping the disabled to lead a fulfilling life.

The problem of one-parent families was even more difficult to solve. This, we knew, was another great source of poverty, and in 1969 Dick Crossman had set up a committee under Sir Morris Finer QC to advise on how to deal with this new and growing phenomenon. The committee's report had landed on my desk, and my heart sank when I read it. It proposed a new cash benefit, the guaranteed maintenance allowance, plus generous child allowances, and it admitted that the cost would be very high unless the new allowances were means tested. I certainly did not want to create a new area of means testing at the heart of our social policy, but I also knew that my spending demands were making me unpopular in Cabinet. Dick Bourton, one of my deputy secretaries, who instinctively sided with the Treasury on everything, had already warned me sourly, 'The trouble, Secretary of State, is that your bids add up to the total amount of public expenditure available for all departments.' I therefore decided that my right course was to concentrate on introducing the party's 'child endowment' scheme designed to absorb both family allowance and child tax allowances in a new universal benefit payable to the mother for every child as of right. Women responded enthusiastically to this idea. As a flat-rate benefit it was more egalitarian than tax allowances. It also had the supreme advantage of diverting some money from the husband's pay packet into the mother's purse, so that she had her own wage at last. Gradually expanded, it could, I believed, play an important part in rolling back dependence on means testing.

The inflationary pressures on the government were already very high. Ted Heath's austerity had left most workers disgruntled and anxious to catch up on the wage increases they had lost.

Michael Foot's first job at Employment had been to settle the miners' strike. It was a simple remit since the Pay Board had found that their claim was just, so Michael was able to meet it in full. The next major wage demand came during the first weeks on my new job. The Royal College of Nursing, never a militant body, sent a deputation to see me. In determined mood, they told me politely but firmly that the nurses, too, had fallen behind and that we might face a mass walk-out of nurses from the NHS unless they were given the independent review of their pay for which they had been asking for some time. The NHS had as emotive an appeal to the Labour movement as the miners, so it was relatively easy for me to persuade Cabinet to let me set up such a review under Lord Halsbury, which would obviously also have to be extended to the professions supplementary to medicine such as radiographers and physiotherapists. I even got agreement that the award would be backdated to 23 May 1974, the date on which this review body was set up.

The Royal College was delighted and so was I. But, to my astonishment, the unions organizing nurses and other health workers reacted belligerently, demanding an immediate increase on account. I was furious when some of them hinted that they could not trust the government, while others argued that the government might fall and that they wanted to have some cash in hand before it did.

Not for the first time I despaired at the short-sightedness of some of the union leaders, who could not see that their interests lay in bolstering up their own government, rather than under-mining it. I had never shared the philosophy of some of my left-wing colleagues: 'My union right or wrong.' Just as I respected the role of the trade unions in our economic life, so I expected them to respect the role of the government and be prepared from time to time to subordinate their sectional interests to the wider interests it was the business of government to represent. The industrial unrest they were now stirring up was sheer sabotage. My frustration came to a head in one memorable scene with Clive Jenkins, the dynamic General Secretary of the Association of Scientific, Technical and Managerial Staff (ASTMS), whose union organized some of the radiographers. In the normal way Clive would have been a left-wing ally. He was a pugnacious little man who was taking trade unionism into the professional workers' field and whose adventurous new methods upset the staider traditional trade unionists. On this issue he was in one of his bloodiest-minded moods. I saw him in my room at the House to explain that Halsbury would be dealing with the radiographers as soon as he had completed his work on the nurses and that they would get an increase too. I appealed to him: 'Will you help me?' He spat out a furious 'No!' and threatened widespread and dis-ruptive industrial action immediately unless I agreed to a payment on account. 'All right then, go ahead,' I told him. 'I can't stop you destroying me and the government. If that is what you want, it is war.' My civil servants sat cowed as we screamed at each other like a couple of fishwives. They had never seen a minister behave like that. But I knew my Clive, and the showdown worked. After that he calmed down and was more reasonable.

But the agitation went on. As I toured hospitals I was greeted by little knots of nurses and radiographers bearing placards demanding: 'Give us our pay increase.' They were surprised when I said to them, 'You've already got it because the award will be backdated.' Nonetheless sporadic action continued, highlighted by the press. I was also having trouble with Lord Halsbury, who was not unnaturally touchy about his dignity. He refused to be hurried, saying he wanted to do a proper job, and I backed him up. When in September his report on the nurses appeared, my

tormentors found that he had indeed done a proper job, rec-
ommending a 30 per cent increase, which the government
accepted in its entirety. Even the Tory press could scarce forbear
to cheer, carrying banner headlines like 'Just What the Doctor
Ordered for the Nurses' (*Daily Mail*), '36,000 Cheers as the Nurses
Taste Their New Pay Tonic' (*Daily Express*). For a few weeks I
basked in public popularity again.

The Halsbury award proved to be one of my enduring
memorials. Seventeen years later when I had to make an after-
dinner speech about the Health Service, one of the guests was the
current President of the Royal College of Nursing, Professor June
Clarke, who greeted me with great friendliness. 'Remember I
gave you a thirty per cent increase,' I teased her. 'I certainly do,'
she replied warmly. 'We have never forgotten it.' It had lifted the
pay and status of nurses on to a new plane. Years later Lord
Halsbury and I were still congratulating ourselves on what he had
done. 'I wanted to give a sister in charge of a ward the same pay
as an inspector in charge of a police station,' he told me proudly.

One of our problems was that after ten years of pay freezes
and pay restraint, a flood of pent-up wage demands on every side
burst over us. The TUC had kept its side of the Social Contract
bargain by issuing a circular to its union members reminding them
that they had agreed to treat the miners' settlement as a special
case and urging their negotiators to 'take account of the economic
and industrial situation and of the policies being pursued by
the Government'. Pay increases, it warned, should only keep
pace with price increases and there should be a gap of twelve
months between pay settlements. But it could not hold the dam
against the flood and, by the end of 1975, inflation was running at
24.5 per cent, a peak not approached again until Margaret
Thatcher achieved an inflation rate of nearly 22 per cent in 1980.
Our peak was not all due to wage demands: increases in the cost
of imports had played a major part. Nonetheless, earnings had
risen over the year by 22.5 per cent, and we all knew that
something had to be done.

It was Jack Jones, fiercest opponent of incomes policies, who
saved the day. He had loyally backed the TUC guidelines, which

got through the General Council by only nineteen votes to thirteen and would not have won even that amount of support if he had not lent them his authority. In a speech at Rothesay he urged unions to be realistic in their wage claims: 'We are not advocating wage control: we are advocating common sense.' Now he was prepared to go further and accept a target figure for wage increases in the next round. When Denis Healey told the TUC that he was prepared to tolerate a target of 10 per cent, Jack concurred, provided that the 10 per cent was turned into the flat-rate figure of £6 a week payable to everyone up to an income limit of £8500 a year, then the equivalent of two and a half times average earnings. Denis agreed thankfully, and inflation fell to 16.1 per cent in the following year, while the increase in earnings was almost halved. The Social Contract had shown its worth.

Jack Jones' egalitarian move changed the whole atmosphere. The unions which organized the lower paid were overjoyed. A woman officer of the General Workers who drove me round my constituency shortly afterwards said to me, 'Our members have never had such an increase before and we did not even have to fight for it.' Obviously, the flat-rate formula could not be permanent since workers were as attached to their differentials as anybody else, but it turned the tide at a crucial time.

A complication among all these economic headaches was Harold Wilson's determination to keep Britain in the European Community at almost any price. He set out with his usual skill to get his own way without a row. It was not an easy task. As soon as we had been elected, he had sent Jim Callaghan to Brussels to renegotiate Heath's terms, but Jim came back with his tail between his legs. We had talked grandiloquently about never accepting taxes on imported food, but Jim reported to Cabinet that the negotiators made it clear that the Treaty of Rome was sacrosanct and that they were not prepared to alter a single line. All he could get was a few minor concessions and the promise that the CAP was being reformed anyway. Harold was not going to risk another all-day meeting at Chequers such as we had held in 1966, at which he had tried to persuade Cabinet to allow him to apply for membership. I have an enduring memory of that long day with the sun streaming in on us and the sunlit park beckoning us outside while a phalanx of officials and advisers, lining the walls behind us, stubbornly refused to give our entry the economic all-clear Harold was hoping for. At that meeting, Sir William Armstrong, guru of the Treasury, startled us all by declaring that the immediate effect of our entry would be a disastrous outflow of capital funds, and he was not too optimistic about the long term either. Harold was not going to let his experts loose on the terms he had renegotiated. Instead he relied on exhaustive and exhausting discussions in Cabinet to get us to accept those terms. Not for the first time his tactics worked, and Cabinet agreed by sixteen votes to seven, the latter including Michael Foot, Tony Benn, Peter Shore and myself, that the government should recommend our continued membership in the coming referendum to which we were pledged.

Sensitive as always to the dangers of a split and knowing how passionately we antis felt, Harold diplomatically agreed that every member of the Cabinet should be free to express his or her views publicly during the campaign. He further subdued unrest by declaring that the battle had to be fought on equal terms and that each side of the argument should be allocated £125,000 of public money to conduct its activities. This was not as generous as it sounded, since we anti-marketeers had paltry outside funds to draw upon, whereas the pro-marketeers received massive financial help from industrialists. A White Paper published when the campaign was over showed that the Britain in Europe movement had received and spent £1,500,000, of which over a million came from industry, while we antis could only scrape together contributions of £8600, of which £1300 came from the Transport and General Workers.

Harold had obviously intended that this unprecedented breach of Cabinet collective responsibility should be merely a gesture to show how scrupulously fair he was. He was outraged when he found that we antis intended to take it seriously. I was the main culprit, since I suggested at one of our private dinners that we should conduct our campaign as a group under the heading 'Cabinet Ministers against the Market'. We should also run brains trusts and hold press conferences together. Tony Benn, Michael

Foot and others demurred at first, but eventually I convinced them with the argument: 'Why should the authority of the Cabinet be thrown behind a line on which it is so split and on an issue on which the country is being left free to choose?' Wedgie was given the job of drawing up a joint statement for us to issue at a press conference opening our campaign.

The press conference as Cabinet Ministers against the Market went with a bang, and I was proud of my idea. Harold however exploded. He had not intended the freedom he had given us to be used so effectively. I was in our Islington flat that evening, hoping for an early night, when he telephoned, angrier than I had ever known him. 'So this is all the loyalty I get!' he snarled, adding that certain ministers were having a meeting in his room at the House. I could come or not as I liked, and he slammed the receiver down. I was totally unrepentant, as well as angry at Harold's attitude, but I knew that I ought to go to the meeting. My patient Ted drove me to the House. I found Harold, Mike and Jim sitting in inspissated gloom. Harold apologized for his earlier rudeness and I went over and kissed him on the forehead. 'Don't I get a kiss?' asked Jim mournfully. 'God knows I need it!' So I kissed him too. 'I can't understand why Barbara is so chirpy,' Jim almost groaned. 'Because I don't think the situation is so tragic,' I replied. 'Harold, you must wear with pride the freedom you have given us.' Michael played his usual emollient role, and gradually he and I soothed Harold down.

Harold need not have worried. Our brave amateur efforts were soon swamped by the professional resources of the pro-marketeers. They called on prominent industrialists and European politicians in their support, even mobilizing members of the Commission to back their case. They used this ploy in the 1983 election when pro-marketeers enlisted Labour's member of the European Commission, Ivor Richard, to declare that Labour's plan to withdraw from the EC would cause unemployment in Britain to reach 5 million. They placed a spy among us who leaked our plans, and they packed our press conferences with hostile critics, some of them recruited from the European press, who uttered their questions almost venomously.

But the star of their side was Edward Heath, who was in his element. At a televised debate on the issues at the Oxford Union he stole the show, standing up before his young listeners without a note and pouring out simplistic certainties. On our side Peter Shore did well and I less well, while Jeremy Thorpe, then Liberal leader, who considered himself something of a wit, showed the shallowness of his personality by merely scoring debating points. He interrupted my speech with the challenge: if the country voted to stay in the EEC, would I resign from the government? Thinking on my feet I retorted, 'If Britain votes to stay in the Common Market, my country will need me more than ever.' The undergraduates jeered and Jeremy stood up to dance a jig, circling a finger round his head to denote the halo I was supposed to have awarded myself. It went down well with that hostile audience, but those who saw the debate on television said that Jeremy had done himself no good at all. It was Ted Heath who captivated his listeners and swept into the division lobby to wipe the floor with us.

The main Tory supporter on our side was Enoch Powell. It could have been politically embarrassing, but Enoch played it straight down the line, scrupulously keeping party politics out of it. He also revealed unexpected old-world courtesy. When, for instance, we found that a press conference we had arranged for him clashed with one I had been hoping to hold, he insisted on giving way to me, postponing his own. In fact, he showed more sense of solidarity than Tony Benn, who like so many politicians with exceptional talents did not like working in a team. On more than one occasion he jumped the gun on our group by calling press conferences on his own account without consulting the rest of us. He always gave scintillating performances but his pieces of private enterprise undermined the concept of an anti-market Cabinet.

Our campaign was not all disaster. We held well-packed public meetings at which the old revivalist spirit of the movement was aroused again. So was the old comradeship. We held conspiratorial meetings in each other's homes. When one such was held in Ted's and my Islington flat, they were all there: not just the regulars like Michael Foot, Tony Benn and Peter Shore but a number of new recruits from the back benches and some of my fiercest former enemies over *In Place of Strife*, notably Ian Mikardo and Jack Jones. They sat cross-legged on the floor while I served them food. Typically Clive Jenkins arrived bearing a magnum of champagne. Despite our efforts the Labour voters' allegiance to Harold held firm. At one of my open-air meetings in my constituency, at which I thought I deployed some powerful arguments, a Labour woman came up to me afterwards and said shyly, 'But Harold's in favour, isn't he? So what do we do?' I knew then that we had lost, as indeed we had, by 68 per cent Yes votes to 33 per cent Noes. Tony Benn immediately issued a statement saying that the people had spoken and he would abide by their verdict. I thought it was a bit premature and so it proved to be, because he later changed his mind.

Despite Tony's conciliatory statement, Harold seized the opportunity to sideline him from his power base at the Department of Industry to Energy. It was a clever move since Tony could hardly argue that it was demeaning to be in charge of the coal industry and nuclear energy. Arthur Scargill, then President of the Yorkshire miners, was already one of his closest allies. Nonetheless, it was intended to clip his wings, and Tony held court behind closed curtains in his room in the House, discussing with his cronies for hours whether he should resign. I for one did not encourage him in this idea because I thought he had brought the move upon himself by the way at Industry he had mishandled one of the key elements in our party's policy. I was as keen as anyone on the idea of 'planning agreements' between government and industry to decide how industry could best be modernized and expanded. Properly handled, the policy could have won the British public over to a new concept of the role of government in a mixed economy. Everyone knew that our manufacturing industry was in decline and conventional policies had failed to get it on its feet. Why, we could have argued, should there not be a partnership between private industry and public policy in achieving nationally important goals? It was an approach which Harold Wilson himself had recommended to party conference.

Tony Benn was a keen advocate of the new policy but once

again his penchant for private enterprise in promoting his own ideas got the better of him. He used his position as chairman of the Home Policy Committee to release his proposals to the press before they had been to Cabinet. To make matters worse he had them drawn up in the most lurid form. Planning agreements would be imposed not only on major firms but on their subsidiaries. The result was predictable. The *Daily Mail* and others quickly made their calculations and the *Mail* came out with the screaming headline 'Benn Grabs 4,000 Firms.' Harold faced merciless questioning in the House on whether these plans had been approved by the Cabinet or were we to be ruled by Transport House, Labour's headquarters at that time. Whatever answer Harold gave, he was in a trap and I was furious with Tony for letting his vanity run away with him.

But the damage had been done. Industry was up in arms. Plagued by economic troubles, it was not surprising that Harold was ready to sue for peace at almost any price. He successfully emasculated Tony's proposals in Cabinet, so the Act which finally emerged had no teeth. The National Enterprise Board did some useful work in promoting modest industrial ventures, but the planning agreements were effectively dead. After two years, only one had been negotiated and that was with Chrysler, which was already being taken into public ownership.

In my continuing struggle for my new social policy I was not prepared to sacrifice the needs of the NHS. Whatever the economic difficulties which faced us, I always tried to defend its principles. Shortly after we came into office, for example, I had announced that the family planning supplies for the new comprehensive planning service which had been set up would be free. This reversed Sir Keith Joseph's decision to impose prescription charges on them and gave the tabloids the chance to have a bit of fun at my expense, the *Daily Mirror* trumpeting 'Barbara's Free Love'. I did not care, because I knew I had common sense on my side.

I had, however, to walk a tightrope to prevent the Treasury from playing one side of my Department off against the other, and my battles with Joel Barnett, who as Chief Secretary of the

Treasury was now in charge of public spending, became legend-ary. I would go along to his room at the Treasury flanked by officials and members of my expert team and bristling with the facts they had supplied. Joel, also flanked by officials, would greet me with a kiss before we got down to the bloodletting. I often had the satisfaction of seeing his officials outfaced by my Depart-ment's statistics. They were not used to their intended victims being so well briefed and found that the boasted infallibility of Treasury calculations was a myth. They were also unaccustomed to the verbal ping-pong at which Joel and I excelled. Sometimes the arguments became acrimonious, but on the whole we remained on affectionate terms, based on respect for each other as adversaries worthy of our steel.

But my struggle for the NHS was rough and tough. In one of his final struggles to ward off economic disaster, Heath had cut the hospitals budget and I faced an uphill struggle, first to restore the cuts and then to get more money for the NHS. Life did not seem too difficult in 1974, when I was given another £400 million to meet the NHS's increased costs, and at the beginning of 1975, when Denis agreed to restore some of the cuts of the previous government. Before long, however, the mood changed and Denis was demanding belt-tightening. Public expenditure, he told us, had increased by nearly 9 per cent in our first year. In the following year we would have to hold the increase down to a mere 0.5 per cent. That was agony enough, but Denis then looked ahead to 1978-9 and produced the old familiar arguments. He told us the economy would be improving by then, so he wanted further cuts to make way for the increased exports and an expansion of investment in industry. Tony Benn and I groaned: this was the old deflationary argument all over again – and deflation, we argued, had never encouraged growth or investment. We should be the last people to discourage public works as the engine of an investment-led recovery. In an interim measure, we should impose import controls as a shield behind which we could modestly expand the economy. But our protests were in vain. Chancellors always win in Cabinet.

We therefore faced a long, exhausting battle over who should give up what. I insisted that, far from accepting cuts in NHS expenditure, I needed a minimum increase of 1.5 per cent merely to keep pace with increased demands due to people living to a ripe old age and due to the spectacular and expensive advances in medical technology. Cabinet's heart was with me, though the Treasury's head was not, and the battle lasted over many weeks. Eventually, thanks to excellent briefing by my departmental team and Harold Wilson's cunning help, I emerged with my 1.5 per cent intact. Harold at any rate realized that I would have resigned rather than accept a cut. It was an immense relief. I even had some applause from the Tory press, typified by Geoffrey Smith's comment in *The Times* that I had got away with 'assault and battery', while Anthony Shrimsley of the *Daily Mail* had a piece headed 'Barbara's Threats Halt Health Service Cuts'.

But there were other troubles in the NHS. We had fought the election on the pledge to put the Health Service on a completely non-commercial basis by phasing pay beds out of NHS hospitals – the beds at the disposal of consultants for their private patients. The right of NHS consultants to supplement their income by treating their private patients in NHS beds was one of the concessions Nye Bevan had had to make to the medical profession to get the service off the ground at all. I for one did not blame him, but the existence of pay beds had irritated NHS patients and staff for years. To most patients, the concept of a free health service in which they would get their turn on the basis of medical priority was precious, and they resented the fact that some patients could jump the queue to an NHS bed by paying the consultant a private fee. Staff too, from nurses to kitchen staff, had become increasingly restive at having to provide special services for patients in private wards for whom the consultants pocketed most of the fee.

I sympathized totally with their view and took my instructions from our manifesto very seriously. It was not that I wanted to outlaw private practice. I believed that the right of individuals to seek private medical care if they wanted to was one of the elements of a free society and I had successfully fought some of our wilder spirits on this point at party conference. I was, however, determined to separate private practice from the NHS because I knew that NHS consultants had too much licence to come and go as they pleased, putting their private patients first, and offloading too many of their NHS responsibilities on to the junior hospital doctors, who were seriously overworked. I knew, too, that the best way of helping the juniors out of their condition of near-slavery was to increase the number of consultant posts and that the fiercest opponents of this move were not my Department or the Treasury but the consultants *in situ* who did not want any more rivals for the pickings of private practice. Above all, I wanted to abolish queue-jumping.

The situation when I took over was complicated by the fact that the consultants were pressing for a new contract to cover their service with the NHS. Sir Philip Rogers, my Permanent Secretary, warned me that they were in an ugly mood because Sir Keith Joseph had kept fending them off. They were very near to downing tools and I ought to see them, which I did.

As soon as I met Dr Walpole Lewin, chairman of the Council of the BMA, and Dr Derek Stevenson, Secretary of the BMA, I knew we were in for a bitter row. They were bristling with anger over our pay-beds policy, for they had come to demand greater freedom to do private practice under their contract, not less. I appeased them by saying I would set up a working party under David Owen's chairmanship to examine their claim for a new contract, but I annoyed them by adding that the working party would also discuss the phasing out of pay beds, to which we were committed. They went off determined to use the working party to get their own way.

The negotiations dragged on for the next two years in a fraught atmosphere. I left David Owen to wrestle with the details, but called him in to report to me regularly as I feared he was giving too much away. David was a curious mixture. On some issues he was excellent, such as preventive medicine and mental health. He had a good mind and his dedication to the NHS was absolute. But he had no stomach for the fight over pay beds and he crumbled too easily when confronted by tough characters like Mr Antony Grabham, who led the BMA's negotiating team. I suspect that as a former registrar he also had a secret awe of the men at the top of the medical hierarchy. What worried me was his lack of consistency as he fluctuated between truculence and a readiness to capitulate. I wrote in my diary that David should only ever be a second-in-command.

When Nye Bevan had agreed to allow consultants pay beds in NHS hospitals, he had said he wanted to 'stuff their mouths with gold'. I, too, believed that the most dedicated consultants deserved a better reward, but I did not think the answer was to stuff their mouths with private gold. It was rather to give them a higher NHS salary plus extra payments on top for those willing to commit themselves to work whole-time for the service, or to work in the under-staffed regions of the country or in less popular specialities like geriatrics and psychiatry. Cabinet, struggling to secure voluntary wage restraint, was horrified at the idea of giving the consultants more. One of the heartbreaks of a minister is to realize that with a little more money he or she could achieve a major reform, only to find that that little bit more money is not there.

The consultants in any case had other ideas. They wanted a new 'closed contract' which would limit the hours they were expected to give in return for their NHS salary, leaving them free to come and go as they pleased and to do more private practice, not less. I resisted doggedly through many a bitter argument late into the night. The consultants finally climbed down in April 1975 when their Pay Review Body recommended a substantial increase in their NHS salary and they wanted my help in getting it through Cabinet. This I did without any phasing in of the increase except for a few consultants at the very top. The relieved negotiators decided to drop the idea of a new contract and turn their attention to improving the existing one. Here I was prepared to meet them halfway, and agreement was quickly reached. David and I were not dissatisfied with what we had achieved. We had strictly defined the hours the consultants were expected to give to the NHS and had preserved the salary differential in favour of those who worked full-time – something the negotiators had done their utmost to eliminate. I had no doubt they would renew their efforts under another government. What interested me was that they had no desire to get rid of the NHS. On the contrary, it provided their bread and butter, but they wanted a liberal serving of private-practice jam on top, and if they were to get it they had to be able to give their private patients some priority. So if they had their way, the NHS patient would become second class.

But the pay-beds issue had not been resolved and this time I was outmanoeuvred by Harold, who was clearly losing his stomach for the fight on this as on other things. I had managed to get my proposals for phasing out pay beds through the Social Services Committee of Cabinet and into the Queen's Speech in November. 'Government Bites Bullet on Pay Beds', wrote John Cunningham admiringly in the *Guardian*, and our backbenchers were delighted. But when the howls came from the consultants I met the same backtracking in Cabinet as I had done over *In Place of Strife*.

The retreat was led by Harold Lever and Shirley Williams. Lever had almost certainly played bridge with some of the consultants, while Shirley was always more radical in words than in deeds. Harold had brought her into the Cabinet as Secretary of State for Prices and Consumer Protection – he was in fact the first Prime Minister to have two women in his Cabinet. Shirley was immensely popular with Labour's rank and file. She had charm, a good brain and great speaking ability, and I hoped she would prove an ally in my battles with the Treasury to protect the poor, but though she usually agreed with my line, she seldom supported me when I pressed it in Cabinet. On pay beds she gave up the battle without a fight.

Her main objection, Shirley told me, was that I was proposing to license the number of private hospitals. The reason was clear: I did not want the phasing out of pay beds to lead to the mushrooming of private facilities round the NHS hospitals which would then try to lure away the nurses and other staff whom the NHS had trained at considerable public expense. I therefore proposed that private facilities should continue at their existing level and that any extensions would have to be approved by me in the light of local needs. This struck me as striking a fair balance between private rights and public needs, but most of the Cabinet did not want to know. They were punch-drunk with economic problems and took refuge in the fallacy that the best way to face a challenge is to run away from it. Harold, in particular, was ready to sue for peace with any vested interest.

My first warning of what was to follow came when Harold Wilson called me in to tell me that Arnold Goodman, who had been retained by the Independent Hospitals Group as their adviser, had offered to mediate in the pay-beds dispute. Arnold, who was Harold's solicitor, was a large man with an imposing presence and a brilliant brain. As chairman of the Newspaper Proprietors' Association, he was called in to advise diverse interests. He had an iron in various liberal fires, such as the arts, and had become one of Harold's closest friends, Harold making him a peer in 1965. Arnold, however, had never taken the Labour Whip in the Lords, preferring to keep his independence to serve any side in any argument which appealed to him. Would I talk to him? asked Harold, and I said, 'Of course,' but I knew I was up against one of the shrewdest operators in public life.

Our weeks of negotiation were a mixture of detailed detective work and French farce. At the outset I decided to keep the talks secret from my officials, except my Private Secretary, and even from David Owen, whom I did not want to have rocking the boat by injudicious surrenders of vital points. So night after night Norman Warner and I repaired to Arnold's roomy flat in Portland Place. Arnold was never there when we arrived at the appointed time. Instead we were greeted by his genteel housekeeper, Mrs Roberts, who plied us with china tea and exquisitely thin cucumber sandwiches. We sat waiting for him in his rather gloomy, if expensively furnished, sitting room with portraits of him by Ruskin Spear and Graham Sutherland propped against the wall. Arnold was courtesy itself when he arrived, offering profuse apologies for being late, but I could not help thinking it was a strange attitude of mind that kept a busy Secretary of State hanging around until he was ready to talk to her. To this day I cannot drive down Portland Place without thinking of those long waits over cucumber sandwiches.

Arnold's technique was to be elaborately conciliatory to each side in turn, which dragged the discussions out endlessly. I knew I was in a trap. The press were waiting to denounce me as unreasonably inflexible, yet I was determined to save something from the wreck. The climax came with a great get-together in Arnold's flat, with the two sides in different rooms and Arnold darting between us with bits of paper in his hand. This time I took David Owen along with me and Sir Patrick Nairne, my new Permanent Secretary, who had come to me from Defence when Philip Rogers retired. Sir Patrick thought like a soldier whose duty it was to obey the orders of his superior whatever he might think of them. His co-operation was impeccable and the constructive suggestions he made were designed to strengthen my hand, not weaken it.

At last, we reached an exhausted compromise. I had taken the precaution of keeping in touch with the health unions at every stage of the talks and they accepted that the compromise was the best that we could get. I had achieved one of my major points when I insisted that 1000 of the existing 4000 pay beds had to go immediately. The phasing out of the rest was to be left to a Health Services Board, including two trade union members, under an independent chairman, acting on strict criteria. The consultants had cavilled at the inclusion of trade unionists, but Arnold for once put his foot down over this. We had wrangled for hours over the criteria and I believed that, if they were scrupulously applied, steady further progress could be made with phasing out. Margaret Thatcher obviously thought so too, for one of her first acts on becoming Prime Minister was to abolish the Board and repeal my Act. She believed in private medicine.

By the beginning of 1976 I was thinking of throwing in my hand. I had had a hostile press over the pay-beds fight. Cummings, still cartoonist of the *Express*, lost no opportunity to portray me as a screaming old harridan. The press was full of stories of Cabinet reshuffles in which it was hinted that I would go. I had already informed my party friends in Blackburn that I did not intend to fight the next election, even though they had pressed me to. I was sixty-six years old and I thought it was time I made way for younger aspirants for power.

I was also disheartened by the changing attitude to public expenditure in Cabinet. It was not so much the cuts themselves which were my stumbling block as the government's overall strategy and the new ideology which was being pressed on us. At one Cabinet meeting I was appalled to hear Roy Jenkins declare that the growth in public expenditure was becoming a 'threat to democracy'; he claimed that it had risen to 60 per cent of GDP. Cabinet was duly impressed, but not for the first time we found later that the statistic (presumably a Treasury one) had been grossly exaggerated and that the real figure was 42 per cent. Those of us who were sceptical about the Treasury brainwashing were later vindicated when the government's think-tank, the Central Policy Review Staff, produced a report showing that the level of public expenditure in Britain was below that of many of our competitors, notably Germany. But when I pressed Cabinet to publish it, Denis angrily refused. He had become truculent and impatient with any talk of our political consciences, and I could see that the Social Contract was being systematically sacrificed.

But I did not want to leave my ministerial job until I had completed some of the major initiatives we had launched at DHSS. Though I had guided the Child Benefit Bill through Parliament I still had to negotiate a reasonable starting figure with Joel Barnett. I also wanted to see the Pay Beds Bill on the statute book without any further watering down of our compromise.

I decided to go and see Harold to find out where I stood. I found that he, too, was in resigning mood, though for different reasons. He had been even more mercilessly persecuted by the press than I had been, this time by a succession of personal smears against him and his entourage. One of the most popular ploys was to get at him through Marcia Williams and even her brother, Tony Fields, who had been the subject of a long press campaign implying that he had been acquiring derelict land and selling it at a big profit for development. Harold had told me more than once that Marcia's flat had been raided, almost certainly by political enemies in MI5 looking for ammunition to destroy the government. At the time I thought he was being neurotic, but the publication of *Spycatcher* some fifteen years later threw a different light on things.

Harold's reaction to the attacks on Marcia was typically cheeky chappie: he put her in the House of Lords as Lady Falkender. She obviously did not particularly want the role since, although she made a dignified figure at her Introduction, she has yet to make her maiden speech. She obviously saw her elevation as Harold did as a gesture of defiance towards his enemies. She and Harold were very much on the same wavelength on matters like this.

Harold was in surprisingly relaxed mood when I went to see him. Pouring me a drink he opened his heart to me. 'Can you keep a secret? I want to talk to you as an old friend who never leaks. I am getting tired of this job and do not intend to go on much longer.' In fact as soon as he became Prime Minister this time he had told the Queen the date on which he would retire. 'She's got the record of it so that no one will be able to say afterwards that I was pushed.' So he had no plans to reshuffle Cabinet. He refused to give me the exact date of his resignation, adding nonchalantly that he might carry on for another six months. When I told him in strict confidence that I wanted to give up my ministerial job in the autumn he looked surprised. I insisted several times that I did not want to go at once because I wanted to get the Pay Beds Bill and child-benefit negotiations through first and to go with dignity. I, too, did not want the press to be able to say I had been pushed out. 'This conversation is proof that you haven't been,' he replied, 'and I will minute it.' He added thoughtfully, 'Your timetable ought to fit into mine all right.' I went away reassured.

But he had been economical with his frankness. Twelve days later he announced his resignation to an astonished Cabinet. Some of us had been warned of his intentions: others had not. Denis Healey complained that the first he had heard of what Harold had in mind was in the lavatory of Number 10 just before the fateful Cabinet. What struck me was the genuine dismay with which my colleagues heard his announcement. I felt that they realized at last how crucial his role had been in keeping us together and leading us to four electoral victories. As we broke up I said to Shirley that Michael Foot was the only possible compromise candidate, but she looked unconvinced.

A number of contestants for the succession were soon in the ring. There was irony in the fact that Jim Callaghan emerged as Harold's chosen heir since Jim had done more than anyone else to undermine Harold's position on *In Place of Strife* and other issues. Although Tony Benn announced he was standing, most of us Tribunites backed Michael Foot and we launched a 'Stop Jim' campaign. Michael did well on the first ballot, gaining ninety votes to Jim's eighty. Roy Jenkins, huffed by his vote of fifty-six, withdrew from the second round, to his followers' dismay. David Owen did not attempt to hide his disgust from me. Denis Healey was of a different mettle. Despite his much more derisory thirty votes, he decided to stay in the fight. 'He is a pugilist, not a patrician,' I noted approvingly, with none of Roy Jenkins' 'political daintiness'. It was soon clear that the Jenkinsites were going to switch to Jim. David Owen admitted to me shamefacedly afterwards that he had done so and was already regretting it. Tony Benn's thirty-seven votes were not enough to save Michael: though his vote rose to 133, Jim scraped home with 141. So near and yet so far.

With Jim ensconced as leader I began to think of my own fate. 'He'll not move you,' David said to me confidently. My friends in the Foot camp assured me that Michael, now in a strong position, would never let Jim get rid of me. But Michael had two main aims. The first was to become Lord President of the Council and Leader of the House, which was fair enough. The second was to obtain for his Minister of State at Employment, Albert Booth, the succession to his job as Secretary of State. He assured me that he had battled for me long and hard, but Jim was adamant. 'I could only get two out of three,' he told me apologetically. I understood the reason for Jim's stubbornness when he announced that David Ennals would have my job. After all, David Ennals had been Jim's campaign manager, while I had been active in the 'Stop Jim' campaign.

On Thursday, 8 April Jim sent for me to break the news that

I was to go. I had, he said, to make way for younger people. I bit back the riposte: 'Then why not start with yourself?' After all, he was only two years younger than I and I was not seeking to be Prime Minister. In any case, Jim went on, Harold had told him I wanted to retire. I was furious. So Harold had not only leaked our private conversation but had leaked it inaccurately. I took the news stiffly. 'Wish me good luck, I shall need it,' said Jim in his most pathetic tones. I did and shook hands. I walked out of Number 10 with my head held high and the waiting crowds gave a cheer as I emerged. I noted in my diary that I did not deserve to be discarded like so much old junk.

Later Ted, having heard the news, phoned me from Brussels where, as a member of the House of Lords, he was serving as an indirectly elected Member of the European Parliament. His comments on Jim Callaghan were unrepeatable. 'I wish I were home to comfort you,' he said. And so did I.

NINETEEN

———————— • ————————

The Unnecessary Defeat

TO BE SACKED from the Cabinet is a humiliating experience at any time. I walked into the Chamber self-consciously, looking for a seat on the back benches and feeling that all eyes were upon me, either sympathetically or patronizingly. I found it hard to believe that I should not be keeping my appointment with Joel Barnett to argue over the starting figure for child benefit or introducing the Pay Beds Bill. I found that, after eight years on the government front bench, the habit of authority died hard.

There were of course consolations, including sympathetic letters from colleagues and friends and party members. The most remarkable one I received was from David Owen. Its generosity astonished me. 'I owe you a debt of gratitude which I will never be able to repay,' he wrote. 'You taught me, trusted me and supported me. . . . You ran a large department as it should be run and your record will never be surpassed.'

There was also comradeship, like Denis Skinner's unexpected display of solidarity when I ran into him in the Commons corridor. 'That man is a shit,' he exclaimed. The poignancy of the situation was heightened by the fact that Brian O'Malley's sudden death had taken place just before my own political demise, and I found myself on a train to Rotherham for his funeral with a large number of his parliamentary colleagues and members of the government. The size and range of this Westminster group was a great tribute to Brian's qualities. It was a strangely comforting occasion. Brian had brought out the best in all of us. Joel Barnett, with whom Brian had crossed swords so many times, was there.

So were Merlyn Rees, busy as he was with Northern Ireland problems, John Silkin and many more. I was particularly pleased when David Owen joined us. I knew he had been deeply distressed by Brian's death, but I thought he would have been kept in the House by the debate on the Children and Young Persons Act, a subject dear to his heart and on which he had himself introduced a Private Member's Bill when we were in opposition. Not for the first time I discovered under his arrogant exterior a warm sense of human priorities. Together we all marched to the church through the streets of Rotherham in a biting April wind. I was not the only one to find that I was under-clothed. At the church, as an ex-minister, I was allocated a seat in the second row of pews with reigning ministers in the front. Merlyn was upset when he discovered it, but I did not care. What did protocol matter? I was among friends and I slept peacefully all the way home in John Silkin's ministerial car, snuggling down next to him.

The transition from power to powerlessness is full of awkward moments. David Ennals was as considerate as possible, telling me not to hurry out of my – now his – ministerial room at the House, so I had time to sort out my papers. One of an ex-minister's duties is to say goodbye to the Queen, and I stood in Speaker's Court at the House wondering about the best way to get to Buckingham Palace – the ministerial car is the first thing to go. I rang Ted Short, also on his way to the Palace, to ask if he would take me in his car. Winnie, Michael Foot's driver, took pity on me as I stood waiting for him in the cold. Did I not know I was allowed to use my ministerial car for an occasion like this? 'It is absurd the way no one explains this to you.'

At the Palace the Queen's secretary, Martin Charteris, greeted us with great friendliness. 'These farewell occasions are always very sad.' He certainly knew how to handle them, chatting to Ted Short, former Lord President of the Council, on first-name terms. The Queen, too, knew how to handle them, as I found when my turn came to go in and say goodbye. From my many contacts with her during my eight years in the Cabinet I had learned to admire this professionalism and the skill with which she managed to combine naturalness with formality, putting people at ease without once letting down her regal guard. She also did her homework with great thoroughness. Now she chatted to me easily and informally, recalling some of the many official visits she had paid in my ministerial company, such as her visit to the new Southampton hospital. After ten minutes she said, 'I want to thank you, Mrs Castle, for all you have done.' I bowed and said goodbye, thinking as I did so that, if we wanted a monarchy, she was a model of how a constitutional monarch should behave.

David Ennals duly piloted my Pay Beds Bill through Parliament. I persuaded the reluctant Whips to put me on the Standing Committee for the Bill, as I wanted to keep an eagle eye on proceedings to ensure that the government did not retreat on any point. I need not have worried. David Ennals stuck scrupulously to the compromise, and the Bill went through unchanged. But it was a different matter on child benefit. One month after my demotion David Ennals announced that the scheme, due to start in 1977, was being postponed indefinitely. Instead a family allowance of £1 a week would be introduced for the first child. There was no attempt to argue that this was being done on economic grounds. Jim Callaghan openly admitted that he had done this to assuage the sensitivities of the male wage-earner, who would find his take-home pay reduced in order to switch the money to his wife. The unions, he claimed, would never accept such a switch at a time when we were urging wage restraint. Jim was a deeply conventional and pragmatic man, who never understood the idealistic values of the left. Decency, yes. Dreaming, no. Some fifteen years later I was to get an illuminating insight into his personality. It was at a party given by Billy Hughes, former principal of Ruskin College, Oxford, who had himself been a Labour MP briefly in the 1945 Parliament. He lived with Beryl, his wife, in an enchanting little old cottage in Islip, not far from Hell Corner Farm, and they were generous with their hospitality. One of the purposes of the party was to celebrate the Labour government of 1945, and Billy had got together as many of the Class of 1945 as he could muster. For the customary photograph I was placed on a sofa next to Jim, who put his arm round me as we smiled into the camera. I did not object because there is nothing more tedious than stale resentment. He then turned to me and said, 'You know, I have never really been interested in politics.' I could believe him, for he was no theorist, merely a skilled practitioner in an interesting game.

Naturally, women MPs and women's organizations were outraged by the dropping of child benefit. Fortunately, I was still on the party's National Executive Committee and so still a member of the Liaison Committee with the TUC. I used the outcry to persuade that body to set up a working party to discuss the issue. I was made a member and I was delighted to be joined by two of my fellow spirits from the trade union side: Alf Allen, General Secretary of the Distributive Workers, and my old friend Terry Parry, General Secretary of the Fire Brigades' Union. These two male trade unionists were to prove Jim Callaghan wrong. They quickly dismissed his alarmist fears. I had a particularly soft spot for Terry Parry, who could be as pugnacious as anyone in defending his members' interests, but he had none of the aridity of some left-wing trade unionists. His union's Christmas parties were a jolly romp, and even as a minister I made a special point of attending them, dancing with abandon until late. Terry, Alf and I joined forces in insisting that child benefit had to go ahead, and Jim was forced to accept a compromise under which it was to be phased in over the next three years. By the time the general election came in 1979, it was in full force at a rate of £4 per week per child and the party was to parade it as one of our flagships.

One result of Jim Callaghan's reshuffle was to make Roy Jenkins politically footloose, with longer-term consequences which were to shake the Labour Party to its roots. Roy had become increasingly detached from the party and made no attempt to hide the fact. I believe, however, that he would have remained attached if he could have seen some hope of achieving the place in its ruling hierarchy he felt he deserved. Roy had been bitterly disappointed by what he considered a humiliatingly low vote in the recent leadership elections. Now Jim Callaghan dealt him another blow, refusing to use the reshuffle to give him the post he really wanted: the foreign secretaryship, while urging him to stay on as Home Secretary. Roy had been in conversation with the right-wing French President, Giscard d'Estaing, for some time about the possibility of becoming President of the European Commission. This attracted him far more than remaining as Home Secretary in a government with which he was out of tune. Salt was rubbed into his wounds when Jim made Anthony Crosland Foreign Secretary. Crosland was Roy's personal friend, charming and often brilliant, but politically of lighter weight than Roy and with even less political stamina. I used to listen to him in Cabinet analysing the government's economic strategy with devastating effect and would feel that at last I had a powerful exponent of my own criticisms. But in the end the analysis always ran into the ground of inaction and he never opposed the Chancellor on any specific points. In the leadership contest, Crosland polled only seventeen votes to Roy's fifty-six, yet he was elevated above him to the post Roy coveted.

Watching from the wings I could not fathom Jim's political strategy, but then I had never been able to follow it when we were together in Cabinet. It was as though in humiliating Roy he was trying to dispose of a dangerous rival, as Harold Wilson tried more than once to do, but Roy had hardly distinguished himself in fighting for the leadership. Perhaps Roy's ardent Europeanism was the cause. Crosland had sat on the fence in our Common Market discussions in Cabinet. Jim himself was no European visionary. He just strung along with whatever he believed to be inescapable. Whatever his motives, they were too much for Roy, a man who had a high estimate of his own abilities, but not enough ambition to fight it through to the leadership.

Roy's decision to go to the Commission was clinched by the high-handed way in which Jim dealt with his appointments and dismissals. I was amused to read in Roy's autobiography, published fifteen years later: 'I realised that the era of Wilsonite consideration was over. . . . I felt glad that I was leaving the Government within a few months.' He hung on as Home Secretary for a bit longer, but when the European Council, consisting of the heads of government of all member states, unanimously offered him the presidency of the Commission to take effect from January 1977, he accepted it.

From the back benches it was difficult to follow what was going on in Cabinet. I was desperately anxious that the aims and spirit of the Social Contract should not be lost. My membership of the NEC and through it of the Liaison Committee of the TUC, enabled me to keep in touch with the mood of the trade unions and it was clear that they were struggling hard to make the Social Contract work. Following the acceptance of his flat-rate pay policy, Jack Jones had become the most loyal supporter of the government, intolerant of its critics to the point of fury. At the 1975 Labour Party conference a few months before I was demoted I had watched Jack's fury explode at the mass rally Tribune always held. In fact I was the innocent cause of it. I ran into Jack in the lobby of the Executive hotel just before Ted and I were due to leave for the rally. Ian Mikardo, one of the speakers, had issued a press handout attacking the trade unions for conniving with the Labour government's wage-restraint policy and I asked Jack whether he had seen it. He had *not* and hurried off to get a copy.

At the rally, Mikardo duly read his speech, piling, as I put it, 'selective statistic upon selective statistic' to condemn the government. We were all electrified by what happened next. I noted in my diary, 'Suddenly out of the crowded aisle where he had been standing leapt Jack Jones up onto the platform, jabbing an accusing finger at Mik like an Old Testament prophet pronouncing his doom.' As Mik had the microphone, we could not hear what Jack said but his menacing presence made his meaning clear enough. He took a seat at the end of the platform and sat there glowering. To me it was the most exciting demonstration of the success of the Social Contract I had ever hoped to see. Only people who like me had lived through anarchical trade union militancy could appreciate the significance of what was happening. Here was the spokesman of one of the most powerful and militant trade unions saying in effect, 'Grow up. Let us remain militant but for positive causes, not destructive ones.' This, I believed, was what the Social Contract was all about. There was plenty of right-wing militancy waiting to destroy the democratic rights of working people, and Jack Jones had realized that the most effective answer lay in political power exercised through a Labour government.

The rally ended harmoniously. Michael Foot made a placatory winding-up speech. Ever since he had accepted the job of Employment Secretary his personality seemed to have changed. The left-wing critic, master of the searing phrase, had given way to a conciliator of the Conrad Heron class. He was later to carry his new role so far that I began to have anxieties. Another highlight of the rally was the appearance of the young Neil Kinnock who, according to my diary, made the funniest fund-raising speech I had ever heard. I commented to Ted: 'He's a find, that boy.'

Neil was, in fact, already emerging as a more serious figure than his witty speeches seemed to indicate. A few months later he outflanked the 'hard left' in the Tribune Group when they plotted to vote against the government's White Paper on Public Expenditure, embodying future cuts. None of us liked the cuts – certainly not the trade unions, though they stood by the Social Contract and did not allow the cuts to prevent them from accepting another round of wage restraint. Neil had become a leading figure in the Tribune Group and set out to prevent it from voting against the White Paper and to abstain instead. His opinion carried a good deal of weight and he used his influence to try to sideline the core of 'hard left' which sought to dominate. He was one of the 'soft left' which, though often critical of the government's policy, as I was myself, had no desire to bring the government down.

Nevertheless, the abstentions were enough to secure the defeat of the motion on the White Paper by twenty-eight votes. This necessitated the government tabling a vote of confidence a few days later, in which the abstainers trooped meekly into the lobby in support of it and gave us a majority of seventeen. Though I was irritated by what I considered the abstainers' empty gesture, I was much more furious at Denis Healey's winding-up speech in the debate, during which he insulted the Tribunites while I sat cringing on the front bench. It was outbursts like this which damaged his chances of the leadership. Those who had abstained, he bellowed, were 'falsifying the hopes of those in the trade union movement who have made sacrifices to help the government and the country in the last few years'.

As I was still in the Cabinet I was obliged to toe the

government line. In fact the White Paper was an appalling document and in his autobiography many years later Denis was to admit as much. A number of us in Cabinet – notably Michael Foot, Tony Benn, John Silkin and I – had queried the need for cuts of the size and range Denis was pushing through, but non-Treasury ministers are at an impossible disadvantage in trying to query Treasury estimates. We did not, however, anticipate that Denis would endorse all our criticism so overwhelmingly in his book. I had been appalled to find that the White Paper reiterated Roy Jenkins' assertion that 'in the last three years the ratio of public spending to gross domestic product [total national wealth] has risen from 50% to 60%'. As I have noted, later calculations proved that the correct figure was 42 per cent. The earlier figures, Denis now claims, were 'unforgivably misleading', and he throws in a superb piece of buck-passing. 'I cannot forgive [the Treasury], or those politicians who preceded me as Chancellor [which, of course, included Jim Callaghan and Roy Jenkins] for misleading the Government, the country and the world for so many years about the true state of public spending in Britain.' It is good to have this admission but at the time Denis contemptuously dismissed the criticisms of the left, ramming these inaccurate figures home as though they were holy writ. His knowledge of his own intellectual strength made the temptation to bulldoze dubious arguments through Cabinet and Parliament irresistible. It was this propensity for bullying which made even admirers, of whom I was one, doubt his suitability for party leadership. He was incapable of realizing that sometimes the instincts of lesser mortals might be nearer the truth than his powerful blockbusting.

But when I left the government the miseries of 1976 had only just begun. If the spending cuts in the White Paper proved to have been unnecessary, so was the run on sterling during the summer of 1976. Here again Denis puts the blame on the Bank of England, which he tells us caused a crisis of confidence by deciding that sterling was overvalued and trying to devalue it. But it seemed to me, watching from the wings, that Denis had to accept some of the responsibility. His Götterdämmerung speeches about the economy had merely created a crisis atmosphere and had given the impression that the government was on the run. Instead I believed we should have been shouting about our achievements from the housetops. We had, for instance, won remarkable co-operation from the trade unions. The Social Contract had held firm because of the sweeping social reforms we had carried through. It was not the unions which broke the Social Contract but the government, as it carried through the deflationary policy Denis had convinced himself was necessary, with further spending cuts, cash limits and all the conventional measures to reduce demand.

I myself believed – and still believe – that the Social Contract is a workable alternative to unemployment and recession for keeping inflation down. But to make it work we had to shake off the arid and by now discredited monetarist doctrines of the Treasury. I had been surprised to read, tucked away in a corner of the White Paper on public spending cuts, the assertion that the 'social wage' was worth £1000 a year at 1975 prices to the average family. The concept of the 'social wage' was something I had pressed on Denis when I was in Cabinet as a means of persuading wage-earners not to press excessive wage demands. I had got my Department to estimate the value to an average family of the social services they received: free maternity care and a good maternity benefit for their wives, home helps and a decent pension for the elderly members of the family, adequate payments for those who suffered from industrial injury, good education for their children, free health care for the whole family and so on. Only in this way, I argued, could we persuade them not to jeopardize these services by concentrating on cash wage increases which could never give them enough income to provide those services privately. Denis assured us he was about to issue a 'popular' version of the Treasury bulletin, a phenomenon I could not wait to see. It never appeared. Now Denis was cynically using my figure to justify his proposed cuts, which would reduce the social wage.

Retrenchment followed retrenchment as the Bank of England did nothing to support the pound. We backbenchers reeled under a succession of blows. In July, Denis told the House he had negotiated a standby loan of some £2.5 billion from the Bank for International Settlements in exchange for which he deflated the economy by over £2 billion. Mutterings grew among Labour MPs and some trade unions. In August, I myself told a trade union rally in Manchester that the cuts were 'a national scandal and a national tragedy'. The run on sterling continued. Some of us suspected, not for the first time, that the Bank of England was playing politics.

The climax came at the Labour Party conference in Blackpool in September 1976. As we arrived the press was full of crisis alarms once again, fuelled by Denis Healey's dramatic turn-round at Heathrow, from where he had been due to fly to Hong Kong for a meeting of the Commonwealth finance ministers. 'Race to Save the Pound' ran the *Daily Mirror* headline in its boldest type. 'Chancellor Denis Healey made a dramatic turn-round at Heathrow airport yesterday and dashed back to London for crisis talks aimed at saving the crumbling pound.' The *Daily Express* called it the Battle of Britain 1976, while the *Sun* trumpeted 'Save Our Sterling! Disaster as the Pound Plunges.' We all wondered what was going on as Margaret Thatcher called for 'stern measures'.

We were even more bewildered when, halfway through the conference, Denis made a surprise dash to Blackpool in a Northolt plane. He arrived in the middle of a debate on the sterling crisis, on which the National Executive had issued a very soothing statement, merely calling on the government 'to meet the crisis within the policies of the Movement'. In his five-minute speech, which was all he was allowed since he was no longer a member of the NEC, Denis delivered a diatribe which did nothing to calm the atmosphere. 'I do not come with a Treasury view,' he stormed at us. 'I come from the battle-front.' Careless speeches could knock £200 million off the reserves in a minute or, if the rate went down, 'it can add up to twenty pence to the price of the goods in your shopping bag in a minute'. It was all good Erroll Flynn stuff and at last the truth came out. He and the Prime Minister, he told us, had agreed to apply to the International Monetary Fund for credit on IMF terms. The credit would merely enable us to continue our existing deflationary policies.

Inevitably the press made a meal of it the following day. 'We Are Up to Our Necks in It' was the *Mirror*'s headline the next day. 'Austerity Britain' shouted the *Daily Mail*. Healey, it said, was asking for a £2300 million loan 'and the conditions could hit everyone'. The picture of Britain holding out her begging bowl was immensely damaging politically and Jim Callaghan's wind-up speech did not help. 'Grim Jim Warns the Nation' said the *Sun*. This was our last chance: Britain could have a dictator if this government sank. I listened angrily. We had put all our money on deflationary policies and the Social Contract had become an irrelevance.

To do him justice, Denis battled hard and long to ensure that the conditions of the loan were as reasonable as possible and boasted that he had managed to keep the immediate public expenditure cuts down to £1 billion, rising to another £1.5 billion in 1978/9. But this was not the whole picture. In November, he had raised bank rate to the then record figure of 15 per cent, cut food subsidies and increased duties on drink and tobacco. The deflationary package had its conventional effect. By 1978, inflation had been almost halved to 8.3 per cent, the balance of payments had moved into surplus by nearly £1 billion and the borrowing requirement was at the manageable figure of just under £8.5 billion, a level often exceeded by Tory governments. But there was a price to pay. The growth rate in manufacturing was down to 1.1 per cent from its peak of nearly 5 per cent in 1976, and unemployment was at the intolerably high figure of 1,383,000. Worse still, the government's popularity had taken a nosedive. By March 1977, its overall majority in the Commons had fallen to one. Its record of by-election losses continued unchecked and, in July 1978, the Liberals walked out of the Lib-Lab pact, which had kept the government alive in the House since March 1977. There was a mood of sullen discontent among the party's activists and the rank and file of the unions which was eventually to spell the party's doom.

The tragedy was that some of the austerity, at any rate, was avoidable. I suspected it at the time, but ironically the proof was to come from Denis Healey's own pen. His account of this period in his autobiography reads like a confessional of Treasury incompetence. 'If', writes Denis, 'I had been given accurate forecasts in

1976, I would never have needed to go to the IMF at all.' For example, in 1976 his estimate in his Budget of the public sector borrowing requirement was, he admits, £2 billion too high, and without this miscalculation it would have fallen within the limits laid down by the IMF 'without any of the measures which the IMF prescribed'. On public expenditure it was the same sad story. 'Here again,' he writes, 'my task was complicated by the Treasury's inability either to know exactly what was happening or to control it.' The estimates he used of the rise in public expenditure proved false. What it all amounted to in Denis's own words was that 'we could have done without the IMF loan . . . if we – and the world – had known the real facts at the time'. Before he left office, he tells us, he changed the Treasury's forecasting methodology, but it was too late. The Labour government had been indelibly imprinted with a reputation for economic profligacy and mismanagement.

Looking back I draw a political moral from the whole tortured IMF episode. The Labour Party's major problem is psychological. We have not got our opponents' arrogant belief in the right to rule. Instead we manage to portray our policies in the most unfavourable light, partly because our chancellors of the Exchequer lean over backwards to create 'confidence' among financial interests by showing how austere they are prepared to be, partly because the left – and I have been guilty of it myself – reacts by exaggerating the amount of austerity we actually impose. After all, we can only go by what those in charge tell us and they are only too anxious to give the appearance of being tough. In any case, the problems of a Labour government are always much greater than those of a Tory one because, thanks to the innate conservatism of the British electorate, we are given the chance to govern only when the other side has got the economy into a major mess. Again, Conservatives are the champions of powerful interests in industry and finance who own and control 95 per cent of newspapers, which obediently manipulate the presentation of the news to distort the economic truth.

There has, therefore, never been equal treatment for Labour and Conservatives. Every piece of economic good luck under the latter is interpreted as their achievement and every economic setback under the former portrayed as a failure of Labour government. The people of Britain were never told, for instance, of the calamitous effect on world trade and our economy of the rise in oil prices in the 1970s. While we were in office during this period the revenues from North Sea oil had not come on stream, and at the very end we were reaping only £1 billion from this asset to offset the rise in oil prices. By 1979, when Margaret Thatcher came to power, the situation had changed dramatically. Our own oil from the North Sea was flowing and revenues from this source gave her an extra £68 billion to play with. She used it to finance the tax cuts which kept her in power for many years.

Inevitably, the succession of government crises swung the party to the left. While I was still in Cabinet my frustration at the seemingly endless retreats from treasured policies was echoed in the party outside, though as a Cabinet minister I could not be active in any group. So I was a bystander as others took up the campaign I had tried to launch way back in the 1940s to make the party constitution more democratic and to give the party workers in the constituencies a greater say. Our target in those days had been the block vote of the trade unions, but the new battlecry was to make Labour MPs more accountable to the local parties which had selected them, and through them to make the government show more respect for the views of the rank and file. The Campaign for Labour Party Democracy (CLPD) launched in 1972 began modestly as the brainchild of a small group of party activists, people like Vladimir Dererer, a university lecturer from Hungary, who with his wife Vera ran the whole modest little show from their own house. They were motivated by the simple desire to give the rank and file more control as the only way of making the government keep in touch with those who worked to put it there. I had a great deal of sympathy with this view.

I also sympathized with the view that the Parliamentary Labour Party was in danger of becoming a law unto itself, hiding behind the Bagehot doctrine that MPs are representatives and not delegates and must be free to vote as they feel fit. It sounds an impeccable principle, but it bears little relationship to a modern

Parliament, which is the product of highly organized party machines backed by expensive propaganda campaigns. If politics are to be controlled by party machines, it is essential that those machines should in turn be democratically controlled. The best medium for this is the Labour Party conference, to which every local party can send delegates, who may be mandated. That MPs once elected should feel free to defy their local party was intolerable to most of us. I had too often been roped in to speak for candidates who, once elected, considered themselves free to ride roughshod over the views of those who had selected and elected them.

The CLPD was to prove one of the pebbles of politics which start an avalanche. Most of the superstars of the left were to climb on to its bandwagon, and from its modest start flowed two major changes. One of its aims was to break the Parliamentary Labour Party's monopoly in choosing the leader and to bring in all sections of the movement through an electoral college comprising representatives of the MPs, the local parties and the trade unions.

Its second aim was to enable local constituencies to get rid of their MP if they were dissatisfied with him or her. This, too, struck me as eminently reasonable. A Labour candidate cannot get elected unless the local party workers throw themselves into the campaign, which they will not do if the candidate is advocating views different from theirs. With the party divided as it was over such issues as the Common Market and the government's deflationary economic policies, it was not surprising that conflicts of view should arise between a local party and its MP. The question was: whose views should prevail?

A typical example of this type of conflict arose in 1975 when the Newham North-East constituency found itself at odds with the right-wing views of Reg Prentice, its MP, then Minister of Overseas Development. It passed, as it was entitled to do, a resolution calling on him to retire at the next election. I was still in the Cabinet and watched angrily as Reg's right-wing allies, led by Shirley Williams, moved in to defend him. The Newham party, they claimed, had been captured by Trotskyists, and even Harold Wilson lent himself to this ploy and tried to persuade the

NEC to rule his deselection out of order. When, however, the NEC conducted an enquiry they found unanimously that the party's proceedings had been conducted properly and that it was within its constitutional rights. I had already had indications from members of the Newham party, among them Anita Pollack, who was later to become my research assistant in the European Parliament for eight years, that this was not a case of Trotskyist entryism, of whose dangers they were well aware: it was a case of genuine local dissatisfaction with the sitting MP. Anita was certainly no Trot, but a hard-working member of the soft left who was later to become a very effective MEP herself. Reg's friends were embarrassed when, two years later, he crossed the floor to join the Conservatives and started voting against their own government. Newham North-East was further vindicated when in 1979 he joined Mrs Thatcher's government. Moved by examples like this, the party conference passed a resolution providing that all Labour MPs should have to go through a process of reselection once in the lifetime of every Parliament. This achievement of 'mandatory reselection' gave local parties greater control of their MPs than they had had before and offered the left a tighter grip on the party machine.

Through all this Tony Benn was rapidly emerging as the most charismatic figure on the left. His capacity for putting mundane issues in a philosophical context was unmatched, and it was what the rank and file hungered for. He could entrance audiences and lift his speeches to dazzling heights which impressed even non-socialists. When in June 1975 the Conservatives at last plucked up enough courage to join Labour in allowing the proceedings of the Commons to be reported on radio, Tony shone. 'Big Benn is the Star of the Air,' declared the *Sun*, while the *Financial Times* endorsed this verdict more sedately with the words 'Commons Radio Starts with Sparkling Benn Cut and Thrust'. Having moved to the top of the constituency section of the NEC for 1974, he stayed there until 1985. A new word had appeared in the political vocabulary: Bevanism had been replaced by Bennery.

At one stage I toyed with the idea of supporting him for the party leadership since I longed for our leaders to talk about the party's values and not just their ability to reduce the balance-of-payments deficit. But I became increasingly uneasy about his skill in manipulating party workers and the party machine to his own ends. Tony was neither a founder nor a member of the CLPD, yet he managed to appropriate most of the credit for the drive to party democracy. He exploited his power as chairman of the Home Policy Committee of the NEC as a sounding board for his own ideas, using party officials as his mouthpiece. I also found his concept of the 'broad left' too indiscriminately broad for me. He welcomed allies from anywhere, from Trotskyists to Stalinists. In my diary, I recorded a revealing little incident at the end of an all-day meeting of the NEC. Tony was sitting next to me and, as we were gathering up our papers afterwards, I overheard his conversation with two hard-left members of the Executive who asked him to address meetings they were organizing. He responded enthusiastically. 'I'm a bit more selective myself,' I wrote.

As Tony's star rose, mine waned. I remained too soft left for the new mood of the rank and file. Though I strongly supported the demand for an electoral college and the right of local parties to get rid of an MP who betrayed their views, I was always unhappy about the idea of 'mandatory' reselection and I could not share uncritically the claim that all conference decisions were sacrosanct. Conference was the right medium for reflecting the party's mood on straightforward issues like unilateralism or Britain's membership of the EEC, but as the instrument for selecting the policy priorities it was meaningless. Faced with the choices governments have to make, delegates refused to choose. Instead they passed every resolution embodying the party's long-term aspirations with overwhelming majorities and the demand for action now. In 1975, when I was still Secretary of State for Social Services, acutely aware of the choices that had to be made, I watched almost with despair as conference passed resolution after resolution demanding the socialist millennium overnight, regardless of the cost. Geoff Bish, the party's head of research, remarked to me that we ought to have a tote at the back of the platform on which the cost of every decision was clocked up, so that conference could see to what it was committing itself.

I was also appalled by the way a flood of resolutions on a particular subject was merged into one comprehensive composite. All the conference managers wanted to do was to get the mass of resolutions reduced to a manageable number. As a result the members of the Conference Arrangements Committee who chaired the compositing meetings tried to get every delegate's pet ideas on a particular subject into one omnibus motion. As a member of the NEC – and not least as a minister – I was not allowed to interfere in the process, so I had to sit biting my nails when the resolutions on the National Health Service were lumped together into an all-embracing whole, including one local party's demand that private medicine should be prohibited by law. When I pointed out to Albert Spanswick of the Confederation of Health Service Employees (COHSE) that the abolition of private medicine was not the policy of his union, he agreed but said that the bulk of the resolution was so good they would have to go along with it. I could only pray that the BMA, which was watching my every move, would understand the subtlety of his argument.

Some ten years later Neil Kinnock as leader was to bring order into this chaos when he persuaded the party to adopt a more structured way of deciding policy. He was attacked by the Bennites for undermining the rights of conference. They were also deeply suspicious of me in 1975 because I held myself aloof from their intrigues. It showed in my vote for the NEC elections: over the next four years I was twice at the bottom of the poll and never came higher than fifth place. It was unpleasant, but I was philosophical. I did not like the mood that was developing.

By the end of 1978 all the economic indicators were in the black, except for unemployment, though this fell slightly to just over 1.3 million. Inflation was down to 8.3 per cent, the growth rate had risen to 3.5 per cent, the balance of payments had moved into a surplus of just under £1 billion and the public sector borrowing requirement was under control at £8.5 billion. It was a scenario of progress of which any government would be proud today and should have been a recipe for electoral victory if the government had been only slightly responsive to the underlying unrest among trade unionists and other wage-earners. The cuts in public expenditure had destroyed the appeal of the Social Contract and the unions were now looking for what they could get. The increase in earnings had been brought down to 8.75 per cent in the previous year, but the pressure for higher increases was erupting in various industries. Faced with this pressure, all the TUC could offer the Chancellor was an attempt to hold the unions within a twelve-monthly round of pay increases. The mutterings within the Liaison Committee with the TUC were obvious enough to me and I was surprised that Labour ministers could not hear them too.

Instead, at one of those tense meetings in the long, panelled board room of TUC headquarters at Congress House, I was horrified when Jim told us that the government had fixed a 'norm' of 5 per cent for pay increases for 1979. The trade unionists sitting opposite to me listened in a state of bewildered shock, obviously believing that the government had gone out of its mind. In his autobiography Denis Healey blames Jim Callaghan for this decision. Jim, he writes, had become obsessed 'with inflation' and had even tried to get a norm of 3 per cent through Cabinet.

Whoever was responsible, the result was disastrous and pre-dictable. The unions on the Liaison Committee listened sullenly as Jim propounded his determination to go into the next election with inflation still in single figures, and that in order to keep inflation down to that level he was going to enforce the 5 per cent norm in the public services. With inflation still running at over 8 per cent and rising, a 5 per cent pay norm would result in a cut in wages. It was a repetition of Roy Jenkins' error in 1970, when he lost the election by refusing to let the man and woman in the street enjoy even a morsel of the fruits of their sacrifices. At the end of a fraught discussion in the Liaison Committee at Congress House Geoffrey Drain, General Secretary of the National Associ-ation of Local Government Officers (NALGO), leaned across the table and said to me earnestly, 'Barbara, we cannot deliver.' I knew Geoffrey quite well as he had been a fellow spirit of Ted's when they were both councillors in their respective North London boroughs in the 1950s, and although he enjoyed having a bash at Tory councillors he was no destructive militant. Advice from reasonable people like him should have been listened to, but Jim stuck rigidly to his chosen formula.

It was a mistake the Tories would never have made. They know when to get out from under unenforceable policies. What astonished me was the continuing metamorphosis of Michael Foot. He who had become the fierce custodian of the prices and incomes policy at Employment now became an even fiercer custodian of the 5 per cent. He had been only narrowly defeated by Jim Callaghan for the leadership, but he carried his loyalty to him almost to the point of idolatry. He would not hear a word against him or the 5 per cent policy. Even the impassioned scenes at the party conference of 1978 could not shake him. I sat next to him on the platform as we watched the battle to defeat the 5 per cent policy going on below, led by Terry Duffy, who had followed Hughie Scanlon as head of the Engineering Workers, and Moss Evans, Jack Jones' successor at the Transport Workers' Union. These changes in trade union leadership had done nothing to help the government. On the contrary Jim must have wished that the 'terrible twins' of trade unionism, Hughie and Jack, were back in charge. When Alan Fisher, speaking for the public employees, made a moving speech on the plight of the low paid and conference rose to him, I turned to Michael and said, 'You can't get away with this five per cent. If you went for something less provocative like nine per cent you might come out in the end with something even lower.' He brushed me aside irritably, muttering, 'The unions just don't understand.' He then went on to make the winding-up speech for the NEC, pulling out every emotional stop of which he was capable, warning of the dangers that would follow the defeat of a Labour government. 'I do not know what is going to happen to my people in Ebbw Vale if we get a Tory government in power. Any chance of our industrial recovery will be wiped off the slate.' So he pleaded with the unions 'in the interests of the whole Labour movement' to remit the issue to the NEC. But it was all in vain. Terry Duffy's resolution rejecting any wage restraint 'totally' and 'specifically the government's 5 per cent' was carried by a vote of two to one.

In the same speech, Mike backed another fateful decision of

Jim Callaghan's: to postpone the general election to the following year and to soldier on into an uncertain spring. It was a misjudgment of colossal proportions. The scene was set for the 'Winter of Discontent'. In January 1979 a nationwide strike of lorry drivers drove a coach and horses through the 5 per cent norm when they received a settlement of 14 per cent. Two weeks later 1.5 million public service workers came out on strike, including water workers, ambulance workers, dustmen and sewerage men. The visible effects of the strike soon appeared on our television screens.

I was in a London hospital during this period for an operation which could have been more serious than it turned out to be. I had successfully resisted the efforts of the delightful sister in charge to put me in a side ward, though she assured me she was doing it on clinical grounds as the presence of a celebrity among them might prove disruptive to other patients. But I knew my British press: they would have been round to the side room like vultures, describing it in their write-ups as a 'private' ward. My prognosis was proved right when not a single press man showed any interest in my presence in the hospital the moment they found I was in a public ward.

In any case, I preferred the public ward. In our ward we were a close community, drawn together by the medical uncertainties which hung over us. We had no resentment whatsoever against the pickets outside, realizing as we did that they too had their problems and struggles. But we also had to survive, so we set about keeping the hospital going by doing our modest bit, those of us who were ambulant trailing along to the kitchen in our dressing gowns to help with the washing up. I knew that the people on the picket lines outside – many of them low-paid manual workers in the NHS – were caring members of caring unions who were stirred into action by a strong sense of injustice, but I felt, not for the first time, that these are the last people who should be driven to use the strike weapon, because it inevitably damages the very people their professions are designed to help. Pictures of overflowing dustbins and striking gravediggers could not help their cause. It was a lesson the unions learned over the years as I was delighted to see when in September 1989 the ambulance workers came out on strike for better conditions and a decent wage. The strike could have caused immense danger and suffering to the casualties they were in business to serve, and public opinion could have turned against them. Instead their chief negotiator, Roger Poole of NUPE, conducted the campaign with consummate skill and won the public's heart by pledging that no patient's health would be placed at risk and that all emergency cases would be handled as usual, even though the workers would get no pay.

The government, its majority in the Commons having evaporated, was already living from day to day, kept alive by Michael Foot's assiduity. He spent his time darting between the little groups – Liberals, Scottish Nationalists and Ulster Unionists – on whose votes the government's survival depended, negotiating with them to keep them sweet. Watching him at work and realizing the little *ad hoc* deals he had to make, I became more convinced than ever that the adoption of proportional representation would be disastrous for any politics of principle. It was a foretaste of the wheeler-dealing I was to see at first hand when I became a member of the European Parliament. The governments of most member states were elected by PR, which often left them at the mercy of quite small minorities and created an atmosphere of instability.

David Steel was a more serious politician than Jeremy Thorpe, whom he succeeded as leader of the Liberal MPs. He was a decent and honourable man, but he could not be sure of delivering the votes of his little band of individualists, even when we had a formal pact with his party. When the pact was disbanded in 1978, the position became even more anarchic, while the Unionists and Nationalists all had their own sectional axes to grind. The possibility of defeat on some quite minor matter hung over us all the time.

The *coup de grâce* for the government was not long in coming. Ironically it did not originate with its critics on the left or with the Opposition. It came from the right-wing and rather pedantic Labour MP for Berwick and East Lothian, John Mackintosh, who was passionately pro-devolution and pro-EEC. Devolution had been exercising the government's mind for a long time and frankly

I was bored by it. By all means let the Scots and Welsh have more control over their own affairs, I used to say to myself when I was still a minister, but do we have to have all these protracted Cabinet discussions, all-day meetings at Chequers, endless analysis of Lord Kilbrandon's and Lord Crowther-Hunt's complicated constitutional alternatives set out in the report of the Royal Commission Harold had set up in 1969? Harold, as always, revelled in the intricacies of constitution-making, but he was also driven by alarm at the havoc the Scottish Nationalists were wreaking in our Labour strongholds in Scotland. Feelings ran astonishingly high among Labour MPs on devolution, both for and against, and it became clear that the issue was not as simple as I had assumed it was. Although Harold had set the ball rolling as far back as 1969, it was 1978 before the government, after many struggles, managed to get the Scotland and Wales Bills on to the statute book.

But there was a time-bomb ticking away in the Acts. The government had persuaded Labour MPs to support the Bills only by providing that referenda would be held in Scotland and Wales before the proposed elected assemblies were set up. Here entered the wicked fairy in the guise of John Mackintosh, who managed to insert a new clause against government opposition which stipulated that a Yes vote in the referendum would not count as effective unless it comprised 40 per cent of the total electorate. On 1 March the referendum in Wales produced a four to one majority against, which most of us had expected for nationalist feeling there was running far less strongly than in Scotland. But in the Scottish referendum the Yes vote, though achieving a narrow majority, failed to reach the statutory 40 per cent, 32.85 per cent having voted for and 30.78 per cent against. Devolution was dead.

Coming after the Winter of Discontent it was a mortal blow. Illogically the members of the Scottish Nationalist Party blamed the government and on 28 March tabled a motion of no confidence, the Conservatives immediately joining in. In the division that day the Liberals voted against the government, as did most of the Ulster Unionists. We might yet have been saved if one of our Members, Alfred Broughton, had not been too ill to vote and if, to our dismay, two Irish Catholics – Gerald Fitt and Frank

Maguire – who normally supported us had not abstained. It was agony to hear Gerry Fitt, who was a member of the Social Democratic and Labour Party (SDLP), explain that it hurt him as much as it did us but he could not vote for the government this time because of the deals it had made with the Ulster Unionists to try to keep afloat. Such are the cross-currents of politics.

As the fateful vote took place, the tension was almost unbearable. I sat in my seat on the third row below the gangway, waiting to read the signs of the result. After a division, the tellers advance slowly in a military line to the Clerks' table in front of the Speaker's Chair to read out the result. If the ayes have it, the tellers in the majority take up their positions on the right, with those for the minority on the left. When we saw that our government tellers were on the left we knew that we had lost and that a general election was inevitable. We sat in stunned silence while the tellers announced that we had been defeated by one vote. It was the most dramatic moment in my thirty-four years in Parliament. Jim Callaghan called a general election for 3 May.

I had made it clear to the Blackburn party some time earlier that I did not intend to stand again. Almost to the last some of my local party officers were pleading with me to reconsider this, urging that I was the only person who could hold the seat. I knew this was a nonsense – the personal vote of a constituency MP, however hard-working, is never as great as we like to flatter ourselves – and I was proved right when Jack Straw, whom the Blackburn party had chosen to succeed me, held the seat with the comfortable majority of 5000 votes. Elsewhere the results were not so happy; fifty Labour MPs lost their seats. As I was not fighting the election I was enlisted by Yorkshire Television to take part in a discussion panel on the election at lunchtime almost every day. This suited me as they provided me with a suite in the Queen's Hotel, Leeds for the duration, from which I made sorties into the surrounding constituencies when my discussion panels were over. Every night I got back to my hotel in time to see the late election news and so could follow what was happening.

From that experience I believe we threw the election away. As it was, the result was not as catastrophic as it might have been, considering the horrors of the Winter of Discontent. Even at that late hour we could have pulled ourselves back from defeat if we had fought the campaign by stressing the sort of society in which we believed, admitting some mistakes while hammering home what we had achieved and would achieve, and vigorously attacking the Tory alternatives. Instead, incredibly, Jim fought the election on his favourite nautical slogan: 'Steady as she goes'. Nothing could have been more inappropriate. Jim was a consummate parliamentarian. I had admired – and envied – his mastery of the House as he ran rings round an uncertain Margaret Thatcher, metaphorically patting her on the head like a kindly uncle. He was incapable of realizing that the scenario had changed. The going had been far from steady in the last few months and we had just been ignominiously defeated in the House. To ask people to vote for more of the same was ludicrous. Night after night I watched Margaret Thatcher on television, shrill but competent and self-confident, offering radical change to solve the country's problems, while all Jim was offering was more avuncular charm. I was not surprised when Margaret Thatcher coasted to victory with an overall majority of forty-three seats and a swing to the Conservatives varying from 4.2 per cent in Scotland to 7.9 per cent in the south of England. Her hour had come and she was determined to make the most of it.

As I heard the result, I said to Ted bitterly that if Harold Wilson had not resigned we would not have lost the election. He had a flexibility and sensitivity which Jim never possessed, and he would never have painted himself into the corner of a 5 per cent norm or have precipitated the Winter of Discontent. Once again I puzzled about why he had resigned. All sorts of sinister explanations had circulated. It was hinted that he had some great secret scandal he was afraid would come to light. I did not believe it and nothing in Harold's subsequent years produced any evidence. Instead he devoted himself to writing books, as he had told me he wanted to do. He was then struck by a cancer which necessitated a serious operation and led to an almost total loss of memory and a ghostly life in the House of Lords. Perhaps his illness cast its shadow before it and had been one of the reasons why he wanted to retire.

I now had to face my own future. I had no intention, I used to tell people jokingly, of declining into senility on the back benches of the House of Commons and had to find a new career before it was too late. I had no idea what that career might be. Jo Richardson, who specialized in women's affairs both in the House and on the National Executive, asked me if I would let her put me forward as chairman of the Equal Opportunities Commission, which the Labour government had set up some years earlier, but I was not interested. Of course, I believed that the Commission was doing important work, but I had never been very involved in single issue politics and wanted to continue to be active on the wider political scene. The question was where and how.

My change of course was decided by the introduction of direct elections to the European Parliament in June that year. Local parties were looking round for candidates in some bewilderment, as Europe was new territory for them, and I was approached by party workers in the north-west asking if I would stand. To some people it seemed an incongruous idea. I had voted No in the referendum and had voted against the Direct Elections Bill in the Commons, because I saw it as another step towards the transfer of power to Brussels, increasing the authority of the European Parliament at the expense of the national one. The Treaty of Rome had visualized the European Parliament as no more than a consultative assembly, and up till then its members had been indirectly elected. In fact, Ted, having been made a life peer by Harold in one of his first acts in 1974, had been a member of it in that capacity. To make the Parliament directly elected would obviously lead to demands for an increase in its powers. How then, some people asked, could I become a member of a body of which I disapproved? But the idea interested me. We anti-marketeers had to face the realities. We had been defeated on both the issues to which we were opposed. If there was to be a directly elected European Parliament, ought we not to be inside it, fighting the creeping federalism we could sense on every hand? I had never believed in vacating any political platform for the Tories to occupy.

I therefore allowed my name to go forward. Since Britain's share of the Parliament was to be a mere eighty-one MEPs, the constituencies were extremely large, comprising eight Commons constituencies and half a million constituents. The selection process was therefore a long one. I came through it successfully. The delegates were as indifferent to, and ignorant of, Europe as most of the electors were, so they jumped at the idea of having a candidate who was nationally known. Thus in June I found myself elected as Member of the European Parliament for Great Manchester North.

I was soon to be glad of the distraction my new life brought to me. A few months later at 2 a.m. on Boxing Day Ted died. I had been worried for some time about his listlessness, but this had not prevented him from presiding over our Christmas dinner as the convivial Great-Uncle Ted. It was the last the children saw of him. Family and friends clustered round to help me bear the shock and misery. He was cremated and I wanted a private service as well in our little Ibstone church, which stands on the crest of the Chilterns like a picture postcard of traditional rural England. Its churchyard had been our joy, where Ted and I used to watch the seasons change: first the expanses of snowdrops and aconites round the graves, then the spread of primroses, followed by wild cyclamen and a bank of white violets. I made it clear that I did not want any nonsense about 'No flowers by request'. Ted was a gardener and I wanted him to be embowered in them. We filled the church with flowers which my secretary–friend, Joan Woodman, arranged in nave and chancel with her usual artistry. When I arrived I was overwhelmed to see that the path from the swing gate to the church door was lined with flowers and tributes every inch of the way. The local hospital had the pleasure of them later that day.

I also made it clear that I did not want the normal funeral service of the Church of England, which I find deadening. I wanted a service of our own in which every member of the family could participate. Neither Ted nor I were orthodox believers, but to us the local church was as much a part of rural life as the country pub, and we contributed to it financially. My nephew-in-law, Colin, took it upon himself to win over the vicar, John Trigg, to my idea. John Trigg proved to be a man I could respect. He agreed to let us take over his church on the condition that he should open the service with a few words. He did so with wit and understanding, including the gentle raillery: 'We must pray for Barbara, whether she wants us to or not.' I gave him full marks for that. The service was supposed to be private, but our neighbours and friends would have none of that. The tiny church was packed to the door and I was fearful at one point that the minute minstrels' gallery would collapse under the weight of its occupants. No one had been specifically invited but they had all wanted to come, from the various phases of Ted's life. I was particularly touched when two of my collagues from the European Parliament, Alan Rogers and Win Griffiths, materialized, having driven from Wales by a spontaneous piece of private enterprise. Ted had already made an impact on our Labour MEPs when he came out with me on our first visit to Strasbourg and spent a lot of time with the wives explaining to them the sort of lives their husbands would now have to lead. The affection for Ted was so tangible at the service that my constituency secretary, Janet Anderson, told me afterwards, 'There was not a dry eye in the house.'

It was certainly an unusual service. It opened with a cello-cum-trombone performance by the younger members of the family, Kate and Paul. At fourteen and twelve years old respectively, they must have been a bit awed by their responsibility, but they were not going to let down Great-Uncle Ted. Sonya read a piece from Dylan Thomas which I had chosen, with its triumphant refrain: 'And death shall have no dominion.' Rachel recited a favourite verse from A. E. Housman. Michael Foot read an extract from William Morris' 'A Dream of John Ball' and John Prescott, with whom Ted had worked in the indirectly elected European Parliament, read from the Declaration of the Rights of Man, 1791.

The service ended with me reciting a poem I had written to

Ted when we had first started our relationship thirty-four years earlier. It ran:

> High love and flaming passion will fall a prey to time,
> For the body's joy must temper as the body leaves its prime;
> And memory must weaken as we move to stranger strands –
> But oh, I shall remember the kindness of your hands.

I scattered Ted's ashes over the field at Hell Corner Farm.

TWENTY

•

Over the Water

USED AS I WAS to the austere and regulated life of the British
House of Commons, my arrival in Europe in 1979 was a cultural
shock. Brussels is a fine city and we British Members of the
European Parliament – sixty Tory, seventeen Labour, one Scottish
Nationalist, three Northern Irish and no Liberals – soon discovered the delights of its many restaurants. The lunch break was
a compulsory two hours and in the evenings we would seek out
the exquisite lobster or a cheaper bowl of mussels cooked in wine
and cream in the restaurants round the fish market. But as far as I
was concerned these delicacies were not enough to offset the
frustrations I felt as someone who had come to do a serious
parliamentary job. In those early days the facilities provided for us
MEPs were laughably inadequate. We were the Cinderellas all
right. While the Commission dominated Brussels with its great
sprawling mass of glass and concrete at the Berlaymont, we MEPs
were corralled in some makeshift cramped quarters in the Boul-
evard l'Empereur a couple of miles away, where we had not even
a locker for whatever parliamentary papers we were able to lay
our hands on, let alone a desk. This was all the more annoying
when I was elected leader of the British Labour group and I
wanted to keep on top of things. I spent my first year in impotent
fury trying to find out what was going on.

Another source of irritation was the nationalist rivalries which
dominated the Community. It was a struggle between the giants
and the pygmies – the giants, of course, being France and
Germany. In theory, under the Treaty of Rome, Luxembourg,

one of the original six signatories and the smallest with a population of 350,000, has legal rights to house certain of the institutions of the Community, notably the Library and Research
Department and the Court of Justice. This did not satisfy her and
she made a pathetic bid to host some at least of the plenary sessions
of the full Parliament to which the committees which meet in
Brussels report monthly, rushing up a building for the purpose at
great expense. Though beyond the means of this tiny state, it was
still quite inadequate. At those monthly meetings, we 410 MEPs
were crammed into our narrow seats in the assembly chamber like
battery hens and in the rest of the building we were not even
allocated tables at which we could write our speeches.

Luxembourg soon dropped out of the race and France moved
in triumphantly to claim her right to the political leadership of the
Community. The modest Palais de l'Europe, which she had built
to accommodate the Community's predecessor, the Council of
Europe, soon blossomed into a massive modernistic building with
the flags of the member states fluttering outside. With one of those
strokes of state interventionism at which it is so good, the French
government had financed the building out of its national pension
funds and was exacting a high rent from the Parliament for its use
while leaving itself with a fine capital asset. At the heart of the
Palais was the vast assembly chamber or 'hemicycle', so called
because the plethora of small parties which the system of proportional representation produces sit in a hemicycle, melting into each
other politically. The architects had given us a magnificent vaulted
panelled ceiling and comfortable seats. They had also given each
MEP a lavish office with two desks, a divan couch and a sanitary
enclave with its own loo and shower. Rumours were soon rife
that the Italians were the worst offenders in spending their nights
there while claiming full hotel costs on their expenses.

Discomfort had given way to comfort and cosseting, but I
continued to sniff suspiciously round what to me was a parody of
a parliament. During my ten years in Strasbourg I pleaded in vain
for our offices to contain closed-circuit television, telling us who
was speaking in the chamber and what point had been reached in
the debate, a facility provided even by the relatively impoverished

House of Commons. My demand for audible division bells to let us know when a vote was imminent went unheeded. I would tear my hair when, having heard a faint tinkle, I would rush into the chamber to find I was too late to vote. Votes did not matter much anyway. There was no government-versus-opposition battle going on, so there was no serious whipping and no pairing. Most MEPs slipped quietly away whenever it suited them, regardless of what was going on in the chamber.

Worst of all was the carving up of our work between the three meeting places – the civil servants of the Commission in Brussels, the Parliament meeting in Strasbourg and the research papers and documents miles away in Luxembourg. It was, as I used to argue, as though we tried to run the British House of Commons with the MPs at Westminster, our civil servants in Newcastle and the crucial documents in Wales. Every month a convoy of cars ferried trunks of material at enormous cost from Brussels to Strasbourg for our debates.

Another frustration came from the wheeler-dealing which accompanies the system of PR. The Socialist Group was the largest political group in the Parliament, the only one with representatives from every member state, but we were not big enough to command a majority on our own. So the group's time was spent in endless backstairs negotiations with other groups which usually produced a watered-down version of the policies in which we believed. This was second nature to my colleagues, who lived in a world of coalition governments in their national parliaments, but it drove me to despair. How could we win the Community over to socialist policies if our message was always muted in this way?

The first meeting of the Socialist Group was my introduction to this alien political environment. Our main job was to decide whom we should support as the President of the first directly elected Parliament. To me it seemed obvious that as the largest group we should push for our own candidate. I argued this with such verve that the lively Member from the Irish Labour Party, Liam Kavanagh, suggested that they should nominate me as their candidate. The consternation among the rest of the group at the idea of making an anti-marketeer their candidate was comical to behold. He then insisted that at the very least I should accompany the group's President, Ernest Glynne, in the negotiations with other parties that the group accepted should take place. Ernest was a delightful Belgian socialist of instinctively liberal views, but he was a product of Belgian politics in which governments formed, fell and reformed almost every month like a political kaleidoscope. To him wheeler-dealing was a way of life and he was appalled to have me attached to him as he went into his backstairs intrigues with Egon Klepsh, leader of the German Christian Democrats, and Martin Bangermann, leader of the Liberals. 'Is she supposed to be here?' they asked Ernest suspiciously as I appeared; Ernest just shrugged. It was soon clear that Ernest was going to ignore the group's desire that we should insist on having a socialist candidate, and a deal was fixed up despite my protests under which Simone Veil, of the Union des Démocrates Français (UDF) on the centre-right, became the first President on condition that her term of office should be limited to two and a half years, at the end of which the socialists would get their turn.

Simone was an impressive but rather reserved figure, a jurist and a Jewess who had suffered in Hitler's concentration camps. I had paid an official visit to her in 1975 when we were both ministers of health in our respective governments and she had won my respect by the skill and courage with which she had piloted reform of the abortion laws through the French Parliament. She was also chic, and I was dazzled when, at a private dinner she gave me, she appeared in a white bouffant evening gown, one of the most elegant I had seen. I had no objection to her as an individual but I was annoyed that coalitionitis had won again.

Another disillusionment came from the lack of cut and thrust in parliamentary debate. In an assembly comprising all the representatives of twelve states, each with three or four political parties demanding to be heard, the number of people wanting to speak vastly exceeded the time available. I would struggle for a small slot in a debate and considered myself lucky to be offered five minutes. Sometimes it was down to two. If one spoke for an extra minute or so, it was taken from the next speaker in one's group. The interjections and challenges which characterize a Commons debate are therefore impossible. Most speakers come with a written speech which they read into the record and then disappear. I was not surprised that the press took little interest in our debates.

The arrival of Roy Jenkins as President of the Commission in 1977 had been hailed as a triumph by the Commission and the Council of Ministers. They had snatched an eminent British politician out of the ranks of the doubters in the Labour government and they were expecting dynamic leadership from him which would improve the running of the Community. When I arrived in the Parliament his presidency did not seem to have made any difference. But if they were disappointed, so was he. He had found that the building of Europe was less simple than he had imagined it and not least that the European Parliament was not the vibrant democratic forum he had hoped for.

I was in the chamber one evening when Roy was due to wind up an important debate, and the true nature of the European Parliament was borne in on him. He sat all day listening to the succession of prim little speeches which Members read into the record from written scripts before disappearing for more congenial activities. When Roy rose to reply at about 10 p.m., there were about five MEPs left in the chamber, including me. Roy was furious and stumbled angrily through his detailed reply. This was not the House of Commons scenario to which he was accustomed, in which the government spokesman delivers a dramatic winding-up speech at the end of a main debate to a crowded and belligerent House. The European idealists have their practical priorities. One of them is the relaxed enjoyment of an evening meal, so the rules provide that the debate does not end with a vote but takes place the following day, by which time the press has lost whatever interest it had. Several years later, I ran into Roy at one of John Mortimer's parties. I teased him: 'You know, Roy, you hated the European Parliament.' He replied with one of those slow smiles of his, 'Barbara, you cannot expect me to abandon the beliefs of a lifetime.'

Perhaps not, I thought, but surely he could learn from

experience. My experience of the European Parliament had taught me that for logistical reasons it can never be turned into an effective instrument of democratic control on anything remotely resembling House of Commons lines. For one thing, too many languages are involved. There are eight official languages in a Community of twelve, and enlargement, for which everyone is pressing, would increase that number, possibly to twenty in due course. In such a situation there can be no flexible response to events as they unfold. Even a horde of translators staying up all night cannot guarantee to produce a translated text of last minute amendments and compromises for Members before they vote on them. I have myself often had to vote on a text I have not even seen. The simultaneous interpretation of speeches has been developed to a high level by skilled interpreters lining the walls in their small glass booths, but even their efforts make for rigidity. MEPs cannot follow the interpretation unless they sit in their seats with uncomfortable headphones clamped over their ears. If they move about they miss the trend of the argument. Last but not least, the size of the European Parliament leads to machine politics. The elaborate system cannot work except by passing the allocation of speaking time and the drafting of compromise resolutions to the political groups and so effectively to their offices. There is no room for the free-booter who in British politics brings so much vitality to our arguments, from Dennis Skinner to Edward Heath.

One of the pleasanter recollections of my ten years in the European Parliament was a letter I received from the English booth of interpreters when I retired. I must often have driven them mad because I never gave them an advance text of what I was going to say because I never knew it myself. I also liked to use irony, which must tax the skill of any interpreter. To my surprise they wrote that they would miss the challenge of interpreting me. I suppose my off-the-cuff remarks were a relief from the monotony of the set speeches and I have always believed that boredom is one of the most dangerous enemies of democracy.

Roy's period of office as President of the Commission was not the success his sponsors had hoped for. For one thing, they found him too aloof and at the end of his first two and a half years, his appointment was not renewed. On almost his last night in December 1981, he sent me a message via his *chef de cabinet* to the effect that the President would be very glad if I would dine with him. When I looked surprised the *chef de cabinet* murmured that the President wanted to discuss my Cabinet diaries, the first volume of which had just been published. I went along intrigued, knowing that I would get an excellent meal. And so it proved.

Roy entertained me at the Zimmer, one of Strasbourg's best restaurants. The wine he had chosen was, as I anticipated, superb, and I seem to remember we got through three bottles of it between us as the evening wore on. He said he wanted to compare notes about our period of office together. He was at his most urbane and friendly, querying one or two of the comments I had made in my diaries but maintaining that on the whole they had been 'very accurate and very fair'. As we talked with great bonhomie of our former days, I wondered why on earth he had split himself from the Labour Party on the ground that it was in the hands of the rabid left, when so many of the colleagues he said he admired were prepared to go on working from inside for the policies in which he believed. It is a mystery I have never solved, though I have often suspected Roy must himself have doubted the wisdom of his change of company.

The main work of the European Parliament is done in its committees, whose reports form the basis of the discussions in the full Parliament. Each MEP is allowed to be a member of one committee, and the British Labour Group was astonished when I said I wanted to go on the Agriculture Committee, which most of them were only too thankful to leave to me. To the majority of them agricultural policy was too technical, but I pointed out that that was where the money went: two-thirds of the Community budget was lavished on the Common Agricultural Policy. I was to fight this situation for the next ten years. In those days, the CAP *was* the Community – France had seen to that. Her peasant population played an important role in her political life and had to be mollified. Ironically, many of her small farmers were communist, which meant that the French socialists in our group were always looking over their shoulders, not to be outdone in demanding that the small farmers should receive still more protection and subsidies.

In my forays into the jungle of the CAP, I found an unexpected ally in Finn Gundelach, the Agricultural Commissioner, a tall, uncharacteristically charismatic Dane who was conducting a one-man campaign to persuade the Council of Ministers that something had to be done to curb the rising costs and absurd excesses of the CAP. On the whole I had a great admiration for the Commission. Although its members are nominated by the national governments, each of which have one or two representatives serving on it, the Commission acts as a unity and its members rise above their national allegiances to a remarkable degree. Of course, Finn had to support the basic principles of the CAP – notably the stimulation of over-production by high prices and the stockpiling or dumping abroad of the resulting surpluses – but he doggedly warned the Council of Ministers that the policy was ruining the Community. I devoured his reports avidly, which confirmed all my worst fears about the inability of the Community to correct the inconsistency at the heart of its policy, under which industry was subjected to the rigours of the market and free trade, while agriculture remained one of the most highly protected in the world.

One afternoon I was given the chance to back his campaign when a slot of seven minutes' speaking time unexpectedly became available in a debate on the CAP. This gave me the chance to launch into an off-the-cuff diatribe against the over-production of butter and the waste as it went slowly rancid in Community stores, having to be sold off cheaply to foreign buyers such as Russia before it became totally unsaleable. I pointed out that 40 per cent of butter disposal was being heavily subsidized, at a cost to the budget of over 2 billion units of European currency (about £1.5 billion), yet there were still over 250,000 tonnes in stock. The situation over skimmed milk powder was still more laughable. Over-production was so great that the Commission was having to sell large quantities of it as feed for animals, including cows. So we had the ludicrous situation in which a cow was lavishly yielding milk at one end of her and being fed it back at the other end in the form of skimmed milk powder. The consumer was paying twice: first through the high price of milk and secondly through the cost of getting rid of the surpluses the high prices produced.

Finn was delighted with my speech, glad to have an ally who could put his points more forcibly than he dared. I believed he would have made some progress with his reforms, but unfortunately he died of a heart attack shortly afterwards. He was followed as Commissioner by Paul Dalsager, whom I affectionately dubbed the 'dull Dane'. Paul was an amiable and well-intentioned man, but he lacked Finn's verve and drive, and did not have the ability to stand up to agriculture's vested interests. When I left the Parliament ten years later a fundamental reform of the CAP had still not been achieved.

During those first five years, I began to realize how deep was the loyalty to the ideal of European union among other member states, despite the Community's maddening inconsistencies. Over supper one evening I argued with a couple of young Belgian socialists. 'Barbara,' they said to me, 'we are as critical of the Community as you are, but we were born into it. We have never known anything else.' To them it was the natural framework for the post-war world. I also realized with what persistence and skill the Commission set out to win over the doubters, particularly among the Brits. I have never known a more accessible civil service than the Commission staff, who were always ready to receive any deputations from local authorities and firms I wanted to bring from my constituency. They would spend hours advising them on how to get some of the tiny pickings from the Social Fund. Local authorities, pressed by the rigours of Margaret Thatcher's economic policies, turned to the Community as to a pot of gold and were won over when they got grants for their activities, even if only a few thousand pounds.

I was also struck by the panoply of inducements the Community authorities held out to us to offset the rigours of endless air travel through fog and snow: generous expense allowances, free language courses, lavish receptions, a lush car service to take us everywhere, subsidized tours of Brussels and Strasbourg for one's constituents. The Strasbourg municipality joined in the conspiracy enthusiastically, the Mayor being always ready to receive groups of MEPs' visitors, welcoming them to the beautiful chamber of the Mairie with a little speech and a *vin d'honneur*, as the complimentary glass of wine was called. Not least there was the enticement of 'Study Days'. Each political group is entitled to a number of these days each year at Community expense, provided they take place in a member state. We northern Europeans had soon had enough of the wet and windy days in Denmark or Germany and plumped for the sunshine of Greece or Italy, where the only serious subject studied tended to be the local beauty spots. Even the toughest anti-marketeer in the British Labour Group softened under such blandishments. The temptation to go native was very great.

At home hostility to British membership of the Community was still running strong. Tony Benn having reversed his initial acceptance of the referendum campaign result had put himself at the head of the uncompromising anti-marketeers. Nothing but total withdrawal from the Community would do. In 1980 Clive Jenkins moved a motion at conference calling for withdrawal from the Community to be included in the next election manifesto: it was carried by 5 million votes to 2 million. This was also the year in which conference decided a special conference should be held to discuss the setting up of an electoral college to choose the leadership, a decision which was duly taken the following year. The dominance of the Bennite left both in conference and on the NEC was soon to be complete.

It was some time, however, before Tony made an open bid for the leadership. When Jim Callaghan, realizing the part he had played in bringing about our electoral defeat in 1979, resigned the leadership in October 1980, the two main contestants for the succession were Denis Healey and Michael Foot. Michael won the contest on the second ballot by ten votes. As an MEP, I had no vote, but I suspect I would have been very torn. The Michael Foot of 1980 was very different from the man I had backed in 1976. For one thing he was five years older and was approaching seventy; for another he had become suspect in my eyes for his uncritical support for Jim Callaghan's rigidities, which had led to the Winter of Discontent. I knew that Denis was ruthless and politically erratic, but he had the intellectual power and authority which we needed in the electoral battles which lay ahead. In the end, however, I would probably have voted for Michael with my left-wing friends.

For a time, the election of Michael Foot as leader mollified the Benn faction, but it was soon clear that he was a changed man politically, anxious for compromise and no match with his simplicities for the sophisticated enemies we faced. From the word go, the Tories set out to make him a laughing-stock, helped by some on our own side who seemed always willing to produce the kind of own-goals the Tories usually manage to avoid. There was something touching in the sight of this honest man, hobbling into view with his walking stick, which he had to use as a result of a serious motor accident, and wearing slightly ill-fitting clothes. His attendance at the Armistice Day ceremony at the Cenotaph in a duffel-coat would probably have gone unnoticed if a sour maverick in Labour's own ranks, Walter Johnson, had not publicly called it an insult to the dead. Michael was frankly bewildered. 'It is a very good duffel-coat,' he said to me ruefully afterwards. Yet the press were to highlight it as proof that he was unfit to be Prime Minister.

But the left soon realized that Michael had no use for Tony Benn, whom he regarded as a self-seeking egotist who never played with the team, preferring to rely on his own personal dynamism and the adulation of a small clique of devotees. When in 1981 Benn announced he was going to run against Healey for the deputy leadership, Michael threw all his weight against him.

There were other people on the left who were agonizing about whether to vote for Benn or not. A few days before the 1981 conference, at which the vote was to be taken, Jack Straw wrote to me asking me for my advice. I replied to him from my hotel in Strasbourg in a long letter in which I set out my political philosophy:

> The position of people like you and me (what Harold, God help us!, would call the 'soft left') is very difficult. We are caught

between our dedication to the ends and our unhappiness about the methods. We are not political Calvinists, but we are not right-wing Jesuits either. We hate the Inquisition from which-ever religious faith it may come. I think we are political William Morris-ites, dreaming of a society in which revolutionary change is achieved by love and tolerance and in which collectivism and the pursuit of aesthetic satisfaction are synonymous. . . . One must never lose sight of the dream. It is the only thing that has kept me going. . . . This brings me back to Tony Benn. You and I distrust him because he is a Calvinist and he carries with him the aura of witch-burnings. But when I stop to think about how you should vote (and how I would vote in your place), I am forced to face the alternatives as you are, and when the chips are down, I know which side of the barricades I am on, even if I don't like some of the company. Denis Healey's reaction to the Benn campaign is a revelation of the fact that at bottom he is a ruthless bully.

In the end, Jack voted on the first ballot for John Silkin, the soft-left candidate put up by the Tribune Group, and, when Silkin was eliminated, voted for Benn. I would probably have followed the lead of Neil Kinnock.

Neil Kinnock too was agonizing over his choice. It was at this conference that he first made his impact on me as a political figure to be taken seriously. Feeling for Benn was running high in the constituencies. Neil's own local party of Bedwellty was Bennite to a man and woman, but Neil made it clear he was going to vote for John Silkin and then, if necessary, abstain. It was a courageous move which put him at odds with the majority of local parties and with his own constituency, and he could only have taken that step as a man of principle. On the first morning of the conference, Ted and I found ourselves behind Neil in the procession waiting to file on to the platform for the opening ceremony. 'There goes a future leader of the party,' I said to Ted audibly. Neil smiled at us over his shoulder and said modestly, 'Thank you, but I do not want the job. It would mean too much disruption of my family life.'

The electoral college voted in three sections: the local parties, the trade unions and Labour MPs. Tony Benn romped home in the local party section while Denis polled heavily with the trade unions and the MPs. The final result showed he had defeated Benn by only 1000 votes and that, if only four of the sixteen members of the Tribune Group who abstained had voted for Benn, he would have won. The fury of the Bennites was uncontained. At the crowded Tribune rally that week, Margaret Beckett, a hard-left aspirant for membership of the NEC, made a vitriolic personal attack on Neil and his fellow Tribunites as 'traitors'. Neil was not there. He told me afterwards, 'She would not have dared to say it if I had been,' and shrugged it off. I realized that this light-hearted, witty, idealistic left-winger had a mind of his own and a will to follow his own course.

Many years later I questioned Neil about this incident. 'So you never set out to become leader of the party?' I asked him. 'Not at that time,' he replied and went on to tell me what happened in the vote for the deputy leadership. The majority of the Tribune group had lost patience with Tony Benn and wanted to put up their own candidate. They asked Neil to stand, but he refused, arguing that it would be divisive and they should abstain. The group therefore nominated John Silkin, who was wiped out on the first ballot. This time Neil persuaded them to abstain. By now he had become the standard-bearer of the sane left and their obvious candidate when the leadership issue came up again.

The defeat of Tony Benn split the left and the Tribune Group. In a breakaway movement, the hard left formed the Campaign Group, whose members were to hound me in the British Labour Group until they managed to unseat me as leader in 1985. But Tony Benn's defeat was also to lead to a split in the Labour Party itself. The introduction of an electoral college administered a fatal blow to the personal ambitions of the leading pro-marketeers, notably David Owen, the extent of whose ambition and self-importance now emerged. He had believed he might one day win over a majority of Labour MPs to give him the leadership, but the electoral college was too tough a nut to crack. He knew he was not trusted by the rank and file. Jim Callaghan's promotion of him in 1977 to be Foreign Secretary – the youngest since Pitt, as the press hastened to point out – had heightened his ambition and deepened his streak of arrogance. His party loyalty, never very strong, could not stand the strain.

We Labour MPs were in Strasbourg when the news broke on the tapes that David Owen, Roy Jenkins, Shirley Williams and Bill Rodgers had left the party to form the Gang of Four, in an attempt to 'break the mould of British politics'. They aimed to create a realignment behind the centre–right, a move welcomed by Liberal leader, David Steel. They had launched a Council for Social Democracy which was later to develop into an independent Social Democratic Party (SDP), splitting the Labour Party. We MEPs went into an anxious huddle, wondering how far this movement would go. Who else would defect? The initial response to the breakaway campaign seemed impressive. Thousands of supporters hastened to enroll. David Sainsbury of the prosperous retailing firm put up generous funds to finance it. Thirteen Labour MPs and one Conservative joined the new party. I was worried about the effects on the British Labour Group. One of the reasons that David Owen had given for breaking ranks was that the Labour Party was anti-Europe, and our group contained a minority of ardent pro-Europeans like Derek Enright and Brian Keays. I need not have worried. They stood firm.

So did the local parties and trade unions. I realized to my relief that, for all its faults, the Labour Party was still founded on a rock of popular support which was not to be taken in by the vanities of a few middle-class intellectuals. It was only the defection of Shirley Williams which really hurt. She was immensely popular in the party for her gentle charm and enlightened views. 'I don't understand why Shirley did it,' one of our party workers said to me. Party workers rightly suspected, as Roy Jenkins revealed later, that she had been the most reluctant member of the Gang of Four. I suspected too that she came to regret it as the SDP, launched so confidently, foundered in a mess of abortive Liberal alliances and on David Owen's inability to co-operate with anyone.

Several years later, when Shirley had lost her parliamentary seat, married an American and gone to lecture at Harvard

University, I ran into her on a television programme in which we were both taking part. She could not have been more affectionate, handing me a greetings card in which she had written 'To Barbara, to whom we owe so much'. When I asked her whether she did not miss the challenge of politics, she replied, 'Of course I do.' She was not to be drawn any further when I asked her whether she had any regrets, but I was convinced she also missed the warmth of Labour Party camaraderie.

But I was worried by the party's mood at this crucial turning point. From my work in the European Parliament I had become convinced that membership of the Community had been accepted by the British people, despite their grumbles, as part of their way of life and that another referendum on the issue would produce an even bigger majority than in 1975 for staying in. Most British people still believed that the Community had a crock of gold from which local authorities and voluntary organizations could top up the depleted funds they got from their own government. The Community had conducted a skilful public relations exercise, putting up large placards along new roads and other developments carrying the slogan 'Built with European Community funds'.

Yet I remained as anxious as ever about the effect of our membership on a Labour government's ability to carry out an expansionary economic policy. In September 1982, I poured out my doubts in an article in the *New Statesman* headed 'Let Them Chuck Us Out'. In it I warned that the party was in danger of fighting on a negative. Margaret Thatcher, I urged, despite the disastrous effects of her monetarist policies, was actually managing to capture the moral initiative because she was positive. The demand for withdrawal was a negative. So we should argue that we wished to remain in the Community but could not allow the Commission to thwart our intention to rebuild British industry. Temporarily at any rate we would introduce the exchange controls and import controls, without which our expansionist policies would merely be an open-sesame for a flood of imports from other EC countries delighted to seize the opportunities our growth policies offered them. We should fight the election on a restatement of our policy for growth and jobs, and challenge the

Commission to tell the British people that it was incompatible with our membership. We would not walk out. They would have to throw us out if they wanted to.

Immediately and predictably the hard-line anti-marketeers in the British Labour Group moved into the attack. Two of our MEPs, Alf Lomas and Richard Balfe, rushed a letter into the *New Statesman* declaring that I had taken a U-turn and was not fit to be leader of the British Labour Group. I went to the party conference a month later in some trepidation, expecting to be denounced on every side. Instead, even those of my left-wing friends who began by shaking their heads over my article – people such as Eric Heffer and Alex Kitson – added that they did not necessarily disagree with it. The attitude of Peter Shore, the most committed of our anti-marketeers, was particularly surprising: he greeted me affectionately with the words, 'Of course you have not done a U-turn.' I was right in a number of things I had said, though he did not agree with all of them. Michael Foot came over to me at breakfast time to say that my article was 'brilliant' but that we must not rush things. I urged on him the need for the party to take an internationalist line and was delighted to hear him do so the next day in an eloquent leader's speech to conference. Paolo Falcone, General Secretary of the Socialist Group, who was sitting in the public gallery, told me that he thought Michael's line had undoubtedly been influenced by my article.

Of course there were some sour critics, notably Clive Jenkins, who was understandably furious since he had moved the successful withdrawal resolution two years earlier. Ian Mikardo nearly spat at me. 'Your name is mud,' he said brutally, though I extracted the confession from him that he had not even read the article. Wedgie Benn was offhand with me at first, but as we talked he did not denounce my ideas outright. I wrote in my diary, 'The most significant thing he said was that to drop withdrawal now would be more than the party could bear.' I added, 'This is Tony's trouble – he has got the rank and file so firmly hooked on his over-simplicities that he has left himself no room for manoeuvre or adaptability.'

But the most remarkable reaction of all came from the visitors to the conference from the Community. They clutched at my article as a lifeline, holding out the hope that Britain might after all remain in the Community. The triumphant delight of our Labour European Commissioner, Ivor Richard, was hard to bear. 'You won't feel like that when you see in practice what my suggestion means,' I warned him. 'Oh yes, I will,' he retorted. 'We can face that.' Paolo told me he was circulating copies of my article to all members of the Socialist Group. Most ecstatic of all was Carlo Ripa de Meana of the Italian Socialists, who almost kissed me: 'Your article is very, very important. We must follow it up.' Carlo was a tall, elegant, well-heeled and cultured man who believed passionately in a united Europe. He was later to make a name for himself as Commissioner for the Environment, in which capacity he hounded the British government for its failure to achieve the EC standards on water purity.

What impressed me in my talks with the Europeans was that none of them seemed to regard as an insurmountable obstacle the freedom of action I had claimed for a Labour government to carry out its industrial policy. Most EC countries were going through economic difficulties and I had the feeling that they would have welcomed a review of the Community's rules to enable them to be applied far more flexibly in accordance with each country's economic needs. After all, as I pointed out in my article, deflation was one of the most drastic import controls of all, since it reduced the capacity of member states to buy from each other. Competitive deflation was a recipe for recession. It was in the interests of the whole Community that each country should be helped to maximize her economic growth instead of being forced into a collective straitjacket. I believe that that was the moment when changes might have been made, given the proper leadership. Instead the Community became locked in by ever more rigid rules, stimulated by the monetarist policies now dominating the British scene.

Despite my efforts, the left remained unconverted and we fought the election of May 1983 on a manifesto of pure Bennery. All the ingredients he and his supporters had been fighting for were there: unilateral nuclear disarmament, more public ownership, withdrawal from the EEC. It helped lose us votes when we should have won. Margaret Thatcher's government had hardly been a triumphant success. She had ruthlessly applied her mone-tarist theories – bring inflation down by cutting the supply of money in circulation and all will be well. The result had been a spate of bankruptcies and a sharp rise in unemployment. At one stage she was rated the most unpopular Prime Minister in history. She was saved by the Falklands war in which she played the role of Boadicea to great effect.

She was also a consummate politician. The dewy-eyed younger woman who had won the Tory leadership had hardened into a practised manipulator of the strings of power, who knew how to play on the lowest common denominator of human emotions on such issues as the restoration of capital punishment. But she had courage, too, and rode the waves of unpopularity like a surfer. While proclaiming that the lady was not for turning, she spun like a top whenever it was necessary for survival. She relaxed her monetary policy, for example, to produce a popular Budget just before the election of 1983.

To pit against her we had Michael Foot. Never has an honourable man been more miscast. The Conservatives spent millions on the PR consultants Saatchi and Saatchi, ritzy rallies and extravagant press conferences in what was later described in a television programme as 'the marketing of Margaret'. Meanwhile the Labour Party, strapped for cash, left Michael to fend for himself. Margaret herself appeared before the cameras immacu-lately groomed, wearing a smart suit enlivened by a dazzling brooch or string of pearls. I watched Michael on one of the election programmes sitting hunched up opposite his interviewer. No doubt he was wearing his most formal suit, but due to the way he was sitting the collar stood out in an ungainly fashion from his neck. I groaned because I knew that appearances are three-quarters of the battle in the age of television politics. I could imagine viewers thinking, probably subconsciously, 'How can he govern the country if he cannot even get his jacket collar to sit properly?' Friends who were desperately anxious for Labour to win said to me, 'He will not do.'

It would be wrong to blame Michael for the amateurish way

in which Labour's press conferences were organized. The party machine had become involved in the left-wing battles then dominating the National Executive, in which politics rather than administrative expertise dictated the running of the party's organization. As leader of the British Labour Group I was brought over from Strasbourg to take part in the early-morning meetings of the party's policy directorate at our new headquarters in Walworth Road. We were supposed to prepare for the press conferences at the more spacious premises of Transport House. The meetings were a shambles. We had no clear campaign and were arguing about what policies to cover and what line to take when we had to dash against the traffic in some disorder to the press conference. We were none of us surprised when Mrs Thatcher swept to victory with a majority of 144 seats, while our share of the poll slumped to 27.6 per cent. The party had not been so demoralized since the débâcle of 1931.

Labour's dismal showing was in no small part due to the campaigning against us of the Alliance of the new SDP and the Liberals, led by Roy Jenkins and David Steel. Although the Alliance won only 23 seats to Labour's 209, it polled 25.5 per cent of the votes, only 2 per cent less than we did, which did not help our morale. The result was also affected by confusion over our policy of unilateral nuclear disarmament.

Michael Foot, who had been toying more than once with the idea of resigning from the leadership, now escaped thankfully from its toils. Denis Healey decided not to stand either for the leadership or for the deputy leadership. One of the significant side-effects of the election was the defeat of Tony Benn at Bristol and voices were to be heard muttering, 'Serve him right.' It was the beginning of the end of his political ascendancy. The way was clear for Neil Kinnock to assume the leadership. He did so at the 1983 party conference capturing 71 per cent of the votes, with a majority in each section of the electoral college. The 'dream ticket' was completed by the election of the right-winger Roy Hattersley as deputy. I decided to watch the result on television in my hotel room, where one could get a much better view of what was happening. All my doubts arising from Neil's lack of ministerial experience melted away when I heard his acceptance speech, one of the most moving and compelling I had ever heard. My spirits rose as he painted a picture of the Britain he wanted to see: brave, realistic and inspired. I already knew Neil to be tough under pressure, but as I listened to him I felt that at last we had an answer to Margaret Thatcher's capture of the moral initiative. The ecstatic audience obviously felt so too.

Back in Strasbourg we Labour MEPs set out to prepare for the European elections of 1984. In the event the party did better than in the domestic election of 1983, bringing our seats in the European Parliament up to thirty-two, while the Tories lost fifteen. I had always seen it as our job to use the European Parliament as a sounding board from which we would flash back messages home to tell our electors what the British government was doing in their name and what its standing was in the European Community. Margaret Thatcher made our job easy.

I was, of course, entirely in agreement with her demand that Britain's net contribution to the Community's budget should be reduced. It was part of the policy on which we had fought the Euro-election in 1979, and I returned to the point time and again in the European newsletters I wrote for some of my local papers. I stressed what a scandal it was that we should be the second-largest net contributor after wealthy Germany, getting less out of the Community than strong economies like France. But the shrillness with which she pressed her claim alienated the rest of the Council of Ministers. I found that the European politicians I met always behaved to each other with great courtesy and often formality. The French language lent itself to such courtesies and I joined in them happily. My reasonable fluency in French and my efforts to learn German endeared me to my pro-market critics even though they disagreed strongly with my view on Europe. But when Margaret Thatcher banged the table and in raucous English demanded '*my* money' back, they shrugged disdainfully at what they considered a piece of Anglo-Saxon vulgarity. At the height of one of her rows I asked my French taxi driver in Strasbourg what he thought of her. He hesitated, then said politely, 'C'est une femme formidable.' The reduction in Britain's budget share which Mrs Thatcher eventually obtained was at the price of a good deal of ill-will.

When I left the European Parliament in 1989 I was touched, if a little puzzled, to receive a letter from Baron von Richthofen, the German Ambassador in London, telling me that the President of the Federal Republic had awarded me the Commander's Cross of the Order of Merit of the Federal Republic of Germany. He asked me to come and receive it from him at a reception he would give in my honour. Baron von Richthofen, a distant nephew of the German pilot known as the Red Baron, was an unassuming and courteous man who greeted me and the friends I was invited to bring with me with liberality. In my acceptance speech I told him I thought the honour had been a recognition of my struggles to master German grammar. 'It is an award for valour, not achievement,' I teased him. When I went on to say I was not afraid of German reunification, I was surprised by the eagerness of his reaction as he came over and thanked me for what I had said. Anti-marketeer I may have been, but never anti-European. I believe the peace of the world depends on nations treating each other's problems with great sensitivity. It was an art of which Margaret Thatcher was incapable.

Nor did the Falklands war bring her the plaudits in the Community which it did at home. I remember the sense of horror with which the European Parliament followed the launch of the British task force against Argentina; I remember too the resolution we got passed urging the need for negotiations for a peaceful settlement. The sinking of the *Belgrano* with the loss of 350 Argentinian lives sent a shudder through the Parliament. 'I would never have believed that a member of the Community would launch a war,' Rudi Arndt said to me angrily. Rudi was the president of our Socialist Group. He was a big blunt German Social Democrat who had been Mayor of Frankfurt and he was a bully of the Denis Healey type, so I knew how to stand up to him. But he was a brave man who had risked his life resisting the Nazis, and his credentials for fighting against racism and for democracy and peace were not in doubt. His reaction to Margaret Thatcher's jingoism over the Falklands war was therefore significant. He was always conscious of Germany's duty to make reparations to the Jews, and on one occasion I stood in line with him and Jesse Jackson at the Stuttgart Memorial to the victims of the holocaust where we were laying our wreaths. It is moments like this which compensated me for the frustrations of Community life.

At home the Labour Party was already modifying its line on Europe. It became clear at the 1983 conference that the party's mood had changed. The NEC had produced a statement in which it declared that Britain had to remain a member of the EEC for the term of the next Parliament and fight inside it for 'the best deal for Britain'. As a sop to the anti-marketeers it added that Britain had to 'retain the option' of withdrawal. This convinced no one. The statement was endorsed by conference without a vote and I was the only one to sound a warning note. In a speech as leader of the British Labour Group I warned conference of the move towards federalism, whose spirit was growing in Europe and which could make it impossible for us to carry out our policies. But I rounded on the local parties which were not even bothering to select candidates for the coming Euro-elections on the ground that they were not interested. 'You had better get interested,' I told them bluntly, because what was happening in Europe was affecting all our lives.

The warning was timely. During my second period in the European Parliament the Community started to change direction dramatically. The federalists, headed by the Italians, had the bit between their teeth. The Italians, who had never been very good at governing themselves, were eager to pass the buck to a European federal government. Under the inspired leadership of the proselytizing Independent MEP, Altiero Spinelli, they pressed for amendments to be made to the Treaty of Rome to enable positive and systematic steps to be taken towards complete economic and political union. I sat helplessly as the Parliament passed Spinelli's draft Treaty of Union.

One of the most dramatic changes was in the attitude of France. In the early years of the directly elected Parliament French MEPs, including the socialists, had shown that de Gaulle's ghost was still abroad, as they defended every aspect of their national sovereignty. They were as reluctant as we Brits to hand over greater power to the Community. I was therefore astonished when François Mitterrand, Socialist President of France, addressed the Parliament in 1984 and gave one of the most pro-federalist speeches I had yet heard. I suspected that the reason was that France, which had entered the Community of Six to contain Germany, had become even more anxious as the Federal Republic emerged as the strongest economy and was increasingly dominating the Community. The French government had become a convert to the need to bind Germany's nationalistic drive in ever tighter shackles of European unity.

Margaret Thatcher was now in a trap. She had allowed herself to be carried along with the new tide as long as she thought it was merely leading to the strengthening of the free market in which she believed. She even signed the Declaration issued by the heads-of-government summit at Stuttgart in 1984 in which they affirmed their determination to transform the whole complex of relations between their states into a European union. She protested later that the other states did not know what they meant by a union, but she herself was to take the process a step further by signing the Single Act, however reluctantly. She even forced the European Communities Bill (which embodied it) through the House of Commons, coercing her own sceptics with a three-line Whip.

The Single Act is a quantum leap in the development of the Community. Its main aim is to establish the 'internal market' – a Europe without internal frontiers in which capital, goods and labour can move freely. In doing so it reverses the assurance Ted Heath gave us when he took us into the Community in 1972 that Britain would retain her veto. The whole aim of the Act is to whittle down the veto and to enable more and more decisions in the Council of Ministers to be reached by a qualified majority. It also claims to give more power to the European Parliament, but it does so by a complicated formula which hides the fact that the power transferred is minuscule. True, this new procedure provides for second as well as first readings of specified measures; it forces the Council to consider amendments by the Parliament, provided they are reached by over half the number of MEPs. If the Commission has approved those amendments the Council must reach its decision on them by a qualified majority: no veto by anyone. This procedure reduced some of the voting chaos I had first experienced, because we were all dragooned by our political groups to be present at the first and second readings to be sure that over half the MEPs were there to vote, but it left me feeling more swamped than ever as the officers of the political groups did their backstairs wheeler-dealing to stitch up the necessary overall majority.

But the major purpose of the Single Act was to give legal backing to the introduction of the internal market at the end of 1992. Margaret Thatcher was all in favour of it, because it was intended to remove all administrative and other barriers to the free trade and the unbridled competition which she advocated. But once again she had not read the small print properly. Ironically it was Lord Cockfield, former Conservative Minister and her nominee for the Commission, who helped to bring her dilemma to crisis point. He was put in charge of producing the 300 odd directives needed to bring the internal market into being, and he threw himself into the job with enthusiasm.

Lord Cockfield was a stocky, indrawn man with few social charms. There were rumours that as a minister he had not been popular in his Department, and his exaggerated English drawl did not go down well with the Parliament, which considered him supercilious. But he made efforts to establish friendly relations with MEPs, particularly over meals. He treated me to an excellent lunch more than once at the Sofitel, because he liked to eat well, but he had no flair for making human contacts. I emerged from these lunches feeling that he was constitutionally incapable of being anything but a technocrat. Nonetheless he won grudging respect for the doggedness with which he worked to get his directives and regulations into place.

He also had a good brain and a logical mind. He could see, as Margaret Thatcher could not, the consequences of creating an internal market in which goods, capital and people could move at will. A Community in which EC nationals could set up a business or a professional establishment in another member state on the same terms as local citizens was already on the high road to European union. Competition policy pushed the process further. No public authority faced with an EC bid would be allowed to allocate its contracts on any but commercial terms. In Britain public contracts formed a considerable part of economic activity. In the North-west, with its high unemployment, it was a tradition among our Labour councils to attach certain conditions to their contract. There had to be no sex discrimination or racial prejudice and above all a certain percentage of local labour had to be used. Under the Single Act the latter stipulation at any rate would be illegal. In Thatcherite Britain privatization made it all the easier for EC firms to buy up any national asset, however essential, such as water or electricity supply. We must no longer think as Britons, but as Europeans.

Cockfield saw clearly what might flow from this. To be effective, an internal market must operate in a unified European economy with a single currency and a central European bank dictating the economic policies needed to keep that currency stable. Taxes must be harmonized. It was unfair competition for Britain to have cheaper food than her competitors by refusing to levy VAT on food. The process would lead logically to political union. When he aired these views publicly Margaret Thatcher was horrified. She felt she had been nurturing a federalist viper in her bosom, and she refused to appoint him for a second term.

Margaret Thatcher also failed to realize that the Treaty of Rome has strong interventionist elements. The most obvious one is the Common Agricultural Policy, under which agricultural production is controlled, managed, subsidized and protected by the Commission. Market forces have nothing to do with it. The CAP is supposed to be merely one of several common policies; another notable one is transport, which is specifically mentioned in the Treaty. The intention there is to regulate road transport, subsidize railways and finance the building of new transport links to provide a comprehensive European network. But the Treaty also has what is called in Euro-jargon a 'social dimension'. The larger market is designed to increase wealth, not for its own sake

542

but to improve working conditions and the standard of living generally. Working people and their trade unions are treated as 'social partners', not as the 'enemies within' of Thatcherite demonology. The Treaty is also concerned with other social issues like legislation for equal pay. It is a far cry from Margaret Thatcher's 'let the market dictate' philosophy.

So when Jacques Delors became President of the Commission and produced his 'Community Charter of Fundamental Social Rights for Workers' it seemed a natural development to most member states. But Margaret Thatcher was horrified. To begin with she disliked Delors as a person. He is a trim little man, bouncing with energy and self-confidence, his poise reinforced by his mastery of the English language, which puts him at a great advantage in international discussions. His lucidity is also remarkable. I have listened enthralled in the Parliament as he has expounded obtuse Commission policies with a compelling clarity. To make matters worse, from Mrs Thatcher's point of view, he is a banker by profession and has served on the board of directors of the Banque de France. How dare such a man, she fumed, propound such socialist views?

And he propounds them with great conviction, too. I watched him on television when he visited the TUC at its annual congress in Bournemouth in 1988, spellbinding his unsentimental audience with his passionate determination not to allow workers to be marginalized in the new people's Europe he was trying to build. They should have the right to join, or not to join, professional organizations or trade unions and to defend their economic interests through collective bargaining. Workers should have the right to information about their firms' activities, consultation over its development plans and participation in certain levels of management. The social charter would give them guarantees of fair wages and fair hours of work; the right to a job and to vocational training to help a displaced worker find one; the provision of sick pay, paid holidays and redundancy pay; better health and safety provision at work, proper care of the elderly, disabled and unemployed; equal pay and equal treatment for women; full childcare, including maternity and paternity leave to help women find their proper place in the world of work. The delegates could barely believe their ears. So the market did not rule, OK?

Margaret Thatcher, too, could barely believe her ears. She stormed over to Bruges, where she was due to address a meeting of Eurocrats, and astonished her audience by the ferocity of her attack on the social charter. 'I have not', she told them, 'worked all these years to free Britain from the paralysis of socialism only to see it creep in through the backdoor of central control and bureaucracy in Brussels.' When in December 1989 the heads of government in Strasbourg adopted the charter, Britain was the only member state which refused to sign. Justifying this on British television Mrs Thatcher remarked grandly, 'If I am in a minority of one the other eleven must be wrong.'

Labour MEPs and the whole Socialist Group backed the proposals enthusiastically. At one of our Study Days meetings in Paris the group called together trade unionists, MEPs, economists and sociologists to discuss how we could make the charter a reality. I got quite excited, because it seemed as if the Socialist Group were ready at last to fight for a socialist Community. One of the keenest supporters of the charter was Germany. The Federal Republic had some of the highest standards of social provision in Europe and was afraid they could be undermined in the internal-market free-for-all unless other member states were lifted into line. The weaker economies like Portugal saw the charter as a lifeline. In one debate in the Parliament I heard a Portuguese socialist point out that a German worker doing a given type of job in a given type of firm got eight times the pay of a Portuguese worker doing identical work. Were Portuguese workers, he asked, to be still further exploited by powerful multinationals roaming at will through the Community seeking to maximize their profits by investing in low-wage economies?

The Delors initiative had a profound effect on the Labour movement. Already Neil Kinnock had switched the Labour Party's line on Europe as part of his root-and-branch overhaul of organization and policy. Not only was any talk of withdrawal dropped but the party enthusiastically embraced the idea of closer co-operation with Europe. The thoroughness of Neil's conversion startled me. For him European unity had become an emotional crusade. I did a good deal of speaking at party rallies, and at a rally in Neil's constituency at the height of his leadership I was intrigued to find that one of the speakers was Laurent Fabius. Fabius had recently been Prime Minister of France and was Secretary of the French Socialist Party, so he was a man of consequence. He flew over from Paris to the local airport in a small private plane especially to take part in the rally. A hefty Welsh gale was blowing and I feared that his tiny plane might not be able to land. He arrived on the platform looking buffeted and a little harassed, greeted Neil with great friendliness, made a short speech and flew back again, Neil embracing him affectionately. There could not have been a more telling proof of the change in Labour's mood.

Indeed, I began to grow worried by Neil's uncritical adoption of the European cause. I was always in favour of closer contacts and co-operation with European socialists, but I felt our job was to remind them incessantly of the threat which developments towards economic and monetary union posed to our socialist ideas. The social charter was a step forward, but it was still more a statement of intent than an actuality. What concerned me was that the moves to complete the internal market were being pressed ahead at record speed, while steps to implement the social charter hung fire, largely due to the blocking tactics of the British government. I urged in the Socialist Group that we should insist that each directive enforcing the internal market had to be matched by one implementing the social charter and that we should refuse to vote for one without the other. But Rudi Arndt turned me down. No doubt he knew that he would never get this through the other groups with whom he had to negotiate his colourless compromises.

Above all I was alarmed by the steady pressure to bring all member states into the Exchange Rate Mechanism as the first step towards a single currency, a European central bank and complete economic and monetary union. By trying to push the weaker economies into the same financial straitjacket as the stronger ones, we were putting the cart before the horse and making it more difficult for the weaker to catch up. We should put 'convergence' first by practical steps to help all member states reach similar levels of economic development. Delors was strongly in favour of economic and monetary union, but he wanted to promote convergence at the same time. When, however, he asked the Council of Ministers to vote more funds for these purposes, they turned him down flatly, led once again by the British government. So convergence is obviously as far away as ever. I listened in vain for Neil to stress these points.

There was more encouraging news on the international front. In 1985 Gorbachev came to power in the Soviet Union and the ice of the cold war began to melt. I was proud of the part which the Socialist Group, free to act on its own instincts and unhampered by timorous allies, played in these developments. One of the characteristics of the old Soviet regime had been her refusal to recognize the existence of the European Community. She had had no ambassador in Brussels, which she considered a stronghold of the capitalist enemy. I was still a member of the bureau, or Executive, of the Socialist Group when all this changed. A few months after Gorbachev's election a message came from Moscow: would we send a delegation to discuss the Soviet government's future relationship to the EC? It was clearly a dramatic turning point, and on a bitterly cold December day I found myself in Moscow with my fellow members of the Executive, complete with fur hat and fur-lined boots.

Gorbachev was canny. He had chosen the Socialist Group as the most appropriate contact with the European Parliament to advise him whether his overtures to the Community would be likely to succeed. He was not going to risk a rebuff himself, so he arranged for his top emissaries to talk to us. The most influential was Vadim Zagladin, deputy head of the International Department of the Central Committee of the Communist Party, who told us that the Soviet Union was anxious to participate in 'our European home'. The message from all of them came over loud and clear. Gorbachev wanted to 'normalize' the Soviet Union's relations with the EC, send in an ambassador and hopefully arrange exchanges of parliamentary delegations. We were only too glad to take the message back.

Moscow in the meantime had left indelible impressions on us with its drabness, poor street lighting, telephones that did not work and empty shop windows. I for one came back convinced that the Soviet Union was in no condition to wage a war and that we had better take Gorbachev's peace overtures seriously, for all our sakes. One of the comical moments in our trip came when our hosts entertained us to lunch in the Kremlin – one of the most architecturally beautiful enclaves in which I have ever been entertained. The table was set with an impressive display of silver and our spirits rose when we saw a row of glasses, graduating down from big to little at every place setting. At last, we hoped, we were going to escape from Gorbachev's stern prohibition of the display and use of alcohol in public. We had already stood in the freezing cold of Red Square and wondered how any Soviet citizen could survive the New Year celebrations there without a flask of vodka in his pocket. At our Kremlin lunch, however, no dispensations were made for us. The row of glasses, we found, were designed to accommodate only fruit juices of different hues. Even the last small liqueur glass, at which we looked hopefully, praying that some vodka might appear in it, was filled to our dismay with blackcurrant juice.

Rudi Arndt followed up our visit vigorously on our return, taking all the other political groups into his confidence, winning them over to the idea of parliamentary exchanges with the Soviet Union. He took the initative in arranging a series of follow-up visits by politicians from Eastern Europe at the Socialist Group's expense to see how far '*perestroika*' had penetrated there and offered to arrange for these visitors to talk to their groups as well. It worked perfectly. Our efforts were crowned with success when in 1988 the Soviet Union officially recognized the EC; in February 1990 the first ever formal delegation from the Supreme Soviet visited the European Parliament. Sadly I was no longer there as I had decided not to run again in the 1989 election.

I wanted to do something worthwhile before I left, so I

launched two initiatives. The first was to organize a massive exhibition on animal welfare in the Parliament building in Strasbourg, bringing in every member state. This was a field in which Community action was essential if cruelty to animals was to be stopped. It was no good, for example, setting good standards in Britain for the conditions under which live animals destined for slaughter were transported if when they passed our frontier they suffered cruel conditions all the way to Spain. One of the main themes of my exhibition was to abolish the iniquitous leg-hold trap in which so many animals suffered a slow death. This meant securing a ban on imports into Europe of furs from animals caught in a leg-hold trap, as they so often were in the United States, Russia and Canada. We had a fierce lobby against us, but also many enthusiastic backers, including the Parliamentary Inter-Group on Animal Welfare, the International Wild Life Fund, the RSPCA and the Princess Aga Khan. Lord Plumb, a genial man, formerly head of the NFU as Henry Plumb and at the time President of the Parliament, gave us his blessing. He made an enthusiastic speech at the opening and liberally entertained the press. The interest shown in the exhibition was considerable. This was the European Community at its best and also at its most typical. As a result of our campaign the Council of Ministers adopted the import ban for which we had asked, but so hedged it round with conditions that no one knows whether it will have any practical effect.

My second initiative was on reform of the CAP. Some of the worst excesses had been curbed over the years and the burden on the budget reduced, but the fundamental flaws remained. Heading these is the system of farmer support based on high prices, which stimulates over-production and results in the dumping of the surpluses on the world market with the help of export subsidies. It is this which has infuriated other exporters of agricultural products and caused the crisis in GATT and the threat of a world trade war. I used to tell the Commission's experts that the only solution lay in returning to a system of income support on the lines of Labour's deficiency-payments scheme for those struggling to survive. They could not deny it, but said it would cost too much. With my two colleagues on the Agriculture Committee, George Stevenson and David Morris, I commissioned Professor Kenneth Thomson, an agricultural economist at the Aberdeen School of Agriculture, to test for us whether a deficiency-payments scheme would be viable. He did a first-class job for us, working out proposals which would give a minimum income guarantee to every farmer at manageable cost without import levies or export subsidies. Inevitably it was a plan to give more to the small and medium-sized farmer at the expense of the rich one, who, as Finn Gundelach used to point out to me, had done excessively well out of the CAP. The plan got lost in the flurry of the Euro-elections, but I think it contains principles which will have to be followed if the CAP is not to continue to disrupt world trade.

My Labour colleagues fought the 1989 European elections with a robust attack on Margaret Thatcher's monetarist concept of the European Community. Though not standing myself I spoke for a number of them and was exhilarated by the response. The social charter made a big impact on our audiences. Our battlecry was: 'Do you want a Europe for the people or for the profiteers?' The result exceeded our expectations. Labour's tally rose to forty-five seats; the Tories' dropped to thirty-two. The most breathtaking victory was that of Anita Pollack, my former research assistant. She won London South-West with a majority of 500, which is about as close as you can comfortably get in an electorate of 500,000. She started firing with great effect the ammunition she once prepared for me.

TWENTY ONE

•

The Thatcher Counter-Revolution

WHEN, ON FRIDAY, 4 May 1979, Margaret Thatcher stood on the steps of 10 Downing Street, shyly waving to the crowd and quoting St Francis of Assisi, few of us realized she was about to launch a change of direction in public policy as fundamental as Labour's revolution in 1945. The difference was that hers was a counter-revolution. She had set her mind and her will on reversing every one of Labour's policies, and Labour's philosophy as well.

Some people argued that she had won and continued to win elections because she gave voice and respectability to a latent discontent with the welfare state, with the scrimshankers it was supposed to have bred, with government interference in people's lives and with the permissive society. The electors, it was suggested, blamed all these on Labour governments, and voted for a complete change of direction. I do not believe that to be true. Looking back, over my many years in Parliament and in government, I am struck by how relatively easily Labour could have avoided defeat in 1951, 1970 and 1979, given even a bit more political stamina, courage of our conviction and flexibility. People were voting not for a fundamental change of direction but for a little more money to spend and a little more colour in their lives. True, the Labour Party had scored a lot of own-goals with its much publicized splits, the trade unions had endangered their own birthright with unnecessary strikes, while the hairshirt brigade and the Calvinists in the party had given it a false killjoy image. But it was remarkable how loyal to Labour's values and the main tenets of Labour's social policy the majority stayed during this period, as the opinion polls showed despite all Margaret Thatcher's attempts to rubbish them.

Nor were people voting against the permissive society. There was no yearning for a return to the 'Victorian values' which Margaret Thatcher espoused. After thirteen years of Thatcher and neo-Thatcher rule there are more women having babies without husbands – sometimes from deliberate choice – than ever before in our history, and they are not social outcasts. If Margaret Thatcher set out to destroy the permissive society, she signally failed. There were more drug-takers and drug-pushers, more muggings, more vandals, more young people on the rampage for a rave at the end of her reign than at the beginning. People voted for her because she was fresh, youngish and vigorous, calling for radical change without being too specific about what it would involve. The Labour Party had thrown the election away.

People certainly had not voted for the monetarist doctrines which Margaret Thatcher proceeded to apply and which caused economic chaos, unparalleled in any Labour government in which I have served. She spent her period of preparation for office in the company of Sir Keith Joseph, the lugubrious monetarist, who loved to set out simplistic scenarios of disaster. He had been lugubrious as long as I had known him. He was lugubrious as Secretary of State for the Social Services when he produced his parsimonious reserve pension scheme, shaking his head all the time over the cost. He was still lugubrious as my shadow when I was in the same job, making gloomy speeches about the 'cycle of deprivation' which, he maintained, condemns some families to inescapable poverty – only for my Department to produce some effective statistics which I used to shoot him down. He had played a bit part in getting Margaret Thatcher into the leadership and brooded over her like an anxious godparent. She also sat at the feet of Milton Friedman, the American Professor who had won the Nobel Prize for Economics in 1976 for his monetary theory, presumably because it proclaimed a simple recipe for growth: cut the amount of money in circulation and the fall in inflation will do the rest. She also drank in the theories of the Austrian-born

economist, Professor Friedrich von Hayek, who carried the monetarist doctrines still further, dismissing with contempt any suggestion that governments could create and distribute wealth and
arguing that their only function was to set free the market forces
which alone could do it.

If the British people had voted for these doctrines they would
soon have regretted it. For once in office, Mrs Thatcher lost no
time in putting them to the test. She cheered on Geoffrey Howe,
her Chancellor of the Exchequer, when in his first Budget he cut
income tax, bringing the top rate down from 83 per cent to 60 per
cent and the standard rate from 33 per cent to 30 per cent, while
increasing VAT from Labour's 8 per cent to 15 per cent. He
sought to close the gap in revenue by raising £1 billion from the
sale of public assets, such as parts of British Petroleum, the start
of a drive for privatization which was to sweep the board. Public
expenditure was slashed by a further £1.5 billion, despite the
trimming which Denis Healey had carried out, and the nationalized industries, such as electricity, were forced to put up their
prices as government subsidies were reduced. Electricity prices
had increased by 50 per cent by the end of 1981. To tighten the
money supply still further, bank rate was raised from 12 per cent
to 14 per cent and the first steps taken to abolish exchange
controls. The medicine of crude monetarism, however, did not
have the desired effect and, despite the cuts in money supply, by
May 1980 inflation had risen from the 10 per cent Mrs Thatcher
had inherited to nearly 22 per cent. All that monetarism had
achieved through Geoffrey Howe's first Budget was a rise in
unemployment of 50 per cent and a drop in manufacturing output
of 9.5 per cent.

But Margaret Thatcher was undeterred. Boasting to the Tory
Party conference that 'The lady's not for turning,' she conspired
with Geoffrey Howe to produce a still more deflationary Budget
in 1981, cutting the public borrowing requirement by another
£3.5 billion. By this time, she had acquired another economic
adviser in Alan Walters, a former professor at the London School
of Economics, but at the time occupying a chair at the Johns
Hopkins University in Maryland, who was to become her favour-

ite. Under his influence, she stood firm against the predictable outcry which Sir Geoffrey's deflationary Budget had produced even among some members of her own Cabinet, whom she increasingly hounded as 'wets'. She was to get rid of anyone she did not regard as 'one of us'. In this way she was to shut herself in to her ideological laager, cut off from any more flexible influences.

But the economic facts were against her. Her theories were playing her tricks. Though inflation had been brought down to single figures (8.6 per cent), this had brought not growth but a dramatic drop in manufacturing output, which had the CBI warning against a slump. By the end of 1982 unemployment in Britain had risen to 3 million and bankruptcies had almost doubled.

I was in Strasbourg during this fraught period, though I visited my constituency as often as I could. Thanks to boundary redistribution, my constituency had changed slightly, giving me a slightly different mix of House of Commons constituencies. As the European elections of 1984 were not far away I told my party workers I wanted to visit every factory in my constituency, as I had done in 1979. 'What factories?' they replied. 'There are none left.' And they were right. I realized why, because I had paid a visit to Courtaulds' mill in Oldham, one of the largest spinning mills in Europe, a short while before. A harassed managing director clutched at my visit as a drowning man does at a straw. 'We are being ruined, Mrs Castle,' he told me in despair. 'Our productivity is unrivalled, but we simply can't compete any more, thanks to government policy. Our electricity charges have been pushed way above those of our competitors. Interest rates have gone up and the government is only concerned with pushing up the value of the pound, which makes our exports too dear. It simply is not interested in industry, and we cannot go on.' I could see what he meant by productivity when I toured the mill. The rows of automated machines stood in what seemed to be a vast empty spinning shed and I discovered that they were being supervised by just two men. There was no fat to squeeze out there. Six months later, this model of modernization had gone the way of the other factories in the area and had been closed down.

In April 1982 Argentina tried to annex Britain's Falkland Islands and all criticism of the government melted away as British serving men were sent thousands of miles across the Atlantic in a task force to recapture them. It was a risky venture which could have destroyed Margaret Thatcher, but her luck held. No Exocet missile sank Prince Andrew's ship, and British casualties were relatively small. She celebrated the first signs of victory on the famous Downing Street steps with a cry of triumphalism, a tendency to which she increasingly succumbed: 'Rejoice, just rejoice!' She was no doubt rejoicing herself, since her opinion poll rating jumped by 20 per cent. She also wisely, though discreetly, did her first U-turn by modifying her monetarist policy, redefining money supply in terms which gave her more room for manoeuvre. Inflation was continuing to fall and in his 1983 Budget Sir Geoffrey was able to give more tax reliefs. The Labour Opposition had not only been constrained by the jingoist fervour aroused by the Falklands war but was struggling with its internal battles, fired by the Campaign Group and the Bennites. Not least, it had to deal with the destructive role of the SDP/Liberal Alliance. The Alliance was expending more of its energies in denouncing the Labour Party, which it hoped to destroy, than the Thatcher government, which it had been persuaded to contemplate joining in a coalition government.

The result was that Margaret Thatcher swept back to power in the 1983 parliamentary election with a majority of 144. Watching from my European base what was happening at home, I soon realized that the second phase of her regime was the more dangerous. The failure of crude monetarism had become apparent to everyone, including her, but she had not given up her aim of transforming the values of British politics. Her guiding inspiration in all this was the Adam Smith Institute, a group of right-wing economists, which had been set up by Dr Madsen Pirie in 1977 as a think-tank for the market economy. It saw that it had a captive convert in Margaret Thatcher, and it remains active to this day, financed by company donations.

Margaret Thatcher was in sympathy with its aim of reducing the role of the government in national life, privatizing everything that could possibly be privatized. We got used to the Institute wanting to privatize education by destroying the state system and giving every parent vouchers to cover the cost of their children's education which they could spend anywhere. Again we got used to its desire to destroy the National Health Service and substitute private insurance schemes to make people dependent on private doctors and private hospitals. Nothing was to be sacrosanct – not even the prison service. Logically, the principle could apply to every aspect of public enterprise: from the Church of England to the monarchy. It is remarkable how many of its policy initiatives – wholesale deregulation of everything from credit institutions to bus companies, the contracting out of local government services to private enterprise, the reduction in the number and intellectual freedom of state universities, the introduction of competition wherever possible, not least in the NHS and education through the opting out of hospitals and schools from the local health and education authorities – were adopted by the Thatcher government and now form part of orthodox Conservative policy, though they had been unthinkable in earlier years. The whole process was backed up by a drastic reduction in income tax, made possible by equally drastic cuts in public expenditure. The Institute is far from satisfied that its job is done and is urging on the No Turning Back Group of the Tory right.

As its name implies, the Institute founded its thinking on the precepts of Adam Smith, Scotland's most prestigious economist. His *Wealth of Nations* is their bible, and I began to think I ought to re-read this book, which I had not looked at since my Oxford days. I was therefore intrigued some time later to be invited to take part in a wide-ranging international conference in Edinburgh organized by World Forum to celebrate the great man's bicentenary. The main theme was the role of government and the future of the world economy.

The conference was designed to give legitimacy, not only to Adam Smith's doctrines, but to the political ideologies which had been built on them. A number of politicians of international repute took part in it, including Ted Heath, who in typical fashion arrived late accompanied by a solitary bodyguard, so that he did not have to talk to anybody. As customary he spoke fluently without a note, about the need for European unity. He reduced the economists to size by declaring that the case for economic and monetary union was not economic but political. He thus gave the entire game away – and then disappeared.

At one of the formal dinners held during the conference I found myself seated next to Raymond Barre, former centrist Prime Minister of France, a lively, interesting man. We conducted our discussion in a mixture of French and English, which he spoke well. He was, of course, in favour of European union, but I was surprised to find how flexible he was. When I asked him if it was wise to press for economic and monetary union before we had achieved convergence of the real economies of the member states, he replied that it was not. 'We must achieve economic unity *de facto*,' he said, 'and then decide whether we need to do it *de jure* as well.' Exactly my point of view!

Thatcherite economists and politicians were well represented at the conference and I looked forward with some trepidation to the final session, at which I was due to speak. The title of that session was 'The Insolence of Government', a phrase from Adam Smith himself, and I could well imagine how the argument would go. I had by then re-read *Wealth of Nations* and, equally important, its companion volume, *Theory of Moral Sentiments*, and had begun to realize the enormity of the con trick which the Adam Smith Institute was seeking to play on the unsuspecting British people, now being dazzled by the self-certainties of the counter-revolutionaries. I had been put on to his track by my old friend Harold Lever, now practically housebound by the after-effects of a stroke but with a mind as acute as ever. Over a drink in his London flat he expounded to me one of his favourite themes: Adam Smith was the most misquoted writer in history. Those who distorted his message for their own ends had never read him properly.

Harold then juxtaposed two quotations: the first being the famous one in which Adam Smith declares that politicians mislead themselves if they imagine they can arrange the 'different members of a great society' like pieces on a chess board to do their economic will. They will follow their own motivations – self-interest and self-love. This was Margaret Thatcher's favourite theme, which led her to exclaim, 'There is no such thing as society' – only an aggregate of individuals the pursuit of whose self-interest was the key to growth. Government should be kept out of the picture to the maximum extent possible. She dismissed with contempt the social reformers, who 'drool and drivel' about caring. But Harold Lever's second quotation put a different light on things. 'Government has a duty', Smith wrote, 'of erecting and maintaining certain public works and certain public institutions' vital to the running of 'a great society', which would never be provided by individuals because 'the profit would never repay the expense to an individual'. I began to wonder why we had allowed Margaret Thatcher to impose her own version of Adam Smith on the British people, and on other countries too.

Thus fortified, I delved more deeply and was astonished by what I found. True, Smith was a firm believer in the market economy, but he was not a doctrinaire advocate of laissez-faire. His ideas for the role of government were obviously limited by the stage of development reached in the eighteenth century, when the state's activities comprised mainly defence, maintenance of the rule of law and the provision and construction of a transport system of roads, bridges and canals. But in one field he was prepared for the government to intervene to the point of being dictatorial – education. This sprang from his recognition of the social costs of the market economy. The growing phenomenon of the division of labour led, he maintained, to the mental mutilation of those condemned to spend their working lives on a few simple and repetitive operations, which bred 'torpor of the mind'. And he added, 'In every improved and civilized society this is the state into which the labouring poor, that is the great body of people, must necessarily fall, unless government takes some pains to prevent it.'

The discovery of these words came like a breath of fresh mountain air. This was William Morris and Ruskin all over again. Why were we socialists allowing the Thatcherites to disguise and distort these revelations of the dangers and inadequacies of the market economy? We were the real custodians of the 'great society'.

I was even more heartened when I discovered I was not alone, even in that right-wing seminar. The session previous to mine was addressed by Professor Andrew Skinner of Glasgow University, Scotland's acknowledged expert on Adam Smith. He cut through the idolatrous atmosphere by pointing out that Adam Smith had argued that men's pursuit of self-interest must be subject to a process of moral scrutiny and that Smith's criteria for government intervention had a far-reaching relevance in our modern society, based as they were on the principle that the government must control the activities of individuals which might damage the interests of society at large. It was therefore nonsense to quote him in favour of the argument that government had only a minor role to play in society. Government must also be prepared to provide the infrastructure of public works which the profit motive would not provide. Thus inspired, I sailed through my own speech the following day, indifferent to the coolness of the audience.

After the conference, Professor Skinner and I congratulated each other on the enlightenment we had introduced and pledged ourselves to keep up the struggle against the intellectual darkness that was clouding British politics.

But Mrs Thatcher, who had probably never read *Theory of Moral Sentiments*, continued to apply her version of Adam Smith's precepts, unmoved. She did not want to hear about Adam Smith's 'great society' because she did not believe in any society at all. Her whole philosophy was to set people free to do what they liked economically as an excuse for not having to do anything for them herself. I watched fascinated as she picked the bits out of *Wealth of Nations* which suited her preconceived prejudices, while ignoring its companion volume with its embarrassing interjections of interventionism. This selectivity dominated her whole approach, for to her economics was not a science but a branch of politics. Far from adapting her policies to economic laws, she invented economic laws to suit her policies. I myself used to argue when I was in the Labour government that making the economy work was a political art rather than the rigid application of certain economic rules. Just before the general election of 1970 I wrote an article for *The Times* about the problems we had to struggle with in implementing our prices and incomes policy. I wrote that inflation was a problem of psychology and could be dealt with only by an understanding of human beings rather than by the application of rigid monetary mechanisms.

Margaret Thatcher's political aims, however, were very different from mine. Because her most influential allies were the wealthy and powerful she evolved the concept of the incentive society in which the rich were to be helped to become richer still, the medium income-earners told to stand on their own feet and the poor at the bottom of the pile made to feel that it was their fault that they had failed. Her most remarkable quality was her ability to make this sound like a moral crusade. I used to listen dumbfounded as she denounced Labour's demand for closing the gap between rich and poor as 'the politics of envy', telling us that the only way to help the poor was to make the top stratum of wealth wealthier still so that a few more crumbs could come trickling down to those below. She even confronted the Churches with the claim that wealth-making was a Christian activity. Reminded of the parable of the Good Samaritan, she would retort that if he had not been rich he would not have been able to help the injured man found by the roadside – a view she managed to get away with at a time when the majority of the British people were pressing for more public money to be spent on their ambulance services; they would have been horrified to have to rely in an emergency on such rich private benefactors as might be passing by.

The mystery which puzzled us all was: how did she manage to get away with it? The longer she stayed in office the more uneasy the majority of people became about the sort of society she was developing, yet they could not break away from her mesmeric grasp. During the Euro-elections of 1989 I went to Chester to address a meeting on behalf of the candidate for the Euro-constituency of Cheshire West, Lyndon Harrison. Chester is a beautiful, relatively prosperous city with a Tory MP. The town hall was packed and some of the local party people on the platform identified half a dozen Tory women councillors in the hall. After reciting a list of Margaret Thatcher's iniquities I turned on the audience and declared, 'You have been like rabbits hypnotized by a stoat.' They took it very well and after the meeting the Tory councillors came behind the platform to shake me by the hand, though I doubt whether I had converted them. Cheshire West was one of our Labour gains in the Euro-elections, but Chester itself remained impregnably Tory in the general election of 1992.

In the meantime I had to sit frustrated in Strasbourg, watching Margaret Thatcher systematically dismantle the social policies Brian O'Malley and I had introduced. Labour's front-bench team in the Commons – notably Michael Meacher and Robin Cook – attacked her mercilessly. But they had not been in at the birth pangs of the policies as I had been, and I longed to be fighting alongside them in the Commons debates. The first casualty was our 'earnings link' for the pensioners. Mrs Thatcher was not too happy with the fact that, thanks to the Labour government, pensioners were for the first time entitled to an annual increase in line with prices – a commitment she dared not repudiate. She found it intolerable, however, that we had legislated to link their increase to the rise in earnings instead of prices if this was more favourable to the pensioners. At a time when earnings were leaping ahead of prices this added to the cost, and she promptly abolished it.

Her second attack was on the state earnings-related pensions scheme (SERPS), which Brian O'Malley and I had launched in 1978. Anything carrying the word 'state' was anathema to her, so this too had to be privatized. She began by trying to abolish the scheme outright, but the uproar was so great – not least among the modest middle class who had just helped to vote her into power – that she had to abandon the attempt and resort to more devious ways of undermining it. In the Social Security Act of 1986 SERPS became a parody of our original scheme. The inspired formula of 'twenty best earning years' was of course too socialist for her tastes, so it disappeared. Widows were allowed to inherit

THE THATCHER COUNTER-REVOLUTION

only half their husband's SERPS rights instead of the full amount as in our scheme. The Treasury supplement was progressively reduced until it was abolished in 1988, Nigel Lawson as Chancellor announcing that in future pension schemes would have to be self-financing. These deterrents were buttressed by bribes to contract out of SERPS and join private, personal pension schemes. Those doing so were given a bonus of 6 per cent for six years on their private pension contributions. By these means the government hoped to persuade enough of SERPS' 10 million contributors to contract out of the scheme to enable them to wind it up.

A private pensions industry hurried to exploit its new opportunities, bombarding potential customers with leaflets and advertisements holding out the vision of a secure old age. What they have carefully not made clear is that our concept of a guaranteed minimum pension had disappeared. The value of the pension to those joining these schemes will depend on what the fund can earn on the market – not a very reliable source of security in recent years. The Equal Opportunities Commission pointed out that women would be the worst sufferers. In a report entitled *Women and Pensions* compiled by Bryn Davies and Sue Ward, it pointed out that people on lower levels of income, such as women, have little to gain from personal pensions and can even lose from them. It estimates that 1 million of them will on average be better off by the magnificent sum of fifty pence a week and that a quarter of a million will end up being worse off 'in some cases by significant amounts'. It is obvious therefore that the aspiration to abolish poverty in old age, which Brian O'Malley and I set out to achieve in our redistributive scheme, has been abandoned.

Mrs Thatcher's counter to criticisms was that Brian and I had been too profligate. The government set out to frighten the voters with warnings about the 'high and rising' costs of provision in old age and how impossible our scheme made it to cut public expenditure. I was as aware as anyone of the limits to what we could ask the taxpayers to fund, and Brian and I had been careful to get the Actuary's assurance that the cost of our scheme was manageable. With the help of Michael Reddin, senior tutor at the London School of Economics, I did some more delving to meet the resurrection of these old arguments. Michael is a delightful man with a lively interest in and expert knowledge about the pensions field, and he pointed out some interesting facts to me. In 1988, when Margaret Thatcher was campaigning against the 'intolerable' burden of public expenditure, the people of this country were spending £300 million a week through taxes and contributions on state schemes of social security, exactly the same amount incidentally as they were spending on alcohol. Far from groaning under this burden, they were spending another £300 million on occupational pension schemes and a further £300 million on private pension endowment schemes and investment for old age in various forms. State provision, therefore, was only one-third of the amount people were prepared to pay for security in old age, and it delivered that security in a far more effective form for all but the most well-to-do.

Margaret Thatcher's third target was child benefit. As a benefit payable to every mother as of right in respect of every child regardless of family income, it was the biggest affront to her philosophy. Everyone, she believed, should stand on their own feet, and the drop-outs should depend on means-tested benefits. Yet here again she was afraid to attack frontally a benefit that was popular. The government's ploy therefore was to downgrade the child benefit by not uprating it every year in line with the cost of living. With another general election safely out of the way John Moore, Secretary of State for the Social Services, denounced the benefit because it did not 'target help to those who most need it'. He would therefore not increase it that year. A new word had come into the Thatcherite vocabulary: 'targeting'. It was used to justify the government's aim of extending means testing over the whole field of social services.

Under this banner child benefit was frozen for the next two years on the ground that it was going to people who did not need it because they were relatively well off. The Adam Smith Institute was demanding that child benefit should be paid only to those in need, arguing that child-bearing was a 'predictable and voluntary choice', so it was entirely reasonable that the burden of child

Top: The mandarins, Alex Jarrett and Denis Barnes, move in on me as I take over at the Department of Employment and Productivity in 1968.

Bottom: I lay down the law to Roy Thompson at a lunch he gave in honour of Governor Ronald Reagan whom I found desperately dull.

"She **WILL** keep bringing it back!"

Best wishes — TrG   Dec 3rd 1969

As Employment Secretary I fight loyally for the prices and incomes policy of the sixties, to the annoyance of Vic Feather, 1969.

No strife with the workers at Rootes factory, Linwood, even at the height of the argument over *In Place of Strife* in 1969.

My new cocker spaniel puppy, Printer, consoles me for the loss of his beloved predecessor, Aldie.

Top: 1970 is not 1945 – election meetings no longer draw a crowd.

Bottom: On the front bench in the House of Commons as Secretary of State for Social Services, 1974.

At a press conference of the Keep Britain Out campaign in 1975 my great-niece Rachel and I demonstrate how much dearer children's clothes are in the EC than in Britain.

Top: Harold Wilson and I exchange friendly banter at the 1975 party conference.

Bottom: Aerial photograph of Hell Corner Farm and its adapted barn – haven for my family for over thirty years.

Top left: With François Mitterrand in 1979.

Top right: I demonstrate the leghold trap at an Animal Welfare Exhibition in Strasbourg
with the aim of outlawing it throughout the world.

Bottom: Indignant French wine growers storm the European Parliament in 1986
and I go out to talk to them.

Ted and I celebrate our silver wedding at Hell Corner Farm in 1969.

support should rest on the parents: 'The state is not justified in interfering in these matters at all.' John Moore declared that the indiscriminate handing out of benefit had undermined the will to self-help and that 'people had become ever more dependent on an ever more powerful state'. The real reason for wanting to means-test child benefit was of course financial. It would save £3 billion a year, equivalent to a reduction in income tax of three pence.

Nigel Lawson, the new Chancellor of the Exchequer, had meanwhile introduced his spectacular give-away Budget of 1988. By this time the government was benefiting from the steady flow of revenue from North Sea oil to the tune of about £5 billion a year and also from what Harold Macmillan in almost his last speech (to the House of Lords) described disparagingly as 'selling the family silver': in other words, the sale of public assets to swell the coffers of the Treasury. Nigel Lawson's Budget was a perfect demonstration of the Thatcherite philosophy. He had some £9 billion to play with, and, shortly before, the Commons all-party Select Committee on the National Health Service had recommended that it needed another £2 billion pumped into it to keep it properly afloat. Instead he diverted some £4 billion to tax cuts, 45 per cent of which went to the country's richest 5 per cent. The wealthy of the country had their top rate of tax cut from 60 per cent to 40 per cent. The middle range of taxpayers who had benefited from the reduction in the standard rate of income tax to 25 per cent, fared more modestly. Only the bottom 30 per cent of the population did not benefit at all, since most of them were on means-tested benefits against which any tax reliefs were offset. Shortly afterwards I was addressing another rally in Neil Kinnock's constituency and I almost spat out, 'They call that targeting!' As far as child benefit was concerned the Budget proved our case. During the 1987 campaign I watched a Tory Party political broadcast featuring a smartly dressed woman in a well-furnished home who said, 'I don't need child benefit, the money should go to somebody else.' It sounded good, but I calculated that the family in question probably had an income of at least £41,000 a year. If so the family would have benefited from Lawson's budget to the tune of £10,000 a year. As I said in a series of speeches, what the woman did not say was 'I do not need it. Give it to the poor.'

One of Margaret Thatcher's most revealing changes was in the social fund. Ever since Beveridge all parties have accepted that there must be state provision to help destitute people in emergencies. It was useless, for instance, to move a single parent or a young couple on a low wage with young children into new accommodation if they had no cooker or even a gas ring on which to prepare their children's food, no bed to sleep in, not even a cot for the new baby. Previous governments, therefore, had given the local Social Security offices discretionary power to make grants to meet these basic needs. With unemployment rising and more people falling into poverty the claims on the fund began to rise steeply, and Margaret Thatcher decided to step in. In 1986 the basis of the fund was changed. A ceiling was set on its annual expenditure and if an emergency case arose when the money ran out it was too bad. Cross-examined on television about what would happen to the applicants in this case, a junior minister in the Social Services Department replied, 'They can always go to charity.' The Churches and the voluntary organizations could not believe their ears: this was taking us straight back to Dickens' day.

Even more grotesque was the decision that two-thirds of the Social Fund payments must be in the form of loans, which merely put off a family's crisis to the moment when the loan had to be repaid. The most notable characteristic of Thatcherite social policy was not so much its meanness as the fact that it did not work. As an MEP I often visited Salford, one of the poorest parts of my Euro-constituency, to talk to the voluntary bodies trying to cope with the problems of the area. They struggled along with the help of small grants from the Labour local authority and hoped I would manage to get them a bit of money from the Euro-pot of gold, which I occasionally did. They did not need any lecturing from Mrs Thatcher about self-help, their efforts being directed towards helping the unemployed to launch modest enterprises which would give them work. Typical were the launderettes I visited which women on a couple of housing estates had opened up with advice and a little financial boost from the voluntary organizations. As I talked to the women, who were full of a mixture of apprehension and pride, I could only hope their launderettes survived the increasing pressures of local poverty.

At one of these gatherings I talked to an eager young woman from the local Social Security office. She was anxious about the upward twist the government's changes in the Social Fund had given to the habit of borrowing. 'The most worrying problem in this area', she told me, 'is debt.' The poorer people were, the more likely they were to be up to their ears in it. Pestered by their children at Christmas time they would take out a small loan from a persuasive moneylender, only to find that rates of interest of 50 per cent or more were beyond their means and they had to borrow more to pay the interest – and that was without repaying the initial debt. They had got themselves into a trap from which they could not escape. The Social Fund loans were interest-free, but they were too sparse and too limited to be much help.

Margaret Thatcher's spectacular victory in 1983 enabled her to carry of these Scrooge-like versions of social policy. In any case she was a past master at covering her reactionary tracks. Michael Meacher laboured in vain to arouse public anger at the way she disguised the real level of unemployment by changing the method by which it was calculated no less than thirty times in twelve years. She brutally pushed all the wets out of her Cabinet, sacking the moderate ˉTory, Francis Pym, and relegating Jim Prior, another moderate, to Northern Ireland, a job he did not want. Lord Carrington resigned over the Falklands war. It was he who had manoeuvred her into a Rhodesia settlement which recognized the strength of African nationalism, as Harold Wilson had failed to do. In Carrington she lost one of the most civilized voices in her government. The resignation of Michael Heseltine, whom she humiliated over the purchase of Westland helicopters, was a different kind of loss. Heseltine, of the brash manner and tawny hair, was still the not-so-young Tarzan who could stir the pulses of Tory Party conferences. By letting him go she had placed a potential rival in the wings.

But Margaret Thatcher did not care. She now considered

herself impregnable. I have seen politicians destroy themselves with '*folie de grandeur*', notably de Gaulle, but her turn was some time away. Supremely confident, she proceeded to introduce an autocratic style of presidential government. All rival centres of power had to be suppressed, including the trade unions, though she weakened them more by means of unemployment than by the legislation she introduced to curb their power. I noted with interest that even she dared not reintroduce Ted Heath's Industrial Relations Act, no doubt wary of the legalistic shambles which had followed it. She also debilitated local government in every way possible, not only reducing the authorities' funds but taking away their powers. She also set out to demote the universities.

Mrs Thatcher had an innate dislike of intellectual independence and intellectual activity for its own sake: everything had to have a commercial purpose and pay its way. One of her first moves was to cut government spending on higher education, a process which she continued so relentlessly that in 1984 the dons of Oxford University delivered her an unprecedented snub. By a large majority they turned down the proposal to give her the honorary degree it was customary for them to award to prime ministers. They issued a statement declaring that she had done 'deep and systematic damage to the whole public system of education in Britain from the provision to the youngest child up to the most advanced research programmes'. She brushed the attack aside with a Mandy Rice-Davies quip: 'They would, wouldn't they?' It was all grist to her mill and she set out to enfeeble powerful sectional interests one by one, implying that they were all living comfortable lives on the backs of the hard-pressed taxpayers. It was part of her appeal to the lowest instincts of her listeners.

The BBC was soon in her sights. It was by definition another institution which she disliked, publicly funded and independent of government. She lost no opportunity to depict it as an inefficient and expensive bureaucracy run by wets. Her weapon was to pare down the BBC's share of the licence fee, which she knew was unpopular anyway, forcing it to sacrifice some of its prestigious productions in an effort to become more 'popular'. She preferred commercial television, because its advertisements encouraged the consumerism which was the mainstay of her economic policy. To its credit ITV has shown that it too can have a mind of its own and a cultural taste to rival that of the BBC. Ironically it was Granada which produced such masterpieces as *Jewel in the Crown* and *Brideshead Revisited*, while the BBC was reintroducing Bruce Forsyth's *Generation Game*.

Margaret Thatcher was never interested in quality. Her final betrayal of standards came in the Broadcasting Bill of 1990, which provided for the new television franchises to be allocated to the highest bidder, with no quality criteria involved at all. Only a revolt by the House of Lords saved television from this crude test: the peers insisted that bidders also had to show they were producing programmes of quality. Nonetheless the process forced up the bids to astronomical heights, and the television companies have been struggling to recoup their costs ever since by increasing their advertising revenue. I was astonished to see the other day that ITV's production of *Rumpole of the Bailey* by my good friend John Mortimer not only had the usual commercial breaks, but was preceded and followed by the legend 'Sponsored by Crofts Port'. This has now become common form. Another favourite programme *Inspector Morse* comes to us by courtesy of Beamish Stout.

Commercial values have now been installed at the centre of our social and cultural life. The government's aim in cutting back public funding for the universities or the BBC is to compel these once intellectually free centres to seek commercial sponsorship. This sometimes reaches comical heights and sometimes dangerous ones. On a recent visit to the Oxford Union to take part in a debate I was astonished to find that sponsorship has penetrated even that establishment. The President announced that the bottle of champagne due to be given to the undergraduate who had been voted the best backbench debater of the year had been donated by a prominent firm whose name of course had to be blazoned forth. The motion for the debate was that 'Freedom in Britain has declined in the past ten years'. In supporting it I said how shocked I was by the creeping commercialization of our universities. 'In my days in St Hugh's,' I told them, 'we were poor, but we were not sponsored. We were free.' I was delighted that, although the motion was opposed by the plausible Mr David Mellor, we carried our motion handsomely.

On another visit to one of our top universities I found forms of sponsorship that were more dangerous. I asked the head of graduate research at the university, to whom I talked over lunch, what piece of research they were currently engaged on. He said Altzheimer's disease. Where did they get their money from? The Medical Research Council? 'A little from the Medical Research Council,' he replied, 'but mainly from the pharmaceutical industry.' 'Do they bring any pressure to bear on you?' I asked. He hesitated and said, 'We are steered.' So much for the vaunted independence of British universities.

The Labour Party had been slow to realize that in Margaret Thatcher we were up against a new phenomenon. The lady, as our bewildered front bench soon found, was no gentleman. This was not the type of politician with whom Clem Attlee, Hugh Gaitskell, Harold Wilson and Roy Jenkins had had to deal. They knew where they were with the Rab Butlers, Harold Macmillans and Ted Heaths, who played within certain accepted parameters. The battles were serious, but they were civilized. This Prime Minister was totally unscrupulous. Those who had been in government were astonished at the way she manipulated her civil service, which seemed too cowed to resist her political appointments in the career service, as they would have done had Labour attempted such partisanship. Bernard Ingham acted more like her personal political bodyguard than as the spokesman for government policy. Spending on government advertising shot up from £67 million in 1986 to £150 million in 1988, and the all-party Select Committee on Treasury Affairs rebuked the government for producing partisan propaganda with public money instead of merely reporting on government activities. Margaret Thatcher obviously agreed with Louis XIV's dictum, 'L'état, c'est moi.'

Under Neil Kinnock's influence the Labour Party had begun to brighten its image and modernize its ideas, but there was a long way to go. Apart from him few of our party leaders and even less of the rank and file appreciated how flexible and adaptable we had to be to combat Margaret Thatcher's populist ingenuity. Most of them yearned for the old, simple battle-lines, particularly the trade unions. This was glaringly apparent when Arthur Scargill launched his miners' strike in 1984. It epitomized the tug-of-war going on in the party between those hankering after the militancy of the past and the realists who recognized that the political ball-game had radically changed and that we had to find new ways to deal with it. The whole party, of course, responded to the miners' appeal for support. Arthur Scargill had brought them out on strike in protest against the intended closure of twenty pits and the loss of 20,000 jobs, a clear reversal of the Plan for Coal which the Labour government had negotiated with the industry and the unions in the 1970s. We must show solidarity.

Money poured in from the rank and file. We MEPs contributed £12 a week from our pay to the Miners' Fund and organized a Christmas whip-round in Strasbourg for the miners' children, to which Members from different groups and countries responded sympathetically, throwing their foreign money into our collecting bag as we sang carols around a Christmas tree which we had strategically placed just outside the debating chamber. All over the country local miners did their stint on the picket lines, while their wives organized support groups, some of which sent deputations to Strasbourg. Others ran food kitchens for the children.

There were strains of pure idealism running through the year-long strike, but my heart was heavy. Scargill had committed the crucial error of calling the strike without a ballot, thus dividing his membership. He had called it in the summer when coal stocks were high, the least propitious time. Margaret Thatcher stood grimly firm in her determination to smash the NUM. Her chosen instrument was Ian MacGregor, the Scottish-born American businessman she had brought in to run the Coal Board. He was a very different type from his predecessor, Derek Ezra, who had helped to draw up the Plan for Coal. This was overt war. Most of the picket lines were peaceful, but the mass pickets Scargill organized at key pits ran into violent clashes with the police. Some police were injured, but so were many miners, thirty-nine of them while picketing the Orgreave colliery. They later won half a million pounds in damages and costs from the South Yorkshire police for the injuries inflicted on them.

Despite these violent scenes relayed on television public opinion remained remarkably sympathetic to the miners' cause. The miners were winning the battle psychologically and the public was looking for a compromise. But I was also worried by the mounting hysteria among the party rank and file whipped up by Arthur Scargill and heightened by Tony Benn. They were not interested in compromise and even talked of extending the dispute into a general strike. At our 1984 conference Scargill excelled himself in an emotional speech which brought the delegates to their feet, spilling over into the aisles, dancing, singing and waving their order papers as though the battle were already won. As I tried to make my way down the aisle to my seat on the platform, a jubilant woman from the trade union section grabbed me and said reprovingly, 'Aren't you cheering, Barbara?' 'I must get to the platform,' I muttered and pulled away. I did not feel like cheering, because I knew we could only win this battle politically and not by open industrial war. In July Scargill had turned down a conciliatory overture into which Ian MacGregor had been forced by public opinion, offering to set up the joint review body on closures which the NUM had been demanding. Apart from its tactical value, this retreat by MacGregor would have been a great political victory for the miners. Instead, faced by Scargill's snub, he decided that the only thing to do was to fight it out to the bitter end. In March 1985, Scargill led his defeated troops ignominiously back to work, with nothing to show for a year's suffering.

Neil Kinnock had no more enthusiasm for Scargill's tactics than I had and was bitterly attacked by the Scargill fans for 'betraying' him. Neil's behaviour during the strike had been perfectly correct, but like me he had little use for a general whose egoism had led his troops into an avoidable defeat and opened the way for the further conquests a triumphant Margaret Thatcher was now planning.

Margaret's triumph was based on an egoism which made Arthur Scargill look like a modest man. After Nigel Lawson had launched his Budget of 1988 I watched her declaim on television, 'This is the death-knell of socialism.' In fact it was the first sounding of her own death-knell.

Few people now deny that this Budget was economically disastrous. Already there were signs that the deregulation of credit which had been introduced in 1986 was leading to the overheating of the economy. For a time, no one cared, as the inevitable boom took place and people rushed into a spending bonanza on borrowed money. The age of the yuppie had arrived. Brilliant young sharebrokers, operating their new electronic links with the world, made fortunes on the Stock Exchange. House prices soared as people rushed to take out bigger mortgages. All this, Margaret Thatcher declared, was the result of 'enterprise', as she toured the country visiting ambitious new projects that confident entrepreneurs had launched, many of which collapsed shortly afterwards. We in the Labour Party could only watch helplessly as the national euphoria took off. Cassandras were not popular.

But it was not to last. The balance-of-payments deficit rose to an unprecedented £20 billion as the hyper-rich bought their yachts and other luxuries abroad. From a low of 3.7 per cent in May 1983, inflation climbed back to 9 per cent. The Treasury was forced to draw in its horns, and by October 1989 interest rates had been raised to 15 per cent. The recession had begun.

Other warnings were sounding which Margaret Thatcher would not listen to. When in opposition, certain that she had an answer to everyone's anxieties, she had promised that she would abolish the rating system, since a revaluation in Scotland had pushed up the rates of many of her supporters, who were consequently up in arms. Finding an alternative had proved a bit more difficult than she had anticipated, but once again her political prejudices produced the simple answer she was looking for. It was the poll tax, which she described as the 'flagship' of her third term, and so it was. It was based on the principle that everyone, however poor, should contribute something to local revenues. The idea was that they should be given an incentive to vote against the very Labour councils which were seeking to provide them with the services they needed most. Once again I marvelled at Margaret Thatcher's ingenuity, but once again she had over-reached herself.

She had no use for redistributive tax systems and it seemed to her perfectly natural that everyone using local services should pay the same community charge per head, though some qualified for rebates – for example, pensioners paid 20 per cent of the charge. The press began to run stories about the resulting anomalies: the dustman in his council house paying as much as the duke on his large estate. The bills of the lower-income groups shot up, while those of the wealthy dropped dramatically.

The young man who did gardening work for me came to see me, white with rage. He had a wife and a small baby and lived in a little low-rated cottage near to mine. He had already been crippled by rising mortgage rates and now faced a poll-tax bill which was as high as mine, though my cottage was four times the size of his. I agreed that it was outrageous, and added sweetly, 'But then I did not vote Conservative.' 'I will never vote Conservative again,' he replied passionately.

The *coup de grâce* came from the least expected quarter – Sir Geoffrey Howe, whom Mrs Thatcher had made Foreign Secretary when she sacked one of the wets in her Cabinet, Sir Francis Pym, some years earlier. Geoffrey was a mild-mannered man whom it was impossible to dislike. He had a good mind, but he was no firebrand and was one of the dullest speakers in the House. He was also a keen European, and Margaret Thatcher's hostile attitude to Brussels and all its works increasingly alienated him and worried the pro-Europeans in her Cabinet. Deceived by his gentle exterior, she believed she could humiliate him with impunity, a process which culminated in her demoting him against his will from Foreign Secretary to Leader of the House. In November 1990 he resigned from the government and a few days later took his revenge in a speech of measured ferocity which shook the House. I regret to this day that I was not in the chamber to hear it, though I had by then become a member of the House of Lords and could have had a vantage point in the peers' gallery. But his controlled hatred came through even in the reported speech, as he told the House he had wrestled with his conscience for perhaps too long and that the time had come for other people to examine theirs. MPs could hardly believe their ears. This was not the man whom Denis Healey had once derided as a 'dead sheep' but a maker of history.

The speech rendered a contest for the leadership inevitable and the following day Michael Heseltine, waiting in the wings, came forward to challenge her. To the end she believed that she would win, but when under the Tory electoral system she was robbed of victory in the first ballot by four votes, a host of once-loyal colleagues crowded in to pressurize her not to go to a second ballot, warning her that she would split the party and might even lose. On 22 November she resigned and the way was open for other contestants to take the field and for John Major to assume the leadership.

In the corridor of the Commons I ran into Elaine Kellet-Bowman, a Tory MP and MEP with whom I had crossed swords several times in the European Parliament. She was jubilant about John Major's victory. 'Did you vote for him?' I asked and she said, 'Of course.' Then she added hastily, 'Of course, I voted for Margaret first. We are old friends.' I realized then that Labour faced a new kind of challenge. The Tories with their usual cleverness had shot our fox and changed to a different type of leadership. We would have to change our tactics too.

TWENTY TWO

———————— • ————————

The Watershed Election

MARGARET THATCHER'S political demise was a blow to Labour. She had been an easy target with her poll tax and the savagery of her social policies. Even her gutsy 'there is no alternative' qualities had become a liability. There are tides in politics which ebb and flow. The tide of toughness had carried her to its peak. Now I believed that it was ebbing and a gentler tide was coming in. Under the exterior of hard materialism which she had clamped on the country, most people wanted to get back to the more caring society.

Overall, therefore, the prospects for Labour were brighter than for many years. True, John Major was an ideal successor from the Conservative Party's point of view. A mild-mannered man with a pleasant smile and humble background, he was able to give credibility to his claim that he represented a 'classless society', but it was soon clear that he was not going to make any serious break with Margaret Thatcher's economic priorities. Michael Heseltine, back in the government at Environment, had taken the sting out of the poll tax, but his proposed new council tax still retained some of the undesirable elements of the original tax, failing to include a clear-cut formula for 'ability to pay'. Norman Lamont, the new Chancellor, stuck stubbornly to deflationary policies, which he could not carry off with Margaret Thatcher's verve. When, in 1991, those out of work reached 2.3 million, he shocked the Labour benches by maintaining that unemployment was 'a price worth paying', a phrase he was never allowed to forget.

As the months went by, a series of disasters befell the new government. Unemployment rose at the rate of 3000 a day. The balance-of-payments deficit reached £4.4 billion, with the government forced to raise its borrowing requirement to the record level of £18 billion in order to finance even reduced expenditure of the social services. Business failures were running at 200 a day and home repossessions at 300 a day. Manufacturing output and investment fell below the level the Labour government had achieved in 1979 and growth was negative for five quarters in succession – the official definition of recession. It seemed that no government could achieve another term of office against such a scenario.

The Labour Party, too, was in better shape than it had been for years. Neil Kinnock had done a Herculean job cleaning out the Augean stables of inefficient organization and out-of-date attitudes. It was an inspired move to appoint Peter Mandelson as director of campaigns and communications to give the party a new look. Peter was a deceptively quiet young man who knew exactly what he wanted to change in order to make Labour more saleable. He was not everyone's cup of tea and I sometimes thought his cosmetic efforts went too far, but I was immensely grateful to find at the first party conference after his appointment that the platform on which we members of the NEC sat had been transformed. Instead of the old trestle table draped with thin red muslin there was a shining white set on modern lines, and I sank thankfully into my place, knowing that I would no longer snag my tights. The simple backdrop was adorned with a red rose – the new party symbol he had chosen. I liked the symbol, which was used by a number of continental socialists, though I remarked that I wished the one on the platform had been painted a bit less pink. It was my first moment of unease.

Within months, Neil moved in on the shambles at party headquarters and carried out a root-and-branch reorganization of the way it was run. He secured the agreement of the NEC to the merging of the Home Policy and International Departments, which had operated as little kingdoms in their own right, into a central policy directorate. One of the results was that Tony Benn lost his power base as chairman of the Home Policy Committee. Although he had been returned to Parliament in 1985 in a by-election at Chesterfield, helped by Arthur Scargill and miners' delegates from the area, Tony had become sidelined by Neil's changes and was increasingly isolated as the mouthpiece of the hard left. By 1985, he was down to third place in the constituency section of the NEC.

Neil also brought order into the chaotic procedures by which policy decisions were made at party conference. He got conference to agree to the setting up of seven policy groups manned by representatives of the NEC and Shadow Cabinet to review the major areas of policy and report on the changes the party should make.

Most remarkable of all was the courage with which he took on Militant. Local parties had been cowering under its intrigues for years. MPs went in fear of it in case its representatives, who had permeated their constituencies, were able to unseat them at their reselection conferences. I had watched in dismay how the mandatory reselection process was abused. Two of my MEP colleagues – Derek Enright of Leeds and Brian Keyes of Yorkshire South – had been its casualties in the reselection of the Euro-election of 1987. Though hard-working and conscientious MEPs, they had fallen victim to the manoeuvrings of the hard left. The Executive's national organizer, Reg Underhill, had been warning the party for some time about the 'entryism' or permeation of the Labour Party, which the Trotskyites through Militant had been practising for some time, but there was a great resistance in the party to intolerance. The Labour Party must be a broad church of the left. In any case, it was argued, not least by Michael Foot, the party could not declare that it was incompatible with membership to buy a newspaper. So *Militant*, with its anti-party message, continued to be sold outside the conference hall with impunity.

Neil decided the time had come to attack this scourge frontally. He did so at the 1985 Labour Party conference in the most courageous and effective speech I have heard a politician make. His target was Derek Hatton, deputy leader of the Militant dominated Labour Group in Liverpool, who had established a bossdom which ran the city. The Council, whose populist policies at first attracted a lot of support, ended in financial chaos, as a result of which the Council had to sack a large number of its staff. Neil pulled no punches. 'You start with far-fetched resolutions,' he told his dazed audience,

> they are then pickled into a rigid dogma, a code, and you go through the years sticking to that, outdated, misplaced, irrelevant to the real needs, and you end in the grotesque chaos of a Labour Council – a *Labour* Council – hiring taxies to scuttle round the City handing out redundancy notices to its own workers. I'm telling you, no matter how entertaining, how fulfilling to short-term egos, you can't play politics with people's jobs and with people's services or with people's lives.

His defiant challenge ran through the delegates like an electric shock. There were shouts of anger from Derek Hatton and his entourage. Eric Heffer, who as an MP for Liverpool had always defended Militant's right to express its views, stalked ostentatiously off the platform. But the protests were drowned by counter-cheers, and delegates streamed out of the hall arguing excitedly. I myself feared that Neil had gone too far, but I was wrong. He had broken the cobweb of sentimentality with which many in the party shrouded Militant, and local parties up and down the country were emboldened to stand up to the entryists.

The Bennites and the hard left watched these developments with growing anxiety. They accused Neil of autocratic leadership, and in one sense they were right. I need not have feared that Neil would be a lightweight. He now moved in with a steely determination to get his own way. He believed that unless the party won the next election it was finished, and he made this his overriding priority. Even some of the soft left, including loyal people like Christine Crawley in the British Labour Group, began to get worried about Neil's high-handedness. In one of my talks with him when I was leader of the British Labour Group I said to him, 'Neil, your job is to detach the soft left from the hard left. Some of them have got confused.' 'Tell them they've got to stand up and be counted,' he snapped back impatiently. Despite some quibbles, however, most members of the party, conscious of its fragile state, were only too glad to welcome strong leadership.

The policy review groups, their membership supplemented by outside experts, worked assiduously. As a member of the Agriculture Committee of the European Parliament, I was made a member of the group dealing with agriculture. I pressed my plan for reform of the CAP with great vigour, but I could not get them to accept my document. This was despite the fact, as I pointed out, that a number of independent economists such as Lionel Hubbard and David Harvey of the Department of Agricultural Economics at Newcastle University had been advocating reform along much the same lines for some time. My proposals were far too radical for a party now cautiously feeling its way to political acceptability. I deplored this timidity. In fact I found most of the review group's reports in their glossy covers too wordy and anodyne. I did not believe that we could win our way back to power by refusing to be bold.

In the first years of his leadership Neil was in ebullient mood, certain that he could purge the party of its past excesses and carry it to power again. Laour's defeat in 1987 shook his self-confidence and he never completely recaptured it. For the Tories to win a majority of 102 seats in that election, despite the great improvement in Labour's organization and image and the toning down of its policies, was shattering.

His reaction was to redouble his efforts to sacrifice the sacred cows of policy he thought had lost us votes. The most obvious of these was unilateral nuclear disarmament, with which the Tories had made great play. Neil was in a trap. He had been an ardent supporter of CND and of the party's line, so if he reversed it now he would be jeered at as a man who ditched his principles to get office. If he did not he would be hamstrung by a policy in which even a large number of our own supporters did not believe. Most working-class people had a simple reflex action on defence: 'As long as they've got the bomb, we must have it.'

I myself had no doubt at all that the time had come to change our policy, not just to win votes, but because the world situation had changed. There is no virtue in sticking to a formula which is outdated by events. Having spoken at a rally with Neil during the 1987 campaign I had flown back to London with him and his entourage in his executive plane. Over a drink I said to him, 'Neil, I see no difficulty at all about our going multilateral. Gorbachev is in power. The cold war is melting like butter in the sun. From my recent visit to Moscow I am convinced that Gorbachev desperately needs to disarm, so much so that he is prepared to go a bit unilateral himself. Our unilateralism was common sense as long as the two nuclear superpowers refused to negotiate. Now the Russians at any rate are only too eager to do so, and our job is to see that the West responds quickly and positively to the possibility of multilateral disarmament.' I believe I helped him to clear his mind and brace himself for the accusations which poured in on him when he persuaded the party to come out unequivocally for a multilateral policy.

I was less happy about Neil's acceptance of the economic doctrine which made currency stability and the reduction of inflation the overriding priorities of economic policy regardless of the effect on growth and jobs. His new devotion to Europe made him an easy prey to the arguments of his economic team, led by John Smith, that Britain should join the Exchange Rate Mechanism as soon as possible. We should then move on to a single currency and a European central bank, with a view to establishing economic and monetary union in due course. Certain conditions were laid down for Britain joining the ERM. The economic circumstances would have to be right and we should join with a realistic valuation of sterling, not an exaggerated one. These not very emphatic caveats, however, were swamped in the front bench campaign to prove that the Tories were dragging their feet over Europe by refusing to join the ERM, while Labour was straining at the leash to prove what good Europeans we were. This political pressure undoubtedly influenced John Major, who had been maintaining quite rightly that the time was not ripe, into deciding to take the plunge.

When, therefore, Norman Lamont announced on 5 October 1990 that he had taken Britain into the ERM at the ludicrously high rate of 2.95 Deutschmarks to the pound, Labour had thrown away its own line of attack. When the news came at the tail end of the Labour Party conference at Blackpool John Smith was unable to exploit the government's economic difficulties by saying we had been too weak to join. Nor could he complain that sterling had been overvalued without provoking the jibe from the government: 'Labour wants to devalue again.' We had put ourselves in the same straitjacket as in 1964–7 when it was taboo to mention the word devaluation, even in Cabinet. Most of the press commentators thought that the rate fixed for sterling was far too high, but when John Smith was asked by an interviewer whether he agreed I was dismayed to hear him brush the question aside as irrelevant. He did not even dare to say that there should be a general realignment of all the currencies in the ERM.

There was a strong section of the party which was deeply unhappy about this policy. At a fringe meeting at the conference the following year I took part in a debate on ERM with Chris Smith, MP for Islington South and Finsbury, one of John Smith's Treasury team. I have always had an affectionate regard for Chris Smith, who is a charming and enlightened man, but I was horrified to hear him repeating all the orthodox arguments as though he believed in them. What industry needed above all, he maintained, was to be able to predict the value of the pound a few years ahead; by giving that stability to the currency our membership would enable us to bring interest rates down. I argued the exact opposite. Being linked in the ERM to the strongest currency in Europe, the Deutschmark, we would be forced to keep putting up interest rates in order to hold our own. This process would merely weaken our industry and make us even less competitive. This argument was justified when in September 1992 a desperate Mr Lamont, faced with a deepening recession, took Britain out of the ERM again.

The party, therefore, went into the general election of May 1992 in a split state of mind. On the one hand we had the satisfaction of seeing the government get deeper and deeper into difficulties in a recession which was worsening all the time. On the other we seemed inhibited by our support of the ERM from exploiting those difficulties to the full. There were plus factors. Our organization was good and I was impressed by the efficiency of the campaign officer, Kathy Sands, who arranged my speaking engagements on visits to constituencies. I also found most local parties' in a good state of preparedness. We oldies were on the campaign trail. I kept getting snatches of reports of Denis Healey glad-handing everyone in market places and cheeking them out-rageously. Michael Foot, too, was on the stumps. Big unions like the General and Municipal Workers and the Transport Workers played an unobtrusive but important role ferrying speakers around, and I struck up brief but warm friendships with the trade unionists who drove me to and fro. The omens were favourable as the polls showed us neck and neck with the Tories with every chance of overtaking them. Yet I found it difficult to gauge the national mood.

One of my tours was of Tory marginals in the south-east, where we had done so badly in the previous election and where we had to make considerable inroads if we were to win. I certainly sensed a swing towards us but not the sort of warm response we had got in London South-East when I campaigned with Anita Pollack in the Euro-elections of 1989. Passers-by then waved to us as we paraded with our posters. They took our leaflets eagerly and said 'Of course' when we asked them if they were voting Labour. This time they were less forthcoming. The reception was warmer in some constituencies than in others. In Ilford South, for example, Mike Gates, our energetic and able candidate, told me exuberantly that his canvass returns showed the 8 per cent swing to us which we needed for victory. His optimism was justified, for he won the seat. In Harlow on the other hand, another of our key marginals, I did not feel the same confidence and despite the valiant efforts of Will Hammell, our candidate, who halved the Tory majority, we did not pull it off.

And yet in some ways the south-east had felt the effects of depression more acutely than my old stamping ground of the north-west, which had always been a depressed area and looked with envy at the prosperity of the south at the height of Margaret Thatcher's boom. I sensed the chill of recession when I visited

Wandsworth open-air marketplace, a famous gathering ground for shoppers from all over the area. It was epitomized by a young man who was sitting in total dejection, head in hands, by his deserted clothing stall. When I spoke to him he said to me desperately, 'They must give the working man more money or we are all finished.' If his attitude was representative we should have walked to victory. Yet I felt the local mood was probably reflected more accurately by another stallholder who, after being very ambiguous about his voting intentions, jumped at the chance of being photographed with me by the photojournalists who were following me around. The March weather had turned against us and I found myself inadequately clothed in a biting wind. A local comrade had hurried to protect me with a warm, if rather shabby, woollen coat which reached to my ankles. As the brash stallholder put his arm round me for the benefit of the cameras, I must have looked like his old moll.

There was ambivalence, too, in the north-west when I went to campaign in parts of my old Euro-constituencies. In Bury South, Hazel Blears, one of the able young Labour women who were coming to the fore, was bursting with self-confidence. The atmosphere seemed good and she could not believe the returning officer when in due course he announced that she had lost by some 800 votes. It also seemed inevitable that we should win Bolton North, where David Crausby, an outstanding young trade unionist with some radical and unorthodox ideas about how the trade union movement should modernize itself, faced a Tory majority of only 800. Yet incredibly his Tory opponent survived, albeit by only 185 votes. Other hopefuls in the area were disappointed, too. We had failed once again to crack the Lancashire Tory nut.

As the campaign progressed it became clear that the Tories' tactic was to concentrate on rubbishing Labour's leadership. They dared not fight on their own policies, which had so abysmally failed, but they had learned from Margaret Thatcher always to turn a defensive position into an aggressive one. Their main target was Neil himself. They knew he was self-conscious about his own lack of ministerial experience, and they played on this mercilessly and on other chinks in his armour to destroy his self-confidence.

In this I believe they succeeded to a considerable extent. He was never as sure of his economic facts as Shadow Chancellor John Smith was, and the Tory ploy was to play off one against the other. This was backed by a persistent refrain in the pro-government press – and to some extent in the opinion polls – that Labour could not win under Kinnock and that, if John Smith were leader, things might be different. There were even some people in our own ranks who were muttering the same thing. Neil continued to appear buoyant through all this, but it inevitably had an effect on him.

The denigration of Neil was not only cruel, it was grossly unfair. John Smith did an impressive job as Shadow Chancellor and had all the Scottish virtues of common sense and competence, but in my view he lacked Neil's political nimble-footedness at the dispatch box and his power to stir the blood of his audiences. I knew Neil's failings as well as anyone. He was given to verbosity at the best of times, and those of us who were close to him shook our heads over it. I often spoke at the same rallies as he, and after one of his speeches I turned to Glenys Kinnock, who was the best supporting spouse any leader could have had, and said, 'If he had cut a quarter of an hour off that speech it would have been twice as good.' She smiled understandingly and said, 'Why don't you tell him? He will listen to you.' I and others dropped our gentle hints to him and they had an effect. He struggled to learn the art of brevity, and the improvement was noticeable.

As the personal attacks on him multiplied, however, with a persistence that would have undermined anyone's self-confidence, the convoluted sentences and conditional clauses crept back in again. The Tories gleefully dubbed him the 'Welsh windbag'. Michael Heseltine amused himself mimicking Neil's accent and his 'boyo' style. The attacks became positively ethnic in tone implying that, because he was Welsh, Neil was not fit to be Prime Minister. They did not go down well in the Welsh valleys, but they were directed at a wider Anglo-Saxon audience.

The greatest mistake, however, was that Neil's advisers would not allow him to be himself. When left to his own instincts no one could match him for inspired and pithy oratory, as he had shown in his acceptance speech to the 1983 party conference. No one had shown greater toughness in overhauling the party's creaking machine and out-of-date attitudes. But the man who was packaged for the election by Labour's campaign team was not the Neil I knew. For a long time I had been disturbed by the front bench's cult of blandness and respectability, designed to reassure a hesitant electorate. Our spokespersons were the picture of conventional acceptability – always well groomed, always sounding reasonable and moderate. I thought John Smith was carrying this tactic a little far when he took to lunching with the magnates of the City, assuring them that nothing much would change under a Labour government and they had nothing to fear. At a time when the City was riddled with scandals and speculators were playing fast and loose with the currency and damaging the real economy, most people were looking for reforms. So I thought this reassurance to the perpetrators of these mischiefs was a little odd.

Neil Kinnock was a captive of this approach. I spoke quite a lot with him at election rallies. The format was always the same: first the local candidate, then a well-known trade unionist, then a stage or other celebrity, with everyone drilled to keep to a timetable which got Neil on his feet in time for the nine o'clock news. Neil would then deliver a carefully prepared speech, with verve but no spontaneity. When the television cameras were switched off, my job was to wind up the proceedings with a clarion call to the faithful sitting in the ticket-only audience. I enjoyed myself, making the same punchy hard-hitting speech I would have made to a street-corner meeting in Blackburn in my earlier days. The audience usually rose to it, delighted to hear something unconstrained. On one such occasion Neil said to me as he listened to the applause, 'You know why I cannot make a speech like that.' 'Yes,' I replied, 'because I am irresponsible.' He nodded and both of us knew what I meant. I was free of the responsibilities of leadership and could make daring, mocking sallies against the government, while Neil was sanitized in case the press should pick out of context a single impulsive phrase they could distort. So he was limited by his advisers to setpiece performances and kept away from informal brushes with the man and woman in the street. Rumour had it that some of them were afraid he might make a gaffe on economic policy. My whole political experience cried out against this approach. I had only got as far as I had done by taking risks. Risks must of course be reasonable ones, but not to take any at all is more likely to bring defeat than victory. Neil, I used to argue, could never begin to make the gaffes the government was making every day. Why should we throw away the asset of his adventurous personality?

Just before the election I went to see Neil in his room in the House. I could talk to him freely because he knew I believed in him. 'Neil,' I pleaded, 'your speeches are too statistical. Why don't you talk more about values?' 'I know,' he replied, 'but they won't let me,' and he looked at the door as though his minders might break in. When the election was over one of them said to me that the trouble had been Neil's lack of self-confidence. That may have been true to some extent, but their job was to build up his self-confidence instead of denaturing him.

As the election progressed I became more desperate. John Major was doing 'meet the people' meetings sitting informally on an upturned box in the middle of a circle of his listeners, fielding any questions which came along. Neil always shone in an environment of 'meeting the people' informally. He was, however, only allowed to appear at carefully stage-managed meetings in a dark suit, collar and tie, close-cropped hair neatly brushed back. 'Our man looks more of a Prime Minister,' his advisers remarked proudly, but I believed they were underestimating the pull of John Major's naturalness. At last I could bear no more and hurriedly wrote a letter to Neil in which my pent-up frustration broke out. 'Neil,' I wrote,

> I can't stand it any longer. What are your image-makers doing to you? You have achieved so much . . . but your advisers are insisting on projecting you in such a denatured form that I for one cannot recognize the man who I know would make a human, warm and daring Prime Minister.
>
> The photograph of you on the front page of the current *Labour Party News* is disastrous. It makes you look like a washed-

out edition of Paddy Ashdown. The photograph in the manifesto allows you a carefully controlled smile but it is still not that of a man who cares passionately about a better society. . . . The result is that John Major is beating you in naturalness and Paddy Ashdown in conveying sincerity. The result could lose us votes. . . . For God's sake let the real you come through more – warts and all, risks and all.

Before I sent the letter I saw him on television making a speech in Birmingham. He seemed to speak without a note and radiated his old spontaneity. The transformation filled me with hope that his style of electioneering had changed, but it did not last. I did not send the letter because his advisers had cast him in the role of calculated respectability and it was too late to change.

I had an opportunity of studying Tory tactics at first hand, having been invited by Sky Television to participate in a bi-weekly election debate with Norman Tebbit and Bill Rodgers. Bill, now Lord Rodgers, was on old Labour colleague, who had defected from the Labour Party a few years earlier to become one of the Gang of Four. Later he became a Liberal Democrat peer. Norman Tebbit was one of the most formidable adversaries in politics: shrewd, forceful, articulate and utterly unscrupulous. He had long had Margaret Thatcher's ear, until he quarrelled with her in 1987 over the conduct of the election campaign that year. He then retired from her government to become a director of British Telecom which he had privatized when he was Secretary of State for Trade and Industry. He was one of Labour's *bêtes noires*. After one of Norman's outbursts in the House of Commons Michael Foot had described him as a 'semi-house-trained polecat'. The Sky producer warned me, 'Norman goes for the jugular.' That suited me, but I noticed with amusement that, with a woman in the team, he changed his style, treating me with great courtesy. This, however, did not deflect either of us from trying to draw blood.

Norman's technique was a highly effective one. He selected one or two subjects on which he thought the Opposition was vulnerable and jabbed away at them, bringing the discussion back to them at the slightest opportunity whatever subject we were supposed to be examining. I enjoyed our duelling. Indeed we found ourselves united more than once in our disdain for the Liberal Democrats' holier-than-thou, a-plague-on-both-your-houses line. Hard hitting we could understand and respect, but we could not abide Bill Rodgers' quiet assumption of moral superiority and his lofty dismissal of both other parties equally.

One of Tebbit's favourite targets was the trade unions. He was helped by the fact that the party had already gone on the defensive about its links with them. Neil himself had taken the lead in demanding a whittling down of the unions' power within the party organization by the introduction of 'one man one vote' particularly in the selection of parliamentary candidates. I was – and am – all in favour of preventing a trade union from moving in to capture a particular seat by suddenly affiliating a large number of local union branches, as Arthur Scargill had done in the Yorkshire South Euro-seat when he displaced Brian Keyes in favour of his own nominee, Norman West. But the unions were by no means the only culprits. Ever since mandatory reselection had been introduced small hard-left cliques had been able to unseat sitting MPs or MEPs by clever back-stairs manipulation of delegates. Certainly the party's selection machinery and the running of the party conference needed overhauling. It was in fact something for which I had been agitating for many years. But it was a fatal mistake to allow this to be used as a weapon to attack the party's special relationship with the trade unions. This was as legitimate as a Conservative government's special relationship with the CBI and was essential for achieving parity of influence on government.

When, therefore, Norman Tebbit turned at every opportunity to the Winter of Discontent, describing the overflowing dustbins and undug graves as though they were the natural symbols of trade unionism, I was ready for him. If Labour were returned, he alleged, life would be one long Winter of Discontent with 29 million days lost through strikes in one year. He knew as well as anyone, I said, that the picture he painted was grotesque and I pointed out that 27 million working days had been lost through strikes in 1984 when Margaret Thatcher had staged her showdown with the miners. Neither the Winter of Discontent nor the miners' strike were typical of the strike record of either government. In fact, these records were broadly similar, until after 1985, when unemployment was bringing industrial workers to their knees. Unemployment was his government's only industrial relations policy. The sole alternative was Labour's policy of co-operation with the trade unions.

I also counter-attacked with the positive case for trade unionism. Unions were needed, I claimed, more than ever in a recession when employers could freely exploit the unorganized and when health and safety provision in the workplace could be the first casualty. What about the horrifying explosion at the Piper Alpha oil rig in the North Sea, I asked, when 166 workers had lost their lives because elementary safety rules had not been followed? Or the loss of 193 lives among passengers and crew on the ironically named car ferry *Herald of Free Enterprise*, because the bow doors had not been closed before casting off? The Sheen report of enquiry had complained that the P & O private management had been 'infected with the disease of sloppiness' and had ignored requests for warning lights to be fitted to tell the masters when the bow doors had not been closed. It was at least possible that neither of the disasters would have taken place if the firms had recognized trade unions and allowed them to place safety representatives on board. As I hammered away at this theme, I could not understand why the party's spokesmen did not hammer away at it as well, instead of being apologetic about Labour's association with the trade unions.

Another of Tebbit's favourite themes was taxation. Labour, he implied, would tax, tax and tax – a theme which John Major was happy to exploit himself. I retorted by quoting the Chancellor of the Exchequer's own published figures which showed that the percentage of people's income taken in tax had been lower under the last Labour government at 35.25 per cent than under the Tories, where it had reached 37.5 per cent by the end of 1991, despite cuts in income tax. The reason was, of course, I told Norman, that the Tories had offset income tax cuts with increases in VAT, which had risen from 8 per cent under Denis Healey to

17.5 per cent under John Major. Heaven knew how much further it would go if he carried out his election pledge to reduce the standard rate of income tax to 20 per cent for everyone. Even the journalists from the more independent-minded press could see this point and flustered John Major at one of his press conferences by pointing out that what mattered to people's incomes was total 'tax take' in whatever form the tax was levied.

This issue should have been central to our whole campaign. Just because it was one on which we might seem vulnerable it was essential that we attacked it frontally. One or two of our moves were excellent such as our poster showing Norman Lamont as 'Vatman' in Batman's costume. But one poster does not make a campaign, particularly when it is given no showing in the ultra-Tory press. The publication of John Smith's alternative Budget was a clever move. I was well aware that a Labour government would not be able to reverse the recession overnight or eradicate the inequalities of our society at a stroke, but John's Budget showed that we could make a start without putting up income tax for any but those earning more than £24,000 a year. No one could seriously object to his raising the top rate of tax to 50 per cent since it had been 60 per cent under the Tories for many years before Nigel Lawson dropped it to 40 per cent in his budget in 1988. Everyone now realized how cruelly that budget had widened the gap between rich and poor and was uneasy about it. Even John's proposals to extend the 9 per cent National Insurance contribution all the way up the income scale was logically unanswerable, though it might have been wiser to phase it in, since it affected everyone earning more than £21,000 a year. As it was, Tories seized on it to support their assertions that we were out to penalize the aspirant middle class. Nonetheless eight out of ten people would have been better off under this Budget; in addition to everyone benefiting from the financial stimulus John Smith proposed giving to small businesses and the construction industry, raising child benefit and increasing funds for the NHS.

The Tory campaigners, however, were not going to let their intended victim get away so easily. Unable to make much mileage out of John Smith's taxation plans, they invented some. They went through every policy commitment Labour had made for future years, costed them and claimed that their implementation would entail a huge tax increase immediately. Chris Patten, who had become chairman of the Conservative Party, had been a favourite Tory of Labour MPs in former years when he was one of Mrs Thatcher's wets. He had now developed a new personality. No distortion was too crude for him if it would enable his government to hang on to power. He plastered prominent hoardings with posters headed 'Labour's Tax Bombshell', claiming that under Labour everyone's tax bill would be increased by £1250 a year, despite the fact that eight out of ten taxpayers would have their tax bill reduced under our policy. The 'nice' Mr Major joined in the deception too, while the tabloids excelled themselves, blazoning it in their headlines every day as polling day drew near. I knew the campaign of distortion was having some effect when I went to talk to a group of old-aged pensioners living in sheltered accommodation. Most of them were responsive to the speeches made by the candidates and me, until one old gentleman remarked, 'But you are going to take twelve hundred pounds a year from us and I couldn't afford that.' When we asked where he got that from, he replied, 'The *Sun*.' He had seen it in print, so it had to be true. It was hard to convince him that in fact we intended to make him better off.

Our campaign managers' strategy in the election was to concentrate on the issues on which we were doing well in the opinion polls: education, training, housing and the NHS. There was sense in this and our frontbenchers undoubtedly scored heavily in their attacks on the government's proposals for the opting out of hospitals and schools, its failure to tackle the need for training and the scandal of homelessness. The strategy's weakness lay in its inflexibility. Our slogan 'It's time for change. It's time for Labour' lost its punch once Margaret Thatcher had gone, and a smiling John Major had replaced her. People felt they had had their change. It was the Tories who offered them a new face, while Neil Kinnock had been leading Labour for the past nine years. They were ready to give John Major, the newcomer, his chance. The Tory slogan 'You can't trust Labour' hit the target of the public mood more effectively.

All this might have been remedied if we had switched our emphasis when the Tory tactic became clear. Everyone in the Labour party later agreed that Bill Clinton won the US Presidential election by riding out similar attacks to ours: personal smears and allegations that he was going to 'tax, tax and tax'. He did it by positive counter-attack and we should have done the same. Instead we stuck to our prearranged themes, and the assault went on unchecked. To his credit, Neil Kinnock wanted to switch the emphasis of the campaign but was overruled.

Yet Neil, too, was to make a fatal mistake. He was one of those who, as part of his 'modernism', was toying with the idea of proportional representation and had encouraged the setting up of the Plant Commission to examine it. When our campaign should have been counter-attacking on the tax issue, he suddenly made overtures to the Liberal Democrats by offering them a place in it. It was a device which did not win over the Liberals. I myself remained against proportional representation fortified by my experience of the fragmentation it caused in the European Parliament. Nor did Paddy Ashdown's performance in the election encourage me to change my mind. His main purpose in the election was to weaken the Labour Party, so that he could hold the balance of power in a hung Parliament. I found it immoral that the leader of alleged Liberals should state, as he did categorically, that if neither party had a majority he would give his support to whichever party – Conservative or Labour – promised to introduce electoral reform if it formed a government. Other social and political issues would not count.

Labour's conciliatory overtures to him made us look weak and increased the public's uneasiness at the prospect of a hung Parliament. Meanwhile John Major scored points by coming out unequivocally against any tampering with our system of first-past-the-post, which he insisted was the only one to guarantee strong government. As the election results showed, it was strong government that the voters were looking for.

Our strategists also failed to realize the ferocity of the resistance we were up against. A blip in the polls temporarily gave our spirits a lift when, on the Sunday before polling day, an NOP poll found that Labour was in the lead by 6 per cent. It looked as though at last our message was getting across, though I did not believe that a one-off boost to 6 per cent was enough to guarantee victory. I was therefore rather taken aback by the atmosphere of euphoria which permeated the highlight of our campaign: an election rally in Sheffield. It was no ordinary rally but a jamboree on an unprecedented scale. The ambitious plan included ferrying 10,000 party workers from all over the north to fill the vast Sheffield arena. A video screen was erected at the back of the platform to enable the audience to watch Neil and Glenys arriving by helicopter, before they marched up the aisle like visiting royalty. Flags waved, balloons descended, celebrities of the musical world sang or played to us on the stage, while others appeared on video. Neil paraded the Shadow Cabinet on the platform as 'our winning team'. The audience loved it, but I was worried about the message we were sending out. As I told the audience in my speech, this area of the north was one of the 'industrial killing fields of John Major's government', so, to me, the elaborate razzmatazz was out of place. The display of triumphalism probably did no harm to us electorally, but it made for a dangerous complacency when we should have been on our toes.

Most serious of all was the failure of our strategists to foresee and prepare against the increasingly vitriolic personal attacks that were made on Neil. As voting day drew near, poisonous misrepresentations poured out of almost every tabloid newspaper, unparalleled in any other Western democracy. We complained about it afterwards, but it was too late. Later analysis showed that these attacks had inspired a marked swing to the Tories in the last few days.

On the eve of the poll, I spoke at the final rally in Neil's constituency, together with Michael Cashman (Colin) and Susan Tully (Michelle) of *EastEnders*. The satirist Ben Elton of BBC's *Auntie* spoke as well and delighted the audience as much as he did me. But it was the last fling of euphoria. Next morning, I breakfasted with Neil and Glenys in the little country hotel where we had stayed the night. Neil was cheerful, as usual, but thoughtful too. The breakfast table was strewn with newspapers and he had been glancing through them to see what final stabs the tabloids had made at him. The previous day the *Sun* had delivered a banner headline: 'Nightmare on Kinnock Street'. It 'reported' what it said would happen under a Labour government: 'Mortgages up 2%. Evictions doubled. House prices crash.' And it then declared vindictively, 'He will have a new home, you won't.' Below this was one of the nastiest appeals to the lowest human emotions I have ever read. 'Gays to rule planning' it claimed and alleged that under a Labour government all planning applications, from loft conversions to garages, would have to be approved by gay and lesbian groups. 'Town chiefs', it stated as a cold fact, 'will be forced by law to consult homosexuals over planning decisions,' adding for good measure, 'as well as ethnic groups.' 'Will this have any effect?' I asked Neil. He shrugged: 'Perhaps with two per cent of the voters and that could be enough.' He told me later he knew by then that we had lost.

On polling day I succumbed to a virus and was running a high temperature. I had intended to stay up all night to hear the results, but my doctor ordered me to bed and I slept through them all. When I awoke at 5.30 a.m. and turned on the radio, the first words I heard were that the FT 100 Share index was up by about 155 points. I knew then that, despite all our economic caution and John Smith's attempts to reassure the City, the speculators and their mouthpieces had beaten us again. Somehow, the Tories had managed to convince the voters despite all the evidence that they were better than we were at running the economy.

When the first shock was over, we began to recover our nerve. The Tories had lost forty-four seats and their majority was down to twenty-one, which was a far cry from the majorities of over 100 which had enabled Margaret Thatcher to behave so autocratically. John Major was to discover this very soon. It was a long way from the Labour majority of which some had dreamed, though I had not. It was even a long way from a hung Parliament, a fact which had its compensations because the Liberal Democrats, despite their twenty seats, had been deprived of the balancing role which they had plotted for. I was sad that so many Labour hopefuls had had their hopes dashed, but we had some heartening victories – notably Anne Campbell in Cambridge and Janet Anderson in Rossendale. They had both won through against formidable odds by sheer weight of personality, persistence and feminine persuasiveness. Janet's constituency included Darwen, my neighbour when I was in Blackburn, which we considered an almost impossible Tory stronghold to capture, so my glee at her victory had a special edge. I was also gratified that Janet was the third of my former secretaries and research assistants to make it to Parliament. Stamina tells – and they had to acquire a bit of that to cope with me.

Nonetheless, we had to face the fact that, despite a swing to Labour of 2 per cent, our share of the national vote was still only 34.4 per cent not even back to the 36.9 per cent we had polled in 1979, when circumstances had been much less in our favour. There was a yawning gap, not only between our figure and the Tories' 41.9 per cent, but between it and the 43 per cent we had polled in 1970 when, all the same, we had lost after six years of Labour government. What did it all mean?

Some people hurried to argue that Labour had not abandoned enough of its old policies. It must, they maintained, break its links with the trade unions, abandon the remaining traces of its belief in public ownership, stop taxing the rich and forge an alliance with the Liberals. I believed this panic reaction would destroy, not only the Labour Party, but the social democratic alternative to both communism and monetarism everywhere.

In my view we lost the 1992 election, not merely as a result of errors in the campaign, but because of the Labour Party's whole psychology in the preceding months and years. In fact, we had never recaptured the confident aggressiveness of the general election of 1964, when Harold Wilson had made himself the mouthpiece of the technological revolution and dismissed the Tories as effete. Yet the Thatcherite and post-Thatcherite Tory economic policies had proved themselves as disastrous as any fumbling with matchsticks by Alec Douglas-Home. Our trouble was that so many of our own party half believed that a lot of the Thatcherite nostrums were right. The voters had not enough confidence in us because we had too little in ourselves.

So I believe that once again we had lost another election we could and should have won. One of our campaign team, Philip Gould, was later invited to America to advise Governor Clinton's team on the pitfalls they were likely to meet in the presidential election campaign in the light of our own experience. He warned them they would be attacked on taxation as we had been and should prepare a vigorous counter-attack and sustain it until polling day. This they did – and they won the day. As I heard Gould describe this on British television on his return, I could not help wondering why we had not followed the same advice at home.

Philip Gould was also struck by the vitality and the unity of the Democrats. Their enthusiastic support kept Clinton buoyant through President Bush's bitter personal attacks. There was no such unity or loyalty to the leader here at home. Some of the whispering about Neil's leadership, which the press was only too anxious to amplify, came from his own side. Some months after the election I was in a taxi taking me to the House of Lords when the taxi driver suddenly said to me, 'I am sorry Neil Kinnock did not make it. I think he would have made a very good Prime Minister.' 'So do I,' I told him. He was not the only man-in-the-street to tell me the same thing. I thought to myself that the Labour Party is the poorer for having failed to give Neil the chance to prove it though I would have been on his tail to detach him from his own right wing.

TWENTY THREE

•

Into the Future

POLITICS HAS been the breath of my life for over fifty years – and a big influence in it even before that. At the end of this long stint, my enthusiasm for my chosen pursuit is as great as ever. The reason is that my political beliefs have strengthened, not weakened with the years. Despite setbacks and disappointments along the way, I have never become cynical. As I look at the shabby, commercialized and demoralized society in which I write this book I am more convinced than ever that the political analysis on which I was brought up was right. I have always believed that the only way to increase wealth is to share it more equally both globally and nationally.

One of the main reasons why the advanced industrial economies are engaged in competitive deflation and in an attempt to undercut each other in trade is that billions of people in the world, including a large number in our own country, are living barely above the subsistence level. They cannot activate their need for the goods we could produce. To insist that we must remedy this situation is not socialist sentimentality. It is common sense.

Without corrective action, Britain will remain in a vicious circle of decline. Unemployment reduces national wealth and tax revenues while the cost of keeping people out of work rises relentlessly. To try to deal with this by cutting public expenditure merely makes matters worse, leaving us with fewer houses, poorer schools, penny-pinched health services, drab cities. It threatens to take us back to 1931 when the axe fell savagely on wages and unemployment benefit.

I am the last to claim, as this book shows, that Labour governments have been perfect. The Labour Party has never been a gathering ground for angels. It is the coming together of normal men and women in an attempt to bring economic sanity and social justice into our national life. Looking back, I am proud of the extent to which we succeeded in changing the mental climate of Britain. It is the direction in which a political party wants to go that matters. As Nye Bevan put it: 'The religion of Socialism is the language of priorities.' Methods may change and compromises be made but the Labour Party's distinguishing mark is – and must remain – its priorities.

Of course, the Labour Party has not had a monopoly of highmindedness. There were great reformers, like Lord Shaftesbury in the nineteenth century, who were horrified by the conditions in which working people lived and worked and who achieved some isolated *ad hoc* reforms. Individuals from other parties than ours agitated for an extension of the franchise in the last century, though they usually accompanied this with the belief that the only people who could be trusted to vote were those who had some property. It was the Labour Party which fought for universal suffrage, to the annoyance of middle-class suffragettes like Christabel Pankhurst, who were prepared to accept any property qualification for the vote as long as women got it on the same terms as men. I was brought up on the philosophy that the political system should reflect the economic changes in society. Nye Bevan once illustrated this with his explanations of the origins of the Civil War, which gave us our constitutional monarchy. 'Why did Pym and Hampden refuse to pay ship money?' he used to ask. 'Because they could not afford to pay? No, because they could.' As members of the rising merchant class they were not prepared to hand over the control of their lives to an autocratic king and the landed nobility of the House of Lords. The working class, Nye argued, had moved into the centre of the economic stage and were similarly demanding a say in how the country was run and a share of its wealth. It was Labour's historic role to secure this for them.

There were also some notable reformers of all parties who

emerged during the Second World War, responsive to the new mood which the war had induced. It was a Tory paternalist, Rab Butler, who carried through the 1944 Education Act in the last throes of the wartime coalition government. The Act established for the first time the right of all children to secondary education and raised the school-leaving age to fifteen. It was a Liberal, William Beveridge, who produced the seminal report proposing a comprehensive system of social security from the cradle to the grave and urged the need for a national health service and for a full employment policy. But it was the Labour Party which endorsed these proposals wholeheartedly and turned them into actuality when it came to form a government. Without that government the egalitarian mood engendered by the war could have melted away with victory, as it had done in 1918 under Lloyd George. If Labour had not been elected in 1945, Britain would never have had the NHS in the form we came to know and love: comprehensive, universal, financed out of taxation and free at the point of use. The trouble Nye Bevan had from the Opposition in getting his scheme through the Commons is proof of that.

For history shows that great reforming movements must be inspired by a philosophy. Individual reformers are important but they cannot change society without the backing of a political machine, as the suffragettes found when they did battle with Asquith for the vote. The Labour Party's belief that the state must intervene to fill the gaps and correct the inadequacies of the free-market economy enabled it to build on the foundations which Beveridge and Butler had laid.

So the Labour Party had to bring Beveridge up to date, as I sought to do through the state earnings-related pensions scheme of 1978. Labour had also to go much further than Butler had in his 1944 Act to create greater equality of opportunity in education. The introduction of comprehensive schools was a step in this direction, though inevitably they vary in quality, mainly due to the inadequacy of the resources some are given to deal with the social problems of the areas they serve. But they embody the principle that all children are precious and that we must establish a system of state education dedicated to breaking down social and educational barriers. The Tories instinctively reject this philosophy. They do not believe in the level playing field they talk about. Instead they believe in divide and rule, setting parent against parent and the bright child against the less bright, so that a few rise to the top while the vast majority remain under-fulfilled. It is no accident that so many Tory leaders come from public schools, misnamed 'charities', in which children from already privileged families enjoy the benefits of a more lavish education with the help of tax reliefs financed by the rest of us.

One of the canards our opponents like to spread about is that socialists want the state to regiment our lives and destroy choice. On the contrary our whole purpose is to emancipate the individual. There is no freedom in unemployment and an impoverished environment or lack of skill so the state must provide the framework of essential services within which all our people can fulfil themselves. Of course, society moves on and circumstances change. Socialism is an organic movement or it is nothing. As Nye Bevan put it, our 'Holy Grail is the living truth and the truth being alive must change'. The fiery policies I advocated in my youth have to be adapted to a more sophisticated economy. The detailed control of industry, for example, which was essential when the post-war Labour government was struggling to share out scarce raw materials and hard currency would be an anachronism today. This does not mean that we should rush to the other extreme and adopt the Conservatives' policy of decontrolling and deregulating everything as a matter of principle. It was the decontrol of credit which helped to turn the Nigel Lawson boom of 1988 into the 'bust' of the longest and deepest recession of this century. It is the deregulation of bus services, as part of a deregulation ideology, which has multiplied the number of buses on city streets while actually reducing the number of passengers, leaving whole areas under-supplied and depriving the rural areas.

The same is true of public ownership. In my young days we believed in the common ownership of the means of production, distribution and exchange as the only way of preventing economic power and wealth from accumulating in the hands of a few people accountable to no one but themselves. The growth of the Labour Party and the trade unions forced industrial magnates and land-owners to accept some curbs on their arbitrary economic power. The Labour government's steps in 1945 to bring key industries and services like coal, electricity, gas, water, and transport and the Bank of England into public ownership hastened the process. They enabled people to see the advantage of public enterprise over the profit motive in certain vital areas. Miners were at last given decent wages and conditions in which to do their dangerous work. The boon of electricity was brought to the most remote rural outposts, in which private profit-makers would not have been interested. The publicly owned water authorities had to conform to national needs on such matters as conservation and access to the beauties of their gathering grounds.

Conservative policy in recent years has been to reverse all that. Thatcherism is not dead. The Tories' path has been made easier by Labour's failure to defend the merits and values of public enterprise. Labour governments have subjected publicly owned industries to rigid and archaic Treasury rules which do not apply to the new private monopolies. It is like expecting a boxer to win with one arm tied behind his back. All capital investment by nationalized industries has to be classified as public expenditure and so entered on the debit side of the national books and be strictly controlled. Investment by private firms, on the other hand, ranks as a productive asset and is encouraged. When water supply was privatized in 1991 I asked the chairman of the North-West Water Group, Dennis Grove, what were the advantages of the change, because real competition was hardly feasible. He replied without hesitation that it was the freedom given the new com-panies to raise capital when and where they wanted. No Treasury interference here. No 'capping' of expenditure, as happens to all public authorities. It was a formula that labelled public bodies as poor relations and kept them poor.

The effect of this policy has been particularly evident in British Rail. Everyone knows that a flourishing railway system is essential if we are to divert freight and private car traffic from road to rail and to bring the blessing of mobility to people who cannot afford to own a car. Yet investment in railways and the recognition that some 'socially necessary' lines will have to be subsidized has for too long been ranked as part of the national debt, rather than as a contribution to a better organized society. So British Rail has never been given the chance to show what it can do. For years I travelled miserably on a down-at-heel Chiltern Line train while British Rail toyed with the idea of closing Marylebone station in a desperate effort to save funds. When it decided that this solution would be untenable in this increasingly important commuter belt and decided to put some money into improving the stock and speeding up the services the transformation was remarkable: clean comfortable coaches and faster trains. It became clear to everyone living along the line that it was quicker and more pleasant to travel to London by train than by private car. Yet the railways have been starved of funds while more and more elaborate road programmes are drawn up. We will never solve the congestion on the roads as long as financial priority is given to widening motorways over the improvement of public transport.

Even Adam Smith realized there are certain needs in a 'great society' which the profit motive cannot meet and that the state must remain responsible for providing them. One of these in the twentieth century is a transport system which serves the needs of all types of citizens and in which therefore the railways must play an essential part. Nationalization created a national rail network comprising less profitable lines and even loss-makers as well as money-making ones. Privatization inevitably breaks that up and produces what the *Observer* has described as 'a structure of Byzantine complexity'. It cannot provide the ease of travel which comes when passengers can take a through train from, say, Scotland to Reading, under the same management, without having to negotiate with a plethora of private companies, and when they know they have benefited from a nationwide scheme of ticket concessions such as British Rail provides.

The Labour Party need never be apologetic about the role of public enterprise. Of course we cannot put back the clock to the days before industry and finance were multinationalized. We must find other ways of making them serve the public interest. But we should vigorously attack the spreading privatization and commercialization of every aspect of our national life. It is infecting all our values and permeating our universities and research centres, our culture and the National Health Service. It threatens public service broadcasting by the BBC. Even the civil service is not immune, and the local authorities' powers have been increasingly transferred to private hands. Democratic control has been handed over to an autocratic central government on the one hand and private interests on the other.

Nor need Labour be on the defensive about its capacity for economic management. Margaret Thatcher has often boasted that socialism is dead, quoting in aid the collapse of the communist command economies. Labour has never believed in a command economy but, in any case, if these systems have failed, so has Thatcherite monetarism. It has produced an era of economic decline in Britain of which any Labour government would have been ashamed. Its sole instrument of economic management has been deflation, which has produced the major problem of modern society – unemployment. With unemployment has come drug-taking, vandalism, rising crime and a sense of hopelessness which has alienated so many of our people from society. Unless we solve it, democracy itself will be at risk.

Monetarism has also produced a shabby poverty-ridden country in which the public services have been run down. Millions of people are enjoying a higher standard of life as a result of the great modern technological explosion which has taken place but millions more are disfranchised from the resulting consumer boom by low wages, unemployment and low benefits. My niece Sonya, whose job it is to help parents who have children with problems, tells me that in some of the homes she visits there is not even a table where she can write her notes. The family sit round the television set with a bag of chips or other convenience food on their laps. Nobody does any cooking. It throws an interesting light on the consumer society.

I believe that the Adam Smith Institute's ideas have run their course. More and more people are disillusioned with what they have produced. They are ashamed to live in a country which cannot even put a roof over people's heads or equip its state schools with books. It is Labour's job to mobilize this unease, and we shall not do it by being bland. As I often told Neil Kinnock when he was leader, the Tories have brought more passion to their materialism than we have to our morality. It is anger that is needed now.

There are swings of public mood in politics. I predict that the pendulum has already begun to swing back against unregulated market economies everywhere. In Eastern Europe, for example, there are signs that disillusionment with the new free-market philosophy is creeping in. The switch to privatization is not proving as simple or as beneficial as the rebels against communism hoped. They find they have let the social democratic baby out with the communist bathwater. On a recent visit to Prague, I found my young Czech guide admiring the greater variety which privatization had brought into the shops and restaurants, but not able to afford to take advantage of them herself because her wages were too low. Nor could she afford any longer to go to the theatre, which the communists had subsidized: with all state subsidies banned under the new regime, ticket prices had risen beyond the reach of local Czechs and the theatres were filled with foreign visitors like myself. She worried about what would happen to the excellent system of public transport which the communists had installed and which had given Prague fast, clean and cheap metro and tram services. Not least, she feared that Czechoslovakia would lose her leading place in the sports world now that sports facilities were no longer subsidized.

Similar fears have been expressed by the Economic Commission for Europe. In its *Economic Survey of Europe 1991–92*, it suggests that in some countries in Eastern Europe the move to privatization has been too wholesale and precipitate. 'A more effective approach', it says, 'might be to consider more active and explicit industrial policies on the part of the government,' including such supply-side measures as better provision for training and increased public investment in the infrastructure necessary to underpin a healthy economy. It is an argument that misinterpreters of Adam Smith refuse to face.

In such a situation it would be folly for Labour to water down its values and principles in pursuit of pacts with centrist groups, such as the Liberal Democrats. History shows that the Liberals are unreliable allies in the demand for fundamental changes in society. They shot their bolt as reformers in Lloyd George's Budget of 1910, and neither he nor they ever reached those heights again. Today there are as many anti-Labour sentiments among the Liberal Democrats as there are anti-Conservative. Proportional representation, by boosting the small parties, would make matters worse. We must seek allies wherever we can find them, but we must attract them as we did in the old days, by the correctness of our economic analysis and the strength of our leadership.

We must also proclaim our own distinctive economic policy. We are the only party which can forge a creative new partnership between the old and the new, because we believe in both and want to combine the best of each. Labour's leaders have already worked out ideas for injecting private capital into public industries in ways which protect the public interest. On economic management we must reject the attempts which have been made to subordinate the needs of the real economy to rigid financial goals, such as zero inflation or the maintenance of a fixed value for the currency. Labour governments have been martyred in the past by attempts to remain on the gold standard or its modern equivalents. Every time, those of us who have opposed these policies have been proved right, as those of us who opposed Britain's entry into the Exchange Rate Mechanism in 1990 were right. Of course 'sound finance' is important, and Labour governments can be trusted more than Tory ones to pursue it. But our experience has shown time and again that 'sound finance' can only be built on the base of a strong economy, and the pursuit of that must be our overriding priority.

People sometimes ask me if I would have liked to become Prime Minister. The answer is yes. Few politicians can resist such a challenge, even though they have secret doubts about their own abilities. But I never schemed for it. Intrigues to promote oneself always bore me and in any case I never for a moment believed I had a chance. In my day the Labour Party was not ready for a woman leader and certainly not one who is as deficient in the arts of flattery as I am.

But I have not spent any time regretting that I did not become Britain's first woman Prime Minister. I have been too fulfilled in the jobs I have been given to do. I would like to have been Foreign Secretary as I believe I am a good negotiator and I enjoy outwitting someone who is trying to outwit me. That apart I found the Ministry of Transport immensely satisfying, though I did not want it in the first place. Helping people to enjoy the great boon of mobility brought by the motor car while curbing the damage it does to the environment is a challenge big enough to satisfy anyone, and I am gratified by how many of the changes I introduced among uproar have survived. It is nice these days, for instance, to be canonized for the breathalyser.

One of the episodes of my political life I do not regret is the production of *In Place of Strife*, even though it destroyed any chance I may have had of the party leadership. From my earliest days I had always joined my appropriate union. To me the idea of standing shoulder to shoulder with my fellow workers against the exploitation I experienced was exhilarating. I have never doubted that the organization of men and women at the work place was an essential element in a pluralistic democratic society. Even the rough handling I got from the unions as a minister did not change this view. So my conscience was clear when I drew up *In Place of Strife*.

Many people think that Labour's rejection of my proposals cost us the election of 1970. It certainly contributed to our defeat, since it revealed us as a movement which refused to face the realities. As my postbag showed, most working people wanted us to do something about the wildcat strikes which were inconveniencing them as well as undermining the work of their Labour governments. The divine right of unions to disrupt the economy was as alien to them as the divine right of kings had been to the Parliamentarians three centuries earlier. I used to tell my left-wing friends that in a sophisticated democracy like ours industrial anarchy was not the way to change society.

I have spent a lot of my political life thinking about what

should be the role of the trade unions. The solidarity of all those in employment against the increasing ruthlessness of the magnates who control their lives remains a sacred principle, a principle whose importance Margaret Thatcher understood as she set out to weaken the trade unions. Her policy was to use unemployment and the free play of market forces to bring wages down. Her monetarist policies were designed to produce a low-wage, 'get on your bike and take any job that offers' economy. The truth, I believe, stands out: the main weapon against such a policy must be political. Public opinion must be won over and the right government elected. In such a scenario industrial action has only a subsidiary part to play.

I believe that this lesson has now been learned by the trade unions. Industrial action should not be ruled out, but it must be used cunningly and sparingly. Unions should be brought round the boardroom table to share in drawing up the decisions of their companies which affect their employees' livelihood. That is still considered a revolutionary principle in this country, where 'management's right to manage' is a hang-over from the privileged education in our public schools. One of the reasons why Britain's attitudes and the attitudes of British management are so out of tune with those in the European Community is that the Treaty of Rome envisages trade unions as 'social partners' and gives them a voice in the Economic and Social Committee of the Community. ECOSOC has not as much power as I would like, but at least it rejects British feudal attitudes.

The biggest problem which faces any government in the advanced and industrialized countries is how to expand the economy without pushing inflation through the roof. The unions have an important part to play in this. By definition they have to exploit the economic situation on behalf of their members. Business managements do this every day on behalf of their shareholders. I believe the Social Contract drawn up by the Labour government of 1970 is still the key. It is designed to persuade wage-earners that their government, given its chance, can do more to improve their standard of living than any wage negotiation can do. Harold Wilson used to say when I was in the Cabinet that people were interested only in 'the jingle in their pockets'. To some extent that is true and it would be folly to ignore the importance of some cash wage increases. But it is also the duty of trade unions to hammer home the importance to their members of the cash value to them of the public services, from the free National Health Service to home helps for elderly members of the family, from a good state education for their children to a rented home at a reasonable price. This is what the Social Contract is all about, and I believe it is the only alternative to holding wages down by keeping people unemployed.

I doubt whether I could have endured the stresses and strains in public life, particularly in government, if it had not been for two things: my family life and Ted's and my shared joy in the countryside. The older Ted grew, the more rustic he became. When he searched out and chose Hell Corner Farm as our base he welcomed the fact that it had an enormous garden. Toiling in it became his hobby and I helped him when I could, though the demands of parliamentary and ministerial life meant I could do far less with him than he wanted me to do. I enjoyed gardening and many a time I have found that the best antidote to the black moods of self-doubt that would descend on me when I had muffed an appearance at the dispatch box or made a poor speech at party conference was to dig vigorously in our backbreaking clay and flint soil. Fortunately for Ted I enjoyed weeding, which he hated. To me it was pure therapy to battle with the bindweed and nettles which encroached insidiously as soon as we turned our backs. Ted loved growing things and even when his heart trouble made it impossible for him to do any heavy work he would be out in the garden sitting on his bottom on a plastic mat somehow managing with the aid of a handfork to make a fine tilth in our heavy ground for sowing his seeds.

It was therapy, too, just to turn off the motorway along our wooded country road, keeping an eye open for the deer which might suddenly dash across it in front of us. I could feel the tensions of office slip away from me as we descended our own narrow lane, which peters out beyond Hell Corner Farm into a bridle path between fields and trees. I have always found the colour green as soothing as the experts say it is, though I also love the elegant tracery of bare black boughs against a winter sky.

So I doubt if I could have kept going without Hell Corner Farm. It helped me to keep the ups and downs of life in proportion. Ted knew how to handle my black moods. Sometimes after a tough day I would moan in bed, 'I'm a failure.' He would reply briskly, 'Yes, we all know you're a failure. Now go to sleep.' Another great salve was our weekend country walks. We both loved the uplands, Ted being a downsman from Berkshire and I a lass from the Yorkshire moors. One of our favourite walks was along the Berkshire Ridgeway high above the Thames, rucksack on back. We would drop down to the valley for the night, finding food and sleep in some country pub. We used to say that when we retired we would live off our six acres of land like a couple of old peasants, getting kindling from our bit of woodland, eggs from our own hens, milk from the goats we would keep in our field, fruit from our orchard and vegetables from the garden Ted cultivated so assiduously. It would have been fun.

Hell Corner Farm remained my great solace when Ted died. I was determined to stay on there, though it has been a struggle to keep on top of it without the head gardener and presiding spirit in charge. But it was vital that I did so, because it has become more than ever the family gathering ground, where congregate the nine great-nephews and great-nieces and their parents, together with the girlfriends and boyfriends who have come into the young people's lives.

Looking back I realize how much I have been influenced by the values of my upbringing. I got them from my parents rather than from my schoolteachers or university tutors. I was brought up to challenge accepted ideas and the conventional assumptions of the establishment, to work out and stand by my own ideas. Our family life was a stormy one. We had our quota of family bickerings, money worries and infidelities, but we were given a deep sense of security, the capacity to look outwards to other people's problems and the wider world. We children might rebel occasionally against our parents' dictates, but we always came back home, the safe haven when things went wrong.

I am delighted that this tradition has seeped down to the younger members of our family. My great-nephews and great-nieces epitomize the sort of richness of life and opportunity socialists would like to ensure for every child. They have been to university or had other training and have a healthy ambition to rise in their chosen job and earn a decent income. They travel the world on a shoestring, but they always turn to their own home – or mine – as the place where they can recharge their batteries. At the great gatherings round the table at Hell Corner Farm at Christmas, at Easter and on Guy Fawkes Night there is no generation gap. Everyone has a place there, from Great-Aunt presiding at the head of the table to the eighteen-year-olds. Often they bring some of the foreign friends they have made in their travels abroad, so the gatherings become international. No one obliges them to come but they gravitate naturally to this common meeting place, staying up half the night to pool their experiences. Some are more political than others, but they all have social consciences and feel instinctively that they must share their privileges. Their common characteristic is their zest for life. As I look at them I renew my optimism and my faith. I know they will fight in their own way the sort of battles that I fought. William Morris comes to mind again:

Is it war, then? Will ye perish as the dry wood in the fire?
Is it peace? Then be ye of us, let your hope be our desire.
Come and live! for life awaketh, and the world shall never
    tire;
And hope is marching on.

INDEX

Macintosh, John, 448
Mackenzie, Bruce, 356
Mackintosh, John, 510–11
Macleod, Iain, 213–14, 434; death, 345;
Minister of health, as, 214; Ministry of
Overseas Development, comment on, 345,
348; Overseas Service Aid Scheme,
introduction of, 345
Macmillan, Harold: annual growth rate
under, 312; Bevan, tribute to, 321;
Chancellor, as, 241; Cyprus, plans for, 290,
293, 298, 307; economic engineering,
326–7; election campaign, manipulative
skills in, 311; family silver, reference to
selling, 563; government, difficulties of,
336; Minister of, Housing, as, 233; Night of
the Long Knives, 336; performer, as, 311;
Profumo affair, effect of, 337; resignation,
338; South Africa, views on, 330–1; wind
of change speech, 330
Macpherson, Duncan, 267, 269–70
Macpherson, Jessie, 282
Maguire, Frank, 511–12
Maizels, Mr, 277–9
Major, John: distortion, campaign of, 590;
election campaign, 585–93; Exchange Rate
Mechanism, joining, 579–80; leader,
becoming, 380, 573; 579; naturalness of,
585; taxation, policy on, 588–9; Thatcher,
as successor to, 574; VAT rate, increasing,
456
Makarios, Archbishop, 292, 294; Castle,
meeting, 301–2, 309; Cyprus constitution,
opinion of, 308; death, 309
Mandela, Nelson, 278–9
Mandelson, Peter, 575
Mangat, Mr, 268
Manning, Leah, 136
Manpower and Productivity Service, 407
Manufacturing output, effect of Tory policy
on, 553
Marples, Ernest, 371, 387
Marris, Robin, 347
Marsh, Richard, 394, 419
Marshall Plan, 147, 160, 185
Martin, Kingsley, 218, 275
Marxism, 25, 66; labour theory of value,
69–70
Massé, M., 332
Matthews, Jim, 303–4
Matthews, Stanley, 217
Maude, Angus, 213
Maudling, Reginald: Chancellor, as, 336, 338
May, Sir Ernest, 56
Mboya, Tom, 259, 268
McAdden, Stephen, 245–6
McMillan, Margaret, 28–9
McNeil, Hector, 173
Meacher, Michael, 560, 565
Melchett, Lord, 415
Mellor, David, 568

Mellor, William, 64–5, 67–8, 82–3, 93, 99,
112; Bevan, not liking, 109; Castle, affair
with, 68–9, 75; communists, negotiation
with, 76; death of, 112; election defeat, 75;
fastidiousness, 68; Fleet Street, in, 98; For
Socialism and Peace, moving amendments to,
73–4; local government paper, launch of,
76; Odhams, reckoning with, 75; Tribune,
editor of, 77–8; Tribune, resignation from,
87
Mendès-France, Pierre, 222, 332–3
Menon, Krishna, 82–3, 112
Middle East, Castle visiting, 244–9
Mikardo, Ian, 157–8, 161, 194, 205, 243; anti-
marketeer, as, 477; Bevanite conspiracy,
participation in, 203; Labour Party,
chairman of, 289; NEC, on, 194, 219;
prices and incomes policy, opposing, 405;
trade unions, attacking, 495; Tribune, use
of, 202; 1957 party conference, at, 255–6;
1959 election defeat, 314
Mikardo, Mary, 243
Militant, 576–7
Miners: overtime ban, 450; strike, Foot
settling, 470; strike, 1984, 569–70
Ministry of Food: Castle working for, 110;
war, in, 110–11
Ministry of Overseas Development: Balogh,
assistance of, 346; Cabinet, in, 339; civil
servants, 343–4; Economic Planning Unit,
372; information team, 357; interest-free
loans by, 356; opposition to, 344; outside
advisers, 346–7; Permanent Secretary,
342–3; setting up, 346; weekend seminars,
347
Ministry of Social Security: concept of social
security, bringing up to date, 462; political
advisers, 460–1
Ministry of Transport: atmosphere in, 366;
Castle taking over, 364–5; economist in,
368; highway engineers in, 366; lavatories,
367; location of, 366
Minty, Abdul, 330–1
Mitchell, Austin, 375
Mitchison, Dick, 220
Mitchison, Naomi, 220
Moffat, Sir John, 286
Monnet, Jean, 332
Moore, John, 563
Moran, Lord, 150
Morley, Miss Headlam, 45
Morris, Alf, 468
Morris, David, 549
Morris, Dr Colin, 284
Morris, John, 388, 390–1
Morris, William, 1, 10, 69–70, 239, 557, 609
Morrison, Herbert, 76, 88–9, 108, 142, 195,
198, 215; Dalton's contempt for, 188;
European Defence Community, reaction
to, 221; foreign secretary, as, 188; illness,
176; leader, running for, 240–1;

Act, rebellion over, 116; unnecessary strikes, asked to avoid, 417

Trades Union Congress: Delors visiting, 543; Liaison committee with, 493, 507; negotiations with, 423; programme for Action, 422; Scottish, 422; Social Contract, keeping to, 472

Traffic and Accident Loss (TAL), 369

Transport Bill, 397; freightliner terminals, 391; integrated policy, production of, 368–70; money-making activities, 395; plan, working out, 387; post-war, 131–2; road and rail, competition between, 370; road-safety issues, 373–4, 378; roads programmes, criteria for drawing up, 368–9; White Papers, 394

Treasury, power of, 342; DEA balancing, 349

Trend, Sir Burke, 341

Trevelyan, George, 87

Tribune: Bevan's frustrations, outlet for, 202; brains trust, 193; circulation of, 86; launch of, 77; pamphlets, 193–4

Trickett, Rachel, 50–1

Trigg, John, 516

Triple Alliance, 13

Truman, President, 137

TSR2, cancellation of, 354

Tully, Susan, 592

Turkey, Castle visiting, 297

Turton, Major, 182

Underhill, Reg, 576

Unemployment: fall in, 506; industrial areas, in, 65; rise in, 575; trade union rights, enemy of, 64

Unemployment benefit, cuts in, 1931, 56

UNESCO, alleged manipulation of, 383

Unfair dismissal, right of appeal against, 424

United States: Castle visiting, 173–6; Lend-Lease arrangements, cancellation of, 137–8; New York, 173–4; policy, subservience to, 184; Soviet Union, deterioration of relations with, 185

Unity Campaign, 77, 82, 86–7

Universities, sponsorship in, 568

Valentino, Rudolf, 33

Value Added Tax: increases in, 588; introduction of, 435

van Hayek, Professor Friedrich, 552

Veil, Simone, 521

Veitch, Marion, 411

Verwoerd, Dr, 332

Vietnam: American policy, lack of condemnation of, 382; Hanoi, mission to, 383–4; issue of, 362; peace initiatives, 383

von Richthofen, Baron, 538

Walker, Harold, 405

Walker, Peter, 328, 395, 434–5

Walker-Smith, Derek, 328

Wall Street Crash, 55

Walters, Alan, 552

Warbey, William, 116–17

Ward, Irene, 274

Ward, Sue, 561

Watkins, Alan, 402

Watkinson, Harold, 323

Watson, Sam, 194, 196, 224

Webb, Sidney, 25–6

Webber, Bill, 237

Wedgwood Benn, Tony, *see* Benn, Tony

Welfare State, creation of, 73

Wells, H. G., 109

West, Norman, 587

Wheatley Housing Act, 31

White, Florence, 134

Whitelaw, William, 457–8

Widows: poverty, living in, 465

Wigg, George, 337

Wigham, Eric, 413

Wilkinson, Ellen, 65, 129

Williams, Marcia, 163, 364, 373; Lady Falkender, becoming, 487; press attacks on, 486–7

Williams, Ruth, 261, 343

Williams, Shirley, 48, 438; Gang of Four, in, 531; pay beds, view on, 483; politics, missing, 531-2; Prentice's deselection, action on, 503

Williams, Tom, 149, 159, 329

Williamson, Tom, 157

Wilson, Harold; 196, 223, 237, 333, 337; Bevan, rift with, 221; Brown, asking to stay as deputy, 336; cancer, 513–14; career of, 162; Castle as PPS for, 162, 165; Castle, relationship with, 162–3; Castle's Shadow Cabinet defeat, anger at, 438–9; Castles' silver wedding party, at, 433; civil servants, not standing up to, 367; constitution-making, 511; conventional approach, 341; Craigie cornering, 161; Crossman, alliance with, 203; devaluation, decision against, 176; EEC, policy on in Opposition, 444–5, 448–9; European Community, determination to keep Britain out of, 473; Feather, discussions with, 421; fighting spirit, recovery of, 454; flirting, 163–4; government, resignation from, 190–1; Hattersley, opinion of, 405–6; humanistic socialism, belief in, 469; *In Place of Dollars*, writing, 194; *In Place of Strife*, approval of, 418; informal government, introduction of, 453; ingratiation, master of, 335; leader of Opposition, as, 443; leadership election, in, 334–6; Macmillan government's difficulties, exploiting, 336; memoirs, writing, 443; Movement for Colonial Freedom, support for, 261; NEC elections, 1956, 252; NEC, voted on in 1952, 205; officials of Board of Trade, discussions with, 181–2; Parliamentary Committee, on, 220; party